Who Built America?

American Social History Project
The City University of New York

Who Built America?

WORKING PEOPLE AND THE NATION'S ECONOMY, POLITICS, CULTURE, AND SOCIETY

VOLUME ONE FROM CONQUEST AND COLONIZATION THROUGH 1877

Christopher Clark, University of Warwick

Nancy A. Hewitt, Rutgers University

Supervising Editor: **Roy Rosenzweig,** George Mason University

Executive Editor: **Stephen Brier,** Graduate Center, City University of New York

Visual Editor: **Joshua Brown,** Graduate Center, City University of New York

Consulting Editor: **Eric Foner,** Columbia University

Based on the original edition authored by:
Bruce Levine, Stephen Brier, David Brundage,
Edward Countryman, Dorothy Fennell, and Marcus Rediker

Worth Publishers

Who Built America?
Volume 1: From Conquest and Colonization Through 1877
Copyright © 2000 by Worth Publishers
All rights reserved.
Printed in the United States of America.
ISBN: 1-57259-302-4
Printing: 5 4 3
Year: 04 03 02

Publisher: Catherine Woods
Development editor: Judith Kromm
Marketing manager: Charles Cavaliere
Production editors: Margaret Comaskey, Tracey Kuehn
Art Director and cover design: Barbara Reingold
Interior text design: Sandra Watanabe
Production manager: Barbara Anne Seixas
Production: Progressive Publishing Alternatives
Composition: Progressive Information Technologies
Printing and binding: R. R. Donnelley and Sons

Worth Publishers
41 Madison Avenue
New York, New York 10010
www.worthpublishers.com

To the late Joe Murphy, former chancellor of the City University of New York, who was a passionate believer in educating the working class and a stalwart supporter of the American Social History Project and *Who Built America?*

Contents

Contents

Contents

Contents

Preface

Who built the seven towers of Thebes?
The books are filled with the names of kings.
Was it kings who hauled the craggy blocks of stone? . . .
In the evening when the Chinese wall was finished,
Where did the masons go?

—Bertolt Brecht,

"Questions from a Worker Who Reads" (1935)

WHO BUILT AMERICA? surveys the nation's past from an important but often neglected perspective—the experiences of ordinary men and women and the role they have played in the making of modern America. It is not merely a documentation of the country's past presidents, politics, wars, and the life and values of the nation's elite, but focuses more on the fundamental social and economic conflicts in our history. *Who Built America?* challenges the notion that the vast majority of its citizens have always been united in a broad consensus about the nation's basic values and shared in its extraordinary prosperity.

In the past three decades or so, historians have made dramatic discoveries about the behavior and beliefs of groups traditionally slighted by their discipline: women; African Americans, enslaved and free; American Indians; factory and white-collar workers; and myriad immigrant groups. They have also unearthed a long and sustained history of conflict among Americans of different classes, races, national origins, and genders over the meaning of the American ideals of liberty and equality and over the distribution of the nation's enormous material wealth. Their findings have enabled historians to think and write differently about familiar topics, including the rise of industrial capitalism, U.S. overseas expansion, successive waves of internal migration and foreign immigration to the nation's cities, depression and war, the rise of industrial unionism, and the widening struggle for civil rights. With this new information, historians have been able to incorporate into the broader narrative of U.S. history the stories of those whose voices had been left out of traditional accounts.

This book grew out of the effort to reinterpret American history from "the bottom up." Its authors and editors are among those whose studies of workers, women, consumers, farmers, African Americans, and immigrants have helped to transform our understanding of the past. The first edition of the book was the work of the American Social History Project (ASHP), which was founded in 1981 by Herbert Gutman (a pioneer of "the new social history") and Stephen Brier to bring this research to the broadest possible audience. In addition to this book, ASHP has produced a wide range of accessible educational materials, in print, video, and digital media, and worked closely with college, high-school, and adult- and labor-education teachers to help them use these resources effectively in their classrooms.

THEMES

Who Built America? thus offers a uniquely wrought history of the United States. Its central focus and organizing theme are the changing nature of the work that built, sustained, and transformed American society over the course of four centuries and the changing conditions, experiences, outlooks, and conduct of the workers themselves. This focus permits the integration of the history of community, family, gender roles, race, and ethnicity into the more familiar history of politics and economic development. Exploring the history of the nation's laboring majority, moreover, also renders more intelligible the beliefs and actions of the nation's economic, political, and intellectual elite.

For the purposes of this book, we have defined the category of "working people" broadly. Throughout much of its history, the nation's actual workforce embraced a wide spectrum of people laboring in very different conditions and settings — free and unfree, small proprietor and propertyless wage earner, agricultural and domestic laborers, as well as industrial, commercial, clerical, service, and technical workers. Answering the question "Who built America?" therefore requires attention not only to wage-earning industrial employees but also to indentured servants, slaves, tenants, sharecroppers, independent farm families, artisans, day laborers, clerks, domestic workers, outworkers, fast food workers and women and children performing unpaid family labor — in short, the great majority of the American population at every phase of the country's development.

Who Built America? departs from convention in other respects as well. Rather than avoiding controversy or strong intepretation, we have not shied away from controversial issues and have offered opinions that are sometimes critical of celebrated figures or dominant beliefs. Our view is that readers would rather encounter a clearly stated perspective, even if they disagree with it, instead of bland platitudes about the past.

STRUCTURE

This study is divided into two volumes. The principal theme of the first volume is the rise and subsequent decline of various precapitalist labor systems, especially racial slavery, and the parallel development and ultimate dominance of capitalism and its system of wage labor. The twelve chapters of this volume are divided into three parts:

- Part One covers three centuries, beginning with the often violent encounters among European, Native American, and African peoples as Europeans first colonized the Americas and subsequently enslaved Africans to work here. It examines the different patterns of European colonization in North America, the growing importance of the English colonies on the continent's Atlantic seaboard, and the evolution of these colonies, North and South. It culminates in the colonists' successful war for independence and the establishment of the United States.

- Part Two spans the six decades following the creation of a national government in the United States, a time of profound economic, social, and political changes, including the industrial revolution, the growth of the cotton kingdom, westward expansion and war with Mexico, and the deepening conflict between the free-labor North and pro-slavery South over the status of slavery in the expanding nation. These developments sparked social and political movements among a wide array of Americans, including many who did not yet have access to formal political rights, but who nonetheless sought to shape the building of the American nation.

- Part Three recounts the intensifying political struggle over the West and the coming of the Civil War — America's Second Revolution. It also looks at the conflict itself and the aftermath of the South's defeat, and the hopes and fears engendered among all Americans, including four million newly freed slaves, during the era of Reconstruction. The volume concludes with the formal end of Reconstruction and the explosive wave of railroad strikes that shook the nation in 1877. Together the dramatic events of that year signal the close of one major epoch in American social, economic, and political history, and the beginning of another.

Volume Two *(From Reconstruction to the Present)* carries the narrative and analysis to the present day. It considers the increasing significance of industrial capitalism and wage labor for the country's economy, social relations, domestic politics, foreign policy, popular culture, and intellectual life during the nation's second century, and focuses on the corresponding growth and continual recomposition of the American working class.

FEATURES

What distinguishes *Who Built America?* from other U.S. history texts is, of course, its point of view. By emphasizing the experiences of the people whose labor shaped the nation and made it prosper, this text gives life to a story that all too often is perceived as having little to do with life in contemporary America. To further counteract the impression that history is little more than names and dates, we have enriched the narrative with excerpts from letters, diaries, autobiographies, poems, songs, journalism, fiction, official testimony, oral histories, and other historical documents. These sidebars convey the experience and often the voices of working people who lived through the events recounted in the text. In the interest of clarity, we have modernized some of the spelling, punctuation, and (especially in the case of the earliest documents) language in these records. To ensure that key events are not lost in the narrative flow and to facilitate review, we have provided timelines at the end of each chapter. These "years in review" reprise the important events covered in the chapter, particularly milestones in political and diplomatic history. Because we believe that history should also be fun, we have included in these chronologies some of the quirkier landmarks in our history—from why the "discovery" of the New World led to the invention of lemonade to why World War II resulted in the popularity of M&Ms.

Each chapter also contains drawings, paintings, prints, and photographs that derive from the era under discussion. Most of the illustrations in this book are images that were reproduced in contemporary books, pamphlets, newspapers, and magazines, individually published broadsides and lithographs, paired photographs sold as "stereoscopic views," and other media. Interpreting the visual record of the past—particularly images of working men and women, immigrants, and people of color—requires great care, and our captions alert readers to distortions and gaps that might not be obvious.

CHANGES IN THE NEW EDITION

The first edition of *Who Built America?* appeared in 1990 and 1992 as a work for a general audience as well as students. For this major revision we began with three main goals in mind. First, we wanted to take account of the vast outpouring of scholarship in the past decade. Where new historical evidence has come to light, we have altered or modified our interpretation. Second, we have sought to increase our coverage of several topics and areas of history — in particular, Spanish America, American Indians, women's history, U.S. foreign policy, electoral politics, consumer culture, and sexuality. To create space for the additional material, we have reduced the coverage of trade union history somewhat. Third, to increase the accessibility of the book we needed to give it a stronger chronological focus. Consequently, we have reorganized a number of chapters to clarify the sequence of events and given more attention to the political context of U.S. history. Fourth, to aid students in understanding the geographical and statistical patterns in American history, we have added charts and maps.

ACKNOWLEDGMENTS

Despite the major changes implemented by the authors and editors of this edition, the narrative of *Who Built America?* rests heavily on the labors of the authors of the original edition, whose names appear on the title page and to whom we are deeply indebted. Bruce Levine, in particular, was the lead author of this volume and also oversaw its research and conceptualization.

In addition, we want to thank the many people who helped bring forth this edition, especially our friends at Worth Publishers, Susan Driscoll and Judith Kromm, who loyally supported and nurtured this project over the past few years. Developmental editors Nancy Fleming, Ann Grogg, Mary Marshall, Mimi Melek, and Betty Morgan provided invaluable feedback through several drafts of the manuscript. Donna King, Tracey Kuehn, Margaret Comasky, and Barbara Seixas ably guided the book through the editing and production stages. Worth art director Barbara Rusin's appreciation of the unique character of *Who Built America?* is reflected in the book's cover and interior design. We also benefited from the collaborative efforts of Charles Cavaliere and Todd Elder on marketing and promotion. And we are deeply grateful to Jim O'Brien for his superb work on the index.

We thank Pennee Bender, Daniel Brown, George Chauncey, Jessica Finnefrock, Ellen Noonan, Linda Shopes, John Summers, Andrea Ades Vásquez, Linda Zeidman, and in particular, Mario Frieson and Gideon Brown, for research assistance and help in locating and captioning illustrations. And we reiterate our sincere thanks to the many people who helped on the first edition (and are acknowledged in those volumes).

To the following colleagues who gave us encouragement and valuable feedback at various stages during the preparation of this edition, we are most grateful:

Preface

Laura Anker, SUNY — Old Westbury

William Blair, University of North Carolina, Greensboro

Kathy Brown, University of Pennsylvania

Richard Burg, Arizona State University

Victoria Bynum, Southwest Texas State University

Kathleen S. Carter, High Point University

Judith L. DeMark, Northern Michigan University

David Engerman, Brandeis University

E. J. Fabyan, Vincennes University

Bradley T. Gericke, U.S. Military Academy, West Point

Gary L. Gerstle, University of Maryland

Julia Greene, University of Colorado, Boulder

Cindy Hahamovitch, The College of William and Mary

David M. Head, John Tyler Community College

Lybeth Hodges, Texas Women's University

Reeve Huston, University of Arizona

Robert P. Ingalls, University of South Florida

Maurice J. Isserman, Hamilton College

Wilma King, Michigan State University

Stephen Kneeshaw, College of the Ozarks

Thomas J. Knock, Southern Methodist University

Nancy Koppelman, Evergreen State College

Gary Kornblith, Oberlin College

Kurt E. Leichtle, University of Wisconsin, River Falls

Molly McGarry, Sarah Lawrence College

John Mayfield, Samford University

Joanne Meyerowitz, University of Cincinnati

Betty Mitchell, University of Massachusetts — Dartmouth

Tiffany Patterson, SUNY — Binghamton

Dolores Peterson, Foothill College

Joseph P. Reidy, Howard University

Bruce J. Schulman, Boston University

Ronald Schultz

Janann Sherman, University of Memphis

Martin J. Sherwin, Tufts University

Rebecca Shoemaker, Indiana State University

Manfred Silva, El Paso Community College

Victor Silverman, University of California, Berkeley

Katherine Sklar, SUNY — Binghamton

David Sloan, University of Arkansas

Herbert Sloan, Barnard College

Michael L. Topp, University of Texas at El Paso

David Waldstreicher, University of Notre Dame
Peter Wood, Duke University
Sherri Yeager, Chabot College
William Young, Johnson County Community College

Finally, we would be remiss if we ended our acknowledgments without noting the role of the late Herbert Gutman in creating the American Social History Project, which gave birth to this book, and in shaping the generation of historical scholarship on which it is based. Our collective and individual debts to Herb are immeasurable. We hope that this new edition of *Who Built America?* meets the high standards he set for himself throughout his rich but too brief career.

Stephen Brier
Joshua Brown
Roy Rosenzweig

ABOUT THE AUTHORS AND EDITORS

Christopher Clark, Professor of North American History at the University of Warwick, received the Frederick Jackson Turner Award from the Organization of American Historians for *The Roots of Rural Capitalism: Western Massachusetts, 1780–1860* (1990). His other publications include *The Communitarian Moment: The Radical Challenge of the Northampton Association* (1995), together with articles on rural history and the social roots of American economic development in the *Journal of Social History, American Quarterly*, the *Journal of the Early Republic* and in several essay collections. He has also been the co-recipient of the Cadbury Schweppes Prize for innovative teaching in the humanities.

Nancy A. Hewitt is professor of history at Rutgers University. A women's history scholar, Professor Hewitt has received many awards and prizes, including the Jerome T. Krivanek Distinguished Teaching Award and the America: History and Life Prize as well as fellowships from the National Endowment for the Humanities, the Andrew W. Mellon Foundation, and the John Simon Guggenheim Memorial Foundation. Currently, Professor Hewitt is Consulting Editor for the "Women in American History" Series, University of Illinois Press; The U.S. Survey on the Web, a joint project of the American Social History Project and George Mason University; and Feminist Studies. Her publications include *Women's Acativism and Social Change: Rochester, New York, 1822–1872* (1984); *Visible Women: New Essays on American Activism,* co-edited with Suzanne Lebsock (1993); and numerous articles on women's history and women's activist in journals such as *Feminist Studies, Radical History Review, Social History,* and *Oesterreichische Zeitschrift F/R Geschichtswissenschaften.* Her current work, *Forging Activist Identities: Latin, African American, and Anglo Women in Tampa, 1870S–1920S,* will be published by University of Illinois Press in 2001.

Stephen Brier, Executive Editor, cofounded the American Social History Project in 1981 with the late Herbert G. Gutman and served as its Executive Director until 1998. He was the supervising editor and co-author of the first edition of the *Who Built America* textbook. He also co-authored the *Who Built America?* CD-ROMs and was the executive producer of the ASHP's award-winning *Who Built America?* video series and the History Matters Web site. Dr. Brier is the Associate Provost for Instructional Technology and External Programs and the co-director of the New Media Lab at The Graduate Center of the City University of New York. He co-edits the "Critical Perspectives on the Past" book series at Temple University Press. Brier has written numerous scholarly and popular articles on race, class, and ethnicity in U.S. labor history and on the educational impact of instructional media.

Joshua Brown, Visual Editor, is the Executive Director of the American Social History Project/Center for Media and Learning at the Graduate Center of the City University of New York. He also co-directs The Graduate Center's New Media Lab. He was Visual Editor of the first edition of *Who Built America?* and, with Stephen Brier and Roy Rosenzweig, co-authored the *Who Built America?* CD-ROMs. Dr. Brown also co-directed and wrote the *Who Built America?* documentary series, including *Heaven Will Protect the Working Girl* and *Savage Acts: Wars, Fairs, and Empire*. He is the creative director of the digital projects *Liberty, Equality, and Fraternity: Exploring the French Revolution* and *History Matters: The U.S. History Survey on the Web*, and co-executive producer of *The Lost Museum*. The recipient of grants from the National Endowment for the Humanities, American Council of Learned Societies, and the Columbia University Bancroft Dissertation Award, Dr. Brown is co-editor of *History from South Africa: Alternative Visions and Practices* (1991), author of *Beyond the Lines*, a social history of the nineteenth-century pictorial press (2001), as well as numerous essays and reviews on the history of U.S. visual culture. His cartoons, illustrations and designs have appeared in academic and popular publications.

Eric Foner, Consulting Editor, is DeWitt Clinton Professor of History at Columbia University and the author of numerous award-winning books on colonial and nineteenth-century America, including *The Story of American Freedom* (1998) and *Reconstruction: America's Unfinished Revolution* (1988). Professor Foner has served as the president of the Organization of American Historians and the American Historical Association.

Roy Rosenzweig, Supervising Editor, is CAS Distinguished Professor of History at George Mason University, where he founded and directs the Center for History and New Media (CHNM). A Guggenheim and Fullbright scholar, Professor Rosenzweig is the author and editor of books on nineteenth- and twentieth-century social and cultural history, including the award-winning book *The Park and the People: A History of Central Park* (1992), which he co-authored with Elizabeth Blackmar, and *Eight Hours for What We Will: Workers and Leisure in an Industrial City, 1870-1920* (1983), as well as numerous articles. His latest book, written with David Thelen, is *The Presence of the Past: Popular Uses of History in American Life* (1998). With Stephen Brier and Joshua Brown, he wrote the award-winning CD-ROM *Who Built America? From the Centennial Celebration of 1876 to the Great War of 1914* (Voyager) and the sequel, *Who Built America? From the Great War of 1914 to the Dawn of the Atomic Age* (Worth). He is also the co-producer of a historical documentary film, *Mission Hill and the Miracle of Boston.*

Who Built America?

Colonization and Revolution

1492–1815

part one

People of many cultures built America. Modern America's beginnings lay in the fifteenth century, with the collision between Europeans and the peoples of the Americas and Africa, as Europeans first explored and then began to establish overseas empires. Spurred by crises in their own societies, European rulers, religious leaders, adventurers, and merchants commenced a frenetic search for new sources of wealth and for souls to convert to Christianity. They created a vast new system of expropriation and trade, centered on the Atlantic. Over the course of three centuries this system linked together and dramatically transformed Africa, the Americas, and Europe itself.

The creation of new overseas empires led to a massive accumulation of wealth for the elites of Europe, and for some colonists, too. It fostered in Europe and North America the development of capitalism—a new economic system with distinctive political ideologies and social values. On the other hand, the colonization of the Americas was a disaster for many of the peoples caught up in it. Land was violently seized from the native inhabitants, and millions of Africans were forcibly enslaved to provide labor for New World colonies. Ordinary Europeans, too, faced hardship, danger, and premature death as they crewed trading vessels and slave ships, or labored in the fields or towns of the New World.

Among European nations, Spain, France, Holland, and England built a significant presence in North America, each fashioning colonies with different patterns of development. From the seventeenth century onward, however, it was the English who would have the most decisive impact on the continent. The English colonies attracted the most settlers, achieved the greatest population growth, and permanently destroyed or disrupted Native American groups who stood in the way of their expanding settlements. In the seventeenth century, the English expelled the Dutch. During the eighteenth century, the character and development of their colonies also gave the English a dominant position over France and Spain in North America.

England's American colonies differed from one another, however, and from their beginnings evolved distinct ways of life. In the South, favorable soils and climate, together with a determined pursuit of wealth, led to the emergence of plantation agriculture sustained by the labor first of indentured servants and then of African slaves. In much of the North, the immigrants' different aspirations led to the creation of smaller-scale farming and craft economies based primarily on family labor, though with some indentured servants, slaves, and wage workers.

All the American colonies, however, faced political, economic, religious, and racial conflicts. As their settlements expanded, colonists struggled with native groups as they tried to drive the natives from the land. Periodically the colonists would provoke full-scale wars with them. Slaveholders, particularly in the South, faced frequent resistance and occasionally outright revolt from the Africans they held in bondage. Above all, many less wealthy European settlers in America harbored their own aspirations for economic independence and liberty from oppression. Those yearnings led them into conflict with wealthier colonists who sought to exploit or control them. Just as slaves tried to resist their enslavement, ordinary colonists adopted methods of protest and political organization to assert what they saw as their rights. English settlers and their descendants, especially, influenced by the radical ideologies of the English Civil War of the mid-seventeenth century, claimed political rights as "freeborn Englishmen" and nurtured a belief in social equality.

By the 1760s, internal conflicts merged with the larger issue of the colonies' continuing relationship with their "mother country." Colonial activists took steps to secure their rights as subjects of the British empire. When their protests led to war with Britain in the 1770s, they found themselves pursuing complete independence from British rule. A broad coalition of Americans — rich, middling, and poor; northern and southern; men and women — supported independence, and finally secured it in 1783, achieving the first successful colonial revolution in modern history.

As they built an independent United States, former colonists established governments based on republican principles, avoiding the formal social inequalities and hierarchies of European societies, with their monarchies and aristocracies. However, particularly in forming a new national government under the Constitution drafted in 1787, Americans disagreed as to who was best fitted to govern in a post-revolutionary society. Advocates of both elite and popular rule disputed this issue well into the nineteenth century. What was made clear, however, was that political rights would extend only to certain Americans. Women, slaves, and even many free men of color would be wholly or partly excluded from the benefits of citizenship in the new republic.

Throughout the colonial and revolutionary periods, then, a tension existed in America between those with full access to economic and political rights, and those who were shut off from them. This tension and the aspirations of laboring Americans—white and black, male and female—shaped America's early history and defined its emergence as an independent nation. Events were never simply always in the hands of famous political leaders. These leaders were constantly challenged, and events were profoundly shaped, by the aspirations and experiences of the ordinary men and women of all cultures who built America.

At the Loom. A late-eighteenth-century anonymous painting of a woman sewing.

Source: Anonymous, *At the Loom,* oil on canvas, c. 1765—American Folk Art Gallery, Downtown Gallery Papers, Archives of American Art, Smithsonian Institution.

"The Voyage of the Sable Venus from Angola to the West Indies." A 1794 British engraving attempts to ennoble the slave trade by mimicking Sandro Botticelli's celebrated fifteenth-century painting, *The Birth of Venus.*

Source: Edwards, *List of Maps . . .* (1764)—Rare Books and Manuscript Division, New York Public Library, Astor, Lenox and Tilden Foundation.

chapter 1

A Meeting of Three Worlds:
Europe Colonizes the Americas
1492 - 1680

In the fall of 1492, the Genoese-born sea captain Christopher Columbus and his Spanish crewmen landed on a small island in the Bahamas after a two-month Atlantic voyage. They met the inhabitants, who called the island Guanahaní. The encounter was friendly enough, but Columbus had plans for these people. He would take some to Spain. When he returned home the next spring, having left a Spanish encampment on an large nearby island he had renamed "Hispaniola," he brought with him six native men whom he had carried off.

Columbus had sailed in the service of King Ferdinand and Queen Isabella of Spain, searching for a western route to the Indies, the Asian source of spices and other valuable goods. He thought he had found the Indies and he, and Europeans after him, called the inhabitants they encountered "Indians." Columbus made three subsequent voyages and apparently believed to his death, in 1506, that he had reached Asia. But other explorers had already questioned this belief. One, Amerigo Vespucci, calculated that these lands were part of a continent unknown to Europeans. In 1507, in Vespucci's honor, a German mapmaker named this continent "America."

Columbus and his fellow explorers were not, in fact, the first Europeans in America. In the eleventh century, Scandinavian seafarers had reached Labrador, building a settlement that may have lasted for three hundred years; other Europeans knew nothing of this, however. To them, Columbus's 1492 voyage marked the "discovery" of a "New World" that they would soon compete avidly to possess. Imagining the possibilities of new wealth or new land, they would begin a process of conquest and settlement that would alter or destroy the lives of the peoples who already lived there. To Native Americans it marked the beginning of a long invasion that would see them colonized, conquered, and almost wiped out.

Europe's encounter with the Americas would transform both continents, and would soon involve Africa, too. Over great distances, traders, warriors, missionaries, and adventurers would forge new commercial, political, and religious patterns that would sweep millions of people into profound changes. Such dramatic developments brought new wealth to some, but also entailed great brutality and misery. By deliberate action or unintended consequence, those involved in the transformation of

America. The natural bounty of the New World was placed on display in this seventeenth-century Flemish painting. On the left of the central panel, America is represented by Indians who lounge alongside the favored object of European desire, a collection of gold weights.

Source: Jan van Kessel the Elder, *America,* oil on copper, 19 1/8 × 26 5/8 inches, 1664-66 — Alte Pinakothek, Bayerische Staatsgemälde-sammlungen, Munich.

continents also brought disease, malnutrition, violence, murder, and destruction in almost catastrophic proportions.

Tragedy tinged even the first contacts. Columbus brought his six captives to the royal court at Barcelona, where they excited much curiosity. Once in Spain, they were baptized into the Catholic Church and given Spanish names, but they did not live long in Spain. Some were taken back to the Caribbean; one man, named for the heir to the Spanish throne, became a page at court but soon died. Meanwhile, Columbus returned to Hispaniola to find his crewmen's camp destroyed and the men vanished.

Europeans dreamed of finding wealth in the New World, but they knew that to make use of their discoveries they would need much labor. Columbus realized this at the outset, noting in his journal that the natives "should be good and intelligent servants." The subsequent history of the Americas would be shaped by the efforts of conquerors and settlers to use first Native American, and then African and European labor to exploit the continent's wealth. Most of these laborers had to endure poverty and untimely death in the process, but they were the people who built America.

Peoples of the New World

None of those involved in the encounter between Europe, the Americas, and Africa were a single people. Most varied of all were the peoples who lived in the Americas at the time of European contact. Archaeologists continue to debate the origin of North American peoples. Most trace it to the last Ice Age, some 14,000 to 20,000 years ago, when dry land linked Alaska with Siberia. Probably for thousands of years, people migrated in many groups from Asia across this "land bridge," before rising sea levels separated the continents. Recent archaeological finds suggest the possibility that people also migrated to the Americas by sea, and from a much earlier period. In either case, for millennia the descendants of migrants spread out across North and South America and to the Caribbean islands, building a vast array of cultures and languages isolated from the rest of the world, and shaping a variety of landscapes. By 1492, there may have been as many as 75 to 100 million people in the Americas, at that time perhaps one-seventh of the world's population.

Among the most developed societies was that of the Incas, centered in present-day Peru and Bolivia. The Inca empire had expanded in the fifteenth century to stretch far down the Andes mountains and along South America's western coast. A royal family surrounded by aristocrats and others of high rank were supported by the obligatory labor of common people. The cloth woven by women was prized in commerce and religious

ritual. Men grew crops and built extensive road and canal systems that united the empire and irrigated arid land.

The Aztecs of Mexico, too, had forged a loosely confederated empire during the fifteenth century. They conquered the descendants of earlier Olmec, Mayan, and Toltec empires, built on their accomplishments, and exacted tribute from outlying tribes. Fifteen to twenty million strong, the Aztecs boasted impressive achievements in irrigation, metallurgy, and city-building. Tenochtitlán, the capital, had over a quarter of a million inhabitants. Aztec society was based on clans that organized farming, much of it on communal lands. Its upper ranks, headed by a figure the Spanish would call an "emperor," included priests, generals, and wealthy merchants. But the vast majority of Aztec people were craft-workers, farmers, laborers, soldiers, or slaves.

North America was more sparsely populated. Although archaeologists disagree as to how many people inhabited its vast stretches of land, many suggest that there were five million or more in 1500. Other estimates range from one to eighteen million. The groups, smaller than those further south, spoke over three hundred different languages, many of which also had mutually unintelligible dialects. For example, on the coast of what would later become California, over eighty separate languages were spoken. Native American societies had long been based on hunting, fishing, and gathering wild plant foods. Starting around 3000 BCE in the Southwest, and spreading northward and eastward over nearly three thousand years, the cultivation of maize (corn) and other crops had also evolved. In most cases, women performed the main tasks of raising and preparing food. The Hohokam culture (300 BCE to 800 CE) of present-day Arizona, and the later pueblo peoples of the highlands north of Mexico, built irrigation systems not unlike those that the Incas and Aztecs would subsequently construct.

Farming meant more dependable food supplies, population growth, and energy to spare for other activities. Groups that cultivated crops became geographically and socially more stable, and often more powerful, than neighbors who still relied on hunting and gathering. Pueblo societies of the Southwest were among the most complex. By the twelfth century, the Anasazi at Chaco Canyon had a network of twelve towns and over two hundred villages, each built of contiguous rooms, that stretched for twelve miles and housed 15,000 people. Corn-cultivating societies in the Mississippi Valley and parts of the Southeast had also built urban centers and become socially stratified. The largest town, at Cahokia near present-day St. Louis, covered up to six square miles and housed as many as 20,000 people before the year 1300.

Some groups, like the Jumanos of the Southwest and the Ottawas of the Great Lakes region, were known as traders. On the plains and prairies of the West, groups hunted buffalo; some, like the Pawnees, exchanged meat for grain with corn-growing societies nearby. Among the Fox and Sauk of what is now Wisconsin, women mined lead while their menfolk hunted. Eastward to the Atlantic coast, where most early encounters with Europeans took place, people sustained themselves through combinations of horticulture, hunting, and trade.

Most of these Eastern woodland peoples lived in family-band societies with little organized hierarchy. Except in the far Northeast, where poor soil and climate prevented farming, they relied on cultivated crops—typically corn, beans, and squashes—for half or more of their food. Women worked the fields, located close to villages so that they could coordinate crop raising with other tasks. Among the Iroquois, men cleared fields for women to plant and harvest. Villages, each with up to a few hundred inhabitants, contained easily moved shelters, and were relocated according to seasonal and ecological changes. Strong kinship ties bound individuals to their villages and groups. Land and water used by each village were the common property of all its members, and all shared in the yield of hunt and harvest. "Every proprietor knows his own," an English observer would note, "yet all things . . . are used in common amongst them."

The absence of accumulated personal property ensured a roughly equal distribution of wealth. The Iroquois, wrote a French missionary, had

Gathering the Harvest. A drawing from Guamán Poma's *Nueva corónica* depicted Incans gathering the annual May harvest before the Spanish came.

Source: Felipe Guamán Poma de Ayala, *El primer nueva corónica y buen gobierno* (1936)—American Social History Project.

Locations of Selected Native American Groups, c. 1500. The map shows just some among the great number and variety of Indian societies in North America at the time of European contact, including several of the East Coast groups that would come into conflict with the first English colonists in the seventeenth century. "Cultural area" is a concept employed by anthropologists and archaeologists to distinguish different regional patterns among native American cultures.

". . . Their Extraordinary Great Labour . . ."

Europeans were quick to note, usually disapprovingly, the work and leadership roles of Indian women. A sympathetic observer was the separatist minister Roger Williams. Williams helped found the colony of Rhode Island after he was expelled from neighboring Massachusetts Bay for questioning its leaders' authority. Critical of English claims to natives' land, Williams set about studying the nearby Narragansett Indians, and he compiled a handbook of their vocabulary and phrases which he published in London in 1643. This *Key into the Language of North America* also contained vivid observations of Indian life.

. . . from their extraordinary great labour (even above the labour of men) as in the Field, they sustaine the labour of it, in carrying of mighty Burthens, in digging clammes and getting other Shelfish from the Sea, in beating all their corne in Morters: &c. Most of them count it a shame for a Woman in Travell [labor and childbirth] to make complaint, and many of them are scarcely heard to groane. I have often knowne in one Quarter of an houre a Woman merry in the House, and delivered and merry againe: and within two dayes abroad, and after foure or five dayes at worke, &c . . .

The Women set or plant, weede, and hill, and gather and barne all the corne, and Fruites of the field: Yet sometimes the man himselfe (either out ouf love to his Wife, or care for his Children, or being an old man) will help the Woman which (by the custome of the Countrey) they are not bound to.

When a field is to be broken up, they have a very loving sociable speedy way to dispatch it: All the neighbours men and Women forty, fifty, a hundred &c, joyne, and come in to help freely.

With friendly joyning they breake up their fields, build their Forts, hunt the Woods, stop and kill fish in the Rivers, it being true with them as in all the World in the Affaires of Earth or Heaven: By concord little things grow great, but discord the greatest come to nothing.

The *Indian* Women to this day (not withstanding our Howes [hoes], doe use their naturall Howes of shells and Wood.

Which they doe carefully upon heapes and Mats many dayes, before they barne it up, covering it up with Mats at night, and opening when the sun is hot. . . .

The woman of the family will commonly raise two or three heapes of twelve, fifteene, or twentie bushells a heap, which they drie in round broad heaps; and if she have helpe of her children or friends, much more.

Source: Colin G. Calloway, ed., *The World Turned Upside Down: Indian Voices from Early America* (1995).

no poorhouses "because there are neither mendicants nor paupers as long as there are any rich people among them. . . . A whole village must be without corn before any individual can be obliged to endure privation." Economic equality and the sharing of goods reinforced the individual's sense of group identity, but there were strong sanctions against unacceptable behavior: from public disapproval, ridicule, and denunciation, to expulsion and exile. Punishment took the form of exclusion from the sources of survival and comfort.

> ## "The Women . . . Join Together for the Heavy Work"
>
> In this description of the Iroquois, a Jesuit missionary details the collective process employed by the tribe's women in planting and harvesting maize (corn), the staple crop of most North American Indian tribes.
>
> The first work done in the fields is gathering and burning the stubble. Then the ground is ploughed to make it ready to receive the grain which they . . . throw there. . . .
>
> All the women of the village join together for the heavy work. They make numerous different bands according to the different quarters where they have their fields and pass from one field to the other helping each other. . . .
>
> The mistress of the field where they are working distributes to each one of the workers the grain or seed for sowing, which they receive in little *mannes* or baskets four or five fingers high and as wide, so that they can calculate the number of grains given out. . . .
>
> They keep their fields very clean. . . . There is also a set time for this [task] when they work all in common. Then each one carries with her a bundle of little sticks . . . with her individual mark and gaily decorated with vermilion. They use these to mark their accomplishments and to make their works show up. . . .
>
> The festival of binding together corn shocks . . . takes place at night in the fields and is the only occasion when the men, who do no work either in the fields or with the harvest, are called upon by the women to help.
>
> ---
>
> **Source:** James Axtell, ed., *The Indian Peoples of Eastern America* (1981).

Many tribes were matrilineal; identity and status descended from mothers to children. Eastern woodland groups tended also to be matrilocal—after marriage men moved into their wives' households. In these groups, leadership was not restricted to men. Some women enjoyed a degree of personal independence and group power. Prominent Iroquois women controlled their own homes and fields, could divorce at will, and had the right to choose sachems from among the men of their clan. They supervised the deliberations and decisions of their appointees and could remove them for misdeeds or incompetence.

Native American societies were not static. They faced long periods of change, upheaval, and conflict. Between the twelfth and fifteenth centuries, large settlements like Chaco Canyon and Cahokia declined and their populations dispersed to villages. Conflicts over access to land and resources often led to war. During the fifteenth century, five groups in the Northeast (the Mohawk, Oneida, Cayuga, Onondaga, and Seneca) formed the Iroquois Confederacy, apparently to minimize such conflicts between them. The Confederacy, though, aggravated tensions with other groups. As a consequence, martial prowess became so prized that Iroquois leadership commonly passed to those with reputations as the best warriors.

Despite their great diversity, two common factors would influence the fate of indigenous North American societies as they faced increasing contact with Europeans. One was that no society had an overarching state comparable to that of the Aztecs and Incas to the south. This had advantages and disadvantages. When the Spanish invaded Central and South America after 1518, Aztec and Inca civilizations rapidly collapsed. Few North American groups faced this outcome. However, the dispersion and disunity of the groups meant that coordinated response or resistance to invasion was difficult.

A second factor that influenced the outcome of contact with Europeans was that native North Americans, in common with those natives to the south, had little immunity to European diseases. The long isolation of the Americas from other continents meant that as soon as European exploration commenced, there began an exchange of flora, fauna, and microorganisms previously unexposed to one another. New World plant and crop seeds were carried to Europe, as well as diseases such as syphilis, which spread there rapidly after arriving from the Americas in the 1520s. But the effect of European organisms on America was more devastating. New grasses drove out existing species, domesticated animals flourished on a continent where they had been unknown, and, worst of all, new diseases had disastrous effects wherever they took hold. According to one Aztec villager, before the Europeans came there had been "no sickness . . . , no aching bones . . . , no high fever . . . , no burning chest . . . , no abdominal pain . . . no consumption . . . [and] no headache. The foreigners made it otherwise when they arrived here." By 1600, in some areas, typhus, influenza, measles, and smallpox had wiped out ninety percent of native peoples. Such devastation—by reducing native populations—would help conquerors and settlers shape their colonies to serve their own purposes.

Europe: The Background to Overseas Expansion

Led by Hernán Cortés, a Spanish expedition set out in 1518 to conquer Mexico. Successive waves of *conquistadores* followed them. In writing that he was doing so "for King, God, and Gold," one conquistador summed up the main motivations that drove Europeans, from the fifteenth century onwards, to explore and seize overseas territory. Changes in

The Beak Doctor. An illustration from a seventeenth-century medical history showed the recommended outfit to be worn by doctors during the "plague years." The long-nosed mask filled with perfumes and disinfectants, along with the goggle-like lenses covering the eyes, was supposed to protect doctors from the deadly air-borne "miasmas" spreading the Black Death.

Source: Thomas Bartholin, *Historiarum anatomicarum medicarum rariorum* (1661)— Prints and photographs Division, Library of Congress.

European societies over the previous few centuries had initiated political consolidation, religious division, and commercial development. These in turn fostered overseas trade and conquest.

Early in the fourteenth century, European population growth peaked. Wars and changes in climate hampered food production just as resources were stretched to their limits. The consequent famine was followed in the 1340s by plague — The Black Death — that ravaged many parts of the continent, so that between 1300 and 1400 Europe lost two-fifths of its people.

Most land in Europe was held by aristocratic landlords, who controlled the labor of peasant serfs legally bound to the land. Population loss weakened these "feudal" ties, and in struggles between rival nobles, and between nobles and peasants, monarchical dynasties were challenged or toppled. In the fifteenth century, however, as population and wealth began to grow again, some monarchs created new military and administrative structures that asserted their power over unruly nobles. The uniting of the crowns of Aragon and Castile in 1469 created a strong Spanish monarchy. The ascent of the Tudor dynasty in England in 1485 ended the long baronial feuding known as the Wars of the Roses and led to the consolidation of royal administration. The French king Louis XI also began consolidating power between 1461 and 1483. These "new monarchies" laid foundations for centrally administered nation states that would soon start to compete for overseas wealth and territory.

While monarchies consolidated, the Roman Catholic church began to fragment. The wealth and corruption of the fifteenth-century papacy and clergy provoked discontent. Religious dissent grew in some regions, but there also began a movement for church renewal and reform. In Spain this produced a revitalized Catholicism symbolized by the piety of King Ferdinand and Queen Isabella. In Germany and other parts of northern Europe from 1517 on, however, it led to the Protestant revolt of Martin Luther and a succession of reformers who broke with Rome and formed new churches. In Sweden and many German principalities, this Reformation quickly secured the adherence of rulers who saw religion as a vehicle for state power. In England, King Henry VIII's conflict with the papacy over his wish to secure a divorce led him to sever ties with Rome in 1534 and declare himself head of a separate Church of England. From mid-century on, as Catholic reform turned into an effort to regain ground lost to Rome, religious wars wracked France, Germany, the Netherlands, and other regions split by the Reformation.

All this added a religious dimension to European overseas exploration and colonization. The pursuit of national power and territory would be clothed in the imperative to convert "heathen" indigenous peoples to Christianity. Spain revitalized religious orders such as the Franciscans and Dominicans to become spearheads of the Faith in the New World. The struggles of the Reformation produced a redoubling of the effort to save souls in the Americas, as priests belonging to new orders, such as the Society of Jesus (Jesuits), also took up the role of missionaries.

Underlying the political and religious impulses for Europe's expansion, however — and making it possible at all — were long-term developments in trade and shipping that marked the continent's recovery from the crisis of the Black Death. Commercial and banking methods originating in Italy spread to northern Europe and formed the sinews of a trading revival that accompanied a growth of urban populations from 1400 onward. Traders accumulated capital to invest in longer voyages that would connect them to the rich trade in luxury goods from Asia. But they still needed the means to obtain the gold and silver that could purchase these goods. Monarchs seeking the means to pay for their governments and armies were also interested in tapping new wealth. Their efforts were hampered by the fifteenth-century expansion of the Islamic Ottoman empire and the dominance over the Asian trade of states such as Venice. Accordingly, they sought alternative routes to the sources of this trade.

West African Societies

The search drew Europeans into increasing trading contact with Africa. Before 1492, trade with West Africa's Gold Coast (now mostly in Ghana) provided two-thirds of Europe's supply of gold. Africa's total population may have exceeded eighty million, four-fifths of it located south of the Sahara. The continent contained a wide diversity of cultures and economies, from the Islamic traders of the Indian Ocean port of Mombasa, to the farmers of the fertile forest regions of what is now Nigeria, to the food-collecting San and cattle-keeping Khoi-Khoi of the south. In complexity and prosperity, many African societies compared with those of Europe and Central America during the same period.

West Africa, the area that would have most importance for New World developments, was home to roughly eleven million people in 1500. Large towns such as Timbuktu, Gao, and Benin were important trading centers and home to merchants, craftsmen, scholars, and priests, who promoted handicrafts, the arts, education, and legal systems. Most West Africans, however, were rural dwellers, belonging to groups orga-

West Africa. This 1606 Venetian map emphasized the coastal trading centers of Western Africa, incorrectly portraying the interior as largely uninhabited.

Source: Giovanni Battista Ramusio, *Della navigationi et viaggi raccolte. . .* (1606)— Rare Books and Manuscript Division, New York Public Library, Astor, Lenox and Tilden Foundations.

nized around family or kinship networks. Families raised livestock, and farmed tubers, bananas, millet, and rice, using iron tools made in the region for more than a thousand years. Family and kin groups owned land communally, and households often cooperated to produce food. Women dominated food production, and they were active in the marketplaces, where they sold surplus produce.

According to a Portuguese observer in Senegambia before 1510, "[t]he houses of the poor are made of stakes stuck in the ground, hardened with mud and covered with thatch. . . [;] the houses of the rich are made of hardened clay and brick . . . and the interior is very well adorned." Polygyny, whereby one man had several wives, was common, especially among the wealthy. Family and clan leaders exercised authority in the collective leadership of villages and larger political confederations. Religious beliefs varied from one place to another, but most West Africans believed they were tied to a larger spiritual world shaped by the cycles of nature, the legacy of ancestors, and an all-knowing Creator. In the

17

"Our Land is Uncommonly Rich and Fruitful . . ."

Olaudah Equiano was kidnapped at age ten from his home in the Benin Empire on the Guinea coast in southern Nigeria. He was sold into slavery and brought to the New World. Equiano was able to buy his freedom within ten years of his capture, from wages earned as a servant to an English naval officer. He then wrote an autobiography, *The Interesting Narrative of the Life of Olaudah Equiano,* published in New York in 1791, which includes this description of the West African world out of which he came.

The Kingdom of Benin . . . is divided into many provinces or districts, in one of the most remote and fertile of which I was born, in the year 1745, situated in a charming, fruitful vale named Essaka. The distance of this province from the capital of Benin and the seacoast must be very considerable; for I had never heard of white men or Europeans, nor of the sea; and our subjection to the king of Benin was little more than nominal. . . .

We are almost a nation of dancers, musicians, and poets. Thus every great event, such as a triumphant return from battle, or other cause of public rejoicing, is celebrated in public dances, which are accompanied with songs and music suited to the occasion. The assembly is separated into four divisions [or age grades]. . . . Each represents some interesting scene of real life, such as a great achievement, domestic employment, a pathetic story, or some rural sport. . . . This gives our dances a spirit and a variety which I have scarcely seen elsewhere. We have many musical instruments, particularly drums of different kinds, a piece of music which resembles a guitar, and another much like a stickado [xylophone].

Our manner of living is entirely plain; for as yet the natives are unacquainted with those refinements in cookery which debauch the taste: bullocks, goats, and poultry supply the greatest part of their food. These constitute likewise the principal wealth of the country, and the chief articles of its commerce. The flesh is usually stewed in a pan. To make it savory we sometimes use also pepper and other spices; and we have salt made of wood ashes. Our vegetables are mostly plantains [bananas], yams, beans, and Indian corn. The head of the family usually eats alone; his wives and slaves have also their separate tables. . . .

Our land is uncommonly rich and fruitful, and produces all kinds of vegetables in great abundance. We have plenty of Indian corn, and vast quantities of cotton and tobacco. . . . All our industry is exerted to improve those blessings of nature. Agriculture is our chief employment; and every one, even the children and women, are engaged in it. Thus we are all habituated to labor from our earliest years. Every one contributes something to the common stock; and, as we are unacquainted with idleness, we have no beggars. The benefits of such a mode of living are obvious.

Source: Olaudah Equiano, *The Interesting Narrative of the Life of Olaudah Equiano* (1791).

towns and grasslands south of the Sahara, there was growing adherence to Islam.

The labor of family members was often supplemented by that of slaves. Slavery was an ancient system with roots all over the globe: in ancient Greece and Rome, in Africa and Byzantium, under Islam and Christianity. Although it had largely died out in Western Europe, it was widespread in West Africa, where slaves were attached to kinship or fam-

Benin. An engraving from a seventeenth-century Dutch survey of Africa featured the royal court of Benin in the foreground, while the expansive city stretched into the distance.

Source: Olfert Dapper, *Naukeurige Beschrijvinge der Afrikaensche Gewesten van Egyptien, Barbaryen, Libyen* . . . (1676)—Rare Books and Manuscript Division, New York Public Library, Astor, Lenox and Tilden Foundations.

ily groups and worked in the fields or at household tasks. Some slaves had been taken prisoner during war; some were debtors, others criminals. The character of slave or servile status varied: the Asante people had at least five different terms to describe slavery. Many slaves had some rights, and slave status rarely passed from parent to child. Some could work for their freedom; some married into the families that held them; some even owned property. But there were also harsher aspects to slavery. In some societies slaves might be put to sacrificial death, and there was an active and growing slave trade with trans-Saharan and Indian Ocean markets, where women and children, especially, were in demand for their labor or for sexual purposes.

Stateless societies were common in West Africa. Warfare and slavery, however, had led villages and kin groups over time to increase their dependence on kingdoms, whose rulers exacted taxes and tribute but could guarantee peace and encourage commerce. The Mali empire, centered on the Niger river valley, was one of the world's largest in the early fifteenth

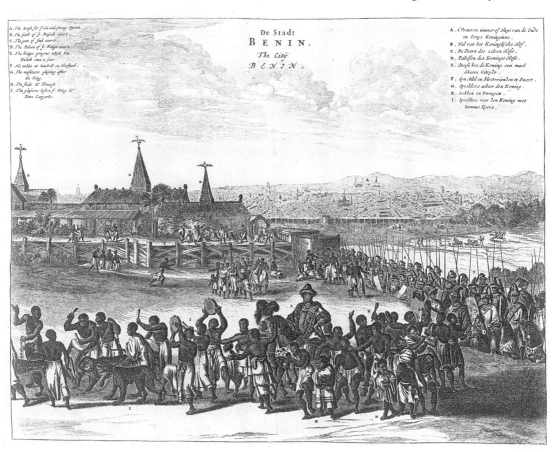

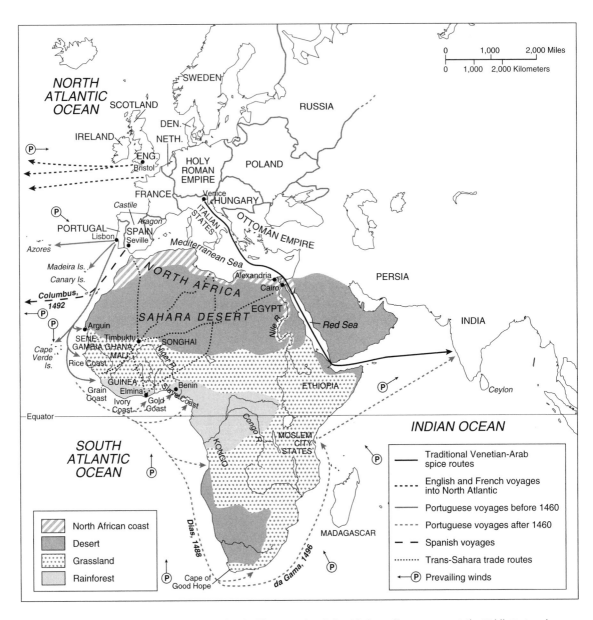

Europe and Africa, c. 1492. Trade centers in West Africa had long-standing links with the Mediterranean coast, the Middle East, and the Indian Ocean. Portuguese explorers established direct European links with West Africa, building trading forts like that at Elmina that would subsequently become important centers of the transatlantic slave trade.

century, but then went into decline. It was eclipsed first by the Songhai empire and then later by smaller but powerful kingdoms—Benin, Dahomey, and Kongo—that rose to prominence after 1600.

Such states encouraged the extension of West Africa's important trading networks. Commercial towns handled a large export trade in gold, ivory, cotton goods, leather, spices, and slaves, to markets in North Africa, the Middle East, and Europe. A European visitor to Benin city found a rich array of goods in its markets:

> Pepper and elephant teeth, oil of palm, cloth made of cotton wool very curiously woven, and cloth made of the bark of palm trees . . . , iron works of sundry sorts, Manillos or bracelets of copper, glass beads and coral. . . . They have good store of soap . . . also many pretty fine mats and baskets that they make, and spoons of elephant's teeth very curiously wrought with divers proportions of fowls and beasts made upon them.

The merchants enriched by this trade exercised significant economic and political power.

Looking for the ivory, gold, and other goods that West Africa's trading networks had to offer, Portuguese sea captains ventured down its coast. In 1470 they reached the Gold Coast, later establishing a trading post at Elmina, and fortifying it against European rivals. By 1600, Portugal was shipping out of West Africa 170,000 gold coins each year—coins that it had obtained in payment for wheat, cloth, and metal goods.

Gold and exotic goods were not all that Europeans wanted from West Africa, however. As early as 1444, Portuguese traders were purchasing slaves for transport to Portugal to become lifelong domestic servants. After they established settlements on Madeira and other islands off the African coast, the Portuguese took slaves there too. To most African rulers and merchants, this trade was merely an extension of existing African slavery and the trans-Saharan slave trade. But as the settlers on the Atlantic islands began developing plantations for growing sugar cane, they purchased African slaves to work them, and so built a prototype for forced labor in the newly discovered Americas.

Portugal, Spain, and American Colonization

Portugal's encounter with the New World grew out of its earlier maritime activities. Since early in the fifteenth century, Portuguese fishing and trading vessels had probed the Atlantic. In time, they established the island colonies of Madeira, the Cape Verde Islands, and the island of São Tomé off the coast of West Africa. Navigational experience and trade with

West Africa after 1470 led to a concerted effort to reach the East Indies. In 1487 a voyage led by Bartholomeu Dias rounded southern Africa; ten years later Vasco da Gama and his crew sailed all the way to India.

Spain's New World empire grew out of conquest at home. On and off since the twelfth century, Spanish rulers and nobles had attempted to drive out or convert Islamic settlers in the south of Spain. This *reconquista,* renewed around 1450, culminated in the defeat of the kingdom of Granada in 1492, and the expulsion or forced conversion of its Muslim and Jewish population. From the 1470s to 1496, Spanish troops also fought to create a colony in the Canary Islands, annihilating the islands' inhabitants in the process.

These conquests set patterns that Spain would follow in the Americas. King Ferdinand and Queen Isabella gave permission for Columbus's voyage just after the fall of Granada. The aim was to extend westward the militancy that Spain had successfully employed close to home. Landing on Guanahaní, Columbus at once claimed the island as a Spanish possession and gave it a Spanish name — an act he and other Spaniards would repeat whenever they came across new territory.

Columbus's voyage spurred Spanish and Portuguese exploration and its associated mission of Christian conversion. In 1493, Pope Alexander VI granted Spain the right to spread the gospels in the Americas. The next year Spain and Portugal signed a treaty in which they divided the entire world between them, an act of arrogance soon marred for Spain when Brazil was discovered in the Portuguese zone. In 1500 Portugal laid claim to Brazil and over the next half-century prepared to extend its Atlantic-island plantation labor system to South America.

Spain, meanwhile, extended its exploration of the Caribbean. In 1502, Spanish families were settled on Hispaniola, and soon were colonizing Cuba, Puerto Rico, Jamaica, and other islands. After 1508 there were even ventures onto the Central American mainland. And in 1513 Vasco Núñez de Balboa confirmed that the Americas were a separate continent when he crossed the Isthmus of Panama and became the first European to see the Pacific Ocean. In the Aztec capital Tenochtitlán, the emperor learned of this Spanish activity as early as 1508, but he punished priest-diviners who foretold an invasion of Mexico. A decade later, however, the

Columbus Discovers . . .?
A plate from a 1493 edition of Columbus's letters depicted an explorer landing somewhere—but not in America. The galley ship in the foreground, which could never have endured an ocean voyage, bore no resemblance to Columbus's vessels. The illustration probably derived from an older publication about Mediterranean exploration.

Source: Christopher Columbus, *Letter to Sanchez* (1493)— Rare Books and Manuscript Division, New York Public Library, Astor, Lenox and Tilden Foundations.

Spanish and Portuguese Possessions in the Americas, to c. 1610. The map conveys the rapidity and scale of Spanish colonization in South and Central America and the Caribbean, and smaller incursions into North America. The 1494 treaty dividing the globe between Spain and Portugal gave the latter Brazil, which the Portuguese turned into an important plantation-slave society in the sixteenth and seventeenth centuries.

conquistador Hernán Cortés and his troops marched on the city and captured it.

Slaughtering and looting by the Spaniards provoked a revolt, and Cortés and his men were driven back. Their recapture of Tenochtitlán in 1521, however, was accompanied by fire and disease, which killed or dispersed much of the population. The capital's fall started a rapid collapse of the Aztec empire itself, which was helped by revolts among tribes the Aztecs had once subdued. The conquerors soon established Spanish rule, set ordinary men and women to forced labor, hunted down nobles and priests, and started wiping out the knowledge and learning that had sustained what the Spaniards considered a "heathen" civilization.

Moving out from the valley of Mexico, the invaders conquered the Maya of the Yucatan and pressed into South America. From 1524 onward, Francisco Pizarro led explorations on the Pacific coast of South America, and in 1532–1533 he invaded the Incas' heartland in the Peruvian Andes. The Spaniards' capture of the Incan capital, Cuzco, provoked a political collapse, and despite rebellions against the invaders, the Incan empire folded as rapidly as that of the Aztecs.

If the conquistadors fought for "King" and "God," they were also envious of Portuguese access to African gold, and wanted their own. Rumors abounded of fabulous wealth in the Americas. "Those lands do not produce bread or wine," claimed a Spanish writer, "but they do produce large quantities of gold, in which lordship consists." The Spanish first looted and shipped off to Spain the treasures from Aztec and Inca temples and palaces. But they soon exhausted these riches and began to search for new sources. In 1545, they were rewarded with the discovery of huge silver ore deposits at Potosí in the Bolivian Andes; smaller ore fields were found in northern Mexico and elsewhere. Many thousands of indigenous people were forced to work in these mines, to supply a flow of precious metals into Spanish coffers that would grow for the rest of the sixteenth century. Between 1500 and 1650 Spaniards extracted more than 180 tons of gold and 16,000 tons of silver from the Americas.

The search for gold also took the Spanish into North America for the first time. Two military expeditions around 1540 failed to find any riches, but soldiers brutally attacked the Indians who resisted them. Francisco Vásquez de Coronado explored from New Mexico as far as Kansas and the Arkansas River.

"Yes, We Eat It." This drawing from Guamán Poma's *Nueva corónica* depicts a meeting between an Incan king and one of the Spaniards left behind by Pizarro after his first voyage to Peru. Curious about the Spanish obsession with gold, the Incan used sign language to ask his visitor if the Spaniards ate the metal. "Yes," the Spaniard answered, misunderstanding, "we eat it." According to Guamán Poma, to satisfy this strange diet, the Indians began to offer gold to the Spaniards.

Source: Felipe Guamán Poma de Ayala, *El primer nueva corónica y buen gobierno* (1936)—American Social History Project.

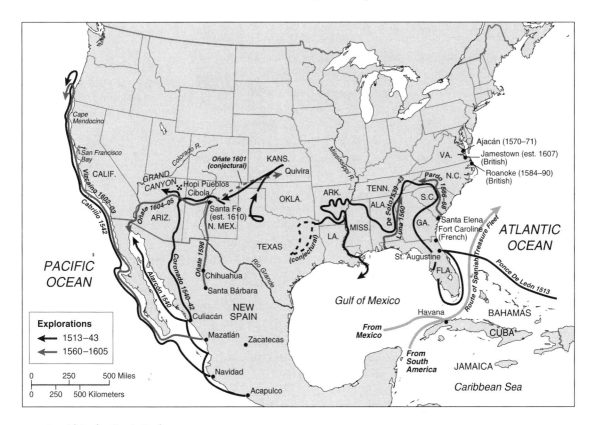

Spanish Exploration in North America, 1513–1610. The gold-seeking expeditions of Hernando de Soto, Francisco Vázquez de Coronado and others before mid-century laid the foundation of settlements in Florida and New Mexico.

Hernando de Soto pushed into Florida, the Southeast, and the lower Mississippi valley, fighting one pitched battle in which thousands of native and Spanish combatants died. These incursions weakened the Indian groups the Spaniards encountered. In central Arkansas, Coronado found thriving towns that, by the time French explorers reached the region in the 1670s, had disappeared.

Spain subsequently ignored North America until other Europeans began to take an interest in it. In 1562 some French Protestants settled on the Florida coast. Fearing attacks on their treasure fleets, the Spanish sent a force to kill them. In 1565 they founded the town of St. Augustine, now the oldest continually occupied European settlement in the United States. Across northern Florida in the following decades, Spanish soldiers and priests established nearly forty mission stations. By 1600 similar efforts were being made north of Mexico. The Spanish pushed into what they named New Mexico, building forts and missions to subdue and convert the indigenous pueblos, and, in 1608, founding the town of Santa Fe.

The Need for Labor

New territory could enhance a nation's power and prestige. Conquered peoples could be converted to Christianity. New land could provide wealth from mining, farming, or trade for governments, investors, and settlers. The Spanish crown, keen to use colonization as a means of rewarding, and thus controlling, Spain's lesser nobility, placed the conduct of overseas conquest under central control, creating the Council of the Indies in 1524 to administer the whole Spanish empire from the port city of Seville. But success depended on obtaining and directing the labor of millions of people.

The conquistadors and noble settlers did not intend to do any work themselves, nor could they attract sufficient emigrants from Spain or Portugal to work for them in the Americas. From Columbus onward they hoped labor would be provided by native peoples who could be subdued and forced to work for their new masters. Whether they were priests seeking souls to convert, planters seeking crops to export, or officials seeking taxes to collect, forced labor systems helped give the conquerors what they wanted.

Adapting methods already used in southern Spain and the Canary Islands, the Spanish crown granted the conquistadors of Mexico and Peru rights to exploit the labor of whole native settlements. Cortés alone had 23,000 workers under this *encomienda* system by the mid-1520s. In parts of Spanish America the system was used until the late seventeenth century to provide labor for missions, mines, and large agricultural settlements. In Florida and New Mexico, Spanish missionaries resettled natives into peasant communities, obliging them to work at erecting mission buildings and growing crops. In Florida, the Spanish missions, with just seventy priests between them, claimed to have over 25,000 Christianized natives working for them by the mid-seventeenth century. Colonial governors exploited native labor to obtain private income while in office. Church and government disputed over the right to put native inhabitants to work for them. In the Southwest, pueblo peoples came into the missions in part to evade harassment by marauding Spanish soldiers.

Implanting a New Faith. A sixteenth-century Spanish drawing approvingly documented the destruction of Aztec temples in Tlaxcala, Mexico.

Source: Glasgow University Library.

But native labor frequently did not fulfill colonists' hopes, even though distance from colonial authority often enabled them to use indigenous populations mercilessly with little fear of restraint. Disease killed large numbers of natives in Spanish America throughout the sixteenth century, and the harsh demands of forced labor helped further reduce their numbers, or wipe them out altogether. The Timucuans of Florida were about 350,000 strong in 1500, but a century later only 7,000 remained; the populations of four out of every five New Mexican pueblos, or villages, declined and the pueblos were abandoned. Harsh enforcement of the *encomienda* system provoked the Indians to resist it. Thus, from the 1570s on, the Spanish partly replaced the *encomienda* with a less harsh system that obliged natives to provide involuntary but compensated labor on public works such as the San Marcos fort at St. Augustine and the town of Santa Fe.

There were also Spanish critics of forced-labor systems. In 1511, the Dominican priest Antonio Montesinos challenged the exploitation of native labor, asking conquistadors "with what right and with what justice do you keep these poor Indians in such cruel and horrible servitude?" He influenced another priest, Bartolomé de Las Casas, who for half a century attacked the slaughter and ill-treatment of New World peoples and rejected the common Spanish assumption that natives were "slaves by nature."

Yet Las Casas knew that the work in the colonies had to be done, and that Europeans could not be found to do it. For him, and for many others in the Spanish and Portuguese colonies, the solution was to import slaves from Africa instead. As they opened up Brazil in the sixteenth century, the Portuguese extended the sugar-plantation system that they had already established in Madeira and the Cape Verde islands. Finding the indigenous people reluctant and impossible to control, they drove them deep into the tropical forests and started bringing laborers from Africa and the islands to work for them. Meanwhile, the Spanish had also begun substituting Africans for native American labor. In so doing they initiated a transatlantic slave trade that would last for almost four centuries.

Africa and the American Slave Trade

Slaves purchased in West Africa were for Europeans an ideal solution to their New World labor problems. In 1510 the Spanish crown legalized the sale of Africans in the Americas, and eight years later a Spanish ship carried the first full cargo of Africans across the Atlantic. By the 1540s slaves were distributed around all the Spanish and Portuguese colonies. Cortés

himself had sixty-eight by 1547, in addition to 169 Mexican slaves. A century later, there were 30,000 African slaves working in the valleys around Lima in Peru, and more in the mines of Mexico and South America. But they would be most used in the plantation economies of Brazil and the Caribbean. By 1600 over 250,000 Africans had been involuntarily removed as slaves to the Americas, and the numbers grew rapidly as French, English, and Dutch merchants began to join in the trade.

The slave trade would prove extremely lucrative. It came to form part of a larger trade pattern that took European goods to Africa, slaves to America, and New World produce back to Europe. The rich pickings, however, were not shared equally among the Europeans who were involved in the slave trade. Many rulers, merchants, and shipowners made money, but most minor officials and the ships' crews endured poor pay and harsh conditions. Of the Dutch West India Company's employees in the slave trade, for instance, only one in twenty made a fortune and another two made more modest profits; the rest made little or nothing.

Some West African rulers, such as the *obas* (kings) of Benin after 1550, curbed the American slave trade. Revolts, such as that by Muslim

"The Spanish Treatment of Fugitive Black Slaves." This is an engraving from the Frankfurt edition of Girolamo Benzoni's widely read sixteenth-century history of America, *Historia del mondo nuovo*. The Milanese author denounced Spanish treatment of Indians and, more unusually, of African slaves in the New World.

Source: Theodor de Bry, ed., *America pars quinta Nobilis & admiratione plena Hieroymi Benzoni . . .* (1595)—British Library.

28

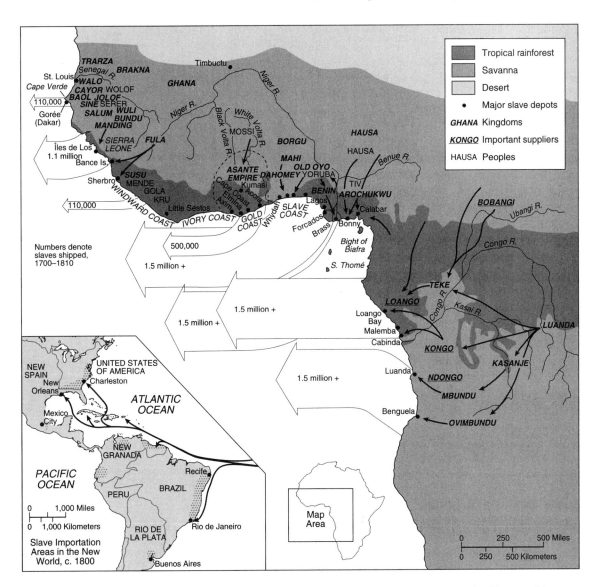

Slave Exports from West Africa to the Americas in the Eighteenth Century. Over 6.5 million people were forcibly removed from Africa as slaves between 1700 and 1810, the majority of them shipped to work on plantations in the Caribbean and Brazil. This map identifies the regions they came from, the main West African kingdoms and slaving ports, and some of the groups from which large numbers of slaves were supplied.

inhabitants on the Senegal River around 1670, grew from resistance to the trade. But many rulers willingly took part. From Senegal to Angola they organized the capture of people, usually from the interior and from ethnic groups other than their own, for delivery to European traders on the coast. They purchased European guns to help fight wars and increase the number of their captives. The King of Dahomey and groups like the Ashanti increased their power and wealth as a result. Some African merchants also did well; at English posts on the Gold Coast, Abee Coffu Jantie Seniees, the leading trader of Cape Coast, and John Kabes, the main middleman between the Ashanti and the port of Komenda, made fortunes selling slaves in the seventeenth century.

". . . Our Country is Being Completely Depopulated"

The slave trade had a profound effect not only on the people enslaved, but also on the African societies they came from. In a 1526 letter from King Nzinga Mbemba of the Congo (baptized King Affonso I) to King João III of Portugal, the African ruler condemned the impact of the slave trade on his own people, an impact that would intensify in the next century.

Sir, your highness should know how our Kingdom is being lost in so many ways. . . . We cannot reckon how great the damage is, since [your Portuguese] merchants are taking every day our natives, sons of the land and the sons of our noblemen and vassals and our relatives. . . . So great, Sir, is the corruption and licentiousness that our country is being completely depopulated, and Your Highness should not agree with this or accept it as in your service. . . . That is why we beg of Your Highness to help and assist us in this matter, commanding your factors [representatives] that they should not send here either merchants or wares, because it is our will that in these Kingdoms there should not be any trade of slaves nor outlet for them. . . .

Moreover, Sir, in our Kingdoms there is another great inconvenience which is of little service to God, and this is that many of our people [are] keenly desirous . . . of the wares and things of your Kingdoms, which are brought here by your people. In order to satisfy their voracious appetite, [they] seize many of our people, freed and exempt men, and very often it happens that they kidnap even noblemen and the sons of noblemen, and our relatives, and take them to be sold to the white men who are in our Kingdoms. . . .

Source: Basil Davidson, *The African Past: Chronicles from Antiquity to Modern Times* (1964).

European nations competed fiercely for a share in the slave trade, but strong local rulers prevented any one of them from monopolizing it. At Ouidah in the kingdom of Dahomey, the king's powerful viceroy kept the port open to all Europeans equally and enforced the rules by which they could do business. The Dahomian state relied on the slave trade, both for the exercise of policy and as a source of revenue.

However, in the long run the slave trade debilitated West Africa. Between the fifteenth and the nineteenth centuries, in one of the largest forced migrations in history, up to twelve million people were sold as slaves to Europeans and shipped to the Americas. Trading economies were ruined as European goods imported to Africa to pay for slaves drove local artisans out of business, and as people fled coastal regions to try and avoid slave hunters. Because European slave traders primarily sought young, healthy men who could be sold in the Americas as field hands, in time women came to outnumber men in West Africa. Family and marriage patterns were altered, and population levels fell. Meanwhile, local demand for women slaves increased. Thus the Atlantic slave trade strengthened African, as well as American, slavery.

Most slaves were seized inland and marched, enchained, by local traders for anything up to a year to the coastal forts. Hunger, sickness, or exhaustion killed many on the way. On arrival at the coast, survivors were locked up to await shipment in prisons known as barracoons, "slaveholds," or "trunks." In the English fort of Cape Coast these were underground caves, each able to hold a thousand or more people. A French trader, Jean Barbot, described the slave pens at Ouidah in the 1680s:

> [T]he slaves . . . are put into a booth or prison, built for that purpose near the beach, all of them together; and when the Europeans are to receive them, they are brought out into a large plain, where the ships' surgeons examine every one of them, to the smallest member, men and women being all stark naked. Such as are allowed [judged] good and sound are set on one side . . . ; [each] is marked on the breast with a red-hot iron, imprinting the mark of the French, English, or Dutch companies so that each nation may distinguish their own property, and so as to prevent their being changed by the sellers for others that are worse.
> . . . In this particular, care is taken that the women, as the tenderest, are not burnt too hard.

Bought and branded by their new owners, captive Africans were chained below-decks in ships designed to carry the largest number of people in the smallest possible space. A German ship's surgeon noted that "some of these poor people obeyed . . . without . . . any resistance," but "others . . . filled the air with heartrending cries which . . . cut me

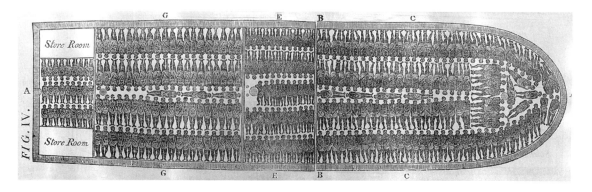

Strange Cargo. A diagram from an 1808 report on the African slave trade showed the interior of a "slaver." Conditions on earlier vessels were even worse.

Source: Thomas Clarkson, *The History of the Rise, Progress, and Accomplishment of the African Slave-Trade by the British Parliament* (1808)—American Social History Project.

to the quick." Barbot recalled one man, a *marabou* or Muslim teacher, who spoke not one word on the two-month Atlantic crossing, "so deep was his sorrow." (He sold him in the Caribbean.)

Shipboard conditions were indescribably horrible. Men, women, and children had to live crammed together among their own excrement—it was said that a slave ship could be smelled downwind long before it came into sight. Traders accepted that on the transatlantic voyage perhaps one in six slaves would die from disease, malnutrition, or suicide. Occasionally they died in shipboard revolts that were brutally suppressed by the European crews. Sailors lived barely more comfortably than the slaves they carried, and their death rates from disease could be even higher. On Dutch vessels one in eight slaves, but one in six crewmen, died at sea. English seamen had a saying:

> Beware and take care of the Bight of Benin
> For the one that comes out there are forty go in.

Slaves went to the Americas not as "Africans," but as members of many different societies and ethnic groups. Even in the 1540s, Cortés's slaves came from many places, from Gambia to Mozambique. Slaves spoke an array of languages and carried with them a variety of customs and beliefs. To reduce the risk of mutiny, shippers often mixed captives from different places. Still, many slaves not only shared common skills, but also assumptions about the nature of religion, kinship, and social life. This often included some connections with the trading cultures of the African seaboard, and some shared knowledge of trading languages. Aboard ship the things they had in common enabled them to begin to cooperate, despite the differences among them. Forcibly shipped across the ocean, they became "African," and started a long, painful transition to a distinctly African-American culture that would be crucial to the history of the New World.

". . . A World of Bad Spirits"

Olaudah Equiano described his West African homeland. Here he recounts in his 1791 autobiography the horrors of the Atlantic crossing. He had been enslaved in Africa and transported to North America as a boy of ten in 1765.

The first object which saluted my eyes when I arrived on the coast was the sea, and a slave ship which was then riding at anchor and waiting for its cargo. These filled me with astonishment, which was soon converted into terror when I was carried on board. I was immediately handled and tossed up to see if I were sound by some of the crew, and I was now persuaded that I had gotten into a world of bad spirits and that they were going to kill me. Indeed such were the horrors of my views and fears at that moment that, if ten thousand worlds had been my own, I would have freely parted with them all to have exchanged my condition with that of the meanest slave in my own country. . . .

I was soon put down under the decks, and there I received such a salutation in my nostrils as I had never experienced in my life: so that with the loathsomeness of the stench and crying together, I became so sick and low that I was not able to eat. . . . I now wished for the last friend, death, to relieve me; but soon, to my grief, two of the white men offered me eatables, and on my refusing to eat, one of them held me fast by the hands . . . and tied my feet while the other flogged me severely. I had never experienced anything of this kind before, and although, not being used to the water, I naturally feared that element the first time I saw it, yet nevertheless could I have got over the nettings I would have jumped over the side. . . .

One day, when we had a smooth sea and moderate wind, two of my wearied countrymen, . . . preferring death to such a life of misery, somehow made through the nettings and jumped into the sea: immediately another quite dejected fellow, who on account of his illness, was suffered to be out of irons, also followed their example; and I believe many more would very soon have done the same if they had not been prevented by the ship's crew who were instantly alarmed. . . . Two of the wretches were drowned, but they got the other, and afterwards flogged him unmercifully for thus attempting to prefer death to slavery.

Source: Olaudah Equiano, *The Interesting Narrative of The Life of Olaudah Equiano* (1791).

The Dutch, French, and English in North America

Spain's colonization of Central and South America extended to the Americas the process of formal conquest that had occurred in Spain itself in previous centuries. In contrast, northwestern Europeans' ventures in America grew out of fishing and commerce. A French-sponsored voyage under Giovanni da Verrazano to the East Coast of North America in 1524 explored from the Carolinas to Maine (where some Abenakis turned their backs on them and exposed their buttocks). A decade later the Frenchman Jacques Cartier explored the St. Lawrence River. French and Dutch ventures looked for furs and other goods to trade. The English began their contact as state-licensed pirates, attacking Spanish shipping in the hope of diverting some of the wealth of the New World into their own hands.

Fishing led to the first semipermanent settlements. From the French and English coasts, men braved the Atlantic to catch cod in the rich fishing grounds off Newfoundland. They established camps on land, for shelter and to process their catches. By 1620 these camps dotted the coastline from Newfoundland and Nova Scotia southwestward to what would become New England.

Meanwhile, interest was developing in more permanent North American settlement. In 1583, Sir Humphrey Gilbert, who had already helped found English colonies in Ireland, claimed Newfoundland for England before his ship sank, with all hands, on its way home. The next year Sir Walter Raleigh planned a base from which to conduct raids on Spanish treasure fleets, and he sent a small force of soldiers to Roanoke Island on North Carolina's outer banks. In 1587, over one hundred settlers arrived to start a colony at Roanoke, but war with Spain delayed a ship bringing supplies to them. By the time it arrived in 1590 the settlers had disappeared without trace.

Warfare in the late sixteenth century hindered ventures to the Americas, but after a peace settlement in 1604, the French, Dutch, and English resumed their efforts to create permanent colonies. The English established a precarious settlement at Jamestown, Virginia, in 1607; the French founded Quebec the following year; and the Dutch established Fort Orange (Albany) on the Hudson River in 1614. In 1620, the English religious dissenters known as the Pilgrims arrived, in the *Mayflower,* at what became Plymouth, Massachusetts. Ten years later, the first fleet of English Puritans, who were also seeking to establish a religious colony, sailed into Massachusetts Bay. By this time, several thousand English settlers were living on the shores of Chesapeake Bay in Virginia. By 1640 tens of thousands more had come to both Massachusetts and the Chesapeake. The English, French, and Dutch vied with one another to establish their claims to parts of North America.

In some ways the French and Dutch colonization efforts differed from one another. France set out to dominate a vast sweep of territory from the St. Lawrence River valley through the Great Lakes region and down the Mississippi River. The French state backed merchants and missionaries who penetrated far into the backcountry, establishing close relationships with native Americans and converting many to Catholicism. Dutch interest, spurred by commercial ventures and organized by the Dutch West India Company, focused on the Mid-Atlantic region, espe-

A New World Beast. Illustrations that appeared in sixteenth-century accounts of European exploration of the Americas often showed exotic wildlife that owed as much to imagination as to observation. This woodcut, from a book by a French Franciscan friar whose two-month visit to Brazil in 1555 was largely spent in a sickbed, probably represented an American bison.

Source: André Thevet, *Les singularitez de la France Antarctique, autrement nommé Amérique* (1557)— Rare Books and Manuscript Division, New York Public Library, Astor, Lenox and Tilden Foundations.

cially the Hudson River valley. Dutch merchants and settlers stayed closer to the coast. They brought their reformed (Protestant) churches with them, but their religious beliefs had less impact on Indian life than those of the French.

In other respects, however, French and Dutch activities in North America were comparable. Both established farming settlements, but though both the French government and the Dutch West India Company tried hard to recruit colonists, social conditions in France and Holland did not induce large numbers of people to want to become farmers in America. Half of the Dutch population were town-dwellers, many of them sharing in Holland's considerable commercial prosperity. France was poorer, and mainly rural, but had low rates of internal migration, and hence relatively few potential overseas emigrants. There were only three thousand French people in Canada by the early 1660s.

More important to both countries was the fur trade. Although Dutch traders stayed close to the coast and to their trading posts at Fort Orange and Nieuw Amsterdam (New York City), they exported large quantities of furs obtained in trade with the Iroquois and other native groups. French fur traders and scouts (known as *coureurs de bois* or "forest runners") traveled far into the interior. The fur trade overwhelmingly employed men, many of whom intermarried with Indians to create a significant mixed-race (*méti*) population.

French and Dutch colonization efforts significantly influenced North American development. Dutch families, legal structures, place names, and expressions helped shape early New York. The French presence in the Great Lakes region and the Mississippi Valley is still marked by hundreds of place names, while the descendants of French settlers still retain their distinct identity in Quebec and other parts of Canada. But the largest and most sustained North American colonies would be English.

Though the English took part in fishing and the fur trade, they became more concerned than either the French or the Dutch with establishing settlements that occupied and cultivated the land. Indeed, after the

New Amsterdam. This satirical English print showed the 1647 arrival of Dutch troops, led by Governor Peter Stuyvesant (left), in New Amsterdam.
Source: Prints and Photographs Division, Library of Congress.

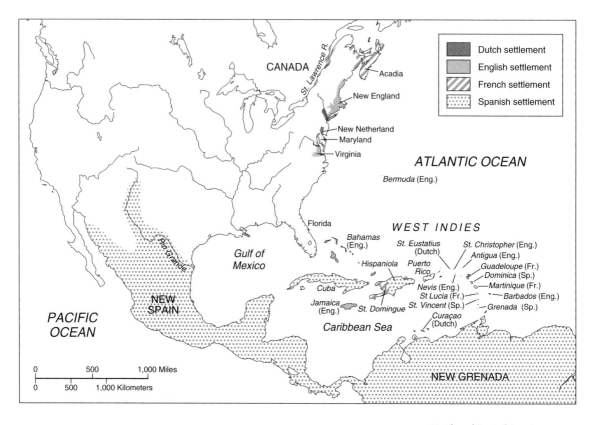

CANADA
St. Lawrence R.
Acadia
New England
New Netherland
Maryland
Virginia
ATLANTIC OCEAN
Bermuda (Eng.)

Florida
WEST INDIES
Bahamas
(Eng.)
St. Eustatius
(Dutch)
St. Christopher (Eng.)
Antigua (Eng.)
Guadeloupe (Fr.)
Dominica (Sp.)
Martinique (Fr.)
Barbados (Eng.)
Grenada (Sp.)
Hispaniola
Puerto
Rico
Cuba
Nevis (Eng.)
St Lucia (Fr.)
St. Vincent (Sp.)
Jamaica
(Eng.)
St. Domingue
Curaçao
(Dutch)

Gulf of
Mexico

Rio Grande

NEW
SPAIN

PACIFIC
OCEAN

Caribbean Sea

NEW GRENADA

Dutch settlement
English settlement
French settlement
Spanish settlement

| 0 | 500 | 1,000 Miles |
| 0 | 500 | 1,000 Kilometers |

English captured New Netherland and renamed it New York in 1664 during one of several wars against Holland's commercial empire, the Dutch gave up their colony to secure more valuable territories elsewhere. Similarly, when British forces seized parts of Canada a century later, the French had richer colonies to safeguard, and they chose to give up New France rather than Caribbean sugar islands that produced more wealth.

By the eighteenth century, English colonies occupied most of the eastern seaboard between Nova Scotia and Florida. These colonies were more than just land claims or commercial outposts. They became permanent homes for streams of migrants from the British Isles and elsewhere. Between 1620 and 1640 alone, almost forty thousand men and women left the British Isles to live in North America. Some English colonists, including the merchants who organized and financed colonial expeditions, sought to make their fortunes from new opportunities in production and trade. But a majority probably had more modest hopes: to achieve economic independence, or religious or political freedoms denied them at home. All were influenced by changes that had been taking place in England over the previous two centuries. The very social and economic

North and Central American Colonies, c. 1660. The map illustrates the land claimed by the major European colonizing powers in the seventeenth century. Though tiny in size, the Caribbean colonies, with their rich sugar plantations, would remain highly important—especially to Britain and France—throughout the seventeenth and eighteenth centuries.

conditions that impelled them to leave for the New World helped shape the character of the English colonies, and the differences between them.

The Roots of English Migration to America

In England, as in many parts of Europe, the Black Death had caused a catastrophic population decline in the fourteenth century. The consequent shortage of labor led, in time, to the collapse of English serfdom. Landlords could no longer compel peasants to carry out compulsory labor services. Serfs resisted, or fled to the comparative freedom of the towns. With no compulsory labor to farm their land, landlords divided their fields up, rented out plots to peasants, and began to live on the rents. Hired laborers benefited from rising wages. Though still condemned to poverty and disease, people working on the land were supported by a web of customary obligations and rights. These included access to common land, where they might graze livestock, grow vegetables, or cut timber. Markets were also regulated, so profiteering was restricted and the price of bread controlled during times of shortage.

But changing circumstances once more undermined peasants' security. Population growth resumed in the fifteenth century, enabling landlords to increase their wealth and political influence. By 1500, landlords were demanding higher rents, usually in cash, and evicting tenants who could not pay. When Henry VIII broke with the Roman Catholic Church in the 1530s, he confiscated vast amounts of church land and granted it to members of the aristocracy and gentry who supported him. In return for political support during the Protestant Reformation, both Henry and — later — his daughter Elizabeth I also enhanced the lawmaking powers of Parliament, in which many nobles and gentry sat. Large landowners found their wealth and status increasing.

"Industry and Idleness." A 1747 engraving by the British artist William Hogarth portrayed two apprentice weavers in a textile workshop. This print was the first in a series that depicted the contrasting careers of two poor young men. The one on the right was always "industrious," while his companion was always "idle." Contemporary viewers recognized that the contrasting behaviors represented, respectively, "virtue" and "vice."

Source: William Hogarth, "The Fellow 'Prentices at Their Looms," engraving (Plate 1 of "Industry and Idleness"), 1747 — Lewis Walpole Library, Farmington, Connecticut.

They also had other opportunities to squeeze higher earnings from their lands. As the textile industry expanded, wool-growing became more profitable, so many landlords evicted tenants to make room for sheep. In a practice called "enclosure," they fenced off the common land on which tenants had relied for part of their livelihoods. Smallholders in Kent petitioned that "they were greatly relieved by [their] common and would be utterly undone if it should be unjustly taken from them." Some tenants moved to woodland or upland areas where they could eke out an existence. Thousands more became hired farmhands or weavers, left the land for the towns, or went to work as miners, sailors, or soldiers. Many single women were obliged to spin wool into yarn in isolated drudgery. By 1600, forty percent of English people were working for wages.

Dislocation from the land and the erosion of customary rights provoked widespread resistance. Crowds, often led by women, rioted against bakers who ignored price ceilings, seizing loaves and leaving money to cover the "just price," while a popular ballad warned of divine punishment for injustice:

> Take heed how they do oppress
> The poor that God obey
> God will not let these long alone
> That do him wrong.

Tenants resisted enclosure, sometimes violently. In 1596, Somerset rioters complained that "rich men had gotten all into their hands and will starve the poor," while another verse condemned property laws that treated rich and poor differently:

> They hang the man and flog the woman
> Who steals the goose from off the Common;
> But let the greater felon loose
> Who steals the Common from the goose.

But despite these protests, the poor faced increasing hardships. Between 1520 and 1580 alone, England's population grew from 2.5 million to 3.5 million, helping keep wages low. Yet the prices of food, rent, and fuel were rising rapidly—fivefold between 1530 and 1640, partly because of inflation caused by the influx into Europe of gold and silver from Spanish America. War in the 1590s disrupted the cloth trade, throwing many in the textile districts out of work, while poor harvests in the 1590s and 1620s caused severe hardship, even famine in a few localities. Young men migrated to find jobs as servants. Destitute men and women seeking work tramped the countryside or flocked to towns. London's population quadrupled between 1500 and 1600, reaching at least 200,000. According to a clergyman in 1622, the city was crowded with "people who rose early, worked all day and went late to bed, yet were scarce able to put bread in their mouths . . . [or] clothes on their backs." To England's governing classes, poverty was a threat that needed controlling. Laws that prohibited vagrancy, punished "idleness" or unwillingness to work by imprisonment or public whipping, had the effect of compelling the poor to work for low pay and long hours in harsh conditions.

Widespread poverty contrasted with the prosperity, not only of landowners but of merchants in London and other towns who had grown rich from textile manufacture or from the expansion of inland and overseas trade, and were willing to invest in new ventures. In return for supporting the monarchy, groups of merchants were granted special privileges, including monopolies of trade with particular parts of the world. Beneficiaries included the founders of the Muscovy Company (1553), the Spanish Company (1577), the Senegal Adventurers (1588), the East India Company (1600), the Virginia Company (1607), and the Massachusetts Bay Company (1629). These companies organized shipping for exploration or trade, and some also began to sponsor attempts at overseas settlement.

From the 1560s onward the government had promoted English and Scottish "plantations" in parts of Ireland, displacing Catholic peasants from fertile land to make way for Protestant settlers. Some commentators came to see overseas colonization as a solution to English poverty. The poet John Donne suggested that it would "sweep your streets, and wash your doors, from idle persons, and the children of idle persons, and employ them," while Sir Francis Bacon saw it as a cure for "rebellions of the belly" brought on by the reorganization of agriculture.

By the early seventeenth century, the significant elements of English overseas colonization were falling into place: merchants, shipowners, and landholders ready to seek out new sources of profit; a Crown keen to promote English and Protestant expansion by granting special rights; and a sizable population of mobile poor, who might provide the labor for schemes of trade and settlement. As the poor flocked to towns in search of work, they met promoters who offered passage to the New World in exchange for a few years' labor as indentured servants. Many men and some women opted to migrate to North America. They took with them a powerful legacy of hardship and social injustice, a suspicion of landlords, a desire for land of their own, a hope for some economic independence, and a determination to defend popular rights.

Colonizing the Chesapeake

The first English settlement at Jamestown, Virginia, organized in 1607 by the Virginia Company of London, mimicked the fantasies of easy wealth that had first driven the Spanish to the New World. Virginia, promoters hoped, would furnish precious metals, or at least valuable herbs, such as sassafras, a supposed cure for syphilis, that was reported to grow in abundance. Explorers' accounts misled settlers into expecting a paradise where they could gather food without effort, would need little clothing or shelter, and could make docile native people work for them when necessary. The one hundred and five men and boys who founded Jamestown had no idea how to build a permanent farming settlement. About one in five were aristocrats, "gentlemen" who considered work beneath them. Most of the rest were unskilled laborers, military recruits, and servants. The few craftsmen included clockmakers, jewelers, and gentlemen's perfumers.

Instead of the paradise they had expected, they found a harsh, disease-ridden place. Even one of its leaders, John Smith, remarked that early Jamestown was "a miserie, a ruine, a death, a hell." Precious supplies dwindled and fields remained uncultivated, but starving gentlemen spent the time playing bowls. Far from being willing to work for them, watching Indians waited for the English intruders to die. Most did. Only thirty-five survived until spring 1608, and they were on the point of abandoning the colony when new settlers and supplies arrived.

A Festive Dance. John White drew a "green corn" celebration in the Indian village of Secoton sometime around 1585. The Indians in his drawings appeared exotic, yet also reassuringly familiar. Their poses, resembling figures in classical antiquity, and their discreetly draped clothes may have been intended to calm English fears of Indian violence and immorality. White, who was appointed governor of the unsuccessful Virginia colony of Roanoke in 1587, underplayed or omitted many aspects of Indian life that would disturb English sensibilities and deter potential colonists.

Source: John White, watercolor over black lead, touched with white, ca. 1585, 10 3/4 × 14 1/8 inches—British Museum.

For the next decade, Virginia Company officers sought to impose order. They tried to recruit morally superior men. They introduced harsh military discipline, dividing servants into work gangs and viciously punishing infractions of the rules. Punishments varied according to rank: gentlemen convicted of capital crimes were hanged or shot, but servants were often mutilated before and after execution. For lesser crimes, the wealthy paid fines while others were whipped, branded, or had body parts cut off. Men labored in the fields while the handful of women, such as Ann Leyden and June Wright, stitched shirts and did other tasks. When their work was judged inadequate, according to an eyewitness, the women were "whipped, and Ann Leyden being then with child, the same night thereof miscarried." Settlers could not return to England without permission, and their often pitiful letters home were censored. Coercive methods maintained the colony in a bleak, precarious existence, setting a precedent for the later introduction of slavery.

Soon, however, the Virginia Company had the chance to use its servants to make money. In 1611 the company began to grow tobacco, popular in England for its supposed medicinal properties. Demand soared. Within a few years the company, and those who acquired land from it, turned wholeheartedly to tobacco cultivation. Virginia began to seem more hospitable. Its fertile soil and a long growing season were suited to tobacco. Tidal rivers made the interior accessible to the vessels that would carry the crop across the Atlantic. The colony boomed. Tobacco exports rose from 2,000 pounds in 1615 to 1.5 million pounds in just fifteen years.

To entice more people to go to Virginia and grow tobacco, the Virginia Company offered land in return for labor or other services. Skilled artisans would receive "a house and four acres as long as they plied their trades." A man willing to cultivate new land could receive fifty acres for himself and another fifty for every person he brought to the colony. Bonded servants were promised land at the end of their terms of service. For a settlement whose population was overwhelmingly male, young, and single, the company even shipped in women to sell as wives to men who could pay 120 pounds of tobacco for them.

The company also took steps to foster support from landowning settlers. It softened martial law. In 1619 it set up an assembly, the House of Burgesses, to which all adult freemen could elect representatives to share government responsibilities with company officers. Between 1619 and 1625 nearly 5,000 new settlers arrived. But such numbers outgrew the Virginia Company's military organization, and in 1624 King James I dissolved the company, making Virginia a royal colony under his direct supervision.

"What Can You Get by War . . . ?"

Powhatan, a leader of the Algonquian-speaking people in colonial Virginia, speaks eloquently about the rapidly deteriorating relations between the first colonists and the Indians upon whom the English were so dependent in the colony's early years. Powhatan's statement was addressed to Captain John Smith, governor of the Virginia colony, in 1612 (only five years after the colony's founding), and was taken down by two of Smith's associates.

Captain Smith, you may understand that I . . . know the difference of peace and war better than any in my Country. But now I am old, and ere long must die. My brethren, namely Opichapam, Opechankanough, and Kekataugh, my two sisters, and their two daughters, are distinctly each other's successors. I wish their experiences no less than mine, and your love of them, no less than mine to you: but this bruit [noise] from Nansamund, that you are come to destroy my Country, so much affrighteth all my people, as they dare not visit you. What will it avail you to take [by force] that you may quietly have with love, or to destroy them that provide you food? What can you get by war, when we can hide our provisions and fly to the woods, whereby you must famish, by wronging us your friends? And why are you thus jealous of our loves, seeing us unarmed . . . and are willing still to feed you with that [which] you cannot get but by our labors? Think you I am so simple not to know it is better to eat good meat, lie well, and sleep quietly with my women and children, laugh, and be merry with you, have copper, hatchets, or what I want being your friend; than be forced to fly . . . , and thus with miserable fear end my miserable life, leaving my pleasures to such youths as you? . . . Let this therefore assume you of our loves, and every year our friendly trade shall furnish you with corn; and now also if you would come in friendly manner to see us, and not thus with your guns and swords, as [if] to invade your foes.

Source: Wilcomb E. Washburn, ed., *The Indian and the White Man* (1964).

Early Virginia was hardly a community. It was rather an armed camp where individualism, competition, and fear prevailed. Men scrambling for wealth had little time for public spirit or civic cooperation. Instead of building towns or villages, tobacco planters scattered along the navigable rivers. The most successful planters owned hundreds of acres, but most of them and their servants lived alike in crude one-room shacks, miles from neighbors or friends. Planters abused servants with "intolerable oppression and hard usage." One servant claimed that he was treated "like a damn'd slave." Death rates remained high. Over seven thousand people migrated to Virginia between 1607 and 1625, but the colony's population was only 1,200 when the Virginia Company was abolished.

In addition to hunger and disease, settlers faced the risk of massacre by Indians. The first colonists had provoked resentment among the local Algonquian-speaking tribes by stealing food from them. Within two years, the natives' leader, Powhatan, declared war, noting that the English "comming hither is not for trade, but to invade my people, and possesse my country." As part of the diplomacy that patched up this dispute in 1614, Powhatan permitted his daughter Pocahontas to marry the Englishman John Rolfe, but during a visit to England in 1617 she fell ill and died. As the Virginia colony grew so grew its demand for land. Conflicts recurred, twice more erupting into war, when Powhatan's brother and successor Opechancanough led campaigns against the settlers. During the first, in 1622, his men killed 347 colonists, prompting the English to promise not to encroach on tribal land. But by 1644, with the Virginia

Pocahontas. This is a portrait of the daughter of Chief Powhatan, at the age of twenty-one, soon after her arrival in London. According to John Smith, Pocahontas saved him from execution when he was captured by the Algonquians in 1607. She subsequently married an English gentleman and became the first Indian of "royal blood" to be brought to England for the edification and entertainment of the nobility— and the first to succumb to England's inhospitable climate, probably dying of tuberculosis.

Source: Anonymous (after an engraving by Simon van de Passe), after 1616, oil on canvas, 30 1/4 × 25 1/4 inches— National Portrait Gallery, Smithsonian Institution.

Ætatis suæ 21. Aº. 1616.

Matoaks als Rebecka daughter to the mighty Prince Powhatan Emperour of Attanoughkomouck als Virginia converted and baptized in the Christian faith, and Wife to the wor.ll Mr Tho: Rolff.

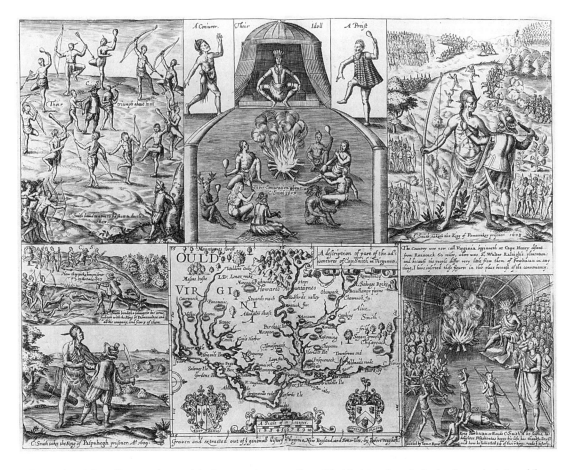

John Smith and the Indians. Smith, one of the first governing councillors of the Virginia colony, took a less benevolent view of the Indians than John White. This engraving from his *Generall Historie of Virginia,* published in 1624, showed the Chesapeake tribes as the threatening giants. Smith recommended repression: "bring them to be tractable, civil, and industrious . . . that the fruit of their labor might make us some recompense."

Source: (Robert Vaughan) John Smith, *The Generall Historie of Virginia* (1624)—Houghton Library, Harvard University.

colony's population at 8,000, increasing encroachment by settlers again caused hostilities. More than five hundred colonists died before Opechancanough was captured and killed in 1646, and the Powhatans signed a treaty acknowledging English authority.

By this time, the colony of Maryland had been established adjacent to Virginia in the upper part of Chesapeake Bay, under a royal charter granted in the early 1630s to the Earl of Baltimore. Lord Baltimore, a Catholic convert, sought a refuge for fellow Catholics facing persecution in England. His family planned to set up feudal manors, with land leased to tenant farmers. But as in Virginia, the promise of land and of profits from tobacco cultivation attracted migrants, both Protestant and Catholic. To obtain support, the proprietors had to modify their plans, offering land to own as well as rent, and permitting the formation of a representative assembly of freemen. The flow of migrants to both Chesapeake colonies continued to grow. By 1660, about 50,000 people had crossed the Atlantic to settle there.

Colonizing New England

The Virginia Company had hoped to attract members of the English gentry to America, and had recruited servants from among the poor, single, and young. But many among the "middling sort," or middle classes, too, were discontented with changes in England. The large number of religious reformers known as Puritans, in particular, distrusted the policies of the Stuart kings James I and Charles I and faced a measure of persecution.

Puritans included members of the gentry, village craftsmen and small landowners, urban merchants and artisans. Their difficulties arose from theological disputes thrown up by the Reformation. They were Calvinists, who believed that God alone determined who would be saved and who would be damned after death; they rejected the "Arminian" doctrine that human actions could earn salvation. Though most Puritans worshiped in the Church of England, they objected to its elaborate rituals, ornate churches, and the authority of bishops. They emphasized the authority of the Word of God in the Bible, and feared that the Stuarts were leading a return to Catholicism. "An Arminian is the spawn of a papist," warned a Puritan member of Parliament in 1629.

Puritans loathed the society taking shape in England: its disorder, its extremes of wealth and poverty, and what they saw as its sinfulness. One wrote that they abhorred "the multitude of irreligious, lascivious and popish affected persons," who had spread "like grasshoppers" across the country. Because they saw churches as communities of the godly, they assembled for preaching, not ritual, and sought to choose their own ministers. Some advocated separation from the English church and had already faced persecution. These included the Pilgrims, who had spent ten years' voluntary exile in Holland before sailing to New England in 1620. After 1625, Archbishop of Canterbury William Laud pressed for conformity to Church of England practices, and some other Puritans began to look for a place where they could avoid England's evils, build their own community, and establish a godly society for the world to see.

In 1629 investors formed the Massachusetts Bay
Company. A group of Puritans led by an East Anglian
gentleman, John Winthrop, promptly turned the company into a vehicle for their plans. The company's
charter granted it political and economic rights in New
England and, unusually, failed to require that company
meetings be held in England. Taking advantage of this
technicality, Winthrop and his recruits sailed in 1630 to
found a colony in Massachusetts armed with the right to
govern their own affairs. The charter would remain the
colony's legal basis until 1684.

Once arrived in Massachusetts, Winthrop and his
followers conducted the colony to suit their own purposes. They abandoned the plan to make profits for the
Massachusetts Bay Company. Membership in the company was closed to investors, but granted only to male
members of an organized Puritan church. The company's governor, Winthrop, and members of its
governing body, the General Court, became the colony's political leaders.
A tax protest in 1632 obliged Winthrop to make the General Court a
representative body. Over the next decade, more than twenty thousand
English migrants, mainly Puritan families with their children and servants, arrived to establish new farms and communities on New England's
rocky soils, aiming to build for themselves a way of life that England
denied them.

They began by establishing Boston and a ring of towns around it.
They incorporated ramshackle fishing camps previously established on the
coast, to form towns such as Salem, Marblehead, and Gloucester. They
also made connections with the Pilgrims' Plymouth Colony, which would
remain separate until 1691. Like the Pilgrims when they founded Plymouth, the Puritans were helped by an epidemic that had killed many
members of the local Massachusett tribe in 1616 and 1617.

By the mid-1630s political disputes and growing numbers led the Puritan colonists to expand south and west. When the government expelled
him in 1635 for questioning its authority, the minister Roger Williams led
settlers into nearby Rhode Island to found a colony that would become a
haven for exiles from Puritan orthodoxy. Migrants from Plymouth and
Massachusetts who settled in the Connecticut River valley helped found
the separate colonies of Connecticut and New Haven. Outbreaks of
smallpox in 1633 once again devastated native settlements in these areas.
"It pleased God to visit these Indians with a great sickness," wrote
Plymouth governor William Bradford; so many died that "many of them
did rott above ground for want of buriall." Keen for fresh land, New

"Mr. Richard Mather." This
1670 portrait of the Puritan
leader was the first woodcut
printed in the colonies.

Source: John Foster, woodcut,
6 1/8 × 4 7/8 inches, 1670—
American Antiquarian Society.

Englanders saw as providential the deaths of so many of the people who stood in their way.

More than profits, Puritans were pursuing religious and community ideals. They were attached to owning their own property, but they set up community institutions to regulate one another. Hardworking men and women bent on self-improvement, for most of them the ideal society revolved around cooperation rather than individualism. When two Puritan noblemen inquired in 1635 about migrating to Massachusetts, they were told that they would be welcome but would receive no special privileges. Neither came. Establishing their towns and farms in a land they saw as a "wilderness," New Englanders created one of the important templates for early American society in the northern colonies.

The English Revolution and Its Effects on the Colonies

In England, by 1642, the combination of social change, economic dislocation, religious conflict, and political instability was doing more than persuading some Puritans to migrate to North America. It brought on a civil war, a period of political upheaval called the English Revolution that was to have important ramifications for people both in England and in the English-American colonies.

By the late 1630s disputes over religion and royal authority were turning into a serious crisis. Since 1629, Charles I had ruled without calling Parliament into session, asserting a monarch's "divine right" to govern and levying taxes on his own authority. He had many supporters, but large numbers of landowners, merchants, and middling folk opposed such arbitrary rule and insisted that Parliament be consulted. Puritans sided with Parliament against the king. In 1640, faced with a rebellion in Scotland and no money to pay for an army to put it down, Charles was forced to recall Parliament in the hope that it would approve taxes. But it resisted him, and two years later, after London apprentices had led crowds to defend Parliament against royal troops sent to suppress it, the crisis turned into open warfare. Puritans stopped leaving for Massachusetts; indeed some returned home from the colony. As one minister put it, England itself could now be "a land of saints and a pattern of holiness to all the world."

After two periods of bitter fighting, the king was arrested and, in early 1649, executed. England became a republic, led by the Puritan Oliver Cromwell until his death in 1658. War brought social upheaval and an extraordinary upsurge of religious and political debate in England.

THE SHEPHERDS ORACLES.

Hope   Charitie

Faith

Obedience

Good workes.

RELIGION

Written by Fran: Quarles.

London Printed for John Marriott and Richard Marriott &c. W. M sculp:

Civil War. The frontispiece illustration from a 1645 book by the English religious poet Francis Quarles portrayed King Charles defending the tree of "Religion" from Cromwell's followers.

Source: Francis Quarles, *The Shepherd's Oracles* (1645)—Henry E. Huntington Library and Art Gallery.

Radicals questioned almost every facet of established society. Poor and middling men and women, calling themselves Levellers, Diggers, Seekers, or Ranters, attacked the Church's right to levy tithes (a one-tenth share of crops or income), and questioned enclosures, wage labor, and even property itself. They asked why more people should not have the vote, and whether heaven and hell were inventions of the rich to keep the poor in subjection. Quakers condemned religious, civil, and social hierarchy, stressing the authority of the divine "inner light" in all believers. Quaker women as well as men preached and prophesied.

The ruling and propertied classes began to unite against what they saw as expressions of anarchy, and they suppressed or brushed aside many of these radical voices. Closing ranks, they arranged for the restoration of the monarchy under Charles II in 1660. Even Puritan gentry sighed with relief at their escape, as one put it, from a "world of confusions . . . [and] unheard of governments." But the civil war period left a rich legacy

"The Poorest He That is in England Has a Life to Live . . . "

English revolutionaries heatedly debated the principles of popular government. In 1647, the "Agreement of the People" was presented to the General Council of the revolutionary army, meeting at Putney, near London. The ensuing Putney Debates revealed sharp divisions among the revolutionaries. Commissary-General Ireton, a close ally of Oliver Cromwell, argued that ownership of property was a necessary qualification for the franchise. Colonel Rainborough and Mr. Petty, leaders of the radical Levellers, asserted that all freeborn Englishmen should be allowed to vote for representatives to the new Parliament. The terms of this debate would reverberate a century and a half later in America's own revolution.

MR. PETTY: We judge that all inhabitants that have not lost their birthright should have an equal voice in elections.

COLONEL RAINBOROUGH: . . . For really I think that the poorest he that is in England has a life to live, as the greatest he; and therefore truly, sir, I think it's clear, that every man that is to live under a government ought first by his own consent to put himself under that government, and I do think that the poorest man in England is not at all bound in a strict sense to that government that he hath not had a voice to put himself under. . . .

COMMISSARY-GENERAL IRETON: I think that no person has a right to an interest or share in the disposing of the affairs of the kingdom, and in determining or choosing those that shall determine what laws we shall be ruled by here—no person hath a right to this, that hath not a permanent fixed interest in the kingdom. . . . But that by a man's being born here he shall have a share in that power that shall dispose of the lands here, and of all things here, I do not think it is sufficient ground. . . . Those that choose the representatives for the making of laws by which this state and kingdom are to be governed are the persons who, taken together, do comprehend the local interest of this kingdom; that is, the persons in whom all land lies, and those in corporations in whom all trading lies. . . .

COLONEL RAINBOROUGH: I do not find anything in the Law of God, that a lord shall choose twenty burgesses and a gentleman but two, or a poor man shall choose none. I . . . am still of the opinion that every man born in England cannot, ought not, neither by the law of God nor the Law of Nature, to be exempted from the choice of those who are to make laws for him to live under, and for him, for aught I know, to lose his life under. . . .

Source: Christopher Hill, ed., *The Good Old Cause: The English Revolution of 1640–60* (1949).

of ideas for those who, in the future, would criticize monarchy or the rule of the wealthy. Even as they put a king back on the throne, English elites accepted the principle that rulers had obligations to their people, and that a people could justifiably depose a monarch who failed to honor these. Popular attachment to traditional rights also survived, particularly the belief that people should be able to live in dignity as economically independent members of their communities. English men and women, including many Quakers, who shared such attitudes, were among those who took passage to America in the later decades of the seventeenth century.

The Revolution also accelerated England's commercial development and social polarization. It limited the monarch's taxing power and abolished many aspects of feudal land-ownership, but it confirmed the property rights of landowners and cleared the way for further enclosure and agricultural improvement. Ties were strengthened between agriculture, commerce, and monied interests.

Under both Cromwell and the restored monarchy, a vigorous foreign policy regulated trade, promoted colonial development, and waged war against commercial rivals, particularly the Dutch. Behind this effort were economic doctrines, loosely known as "mercantilism," that aimed at enriching the state by ensuring a net inflow of wealth into the country. Trade laws, colonies, and naval power were all instruments used in the effort to increase national prosperity by competing with other European powers to increase England's share of total wealth, which mercantilists believed remained roughly fixed.

Economic policies at first aimed to expand England's share of the commodities and raw materials produced in the colonies, but they would later also seek to expand colonial markets for English goods. The Crown granted trading monopolies, which Parliament protected from competition, and the king granted economic privileges, land, and even entire colonies to his favorites. A web of monopolies, restrictions, subsidies, and tariffs linked these colonies to England, all aimed at assuring profits for the mother country.

Native Americans: Collapse, Resistance, Exchange

America had not been the first place the English colonized. English attitudes were shaped by their conquest and settlement of parts of Ireland since the mid-sixteenth century. "Planters" in Ireland asserted their superiority over the people whose land they took over. They disdained the Gaelic Irish peasants, whom they viewed as savages. Some early settlers in

"They Live Like Beasts, Voide of Lawe and All Good Order." England's subjugation of Ireland during the reign of Elizabeth I served as a rehearsal for the colonization of Virginia in the seventeenth century. As in the later New World colony, the crown licensed private individuals and companies to undertake conquest and settlement for their own profit. Colonists expropriated Irish lands and rationalized their violence against the Irish by viewing them as savage pagans. In this sixteenth-century woodcut, English soldiers returned to their camp carrying a grisly trophy of conquest.

Source: John Derricke, *The Image of Irelande* (1581) — Folger Shakespeare Library.

America compared the native peoples they encountered favorably with the hated Irish, but too often the settlers' view of the Irish prepared them to hold similar contempt for Native Americans.

This outlook influenced their reaction to the Indians' destruction by disease. Local inhabitants, wrote one of the first Massachusetts settlers in 1630, "above twelve years since were swept away by a great & grievous Plague . . . so that there are verie few left." Like many Puritans he saw the epidemic as part of God's design to clear the land for His chosen people. Many Virginians and New Englanders perceived native Americans as inferior, because they spoke in strange tongues, cultivated with hoes rather than plows, and had no concept of property accumulation. William Simmonds wrote of Virginia in 1612 that "we found only an idle, improvident, scattered people, ignorant of the knowledge of gold, or silver, or any commodities; and carelesse of anything but from hand to mouth." Such attitudes would justify, to the English, the seizure of native land, misunderstandings over theft, and the subjugation or expulsion of Native Americans, whom colonists found in their way.

Yet Indians were not simply victims of disease and conquest. Even in eastern North America, where native cultures were largely eradicated by the nineteenth century, there were over two hundred years of contact, conflict, and negotiation. What actually happened to Native American groups depended not just on what settlers demanded of them, but on their own actions and the character of their own societies.

51

Indians tried to incorporate settlers into their own systems of authority. At Jamestown in 1607 and 1608, Powhatan treated John Smith and the Virginia leaders just like the other local chiefs who owed allegiance to him, and his offer of Pocahontas in marriage to John Rolfe in 1614 was part of an effort to control the English. The aim of Opechancanough's challenges to the growing Virginia settlements was to set bounds on both the colony's expansion and unreasonable English behavior. A Wicomesse leader told Maryland's governor in 1633 that "since . . . you are heere strangers and come into our Countrey, you should rather confine yourselves to the Customes of our Countrey, than impose yours upon us."

For some groups, hostile neighboring tribes posed more problems than Europeans. In the Southwest, Apaches attacked pueblo tribes, making them susceptible to Spanish domination. In the eastern Great Lakes region, the Hurons lost half their numbers to disease in the 1630s and were then attacked by the Iroquois; by 1649, they were scattered. Algonquian-speakers in the St. Lawrence valley, also pressed and defeated by the Iroquois, turned to the French for help. Over several decades the two built an alliance that enabled the Algonquians to hold the Iroquois back and reach an agreement with them in the 1690s.

Yet the European settlements did oblige native cultures to adapt. From bands based on kin groups they formed more structured "tribes." The fur trade also brought irreversible changes. Some groups, like the Micmacs of Nova Scotia, found themselves trapped by it. Dependent entirely on hunting and fishing, the Micmacs had ensured their survival by avoiding overhunting. But when European traders offered guns, cloth, ironware, and drink, they increased their hunting to obtain the pelts to trade for these goods. Soon their beaver were gone, the traders and their goods moved on, and the Micmacs were unable to support themselves.

As the beaver population of the coastal regions was depleted, the hunters moved inland to search for fresh supplies, in the process colliding with other groups. Demand for pelts set tribe against tribe, and competing groups of Europeans were usually pleased to sell arms to the rivals. Along the Hudson River, Dutch traders at first obtained furs from local Mahicans. But as their beaver dwindled, the Mahicans were pushed aside by Mohawks, who set up a regular supply of furs from the Iroquois interior.

Wars between tribes not only caused many deaths, but also reshaped tribes' territories and alliances. An increased reliance on hunting and warfare widened the gap between male and female roles, reducing the importance of agriculture, strengthening the power of men at the expense of women, and enhancing the claims of hunters and warriors to leadership.

The alteration of many Indians' methods of sustaining and governing themselves often left them with stark alternatives. They could labor for their European conquerors, or they could move inland and be assimilated into more powerful groups that might successfully resist European encroachment. Natives of Nantucket Island, off Cape Cod, took the first path. In 1600 they were about twenty-five hundred strong; two centuries later only twenty-two of them remained. Puritan traders advanced them goods, but they fell into debt, which they were obliged to work off by going to sea as crewmen on fishing vessels or whaleboats. But they found that they could never earn enough to settle their accounts, and were thus trapped in a cycle of debt and forced labor. Other eastern groups, like the Catawba of the Carolinas, negotiated their survival by making themselves useful to colonists, accepting in the process significant changes to their own culture and forming alliances with the English against neighboring tribes.

Few coastal peoples managed to resist colonial encroachment. Their groups were small and fragmented. A Narragansett sachem, Miantonomi, called for unity among them: "so are we all Indians as the English are, and say brother to one another; so must we be one as they are, otherwise we shall be all gone shortly." But such unity proved elusive or only temporary. In southern New England, the Pequots were at first strengthened by European contact. Trading with Dutch and English shippers, they became a conduit for furs from the interior and built up their military power. The 1630s, however, brought epidemics and then encroachment by English

"We Must Burn Them." An engraving from a contemporary account of the Pequot war showed the dawn raid on the Pequot fort at Mystic, Connecticut, on May 26, 1637. "Many were burnt in the fort, both men, women, and children. Others forced out, . . . twenty and thirty at a time, which our soldiers received and entertained with the point of the sword. Down fell men, women, and children; those that scaped us fell into the hands of the Indians that were in the rear of us."

Source: John Underhill, *Newes from America: or a New Discoverie of New England* (1638)—Rare Books and Manuscript Division, New York Public Library, Astor, Lenox and Tilden Foundations.

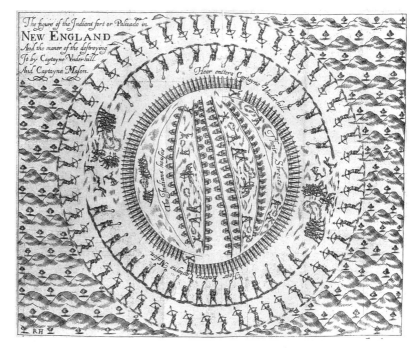

settlers moving west from Massachusetts Bay. Seeking to resist the English, the Pequots joined with other tribes and attacked colonists' farms and towns. But the English made their own alliances among other groups pressed by the Pequots, including the Narragansetts. In an assault on a Pequot village in 1637, English soldiers burned or hacked to death more than four hundred men, women, and children, while their Indian allies encircled the site to prevent any Pequots from escaping. When the Pequot War ended, the English executed many captured warriors, sold others into slavery, and dispersed the remaining Pequots to other tribes.

In the Spanish territories, extreme labor demands and excessive missionary efforts provoked more effective resistance. Florida tribes rebelled against missions repeatedly from the 1590s to the 1650s. Although it was difficult to coordinate their attacks, the tribes nevertheless survived in the swamps. At length, after 1680, they began to drive the missions out. Similarly, New Mexican pueblo groups resisted complete submission to Spanish conversion efforts and demands for forced labor. Christian "converts" covertly adhered to their native beliefs despite harsh attempts at suppression by the Spanish. Sporadic revolts from the 1630s onward took advantage of the Spanish remoteness from their Mexican bases and the rivalry between missions and farming estates.

In 1680 a concerted uprising under a leader called El Popé swept the eastern pueblo villages, killing settlers and priests and driving the Spanish out of New Mexico in panic. For over a decade the pueblos were free from intrusion, until a campaign in 1692–1693 reconquered them. Even then, the pueblos continued to resist, rebelling when participants in the revolt were executed, and preventing the reimposition of the *encomienda* system. As a result, Spanish settlers took to ranching rather than farming. The pueblos, now weakened by population decline and by raids by Apache and Comanche groups from the north, worked out a degree of coexistence with the Spanish that would largely preserve their own identity.

Coexistence, rather than collapse or resistance was, indeed, common for Indians whose lands were not directly subject to European settlement. Among those most successful at holding settlers at arms' length were the Iroquois, whose organization and coherence increased under European pressure. Until the mid-eighteenth century, much of upland eastern North America, the Great Lakes, and Mississippi Valley formed an arena of exchange and interaction between natives and Europeans. After early setbacks and consolidations, some tribes stabilized control over their fields and hunting grounds, and probably even achieved modest population growth. Many continued to regard themselves as superior to the invading Europeans, whose actions they thought of as uncivilized. In these societies, too, women initially retained much of their status and authority.

"Now They Were as They Had Been in Ancient Times"

The Pueblo Revolt of 1680 against Spanish rule in New Mexico was probably the most successful of all Native American efforts to turn back the European colonists of North America. As the Spanish sought to retake the territory they had lost—and punish the rebels harshly—they captured and interrogated Indian prisoners. Though we only have the Spanish versions of their evidence, the prisoners' explanations of the rebellion and its causes come across powerfully, as in this testimony of a Keresan Pueblo man called Pedro Naranjo:

Finally, in the past years, at the summons of an Indian named Popé who is said to have communication with the devil, it happened that in an estufa [kiva] of the pueblo of Los Taos there appeared to the said Popé three figures of Indians who never came out of the estufa. They told him to make a cord of maguey fiber and tie some knots in it which would signify the number of days that they must wait before the rebellion. He said that the cord was passed through all the pueblos of the kingdom so that the ones which agreed to it [the rebellion] might untie one knot in sign of obedience, and by the other knots they would know the days which were lacking; and this was to be done on pain of death to those who refused to agree to it. The said cord was taken from pueblo to pueblo by the swiftest youths under the penalty of death if they revealed the secret. Everything being thus arranged, two days before the time set for its execution, because his lordship had learned of it and had imprisoned two Indian accomplices from the pueblo of Tesuque, it was carried out prematurely that night, because it seemed to them that they were now discovered; and they killed religious, Spaniards, women, and children. This being done, it was proclaimed in all the pueblos that everyone in common should obey the commands of their father whom they did not know, which would be given through El Caydi or El Popé. This was heard by Alonso Catití, who came to the pueblo of this declarant to say that everyone must unite to go to the villa to kill the governor and the Spaniards who had remained with him, and that he who did not obey would, on their return, be beheaded; and in fear of this they agreed to it. Finally, the señor governor and those who were with him escaped from the siege, and later this declarant saw that as soon as the Spaniards had left the kingdom an order came from the said Indian, Popé, in which he commanded all the Indians to break the lands and enlarge their cultivated fields, saying that now they were as they had been in ancient times, free from the labor they had performed for the religious and the Spaniards, who could not now be alive. He said that this is the legitimate cause and the reason they had for rebelling.

Source: Albert L. Hurtado and Peter Iverson, ed., *Major Problems in American Indian History* (1994).

Many Indian groups traded with English, French, or Dutch merchants, providing furs and other goods in exchange for metalwares, guns, blankets, or rum. These exchanges often led to dependency, and, in the view of many Europeans and some native leaders, alcohol in particular made natives more susceptible to exploitation. Settlers told stories of natives' accepting trinkets in payment for furs or even land. But trade was often not as one-sided as it appeared. The Indians chose goods that were useful to them; knives, guns, pans, and cloth made hunting or survival easier. And Europeans could seem naive. "[T]he English have no sense," laughed a member of the Montagnais tribe on the St. Lawrence River; "they give us twenty knives for this one beaver skin." Some native groups continued the fishing, hunting, and crop-growing that provided the necessities of life, and chose when and on what terms they would trade with Europeans. Although frontier exchange often provoked antagonism and conflict, the natives conducted their dealings with whites as equals or superiors, and demanded a measure of deference from them. Until circumstances changed, many Indians would hold their ground.

Worth Its Weight in Copper?
This small copper beaver was equal in value to one beaver pelt in the Hudson Bay fur trade.

Source: George Gustav Heye Center of the National Museum of the American Indian.

The Remaking of Three Worlds

The European invasion of the Americas profoundly altered societies and ways of life on three continents, linking the peoples of Europe, Africa, and the Americas in patterns of commerce, conflict, and labor coercion.

Africa was the most evident loser. The slave trade, with its grievous drain of population and cultural dislocation, profited some powerful Africans, but few others except Europeans benefited. It impoverished much of the African continent, disrupted established commercial patterns, and altered political structures. Before 1500, West African economies had living standards comparable with much of Europe. Slavery, external and internal, greatly weakened them, helping prepare Africa for its own colonization by European powers in the nineteenth century.

The removal of millions of men and women as slaves produced an involuntary mass migration from Africa that for over two centuries much exceeded the scale of European migration to the New World. Until about 1800 fully six out of every seven people arriving in the Americas were enslaved Africans. Most were taken to Brazil, Central America, or the West Indies. Only about five percent went to British North America.

The European invasion's effects on the Americas were mixed. Major Central and South American cultures collapsed and were rapidly incorporated into colonial societies. As new European settlements were established, vast numbers of Native Americans were killed by disease or war, or driven to find new places to live. In North America, most eastern seaboard groups declined or retreated in the face of invasion, disease, and dispossession. Those in the interior or in the Spanish borderlands had some success in resisting deeper invasion, and at adapting their cultures to the new situation. But even peoples who had little direct contact with Europeans felt their influence.

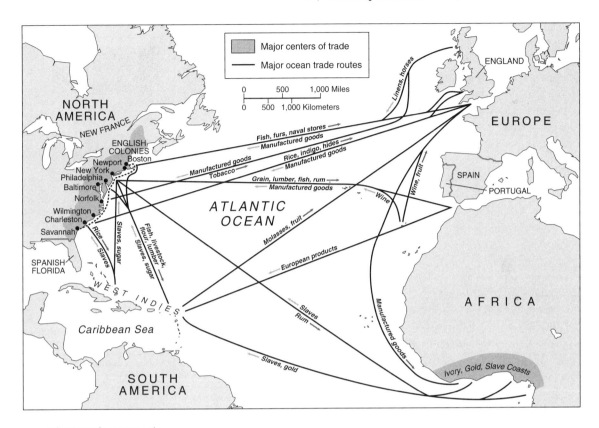

Atlantic Trade Patterns. The map shows the principal routes by which slaves, colonial products, and manufactured goods were carried around the Atlantic trade system by the eighteenth century. At this stage the British North American colonies were primarily oriented toward oceanic trade, not inland to the North American continent.

Not surprisingly, Europeans were the main beneficiaries of colonization. To notables who received land grants, absentee planters who controlled crop production, and merchants in the Atlantic trade, it brought new wealth. Colonial goods literally changed European tastes. Virginia tobacco swept Holland and England early in the seventeenth century, and its popularity continued to mount. Sugar from the Caribbean and Brazil brought confections to Europeans of middling rank that were once enjoyed only by the very wealthy. There was pain as well as pleasure, of course: sugar caused tooth decay and gum disease. But the period of early colonial settlement initiated a lasting dependence on overseas commodities that would affect all levels of European society in the centuries to come.

Profits from colonial trade and commodities also helped transform European economies. By 1600, two hundred ships each year were arriving at Seville in Spain, laden with treasure from the Spanish empire. This increasingly found its way to the trading cities of northern Europe, inflating prices but boosting commerce and urban growth, and helping to finance further overseas expansion.

57

Colonization had arisen from a series of national and social struggles in Europe that had caused rulers to look for new sources of wealth and led to enough discontent among their peoples that many were willing to venture to strange lands. Acquiring colonies only altered these struggles rather than ending them. Spain, France, and Britain all saw North America as an arena for territorial acquisition and rivalry; throughout the eighteenth century they would fight wars to gain greater control of the continent.

White settlers in Spanish, French, and English America, meanwhile, built an array of new societies. All started to see their interests as different from those of the countries they had come from. In Spanish colonies, where high officials rotated through offices in order to make careers back home, distinctions emerged between Spanish-born *peninsulares* and American-born *criollos* (creoles). There was a high rate of intermarriage between settlers and Native Americans. Mixed-race *mestizos* outnumbered the Spanish in Mexico after 1650 and among the "Spanish" who migrated northward into New Mexico.

In the English colonies the distinction between English- and American-born settlers was never as formal as in the Spanish empire. English–Native American intermarriage was also much rarer. Still, population growth and migration increased the proportion of American-born "English" people with no direct ties to England. In the context of colonial rivalry and wars from the mid-eighteenth century on, these American-born colonists would radically alter their relationships both with England and with Native Americans.

The settlers of North America continued, above all, to need labor. The differences in the ways they procured it would have profound implications for the future. This was particularly true of the different labor patterns that developed in the northern and southern colonies of British North America.

The Years in Review

18,000–12,000 BCE

- Asian peoples, who are later called Indians, migrate to North America.

3000 BCE

- Settled agriculture begins among Indians of the Southwest.

1000 CE

- Norsemen led by Leif Ericsson "discover" the Western Hemisphere. They call it "Vinland" (Wineland) because of the grapes growing there.

1340

- Plague ravages Europe, which loses two-fifths of its population between 1300 and 1400.

1444

- Portuguese traders purchase West African slaves to work as lifelong domestic servants in Portugal — beginnings of European slave trade.

1492

- Christopher Columbus sails in search of a westerly route to the East, to Asia, but instead lands in the Bahamas, "discovering" a "New World." This leads to the European exploration of the Americas, home to 75 to 100 million people, perhaps one-seventh of the world's population.

1493

- Europeans first taste pineapples, which have been brought back by Columbus; other foods and crops discovered by Columbus are maize, sweet potatoes, and tobacco.

1497

- Vasco da Gama of Portugal rounds Africa and reaches India.

1507

- German mapmaker names New World "America" in honor of explorer Amerigo Vespucci.

1513

- Balboa becomes first European to see the Pacific Ocean.

1517

- The Protestant Reformation begins in Germany.

1518

- Spanish ship carries the first full cargo of Africans across the Atlantic, initiating the highly lucrative slave trade and one of the largest forced migrations in history.
- Hernan Cortés and Spanish conquistadors set out for Mexico; within three years they conquer the Aztec Empire. Within thirty years, the native population drops by almost half as the result of Spanish exploitation and new diseases.
- Conquistadors discover foods that will transform the European palette, including chocolate, peanuts, tortillas, turkeys, and tomatoes.

1524

- French expedition led by Giovanni da Verrazano explores east coast of North America; he is "mooned" by Maine's Abenaki Indians.

1532–1533

- Spanish conquistador Francisco Pizarro, aided by horses and firearms and facing Indians weakened by civil war, invades Peruvian Andes, defeats the Incas and conquers Peru.

1545

- Spanish discover silver in Andes; between 1500 and 1650, Spaniards (often using forced labor of indigenous peoples) extract 180 tons of gold and 16,000 tons of silver from Americas.

1565

- Spanish found St. Augustine (Florida), which has become the oldest continually occupied European settlement in North America.

1588

- English Navy defeats the Spanish Armada; New World opened up to colonization by Northwestern European nations.

1607

- First permanent English settlement in the New World created at Jamestown (Virginia); fewer than half of new arrivals survive their first year.

1608

- French establish colony of Quebec.
- Spanish, heading north from Mexico in effort to subdue and convert Indians, found Santa Fe in what they call "New Mexico."

1614

- Dutch establish Fort Orange (Albany) on the Hudson River.

1619

- Virginia House of Burgesses (first colonial legislature) meets for first time; colonists have discovered tobacco and the colony is booming; Indians teach them how to cultivate tobacco which is popular in England as medicine.

1620

- Pilgrims (religious dissenters) establish a colony at Plymouth, Mass.

1624

- James I dissolves the Virginia Company and establishes Virginia as a royal colony.

1626

- Dutch settlement of Nieuw Amsterdam established on Manhattan Island.

1630

- Massachusetts Bay Company establishes colony of English Puritans.
- Lemonade is invented in Paris; one of many effects of the availability of

cheap sugar grown by slaves and imported from the West Indies; in the eighteenth century, per capita British sugar consumption will more than triple.

1635

- Roger Williams, expelled from Massachusetts, founds Providence, Rhode Island.

1637

- English and Indian allies wage war against Pequot tribe of Connecticut, leading to the Pequots' virtual extermination.

1638

- Swedish settlers create a short-lived colony at Fort Christina (Wilmington).

1640

- First book published in New England: *The Whole Booke of Psalmes faithfully Translated Into English Metre* (commonly called *Bay Psalm Book*).

1642–46

- First English Civil War occurs.

1648

- Second English Civil War begins; King Charles I is beheaded in 1649 and Commonwealth with Cromwell as leader is created; Cromwell dies in 1658.

1660

- Charles II restored to monarchy.

1670

- Muslim inhabitants on Senegal River revolt in resistance to slave trade.

1680

- Pueblo Indians led by El Popé drive the Spanish from New Mexico; Spanish do not reconquer pueblos for a dozen years.

Suggested Readings

Axtell, James, *After Columbus: Essays in the Ethnohistory of Colonial North America* (1988).

Barry, Bonbacar, *Senegambia and the Atlantic Slave Trade* (1998).

Blackburn, Robin, *The Making of New World Slavery: From the Baroque to the Modern, 1492–1800* (1997).

Calloway, Colin G., *New Worlds for All: Indians, Europeans, and the Remaking of Early America* (1997).

Canny, Nicholas P., and Peter J. Marshall, eds., *The Oxford History of the British Empire,* vol. I (1998).

Countryman, Edward, *Americans: A Collision of Histories* (1996).

Cressy, David, *Coming Over: Migration and Communication between England and New England in the Seventeenth Century* (1987).

Crosby, Alfred W., *Ecological Imperialism: The Biological Expansion of Europe, 900–1900* (1986).

Curtin, Philip D., *The Rise and Fall of the Plantation Complex: Essays in Atlantic History,* 2nd edition (1998).

Davidson, Basil, *West Africa before the Colonial Era: A History to 1850* (1998).

Davies, Norman, *Europe: A History* (1996).

Fischer, David Hackett, *Albion's Seed: Four British Folkways in America* (1989).

Hall, Thomas D., *Social Change in the Southwest, 1350–1880* (1989).

Horn, James, *Adapting to a New World: English Society in the Seventeenth-Century Chesapeake* (1994).

Josephy, Alvin, F., ed., *America in 1492: The World of the Indian Peoples before the Arrival of Columbus* (1993).

Kennedy, Roger G., *Hidden Cities: The Discovery and Loss of Ancient North American Civilization* (1994).

Klein, Herbert S., *The Atlantic Slave Trade* (1999).

Kupperman, Karen Ordahl, *Roanoke: The Abandoned Colony* (1984).

Law, Robin, *The Slave Coast of West Africa, 1550–1750: The Impact of the Atlantic Slave Trade on an African Society* (1991).

Manning, Patrick, *Slavery and African Life: Occidental, Oriental and African Slave Trades* (1990).

Martin, Calvin, *Keepers of the Game: Indians, Animals, and the Fur Trade* (1978).

Meinig, D. W., *The Shaping of America: A Geographical Perspective on 500 Years of History,* Vol. 1, *Atlantic America, 1492–1800* (1986).

Morgan, Edmund S., *American Slavery, American Freedom: The Ordeal of Colonial Virginia* (1975).

Nash, Gary B., and Richard Sweet, eds., *Struggle and Survival in Colonial America* (1982).

Pagden, Anthony, *European Encounters with the New World: From Renaissance to Romanticism* (1993).

Richter, Daniel K., *The Ordeal of the Longhouse: The Peoples of the Iroquois League in the Era of European Colonization* (1992).

Salisbury, Neal, *Manitou and Providence: Indians, Europeans, and the Making of New England, 1500–1643* (1982).

Schama, Simon, *The Embarrassment of Riches: An Interpretation of Dutch Culture in the Golden Age* (1987).

Seed, Patricia, *Ceremonies of Possession in Europe's Conquest of the New World, 1492–1640* (1995).

Thomas, Hugh, *The Slave Trade: The History of the Atlantic Slave Trade, 1440–1870* (1997).

Thornton, John, *Africa and Africans in the Making of the Atlantic World, 1400–1680* (1992).

Underdown, David, *A Freeborn People: Politics and the Nation in Seventeenth-Century England* (1996).

Weatherford, Jack, *Indian Givers: How the Indians of the Americas Transformed the World* (1988).

Weber, David J., *The Spanish Frontier in North America* (1992).

White, Richard, *The Middle Ground: Indians, Empires, and Republics in the Great Lakes Region, 1650–1815* (1991).

Wrightson, Keith, *English Society, 1580–1680* (1982).

And on the World Wide Web

John Kantner, *Sipapu-Cheto Ketl Great Kiva Model*
(http://sipapu.ucsb.edu/html/kiva.html)

Millersville University, *Columbus and the Age of Discovery*
(http://marauder.millersv.edu/~columbus/aod.html)

Virginia Polytechnic Institute, *Virtual Jamestown*
(http://jefferson.village.virginia.edu/vcdh/jamestown/)

Colonial Williamsburg Foundation, *Historical Almanack*
(http://www.history.org/almanack.htm)

chapter 2

Servitude, Slavery, and the Growth of the Southern Colonies
1620–1760

Anthony Johnson arrived in Virginia early in the 1620s, one of the first African slaves to be brought to the colony. Like other Africans and thousands of English servants, he was set to work on the land. Here he met Mary, another slave, whom he married. By the 1650s, both Anthony and Mary had obtained their freedom, and Anthony owned 250 acres of land on Virginia's Eastern Shore. He may have been the first black Virginian to possess a slave of his own. Anthony and Mary's son also became a landowner, and a grandson would name his small farm "Angola" to mark his African heritage. The Johnsons used opportunities available in early Virginia to throw off their slave status. When Anthony asserted that "I know myne owne ground[.] I will worke when I please and play when I please," he was summing up the aspirations of many early migrants who hoped to achieve economic independence in English North America.

The Johnsons' story was not unique, but it was far from typical. Of early colonists in Virginia and Maryland, relatively few Europeans, and very few Africans, were as successful as they were. After the mid seventeenth century, too, what opportunities did exist were increasingly reserved for whites. Harassment by white landowners increased, and in the 1660s Anthony and Mary sold up and moved to a settlement in Maryland where they were more welcome. Their experience was illustrative of a tightening of opportunities in the coastal regions of the Chesapeake, and of a growing racial rigidity. The second half of the seventeenth century would see the emergence of racially based slavery as a distinctive labor system, and the eighteenth century would see its extension from Virginia and Maryland into the new English lower South colonies of North and South Carolina and Georgia.

England's North American colonies developed in varied ways but shared a common context. Originating as commercial ventures, they were all open to settlers from the British Isles and other parts of Europe. Economic, social, and religious pressure in England and elsewhere led tens of thousands of Europeans to cross the Atlantic to America in the seventeenth century. By 1700, an estimated 130,000 migrants had journeyed from the British Isles to the Chesapeake colonies of Virginia and Maryland alone.

Belowdecks. This is a sketch of the interior of a Spanish slave ship called the *Albanez,* bound for the West Indies. After a British naval frigate captured the slaver, one of its officers descended belowdecks to record the horrible conditions of the Africans' Middle Passage.

Source: Francis Meynell, *The Slave Deck of the Albanez,* watercolor, c. 1860—National Maritime Museum.

Such an expansion of the population meant that none of the colonies evolved as their founders had intended or expected. This was especially so in the southern colonies, which emerged as producers of staple agricultural crops for export to Europe. After the near-disastrous early settlement in Virginia, English men and women learned to survive in this region, to make their colony and its neighbor, Maryland, economically viable, to organize local governments, and to adapt their Old World values, habits, and expectations to New World realities. They used the land to grow tobacco, the crop around which their entire economy revolved. Tobacco was a "poor-man's crop" in that it could be produced on small landholdings with a limited supply of labor. Most tobacco farmers were men of modest but independent means, although some were tenants of larger landholders, and a few were servants who hoped eventually to acquire land of their own. At the top of the social hierarchy were the largest tobacco growers: planters who could harness the labor of others to grow their crops for them.

Tobacco Plant. This woodcut in *Stirpium Adversaria Nova*, a botanical study published in 1570, was the first published illustration of the plant.

Source: (Pierre van der Borcht?) Pierre Pena and Mathias de Lobel, *Stirpium Adversaria Nova* (1574)—Arents Collection, New York Public Library, Astor, Lenox and Tilden Foundations.

For half a century or so after 1620 most of these laborers were indentured servants; only a relatively small number were African slaves. But the harshness and injustice of early colonial life produced deep social instability, leading, in Virginia, to open rebellion in the 1670s. Subsequently, planters began to rely increasingly on African slave labor, and the number of slaves grew rapidly. Early on, the Chesapeake had been what historians call a "society with slaves," but by the early eighteenth century it had been transformed into a "slave society," one in which slavery was essential to the economic and social fabric, and in which the two most important groups were slaves and the master class who owned and employed them. This change was the single most significant development in the early history of the Chesapeake region, and it set a pattern for the other English southern colonies as they too expanded.

By the time David George was born into slavery in Surry County, Virginia, around 1740, the slave system was well entrenched. Put to work in the tobacco fields with members of his family, he felt and witnessed slavery's cruelty. Not only was he whipped by his owners "many a time on my naked skin . . . sometimes until the blood has run down over my waist band," but he had to watch his mother and sister being whipped, and see a brother tortured for trying to run away. David himself escaped, but was re-enslaved, first by Indians and later by a South Carolina planter. Growing up during the era of religious revivals known as the Great Awakening, which stirred both white and black communities, David George was one of a growing number of slaves who embraced Christianity. In due course he became a pioneering Baptist minister. His life marked one of the many ways in which, even as they were constrained by the legal and economic shackles of slavery, African Americans in the South carved out a degree of cultural autonomy.

The Southern Colonies in Context

The southern colonies did not evolve their distinctive social and economic systems in isolation. Their reliance on the exporting of crops tied them closely to the broader trading patterns of the Atlantic, to British policies for regulating commerce, and to overseas sources of labor and manufactured goods. They had important links with the growing number of British colonies on the islands of the West Indies, most of which became dominated by sugar plantations worked by African slaves. Along with all British American colonies, they shared a geographical relationship with Native American groups and with the territories of other European powers, especially France and Spain. Despite crucial differences between the French, Spanish, and British colonies, their proximity to one another would influence the British colonies' development.

Britain permitted unrestricted emigration to its colonies, and this distinguished them from French and Spanish colonies in the Americas. Migration from Europe and the West Indies, and the importation of African slaves ensured that populations grew much more rapidly than those of French or Spanish settlements. On the other hand, population growth increased demand for land, which in turn fueled the potential for conflict with Native Americans. Plans were laid to establish missions and schools for southern tribes, but these rarely came to anything. Often uninterested in saving Indians' souls and frequently unable to exploit their labor, English settlers became increasingly bent on removing or destroying them. Seventeenth-century Virginians, for example, pushed well to the west most of the Indians who had once occupied the land they settled.

The French and Spanish monarchies sought closer direction over their empires than the British did and were unwilling to permit free migration. However, neither government was successful in their efforts to promote settlement or in encouraging large numbers of their people to move to the colonies. The Hispanic population of Spanish North America, in particular, remained tiny and predominantly male.

France established permanent agricultural settlements in Quebec and an extensive trading network. This network extended far across the Great

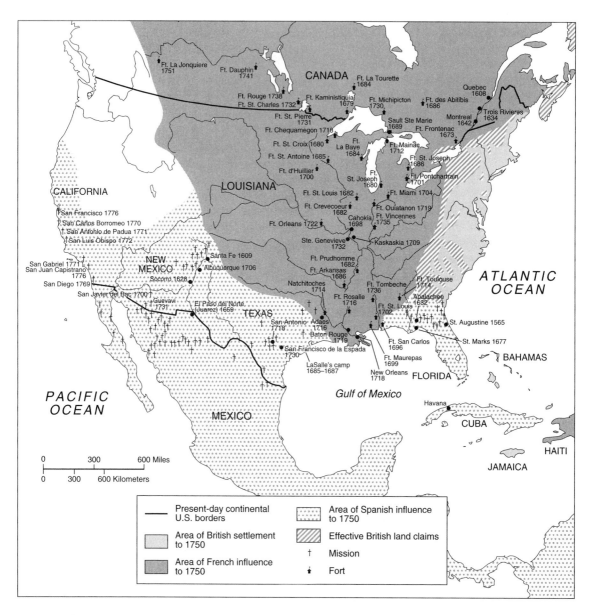

Spanish and French Settlements in North America before 1750. Early Spanish mission-building in Florida and New Mexico was followed in the first half of the eighteenth century by the occupation of parts of Texas (and from 1769, of the coast of California, too). Meanwhile, the far-flung activities of French fur traders in the Great Lakes and Mississippi Valley led to the establishment of numerous forts and trading centers, such as New Orleans. British colonies were confined to the eastern part of the continent.

Lakes region and ultimately down the Mississippi Valley to the colony of Louisiana. The port and administrative center of New Orleans was established in 1718. French missionaries sought to convert to Christianity Indians across this vast territory. Since, except in Quebec and in parts of Louisiana, the French were not primarily settlers on the land, they often established reciprocal and harmonious relations with the indigenous peoples they encountered.

Spanish missionaries also sought religious converts in New Mexico and Florida, but with less harmonious consequences. As we saw earlier, Spain's policies of military conquest and efforts to harness native labor often provoked resistance, including the Pueblo Revolt of 1680 that temporarily drove Spanish settlers out of New Mexico. From the viewpoint of the Spanish government, the fortifications and missions of Florida and New Mexico were marginal northern outposts of its richer, more important colonies in Mexico and South America.

Nevertheless, European powers jockeyed for position in North America, not least to restrain their rivals' influence. French traders in the Mississippi Valley and Louisiana, for instance, made contact with native Apaches and Comanches of the Southwest, providing them with horses and firearms that they used to attack settlements in New Mexico. Partly to counter the French, Spain extended its military and missionary activity into Texas in the eighteenth century. Spain and Britain, meanwhile, eyed one another warily over Florida, the Spanish keen to protect its sea routes to the Caribbean and Central America, the English anxious over the vulnerability to Spanish influence of their colonies in the Carolinas and Georgia. Early in the eighteenth century, the English helped Florida Indians attack and roll back the Spanish network of missions. The Spanish towns of St. Augustine and Pensacola, however, for a while remained potential refuges for fugitive slaves from the lower South colonies.

The Demand for Labor: Servitude in the Chesapeake

The new colonies throughout North America faced a fact inescapable in frontier societies: easy access to land and resources made gathering and keeping a labor force difficult. People who could make their own living from the land had little reason to work for others. This posed little problem for hunters and small farmers whose family members provided sufficient labor, but owners of large plantations could not work their fields solely with the labor of wives and children. The leaders of the Chesapeake colonies sought wealth from their lands and, in establishing tobacco as a staple crop, had found a major source of it since fortunes might be made growing tobacco on a large scale. However, no planter, no matter how hard he worked or how large his family, could accumulate riches without inducing others to till his fields. The first two generations of planters, rich in land but poor in workers, had to find and discipline a labor force in order to make their land yield its wealth. Frontier "freedom" actually gave rise to various forms of coercion.

Virginia's first promoters expected to make the Indians the colony's labor force. Settlers believed that English goods and civility would seduce and domesticate a native population they regarded as inferior to themselves. When the native Powhatan people refused to play this role, planters considered enslaving them. But for four decades after 1607, the Chesapeake tribes were too well armed, too numerous, and too familiar with the countryside to be easily enslaved. After wars with the Powhatans in 1622 and 1644, planters resolved to remove them—a decision they implemented with increasing severity over the rest of the seventeenth century.

"Excellent Fruites." This is the title page of a 1609 pamphlet, published in London, that promoted investment in the Virginia Company.

Source: Robert Johnson, *Nova Britannia* (1609)—Rare Books and Manuscript Division, New York Public Library, Astor, Lenox and Tilden Foundations.

So planters had to look elsewhere for laborers. English authorities offered a helping hand by forcibly transporting some of London's orphans to work in the tobacco fields. Between 1617 and 1624, several hundred orphans, scores of whom had declared "their unwillingness to go to Virginia," were turned over to planters to be worked until they reached the age of twenty-one. Having been "brought to goodness under severe Masters," they could then be set free. Crown and planters alike applauded this arrangement, since it promised to turn troublesome or financially burdensome orphans into productive assets. Most of these involuntary migrants, however, died prematurely after months or years of hard labor. The Crown also proposed shipping convicts to Virginia, but planters opposed the plan. Not wishing to employ men and women who had already demonstrated a readiness to break the law, they were able to limit the number of convicts transported to Virginia until the next century.

Planters had little choice but to recruit young, poor English adults as servants. Prompted by the prospect of persistent poverty and unemployment in England, recruits signed an indenture, a contract by which they agreed to work for a term of four to seven years in exchange for passage to the New World. At the end of the period, each would get freedom, a

". . . To Be in England Again"

The dangers posed by disease and hostile Indians, the pain of separation from home, and the persistent problem of securing adequate food left many new settlers in a state of despair. This letter, dated March 20, 1623, is
from Richard Frethorne, an indentured servant, to his parents in England. Frethorne had landed in Virginia
three months earlier. Two-thirds of his fellow ship passengers had died *since* arriving in the colony. Frethorne
asks his parents to "redeem," that is, buy out, his indenture.

Loving and kind father and mother . . . this is to let you understand that I your child am in a most heavy case by reason
of the nature of the country [which] is such that it causeth much sickness, [such] as the scurvy and the bloody flux, and diverse other diseases, which maketh the body very poor and weak. And when we are sick there is nothing to comfort us, for
since I came out of the ship, I never ate anything but peas and loblollie (that is water gruel); as for deer or venison I never
saw any since I came into this land; there is indeed some fowl, but we are not allowed to go and get it, but must work hard
both early and late for a mess of water gruel, and a mouthful of bread and beef. A mouthful of bread, for a penny loaf must
serve for 4 men which is most pitiful if you did know as much as I, when people cry out day and night—Oh! that they were
in England without their limbs—and would [sacrifice] any limb to be in England again. . . .

   We live in fear of the enemy every hour, yet we have had to combat with them . . . and we took two alive, and make
slaves of them . . . for we are in great danger, for our Plantation is very weak, by reason of the dearth, and sickness, of
our company. . . .

   But I am not half, a quarter so strong as I was in England, and all is for want of victuals, for I do protest unto you that
I have eaten more in a day at home then I have allowed me here for a week. . . . If you love me you will redeem me suddenly, for which I do entreat and beg, and if you cannot get the merchants to redeem me for some little money then for
God's sake get a gathering or entreat some good folks to lay out some little sum of money, in meal, and cheese and butter,
and beef. . . .

   Good father do not forget me, but have mercy and pity my miserable case. I know if you did but see me you would
weep to see me, for I have but one suit, but it is a strange one, . . . and as for my part I have set down my resolution that
. . . the answer of this letter will be life or death to me, therefore good father send as soon as you can . . .

Source: Susan Kingsbury, ed., *The Records of the Virginia Company of London* (1935).

new set of clothes, a few tools, and fifty acres of land. Over half of early
indentured servants came from agricultural backgrounds, and another
twenty percent were from the textile or clothing trades. Few of them had
any other prospect of acquiring that much land. Between seventy-five and
eighty-five percent of those who migrated to Virginia and Maryland in the
seventeenth century did so as indentured servants.

   Single men between the ages of fifteen and twenty-four accounted for
three-fourths of them. Most worked with one or two other indentured
servants on tobacco farms, performing the delicate but routine tasks of
sprouting, transplanting, and curing tobacco. During the growing season

the fields had to be hoed often, and much additional work was required to eke out a subsistence through gardening, hunting, and foraging.

Indentured women, who accounted for nearly all unmarried female immigrants from England, comprised only a small percentage of the population. Only a few hundred went to Maryland, where in the early decades of settlement men outnumbered women six to one. More women went to Virginia, but the sex ratio was still imbalanced; men outnumbered women by four to one in 1625 and remained in the majority for most of the century. An indentured woman's work depended on the social status of her employer. If indentured to a small planter, she labored in the fields. Wealthier planters and merchants employed their female servants at domestic tasks such as washing clothes, sewing, "dressing the victuals," "righting up the home," and child rearing.

Some planters also purchased slaves and set them to work alongside English indentured servants. Nearly all the earliest slaves in North America were male Africans who had been enslaved for several years on the tobacco or sugar plantations of the Caribbean, and so arrived in the Chesapeake already "seasoned." Many of this first generation of American slaves were from the trading societies of the West African coast, and had some familiarity with the commercial system that had ensnared them, as

From Rags to Riches. This British engraving represented a fictional colonial success story. Polly Haycock, pregnant and unmarried, was sentenced to transportation to Virginia as an indentured servant. Brutalized by her master, Polly was released from her servitude by a Virginia magistrate. She married her rescuer, and the tale ended with Polly a rich plantation mistress who now mistreated her own servants.

Source: Anonymous, "The Fortunate Transport. Rob Theif: or the Lady of ye Gold Watch Polly Haycock," engraving, 1760–80, 11 1/4 × 15 3/4 inches—Colonial Williamsburg.

well as with the languages (English or various pidgins) that were spoken in the English Atlantic world.

But the number of slaves was still relatively small in the mid-seventeenth century South. By 1660, when the English population of the Chesapeake had reached thirty thousand, there were probably fewer than fifteen hundred people of African birth or descent in the region. Most of these labored as slaves for life. Some, however, worked as indentured servants and were freed when their terms of service expired. Black and white servants worked together, but they were not always treated equally. Black servants' terms of service tended to be longer, and punishments for infractions more severe. In 1640 an African servant, John Punch, ran away from Virginia to Maryland with two white servants. When the three were caught, the whites were punished by having their terms extended, but Punch was condemned to service for life. Nevertheless, there were still chances to obtain freedom. By 1650, a small free black population had grown up in the Chesapeake, finding employment as craftsmen, laborers, and tenants, or — like Anthony Johnson — acquiring land and becoming independent farmers.

Between the 1620s and the 1650s, as the tobacco economy expanded, thousands of English immigrants flocked to Virginia and Maryland. Servants and slaves found themselves scattered on farms and plantations across the Tidewater, the low-lying region that lay close to Chesapeake Bay's many navigable rivers and inlets, where crops could easily be loaded onto ships. Virginia's elected assembly, the House of Burgesses, emerged as the protector of the interests of large planters. Yet, because planters' lives revolved so completely around the competitive scuffle for tobacco and money that they had little time or energy for anything else, public institutions often remained scanty or neglected. One member of the House of Burgesses was so busy getting rich from tobacco that he attended only one session in eight years. Schooling was poor or nonexistent, and no public provision for education would be made for generations. Some planters could not even be persuaded to organize, much less to participate in, a militia.

Colonial conditions loosened English social conventions. Some early leaders fretted at what they saw as the indiscipline of servants who dressed "above their station" or addressed masters without due deference. English social class prejudices prevailed. The propertied felt contempt for the poor who were obliged to labor for them. One writer described indentured servants as "idle, lazy, simple people such as have professed idleness and will rather beg than work."

To make sure servants did work, masters exercised considerable power; colonial laws gave them wider authority over their servants than they would have had in England. Unlike English servants, for instance,

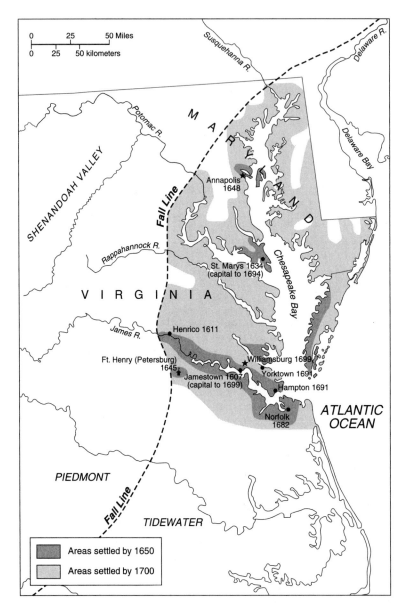

0 25 50 Miles
0 25 50 kilometers

Susquehanna R.

Delaware R.

M A R Y L A N D

Potomac R.

SHENANDOAH VALLEY

Delaware Bay

Fall Line

Annapolis 1648

Rappahannock R.

St. Marys 1634
(capital to 1694)

Chesapeake Bay

V I R G I N I A

James R.

Henrico 1611

Ft. Henry (Petersburg) 1645

Williamsburg 1699

Yorktown 1691

Jamestown 1607
(capital to 1699)

Hampton 1691

Norfolk 1682

ATLANTIC
OCEAN

PIEDMONT

Fall Line

TIDEWATER

Areas settled by 1650

Areas settled by 1700

The Chesapeake Colonies, 1607–1660. Early English settlements in Virginia and Maryland kept close to the coastal inlets around Chesapeake Bay that provided easy navigation. As Native Americans were pushed back and the colonial population expanded, settlement spread across much of the low-lying region known as the Tidewater. By the eighteenth century, small farmers and larger planters were settling land in the higher piedmont region above the Fall Line.

those in Virginia lacked the right to take masters to court for maltreatment or breach of contract. Indeed, the local magistrates to whom they might appeal were often the very men who employed them. As a result, labor discipline was largely maintained by brute force. One woman was beaten "like a dogge," another "sore beaten and her body full of sores and holes." Even when the authorities did act to protect servants, masters

Inconvenience. Directed to English free men and their families, this 1622 notice listed the necessities that prospective voluntary immigrants should obtain before embarking for Virginia.

Source: John Carter Brown Library, Brown University.

THE INCONVENIENCIES
THAT HAVE HAPPENED TO SOME PER- SONS WHICH HAVE TRANSPORTED THEMSELVES

from *England* to *Virginia*, vvithout prouisions necessary to sustaine themselues, hath greatly hindred the *Progresse* of that noble *Plantation*: For preuention of the like disorders heereafter, that no man suffer, either through ignorance or misinformation; it is thought requisite to publish this short declaration: wherein is contained a particular of such necessaries, as either priuate families or single persons shall haue cause to furnish themselues with, for their better support at their first landing in *Virginia*; whereby also greater numbers may receiue in part, directions how to prouide themselues.

Apparrell.	li.	s.	d.
One Monmouth Cap	00	01	10
Three falling bands	—	01	03
Three shirts	—	07	06
One waste-coate	—	02	02
One suite of Canuase	—	07	06
One suite of Frize	—	10	00
One suite of Cloth	—	15	00
Three paire of Irish stockins	—	04	—
Foure paire of shooes	—	08	c8
One paire of garters	—	00	10
One doozen of points	—	00	03
One paire of Canuase sheets	—	08	00
Seuen ells of Canuase, to make a bed and boulster, to be filled in *Virginia* 8.s.			
One Rug for a bed 8.s. which with the bed seruing for two men, halfe is	—	c8	00
Fiue ells coorse Canuase, to make a bed at Sea for two men, to be filled with straw, iiij.s.			
One coorse Rug at Sea for two men, will cost vj.s. is for one	—	05	00
	04	00	00

Apparrell for one man, and so after the rate for more.

Victuall.			
Eight bushels of Meale	02	00	00
Two bushels of pease at 3.s.	—	06	00
Two bushels of Oatemeale 4.s. 6.d.	—	09	00
One gallon of *Aquauite*	—	02	06
One gallon of Oyle	—	03	06
Two gallons of Vineger 1.s.	—	02	00
	03	03	00

For a whole yeere for one man, and so for more after the rate.

Armes.			
One Armour compleat, light	—	17	00
One long Peece, fiue foot or fiue and a halfe, neere Musket bore	01	02	—
One sword	—	05	—
One belt	—	01	—
One bandaleere	—	01	06
Twenty pound of powder	—	18	00
Sixty pound of shot or lead, Pistoll and Goose shot	—	05	00
	03	09	06

For one man, but if halfe of your men haue armour it is sufficient so that all haue Peeces and swords.

Tooles.	li.	s.	d.
Fiue broad howes at 2.s. a piece	—	10	—
Fiue narrow howes at 16.d. a piece	—	06	c8
Two broad Axes at 3.s. 8.d. a piece	—	07	c4
Fiue felling Axes at 18.d. a piece	—	07	06
Two steele hand sawes at 16.d. a piece	—	02	08
Two two-hand-sawes at 5.s. a piece	—	10	—
One whip-saw, set and filed with box, file, and wrest	—	10	—
Two hammers 12.d. a piece	—	02	00
Three shouels 18.d. a piece	—	04	06
Two spades at 18.d. a piece	—	03	—
Two augers 6.d. a piece	—	01	00
Sixe chissels 6.d. a piece	—	03	00
Two percers stocked 4.d. a piece	—	00	c8
Three gimlets 2.d. a piece	—	00	06
Two hatchets 21.d. a piece	—	03	06
Two frowes to cleaue pale 18.d.	—	03	00
Two hand-bills 20. a piece	—	03	04
One grindlestone 4.s.	—	04	00
Nailes of all sorts to the value of	02	00	—
Two Pickaxes	—	03	—
	06	02	c8

For a family of 6. persons and so after the rate for more.

Houshold Implements.			
One Iron Pot	—	07	—
One kettle	—	06	—
One large frying pan	—	02	06
One gridiron	—	01	06
Two skillets	—	05	—
One spit	—	02	—
Platters, dishes, spoones of wood	—	04	—
	01	08	00

For a family of 6. persons, and so for more or lesse after the rate.

For Suger, Spice, and fruit, and at Sea for 6.men—— 00 | 12 | 06

So the full charge of Apparrell, Victuall, Armes, Tooles, and houshold stuffe, and after this rate for each person, will amount vnto about the summe of —— 12 | 10 | —
The passage of each man is —— 06 | 00 | —
The fraight of these prouisions for a man, will bee about halfe a Tun, which is —— 01 | 10 | 00

So the whole charge will amount to about —— 20 | 00 | 00

Nets, hookes, lines, and a tent must be added, if the number of people be greater, as also some kine. And this is the vsuall proportion that the Virginia Company doe bestow vpon their Tenants which they send.

Whosoeuer transports himselfe or any other at his owne charge vnto *Virginia*, shall for each person so transported before Midsummer 1625. haue to him and his heires for euer fifty Acres of Land vpon a first, and fifty Acres vpon a second diuision.

Imprinted at London by FELIX KYNGSTON. 1622.

could show their contempt. A Captain William Odeon, on being convicted in 1662 of repeated maltreatment of servants, promptly "struck and abused his servant" right there in the courtroom.

Colonial indentured servants, unlike English servants, could be repeatedly bought and sold. Those accused of insubordination could be fined, branded, whipped, or have their terms of service extended. Serious offenders faced execution, usually at a public ceremony attended by fellow servants, staged to act as an example to the discontented among them. The Virginia House of Burgesses required each county court to install a ducking-stool with which to punish misbehaving women. Such conditions, combined with the fact that most servants had no family in the Chesapeake, often resulted in lives of abject misery. "So the truth is," the servant Edward Hill complained to his brother in England, "we live in the fearfullest age that ever Christians lived in."

The disease, poor diet, and maltreatment that servants were subject to meant that before 1650 nearly two-thirds of them died before their indentures expired. Planters thus frequently escaped the obligation to provide land to servants on completion of their terms. Even in Maryland, where survival rates were more favorable than in Virginia, only one in three of the servants who arrived before 1642 eventually acquired land. After mid-century, however, although labor remained harsh, improvements in diet and living conditions did produce a higher survival rate among indentured servants.

The Chesapeake colonies also faced the problem of regulating sexual contacts and marriages with scarce white women in a predominantly male society. Unmarried women servants who became pregnant, as did an estimated twenty percent, were punished by additional years of service. It took Virginia until 1662 to recognize the obvious incentive this gave owners to impregnate their own servants; the House of Burgesses then passed a law requiring that the extra service be with a new master. Some women had their infants taken from them and sold, for a few pounds of tobacco, to another master. Masters permitted these female servants to marry only if the servants compensated them for the loss of their labor, a financial obligation beyond most servants' means.

Female servants very rarely acquired property or political rights after gaining their freedom. For a time, however, it was possible for freed men who obtained land to aspire to minor political offices, and to vote for the prominent planters who filled nearly all important public positions. Nevertheless, the planter elite continued to protect its own interests. Both in Virginia and in Maryland, new laws lengthened the years of indentured service. Other measures denied freed men their promised fifty acres, or narrowed economic and political opportunities for small landowners. As more servants survived their terms and clamored for the land they had been promised, the system of indentured servitude began to lose its attractiveness to planters. Unwilling to share wealth and power with their former servants, planters found this growing group of free, landless people menacing. Their geographical isolation on Tidewater plantations heightened planters' sense of vulnerability. After midcentury their lives would be dominated by a constant balancing of their need for labor against their fear of social disorder.

Conditions in the Chesapeake: 1650s to 1670s

At the top of this fragile new society were the men who had been most successful at reaping wealth from the fertile soil through the hard work of their servants. Those who sat in the House of Burgesses and on the judicial bench had scratched their way to the top. These shrewd and often ruthless men had married the widows of wealthy planters, made the best deals, or paid the highest bribes to force other men to do their bidding. By midcentury, many such men had obtained thousands of acres of land apiece. Colonel Philip Ludwell acquired his land simply by altering documents so that he received ten times the acreage he was entitled to. The planter elite's exercise of power through government and law was an undisguised attempt to use the tools of civil authority to keep the upper hand in an ongoing battle for profit.

As the southern colonies achieved a measure of stability, their reputation improved. An English pamphlet of 1656 noted, rather backhandedly, that the Chesapeake was no longer an "unhealthy place, a nest of Rogues, whores, desolate and rooking persons," but one where planters might prosper. The earliest planters were now joined by a new group of men, immigrants who were richer and better connected with the aristocracy in England. These newcomers acquired assembly seats, joined court benches, and obtained other important positions. Many were the younger sons of English gentry. Barred from the status and wealth of their fathers by England's laws of primogeniture — by which the eldest son inherited

Plantation House. The architect Benjamin Latrobe sketched Virginia's first great plantation house in 1796. At the time, the principal part of the house, built by Sir William Berkeley, was more than 147 years old.

Source: Benjamin Henry Latrobe, *View of "Greenspring," home of William Ludwell Lee,* —Maryland Historical Society.

his father's whole estate — these men found in America the chance to begin life at the top of society. Some had inherited thousands of acres originally purchased from the Virginia Company. Others came with enough cash to buy plantations or uncleared land. In the 1660s and 1670s, these men formed a new ruling elite, using their wealth as tobacco planters to make political connections, and filling political offices with relatives. By 1700, ninety percent of Virginia's burgesses were linked by ties of blood or marriage. Descendants of this new landed gentry would be found among the South's leading families for generations to come.

This rise of a new colonial elite took place during a time of great turmoil in England. Between 1640 and 1660, England was too preoccupied with its civil war and revolution to pay much attention to what was going on in the colonies. Virginia planters turned to Dutch merchants to carry their tobacco to Europe and their cattle to the West Indies. Access to the Caribbean market encouraged landowners to shift more of their land from growing tobacco to raising cattle and cereal grains, which they traded for rum, sugar, and slaves, largely without paying duties to the English government. Planters came to think of free trade as a political right and to regard any English law as invalid unless it had been ratified by their own assemblies.

Neither of these notions withstood direct challenge from England. Commercial rivalry between England and Holland had provoked one war with the Dutch in the 1650s. After Charles II was restored to the English throne in 1660, he continued the policy of hostility to the Dutch and reasserted the crown's authority over those American colonists whose trade conflicted with England's interests. Planters grumbled but obeyed new trade regulations — known as the Navigation Acts — first introduced in 1651 but extended in the early 1660s. Colonial products now had to be carried in English vessels — vessels built, owned, and crewed by Englishmen or English colonials. All tobacco had to be shipped first to England or Ireland, or to another English colony, where it was assessed an import duty. If the cargo was shipped on from there, it now cost the planter an export duty as well. Such regulations greatly enriched the crown and London merchants, but burdened the Chesapeake planters. To make matters worse, overproduction of tobacco in the 1660s and 1670s drove the price of the crop to an all-time low, just as further Anglo-Dutch wars disrupted trade and colonists were obliged to raise taxes to pay for forts and troops.

To make sure planters paid their taxes despite these difficulties, Charles II relied on his friend and loyal supporter, Virginia's governor William Berkeley. Berkeley, and those he chose to favor with office, comprised the colony's royal officialdom, which was often at loggerheads with the House of Burgesses. Though these two ruling groups overlapped somewhat in membership and goals, they were divided by a fundamental conflict. The amount of revenue the crown collected depended solely on how much tobacco was shipped, not how much it sold for. Thus the crown had little interest in diversifying Chesapeake agriculture or curbing tobacco production. The fortunes of the planters, however, rose, and fell with the price of tobacco. Overproduction, which drove the price down, was a major concern to them.

Nevertheless, the mid-seventeenth-century Chesapeake colonies were becoming successful. The disease and malnutrition of Virginia's first years was being overcome. The life expectancy of the second generation of American-born colonists was at least as good as the forty years their English counterparts enjoyed. Above all, the colonies were a financial success, attractive both to the crown for the tobacco taxes they provided and to the immigrants who came in search of opportunities that eluded them in England.

Still, the Chesapeake around 1660 was very far from idyllic. It looked nothing like the rural society of small family farms that an earlier generation of English writers had thought possible in the New World. To a shocking extent, the quest for tobacco profits justified an individualistic adventurism that was unknown in most English communities. Death rates remained sufficiently high that twenty-five percent of newborn white children died in their first year, and fifty percent of white Virginians died before they reached twenty-one. Community and family life were still more the exception than the rule. Men outnumbered women by at least three to one, and in some areas by as much as six to one. The high mortality meant that many of the marriages that did occur were short-lived; only one in three lasted ten years or more. Orphaned children were common: half the children in seventeenth-century Virginia had lost one or both of their parents by the age of nine. All these factors made society seem crude and unstable.

The great majority of colonists were either landowners or servants. The need of the planters for a larger workforce did not lead them to improve conditions for their laborers. Instead, like most English employers of the period, they tried to exploit to the full the men and women they could recruit. Wealthy planters stacked the odds in their own favor and against their poorer neighbors. They made up five percent or less of the landowners, but for themselves and their children they reserved the best land, including much of the fertile Tidewater. They had pushed westward most of the region's Indians, who maintained uneasy contacts with English traders and the colonists who settled near them.

Only a small number of freed servants were able to acquire land. By the 1670s in Virginia, the proportion from county to county varied between nine and seventeen percent. Even these fortunate ex-servants were often obliged to take marginal land with poor soil, controlled by Indians or too distant from navigable water to permit tobacco to be marketed. Small landholders close to waterways were at the mercy of large planters, whose control of the ships that carried tobacco to market enabled them to gouge more marginal competitors. Those who overcame these obstacles still faced high taxes and fees imposed by the planter-dominated House of Burgesses, as well as skirmishes with Indians living near their hard-won properties. All these conditions combined to produce a large group of frustrated, debt-ridden small landowners.

Bacon's Rebellion of 1676: A Turning Point in the Chesapeake

Discontent among former servants posed a problem for wealthy planters. The anger of small landowners, Governor Berkeley told the Privy Council in London, set a bad example for those who were still bound as servants. Neither group supported the Virginia government, which, Berkeley complained in 1667 during one of the Anglo-Dutch wars, was "pressed at our backes with Indians, in our Bowills with our servants . . . and invaded from without by the Dutch." He feared that if the Dutch invaded Virginia, "at least one-third" of the single freemen "would revolt . . . in hopes of bettering their condition by sharing the Plunder of the Country with them." By 1673 he thought that even without outside provocation, the population, of whom "Six parts of Seven at least are Poore, Indebted, Discontented, and Armed," might rebel at any time.

Berkeley's fears were not groundless. The number of runaway servants had steadily increased since 1650. Servants in two separate Virginia counties had already taken up arms and demanded freedom. In the first incident, in 1661, York County servants complained of "hard usage"

Governor. This portrait of Sir William Berkeley, governor of Virginia, was painted around 1662.

Source: Sir Peter Lely, c. 1662—Trustee of the will of the eighth earl of Berkeley, deceased.

and poor diets. Isaac Friend, their leader, planned to assemble forty or so servants, who would arm themselves and march through the country, raising recruits by urging those "who would be for liberty, and free from bondage," to join them. Once a large enough force had been gathered, the rebels "would go through the Country and kill those that made any opposition, and they would either be free or die for it." An informer enabled officials to nip this plot in the bud, and they put Friend under surveillance. A second rebellion of servants in Gloucester County in 1663 met with harsher punishment. Several men were executed for their "villainous Plot to destroy their Masters, and afterwards to set up for themselves." Across the colony, curbs were placed on servants' and slaves' freedom of movement, and new laws tightened their conditions of service.

But propertied elites were not the only group indentured servants and discontented freemen saw as blocks to their economic independence. Indians, whom they viewed as heathens who had no just claim to the land, also posed an obstacle. In 1675, Maryland forced a group of Susquehannocks to resettle across the Potomac River in Virginia. The following year, Governor Berkeley planned with powerful planters to pass a measure to enslave all Virginia's Indians, but before he could act, angry settlers took matters into their own hands. That May, Nathaniel Bacon, a planter who thought Berkeley too lenient with local tribes, led a mixed band, including prosperous neighbors from the north bank of the James River and indebted farmers from the south, in an unauthorized assault on a friendly native village. Fourteen of the Susquehannocks from Maryland were among those they killed.

Young and well-to-do, Bacon had arrived from England a few years before. Although his resentment of Berkeley's control of power and patronage was fueled by a haughty contempt for a colonial elite he considered socially inferior, he nevertheless built a following among the discontented at all levels of Virginia society. His action in May 1676 unleashed their fury. Middling frontier farmers joined with poor freemen, indentured servants, and slaves to form a rebel army. When Berkeley's militia captured Bacon in June, the governor made Bacon write a confession and then pardoned him, in an effort to conciliate Bacon's followers and reestablish the ruling elite's authority. But Bacon, who "heard what an incredible Number of the meanest [poorest] of People were everywhere Armed to assist him and his cause," soon renewed his attacks.

Over the summer and into the fall of 1676, Bacon's supporters drove Berkeley out of Virginia, tried to capture the governor of Maryland, plundered the estates of their prosperous adversaries, and massacred hundreds of Indians. The rebels did not distinguish between friendly and other native groups. "We find them all alike," Bacon declared; "they are all our enemies." In September, when Berkeley tried to reassert his authority in

"The Declaration of the People"

In announcing the rebellion in 1676, Nathaniel Bacon issued "The Declaration of the People," in which he detailed a set of grievances of the common people against Governor Berkeley's administration and argued the revolutionary notion that Berkeley's authority could not be considered legitimate without the consent of the people.

For having upon specious pretenses of Public works raised unjust Taxes upon the Commonality for the advancement of private Favorites and other sinister ends. . . .

For having abused and rendered Contemptible the Majesty of Justice, [by] advancing to places of judicature scandalous and Ignorant favorites.

For having wronged his Majesty's Prerogative and Interest by assuming the monopoly of the Beaver Trade.

By having in that unjust gaine Bartered and sold his Majesty's Country and the lives of his Loyal Subjects to the Barbarous Heathen [the Indians].

For having protected, favored, and Imboldened the Indians against his Majesty's most Loyal subjects, never contriving, requiring, or appointing any due or proper means [to prevent] their many Invasions, Murders, and Robberies Committed upon us. . . .

For having . . . forged a Commission by we know not what hand, not only without but against the Consent of the People, for raising and effecting of Civil Wars and distractions. . . .

Of these the aforesaid Articles we accuse Sir William Berkeley, as guilty of each and every one of the same, and as one, who has Traitorously attempted, violated and Injured his Majesty's Interest here. . . .

These are therefore in his Majesty's name, to Command you forthwith to seize the Persons above mentioned as Traitors to your King and Country, . . . and if you want any other Assistance, you are forthwith to demand it in the Name of the People of all the Counties of Virginia.

Source: *Virginia Magazine of History and Biography,* I (1893–94).

Virginia, Bacon, with an armed force of 120 horsemen and 400 men on foot, attacked Jamestown and burned it to the ground. Bacon's ranks had been swollen by the servants and slaves of Berkeley loyalists, who had joined the campaign on being offered their freedom, while women joined the rebellion too.

For another four weeks, the rebels looted the estates of Berkeley's backers and collected tribute from other wealthy planters. Then, on October 26, Bacon unexpectedly died of dysentery. The arrival in November of

"Bacon's Castle, Surrey, Va."

No portrait of Nathaniel Bacon survived. This engraving in an 1866 weekly newspaper showed a house that Bacon and his followers reputedly used as a stronghold in 1676.

Source: (Albert Berghaus), *Frank Leslie's Illustrated Newspaper*, September 8, 1866—General Research Division, New York Public Library, Astor, Lenox and Tilden Foundations.

armed vessels from England cooled the rebelliousness of some of Bacon's more prosperous followers, but hundreds of indentured servants, armed slaves, and "Freemen that had but lately crept out of the condition of Servants" fought on until they were captured or killed. By late January of 1677 the rebellion was over, and Berkeley's government exacted its punishment by hanging twenty-three rebels. The women who had joined the campaign included affluent ladies such as Sarah Drummond, who had helped stir Bacon's supporters to action. Her husband was among those hanged.

An inquiry blamed Bacon's Rebellion on a "giddy-headed multitude," but it had given Virginia's most oppressed whites and blacks an opportunity to turn their world upside down. According to its opponents, this "Rabble of the basest sort of People" had sought "the subversion of the Laws and to Levell all." It is estimated that ten percent of all Virginia's black males joined the rebellion. Eighty slaves were, with four hundred white laborers, among the last rebels to surrender. Bacon's rhetoric had drawn no distinction between whites and blacks, free men and slaves. He had spoken only of the "common people," united by poverty and their oppression at the hands of wealthy planters, "unworthy favourites and juggling parasites." The spectacle of concerted action by a combination of

free men, servants, and slaves, with its interracial as well as interclass solidarity, terrified leading planters. They were determined that no such
challenge should threaten them again.

Although Bacon's Rebellion collapsed, it marked important changes
in the Chesapeake that would lead to the emergence of an increasingly
distinctive "southern" form of colonial society. Population growth and the
westward migration of former servants, who settled in the back country,
increased pressure on the frontiers and intensified demands from white
settlers for military action against Indians. Tensions between rich and
poor, and between backcountry settlers and Tidewater inhabitants, threatened to divide Chesapeake society along class lines. The elite saw
particular danger in the potential for a union of poorer whites and blacks
to rise up against them. They resolved to place less reliance on white servants and to recruit increasing numbers of black slave laborers. In
previous decades, Virginia and Maryland had been societies with slaves, in
which slaves had provided some of the labor. By the end of the seventeenth century they were being transformed into slave societies, in which
slaves formed the bulk of the subordinate labor force. Demographic
changes and a new sense of permanence also contributed to the emergence of a new labor system. White farmers, artisans, tenants, and
laborers—the men among them, at least—won civil rights and economic opportunities denied to the growing number of black slaves, who
would be kept in racially based subjugation.

From Servitude to Slavery

Among the first steps taken after Bacon's Rebellion were efforts to reduce
social tensions among whites. Disagreements between local and royal authorities became less heated as Charles II limited the power of his council
in Virginia and extended that of the House of Burgesses. Freed servants'
access to land was improved. New legislation curbed wild and often illegal land speculation—such as that practiced by the king himself when he
had granted two friends all the public lands in Virginia. There was a campaign to drive the Indians over the mountains into present-day Kentucky
and Tennessee. In addition, the English Parliament began investigating the
treatment of indentured servants. The Crown now prosecuted recruiters
who used illegal tactics such as kidnapping, misrepresentation, and fraud.

Meanwhile, continuing a process begun before the rebellion, a series
of measures sought to place black people—both free and slave—in
greater subjection, and to break the ties between white and black laborers. Free blacks now faced restrictions on their legal and political rights.
Laws passed in the 1660s had formally recognized slavery and begun to

define it in racial terms. Any child born to a slave woman would be enslaved, too. Although "Christians" could not be slaves, Africans were to be excluded from this principle. Conversion, it was held, "doth not make a man free," and in 1682 those whose parents or homeland were not Christian at the time of their purchase were defined as slaves. Other laws prohibited interracial cohabitation or marriage, banned "Negroes and other slaves" from carrying arms or joining the militia, made freeing slaves more difficult, and prevented slaves from owning land. Slave women were excluded from the protection of laws against rape. A Virginia law of 1699 even declared that an owner who killed his slave could not be guilty of murder because he would not intentionally destroy his own property. By 1705, the contempt earlier generations of planters had shown for Indians and English indentured servants had reached its logical culmination in a slave code that gave masters unrestricted power over a labor force that would never be free.

As many blacks lost what freedom they had, whites now benefited from preferential treatment. Guaranteed their own freedom, even poor whites could see themselves as superior to blacks who were increasingly enslaved. With laws that placed all whites above and separate from blacks, Virginia's elite fostered racial bonds among whites that overcame the economic and political inequalities between them, and reduced the chance that poor whites would join blacks against their masters. Planters thus drove a wedge between slaves and white servants and so ensured their own continued dominance.

Other changes reinforced these efforts to differentiate white from black labor. Opportunities elsewhere curbed both the free white migration to the region and the supply of new white indentured servants. A revival of the English economy improved opportunities for the poor in England, while the attraction of newly opening colonies, such as Pennsylvania, also reduced the flow of servants available to do farm and craft labor in the South. Indentured servants continued to come to the Chesapeake, but an increasing proportion were young women, purchased to perform domestic work in prosperous households.

Such changes also altered landowners' plans for working their properties. Thomas Gerard, lord of the manor of St. Clement's in St. Mary's County, Maryland, had expected to make his money from renting land to tenants, as he might have done in England. Like other landowners, he purchased indentured servants to work on his farms, and recruited settlers and freed servants willing to rent land from him. But this became increasingly difficult to do. Freed servants with means sought to purchase their own land, and the poor could neither buy nor rent. By 1670, Gerard had sold much of his manor to freeholders, and was now preoccupied with purchasing slaves to work other land he owned in Virginia.

With white labor becoming increasingly scarce, more and more planters followed Gerard's lead in buying slaves to work as field hands. After 1672, the Royal Africa Company, which held a monopoly on the slave trade with the English colonies, increased its slave shipments from Africa. Even so, demand outstripped supply, and Chesapeake planters resorted to the illegal purchase of slaves whenever they could. Abolition of the slave-trade monopoly in 1698 increased the supply, and the number of slaves imported from Africa continued to rise markedly. Virginia's slave population rose from 3,000 in 1680 to 13,000 in 1700. Of that 13,000, half had been brought from Africa. Another twenty years later there were 27,000 slaves in Virginia, and imports from Africa exceeded one thousand a year. In 1680 in St. Mary's County, Maryland, servants outnumbered slaves by almost four to one, but by 1710 slaves outnumbered servants by five to one. Instead of the society of landlords, tenants, and servants Gerard and other wealthy settlers had once envisioned, the Virginia and Maryland Tidewater was turning into something quite different: a society of large and small landowners, poor white laborers, and African slaves.

Unlike many of the first generations of American slaves, the newly imported slave men and women spoke no English, and had had no experience even of near-equality with whites. Unlike their predecessors, who had come mainly from coastal West Africa, most were from the African interior, where they had had little contact with the languages or commerce of the Atlantic trade system. After being captured and suffering a brutal voyage, they reached the Chesapeake to be put on sale. According to one observer around 1700, "slaves can be selected according to pleasure, young and old, men and women. They are entirely naked when they arrive, having only corals of different colors around their necks and arms." They were usually dispersed singly or in small groups among different slaveowners.

The strange society into which they were forced was, meanwhile, becoming increasingly comfortable for its white inhabitants. By the late seventeenth century, after two generations of imbalanced sex ratios and high mortality, the Chesapeake's white population was growing of its own accord. The proportion of women increased.

"To Be Sold." This handbill announcing an auction of African captives was posted around the city of Charleston in 1769.

Source: American Antiquarian Society.

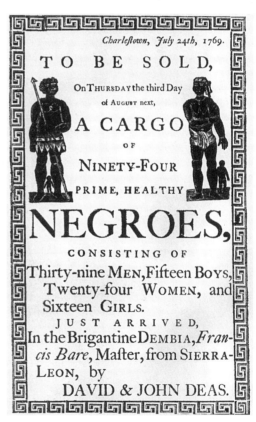

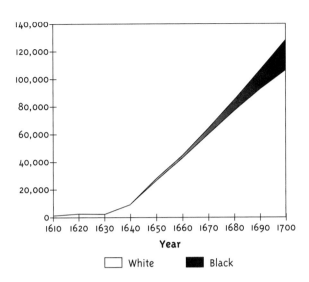

Population in the Seventeenth-Century Southern Colonies. The chart illustrates the slow population growth of the early decades of white settlement; the steady growth after 1640; and the small black population up to the 1670s and its increase from then on as slavery expanded.

In St. Mary's County, Maryland, for instance, where before 1670 men outnumbered women by three or four to one, by 1712 the ratio had reached 1.22:1. Marrying young, women bore considerable numbers of children, an increasing proportion of whom survived infancy. A better food supply and improved living conditions also improved life expectancy. Planters and small farmers began to build more permanent houses and farm buildings. Marriages, now less frequently broken by death, lasted longer; among the gentry, the average length of marriages rose from fifteen years in the late seventeenth century to twenty-five for those beginning after 1700. A settled southern society, based on slavery, was starting to take shape.

The Spread of Slavery to the Carolinas and Georgia

As these changes were taking place in the Chesapeake, immigrants began to colonize the lower South. They settled in the area that at first was called Carolina, granted to a company of proprietors by Charles II after his restoration to the throne in 1660. From this original grant, the colonies of North and South Carolina (formally separated in 1719) and Georgia would eventually be formed.

At first, the lower South differed from the Chesapeake in several ways. Although migrants from Virginia brought tobacco and slavery to the Albermarle region, which became North Carolina, early South Carolinians rejected both tobacco and exclusive reliance on slave labor. They grew a variety of crops with a mixed workforce that, in addition to slaves, included family members, indentured servants, and wage laborers. By the early eighteenth century, however, South Carolina too was making the transition from a society with slaves to a slave society.

The original principles of government for Carolina, the Fundamental Constitutions, were drawn up for the proprietors in the late 1660s, chiefly by the English political philosopher John Locke. He envisaged a harmonious agricultural society with an economy based on mixed farming, cattle raising, and a trade in deerskins with local natives. Though his subsequent writings helped to inspire, among a later generation of Americans, the belief that all men were created equal, here Locke proposed an ordered, hierarchical society in which the right of large landowners to govern would receive the formal assent of the majority of settlers. However, prevailing conditions prevented the colony from conforming to this vision. Despite repeated attempts, the proprietors failed to persuade colonists to approve the Fundamental Constitutions. Carolina society would indeed be unequal and hierarchical, but in ways different than Locked had envisioned.

The Carolina proprietors planned to recruit only "seasoned" colonists from the Caribbean who could pay their own passage. These colonists would be offered land at a low price and encouraged to form communities of self-sufficient family farms. The Crown granted all colonists political and religious freedom, and adult white males were promised the right to vote for assemblymen who were to govern the colony with the help of noblemen drawn from England.

Migrants flocked to Carolina. The children of some of the richest planters of the Caribbean sugar islands came, bringing with them hundreds

Sugar Making. An illustration in a seventeenth-century history of the Caribbean islands showed the role of slave labor in the production of sugar.

Source: Charles de Rochefort, *Histoire naturelle et morale des Iles Antilles de l'Amerique* (Rotterdam, 1665)—Library Company of Philadelphia.

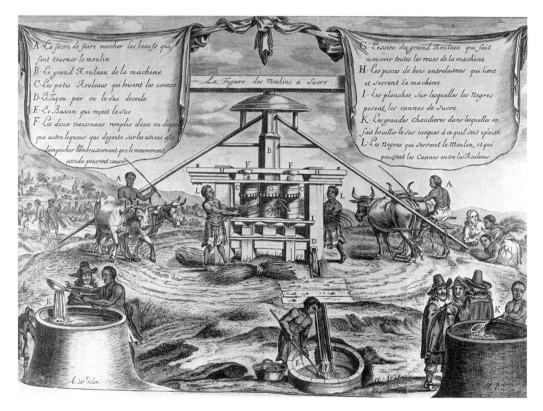

of slaves and the customs of the West Indian gentry. Nevertheless, independent, non-slave-owning white farmers at first outnumbered slave owners, indentured servants, propertyless laborers, and slaves. Many migrants were Barbadians who owned too few slaves and too little land on Barbados to make a successful transition from cultivating the traditional tobacco to sugar-growing. By the 1650s, they had few prospects on their already over-populated, overcultivated island. They were also generally older than the first Chesapeake colonists, and many had families. Immigrant families from Scotland, Germany, and Ireland likewise took up mixed-crop farming in Carolina. Most colonists lived on modest farms, close to the coast, where they grew their own food and raised cattle for export to the Caribbean.

However, mixed subsistence farming generated little revenue. The lucrative deerskin trade with the Indians did not materialize. Instead, some colonists organized a new slave trade, capturing Indians to sell in the West Indies in exchange for rum and sugar. Meanwhile, the tiny minority of wealthy migrants acquired huge tracts of land and seized political control. Many of these leading families settled in Charleston, which soon became the largest port town in the South. Before 1705, these Charleston families owned most of the colony's slaves. But successful traders and farmers also employed laborers, some American-born whites, some indentured servants from England and Ireland, and some African-born slaves brought from the Caribbean.

Settling the Carolina coastal region, or lowcountry, involved interactions with successful Indian groups. As elsewhere, early cooperation was followed by colonists' provocations that caused, first, resentment against whites and then resistance to them. In what would become North Carolina, settlers captured Tuscarora women and children to sell as slaves, and then encroached on the group's lands. After a two-year war, beginning in 1711, the Tuscarora were defeated and displaced inland. In South Carolina, the Westo people who were present at the start of white settlement there were removed in the 1680s with the help of the neighboring Yamassees, who then formed a thirty-year-long alliance with English governments, directed in part against Spanish Florida further down the coast. But English demands and encroachments eventually sparked Yamassee resistance too. Now allied with the Spanish and the Creeks, the Yamassee attacked South Carolina settlements in 1715, but they were defeated and the survivors sold into slavery. The English formed a new alliance with the stronger inland Cherokees, who for another half-century held their position, trading in slaves and establishing settled agriculture, while maintaining some of their traditional ways; Cherokee women, for instance, maintained rights over land and agricultural produce. By the 1760s, however, the English and the Cherokees were themselves coming into conflict.

For white and black settlers alike, conditions in early South Carolina were difficult. Work was hard. Everyone suffered from inadequate shelter, poor nutrition, and semitropical diseases. Judith Manigault, who settled with her husband on the Santee River in 1689, and worked with him to clear and plant land, later wrote: "I have been for six months together without tasting bread . . . and I have even passed three or four years without always having it when I wanted it." Even those who survived their first few years had a relatively short life-expectancy. Judith Manigault died in 1711, aged 42. Though mortality rates fell with each generation, only after 1750 did births outnumber deaths among free men and slaves.

Some harsher aspects of the Chesapeake's labor regime were absent from South Carolina, however. Restrictions placed on masters in 1676 and the availability of land in other colonies gave prospective indentured servants some bargaining power. Slaves, too, had slightly more freedom of action than in Virginia or Maryland. Commercial cattle farmers, unlike tobacco planters, needed a mobile, self-reliant labor force, and they recognized the skill of Africans at raising livestock in a subtropical climate. Cattle were unfenced, and slaves who tended them had to move with the herds and run down strays. Male servants and slaves also had some access to public life. As late as 1706, petitioners complained that in "the last election Jews, Strangers, Sailors, Servants, Negroes, and almost every French Man came down to elect, and their votes were taken." The need to defend the colony from hostile Spanish troops in Florida even required — in contrast to Virginia — that slaves sometimes be mobilized and armed. A Carolina official noted in 1710 that "enrolled in our Militia [are] a considerable Number of active, able, Negro Slaves; and Law gives everyone of those his freedom, who in Time of an Invasion kills an Enemy."

But in South Carolina, as in the Chesapeake, during the late seventeenth and early eighteenth centuries various factors led to the expansion and tightening of slavery. After 1680, the number of arriving white indentured servants fell, and those who did come to the lower South refused to accept terms longer than five years. Determined to reap profits from staple-crop production, the wealthy planters who had settled in Carolina from Barbados consolidated their lowcountry farms into large plantations and concentrated on growing rice, thus squeezing out mixed-crop farmers and cattle raisers. By the early eighteenth century, the rice grown on these plantations became South Carolina's chief export, and planters turned almost exclusively to imported African slaves for their workforce. Some of these slaves had grown rice as free men and women in West Africa. South Carolina's slave population rose from 2,400 in 1700 to 12,000 in 1720, of whom nearly three-fifths were African-born. Moreover, by 1708, for the first time in any North American colony, Carolina's blacks outnumbered the white population.

90

"Slaves, To All Intents and Purposes"

Carolina's Slave Code, enacted in 1712, was one of the first comprehensive acts regulating slave life in the North American colonies. Note the racist arguments used explicitly to justify the permanent enslavement of "negroes, mulattoes, mestizoes [mixed Indian and European people], and Indians" and their children.

Whereas, the plantations and estates of this province cannot be well and sufficiently managed and brought into use, without the labor and service of negroes and other slaves; and forasmuch as the said negroes and other slaves brought into the people of this Province for that purpose, are of barbarous, wild, savage natures, and such as renders them wholly unqualified to be governed by the laws, customs, and practices of this Province; but that it is absolutely necessary, that such other constitutions, laws and orders, should in this Province be made and enacted, for the good regulating and ordering of them, as may restrain the disorders, rapines and inhumanity, to which they are naturally prone and inclined, and may also tend to the safety and security of the people of this Province and their estates; to which purpose,

Be it therefore enacted . . . that all negroes, mulattoes, mestizoes or Indians, which at any time heretofore have been sold, or now are held or taken to be, or hereafter shall be bought and sold for slaves, are hereby declared slaves; and they, and their children, are hereby made and declared slaves, to all intents and purposes. . . .

As the rice economy spread and frontier conditions gave way to a more settled, structured, race-bound society, slavery itself became more rigid. An English immigrant wrote home in 1711 that farmers or craftsmen could do well in the colony if they could "get a few slaves and beat them well to make them work hard." Slaves had little chance of obtaining freedom. Free black servants, too, could expect extended terms of bondage, and free black women were forced to "apprentice" any children they bore during their servitude, which often lasted into their early thirties. Even opportunities for escape became scarcer, as the loose supervision of cattle farms gave way to a tighter plantation regime, and the Yamassee war wiped out the runaway slaves' chief allies.

In 1732, the southernmost territory of the original Carolina grant was organized as the new colony of Georgia. Initially Georgia was to be a military buffer between South Carolina and Spanish Florida. Its founders hoped to build a colony that was not based on plantation slavery. Early

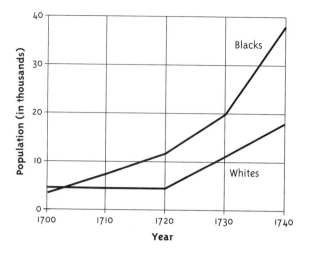

The Emergence of a Black Majority in South Carolina. As planters imported more and more slaves to grow rice and other crops, South Carolina's black population quickly exceeded that of whites, and it grew more rapidly into the mid-eighteenth century.

settlers were Englishmen who had signed up for the colony's militia as an alternative to debtor's prison. The colony's promoters recruited skilled workers from Italy, with whom they wanted to develop a silk industry, and unskilled laborers from Scotland, Ireland, and Germany. Women and children were not included in their original plans because they could not contribute to the colony's defense. In 1735 slavery was also prohibited on military grounds as a potential source of internal rebellion. A few Georgia settlers also expressed moral objections to slavery. Some petitioned the king in 1738 to ignore other Georgians' requests to admit slaves, arguing that "perpetual slavery" was "shocking to human Nature," and that whites would one day pay a heavy price for enslaving men and women who held freedom as "dear" as they did. But rice cultivation soon spread to the

"Establishing the Colony of Georgia." An illustration from a 1733 book that advocated colonization depicted Georgia as an idyllic, bountiful land—the perfect setting for the creation of a well-ordered, hierarchical society. Note the gentleman in the lower right corner supervising the work.

Source: B. Martyn, *Reasons for Establishing the Colony of Georgia* (1733)—Rare Books and Manuscript Division, New York Public Library, Astor, Lenox and Tilden Foundations.

92

Georgia lowcountry, and in 1749 the colony rescinded its ban on slavery. A plantation economy then developed, and the lure of profits helped overcome the original proprietors' military and moral objections to slavery. Slaveowners in other colonies had also objected to Georgia's prohibition of slavery, viewing it as an enticement to their own slaves to escape.

Slaves growing rice were not subject to the regimentation and close supervision imposed on those in the tobacco regions. Rice did not, like tobacco, require constant daily attention. Slaves spent part of the year repairing dams, building canals, and mending fences. Many had done similar work in Africa, and their experience helped both to shape the system of labor and to enhance their bargaining position with English masters who did not know how to grow rice. Even so, conditions were very difficult. Planting and harvesting rice in water-filled fields was backbreaking, unhealthy labor; work on dikes and canals was heavier still. Hard work, poor diet, disease, and maltreatment contributed to high mortality rates. Masters had unrestricted authority over their slaves and did not hesitate to use it. Brute force maintained discipline. In South Carolina the law prescribed amputation as the punishment for recaptured runaway slaves: females could have their ears cut off, males their testicles.

Beginning in the 1720s, the most successful South Carolina rice planters left overseers in charge of their plantations and moved to Charleston, where the climate was pleasanter, diseases like malaria less

View of Mulberry House and Grounds. In this painting of a rice plantation near Charleston in the 1770s, the master's house was framed by the slave quarters. The size of the slave cabins was probably inaccurate, suggesting a height and spaciousness that the one-room cabins did not possess.

Source: Thomas Coram, oils on paper, after 1775—Gibbes Art Gallery/Carolina Art Association, Charleston.

prevalent, and the society more stimulating than in the countryside. There they formed an aristocracy at least as wealthy and elegant as that of Virginia. Many slaves in Charleston were hired out, working for master craftsmen as shipbuilders, ropemakers, leatherworkers, and carpenters, or as dock workers or general laborers. In contrast to those on plantations, many urban slaves worked as artisans, were literate, and of mixed English and African origin. Women also formed a higher proportion of them than in the countryside. By 1776, half of Charleston's twelve thousand inhabitants were black. Interaction with their masters, more frequent than on the plantations, also provided the occasional opportunity to buy or be granted freedom.

African-American Culture in the South

By 1760, the American slave system, which would last another century, was firmly in place. It defined most black people as the property of white men, yet within the confines of the system blacks created their own fragile institutions through which they asserted their dignity and humanity. They established family, kinship, and community networks that extended beyond the limits of any one plantation and strove to survive the slave sales that separated husband from wife and parent from child. African-Americans also practiced their own religions, composed songs, created dances, devised ceremonies, and established ways of living and thinking that distinguished them from both their masters and their African ancestors. African-American culture evolved as some half-million transported Africans and their descendants learned to resist the degradation and oppression of their enslavement and to assert some control over their day-to-day existence. This culture was neither English nor African, neither imposed by the master class nor imported as a relic of an irretrievably lost past. It was instead a cultural blend, adapted to the peculiar needs of a people in bondage. Slaves retained what they could of their African heritage and reconciled it with what they were forced to do or had learned to do to survive in America.

This evolving African-American culture contrasted with the experiences of the first two generations of slaves and free blacks in the Chesapeake. For those early slaves a distinctive new culture had not been possible. Their numbers had been small, and contact between them was limited by their dispersal among a much larger English population. Closely supervised by their masters, slaves had little time for themselves. There were also as yet no rigid barriers dividing white and black laborers, and some slaves could still expect to gain their freedom. So slaves easily adopted the culture of their English fellow servants, with whom they con-

"Group of Negroes Imported to Be Sold as Slaves." A late-eighteenth century engraving showed newly arrived captive Africans being driven to an auction.

Source: (William Blake) John Gabriel Stedman, *Narrative of a five-years expedition against the revolted Negroes of Surinam . . . from the year 1772, to 1777* (1796)— Rare Books and Manuscript Division, New York Public Library, Astor, Lenox and Tilden Foundations.

spired, drank, ran away, and "frolicked." A distinctly African-American culture began to emerge only as the number of Africans increased, as racial laws began restricting their contact with whites, and as the chances of freedom from slavery dwindled.

Wrenched from different societies in Africa, the newly arrived slaves usually faced a life among strangers. Before taking them from Africa, traders often mixed captives from different regions to reduce the opportunity for concerted resistance. Forcibly separated from their families, most slaves faced life in America without kin or other acquaintances around them. They had been robbed of their land, tools, and possessions, so they could not ply their trades or even dress as they had previously done. Separated from others from their own societies, they could not speak their native languages, play their assigned kinship roles, or practice their religions—the things that had distinguished them as belonging to diverse African villages and regions.

As the number of slaves grew rapidly in the first half of the eighteenth century, the different circumstances in the Chesapeake and the lower South determined how long it would take for new arrivals to establish relationships with one another, and with those who had preceded them. In the Chesapeake, many slaves were sold to small planters and so tended to live in small groups, separated from each other. Perhaps as many as one in three Chesapeake slaves lived in groups of five or less, and they had quite close contact with whites. As slavery spread inland, across the Virginia piedmont region in the eighteenth century, only about one-third of slaves lived on plantations with more than twenty slaves each. South Carolina rice plantations were larger, on average, than Chesapeake tobacco farms. There, newly imported slaves were more frequently sold in large groups to single planters, so they were less likely to be isolated from one another and more likely to live separately from whites. As a result of these differences, slaves in the Chesapeake tended to speak English, while those in South Carolina and Georgia combined various similarly structured African languages with English to form Gullah, which became the lowcountry slaves' common and unifying language.

The organization of tobacco and rice production also played an important role in creating different regional patterns in slave life. Work on large Chesapeake tobacco farms was fairly continuous, conducted by gangs of slaves who worked for long hours under the supervision of overseers. Carolina rice cultivation, by contrast, involved more strenuous but more varied work and was not amenable to gang labor. Rice planters therefore introduced a task system, in which slaves were required to complete allocated jobs, but were freer of direct supervision. The task system also gave slaves more time to cultivate their own "provision grounds" (garden plots), or to hunt and fish. As a result, South Carolina slaves found themselves with greater relative autonomy and greater responsibility for providing their own food than those in the Chesapeake. At the same time, though, they were more vulnerable to the whims of overseers left in charge by absentee planters who had taken up residence in Charleston.

Despite these differences, slave cultures throughout the South also acquired much in common with one another. The strong emphasis African societies placed on kinship, and especially on ties between brothers and sisters, helped uprooted people survive enslavement. Although kinship systems varied among African societies, family bonds were universal, providing an important context in which an African-American culture could unfold. Even on slave ships unrelated captives began to refer to each other as brothers and sisters, and sexual intercourse between such "siblings" was forbidden. Children were taught to call former shipmates aunts and uncles. Over several generations, kinship practices helped slaves from diverse backgrounds order their lives and maintain connections that extended beyond a single slave quarter, plantation, or county.

These bonds were not easily developed. The constant arrival of new immigrants strained the resources of whatever collective institutions already existed. Slaves were frequently sent from one plantation to another, fracturing communities. Nevertheless, since such movement was often

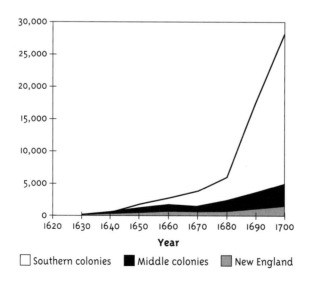

The Distribution of African Americans in the Seventeenth-Century Colonies. Even though slavery existed throughout the colonies, its rapid expansion in the South after the 1670s meant that the great majority of African Americans lived there, rather than in New England or the Middle Colonies.

within the same geographical area, kin connections and knowledge of family histories could be maintained with some effort. In southern Maryland in the 1760s, between 120 and 300 slaves claimed their descent from a couple called Butler, who had started having children eighty years before. After 1720 in the Chesapeake and 1760 in the lower South, many impediments to family life disappeared: death rates fell, the number of men and women equalized, and slave importation from Africa declined in relative importance. Among Robert "King" Carter's slaves in Virginia, over half lived in households with children by 1733, including almost all the women. Of fifty-five slaves belonging to a North Carolina owner in 1761, only eight were single; the rest lived in six families.

The Chesapeake slave population became the first anywhere in the New World to sustain its numbers by natural increase. The majority of Chesapeake slaves were native-born by the 1740s, and this would be the case throughout the South by the end of the century. Young black Americans were increasingly raised by African-American parents in an emerging African-American culture, not "seasoned" by white masters as their predecessors had been.

But masters still defined the context of daily life and limited the ways in which slaves could act. Masters determined working conditions, enforced slave codes, and ultimately held the power of life and death. They could break up slaves' families at will, and their indebtedness, bankruptcy, or death could do so unintentionally. Yet, if the system was to work, they had to be able to depend on their slaves' ability to take care of each other, to raise children, to learn English, to perform a variety of tasks, and, in some cases, to manage other slaves. Slaves did all of these things, and taught their children to do likewise.

Slaves' living arrangements also evolved with the slave system. During the early eighteenth century, when the majority of field hands were men, many slaves lived together in rough dormitories or barracks. However, as the sex ratio among slaves became more balanced and many established families, an increasing number lived in separate dwellings. Cabins sprang up in the slave settlements near plantation houses. They reminded one visitor to South Carolina of the "wooden cottages [of] poor villagers" in England, but many built by slaves themselves reflected an African influence. Often scantily built, these dwellings offered basic shelter, but little material comfort or adornment. Still, in the family cabin, slaves enjoyed a space that was mostly theirs, where to some extent they could shape their own lives. Here they determined the range of their kinship group, provided for "outsiders"—unrelated slaves acquired by the master—and even sheltered runaways from other plantations. Within this private sphere, they took last names different from their masters', and bestowed the names of grandparents and great-grandparents—Cuffee, Quash—on

Advertisements for Slaves in the *Maryland Gazette*

Although most slaves worked as field hands, there was also demand for men and women slaves with craft skills, particularly in districts with large plantations. Some male slaves were trained as carpenters, shoemakers, blacksmiths, and masons, or as coopers who made barrels for shipping tobacco and other goods. A smaller number of women slaves escaped field labor to become household servants or to work at spinning yarn and weaving cloth. These advertisements from the *Maryland Gazette* reflect the market in skilled slaves.

[April 27, 1748]

TO BE SOLD BY THE SUBSCRIBER, IN ANNAPOLIS

A brisk likely Country-born Negro Wench about 18 or 19 years of Age, who is a good Spinner; with a Child, about 18 months Old.

William Reynolds

Very good Nutmegs, by the Pound, or Ounce, to be sold by the same Reynolds.

[May 29, 1751]

TO BE SOLD

A likely, strong Negro Girl, about 16 Years of Age, fit for Plantation Work, or very capable of making a Good House Wench, having for some Months served as such in a small Family. For further Particulars, Enquire of the Printer Hereof.

their children, linking them to an African past and to a memory of freedom.

Many masters, intent on destroying the remnants of their chattels' free identities, discouraged African customs and languages. As a result, the work habits, family arrangements, and religious beliefs that were most similar to English practices were the ones most likely to survive. Yet slaves retained non-Christian beliefs, dances, songs, "revels," and funeral practices. African influences persisted in foodways too, in the child-rearing practices of mothers and female kin, in the work of artisans who made pottery, in musical instruments and metal goods, and in the objects slaves placed in the graves of their dead. By building bonds of family and kinship, and by preserving aspects of African culture, slaves fashioned a

[May 28, 1752]

TO BE SOLD BY PUBLIC VENDOR

At the House of Mr. Samuel Middleton, in Annapolis, on Wednesday the 10th Day of June next at 4 o'clock in the afternoon:

The Hull of a New Vessel lying now at the Town Dock, together with her Masts, and some of her Yards. . . .

Also at the same time will be sold a Blacksmith and a Wheelright, with their Tools; both being excellent workmen. Also a Collier and a Sawyer, who have each about 5 Yeares to Serve. . . .

Likewise a Country-born Negro Wench, About 27 Years of Age, very sober and healthy; and understands Household Business very well, with a Mulatto Boy about a year and a half old, who is the said Negro's Child.

Whoever is inclinable to purchase, on giving security (if required), may have two Months time for Payment.

[December 17, 1761]

TO BE SOLD BY THE SUBSCRIBER, being near Upper Marlborough, in Prince George's County, on the Second Day of January next, for good Bills of Exchange:

A Choice Parcel of Country-born Slaves, consisting of Men, Women, Boys, and Girls, all Young and healthy, chief between 10 and 20 years of Age; among these Slaves there are two Wenches about 16 or 17 Years of Age, who Understand Spinning and Knitting, and a young Fellow of 20 Years of Age, a good Plowman and Cartman.

The Sale to be on a Plantation now Mr. William Beall's.

William Parker

Source: Nancy Woloch, ed., *Early American Women: A Documentary History, 1600–1700* (1992).

social identity that enabled them to maintain their dignity despite captivity and oppression.

The Fear of Slave Rebellion

Slaves also tried to resist their captivity. Slave owners, by reducing men and women to property, sought to deny the humanity of their slaves. Slaves, by creating their own institutions and social practices, reasserted that humanity. By 1760, African-Americans accounted for well over one-third of the South's total population. In the Chesapeake they constituted about two-fifths of the population. In South Carolina, with its larger rice

The Old Plantation. This unusual late-eighteenth-century painting by an unknown artist indicated the blending of cultural influences in the slaves' quarters. African and American culture merged in the slaves' dress, dance, and musical instruments (a drum and banjo). The ceremony was probably a wedding where, by African custom, the bride and groom jumped over a stick.

Source: Anonymous, watercolor, c. 1800—Abby Aldrich Rockefeller Folk Art Center, Williamsburg, Virginia.

plantations, they were a substantial majority, and here, particularly, the threat of slave rebellion led to repressive arrangements. But wherever slavery existed, the fear and actuality of resistance produced harsh laws and institutions designed to impose order on potentially unruly slaves.

From time to time slaves did resort to overt rebellion. As many as two hundred slaves took part in a revolt around Norfolk, Virginia, in 1730. Four of them were executed and local militias were enlarged. In 1769, when whites exposed a planned uprising in Hanover County, Virginia, armed slaves confronted them in a pitched battle before being overwhelmed. The Stono Rebellion in South Carolina in 1739 began when about twenty slaves marched off in the direction of Florida from the Stono River, not far from Charleston. Many of them were recently arrived from Angola and may have been prompted to resist their enslavement by the outbreak of war between England and Spain. After stealing arms and decapitating two storekeepers, they began burning buildings and murdering whites at the plantations they passed, while recruiting a further fifty or more slaves into their ranks. At the Edisto River, a white militia confronted them, shooting fourteen slaves dead immediately and killing two dozen more after they had surrendered. In the brutal repression that followed, fleeing rebels were rounded up and executed. Their heads were displayed at mileposts along the roadsides as a warning to others.

Such outright rebellion was rare. But fear of it was common, and periodic panics gripped the white population. Planters were wary of "intestine enemies" and "dangerous domestics." Women employed as

"Barns Being Burnt . . ."

Slaves' resistance took many forms. In South Carolina, slaves involved in rice production often burned down the barns where the harvested rice was stored. This October 14, 1732, letter, printed in the *South Carolina Gazette*, reveals how common the slave "custom" of barn-burning had become in one part of the colony.

I have taken notice for Several Years past, that there has not one Winter elapsed, without one or more Barns being burnt, and two Winters since, there was no less than five. Whether it is owing to Accident, Carelessness, or Severity, I will not pretend to determine; but am afraid, chiefly to the [latter two causes]. I desire therefore, as a Friend to the Planters, that you'll insert the following Account from Pon Pon, which, I hope, will forewarn the Planters of their Danger, and make them for the future, more careful and human:

About 3 Weeks since, Mr. James Gray worked his Negroes late in his Barn at Night, and the next Morning before Day, hurried them out again, and when they came to it, found it burnt down to the Ground, and all that was in it.

Source: *South Carolina Gazette,* October 14, 1732.

cooks, who were intimately connected to their white owners and in a unique position to harm them, came under suspicion. Slaves were known to have brought the knowledge of poisons from Africa, and those suspected of plotting to use it faced savage punishment. In South Carolina, this included execution by being burned alive.

Slaves resisted in many other ways, too. As their numbers grew and a sense of community developed among them, they worked together to protect one another and reduce the harshness of labor. Though whippings for disobedience or insolence were a near-certainty, slaves conspired to break tools, feign illness, slow down or neglect work, and avoid learning new tasks. When a Virginia planter skimped on his field hands' clothing so that they were almost naked, one of his neighbors noted that he got "nothing by his injustice but the scandal of it," because the slaves produced poor crops. The Virginia slaveowner Landon Carter railed at the frequency with which his slaves fell ill on Mondays.

Slaves also made bids for freedom. Running away, individually or in small groups, was common. Most did it only for short periods, to visit spouses or relatives on other farms, or to escape punishment. Much truancy occurred in planting, hoeing, or harvesting seasons. The majority of runaways were men, though women were as important as men in harboring fugitives. When a slave called Caesar absconded for several months on Virginia's Eastern Shore in 1724, Alice Cormack, a white widow, was

---

". . . A Bloody Tragedy"

Full-scale rebellion was rare, but the very possibility of such insurrection terrified southern whites, as this letter, printed in the October 22, 1730, issue of the *Boston Weekly News-Letter,* reveals. A slave uprising planned
to begin in Charleston, South Carolina, on August 15, 1730, was uncovered in advance. This report hints at how
slaves planned to spread their actions out of the city into the countryside.

I shall give an Account of a bloody Tragedy which was to have been executed here last Saturday night (the 15th Inst.) by the
Negroes, who had conspired to Rise and destroy us, and had almost brought it to pass: but it pleased God to appear for us,
and confound their Councils. For some of them proposed that the Negroes of every Plantation should destroy their own Masters; but others were for Rising in a Body, and giving the blow at once on surprise; and thus they differed. They soon made
a great Body at the back of the Town, and had a great Dance, and expected the Country Negroes to come & join them; and
had not an overruling Providence discovered their Intrigues, we had been all in Blood. . . . The Chief of them, with the others, is apprehended and in Irons, in order to a Tryal, and we are in Hopes to find out the whole Affair.

Source: *Boston Weekly News-Letter,* October 22, 1730.

---

jailed for a month and given twenty-five lashes of the whip for aiding him.
Returned fugitives could also expect a whipping, but some persistent
runaways had their toes cut off: one planter wrote that "nothing less than
dismemberment" would "reclaim" an "incorrigeble rogue" who kept ab-
sconding. Some escapees paid with their lives. Twenty-one-year-old
Henry Carter, sold to a new master with a fearsome reputation, ran off.
An overseer caught him crossing a river and stoned him to death.

Unlike some Caribbean islands whose black majority populations and
mountainous terrain sheltered communities of escaped slaves (known as
maroons), the southern colonies provided only slender chances for permanent escape. Inland from the Chesapeake plantation districts, for
example, lay land occupied by hostile whites. Near present-day Lexington, Virginia, in 1728–1729 one group of runaway slaves did create a
village. They built homes like those they had known in Africa, established
a tribal government under a chief, and (with stolen implements) used
African farming techniques to grow crops. Whites soon destroyed the village, killed the chief, and returned the residents to their masters. The
Carolinas held somewhat more promise, but not much. Escape to Indian
groups such as the Cherokee or Creeks might provide a chance for assimilation, but would equally likely lead to reenslavement. Small groups of

Ran Off. The September 18, 1762, edition of the *South Carolina Gazette* included notices about escaped slaves, stray animals, and runaway wives.

Source: *South Carolina Gazette,* Supplement, September 18, 1762—Prints and Photographs Division, Library of Congress.

To be sold by the subscribers,

A Valuable tract of land near the river May, in St. Helena parish, belonging to the estate of James Macpherson, jun. deceased, containing 500 acres; 200 acres of which is very good rice-land, and may be kept under water by two short dams, 100 acres is pine-land, and the other 200 acres exceeding good for corn or indico ——All persons having any demands against the above estate, are desired to make them properly known to us; and all those who stand any wise indebted to the said estate are desired to settle with
SARAH MACPHERSON, Executrix.
ISAAC MACPHERSON, Executor.

A Few Hogsheads of exceeding good Jamaica muscovado and prize sugars, just imported, to be sold reasonably by   JOHN DART.

Henry Smith at William Glover's cow-pen, informs me of a bright bay horse, about 14 hands high, has an obscure brand on the near buttock, and on the off shoulder and buttock L, with a flower de luce on the top, a scar on the right cheek, a small blaze in his forehead, and has three white feet.   CHARLES LOWNDES.

Whereas my wife Hannah hath absconded from me, without any just cause; This is to give public notice, that I will not pay any debts she may contract, and desire all persons not to harbour her, as this is the second time of her elopement.   THOMAS NEILSON.

Run away about the end of July last, from my plantation on the Five and twenty-mile Creek, on the Wateree-river, a new negro girl about 12 years old, named ROSE, speaks pretty good English. Whoever takes up said negro, and delivers her to me at the aforesaid plantation, or the warden of the work-house in Charles-Town, shall receive a reward of *five pounds*. And any person giving information of her being harboured by a white person, shall, on conviction of the offender, be entitled to a reward of *twenty pounds*.   SAMUEL SCOTT.

John Tucker, of Wassamsaw, informs me of two small stray'd creatures, one a roan mare with a white down her face, a bow mane, one hind foot white, and has the mark of an old sore on her withers, branded on the off shoulder y turned upside down, with a flower de luce joining it, and on the off buttock MO.—A bay gelding, his hind feet white, and branded on the off buttock Y with a heart, and on the off shoulder the same brand turn'd sideways. The owner of said strays may apply to   BENJ. WARING.

maroons did survive in the swamps behind the rice plantations, but in isolated and harsh conditions.

The presence of the Spanish in Florida did give Carolina slaves one other chance of escape. In 1693 Spain offered freedom to fugitive slaves who would convert to Catholicism. Some evaded capture on the long, dangerous march south, and in Florida groups of runaways lived among

Suppression of a Runaway Slave Community

In a letter to the Board of Trade in London, written in 1729, Virginia's lieutenant-governor, Sir William Gooch, describes measures taken by planters and colonial governments to curb slave runaways.

My Lords:

. . . Sometime after my Last a number of Negroes, about fifteen, belonging to a new Plantation on the head of James River formed a Design to withdraw from their Master and to fix themselves in the fastness of the neighboring Mountains. They had found means to get into their possession some Arms & Ammunition, and they took along with them some Provisions, their Cloaths, bedding and working Tools; but the Gentleman to whom they belonged with a Party of Men made such diligent pursuit after them, that he soon found them out in their new Settlement, a very obscure place among the Mountains, where they had already begun to clear the ground, and obliged them after exchanging a shot or two by which one of the Slaves was wounded, to surrender and return back, and so prevented for this time a design which might have proved as dangerous to this Country, as is that of the Negroes in the Mountains of Jamaica to the Inhabitants of that Island. Tho' this attempt has happily been defeated, it ought nevertheless to awaken us into some effectual measures for preventing the like hereafter, it being certain that a very small number of Negroes once settled in those Parts, would very soon be encreas'd by the Accession of other Runaways and prove dangerous Neighbours to our frontier Inhabitants. To prevent this and many other Mischiefs I am training and exercising the Militia in the several counties as the best means to deter our Slaves from endeavouring to make their Escape, and to suppress them if they should.

Source: Karen Ordahl Kupperman, ed., *Major Problems in American Colonial History* (1993).

Native Americans or in their own communities. But even here they were vulnerable. The largest village of escaped slaves, Santa Teresa de Mose near St. Augustine, was captured by English troops in 1740. Although the Spanish later recaptured it, Mose did not regain its former size and disintegrated when Florida became a British possession in 1763.

Slave Societies: Material Prosperity and Inequality

By the middle of the eighteenth century, the population of the southern colonies numbered just over 300,000 whites and about 200,000 black slaves, together with small numbers of free blacks and the remaining Indians. Nearly two-thirds of all southerners lived in Virginia and Maryland, and a third in the two Carolinas; only about 5,000 people had settled in Georgia up to this time. Each of the five southern colonies had a colonial assembly and a system of courts that governed in accordance with English political and legal precedents. The king's representatives in each colony included a royal governor, customs collectors, and a host of other officials charged with overseeing colonial trade. The Church of England had become part of the fabric of life; as in England it was closely identified with the elite, and with the enforcement of social hierarchy.

Southern customs and lifestyles no longer horrified English visitors as they had in earlier decades. Though few of the increasing numbers born in the South would ever see England, many shared an English cultural identity, and to some extent duplicated the social norms of their English peers. Men no longer outnumbered women in the southern colonies, and the family became the center of social life. Like their counterparts in England, many southern white women contributed to the family income by spinning, weaving, gardening, and selling dairy products. Slavery and the plantation economy were securely in place. There had been some diversification of agriculture. Chesapeake farmers and planters exported cattle and wheat. From the deep South went out shipments of the dyestuff indigo—first grown on the plantation of a resourceful young woman planter, Eliza Lucas Pinckney—as well as naval stores such as pitch, tar, and timber. But the main staple crops of each region remained dominant. In the Chesapeake, tobacco production rose from 28 million pounds in 1700 to 80 million in 1760; from the coastal regions of the lower South, rice exports rose from ten thousand barrels in 1720 to one hundred thousand in 1760.

Exporting Tobacco. A detail from a 1775 map showed slaves packing tobacco in barrels on a Virginia wharf for shipment abroad.

Source: Joshua Fry and Peter Jefferson, *A Map of the Inhabited Part of Virginia* . . . (1775)—Maryland Historical Society.

Staple export crops and slave labor enabled the southern colonies to achieve a prosperity unmatched elsewhere in eighteenth-century North America. Per head of population, white wealth in Virginia and South Carolina was double that in New England or the Middle Colonies. Land was easier to acquire in the South than in England and few European visitors failed to note the abundance of food and the prevalence of landownership. In Virginia, for example, about two in three white families farmed their own land in 1750, consuming roughly sixty percent of what they produced and bartering the surplus for tools and other goods they could not make. In North and South Carolina the proportion of white households with land was even higher.

Yet slavery and staple crop production also ensured that the South's wealth was very unequally distributed. Owning slaves enhanced the advantages of the rich over the poor. Those at the lower end of the scale slipped easily into poverty, and at least one-fifth of the white population owned little more than the clothes they wore. Dramatic distinctions existed between rich and poor. Tobacco and rice, speculation in western land, slave trading, and shipping had made a few southerners very wealthy. When he died in 1732, Virginia's richest planter, Robert "King"

Charleston Entertainment, 1760. Having served supper and then after-dinner drinks, a young slave dozed while members of Charleston's merchant-planter elite caroused around the dining-room table. The drawing was set in the home of Peter Manigault (seated at the left center), scion of one of the wealthiest families in colonial Carolina.

Source: George Roupell, *Peter Manigault and His Friends,* c. 1760, black ink and wash, 10 3/16 × 13 3/16 inches—Henry Francis duPont Winterthur Museum.

Carter, owned 300,000 acres and almost one thousand slaves; one of his sons alone held 500 slaves. Across the southern colonies the richest ten percent of the population owned half of all wealth, including one-seventh of the people.

Planter elites mimicked the style of the English gentry. By the 1720s they were building spacious brick mansions in parklike surroundings; Charleston's wealthy planters and merchants built elegant townhouses too. The rich imported elaborate furnishings, adorned their wives and daughters in European fashions, and maintained large numbers of slaves as house servants. They hired tutors for their sons or, in many cases, sent them to be educated in Scotland or England. They brought up their children to exercise authority. In 1728 Robert "King" Carter planned to buy slave girls to give to each of his grandsons.

The majority of white southerners lived in humbler surroundings. Their houses were small and built of wood; they had no servants, slaves, or silverware, and relied on their own labor. Though many owned their own land, significant numbers of whites in the Chesapeake owned none. In Maryland, a majority of small farmers were tenants, renting land from large landholders, and living in relative poverty. Landless whites relied on intermittent work, or settled and hunted on marginal land or in frontier areas. Many landless men worked as tenants on the large estates or as wage laborers in agriculture, shipping, or the crafts; most landless women had to work as domestic servants.

Nondescripts . . . near Oaks, Virginia. "A family of poor White children," architect Benjamin Henry Latrobe noted in his sketchbook, "observed from the Stage carrying peaches to a neighboring Barbecue for Sale." The woman and children in this 1796 sketch wore large, stiff bonnets common to that part of Virginia.

Source: Benjamin Henry Latrobe, *Nondescripts attracted by a neighbouring barbecue, near the Oaks, Virginia,* 1796, pencil, pen, and ink, wash, 6 15/16 × 10 15/16 inches — Maryland Historical Society.

"Pity Your Distressed Daughter"

Well into the eighteenth century, many women committed themselves to indentured servitude in exchange for passage to the North American colonies. In this 1756 letter to her parents in England, Elizabeth Sprigs, a female servant in Maryland, describes her life and labor.

Honored Father
     My being forever banished from your sight will I hope pardon the boldness I now take of troubling you with these [words]. . . . O Dear Father, believe that I am going to relate the words of truth and sincerity, and balance my former bad conduct [to] my sufferings here, and then I am sure you'll pity your distressed daughter. What we unfortunate English people suffer here is beyond the probability of you in England to conceive. Let it suffice that I, one of the unhappy number, am toiling almost day and night, and very often in the horses' drudgery, with only this comfort that "you bitch you do not half enough," and then tied up and whipped to that degree that you'd not serve an animal. Scarce anything but Indian corn and salt to eat and that even begrudged nay many Negroes are better used, almost naked no shoes nor stockings to wear, and the comfort after slaving during Master's pleasure, what rest we can get is to wrap ourselves up in an blanket and lay upon the ground. This is the deplorable condition your poor Betty endures, and now I beg if you have any bowels of compassion left show it by sending me some relief, clothing is the principal thing wanting, which if you should condescend to, may easily send them to me by any ships bound to Baltimore Town, Patapsco River, Maryland, and give me leave to conclude in duty to you and Uncles and Aunts, and respect to all friends, Honored Father

Your undutiful and
disobedient child
ELIZABETH SPRIGS

Also found in humble surroundings were most of the growing numbers of white men and women who lived in the less-settled areas of the South, away from the coast. This "backcountry" attracted both the children of poor-to-middling native-born southerners and the most recent immigrants from Ireland, Scotland, and Germany. Frontier dwellers were generally poorer than their coastal counterparts. A mid-century visitor to the South Carolina backcountry found many inhabitants who "have nought but a Gourd to drink out of, nor a Plate, Knive or Spoon, a Glass, Cup, or anything." Many were tenants who rented from large landowners and speculators. Society itself was less structured than on the coast, authority less established. There were few great plantations here or large concentrations of slaves. In the western counties of North Carolina, for example, only about twelve percent of the white population owned slaves, and very few of those owned more than five.

Land on the frontier was cheaper than on the coast, and thousands obtained legal title through squatter's rights—that is, by building a cabin, clearing a number of acres, and planting a crop. Permitting settlement to expand in this way could help a colonial government bolster its claims to the interior against the counterclaims of Indians, English speculators, or other colonies. Though few of these modest settlers achieved more than a decent subsistence, they established communities in which a rough frontier equality prevailed. The backcountry could also provide the opportunity for social mobility. In Lunenburg County, part of Virginia's newly settled Southside, for instance, John Hix and George McLaughlin were both landless laborers in 1748. By 1769, Hix had acquired almost four hundred acres and owned two slaves. Though McLaughlin had not joined the ranks of slave owners, his 250 acres of land made him an independent farmer.

Slave Societies: Deference and Conflict

Alongside the Crown's officials, wealthy men in the South controlled the government, the courts, and the church. Leading planter families had from the first dominated political life in the southern colonies, and the growing permanence and prosperity of settlement merely reinforced their position as a stable gentry class. By the eighteenth century, the Beverlys, Randolphs, Carters, Harrisons, Lees, and Byrds, with their relatives and connections, had secure hold of seats in the Virginia House of Burgesses. Between 1700 and 1760, one-third of the places on the Virginia governor's council were held by members of just nine families. Pinckneys, Rutledges, Draytons, and a handful of others obtained even greater relative prominence in South Carolina. John Randolph of Virginia wrote that "person[s] of note in the Colony . . . either by blood or marriage, . . . are almost all related, or so connected in our interests, that whoever of a Stranger presumes to offend any one of us will infallibly find an enemy of the whole."

The gentry's power was rooted at the local level. They controlled the vestries, or governing bodies, of the churches. The established church throughout the South was the Church of England (or Anglican church), and individual communities levied taxes to pay the salaries of clergymen, who had often been educated and ordained in England. The gentry also dominated the county courts—the centers of local political as well as legal power. Their houses were centers of social and political activity, of hospitality and patronage for farmers and voters. They engaged in sociable rituals of gambling, horse racing and other entertainment.

These institutions and practices reflected the assumption that, in an unequal society, the wealthy and powerful were owed deference and respect by the majority. As one Virginian recalled, "we were accustomed to look upon what were called *gentle folks* as beings of a superior order." To some extent the ways in which non-elite white men could participate in the benefits of privilege sustained such a notion of deference. By the mid-eighteenth century, the proportion of small slaveholders was rising, particularly in coastal regions. About half the white farmers in coastal Maryland owned one or more slaves, as did a majority of Charleston's white artisans. Propertyholding or taxpaying was widespread enough that many white men qualified for the vote—between sixty and ninety percent across the South, according to some estimates. The ten to forty percent of the population who could not meet the qualifications for voting were disenfranchised, as were all blacks and women. Even elite single women, like the pioneer landowner Mistress Margaret Brent, were unable to translate financial and political influence into the formal right to vote. No white men, however poor, shared the inferior economic and political status of women or the burdens and penalties of slavery.

But powerful as the gentry were, their relationship with the poorer whites around them was not just one of domination. The Chesapeake gentry, for instance, largely noted the lessons of Bacon's Rebellion, dispensing credit and employment to the less affluent, and making court sessions and elections a theater in which white property owners large and small enjoyed a measure of equality. Poorer men's social distance from the gentry was bridged by occasions at which classes would mingle. Sociability at taverns, racecourses, militia musters, and court-days, and the hospitality of the planter houses reflected the interdependence of rich and poor.

Even so, sharp conflicts arose within white society over religion, politics, and economic issues. Elites were divided by political differences among themselves. Wealthy planters and representatives of the king vied for power and the spoils of office. Planters complained about the "exorbitant" salaries they had to pay governors and other Crown officials, and thought them too eager to exploit the region and its public lands for quick speculative gains, regardless of the long-term effect on the economy. Conflict with other groups was common, too. Struggles over land and markets often pitted wealthy landowners and speculators against middling and poorer whites. In the 1730s, wealthy Virginia planters secured the passage of tobacco inspection laws that threatened to squeeze out smaller growers of the crop. Small planters protested, burning down tobacco warehouses in several counties, but in vain.

In the Carolinas, conflict emerged between wealthy, politically dominant coastal elites and the poorer inhabitants of the backcountry. Frontier
settlers claimed the right of all freeborn Englishmen to oppose authority
they saw as illegitimate. People expected the wealthy to rule, but also to
protect the larger interests of the community. When they did not, ordinary men and women claimed the right to take collective action on the
community's behalf. Backcountry people in the lower South seriously
challenged the coastal elites in the 1760s. Grievances varied from one
colony to another, but most concerned access to the land and representation in colonial assemblies. Complaints readily escalated into violent
confrontations, because frontier dwellers were already organized into
armed—usually democratic—militias for action against the Indians in
the area. Though coastal authorities in the Carolinas and Georgia accused
frontier dwellers of living "out of the bounds of the law," such people
were not overly violent or reckless. They were simply less deferential,
more irreverent, and more egalitarian than their lowcountry peers.

The Challenge of the Great Awakening

Throughout the South a less violent but broader challenge emerged in the
1740s, when poor and politically disenfranchised whites joined an evangelical religious movement that became known as the Great Awakening.
For decades the Anglican clergy and other well-educated colonists had begun to take the "enlightened" view, then current in Europe and England,
that God was rational and kind. This fitted well with elite concepts of a
decorous form of religious observance in which popular participation
would pose no threat to social order or the authority of rulers. But evangelicals, many from the middling and lower classes, rejected the
rationalists' increasingly refined, polite, and philosophical religious dis-
course. Their God was wrathful and disgusted with the sinfulness of
mankind. Individuals could be saved only be recognizing their own help-
lessness and depravity in the face of an almighty God. Salvation was
available only to those who surrendered to God, through an emotional
conversion, and asked for his forgiveness.

The Great Awakening was touched off by visits to America of figures
who were at the heart of profound changes in the English churches during
the 1730s. John Wesley, the founder of Methodism, preached in Georgia
in 1736, while a tour of the American colonies three years later by his
colleague George Whitefield prompted widespread revivals. From the
early revival meetings grew new Christian sects that challenged the Anglican church and appealed to men and women of moderate and poor
means. "New Lights," as they were known, disputed with the clergy, at-

tacked the sinfulness of gambling, horse racing and other leisured activities, and proclaimed the spiritual equality of all men and women before God. The eruption was particularly intense in Virginia, where the colony's small farmers enthusiastically denounced the gentry's way of life and social values. Itinerant preachers, little-educated but steeped in the oral traditions of the poorest people in the South, taught their growing flocks that ordinary men and women were more likely candidates for divine inspiration than the gentry and educated clergymen who led them. Ordinary folk increasingly relied on vivid religious imagery and language in confrontations with their elite antagonists.

The egalitarianism of the Great Awakening challenged more than planters' habits. It called their control into question, and it also threatened to break through the racial barriers that had become an essential facet of the South's slave societies. Although Whitefield did not question slavery itself, he did condemn the mistreatment of slaves and referred to the recent Stono Rebellion as God's judgment on planters. Others went further. In 1741, Hugh Bryan, a South Carolina planter and politician converted in the revival, began prophesying a day of doom that would bring "Deliverance of the Negroes from servitude." The colonial assembly forced him to retract and apologize for his remarks because, as another planter put it, "we dreaded the consiquence of such a thing being put in to the head of the slaves and the advantage they might take of us." The doctrine of spiritual equality had subversive potential in a slave society.

Nevertheless, it was revivalist religion, not Anglican hierarchicalism, that spread Christianity rapidly among slaves, as well as poor whites, in the middle decades of the eighteenth century. Slaves like David George converted in significant numbers, and the proportion of Christianized slaves would rise from the mid-eighteenth century onward, though the growth occurred faster in the Chesapeake than it did in the lower South. Some evangelicals—considered by Virginia's well-to-do to be "continual fomenters of discord"—held the radical belief that equality before God extended to all men and women, black and white; all could surrender to God and be saved. In the Virginia backcountry, the Presbyterian preacher Samuel Davies attracted growing numbers of black and white members to his churches in the 1750s, while Methodist churches regularly became forums of biracial worship. The evangelical movement as a whole, white and black, raised the level of religious involvement in the colonies, though its influence was greater among women than men.

Davies was careful to assure leading Virginians that he was not seeking to undermine the social order. As a channel for turning human minds to spiritual matters, revivalism was potentially a conservative force. But by democratizing salvation, preachers helped erode some of the deference with which blacks and most whites were expected to regard the gentry

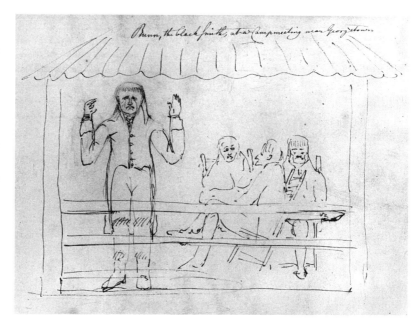

Bunn, the Blacksmith, at a Campmeeting near Georgetown. In 1809, Benjamin Henry Latrobe attended a Virginia Methodist revival meeting, where he sketched the effective performance of a self-educated, artisan preacher. "A general groaning was going on," Latrobe wrote in his journal, "in several parts of the Camp, women were shrieking, and just under the stage there was an uncommon bustle, and cry, which I understood arose from some persons who were under conversion."

Source: Benjamin Henry Latrobe, *Bunn, the blacksmith, at a Campmeeting near Georgetown,* August 6, 1809, pencil, pen, and ink, 8 × 12 3/4 inches—Maryland Historical Society.

and its institutions. Groups like the Separate Baptists became open critics of slavery and the slave trade. Both in calling slavery into question and in bringing white and black worshippers together on an equal footing, the Awakening weakened the gentry's formula, worked out in the aftermath of Bacon's Rebellion, for preserving order in a slave society.

The evangelical movement also helped to popularize the belief that government was merely the human mechanism through which God would ensure equality among individuals from various classes. In this belief, illiterate craftsmen, backwoods farmers, and female servants sought salvation for themselves and for society. Looking down on what they considered the planters' excessive comforts and pleasures, evangelicals questioned the legitimacy of their rule and the superiority of their culture.

Southern Society at Mid Eighteenth Century

Midcentury social tensions in the English southern colonies did not undermine their position with regard to the Indians or other European powers whose territory lay adjacent to them. Population growth and frontier settlement maintained pressure on Native American groups. Wars and skirmishes across the border to the South weakened Spanish control of Florida and would lead to the British acquisition of East Florida in 1763. Meanwhile, in the Mississippi Valley, the French were also having

An Overseer Doing His Duty. A relaxed overseer watched two slave women at work in a Virginia scene sketched by Benjamin Henry Latrobe in 1798. Latrobe (who would become one of the most influential architects in nineteenth-century America) had been in the United States only two years, but during that brief time he grew to detest slavery (suggested in the sarcastic title of the sketch).

Source: Benjamin Henry Latrobe, *An overseer doing his duty. Sketched from life near Fredericsburg, March 13, 1798,* pencil, pen, and ink, watercolor, 7 × 10 1/4 inches — Maryland Historical Society.

difficulty sustaining their projected plantation society. Having imported several thousand African slaves to Louisiana in the decade or so after founding New Orleans, they found themselves unable to build the kind of slave society that had emerged in the English South. Slaves and members of the local Natchez tribe revolted in 1729, weakening an already tenuous French control of society. The European population grew more slowly than the African, and Louisiana soon had a black majority. Slaveholding was concentrated in the hands of a small elite of planters and merchants, but racial distinctions were weakly defined and intermarriage became frequent. In contrast with the English slave colonies, Louisiana ceased to be dominated by the existence of slavery; it became a "society with slaves."

From Maryland to Georgia, by contrast, wealthy landowners could convince many poor whites that the division between white and black meant more than that between rich and poor. The existence of slavery shaped virtually all social relations in the English southern colonies, where planters held sway over economic and political activity and exercised relatively unconstrained power. This made the South different, not only from Florida and Louisiana, but from the other English settlements that lay to the north.

The Years in Review

1607

- First permanent English settlement in the New World created at Jamestown (Virginia).

1609

- First wedding in American colonies is held in Virginia.

1611

- Tobacco production introduced in Virginia; Indians teach whites how to cultivate it.

1617

- Several hundred London orphans forcibly transported to Virginia to work in tobacco fields.

1619

- First African slaves arrive in America.
- Virginia House of Burgesses (first colonial legislature) meets for the first time.

1622

- War of 1622: Powhatan Indians attack white settlers in Virginia.

1633

- Galileo is put on trial in Rome for insisting that the earth revolves around the sun.

1634

- Lord Baltimore establishes colony in Maryland that welcomes Protestants and Catholics.

1636

- Dutch introduce sugar cane into Barbados; it soon becomes the major crop in the West Indies; by 1645, Barbados has 6,000 slaves, most of them working on sugar plantations.

1638

- Colonists introduce honeybees to New World; Indians call them "the white man's fly."

1651

- First of the English government's trade regulations on colonists known as Navigation Acts; they are extended further in 1660s.

1660

- Slavery gains official sanction in colonial law.
- Charles II restored to English throne after Civil War and the Commonwealth; he reasserts Crown's authority over American colonists.

1661

- Indentured servants in Virginia led by Isaac Friend plan rebellion, but this is quashed when officials learn of plot.

1663

- Carolina colony chartered.
- Officials stop rebellion of indentured servants in Gloucester County, Virginia, and execute several of the conspirators.

1666

- In a busy year, Isaac Newton discovers calculus and establishes the laws of gravity.

1672

- Royal Africa Company, which has monopoly on the slave trade with the English colonies, increases its slave shipments from Africa.

1673

- A York County (Virginia) tailor is unable to collect money on his horse's victory in race because court declares "racing to be a sport for gentlemen only."

1676

- Indentured servants, discontented free farmers, slaves, and others led by Nathaniel Bacon rebel against propertied elites and Indians whom they see as keeping them from land they want; Bacon's Rebellion is crushed and twenty-three are hanged.

1693

- Spanish government offers freedom to slaves in their territory who convert to Catholicism.

1699

- Virginia law declares that an owner who killed his slave could not be guilty of murder because he would not intentionally destroy his own property.

1700

- Samuel Sewall publishes *The Selling of Joseph,* probably the first antislavery tract in the colonies.

1703

- The first group of professional actors in the colonies performs in Charleston, South Carolina, but generally the theater is viewed as immoral.

1708

- Blacks outnumber whites (in Carolina) for the first time in any of the colonies.

1711

- Tuscarora Indians in northern Carolina defeated and pushed inland.

1715

- Yamasee War: Yamasee Indians attack English settlements encroaching on their territory. Yamasees defeated and sold into slavery.

1718

- Virginia's governor offers a reward for capture of the pirate Blackbeard (Edward Teach). North Carolina's governor (who shares in Blackbeard's booty) protects him, but the pirate is caught and hanged.

1719

- North and South Carolina formally separated.

1728

- Runaway slaves create a village, establish tribal government, and grow crops in Lexington, Virginia; whites destroy it the following year.

1730

- Two hundred slaves revolt near Norfolk, Virginia; the defeat leads to enlargement of local militias.

1732

- Colony of Georgia established.

1735

- Slavery banned in Georgia.

1739

- Stono Rebellion: Uprising of South Carolina slaves, which is brutally suppressed with executions and the display of severed heads as warning to others.
- Preaching by the Methodist George Whitefield helps set off religious revivals known as the Great Awakening.

1740

- English troops capture village of escaped slaves near St. Augustine, Florida.

1749

- Georgia's ban on slavery rescinded.

1760

- Students at William and Mary College (founded 1693) petition for better food, seeking salt, fresh meat, and dessert at least three times per week.

Suggested Readings

Beeman, Richard R., *The Evolution of the Southern Backcountry: A Case Study of Lunenburg County, Virginia, 1746–1832* (1984).

Berlin, Ira, *Many Thousands Gone: The First Two Centuries of Slavery in North America* (1998).

Breen, T. H., *Tobacco Culture: The Mentality of the Great Tidewater Planters on the Eve of Revolution* (1985).

Brown, Kathleen M., *Good Wives, Nasty Wenches, and Anxious Patriarchs: Gender, Race, and Power in Colonial Virginia* (1996).

Carr, Lois G., et al., *Robert Cole's World: Agriculture and Society in Early Maryland* (1991).

Fischer, David Hackett, *Albion's Seed: Four British Folkways in America* (1989).

Frey, Sylvia, R., and Betty Wood, *Come Shouting to Zion: African American Protestantism in the American South and British Caribbean to 1830* (1998).

Hall, Gwendolyn M., *Africans in Colonial Louisiana: The Development of Afro-Creole Culture in the Eighteenth Century* (1992).

Hatley, Tom, *The Dividing Paths: Cherokees and South Carolinians through the Revolutionary Era* (1993).

Horn, James, *Adapting to a New World: English Society in the Seventeenth Century Chesapeake* (1994).

Innes, Stephen, ed., *Work and Labor in Early America* (1988).

Isaac, Rhys, *The Transformation of Virginia, 1740–1790* (1982).

Kulikoff, Allan, *Tobacco and Slaves: The Development of Southern Cultures in the Chesapeake* (1986).

Lewis, Johanna Miller, *Artisans in the North Carolina Backcountry* (1995).

Littlefield, Daniel C., *Rice and Slaves: Ethnicity and the Slave Trade in Colonial South Carolina* (1981).

Merrell, James H., *The Indians' New World: Catawbas and Their Neighbors from European Contact through the Period of Removal* (1989).

Morgan, Edmund S., *American Slavery, American Freedom: The Ordeal of Colonial Virginia* (1975).

Morgan, Philip D., *Slave Counterpoint: Black Culture in the Eighteenth-Century Chesapeake and Lowcountry* (1998).

Mullin, Gerald W., *Flight and Rebellion: Slave Resistance in Eighteenth-Century Virginia* (1972).

Olwell, Robert, *Masters, Slaves, and Subjects: The Culture of Power in the South Carolina Low Country* (1998).

Silver, Timothy, *A New Face on the Countryside: Indians, Colonists, and Slaves in South Atlantic Forests, 1500–1800* (1990).

Usner, Daniel H., Jr., *Indians, Settlers, and Slaves in a Frontier Exchange Economy: The Lower Mississippi Valley before 1783* (1992).

Walsh, Lorena S., *From Calabar to Carter's Grove: The History of a Virginia Slave Community* (1997).

Weber, David J., *The Spanish Frontier in North America* (1992).

Wood, Peter H., *Black Majority: Negroes in Colonial South Carolina from 1670 through the Stono Rebellion* (1974).

Wood, Peter H., et. al., eds., *Powhatan's Mantle: Indians in the Colonial Southeast* (1989).

And on the World Wide Web

Colonial Williamsburg Foundation, *Historical Almanack* (http://www.history.org/almanack.htm)

Virginia Polytechnic Institute, *Virtual Jamestown* (http://jefferson.village.virginia.edu/vcdh/jamestown/)

chapter 3

Straw Hat Maker.

A Cooper

Spinner.

A Carpenter.

A Bricklayer.

Type Founder.

Shipwrights.

Hat-maker.

Family Labor and the Growth of the Northern Colonies
1640–1760

Michael and Hannah Emerson married in 1657 and settled on a small farm in Haverhill, Massachusetts. In addition to running the farm and household, Michael Emerson also practiced his trade of shoemaking, and Hannah may have assisted him. They began to have children, and it fell to Hannah to do much of the work of raising a growing family. For her this task must have been long and arduous, for in time she gave birth to fifteen children. Even for colonial New England, where large families were the norm, this was unusual. Five of the children died before they reached adulthood, but the other ten survived to an age at which they could expect to marry and begin their own families. In New England, as in much of the northern part of British America, family households were at the center of economic activity and the basis on which society itself was built.

The New England colonies that grew up from the Puritan settlements of the 1620s and 1630s developed differently from those of the Chesapeake and Lower South. There were no tobacco or rice plantations, as in Virginia or South Carolina, just as there were no great silver mines, as in Peru or Mexico. Rather than extracting wealth through the forced labor of others, the majority of colonists achieved at least a "decent competency" by steady family toil on the land.

Family labor was also important in the "Middle Colonies," including New York, New Jersey, and Pennsylvania, that developed to the south of New England. New York became an English possession when, in 1664, the English seized the Dutch territory of New Netherland, and King Charles II gave it to his brother the Duke of York, who renamed it after himself. In the 1670s and 1680s further land grants by the English crown led to the settlement of New Jersey and Pennsylvania. Though the Middle Colonies differed from New England in important respects, all the northern colonies came to share the same economic foundation: family-run farming.

Like the colonies to the south, the northern colonies attracted diverse peoples. Most were from the British Isles, including not just English, but Highland Scots, Scots-Irish, Welsh, and a few Catholic Irish. Substantial numbers of new colonists came from mainland Europe: Dutch settlers (in New Netherland), Huguenot (Protestant) French, and many Protestant Germans. A few Sephardic Jews also made their way from the Mediterranean. The Scandinavians who settled the forests of the Delaware Valley introduced their version of the log house to North America. Many

Colonial Trades. These illustrations were published in the American edition of *The Book of Trades*, a British survey of crafts that were practiced in the colonies.

Source: *The Book of Trades, or Library of the Useful Arts* (1807)—American Social History Project.

121

northern settlers were working people of moderate means who came to America more or less willingly, in search of a new start. They hoped to obtain land and become independent "yeomen" farmers, or to secure independence as skilled artisans, as small merchants, midwives, or dressmakers. Puritan migrants to Massachusetts Bay, and the Quakers who later settled Pennsylvania, sought to build societies that would exemplify their religious ideals. Religious separatists, like the original Pilgrims of the *Mayflower* and the Amish and other Germans who settled in Pennsylvania, chiefly wanted the world to leave them alone.

By the eighteenth century, most European Americans in the northern colonies lived in the countryside, the majority supporting themselves reasonably well on modest-sized farms. But though rural families formed its backbone, northern colonial society was not made up just of yeomen farmers able to enjoy independence, as a much-quoted Biblical phrase put it, "under their own vine and fig-tree." In some areas, such as New York's Hudson River Valley, ambitious, privileged men were assembling great estates on which they would earn wealth from the labor of tenants. There were also, dotted along the coasts and estuaries, port towns whose inhabitants linked the rural interior to the commerce and fishing grounds of the Atlantic Ocean.

In 1700, even the largest of these towns — Boston, New York City, and Philadelphia — were little more than overgrown villages, with a few thousand inhabitants each. But by 1760, they would be substantial places, whose inhabitants lived differently from their rural counterparts. In these port towns merchants and shipowners rubbed shoulders with professional men, with master artisans and their apprentices, with the day laborers who worked on the wharves, and with seamen from many places who crewed cargo ships and fishing vessels. Public emblems still commemorate the work of these early colonists. In Boston's State House hangs the gilded image of a codfish, symbol of New England's early wealth from fishing and the sea. New York City's official seal bears the sails of a windmill, two barrels, a beaver, and the figures of a Native American and a white man. It recalls the port's initial prosperity from native-trapped furs, and from grain grown by farmers, ground by millers, and shipped in barrels made by coopers. In towns, as in the country, many economic activities were organized around families and households.

Although most northern working people were free, there were unfree people, too. Many poorer white immigrants, especially in Pennsylvania and the northern Chesapeake area, had signed on for periods of indentured service in return for their transatlantic passage or the promise of land after their service was up. At times in the eighteenth century, indentured servants made up half of the immigration from Europe, though their numbers eventually started to dwindle. There were also slaves in the northern colonies. In 1645, Emmanuel Downing of Salem, Massachusetts, urged Governor John Winthrop to sponsor slave imports, arguing: "I do not see how we can thrive until we get a stock of slaves sufficient to do all our business." New York imported sizable numbers of slaves, and in the mid eighteenth century over one-fifth of New York City's population was of African origin, either slave or free. Northern slavery could be as harsh and oppressive as that in the south, but it was nothing like as widespread. Partly because of the absence of "staple" cash crops, and partly because of the prevalence and success of family farming, slavery never became the crucial underpinning of society that it did in the southern plantation regions. For most northerners, the labor to do what Downing called "all our business" would come, not from slavery, but from their own families and children.

Many parts of the northern colonies grew rapidly in population, and some became very prosperous. As in the South, growth often entailed conflict. Population expansion and the spread of settlements across the land provoked confrontations with Indians, many of whom resented the European incursion and took steps to resist it. Native groups in the main areas of white settlement were largely defeated and dispersed, but those well inland, such as the Iroquois, held off the colonists' encroachment. Conflict with Indians became entwined with fierce international rivalries, first between the Dutch and the English and then, for almost a century, between the English and the French in Canada. Repeated wars put New Englanders and other colonial frontier settlers under arms. There were religious and social conflicts, too, as well as disputes between colonies. New York and New Hampshire, for instance, quarreled over what is now Vermont until 1764. More was at stake than lines on a map; the lives of individuals and entire communities were affected.

Freeholders in Early New England

From the start of European migration to the northern colonies, most settlers found themselves in a healthier, less economically exploitative environment than their counterparts in the South. While early migrants to the Chesapeake faced frightful conditions and high mortality from disease and harsh treatment, those reaching New England soon established stable, flourishing societies. The availability of land and food enabled the first generation of Massachusetts settlers to enjoy life expectancies longer than any in Europe. People who might have died in middle age now lived to be elderly. Even as Indians died from Europeans' diseases, white northern settlers began to multiply rapidly, doubling their numbers every twenty years or so.

Different goals also help explain why the northern colonies became established more rapidly than those in the South. Virgina's founders had come to the New World intending to get rich and get out. Their aim was to harness the labor (of natives, white indentured servants, or slaves) to do this, and they built a society in which, for much of the seventeenth century, there was little scope for settled family life. But the founders of New England—and later, Pennsylvania—intended to build stable communities, for which families were essential. In the 1630s, seven out of eight migrants to Massachusetts traveled with at least one relative, and three out of four came in a family group. Both their social backgrounds and their religious ideals led the Puritans to promote the rapid establishment of family life in New England.

Women were present in significant numbers from the start. Whereas in the Chesapeake, men outnumbered women by three to two even in 1700, in New England the ratio was almost balanced half a century earlier. This was another reason for rapid population growth. Most men and women in the northern colonies found marriage partners. Women bore an unprecedented number of children, and children survived the hazards of infancy at an unprecedented rate. Marriage and children supplied many farmers' and tradesmen's basic requirements for labor. Men and women divided tasks between them, and older children worked for the family,

Harvesting. A woodcut from a Pennsylvania almanac published in the 1760s showed a farm family at work in the fields.

Source: *Father Abraham's 1760 Almanac* (1759)— American Antiquarian Society.

too. If a husband and wife obtained other assistance, as they often did, this was usually to supply a need that the family could not for the time being meet.

The flow of English emigrants to the New England colonies ceased in about 1640. As England became embroiled in political crisis and civil war, English Puritans sided with Parliament against the King, seeing the chance that they had long sought to reshape England into a godly commonwealth. They no longer felt it necessary to journey to the New World to establish the kind of society they sought to live in, because the opportunity was now opening up for such a society at home. Nevertheless, the New England settlements survived because low mortality rates enabled the population not just to sustain itself but to grow rapidly.

The other key to New England's survival was the widespread availability of land to settlers. Land there was not just monopolized by the wealthy or by those with the right connections. Largely rejecting competitive individualism, and aiming to shape their lives to achieve the goals of spiritual grace and social harmony, most early new Englanders avoided the kind of free-for-all that had marked planters' acquisition of land in Virginia. In Massachusetts the government usually made grants of land not to individuals, but to whole communities, known as "towns."

Just west of Boston, for example, the town of Dedham was founded when a group of family heads petitioned the General Court (the colony's assembly) in 1636 for a grant in common. They had spent months working out a town covenant that would establish the terms on which they would live. Their basic premises were that the town and the family were more important than the individual, and that social peace was more important than personal gain. With social harmony in mind they had at first planned to call their town "Contentment," and though the Dedhamites changed their minds, other nearby settlers did call their town Concord.

Sometimes at meetings of the whole town, sometimes through special committees, townsmen themselves decided how to allocate the grant. At Dedham and elsewhere, they divided the land into large open fields rather than separate enclosed farms, a longstanding pattern familiar especially to those who had come from eastern England. People lived together in central villages, offering one another mutual support and defense. Each landowner had individual strips in the different fields, but townspeople worked together as a group, from the first plowing to the harvest. Which field to use and which crops to plant were to be decided by the whole community.

Requests for town grants met with generous response from the colonial government. Andover's founders received more than 38,000 acres of land for a population that, as late as 1662, numbered only forty families. Often the towns held most of their land in reserve. When the town of

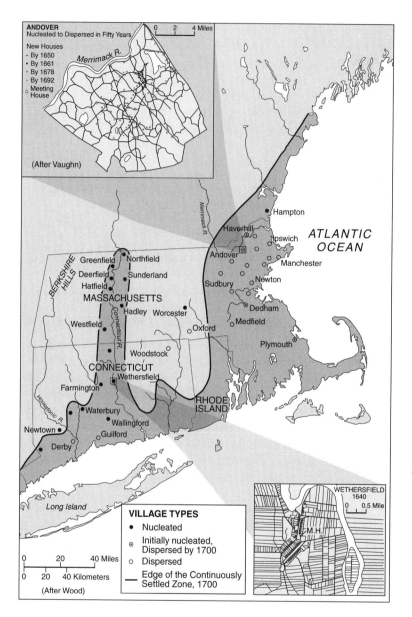

ANDOVER
Nucleated to Dispersed in Fifty Years

New Houses
• By 1650
• By 1661
• By 1678
• By 1692
▪ Meeting House

(After Vaughn)

Merrimack R.

0 2 4 Miles

Merrimack R.

• Hampton

Haverhill
Ipswich

ATLANTIC
OCEAN

Andover
Manchester

BERKSHIRE HILLS
Greenfield Northfield
Deerfield Sunderland
Hatfield
MASSACHUSETTS
Hadley Worcester
Westfield
Oxford
Woodstock

Sudbury
Newton

Dedham
Medfield

Plymouth

Connecticut R.

CONNECTICUT
Wethersfield
Farmington
Waterbury
Wallingford
Newtown
Guilford
Derby

Housatonic R.

RHODE ISLAND

Long Island

0   20   40 Miles
0   20   40 Kilometers
(After Wood)

VILLAGE TYPES
• Nucleated
◉ Initially nucleated, Dispersed by 1700
○ Dispersed
— Edge of the Continuously Settled Zone, 1700

WETHERSFIELD 1640
0   0.5 Mile

M.H.

Settlement in Seventeenth-Century New England. New England colonists quickly spread out from their initial settlements of Plymouth and Boston, reaching down to Long Island Sound, up the Connecticut River valley, and up the coast toward what became New Hampshire and Maine. But warfare and continued Indian resistance helped prevent the further spread of settlement beyond these areas until the next century. Meanwhile, within New England, settlement patterns changed. Early nucleated towns like Wethersfield were succeeded by towns such as Andover, where most residents lived on dispersed farms.

Sudbury made its first division, it handed out only 751 acres, in grants ranging from four acres to 76 acres. Individuals—almost always male household heads—received their land on the basis of the whole town's judgment about how much each man or family needed. A man's prestige (being the minister or having a good name from England), community need (for a miller or a blacksmith), and individual necessity (the number of children in a given family) all influenced the outcome of the decision. Undivided land was held back, for allocation to newcomers and, especially, for the next generation of townspeople.

The towns' distribution of land helped secure the authority and economic position of male property owners, who used their own labor and that of their families and servants to work the land they were given. Landownership in New England usually conferred outright title, or "freehold," in a property. In England, most land had been held by large landholders, who might lease it in portions to tenant-farmers in return for rent, or who might even retain feudal or manorial rights to payments, labor services, and other obligations from the people who occupied and worked it. New Englanders took pride in their absolute property rights, and in the freedom this conferred to pass on their land as they wished, without owing tribute to aristocratic landlords. They saw this as an essential part of their "English liberties."

Equality and Inequality in Puritan Society

But towns were much more than devices for managing land. To Puritan leaders they were the means for gathering communities of believers. Each town had its independent Congregational church, based on a carefully worked-out covenant, and with power to appoint its own minister. Although town membership and church membership were never identical, Puritans saw their churches as central to the creation of an ordered commonwealth. Puritan society had both egalitarian and hierarchical aspects. It avoided extremes of wealth and poverty, and rejected ostentation or formal hereditary distinction. Yet it also stressed authority and hierarchy as instruments of social order. Even in New England, wrote Governor John Winthrop, "as in all times some must be rich some poore, some highe and eminent in power and dignitie; others meane and in subjeccion." At public worship, people were seated according to their rank in town. Respect was expected to be accorded to age, gender, piety, and social standing. Clergy and magistrates were cast as "fathers" to the community. Only men with property exercised influence in towns and churches, and the voices of women and of youths were curbed.

Though Puritans regarded men and women as spiritual equals, and although women were vital to the economic system, this did not mean that women and men were socially equal. Along with other early settlers, Puritans held the patriarchal assumptions that men were superior to women and that property-owning men had the right and the obligation to exercise authority over the women, children, and other dependents of their families. They saw orderly and obedient households as the germ of social order; individuality and personal freedom were minor considerations.

Single people merited suspicion. New England laws discouraged "solitary living" to ensure that everyone resided under the discipline of family life. Young single men and women were obliged to live with families as servants. They formed up to one-third of New England's workforce before 1650, although their relative importance declined after that. But even in colonies without such laws, few lived outside families, because belonging to a household was crucial for economic survival.

Law and custom gave the male head of a family authority over his wife, and both parents had authority over their servants and children, at least until the children were well into adulthood. Parents or employers could lawfully administer whippings or beatings as punishment for wrongdoing, as long as they did not overdo things. After Judith Weeks of Kittery, Maine, cut off the toes of her servant in 1666, and the young man later died, she was prosecuted. But the courts also admonished masters or parents if they showed too much laxity. Servants were expected to remain with uncongenial employers, and could be returned to them if they ran away. Similarly, the law looked with disfavor on wives who sought to escape cruel husbands, or refused their husbands the services they were expected to provide them.

Women who spoke up or stood out posed a threat to social order. In 1637, Anne Hutchinson, a prominent Boston woman, was tried and banished from Massachusetts after attracting a religious following and "casting reproach upon the faithful Ministers of this Country." Winthrop claimed that she had "a very voluble tongue, more bold than a man," which the authorities feared would "spread like a Leprosie, and infect farr and near." For expressing "unorthodox opinion" in 1644, Anne Yale Eaton, wife of the governor of the newly formed colony of New Haven, was excommunicated from the church. When a few Quaker preachers, including women, entered Massachusetts in the late 1650s, they were jailed, whipped, and banished. Four of them were executed, including Mary Dyer, who was hanged in 1660 after she defied the courts and returned to Boston from exile to preach.

Women seen as too independent or assertive also faced suspicion of witchcraft or complicity with the devil, a crime punishable by death. Ann Hibbens was excommunicated from Boston's church in 1641 for "usurping" her husband's role in giving directions to some workmen. While her husband was alive, Hibbens was protected from further harm, but his death in the early 1650s put her in great danger. Still regarded as "quarrelsome," she was accused of witchcraft, tried, and hanged. Eighty percent of accused witches in seventeenth-century New England were women, many of them widowed or in some sense independent. The fear of disor-

Witchcraft. Women were accused, prosecuted, and occasionally executed for the crime of witchcraft in seventeenth-century New England. Although Anne Hutchinson was never accused outright of being a witch, the delivery of a deformed, stillborn infant to one of her female associates in 1638 was interpreted by the Puritan fathers as the Devil's work. This illustration from an eighteenth-century chapbook (a cheaply printed pamphlet) presented a "monstrous" birth as a sign of witchcraft.

Source: John Ashton, *Chapbooks of the Eighteenth Century* (1882) — Prints and Photographs Division, Library of Congress.

der such women instilled helped bring about the notorious Salem Village trials of 1692, when magistrates put credence in rampant accusations of witchcraft in a local community. Of nineteen alleged witches eventually hanged at Salem, fourteen were women. The first three to be accused — a West Indian slave, a poor widow, and an old semi-invalid woman who lived on the edge of town — were at the margins of Salem society, but among the others were women of means who had exercised some discretion over their own affairs.

Though men headed New England's social hierarchy, there were also substantial inequalities among them. Not all towns developed in the manner of Dedham, Sudbury, or Andover. For instance, the ports and fishing camps that lay northeast of Boston were dominated by traders and shipowners, for whom poorer men worked as crews on fishing boats and as seamen. Such places were never as egalitarian as some of the inland towns. In one of them, Ipswich, Massachusetts, in the mid-seventeenth century, 75 percent of families owned less than 90 acres of land each, almost 25 percent owned more than 100 acres, and just five men owned over 1,000 acres.

Inequality was even greater in Springfield in western Massachusetts, founded in 1636. A single father and son, William and John Pynchon, turned a large initial land grant into near-domination of the town, as they acquired much of its best land in the fertile Connecticut River valley. By 1685 John Pynchon owned eighteen hundred acres, almost five times as much as Springfield's next-largest landowner. Many townsmen had become the Pynchons' tenants. Others, particularly craftsmen and small farmers, became reliant on them. At some time or another almost everyone in town fell into John Pynchon's debt. Pynchon never hesitated to call in a debt if it suited him, and he would acquire the debtor's land if the debt could not be paid. Their successful pursuit of wealth and power enabled the Pynchons to control seventeenth-century Springfield and its life.

Springfield, however, was not typical, and even there the Pynchon family's influence declined after 1700. Most New Englanders upheld the ideal of a society based on widespread freehold landownership by independent households. This ideal helped seal the fate of New England's Indians, and it also shaped colonists' attitudes to English rule in the later seventeenth century.

Conflict with Indians

The destruction of the Pequot tribe in the late 1630s did not end the friction between growing populations of settlers and native groups. The spread of colonial settlements, coupled with the conception that land could be held by absolute right of ownership, sustained tension with Indians. Early colonial settlements were small and scattered, separated by great swathes of forest and linked by rough pathways that were quickly turned into mud wallows by rain or the spring thaw. To most settlers, the land seemed a "howling wilderness," and they did what they could to start changing it. They wanted to clear the forest; fence in their fields; build houses and barns, meetinghouses and stores; plant English crops; and raise livestock.

Native Americans and Europeans had very different understandings of what it meant to possess the land. For most Native Americans a land title was collective and relative. All members of a tribe owned the land; there was no such thing as rent or purchase. Especially for the freeholders of New England, ownership was individual and absolute. The holder could forbid any use of the land by someone else, or could rent it out or sell it at will. Colonists asserted that Indians did not, according to English law, actually own their land. They were considered to merely occupy it, because they built no permanent houses or churches and used no draft animals to plow fields. Their men, settlers claimed, lazed about all day while women scratched away on patches of ground where corn, beans, and squash grew wildly. There were no fences and hedges to indicate where one person's property ended and another's began. Native men, they believed, exerted themselves only to hunt or fish, activities inferior to those of cultivating fields, suitable for aristocrats or poachers but unworthy of sturdy independent yeomen.

These differing assumptions had tragic consequences. For Europeans, land that natives had not actually cleared was not considered really theirs. For natives, "selling" the land to Europeans meant no more than allowing them to use it. Conflict developed not simply over ownership, but between two completely different ways of understanding peoples' place in the landscape. Even the settlers' introduction of livestock had huge effects. Following English custom, colonists let their animals roam free in the woods, to be rounded up when needed, and they built fences to keep them out of their own crops. But their pigs and cattle invaded Indians' unfenced fields and destroyed their crops. Roger Williams, a founder of the province of Rhode Island, was one of the few first-generation colonists to acknowledge the violation of natives' rights: "the Swine," he noted, "are most hateful to all Natives, and they call them filthy cutthroats." But many colonists, attached to their absolute property rights, convinced themselves that the natives would have to move out of their way, or be removed.

The colonists' defeat of the Pequots helped them expand across southern New England. They established Connecticut, and the small colony of New Haven, and soon began to settle Long Island. By making alliances with some native groups against other groups, the colonists were able to hold off any united resistance to their expansion. They made deals, often with minor sachems or chiefs, by which native groups agreed to cede land for settlement or pay tribute in return for protection.

The responses of natives to this intrusion varied. Some ceded land simply because they were outnumbered. At New Haven, five dozen or so Quinnipiacs and others, their population depleted by disease and displacement, faced 2,500 arriving colonists. In eastern Connecticut, however, the large Mohegan tribe made an alliance with the English so as to strengthen their own hold over smaller native groups, and in hope of protecting themselves against encroachment.

Some native leaders tried to form a defensive alliance among the remaining tribes. The Narragansetts, who had helped the colonists destroy the Pequots, soon began to ponder their own prospects for survival. One sachem, Miantonomi, traveled across southern New England and Long Island in the early 1640s to arrange a pact, warning of what would be lost if the English were not turned back. But the colonists, helped by their new Mohegan allies, silenced Miantonomi. The Mohegans captured him, delivering him to a Massachusetts court for trial on a trumped-up murder charge. The court convicted him, and then handed him back to the Mohegans for execution.

Other natives accepted greater association with the colonists. Puritan missionaries in Massachusetts established towns for "praying Indians," who were converted to Christianity and settled on farms. There were fourteen such towns by the early 1670s. Yet even these converts never allayed English suspicion of Indians. In time the choice of the "praying Indians" to seek a form of assimilation with the colonists would help little better than other options to preserve their own communities.

The Wampanoag tribe, which had so far maintained cordial relations with both the Massachusetts and Plymouth colonies, came under

"We Must Be One as They Are . . ."

In the Pequot War of the late 1630s, the Narragansett Indians of Rhode Island had allied with the English, and they had absorbed some of the surviving Pequots into their settlements after the war ended. Soon, however, Narragansett leaders became alarmed at continued English incursions on their land and hunting grounds. In 1642 the sachem Miantonomi traveled to Long Island to forge alliances with members of the Montauk and other groups. Outmaneuvered by the English and their Mohegan allies, Miantonomi was eventually captured, tried, and executed. Though this English account of Miantonomi's efforts to form an Indian alliance was part of the case against him, it amply summarizes New England Indians' grievances.

A while after this came Miantenomie from Block-Island to Mantacut with a troop of men . . . ; and instead of receiving presents, which they used to do in their progress, he gave them gifts, calling them brethren and friends, for so are we all Indians as the English are, and say brother to one another; so must we be one as they are, otherwise we shall be all gone shortly, for you know our fathers had plenty of deer and skins, our plains were full of deer, and also our woods, and of turkies, and our coves full of fish and fowl. But these English having gotten our land, they with scythes cut down the grass, and with axes fell the trees; their cows and horses eat the grass, and their hogs spoil our clam banks, and we shall all be starved; therefore it is best for you to do as we, for we are all the Sachems from east to west, both Moquakues and Mohauks joining with us, and we are all resolved to fall upon them all, at one appointed day; and therefore I am come to you privately first, because you can persuade the Indians and Sachem to what you will, and I will send over fifty Indians to Block-Island, and thirty to you from thence, and take an hundred of Southampton Indians with an hundred of your own here; and when you see the three fires that will be made forty days hence, in a clear night, then do as we, and the next day fall on and kill men, women, and children, but no cows, for they will serve to eat till our deer be increased again. . . .

Source: Karen Ordahl Kupperman, ed., *Major Problems in American Colonial History* (1993).

increasing pressure from new settlements in the 1650s and 1660s. Under their leader Metacom, whom the English called "King Philip," they took a decisive step to reverse colonial encroachment. In 1675, after repeated provocations, the Wampanoags launched fierce attacks on outlying eastern Massachusetts towns. At first they acted alone, but

The Causes of "King Philip's War"

John Easton, as Deputy Governor of Rhode Island, met the Wampanoag leader Metacom ("King Philip") in June 1675 in an attempt to avert the impending English-Indian war in eastern New England. His account of the discussions provides the most direct surviving statement of the Indian grievances that led them to try and dislodge the English colonists by force. The English often called Indian leaders "kings" or "queens," suggesting that they recognized the sovereignty of the people these sachems led. War began a week after Easton's meeting with Metacom ended.

They said they had been the first in doing good to the English, and the English the first in doing wrong, said when the English first came their king's father was as a great man and the English as a little child, he constrained other Indians from wronging the English and gave them corn and showed them how to plant and was free to do them any good and had let them have a 100 times more land; then now the king had for his own people, but their king's brother when he was king came miserably to die by being forced to court as they judged poisoned, and another greivance was if 20 of their honest Indians testified that a Englishman had done them wrong, it was as nothing, and if but one of their worst Indians testified against any Indian or their king when it pleased the English that was sufficient. Another grievance was when their kings sold land the English would say it was more than they agreed to and a writing must be proof against all them, and sum of their kings had done wrong to sell so much. He left his people none and some being given to drunkeness the English made them drunk and then cheated them in bargains, but now their kings were forewarned not for to part with land for nothing in comparison to the value thereof. . . . Another grievance the English cattle and horses still increased that when they removed 30 miles from where English had anything to do, they could not keep their corn from being spoiled, they never being used to fence, and thought when the English bought land of them that they would have kept their cattle upon their own land. Another grievance the English were so eager to sell the Indians liquors that most of the Indians spent all in drunkeness and then ravened upon the sober Indians and they did believe often did hurt the English cattle, and their kings could not prevent it. We knew before these were their grand complaints, but then we only endeavored to persuade that all complaints might be righted without war, . . . We endeavored that . . . they should lay down their arms for the English were too strong for them. They said then the English should do to them as they did when they were too strong for the English.

Source: Mary Rowlandson, *The sovereignty and goodness of God: together with the faithfulness of His promises displayed,* ed. Neal Salisbury (1997).

Metacom was soon able to forge alliances with other native groups. The Nipmucks attacked towns in the Connecticut Valley, and the Abenaki and others took up arms on the Maine coast.

Reeling from the outbreak of what they called "King Philip's War," the colonists' response at first only strengthened Metacom's position. Soldiers searched for Wampanoags said to be hiding in Narragansett settlements. They massacred three hundred people, mostly women and children, pushing the Narragansetts into the alliance against the colonists. Colonial settlements suffered heavily. Of ninety towns, twelve were wiped out and forty more damaged. One-tenth of the adult white male pop-

A

NARRATIVE

OF THE

CAPTIVITY, SUFFERINGS AND REMOVES

OF

Mrs. *Mary Rowlandson,*

Who was taken Prisoner by the INDIANS with several others, and treated in the most barbarous and cruel Manner by those vile Savages : With many other remarkable Events during her TRAVELS.

Written by her own Hand, for her private Use, and now made public at the earnest Desire of some Friends, and for the Benefit of the afflicted.

B O S T O N

Printed and Sold at JOHN BOYLE's Printing-Office, next Door to the *Three Doves* in Marlborough-Street. 1773.

Captivity. In 1676, during King Philip's War, Mary Rowlandson was captured by Indians raiding Lancaster, Massachusetts; after being held for three months, she was ransomed and freed. She later wrote *The Sovereignty and Goodness of God: A Narrative . . .* , which was published in 1682 and often reprinted (here in a 1773 edition). It was the first of many "captivity" narratives, which portrayed captivity as a test of the protagonists' Puritan faith.

Source: Mary Rowlandson, *A Narrative of the Captivity, Sufferings and Removes of Mrs. Mary Rowlandson* (1773)—Rare Books and Manuscript Division, New York Public Library, Astor, Lenox and Tilden Foundations.

ulation was killed or captured. It looked as if Metacom might succeed in turning back English settlement.

Yet the colonists proved too well-established to dislodge. New Englanders forged their own alliance with New York's governor Edmund Andros. Motivated by fear and racial hatred, the colonists took harsh measures. The Massachusetts government distrusted even the Christian "praying Indians" and forcibly interned them on an island in Boston Harbor. Metacom's forces were weakened in a battle with Mohawks allied to Andros. In 1676, colonial fighters cornered Metacom in a swamp and killed him. Most native resistance then collapsed, although in Maine the Abenaki sustained their attacks into 1677.

For the Wampanoags and their allies, the war's effects were devastating. Five thousand or more died in the fighting. Many survivors, including Metacom's own family, were sold in the Caribbean as slaves.

King Philip. This fanciful 1772 engraving by the Boston silversmith Paul Revere was copied from a portrait of the Mohawk chief Thayendanega, or Joseph Brant (see page 246). Despite its inaccuracy, Revere's picture influenced print and stage portrayals of Metacom through the mid nineteenth century.

Source: American Antiquarian Society.

PHILIP. *KING* of Mount Hope.

Only four of the fourteen "praying Indian" towns were reestablished. Across southern New England, native peoples were dispersed, obliged to live on marginal lands, hunting and fishing where they could, or supporting themselves by laboring for white communities, their children often put into white families as servants. As a Mohegan memoir later put it:

Yea the Times have turn'd everything Upside down, or rather we have changed the good Times, Chiefly by the help of the White People. For in Times past our Fore-Fathers lived in Peace . . . and had everything in Great plenty . . . and now we plainly see that . . . poor Widows and Orphans Must be pushed to one side and there they Must set a-Crying, Starving, and die.

By the eighteenth century many Indians lived like the family of the Mohegan Samson Occom, who wrote that his parents "Chiefly Depended upon Hunting, Fishing and Fowling for their Living and had no connection with the English except to Traffic with them in their small Trifles." They preserved a degree of independence, but had largely lost control of their lands.

Early Proprietors in the Middle Colonies

Defeating the Wampanoags did not, however, assure New Englanders that they would be secure on their freehold lands. The restoration of the monarchy in England brought renewed aristocratic visions of great landed estates in the New World, threatening the freehold ideal.

New Englanders had sympathized with the English revolution and its vision of a Puritan commonwealth. After King Charles I was beheaded in 1649, England became a republic, first under Parliament then under the "Lord Protector" Oliver Cromwell. But royalists remained active, and Cromwell's death in 1658 prepared the way for them to restore the monarchy two years later, bringing Charles II to the throne. English Puritans now faced a hostile political climate, and the New England colonies offered support. They gave refuge to some of the "regicides," Charles I's executioners, whose lives were now in danger. Puritans fleeing persecution briefly renewed the Great Migration of the 1630s.

A newly restored monarchy unsympathetic to Puritanism seemed likely to undermine New England's distinctiveness and relative independence, including its freehold land titles. The control of vast tracts of land by hereditary lords or proprietors had been envisaged in America before the English Civil War. In granting Maryland to Lord Baltimore in the 1630s, Charles I had envisaged the creation of manorial estates. Now interest centered on the Middle Colonies, along the Hudson, Delaware, and Susquehanna Rivers, that for half a century had been mainly under Dutch influence. In the 1660s and 1670s these looked likely to become sites for a kind of feudalism. Twice in the early 1660s, the English attacked the Dutch colony of New Netherland, and in 1664 they captured it. Charles II granted the conquered province to his brother James, Duke of York, and gave him New Jersey as well. The Dutch had already created proprietorships, known as *patroonships,* in New Netherland. The English did the same, granting large tracts of land on feudal terms to manor lords who gained the right to hold court and sit in judgment over their tenants. No landowner actually exercised that right, but three manorial families would control what amounted to private seats in the New York colonial assembly.

The Duke of York meanwhile gave New Jersey to his close associates, Lord John Berkeley and Sir George Carteret. In 1676, William Penn and three other Quaker gentlemen acquired Carteret's share. By the early 1680s, the well-connected Penn had negotiated control of even more territory. Owed the huge sum of £16,000 by the king, Penn agreed to forgive the debt in exchange for the grant of a large mass of land, which he named Pennsylvania. The Penns became hereditary proprietors of their new province, and, until the American Revolution, its governorship would descend in their family. Having created an American proprietorship on a grand scale, William Penn drew up an ambitious scheme of settlement, advertising for colonists in 1681. A year later his first party of emigrants arrived on the Delaware River to found the city of Philadelphia and settle the land nearby.

The creation of great proprietorships in the Middle Colonies suggested that English North America might become a society of great estates in which aristocrats would, for their own benefit and profit, employ tenant farmers and other dependents to cultivate the land. This was

The Middle Colonies in the Late Seventeenth Century. The map shows the principal land grants made by the government of King Charles II after the English capture of Dutch New Netherland, with some of the main Indian groups that lived there. Colonial settlements soon surrounded or displaced the Mahicans and Delawares, but the Iroquois successfully resisted white encroachments until the American Revolution in the 1770s.

Source: Robert A. Divine, et al., *America: Past and Present* 5th edition (1999).

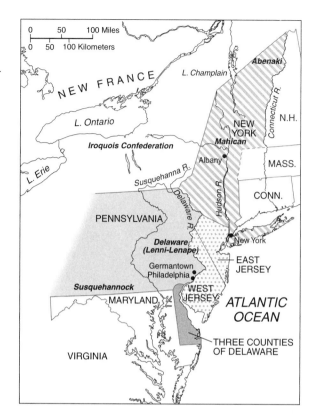

the English pattern. Developments in New York seemed to suggest that it might become the American pattern, too.

Over the next several decades, the creation of great estates in the Hudson and Mohawk river valleys was one of the most notable features of New York society. Families like the Van Rensselaers, the Johnsons, the Livingstons, the Schuylers, the Philipses, and the Morrises acquired large manors derived from Dutch or English land-grants. Livingston Manor, some forty miles south of Albany, grew to occupy 160,000 acres of prime farmland. Landlords rented farms to tenants over whom they acquired considerable power. The result was class division and landlords' expectation of deference from their tenants. Sir William Johnson, the eighteenth-century "Mohawk Baronet," actually owned the local courthouse, jail, and Anglican church on his estate. A tenant could seek permission to sell his leasehold, but only "provided your Honnour consents." One landlord's daughter was married "under a crimson canopy emblazoned with the family crest in gold," while "the tenants gathered before the manor hall" in deferential attendance, "as on rent day."

137

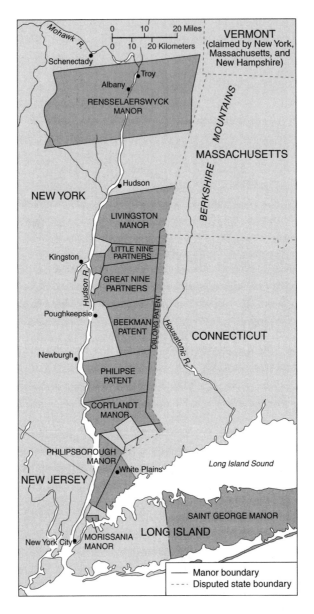

The Manors of the Hudson River Valley. From the seventeenth century large manorial grants occupied most of the eastern side of the Hudson River valley after first the Dutch, then the English awarded them to wealthy landowners. Farmed by tenants, not freeholders, the existence of the manors both blocked migration from crowded parts of New England and fed New England farmers' greatest fear—that they, too, might be "reduced to lordships."

Pennsylvania, however, followed a different pattern. William Penn was primarily concerned with creating a colony that could serve both as a prosperous haven for oppressed Quakers and as an experiment in religious toleration. Accordingly, he and his family never set up the lesser lordships permitted by their charter. Instead they encouraged settlers to migrate to Pennsylvania by selling them land directly, fixing only modest

sums for the annual "quitrents" to which their grant entitled them. They also set aside fifty-acre allotments of land for male servants completing their terms. In practice, Pennsylvania's land system worked little differently from the freehold tenure of New England. Some purchasers became landlords in their own right, but they never enjoyed the power of a New York manor lord, or even a John Pynchon.

Farmer at the Plough. This woodcut appeared in a Pennsylvania almanac published in the mid eighteenth century.
Source: *John Tobler's Almanack* (published by Christopher Sower, Germantown, Pennsylvania, between 1742-59)—Library Company of Philadelphia.

The Glorious Revolution of 1688–1689

Even so, after 1660 New Englanders were increasingly apprehensive that the crown would seek greater control of their colonies. They worried that aristocracy in some form, or the Anglican church governed by bishops, would be imposed upon them. Royal officials began to scrutinize colonists' conformity to English trade regulations, as well as the close connections—except in Rhode Island—between the Puritan churches and colonial governments. Complaints reached England from people denied political rights because they were not members of a Puritan church, or from those who had been harshly punished for infractions of tight Puritan laws. In Massachusetts in particular there was mounting concern that the crown would overturn the colony's original charter and bring the Puritan experiment in godly government to an end.

In 1684 the Massachusetts charter was suspended. The following year, the colony was placed with Plymouth, Maine, and New Hampshire in a united "Dominion of New England" that Connecticut and Rhode Island were also pressed to join. With Sir Edmund Andros as the Dominion's governor, it seemed possible that New England would be joined with New York as well. Massachusetts lost its elected General Court and would now be ruled by a council that Andros appointed. The New Englanders' political autonomy seemed doomed. The fact that the Dominion's creation followed the succession of the Duke of York to the English throne as James II in 1685, and that James was suspected of autocratic

139

designs and Catholic sympathies, underscored colonists' anxiety for the future of their property and religion.

But events in England helped the colonies evade disaster. English opposition to James mounted, and in 1688 he was deposed and forced to flee to France, in what came to be called the "Glorious Revolution." Parliament confirmed James's son-in-law, the Protestant Dutch ruler William III, as the new king, passing laws to secure its own powers and exclude Catholics from the English throne. The news touched off rebellions in several American colonies. Massachusetts provincial leaders ousted Governor Andros, reinstituted their own government, and petitioned London for a new charter. By 1689 the Dominion of New England was shattered. In New York, a militia officer called Jacob Leisler took charge of the government, backed by Dutch farmers and other small property owners against the colony's leading families. All awaited a new political settlement.

Two years later, Massachusetts received its new charter, which ended the Puritans' autonomy, reduced the churches' influence in government, and created a royal governorship, like those in New York and Virginia. But the charter also restored Massachusetts' elected assembly, the General Court, and confirmed the colony's freehold land titles. After decades of uncertainty, New Englanders could celebrate their escape from the "reduction to lordships" that the English Restoration had threatened. In New York, Jacob Leisler was less fortunate. The new royal governor sided with Leisler's enemies, who had him tried for treason in 1691 and executed.

How the Iroquois Set Limits on Settlement

By the early eighteenth century many Indians along the East Coast acknowledged the king of England's sovereignty over his colonies, but they also insisted that this sovereignty did not bestow control over native peoples or how they used their lands. In 1727, a leader of the Penobscots of Casco Bay, Maine, declared: "God hath willed that I have no king, but that I be master of my lands in common." Such claims, unfortunately, did little to prevent conquest and near-destruction of Indians in many seaboard regions.

In the interior, however, the more powerful native groups held off European settlement remarkably well. In the 150 years between the landing of the Pilgrims and the American Revolution, the boundary of white settlement moved inland by at most a few hundred miles. Beyond that, Native Americans imposed effective limits on the seizure and occupation of their land.

The English and French used Indian allies to help fight their colonial wars for them. In northern New England, protected by remote forests

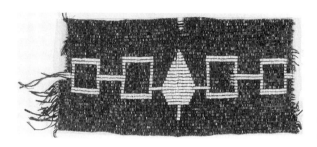

Hiawatha Wampum Belt. This belt depicted the Haudenosaunee, "the people of the Longhouse," called the Iroquois Confederacy by the French. The Great Tree of Peace was the central symbol, unifying the Mohawk, Oneida, Onondaga, Cayuga, and Seneca nations.

Source: Courtesy of the Onondaga Nation and the New York State Museum.

and supported from nearby Canada, native groups harassed outlying colonial villages and held back the spread of settlement until the 1720s and 1730s. Raids like the one on Deerfield in western Massachusetts in 1704 caused the death or capture of dozens of white men, women, and children, and discouraged frontier expansion. Some three hundred people were captured from northern New England in the four decades up to 1730. Although many returned, over one in ten of the males and one in four of the females chose to adopt their captors' way of life. Eunice Williams, the young daughter of Deerfield's Puritan minister, remained in Canada, forgot the English language, became a Catholic, married a Mohawk, and refused to return to live in New England.

The Iroquois-speaking Mohawks, Senecas, Onondagas, Oneidas, and Cayugas played a key part in containing white settlement. Their territory stretched from Canada to New York's Finger Lakes region, and the confederacy they had already formed before the first whites arrived provided the kind of stable alliance that the New England tribes found hard to achieve. In the seventeenth century, the Iroquois used their power mainly to expel other native groups from the region. By the time European settlers were pressing on their lands, they had consolidated a strong position. Controlling the fur-rich Adirondack Mountains and key routes toward the west, they could induce both the French in Montreal and the Dutch and English at Albany to pay court to them.

The Iroquois' numbers, estimated at ten thousand around 1600, also sustained their strength against smaller settler groups. In 1716, they adopted a sixth Iroquois-speaking tribe, the Tuscaroras, who had been driven out of North Carolina by white settlement. By the 1740s and 1750s, after a deal with the Pennsylvania government, the Iroquois were taking Delawares under their supervision in the upper Susquehanna valley.

The Iroquois grasped many of the lessons taught by the subjugation or destruction of other tribes. Because French Jesuit missionaries respected Iroquois culture, they had some success converting them to Christianity. One Mohawk woman, Kateri Tekakwitha, noted for her penitent life, became an object of Catholic pilgrimage after her death in Canada in 1680. But knowing how the "praying Indians" of Massachusetts had been crushed by Puritans who had converted them and then changed their way of life, the Iroquois remained wary of Protestant missionaries. When a Yankee preacher named Samuel Kirkland approached the Senecas in the mid-eighteenth century, he was denounced and shot at. A man known as Onoogwandikha told his fellows: "Brethren attend! . . . If we

Senecas . . . receive this white man, and attend to the Book which was made solely for white people, we shall become a miserable abject people . . . we shall soon lose the spirit of true men."

The Iroquois could fight fiercely, and might severely torture men they captured in war, but they also adopted captives into the tribe. Such people might rise to high rank. Hendrick Peters, born around 1680, adopted by the Mohawk as Tee Yee Neen No Ga Row, became a prominent leader at Canajoharie, west of Albany. Women elders usually determined the fate of captives. Female prisoners were not sexually molested, and those who accepted adoption sometimes became honored matriarchs in a society in which women wielded considerable power.

Using the advantages of their position, the Iroquois became as adept at diplomacy as any European nation, playing off the rival contenders for their lands against each other. For well over a century, they balanced the Dutch against the French, then the French against the English, and finally the English against their own colonists. Iroquois fighters played an important part in the succession of wars between English and French colonies that took place from the 1680s to the 1760s. The Iroquois confederacy held together and managed to curb colonial expansion. Only later, when the American Revolution decisively altered the balance of power against them, would the Iroquois' diplomacy finally fail.

Patterns on the Land: The Eighteenth Century

By the eighteenth century the rural population of the northern colonies was growing, both in absolute numbers and as a proportion of the total. The rural North was divided between the relatively small areas of New York and New Jersey, where tenancy and large estates were common, and the bulk of New England and Pennsylvania, where most land was controlled by independent farmers.

At first, when their land was empty, New York's proprietary landlords made tenancy attractive so as to secure scarce labor. Mills, roads, help with livestock, years of free rent for new arrivals—all of these were used to lure people to do the hard work necessary to transform a grant of uncultivated land into a productive estate. But such benefits came at a price. Rent payments on some manors included obligatory days of work that the tenant owed the landlord. Tenants also had to give the landlord first option to buy their crops and they had to grind their grain at his mill. The landlord could require tenants to plant certain kinds of fruit trees or build certain kinds of houses; he, not they, would be the long-term beneficiary. Tenants could not buy the land they farmed. They could expect payment from the landlord for any improvements they made, but if they wanted farms of their own, they were obliged to sell their leases and move to freehold land elsewhere. When a lease was sold, the landlord could demand up to one-third of the purchase price.

For some landlords the manorial system created immense wealth. By the 1770s, Philipse Manor, near New York City, was alone valued at £500,000 (at least $50 million today). Landlords' relations with their tenants varied. Some, including Frederick Philipse at Philipse Manor and Sir William Johnson in the Mohawk Valley, tried to create stable, paternalistic communities. Although Philipse raised rents when he inherited his manor in 1760, he promised never to do so again, and kept his word. But others were out to gain all they could. While Philipse held rents steady, his brother-in-law Colonel Beverly Robinson raised his rents three times. Not surprisingly, Philipse's tenants proved loyal to him; Robinson's did not. Tenants' resentment also focused on the shaky legal basis of some estate grants. Only 6,000 of Livingston Manor's 160,000 acres had been included in the original grant to the first manor lord. Ill-drawn surveys and outright fraud had contributed the rest, and the tenants knew it.

Poor conditions for tenants on many manorial estates helped limit New York's overall expansion. By 1770, the colony's population stood at approximately 162,000. In contrast, Pennsylvania, founded decades after New York, had already surpassed 240,000 by that date. By making land relatively attractive and affordable, William Penn had sown the seeds of rapid growth. By the mid eighteenth century, Pennsylvania's accessibility and prosperity gave it a reputation as "the best poor man's country in the world." Most settlers created small or moderately sized family farms. At first they raised cattle and other livestock, but soon switched to grain farming, because on modest farms this could better provide livings for their children. The sex-ratio was relatively even, and family patterns among the colony's various groups converged during the eighteenth century. To a significant degree settlers realized William Penn's founding vision of a middling rural society in which family and neighborhood cooperation would be complemented by the commerce generated by grain exports.

Pennsylvania's people were especially diverse. Its English Quakers were of the "middling sort," many of them skilled artisans who came to the colony to ply their trades and live in religious harmony. Germans of peasant origin also came to found communities on Pennsylvania's rich farmland. Many were members of religious sects such as the Moravians and the Amish who, like the Quakers, were pacifists. Between 1717 and 1740 they were joined by tens of thousands of "Scots-Irish" migrants from the northern part of Ireland, many of whom came as indentured servants, as the Germans did. Many Scots-Irish were accustomed to conflict. They had known it in Ireland, both with the English overlords who brought them there from Scotland in the first place, and with the Gaelic Irish, who did not want them. As they migrated to the colonial frontier, friction with Indians and other settlers often led to trouble. Pennsylvanians had a reputation for sturdy independence. When the gentleman-pamphleteer John Dickinson wanted to emphasize Americans' independence of spirit during one of the 1760s disputes with Britain, he could find no better way than to style himself "a farmer in Pennsylvania."

Rural Societies

Whether they were tenants or freeholders, whether they lived in New England, New York, or Pennsylvania, northern farm families faced many similar circumstances. Only in the early years of settlement and in some frontier regions had New England towns been arranged on the open-field system like that adopted by the settlers of Dedham. In most places, rural settlements became based on scattered farmsteads, rather than village centers, but ideals of social harmony persisted. Church membership, town government, family ties, and the mutual exchange of goods and labor sustained a sense of "neighborhood" and community in much of New England. In the Middle Colonies, too, tenants and farmers lived on dispersed farmsteads, but maintained ties to their neighborhoods and to the wider commercial world. For all farm families, a central concern was how to pass on land and livelihoods to their children.

In a precontraceptive age, almost every married woman spent a good part of her life pregnant and caring for children. The women of Andover, Massachusetts, experienced more than five births per marriage in every decade between 1650 and 1720, and between 1690 and 1710 the rate was higher than seven. Yet, though childbirth risked women's lives in a proportion of cases, the life expectancy of New England women was much better than those of women in England or in the southern colonies, and almost as good as those of men in the same age groups. In four out of every five early New England marriages, both partners survived to the end of their childbearing years.

In strictly legal terms, a colonial women ceased to exist as an independent being when she married. Unless she made special arrangements, a wife did not control her own property, nor was she able to make a binding contract. Her husband was the head of the family, and both church and government insisted that she obey him. He controlled the family's property, whether he had earned it, inherited it, or acquired it through her.

In reality, however, a wife was her husband's partner. The operation of a household depended heavily on women's work, not just at raising children, but at a host of other tasks. A woman's work in the kitchen and the garden, in the dairy, or at the spinning wheel was just as essential to

A Farmer's Diary, 1660

Thomas Minor was a prosperous farmer in the coastal Connecticut town of Stonington, who attended to town and other public affairs as well as his own farm. His diary for the summer and autumn months of 1660 reflect the variety of farming tasks, the produce and livestock Minor traded, the use of family and locally hired labor, and exchanges with neighbors. The butter Minor delivered will have been made by his wife, Grace, or another female member of the household. Until the mid eighteenth century the English and English colonists started the New Year in March—hence Minor's numbering of the months in his diary.

The fifth month is July 31 days & Sabbath day the first. This week I agreed with Rogers about John's 2 Cows & a calf & Sabbath day the 8. The 7th of this month I sowed turnips. The 13 there was a town meeting & Sabbath day the 15. I pulled hemp. Ephraim & Joseph [Thomas Minor's sons] mowed in the orchard Friday & Saturday 20 and 21. We had a court at Captain Denison's Sabbath day 22. 23 I looked horses fetched one load of hay & Saturday the 28 I cut peas & Sabbath day 29 & Tuesday the 31.

The sixth month is August 31 days and Wednesday the first. I cut fence & carried them Wednesday the 8. I carried my wheat Thursday the 9. I carried the Ram to the Island & Wednesday the 15. Friday 17 Thomas & Ephraim [Thomas Minor's sons] was at Samuel Cheesbrough's. The 13 day I had the gelding at Captain Denison's. The 20th day John Tower came here & Wednesday the 22 we Carried 5 loads of hay & made a rick next to the barn. Wednesday 29 I was at town & took up things for John. I was at Prentice to show the horse Friday 31.

The seventh month is September 30 days & Saturday the first. Mr. Winthrop [John Winthrop, Jr., son of the Massachusetts Bay leader and a governor of Connecticut] was at New London. The 4th day the horses were at Culver's. John Moore began to work for me Saturday the 8. The 12 I reckoned with Mr. Picket and made all even being Wednesday & Saturday the 15 Clement & John Moore went to New London. I & Joseph was at Borden's & the 2 horses were gone. The 12th day also I paid Toung his silver before Josias Willkins and quite freed the horse & Saturday the 22 I clove Clapboards. Sabbath day 23 we first did see Carrie's cow to spring udder. John was here. The last of September we came home from Narraganset & Master Brigden first taught here.

The eight month is October 31 days & Monday the first. This day Hannah her child [possibly Grace Minor's sister Hannah] died before day & Monday the 8 the moon was Eclipsed. I was to go with Mr. Bridgen toward Mohegan & Monday the 29 I carried the firkin or butter to Mr. Smith for Amos. I marked the Colt a bay mare without any white. The mare have a white face, a slit in the right ear, 3 white feet part of the 42, a white ring about each ear, a halfpenny on each ear Wednesday the 31.

The ninth [month] is November 30 days & Thursday the first. Friday the 2 I weighed Amos his firkin of butter at Mr. Smith's. It was 70 pounds & there is 13 pounds to pay. The 8 day being Thursday we had Carried 45 loads of muck out of the yards. There was a meeting to be at Smith's of the whole Town & Thursday the 15. This week we killed the steer. I was at New London & had the axes & guns mended. The steer came to six pounds. The 20 we began the little house. Thursday 22 it snowed the second time. Thursday the 29 we appointed a meeting to be at Cheesbrough's. That day fortnight I began to clean clapboards. Friday the 30 we had home all the timber for the little house.

Source: Karen Ordahl Kupperman, ed., *Major Problems in American Colonial History* (1993).

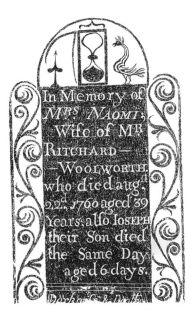

Untimely Deaths. The grave-yards of colonial New England testified to the hazards of childbirth for colonial women and their babies.
Source: Edmund Vincent Gillon, Jr., *Early New England Gravestone Rubbings* (1966).

the family's well-being as what a man did in the fields or the shop. Women made cheese and butter, which were vital sources of cash income; they also made the beer or cider and much of the food that sustained the family's members. Women made and repaired clothing, produced the soap that kept the family clean, and made the tallow candles that provided lighting. Undoubtedly women's work was undervalued, and often overlooked. In practice, however, women and men frequently worked side by side. During the harvest, northern farmwomen joined in gathering crops. An artisan's wife was likely to acquire some of her husband's craft skills and to take a hand in production.

Women's work was indeed hard. When, for example, she found herself without a servant to assist her in 1782, Ruth Belknap of Dover, New Hampshire, reflected on the burden of her chores:

> Up in the morning I must rise
> Before I've time to rub my eyes.
> With half-pin'd gown, unbuckled shoe,
> I haste to milk my lowing cow.
> But, Oh! it makes my heart to ake,
> I have no bread till I can bake,
> And then, alas! it makes me sputter,
> For I must churn or have no butter.
> The hogs with swill too I must serve;
> For hogs must eat or men will starve.

Belknap was a minister's wife, but her status did not spare her toil and drudgery, nor the misery on butchering-day of looking "like ten thousand sluts, / My kitchen spread with grease and guts."

Some women did venture outside the conventional expectations of their roles, daring (as one put it) to be "as independent as circumstances will admit [i.e., permit]." But in a rural community, unmarried women faced great hardships. Often the best they could hope for was to have a room in a relative's house, paid for by performing household chores. Widows also often found life trying. The law guaranteed the "widow's portion," usually one-third, of a husband's real estate, but her right was not to the freehold, only to the use of it during her lifetime. In some colonies, even this right eroded over time. Many widows were as dependent on their sons or sons-in-law as they had once been on their fathers and husbands. For the single or widowed rural women who were literate, the one other possibility was to open a "dame school," teaching village children for a pittance.

Children were expected to submit to parental authority. As they grew older, children became important to the work of most rural households, first performing simple tasks, then assuming the roles that, according to their sex, would fall to them as adults. Unmarried daughters usually assisted with household and garden tasks and undertook dairy work or home manufacturing. Boys and young men, as well as helping with regular farm work, often provided crucial labor for felling trees, clearing land, and other heavy tasks associated with new settlements. Fathers could use the promise of land to keep their sons at home and working for the household until well into the sons' early adulthood. It was a form of labor control that shaped and fitted the family life cycle, and the transmission of economic power from one generation to another. It favored those with property, of course. Poor or orphaned children were often put out to live and work in other families, where their labor earned them no future security. In Connecticut in 1703, for example, when her mother and stepfather were convicted of incest, Hannah Rood was sent to work "as a drudge sometime in one house and sometime in another."

Some farm neighborhoods were largely self-sufficient, with families growing or making much of what they needed, and swapping labor, or " 'changing works," among households. Much of what they had derived from the land. As one writer put it: "What should we American farmers be without the distinct possession of that soil? It feeds us, it clothes us, from it we draw even a great exuberancy, our best meat, our richest drink; the very honey of our bees comes from this privileged spot." Farmers grew mixed crops to give their families a degree of autonomy. They built local networks of barter and mutual exchange, in which a tradesman might accept "wheat, rye, Indian corn, as well as cash, or anything that is good to eat," in return for his services. Farm wives traded cloth, butter, and beer, as well as nursing, midwifery, and child-care. Many farmers also bought and sold land, usually not out of greed, but to build holdings large enough to provide for their children. For every John Pynchon or Robert Livingston who avidly pursued wealth, there were many people who held a more modest idea of prosperity, independence, and "competency."

For most country people, competency also involved producing surpluses to be marketed at the best prices that could be found. The role of this surplus produce in broader patterns of commerce, and in farm families' own strategies, varied according to circumstances. In much of

T Young *Timothy* Learnt Sin to fly.

V *Vashti* for Pride, Was set aside.

W Whales in the Sea, GOD's Voice obey.

X *Xerxes* did die, And so must I.

Y While youth do chear Death may be near.

Z *Zaccheus* he Did climb the Tree, Our Lord to see.

New England Primer. As demonstrated by a page from a 1767 edition of the widely used schoolbook, children learning the alphabet also received lessons in obedience and restraint.

Source: *New England Primer* (1767)—Rare Books and Manuscript Division, New York Public Library, Astor, Lenox and Tilden Foundations.

eastern and southern New England by the mid eighteenth century, settlements were becoming crowded and landholdings were being divided up. Of farms in Andover, Massachusetts, only one in three exceeded 200 acres in size. The land in many parts of New England was relatively poor, and crop surpluses there were low. Families seeking land on which to settle their offspring might well look to frontier regions. From the 1730s onward, their demand for land led to a powerful outward migration from old to new areas.

In Pennsylvania and elsewhere, many landholdings were larger, and more fertile land was available. In the mid eighteenth-century Delaware Valley, two-thirds of farms exceeded 500 acres in size. Farmers here, by concentrating their effort on grain production, were able to raise market income from the sale of wheat and other crops, using these resources to provide for their children. On eighty percent of Pennsylvania farms there were crop surpluses, and forty percent of the total crop was sent to market for export. By the third quarter of the eighteenth century, wheat from New York, Pennsylvania, and the northern Chesapeake fed people all around the Atlantic basin. Farmwomen, too, contributed to both household consumption and marketable surpluses by their work at dairying and other functions.

Samuel Swayne and his family of East Marlborough township were typical small Pennsylvania farmers. Samuel had inherited a 91-acre farm by the time of his marriage in 1756. The Swaynes grew wheat and other grains, cut hay, and picked fruit trees; Hannah Swayne milked cows and made butter and cheese. They had no household servant, but hired local labor intermittently when they needed help. Some years they boarded laborers at their house, later reducing their reliance on outside labor as their own children became old enough to work.

But by the 1750s, the demands of wheat farming were altering patterns of labor, especially on the larger farms in Pennsylvania's English-speaking areas. A steadily increasing number of servants, some of them indentured to work off the cost of transatlantic passages, were employed on farms to assist with crop-raising. Many were German or Scots-Irish, unrelated to their employers. Conflicts arose over harsh treatment or monotonous work. Servants frequently ran away. George Owens of Chester County, Pennsylvania, driven to despair because his only work was chopping wood, absconded. Married servants known as "inmates" occupied cottages on farm lands. Others worked as day laborers according to the varied seasonal demands of plowing, sowing, and harvesting. In Chester County in 1750 there was roughly one inmate or free laborer for every four householders, but a decade later the proportion had risen to nearly one in two. Wage labor was becoming a growing part of the grain-exporting rural economy.

149

"Oak Tree Stumps Are Just as Hard in America . . ."

Though many poor Europeans were attracted to Pennsylvania, some travelers warned that the vision of prosperity there was exaggerated. Gottlieb Mittelberger came to America from Germany in 1750, experiencing the hardships of the Atlantic crossing and of indentured servitude in Pennsylvania. He returned home after four years and wrote a book urging his countrymen not to emigrate to America. His descriptions of shipboard conditions, the sale of servants at Philadelphia, and farm work bear strong similarities to accounts of the African slave trade.

When the ships have weighed anchor for the last time, usually off Cowes in Old England, then both the long sea voyage and misery begin in earnest. For from there the ships often take eight, nine, ten, or twelve weeks sailing to Philadelphia, if the wind is unfavorable. But even given the most favorable winds, the voyage takes seven weeks.

During the journey the ship is full of pitiful signs of distress—smells, fumes, horrors, vomiting, various kinds of sea sickness, fever, dysentery, headaches, heat, constipation, boils, scurvy, cancer, mouth-rot, and similar afflictions, all of them caused by the age and the highly salted state of the food, especially of the meat, as well as by the very bad and filthy water, which brings about the miserable destruction and death of many. Add to all that shortage of food, hunger, thirst, frost, heat, dampness, fear, misery, vexation, and lamentation as well as other troubles. Thus, for example, there are so many lice, especially on the sick people, that they have to be scraped off the bodies. All this misery reaches its climax when in addition to everything else one must also suffer through two to three days and nights of storm, with everyone convinced that the ship with all aboard is bound to sink. In such misery all the people on board pray and cry pitifully together. . . .

When the ships finally arrive in Philadelphia after the long voyage only those are let off who can pay their sea freight or can give good security. The others, who lack the money to pay, have to remain on board until they are purchased. . . .

This is how the commerce in human beings on board ship takes place. Every day Englishmen, Dutchmen, and High Germans come from Philadelphia and other places, some of them very far away, . . . and go on board the newly arrived vessel that has brought people from Europe and offers them for sale. From among the healthy they pick out those suitable for the purposes for which they require them. Then they negotiate with them as to the length of the period for which they will go into service in order to pay off their passage, the whole amount of which they generally still owe. When an agreement has been reached, adult persons by written contract bind themselves to serve for three, four, five, or six years, according to their health and age. The very young, between the ages of 10 and 15, have to serve until they are 21, however. . . .

Our Europeans who have been purchased must work hard all the time. For new fields are constantly being laid out, and thus they learn from experience that oak tree stumps are just as hard in America as they are in Germany. . . .

Source: Linda R. Monk, ed., *Ordinary Americans: U.S. History Through the Eyes of Ordinary People* (1994).

Although independent farm families dominated northern agriculture, there were a few localities in which slave labor also became important. Along Rhode Island's Narragansett Bay, large slave-worked dairy farms grew up by the end of the seventeenth century. Around Fairfield, Connecticut, and in parts of Long Island and New Jersey, rural household slavery also became common. In 1700 thirteen percent of Long Island's people were slaves; slaves and free black people accounted for one-fifth of the population of Bergen County, New Jersey, in the early eighteenth century. In contrast to southern plantations, however, most northern slaveholders had only one slave. As a result, northern slaves often lived separate lives, without their own families or distinctive culture.

While the North's rural slave population grew in the early eighteenth century, so did social stratification among rural whites. Some parts of new England, such as the Connecticut River Valley in western Massachusetts, became dominated politically by wealthy families, whose influence earned them the title of "River Gods." Members of these families intermarried, filled town delegations to the General Court in Boston, secured provincial appointments as colonels of militia or county-court judges, and became pastors of some of the region's churches. Although none achieved the power that the Pynchons had held in seventeenth-century Springfield, and although the New England ethos sometimes bred resentment against the powerful and well-to-do, deference toward age, wealth, and family remained common. Only during times of crisis was it sometimes disrupted.

Cities by the Sea

By 1770, about ninety-three percent of all colonists lived in places with populations under 2,500. However, one of the ways in which the northern colonies were distinct from those in much of the South was in the relative significance of the port towns that grew up along their coasts and river estuaries. By the eighteenth century, the people of Boston, New York, Philadelphia, and smaller ports lived differently from their country cousins. Each town had established itself as a place where trade and manufacturing, rather than farming, formed the essential basis of life. Lesser centers, such as Newport, Albany, and Baltimore, which expanded in the eighteenth century, developed in the same direction. None was large by modern standards. Even the biggest were "walking towns," easily crossed on foot, full of places and faces familiar to their residents.

Boston, for example, occupied no more than a small peninsula that jutted into Massachusetts Bay, linked to the mainland by a narrow spit called Boston Neck. Although the town grew steadily for a century, around 1750 it began to stagnate, and its population leveled off at about 15,000. It governed itself by the same open town meetings that were used in the tiniest New England settlements. Ordinary Bostonians valued those open meetings highly. As early as 1708 a proposal to abandon them and create a mayor and a board of aldermen was resoundingly defeated, not least because people objected to the £1,000 wealth qualification for holders of the new offices. As one pamphleteer argued, "The rich will exert that right of Dominion, which they think they have exclusive of all others . . . and then the Great Men will no more have the Dissatisfaction of seeing their Poorer Neighbours stand up for equal Privileges with them."

New York and Philadelphia exceeded Boston in size, but not by much. As late as 1770, New York filled only the southernmost part of Manhattan Island, where the financial district now stands, and boasted a mere 21,000 inhabitants. Philadelphia was North America's fastest-growing city. Its population of 25,000 in 1770 made it, after London, one of the largest settlements in the English-speaking world. Even so, its people occupied little more than the modern downtown area. Both cities were governed differently than Boston. In New York, a mayor was picked by the colony's royal governor, but aldermen were chosen by election. Philadelphia, like many English boroughs, was run by a "closed" corporation, a body of officials who picked their own successors.

Small though they were, the colonial port towns fulfilled many functions. They were important commercial centers, whose merchants

British and American Atlantic Trade Patterns in the Eighteenth Century. American merchants based in the North carved out for themselves a substantial share of Anglo-American trade. The Navigation Acts gave British traders dominance over many routes, but merchants from the northern port towns captured business with the Mediterranean and the West Indies, shipping crops produced in the southern colonies, and importing slaves for sale there.

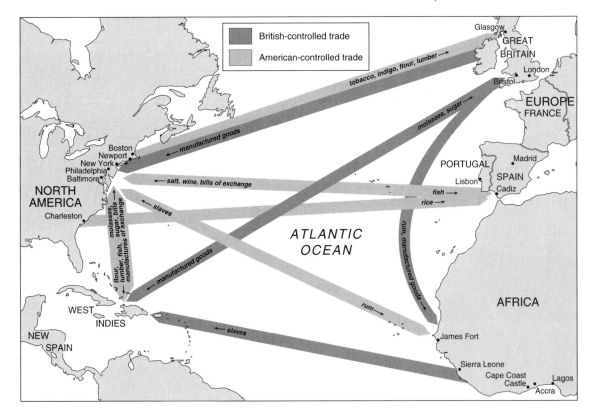

dispatched and received ships and their cargoes over thousands of miles, to and from Britain, mainland Europe, Africa, the Caribbean, or the Azores. Colonial ships carried fish from the Grand Banks, flour from Pennsylvania, barrel staves from New York's forests, flaxseed for Irish linen growers, lemons, salt, oil, and wine. They also carried slaves: from the 1720s onward merchants in Boston, Providence, Newport, and other New England ports became active in the Atlantic slave trade. After mid-century, Newport was the largest slave port in North America, its ships carrying slaves from Africa either to the West Indies, or to the mainland for sale to southern planters. As their commerce grew, the port towns increasingly became centers of wealth as well. By the mid eighteenth century some of their richest merchants enjoyed fortunes respectable even by lofty British standards.

The main ports were also centers of politics and the arts. They were political capitals where men with a claim to rule gathered to conduct their province's business, and were centers of upper-class culture, with colleges, playhouses, concerts, and artists that imitated Europe's best. Two American artists, the Philadelphian Benjamin West and the Bostonian John Singleton Copley, would influence the course of eighteenth-century art. Philadelphia in particular was emerging as an intellectual center, noted for its contributions to science and high-quality craftsmanship.

Colonial towns were also manufacturing centers. New England ports became important for shipbuilding. The earliest Bostonians had recognized the riches of the nearby ocean: "Here is good store of fish," one migrant said, "if we had boates to go 8 or 10 leagues to sea to fish in." Fish, salted and dried, would have markets in the West Indies and across the Atlantic. Shipyards, ropewalks, iron foundries, and sailmaking shops grew up in Boston and elsewhere to build, equip, and supply the fishing boats and larger vessels that landed and transported the catch, and then to build other cargo-carrying vessels. Skilled artisans and laborers ran the yards and shops, and the ships they built earned a high reputation around the Atlantic. By 1760, American shipyards were building one-third of all new British commercial shipping. Shipbuilding and related activities attracted other occupations. Towns became hives of activity, where wagoners, seamstresses, craftsmen, laborers, coopers, dressmakers, midwives, and prostitutes plied their trades.

Urban Elites

Northern towns developed their own social order, with different classes living in distinctly different ways. Wealthy "elites," or upper classes, emerged, well connected to international networks and to colonial administrations. The richest were likely to be merchants trading across the Atlantic; others, usually less wealthy, were involved in trade along the American coast and to the Caribbean. A professional class, too, began to take shape, starting with the Protestant ministry. In the eighteenth century, lawyers emerged as a separate group, using their specialized skills to serve landowners and merchants as laws became more elaborate and business expanded. Ministers and lawyers formed an intellectual elite, producing the bulk of early America's writing and scholarship.

Merchant elites varied in character. Boston's divided between Puritan descendants of early settlers and more recent arrivals, many of whom were Anglican. Philadelphia's early Quaker merchants were also joined later by other groups. Boston and Philadelphia merchants were relatively uninvolved in rural landholding, since the independent farming economies of New England and Pennsylvania kept them at arms' length. By contrast, some of New York's prominent merchant families were also

Clothes Make the Man. In colonial New England, merchants commissioned paintings that would display not only their faces but their place in society as well. Boston merchant Joseph Sherburne ostentatiously indicated his rank and wealth in this portrait by John Singleton Copley painted in the late 1760s.

Source: John Singleton Copley, *Joseph Sherburne,* oil on canvas, 1767-70, 50 × 40 inches—Metropolitan Museum of Art.

Commerce Makes the Man.
Other merchants, such as James Tilley in this 1757 painting attributed to Copley, preferred to emphasize the source of their wealth in their portraits.

Source: John Singleton Copley, *James Tilley,* oil on copper, 1757, 13 3/4 × 10 1/4 inches— M. Knoedler and Company, New York.

among the leading holders of the colony's manorial estates.

Some women, mostly widows, succeeded in business, most of them running small stores. A few of these "she-merchants" prospered as long-distance traders. Perhaps the most notable was the Bostonian Elizabeth Murray Smith, whose wealth enabled her, as she proudly put it, "to live and act as I please." She celebrated herself by commissioning a portrait from John Singleton Copley. Though Copley depicted her in a conventional feminine mode, in elegant costume and holding a bunch of fruit in her hands, her bearing and expression belied any thought that this woman was either submissive or decorative. But even women such as she did not attain public positions. In 1733 some New York businesswomen

Growing Inequality in the Northern Port Towns. The chart illustrates the urban elites' expanding share of wealth, and the decreasing shares enjoyed by the middling and poorer sections of the towns' populations. By 1775 the poorest three-fifths of urban inhabitants owned less than one-twentieth of taxable wealth.

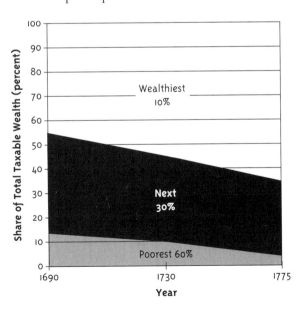

155

complained to the governor that "We are Housekeepers, Pay our Taxes, carry on Trade and most of us are she Merchants, and as we in some measure contribute to the Support of Government, we ought to be entitled to some of the Sweets of it."

During the eighteenth century urban elites increased their share of colonial wealth. In 1687 in Philadelphia, the top 5 percent of taxpayers owned 30 percent of all property, but by 1774 they owned 55 percent. In Boston, the share of wealth held by the top 10 percent of taxpayers rose from 46 percent in 1687 to 63 percent in 1771. As merchants built their fortunes, they acquired partners in faraway ports, thus becoming part of a transatlantic elite. Some had connections to the highest circles in England. By 1750 a daughter of New York's DeLancey family had married a knighted British admiral, and one of the DeLancey sons was close to the Archbishop of Canterbury. Such families lived in a cosmopolitan world in which events thousands of miles away were just as important as what was happening close at hand, and where men and women adopted European customs and fashions to indicate that they were not mere colonists.

Artisans, Laborers, and Seamen

Most townspeople, however, were not merchants or ministers or lawyers. They belonged instead to the "laboring classes," and they worked with their hands. Workmen's dress — leather work-aprons, plain hair, and long trousers — signaled that their wearers did not belong to an elite whose male members wore satin coats, powdered wigs, and knee breeches. Women's clothing that could withstand the rigors of kitchen work, sewing, washing, and scouring was readily distinguishable from the silk garments of well-to-do women.

Seamen lived in a world with its own special conditions and customs. Inhabitants of the ocean as much as any port town, they developed friendships that spanned great distances. They faced danger from storms and shipwreck, the fear that the British navy might impress them into service for the king, or that a privateer or enemy man-of-war might capture them. They faced low pay, constant discomfort, and the captain's sometimes harsh discipline. Many landsmen, too, worked in connection with maritime commerce. Shipwrights and ironmakers employed in the largest manufacturing establishments had skills and status that gave them considerable freedom and control of their own time.

The goal of most laboring townsmen was to become master artisans or "mechanics," which meant serving several years of apprenticeship, learning the skills and secrets of a trade while legally bound to serve their

Crafts Make the Man. Boston silversmith Paul Revere was one of the few colonial craftsmen painted by Copley. In this painting, dating from about 1770, Revere posed at his workbench, wearing the artisan's plain linen shirt and vest, and displaying his engraving tools and an unfinished teapot.

Source: John Singleton Copley, *Paul Revere,* oil on canvas, 1768-70, 35 × 28 1/2 inches — Gift of Joseph W., William B., and Edward H. R. Revere, Museum of Fine Arts, Boston.

masters. Having completed his apprenticeship, the laborer became a journeyman, hired for a time as he saved to open a shop of his own. If a man did become a master in his own right, he had to be many things: a producer, using his own tools to turn out goods; a businessman, buying raw materials and selling finished products; a teacher, training apprentices; and an employer, hiring journeymen as perhaps he himself had once been hired.

Just as much as farmers, urban workingmen based their activities in their households. "Mastery" was a source of pride. It meant the ownership of a shop, command of a respected set of skills, a good measure of independence, and control of one's working environment. The Boston silversmith Paul Revere proudly had John Singleton Copley paint him in his work clothes, the tools of his trade in front of him, while he fingered a fine silver teapot he had made. Most master craftsmen also had the support of a hardworking wife, to provide housing, food, clothing, and laundry services for himself and his apprentices.

Some master artisans, like Revere, achieved considerable comfort. Revere's North End house, still standing, was no mansion, but clearly he did not live in poverty. Under special circumstances an artisan might claim international fame: the Philadelphia printer Benjamin Franklin became one of the foremost scientific figures of the eighteenth century. Men like Franklin and Revere were relentless self-improvers. The mottoes Franklin printed in *Poor Richard's Almanac* showed his belief that hard work and self-discipline would carry a man far in the world. Franklin's own progress seemed to prove the point.

Yet much more typical of an artisan's life was the course followed by the Boston shoemaker George Robert Twelves Hewes, who never grew wealthy. He did win fame, but only in very old age, as one of the last survivors of the American Revolution. Problems like insecurity and poverty did not directly affect men like Franklin or Revere, but were very real for someone like Hewes, for whom one bad year could mean the humiliation of debtors' prison or the poorhouse. Such difficulties were worse still for the ordinary laborers who loaded and unloaded ships, carted goods, and sold their labor from day to day, and for the growing numbers of widows and orphans in eighteenth-century cities, who could barely support themselves adequately in the absence of a male wage earner. For them economic insecurity was part of life.

". . . Plough Deep, While Sluggards Sleep"

Benjamin Franklin's *Poor Richard's Almanack* was perhaps the most popular advice book published in colonial America. Although many of Franklin's proverbs and homilies are now clichés, at the time they reflected the abiding belief of farmers and skilled artisans in the dignity and importance of their labor in northern colonial society.

Industry need not wish, as Poor Richard says, and he that lives upon Hope will die fasting. There are no Gains without Pains; then Help Hands, for I have no Lands, or if I have, they are smartly taxed. And, as Poor Richard likewise observes, He that hath a Trade hath an Estate; and he that hath a Calling, hath an Office of Profit and Honour; but then the Trade must be worked at, and Calling well followed, or neither the Estate nor the Office will enable us to pay our taxes. If we are industrious, we shall never starve; for, as Poor Richard says, At the working Man's House Hunger looks in, but dares not enter. Nor will the Bailiff or the Constable enter, for Industry pays Debts, while Despair encreaseth them, say Poor Richard. What though you have no Treasure, nor has any rich Relation left you a Legacy, Diligence is the Mother of Goodluck, as Poor Richard says, and God gives all Things to Industry. Then plough deep, while Sluggards sleep, and you shall have Corn to sell and to keep, says Poor Dick. . . . If you were a Servant, would you not be ashamed that a good Master should catch you idle? Are you then your own Master, be ashamed to catch yourself idle, as Poor Dick says. When there is so much to be done for yourself, your Family, your Country, and your gracious King, be up by Peep of Day; Let not the Sun look down and say, Inglorious here he lies.

Source: Richard Saunders, ed., *Poor Richard: The Almanacks for the Years 1753–1758* (1964).

The larger towns offered women more options than they had in the countryside. They took in lodgers, ran taverns, made fashionable clothes for the well-to-do, or practiced midwifery. One Boston midwife, a Mrs. Phillips, was said to have delivered over 3,000 babies by the time she died in her early forties in 1761. It was not unusual for widows of artisans to take charge of their husbands' shops. Elizabeth Holt succeeded her husband as the publisher of the *New York Journal,* and she became New York State's official printer during the Revolution.

Working women, though, were often confined to poorly paid tasks—sewing, washing, cleaning, and cooking for wages or sometimes just for bed and board. Some women worked as prostitutes. In smaller ports, like Salem, Massachusetts, women formed a majority of the working population, because many men were at sea on fishing or trading voyages. Often obliged to support themselves and their children, but rarely able to obtain well-paid employment, women formed a significant proportion of the poor in many port towns. With menfolk at sea amid the hazards of accident, disease, and shipwreck, many of these women could also expect to face the trials of premature widowhood.

The Centenarian. Despite its title, George Robert Twelves Hewes was ninety-three when Joseph G. Cole painted this portrait in 1835. Based on Hewes's clothes and demeanor, viewers of the painting probably did not know about his artisanal background or that he was destitute.

Source: Bostonian Society, Old State House, Boston.

Indeed, poverty was increasingly common among both men and women in eighteenth-century towns. If the goal of most young artisans was to acquire a "decent competency"—sufficient property and skill to stand on their own two feet—many could not be sure that they ever would. In Boston, the problem was economic stagnation. The town's expenditure for poor-relief in the 1760s was almost six times as much per head of population as it had been forty years before. Philadelphia's expanding economy provided no less of a struggle for laboring people, as a constant flow of migrants from the countryside and overseas competed for jobs. Of Philadelphia laborers and journeymen who got married in 1756, for example, one-fifth owned no property at all, and another three-fifths owned only the bare necessities for setting up a home. Over the next eleven years only just over a fourth of them improved their position. The great majority either merely hung on, or slipped down the economic slope. The share of property held by the bottom 30 percent of Philadelphia taxpayers fell from 2.6 percent in 1687 to barely 1 percent in 1774.

Poorer Bostonians expressed many of their concerns every year on November 5, when—like people in parts of England—they gathered to commemorate "Pope's Day," the anniversary of the discovery in 1605 of the Gunpowder Plot, in which a group of English Catholics had conspired to blow up Parliament while King James I was in the building. Bostonians paraded effigies of the pope, the devil, and of Guy Fawkes, the best-remembered of the plotters. Rival groups from Boston's North and South Ends brawled, and the victors threw the losers' effigies into a bonfire. The cobblers, apprentices, and seamen who took part were showing their identification both with Protestantism and with the seventeenth-century upheavals that had secured the "English liberty" they shared. They were also celebrating a day of misrule when the streets were theirs, a brief carnival when people like themselves took control.

The Unfree: Servants and Slaves

Poor though they might be, laborers and journeymen might console themselves that they were at least free. At the bottom of the colonial social scale were many people—white and black, indentured servants and slaves—who were not.

"Forty Shillings Reward"

The lot of indentured servants was extremely difficult in colonial America, as evidenced by the number of servants who ran away from their masters. Masters were often reduced to placing advertisements in local newspapers to announce the disappearance of their servants, as these notices—from a shipmaster in New York in 1737, and from a merchant in Albany in 1761—suggest.

Run away from the Brigantine Joanna . . . an Irish Servant man, named Charles McCammel, aged about 25 Years, a tall lusty Man, wearing his own black Hair. . . . N.B. The Servant having been offr'd 8 shillings for his Hair, it's suppos'd he may have cut it off. He speaks very good English.

Source: *New York Weekly Journal,* August 29, 1737.

FORTY SHILLINGS REWARD. For taking up and securing Mary Brown, alias Edwards, a Pennsylvania born indented Servant, who ran away from the Service of . . . her Master a few days ago: She is a so-so-sort of a looking Woman, inclinable to Clumsiness, much Pock pitted, which gives her an hard Favour and a frosty Look, wants several of her Teeth, yet speaks good English and Dutch, about 26 or 28 Years old, perhaps 30. Had on and about her when she went off a red quilted Pettycoat, a crossbarr'd brown and white Josey [jersey], a sorry red Cloak and the making of a new stuff Wrapper, supposed to be gone towards Philadelphia, via New York.—James Crofton, Albany

Source: *New York Mercury,* March 19, 1761.

Indentured servants came to the middle colonies, as they did to the South, throughout the colonial period. At first most were single males from London and the south of England. They entered America through colonial ports like Philadelphia, where they worked off their indentures and tended to stay on. More than half were artisans and craftsmen, and another quarter were laborers and personal servants. The colonial iron and construction industries were hungry for skilled workers, and occasionally servants bargained themselves into good situations. By the mid-eighteenth century a substantial proportion of bound servants arriving in Pennsylvania were from places other than England, especially from the north of Ireland and from Germany.

Young families, typically from rural areas in the north of England, Scotland, and other parts of Europe, also came as indentured servants. They tended to work off their indentures in agricultural areas such as western New York, at the edges of colonial settlement, where they hoped to find land to farm on their own when their service was complete. These were people whose circumstances in Europe were so hard that they were willing to sell a portion of their adult lives to escape, knowing that in America they would be sold to a stranger who would govern them for

FIVE SHILLINGS REWARD.

RUNAWAY from the subscriber living in Fourth-street, a little above Race-street, the 25th ult. a girl named Christiana Lower, 13 years of age: Had on a blue calimancoe cap, blue and white checked handkerchief, a short red gown, blue and white striped linsey petticoat, an old pair of black stockings and new shoes. Whoever takes up said girl and brings her home, shall have the above reward and reasonable charges.

CHRISTIAN LOWER.

THREE POUNDS REWARD.

RUN AWAY from the Subscriber, living at Warwick furnace, Minehole, on the 23d ult. an Irish servant man, named DENNIS M'CALLIN, about five feet eight inches high, nineteen years of age, has a freckled face, light coloured curly hair. Had on when he went away, an old felt hat, white and yellow striped jacket, a new blue cloth coat, and buckskin breeches; also, he took with him a bundle of shirts and stockings, and a pocket pistol; likewise, a box containing gold rings, &c. Whoever takes up said servant and secures him in any goal, so as his master may get him again, shall have the above reward and reasonable charges paid by JAMES TODD.

N. B. All masters of vessels, and others, are forbid from harbouring or carrying him off, at their peril.

four to seven years. Not surprisingly, their "fondness for freedom" often led to disputes with their masters, complaints of harsh treatment, or bids to run away.

Slaves in the northern colonies were in a worse position than servants. Although some worked on farms, most northern slaves were town-dwellers. In the late seventeenth century, they were often employed as domestic servants, but their numbers and functions grew with the North's involvement in the slave trade. From 1710 to 1742, the number of slaves in Boston quadrupled, to about thirteen hundred, or 8.5 percent of the population. Slaves made up 18 percent of New York's population in 1731 and 21 percent in 1746. Perhaps half of New York City households owned a slave by the 1740s.

The majority of slaves were men, working as general laborers, or as porters, cartmen, dockworkers, and stockmen; many women slaves worked in domestic service. Most lived alone, in the attic or back room of their master's house. Particularly for women, this often meant considerable isolation. When one New Yorker advertised his slave for sale, he noted that "she drinks no Strong Drink, and gets no Children" and was, consequently, "a very good Drudge." A few blacks also lived as freemen in northern cities, although they could neither vote nor own property. In the port towns, African-American men — slave and free alike — had extensive contact with whites at workplaces, taverns, and fairs.

Many northern whites were hostile toward this African-American population, fearing slave insurrection. In 1712, a band of twenty New York slaves set a blaze and then fired on a group of whites who arrived to put it out, touching off a major panic. The white militia quickly routed the armed slaves, but for weeks there were arrests, trials, suicides, and executions. Nineteen convicted slaves were hanged, or burned alive and cut into pieces. New York's governor boasted that these were "the most exemplary punishments that could possibly be thought of." But even such brutal punishment did little to quell the fear of slave revolt. For instance, the New York events spurred efforts by Pennsylvanians to curb slave imports into their province. In another episode in 1741, New York slaves accused of arson and theft were alleged to have conspired with Irish and free black laborers to kill white inhabitants. Eighteen blacks were hanged or burned to death, along with four whites implicated in the conspiracy.

Despite such treatment, slaves living in northern colonial towns found ways to affirm their dignity and sustain their own communities. Like their southern counterparts, they adapted remnants of African culture and rituals. In New York City and Albany each spring, slaves celebrated the festival of Pinkster, whose name derived from the Judeo-Christian feast of Pentecost, but which they marked with dances and music drawn from African tradition. By the mid-eighteenth century, slaves in several New England towns had initiated an annual "Negro Election

Head of a Negro. This portrait painted in the late 1770s by John Singleton Copley, possibly of a London dockworker, was unusual in this era for portraying a person of color as an individual.

Source: John Singleton Copley, *Head of a Negro,* oil on canvas, 1777-78, 21 × 16 1/4 inches — The Detroit Institute of the Arts. Founders Society Purchase, Gibbs-Williams Fund.

Day," which the slave community celebrated with feasting and dancing, and by "electing" its own governors, judges, sheriffs, and magistrates. Like the popular "mock elections" that took place in parts of England at the same time, Negro Election Day enabled those who could not vote to satirize the political system that excluded them from participation.

Government and Power in the Colonial North

By modern standards, the northern colonies were not democratic. Most people had no part in public life. Only men who owned some property and who could claim to be independent of others' authority had the right to vote or hold political office. This excluded slaves, servants, women, youths, and adult men who did not meet the minimum property requirements. The last group amounted to almost half of free adult males. Altogether, up to 80 or 90 percent of the population was disenfranchised.

Even those men who did vote frequently deferred to their social "betters"—the merchants, planters, lawyers, and large landowners who occupied most seats in the colonial assemblies. Rarely did genuine farmers or artisans reach the circles where real political power was wielded. In New England, where each organized town normally chose its own assembly delegate, farmers did frequently get elected, but even there the voices that counted most belonged to great merchants, to graduates of Harvard and Yale, and to the well-connected "River Gods" of the Connecticut Valley. In New York's provincial government there was little pretense of democracy. The assembly had fewer than thirty seats, three of them

Poverty Incarcerated. Increasing numbers of urban poor taxed the resources of northern colonial towns and cities. Many were incarcerated in almshouses and workhouses, but these institutions grew overcrowded. This 1767 engraving commemorated the opening of new facilities on the outskirts of Philadelphia. Typically, the print emphasized the institution's bucolic setting rather than the less picturesque activities within its walls.

Source: James Hulett, "A View of the House of Employment, Almshouse, Pennsylvania Hospital, & part of the City of Philadelphia," line engraving, c. 1767, 13 1/2 × 18 5/8 inches—Library Company of Philadelphia.

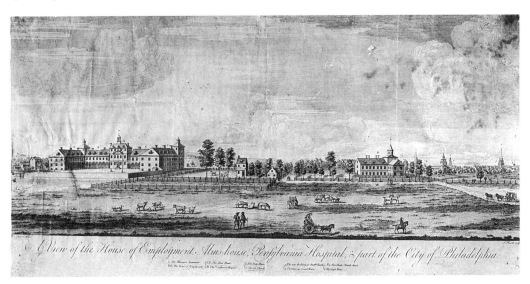

effectively hereditary, and members of the landed and mercantile elite expected to fill them. In 1761, Abraham Yates, an Albany shoemaker-turned-lawyer, tried to win a seat in the New York assembly, but was defeated by no less a figure than Sir William Johnson. This rebuff would later spur Yates to try to overturn the elite's hold on government.

Much power in fact lay with wealthy men who held appointive, rather than elective offices. These included the royal governor in most colonies, whichever member of the Penn family occupied the Pennsylvania proprietorship, members of the governors' councils (except in Massachusetts, Connecticut, and Rhode Island), as well as mayors, judges, sheriffs, and the members of Philadelphia's closed corporation.

Yet compared with almost anywhere else in the eighteenth century, the northern colonies were quite democratic. Once voting rights in New England were no longer tied to church membership, eligibility to vote followed the same basic rule that held in England: a man had to have a freehold valued at forty pounds or a tenancy worth forty shillings per year. In England this limit was high enough to deny the vote to the vast majority, but in America, where land was more easily obtained, a little over half of free adult males met the requirement. This included most of the tenants on New York's great estates, although there was no secret ballot and voice voting meant that the landlord's candidate rarely lost. There were other ways to be eligible to vote as well. In New York City and in Albany the status of "freeman," open to most craftsmen, conferred voting rights and was an important avenue to political expression among urban workingmen.

For women no such possibilities for voting existed. They found their best arena for public involvement in the churches. The radical sects of seventeenth-century England had flirted boldly with the idea of gender equality. Quaker women could preach. Even some mainstream Puritans leaned toward the notion of equality. Puritan women were sometimes members of a church while their husbands were not. Unlike men, they had no formal voice in church affairs, but they had the prestige of being "visible saints." By the eighteenth century, church membership in New England was far more common among women than among men, and women took informal part in church leadership. But they still risked censure if they overstepped their "proper" roles, and they remained unable to preach or to exercise formal authority.

Outside their churches, colonists governed themselves under their own version of the British political system. In each colony a governor represented the king, and except in Rhode Island and Connecticut (where the governor was elected) and in Pennsylvania (where the Penns chose him), he was appointed by the king. Often he was a fortune hunter intent on increasing his own wealth. But he found himself having to placate both his royal master, who issued detailed instructions, and the leading figures of the province, who often had distinct interests of their own. The other main political institutions were the council, a pale imitation of the House of Lords, and the assembly, whose members liked to compare themselves with the House of Commons and to assert similar constitutional privileges. The governor had an absolute veto on colonial laws, as did the crown (a power it ceased to exercise in Britain itself after the early eighteenth century). The governor also had great patronage in matters of office-holding and land distribution, but wily colonial politicians frequently outwitted him in such matters.

Although most colonists, particularly urban dwellers, depended in one way or another on commerce, they were not free to organize trade as they chose. From the passage of the Navigation Acts in the 1650s and 1660s, Parliament sought to arrange colonial economic activity for the mother country's benefit. Foreign vessels were barred from colonial ports, and colonial goods were to be carried only in British or colonial vessels. Many types of colonial produce could not be sold or shipped other than to Britain. The theory was that the colonial economies should complement Britain's economy and supply the mother country with goods and materials it needed, not compete with it by making or trading in similar products.

While the southern colonies conformed to this pattern fairly well by producing staple crops for export, the northern colonies posed more of a challenge to Britain. Lacking plantation staple crops, a higher proportion of their output was either of little use to Britain or duplicated goods produced there. As colonial manufacturing grew, and threatened to undercut British producers, Parliament sought to restrain it. An act of 1699 banned the export of woolen goods from the colonies, and in 1732 Parliament prohibited the sale of hats across provincial boundaries. By 1750, colonial ironworks, mainly in the Middle Colonies, were producing one-eighth of the world's crude iron. Parliament that year prohibited them from refining iron, requiring that it be shipped to Britain for further processing. Yet these restrictions did little to alter the pattern of colonial work or production. The laws were poorly enforced. In some cases they benefited the colonies. Defining colonial-built ships as "British," for instance, they enabled American shipyards to become important suppliers to British as well as colonial shipowners.

Colonial governments also regulated commerce, particularly in urban areas. European thinkers debated the advantages of letting an open market determine supplies and prices. The foremost proponent of free markets, the Scottish political economist Adam Smith, would publish his arguments in a book called *The Wealth of Nations* in 1776. But these were new and uncommon ideas. Most colonists accepted an older view of trade, that government had an obligation to see that the market provided what people needed, at a quality they would accept, and at a price they could afford.

In New York both the Dutch and English authorities set up controlled markets, in which it was illegal to "engross" (buy a crop that was still in the fields), "forestall" (buy provisions on their way to market), or "re-grate" (buy in the market in order to sell again). The city authorities also regulated the price and weight of an ordinary loaf of bread. Such measures aimed to provide farmers and bakers with a decent return on their work, and also to protect purchasers — especially the poor — against sudden price rises or unscrupulous dealing when supplies were scarce. In crises, the authorities took even stronger measures. In 1748 New York's mayor and aldermen warned that "great and unusual exportations" of wheat had made it "most excessive dear, to the very great oppression of all degrees of people, but more especially to the industrious poor" of the city and its surroundings. They asked the provincial assembly to lay an embargo on shipments to conserve the city's supplies and keep the price of wheat within peoples' means. Their call expressed a traditional concept of justice, that private profit should not take priority over public needs.

Direct Action and Popular Politics

If authorities failed to uphold this principle, ordinary people sometimes did so instead. "Food riots" were common in the eighteenth century, not only in the North American colonies, but also in South America, in continental Europe, and in England. Most often food rioters aimed to prevent suppliers from taking advantage of scarcity at the expense of the poor. In 1713, when a Boston merchant named Andrew Belcher learned of grain shortages and high prices in the Caribbean, he planned to export his own stocks there to profit from the situation. When he ignored Boston selectmen's pleas not to ship his grain out and so create scarcity in the town, two hundred women and men broke into Belcher's stores and seized it. The lieutenant-governor was shot and wounded when he tried to stop the crowd. Usually the rioters' object was not to steal supplies outright, but to regulate distribution at a price they deemed fair.

Crowds expressed popular opinion or notions of justice about a variety of public causes. As in many food riots, crowd violence was rarely indiscriminate, and participants often included women. Angered at colonial losses in King Philip's War, some Marblehead women in 1676 seized two Indian captives and tore them limb from limb. In 1704, Boston women fed up with a failed military campaign soused returning soldiers with the contents of their chamberpots. Bostonians resisted elite efforts to curb street vendors and restrict the sale of produce to public market-

Crowd Justice. Public executions were occasions for common people to express approval of the punishment of those who broke the moral code. This broadside, printed and distributed in Boston in 1773, tells the story of a twenty-one-year-old convicted burglar, Levi Ames. The ritual of execution extended over a period of two months: on Sundays, Ames was conveyed in shackles through the streets of Boston, followed by crowds of men, women, and children. Each Sabbath journey ended at a different church, where Ames stood while the minister delivered a moralizing sermon.

Source: Historical Society of Pennsylvania.

An Exhortation to young and old to be cautious of small Crimes, left they become habitual, and lead them before they are aware into thofe of the moft heinous Nature. Occafioned by the unhappy Cafe of *Levi Ames*, Executed on *Bofton*-Neck, *October* 21ft, 1773, for the Crime of Burglary.

I.

BEWARE, young People, look at me,
  Before it be too late,
And fee Sin's End is Mifery:
  Oh! fhun poor *Ames*'s Fate.

II.

I warn you all (beware betimes)
  With my now dying Breath,
To fhun Theft, Burglaries, heinous Crimes;
  They bring untimely Death.

III.

Shun vain and idle Company;
  They'll lead you foon aftray;
From ill-fam'd Houfes ever flee,
  And keep yourfelves away.

IV.

With honeft Labor earn your Bread,
  While in your youthful Prime;
Nor come you near the Harlot's Bed,
  Nor idly wafte your Time.

V.

Nor meddle with another's Wealth,
  In a defrauding Way:
A Curfe is with what's got by ftealth,
  Which makes your Life a Prey.

VI.

Shun Things that feem but little Sins,
  For they lead on to great;
From Sporting many Times begins
  Ill Blood, and poifonous Hate.

VII.

The Sabbath-Day do not prophane,
  By wickednefs and Plays;
By needlefs Walking Streets or Lanes
  Upon fuch Holy days.

VIII.

To you that have the care of Youth,
  Parents and Mafters too,
Teach them betimes to know the Truth,
  And Righteoufnefs to do.

IX.

The dreadful Deed for which I die,
  Arofe from fmall Beginning;
My Idlenefs brought poverty,
  And fo I took to Stealing.

X.

Thus I went on in finning faft,
  And tho' I'm young 'tis true,
I'm old in Sin, but catcht at laft,
  And here receive my due.

XI.

Alas for my unhappy Fall,
  The Rigs that I have run!
Juftice aloud for vengeance calls,
  Hang him for what he's done.

XII.

O may it have fome good Effect,
  And warn each wicked one,
That they God's righteous Laws refpect,
  And Sinful Courfes Shun.

houses; in the 1730s women led protests to get the public markets abolished, culminating in a riot in 1737.

Private actions, such as a creditor's efforts to collect debts, also provoked collective resistance if they were perceived as unjust. In 1719 a sheriff trying to serve a writ, or legal order, at a house in Exeter, New Hampshire, was blocked by a crowd of neighbors. When he returned with reinforcements, he found the house defended by thirty or forty men. The notion that crowd action could be justified despite being outside the law was strong. Even the Massachusetts chief justice and lieutenant-governor Thomas Hutchinson observed that "Mobs, a sort of them at least, are constitutional."

Rioters often made their point with more than just force or weight of numbers. Like Pope's Day celebrants or participants in mock elections, they employed ritual to symbolize their cause, or to ridicule or invert the social order against which they were protesting. Rioters paraded effigies of their targets, or conducted mock trials or funerals. Men blackened their faces or disguised themselves as women. Of the men defending the house in Exeter in 1719, many were reported to be blacked up or dressed in women's clothing. Some of the Boston market rioters of 1737 blacked their faces, or dressed as ministers to parody a clergyman who had supported the market reforms.

Crowd actions in some ways merely extended other avenues by which ordinary people — men in particular — could take part in northern public life. Militia units, sheriff's posses, and volunteer fire companies were other vehicles for popular public involvement. So were the craft societies that began to be formed. The "Carpenters' Company" founded by Philadelphia builders in 1724 began as a friendly society to assist members in difficulty. But similar organizations began to regulate prices, to decide who could enter the trade, and to set the rules for apprenticeship. Organizations set up for one purpose branched into others. By 1760 a Philadelphian whose house caught fire had a choice of companies to put out the blaze, including the Hibernia Fire Company, whose members were all Irish, and the Cordwainers' Fire Company, made up exclusively of shoemakers.

There was popular involvement in politics, too. In New England town meetings, participants could discuss whatever issues they chose. Several times in eighteenth-century Boston, popular efforts prevented the town meeting from becoming a preserve of the wealthy and privileged. After 1718, the physician Elisha Cooke, Jr., emerged as an advocate of popular interests in Boston politics. He helped form the Boston Caucus to represent artisans and small shopkeepers in the town meeting, backed policies to promote local manufacturing, and helped mobilize opposition to market reforms in the 1730s. At Cooke's death in 1733, the Massachusetts governor tacitly acknowledged his success at being a thorn in the side of privilege, referring to him as "the late . . . head of the scum." After 1750, however, Boston's economic decline put popular participation at risk by sinking many men below the property qualification for voting.

In Philadelphia and New York, assembly elections could be raucous, even violent affairs, with candidates treating the voters to strong drink, and the air filled with brickbats and heated words. New York had no town meeting, but public life there was more open than in any other city. It had the highest proportion of men able to vote, and laboring men were a powerful presence at elections. Handbills signed "Jack Bowline and Tom Hatchway" or "Mr. Axe and Mr. Hammer" were printed and distributed by men drawing attention to their trades. Unlike voters in Philadelphia or Boston, New Yorkers often elected workingmen to city office. Fully thirty percent of the councilmen chosen in New York in the early 1760s were artisans — three times the proportion in Boston.

The tone of political life in the three major cities, as in the separate northern colonies, differed, but the basic facts were similar. Workingmen found themselves neither wholly in nor wholly out of the political arena. They might be courted at election time by popular politicians like Cooke, or even by rich men like New York's Morrises, DeLanceys, and Livingstons. They made their voices heard in "Mobs, Bonfires, . . . Huzzas," and in their parades that often accompanied elections. A politician who scorned the popular element, such as Boston's Thomas Hutchinson, might find himself despised. "Let it burn," a crowd shouted when Hutchinson's house caught fire in 1750. More prudent political leaders let it be known that they would find it "an honour to receive a visit from the meanest freeholder, nay condescend to shake hands with the dirtiest mechanic in the country." Public power remained a privilege of elites, but popular politics was becoming more important.

Growing Tension: Northern Colonies in the Mid Eighteenth Century

By 1760 the northern colonies were mature societies, with rapidly growing populations. The astute Benjamin Franklin observed that the number of Americans was doubling every twenty-five years, and he took this as a sure sign of America's rising glory. Two of the great ports in particular, New York and Philadelphia, grew increasingly prosperous as international and domestic trade increased dramatically in midcentury.

A colonial elite of landlords, lawyers, and merchants had emerged and was busily consolidating its power. Its members treated themselves to

Estimated Population of the British American Colonies, 1720–1760

Year	Race	New England Colonies	Middle Colonies	Southern Colonies
1720	White	166,937	92,259	138,110
	Black	3,956	10,825	54,098
1730	White	211,233	135,298	191,893
	Black	6,118	11,683	73,220
1740	White	281,163	204,093	270,283
	Black	8,541	16,452	125,031
1750	White	349,029	275,723	309,588
	Black	10,982	20,736	204,702
1760	White	436,917	398,855	432,047
	Black	12,717	29,049	284,040

New England Colonies   New Hampshire, Massachusetts, Rhode Island, and Connecticut
Middle Colonies   New York, New Jersey, Pennsylvania, and Delaware
Southern Colonies   Maryland, Virginia, North Carolina, South Carolina, and (after 1740) Georgia

Source: *The American Colonies* by R. C. Simmons. Copyright © 1976 by R. C. Simmons. Reprinted by permission of Harold Matson Company, Inc.

elegant houses, fine furniture, and imported carriages. The new colleges they founded—Princeton, Brown, the College of Philadelphia, King's College in New York—joined Harvard and Yale as places at which to educate their sons. Colonial writers praised America as a good place to live, and Europeans responded by migrating there in larger numbers.

But maturity brought poverty and conflict as well as prosperity. War was part of the problem. Since the 1680s a great struggle had been under way between England and France for mastery of the Atlantic world. American colonists, especially northerners, found themselves repeatedly embroiled in it. Four major wars occupied no less than forty-one of the seventy-five years from 1689 to 1763. Farmers' sons and workingmen fought in all of them, but their involvement grew over time. In the French and Indian War that began in 1754, one-third of all Massachusetts men of fighting age served in the military. Some folks perceived that wartime suffering was not shared equally, that some grew rich—or even richer—in war years, and that some of the achievements of the elite were at the expense of working people.

Population growth and the emergence of an increasingly commercial way of life were also sources of tension. In eastern New England, population densities neared English levels, and the agricultural system could not support all the inhabitants. Farming techniques had never been especially efficient, and, except for places like the Connecticut Valley, the soil was stony and thin. New Englanders found that, unlike their parents and grandparents, many had no prospect of living their lives in the places where they had been born. The tiny, worn-out farms some would inherit would not permit it. Many had not even an exhausted plot of land to call their own. Laborers without property or regular work, male and female servants seeking employment, all swelled the slowly rising numbers of the "strolling poor."

New Englanders opened up new town sites in the Massachusetts and Connecticut highlands, and trekked northward to New Hampshire and northeastward into Maine. They wandered into an ill-defined region, claimed by both New Hampshire and New York, which lay between the upper Connecticut Valley and Lake George and Lake Champlain. Moving helped solve some of their problems, for they found land in abundance. But migration created new problems, too—disputes over control of newly settled land and conflict with the natives already living there.

From the second quarter of the eighteenth century, rigid patriarchal controls over women and children were also starting to weaken. In longer-settled regions, such as eastern Massachusetts and the outskirts of Philadelphia, few household heads now controlled enough land to promise farms for all their sons. Young men had to turn to other occupations than their fathers' to seek their livelihoods. This led many young people to challenge their parents' authority.

Parents, for instance, expected to control their children's choice of marriage partners, but many sons and daughters circumvented them and chose for themselves. In Pennsylvania and elsewhere, a growing number of young Quakers were "disowned" by the sect for marrying outside it. In Massachusetts by the 1720s and 1730s, between one-third and one-half of brides were pregnant at marriage, almost always by the prospective husband, obliging parents to accept spouses of whom they would otherwise have disapproved. Where land remained available, or where families had moved to provide farms for their sons, this trend was less apparent. When western Massachusetts households ran short of land by the early eighteenth century, they moved into unsettled areas of eastern Connecticut. Rates of premarital pregnancy in both regions remained lower than those in the more crowded parts of eastern Massachusetts.

Whether they moved or stayed, New Englanders found that the quality of life was changing around them. In the seventeenth century and the early decades of the eighteenth, they had established and conducted their town meetings on the premise that consensus was valued above all else. But now the meetings grew contentious, even bitter. Selectmen who had held office for years, even decades, were unseated. Hamlets remote from village centers petitioned colonial assemblies to be made towns in their own right.

Social tensions were among both the causes and effects of the northward spread of the Great Awakening, the evangelical religious fervor that swept like a firestorm from Georgia to New Hampshire in the late 1730s and early 1740s. Most strongly affected by the Awakening was New England. One of the Awakening's key figures was Jonathan Edwards, pastor of Northampton, Massachusetts, whose sermon "Sinners in the Hands of an

---

"There Was a Great Multitude . . . Assembled Together"

This account by a Connecticut farmer, Nathan Cole, captures the spiritual frenzy of the Great Awakening, as thousands flocked to hear the preaching of the English evangelical preacher George Whitefield in 1740. Cole and his wife, riding double, dashed twelve miles on their horse in little more than an hour to join the throng gathered at Middletown.

Now it pleased God to send Mr. Whitefield into this land; and my hearing of his preaching at Philadelphia, like one of the old apostles, and many thousands flocking to hear him preach the Gospel, and great numbers were converted to Christ. I felt the Spirit of God drawing me by conviction; I longed to see and hear him and wished he would come this way. . . .

Then on a sudden, in the morning about 8 or 9 of the clock there came a messenger and said Mr. Whitefield preached at Hartford and Wethersfield yesterday and is to preach at Middletown this morning at ten of the clock. I was in my field at work. I dropped my tool that I had in my hand and ran home to my wife, telling her to make ready quickly to go and hear Mr. Whitefield preach at Middletown, then ran to my pasture for my horse with all my might, fearing that I should be too late. . . .

When we got to Middletown old meeting house, there was a great multitude, it was said to be 3 or 4,000 of people, assembled together. We dismounted and shook off our dust, and the ministers were then coming to the meeting house. I turned and looked towards the Great River and saw the ferry boats running swift backward and forward bringing over loads of people, and the oars rowed nimble and quick. Everything, men, horses, and boats seemed to be struggling for life. The land and banks over the river looked black with people and horses; all along the 12 miles I saw no man at work in his field, but all seemed to be gone. When I saw Mr. Whitefield come upon the scaffold, he looked almost angelical; a young, slim, slender youth, before some thousands of people with a bold undaunted countenance. And my hearing how God was with him everywhere as he came along, it solemnized my mind and put me into a trembling fear before he began to preach; for he looked as if he was clothed with authority from the Great God, and a sweet solemn solemnity sat upon his brow, and my hearing him preach gave me a heart wound. By God's blessing, my old foundation was broken up, and I saw that my righteousness would not save me.

Source: Karen Ordahl Kupperman, ed., *Major Problems in American Colonial History* (1993).

Angry God" remains one of the masterpieces of American preaching. Edwards, along with such men as the Englishman George Whitefield and the Americans Gilbert Tennent and James Davenport, abandoned the dry, logical, rationalistic arguments of the traditional Puritan sermon style and reached straight for the heart. Their message was simple: only sinners who cast themselves on God's mercy would be saved. This message was particularly appealing to people whose communities were undergoing upheaval, and who were conscious that they might not measure up to the standards of an earlier generation.

The Great Awakening questioned the assumptions of orthodox Congregationalism. Preachers and worshippers influenced by the revival challenged the authority of their established ministers. Though Edwards was pastor to his own congregation until it fired him, Whitefield, Tennent, Davenport and others were "itinerants," who traveled from place to place to preach. Their audiences could be huge. Whitefield's last appearance in Boston in 1740 was before a crowd of 20,000 on the Common. Where itinerants went, disruption often followed. Connecticut passed a law against wandering preachers, and a number of them were jailed.

Tennent, Davenport, and others began to recapture the visions of equality that had seized the poor of England during the Civil War a century earlier. Their sermons began to address contentious political and economic questions, especially whether Massachusetts should set up a land bank, which would serve ordinary people, or a silver bank which would serve the rich. Men without formal religious training became exhorters and preachers; in some cases women also did so. Antirevivalist ministers were outraged at the challenge that the Awakening posed to their position. The minister of Salem, Massachusetts, complained in 1742 that Richard Ewins, a local baker, preached "every Thursday, and tho' a fellow of consummate ignorance is nevertheless followed by great multitudes."

Churches split. New denominations like the Baptists began to grow, challenging the established Congregational churches. Church separations exacerbated the divisions within towns and spurred migration to new regions. Ewins, the baker-preacher from Salem, moved to the Maine coast with some of his followers and set up a church there in 1744. Groups setting up Baptist and other separate churches migrated to the Maine, New Hampshire, and New York frontiers in the 1750s.

Yet even as tensions spread in the northern colonies, the colonies themselves continued to expand. Population and trade grew. Pressure to occupy more land for farm settlements remained strong. Traders, farmers, and artisans with control of their own property and households valued their personal independence and their "English liberties." They carefully guarded their freehold rights. They sought obedience and respect from the dependents in their own households, and this helped preserve

their deference for officials and colonial rulers. But this public deference was conditional upon the recognition of their own rights and interests. As prosperity and inequality grew in the eighteenth century, challenges to authority became more common. In politics, in their churches, in direct action to uphold what they saw as just, ordinary people had started to make their influence felt.

The 1750s would bring renewed war between Britain and France, the climax of their long rivalry for empire in North America. The war would tie the people of the colonies more closely than ever before to the web of British colonial interests, but it would also intensify the inequalities and disputes that had been growing in colonial life. People already used to challenging others' power would start to question the very nature of their colonies' connections with Britain. Ordinary people and popular politics would play a crucial part in the crisis that ensued.

"Baptism on the Schuylkill." The frontispiece to *Materials Towards a History of the American Baptists,* published in Philadelphia in 1770, showed the ritual immersion of adults baptized into the church.

Source: (James Smithers) Morgan Edwards, *Materials Towards a History of the American Baptists,* I (1770)— Library Company of Philadelphia.

The Years in Review

1637

- Massachusetts Bay Colony banishes Anne Hutchinson for religious heresy.

1638

- Swedish settlers of Delaware erect the first log cabin—the building form that came from Finland.

1642

- First B.A. degree awarded in North America at Harvard College.

1643

- Indians kill Anne Hutchinson and Puritans rejoice.

1647

- Believing that smoking in groups leads to dissipation, Connecticut passes a law which only allows people to smoke in their own homes.

1648

- Massachusetts Bay Colony authorizes shoemakers to create first labor organization in America.

1649

- English Civil War results in arrest and beheading of King Charles I by parliamentary forces; England becomes a republic under Oliver Cromwell.

1652

- Residents of New Netherland begin playing a kind of miniature golf, using a small ball and a crooked club.

1653

- Dutch colonists in Nieuw Amsterdam build a wall across Manhattan to stop English attacks; later becomes the source of the name "Wall Street."

1658

- Oliver Cromwell dies.

1660

- Charles II restores English monarchy.
- A Massachusetts law forbids the celebration of Christmas.
- Mary Dyer, a Quaker, is hanged after she defies courts by trying to preach in Boston.

1664

- New Netherland captured by English, renamed New York.

- New Jersey chartered.
- Horse racing becomes the first organized sport in America with the opening of Newmarket Course on Long Island.

1670

- First American coffee house opens in Boston.

1675

- King Philip's War: Mohawk Indians led by Metacom (called "King Philip") attack English settlements in New England in an effort to reclaim their land; one-tenth of adult white male population is captured or killed, but colonial forces ultimately triumph.

1680

- New Hampshire chartered.

1681

- William Penn founds colony of Pennsylvania.

1684

- Massachusetts' charter suspended; the next year Massachusetts is placed with Plymouth, Maine, and New Hampshire in a united "Dominion of New England."

1685

- King James II succeeds to the English throne; he is suspected of autocratic designs and Catholic sympathies.

1688

- Glorious Revolution: Parliament removes James II from the throne and replaces him with a new Protestant king, William III.

1689

- Leisler's Rebellion: During the upheaval caused by the Glorious Revolution, Jacob Leisler declares himself governor of New York. His authority is strongly resisted in New York and he is executed for treason in 1691.

1691

- Massachusetts receives new colonial charter, which ends Puritan autonomy but restores elected assembly.

1692

- Salem witchcraft trials result in hanging of nineteen alleged witches, fourteen of them women.

1699

- In effort to restrain colonial manufacturing, England bans the export of woolen goods from colonies.

1700

- Massachusetts orders all Roman Catholic priests out of the colony within three months.

1704

- Indian raid on Deerfield, Massachusetts, leads to death or capture of dozens of whites and discourages frontier expansion.

1705

- Thomas Odell is arrested in Boston for counterfeiting; this new crime emerges along with paper money.
- Massachusetts outlaws intermarriage between blacks and whites; law is not repealed until 1843.

1712

- Twenty New York slaves light a blaze and then fire on a group of whites who try to put it out; in aftermath, nineteen convicted slaves are hanged or burned alive.

1719

- America's first streetlight (a single lantern in Boston) is sign of growth of towns in the New World.

1739

- Ben Franklin's *Poor Richard's Almanack* declares: "He that falls in love with himself will have no rivals."

1740

- Great Awakening, a wave of evangelical religious fervor, sweeps over the American colonies in late 1730s and early 1740s.

1741

- New York slaves are accused of arson and theft, and of conspiracy to kill whites; eighteen blacks are hanged or burned to death.
- Jonathan Edwards preaches his famous sermon, "Sinners in the Hands of an Angry God" at Enfield, Connecticut.

1752

- Ben Franklin flies a kite and proves that lightning is a form of electricity.

1776

- Adam Smith's *The Wealth of Nations* makes arguments for a free market.

Suggested Readings

Anderson, Virginia deJohn, *New England's Generation: The Great Migration and the Formation of Society and Culture in the Seventeenth Century* (1991).

Bailyn, Bernard, and Philip D. Morgan eds., *Strangers within the Realm: Cultural Margins of the First British Empire* (1991).

Berlin, Ira, *Many Thousands Gone: The First Two Centuries of Slavery in North America* (1998).

Bolster, W. Jeffrey, *Black Jacks: African American Seamen in the Age of Sail* (1997).

Burrows, Edwin G., and Mike Wallace, *Gotham: A History of New York City to 1898* (1999).

Bushman, Richard L., *The Refinement of America: Persons, Houses, Cities* (1992).

Calloway, Colin G., *New Worlds for All: Indians, Europeans, and the Remaking of Early America* (1997).

Cressy, David, *Coming Over: Migration and Communication between England and New England in the Seventeenth Century* (1987).

Dayton, Cornelia H., *Women before the Bar: Gender, Law, and Society in Connecticut* (1995).

Demos, John, *The Unredeemed Captive: A Family Story from Early America* (1994).

Fischer, David Hackett, *Albion's Seed: Four British Folkways in America* (1989).

Gildrie, Richard P., *The Profane, the Civil, and the Godly: The Reformation of Manners in Orthodox New England, 1679–1749* (1994).

Innes, Stephen, *Labor in a New Land: Economy and Society in Seventeenth Century Springfield* (1983).

Kamensky, Jane, *Governing the Tongue: The Politics of Speech in Early New England* (1997).

Karlsen, Carol F., *The Devil in the Shape of a Woman: Witchcraft in Colonial New England* (1987).

Lambert, Frank, *"Pedlar in Divinity": George Whitefield and the Transatlantic Revivals* (1994).

Lemon, James T., *The Best Poor Man's Country: A Geographical Study of Early Southeastern Pennsylvania* (1972).

Lepore, Jill, *The Name of War: King Philip's War and the Origin of American Identity* (1998).

Levy, Barry, *Quakers and the American Family: British Settlement in the Delaware Valley* (1988).

Mancall, Peter C., *Valley of Opportunity: Economic Culture along the Upper Susquehanna* (1991).

Matson, Cathy, *Merchants and Empire: Trading in Colonial New York* (1998).

Merwick, Donna, *Possessing Albany, 1630–1710: The Dutch and English Experiences* (1990).

Nash, Gary B., *The Urban Crucible: Social Change, Political Consciousness, and the Origins of the American Revolution* (1979).

Norton, Mary Beth, *Founding Mothers and Fathers: Gendered Power and the Forming of American Society* (1996).

Rediker, Marcus, *Between the Devil and the Deep Blue Sea: Merchant Seamen, Pirates, and the Anglo-American Maritime World, 1700–1750* (1987).

Reis, Elizabeth, *Damned Women: Sinners and Witches in Puritan New England* (1997).

Richter, Daniel K., *The Ordeal of the Longhouse: The Peoples of the Iroquois League in the Era of European Colonization* (1992).

Roeber, A. G., *Palatines, Liberty, and Property: German Lutherans in Colonial British America* (1993).

Steele, Ian K., *Warpaths: Invasions of North America* (1994).

Ulrich, Laurel Thatcher, *Good Wives: Image and Reality in the Lives of Women in Northern New England, 1650–1750* (1982).

Vickers, Daniel, *Farmers and Fishermen: Two Centuries of Work in Essex County, Massachusetts, 1630–1830* (1994).

Wall, Helena M., *Fierce Communion: Family and Community in Early America* (1990).

And on the World Wide Web

Colonial Williamsburg Foundation, *Historical Almanack:* (http://www.history.org/almanack.htm)

DoHistory, *Martha Ballard's Diary Online* (http://www.dohistory.org/)

Toward Revolution
1750–1776

George Robert Twelves Hewes was born in Boston in 1742. His father, who had come from a country town nearby, had been sent to Boston "to learn a mechanical trade" because his family lacked the means to support him. However, the elder Hewes did not prosper, so when George was fourteen he had to apprentice himself to any artisan who would take him on. He became a shoemaker. Although he eventually obtained his own shop, in the Boston of the 1760s he could make only a meager living. He even went on fishing voyages to supplement his income. By 1771 he was living in lodgings with his wife and children, and owned no taxable property. Elsewhere in town, Jane Mecom struggled to raise her children and earned money by making soap and selling clothes. She, too, was from an artisan family. Unlike Hewes, however, she was able to get help from a successful brother, Benjamin Franklin, the printer who had left Boston to find his fortune in Philadelphia. Hewes's and Mecom's paths may never have crossed. But in the 1770s, like thousands of other working men and women, they were both drawn into the shattering events of the American Revolution and the colonies' pursuit of independence from Britain.

Neither Hewes nor Mecom was prominent (although at the end of his long life Hewes would be fêted as one of the last survivors of the revolutionary generation). Fame was reserved for the political and military leaders who were honored as the founding fathers of a new nation. But the Revolution could not have begun, nor independence been achieved, without the actions and sacrifices of countless ordinary American colonists.

By the middle of the eighteenth century, the British colonies in North America were achieving social and political maturity. The seaboard regions were no longer harsh frontier settlements: they sported well-settled farming and plantation districts and burgeoning port towns, with established social and political networks and institutions. The population was growing fast. In New England, immigration was low, so a high birth rate and good life expectancy accounted for most of its growth. Elsewhere, the arrival of European settlers and the forced importation of African slaves contributed to population increase. Such rapid growth led Benjamin Franklin and a few other colonists to predict that within a century America, not the British Isles, would be the center of the British empire.

To Britain, the North American colonies were economically important, a stable and prosperous portion of an expanding empire. Their shipping,

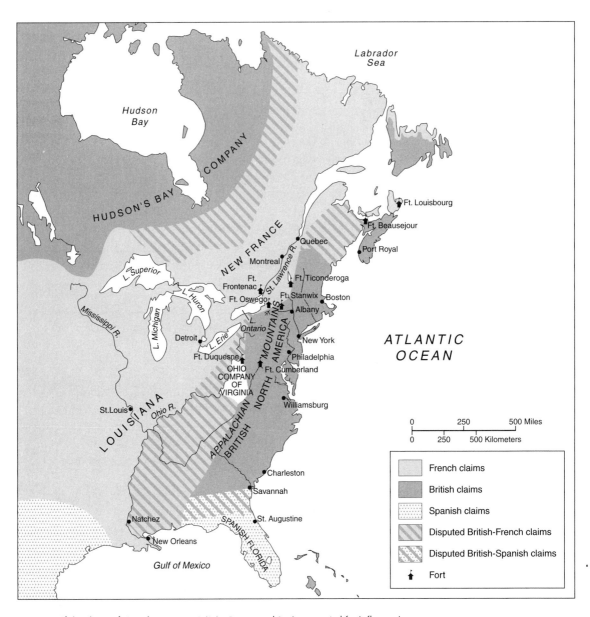

European Claims in North America, c. 1750. Britain, France, and Spain competed for influence in North America, each laying claim to vast areas of land, and seeking alliances with the American Indians who occupied most of it to secure their positions. The Indians, for their part, played the Europeans against one another, as part of a strategy for holding on to their territories. Note the comparatively small area occupied by the thirteen colonies of mainland British North America.

their agricultural exports (rice and indigo from the Carolinas, tobacco from Virginia, wheat from the middle colonies), their demand for manufactured goods, and their imports of African slaves all contributed to a steadily growing Atlantic economy. After 1750, Britain's trade with North America exceeded that with its Caribbean sugar colonies. By the 1770s the Americas would contribute two-fifths of Britain's total overseas trade.

The mainland colonies also gave Britain a strong foothold on the North American continent with which to pursue rivalries with other European powers. In the war fought between 1754 and 1763, known in North America as the French and Indian War, Britain used this foothold successfully to extend its influence. With active help from the colonies and Native American allies such as the Iroquois, British forces conquered New France, driving the French out of Canada and establishing control over much of the eastern part of the continent. It was a triumph that, with other gains in the Atlantic and Indian Oceans, consolidated what is often called the "First British Empire."

Yet within little more than a decade, Britain's hopes of power in North America were shattered. In 1775, thirteen of the American colonies rose in rebellion against British rule and joined together in another war, this time to achieve their independence. How did Britain's American triumph turn so quickly to disaster? The story centers on two themes: the conflicts that arose in colonial society itself, and the impact on the colonies of imperial wars and policies. In a colonial society already wracked by tensions, and whose citizens were mindful of their political rights, British policies provoked increasing popular unrest and protest. When popular movements became allied with colonial elites, resistance became revolution. The goals and actions of people such as George Hewes helped to undermine Britain's rich transatlantic empire and bring into being a new, vigorous republic.

Conflict with Britain would force colonists to decide whether they were Britons who happened to live in America, or whether they were Americans separate from the mother country. A sizable minority chose to remain loyal to Britain. Many others tried to stay neutral, but could not always do so. Those who embraced independence did so for a wide array of reasons. The Revolution was not a single movement, but a series of coalitions that formed, dissolved, and re-formed in the heat of events.

Why Were the Thirteen Colonies Primed for Rebellion?

When, in 1776, the people of the thirteen colonies declared independence from Britain and formed the United States, they transformed both the history and the geography of North America. As the United

States secured its independence, grew, and prospered, its presence on the map would come to seem inevitable. But to most people in the middle of the eighteenth century, the union of Britain's North American colonies into a single nation would have seemed almost inconceivable. The colonies that would later form the United States were all separate. There was no unity between them, or institutions to foster it: Benjamin Franklin's Albany Plan of 1754, which proposed a colonial union to conduct defense and Indian affairs, came to nothing. There were many contrasts between the colonies, and many sources of dispute. Most had closer, more regular ties with Britain than they had with each other, and to leading colonists the British connection seemed largely beneficial. Moreover, they were only thirteen among dozens of colonies—belonging to Britain, Spain, France, or other European countries—strung out across the Americas and the Caribbean. Why did these colonies in particular, and not the others, come to rebel against European rule in the 1760s and 1770s?

The answer to that question lies in the varied character of colonial societies and economies, and in the different relationships these societies had with their mother countries in Europe. Although there were many contrasts among them, the thirteen colonies that rebelled did have things in common—characteristics that they shared with no other New World colonies at the time. By the mid eighteenth century they displayed simultaneously several traits that other settlements in the Americas shared only partly, or not at all.

The thirteen colonies were successful centers of European settlement and economic activity. British policy had permitted virtually unlimited immigration to the American colonies. Many people from the British Isles and parts of Germany, pressed by population growth, agricultural change, and political events, had taken the risk of resettling there. The thirteen colonies had their own political institutions, and they had ruling groups whose homes were in America, rather than in Europe. Since the late seventeenth century, British governments had largely left these colonies to their own devices and relatively free of political direction or interference from the mother country. Political liberty and colonial expansion were connected. According to South Carolina's Christopher Gadsden, the colonists proudly shared the "natural liberties of British subjects." Without these, "no free men would have ever thought of coming to America" and "the sons of Britain would have been . . . very thinly scattered on this side of the Atlantic."

A brief look around the mid-eighteenth-century Americas demonstrates the thirteen colonies' distinctiveness. Spain's empire remained under central control and Spanish colonial governors were expected to follow instructions from the royal Council of the Indies in Seville. Although

"How Blest Is That Interpreter of Laws." Colonists' pride in the institution of the law was demonstrated by this woodcut depicting a courtroom scene (with the presiding judge seated on the right). An accompanying poem celebrated the impartiality of the colonial court system:

How blest is that INTERPRETER OF LAWS
Who rich and Poor make equal in a Cause!
Who dares with steady hand the Balance hold,
And ne'er inclines it to one Side for Gold.

Source: Prints and Photographs Division, Library of Congress.

distance often enabled governors to adapt or ignore their orders ("I obey, but I do not comply" was the legendary evasion), autonomous political institutions were weak or nonexistent in the Spanish colonies. Ruling groups remained divided between colonial-born creoles and Spanish-born *peninsulares.* Most prominent merchants were based in Spain, unlike many leading traders in British North American ports, who were colonials.

To Spanish administrators, the North American provinces still seemed peripheral to their main possessions in Central and South America and the Caribbean. Forced by defeat to give up some territory at the peace negotiations of 1763, they let Florida pass into British control. Nevertheless, Spain took over French Louisiana in the same year, and in 1769 began to establish missions and military settlements on the coast of California. Neither of these new possessions, however, nor the older Spanish provinces of New Mexico or Texas, attracted large numbers of settlers. Spain's government in Louisiana soon faced a rebellion by French inhabitants, which it suppressed by calling in a Spanish occupation force. None of the Spanish colonies was yet ripe for rebellion against Spain itself.

French colonies, similarly, lacked the conditions for political independence. The one settler society, Quebec, had a small mercantile and landed elite, but little political autonomy. Elsewhere, across the Great Lakes and down the Mississippi Valley, France had built notable missionary and trading networks, but except at the port of New Orleans there was no settler society or basis for a political culture. After France lost its American territories during the war of 1754–1763, most French inhabitants came under foreign control, but no independence movements resulted. While Spain ruthlessly put down rebels in Louisiana, the British occupiers of Quebec pursued policies designed to avoid revolt among their new French Canadian subjects.

Preconditions for political independence were also scarce in British America outside the thirteen colonies. Newfoundland remained a colony of fishing outposts, with little political cohesion. Nova Scotia was only recently and sparsely settled. Many of Britain's Caribbean island possessions, however, were well populated. The largest, Jamaica, had its own provincial assembly that, like those in North America, was often in dispute with the government in London. Even so, there was little chance that Jamaica or other island colonies would rebel against British rule. White elites in the Caribbean were much more closely tied to Britain than those on the mainland. Unlike planters in the Chesapeake or the Carolinas, many wealthy Caribbean planters lived in England and had relatives or agents manage their plantations. The vast majority (ninety percent, in some cases) of the sugar islands' populations were African slaves. In economies dominated by sugar plantations, there was little land or activity to sustain individual farmers, artisans, or laborers, so the islands attracted few European settlers. Living in perpetual fear of the slave insurrections that periodically broke out, the islands' small white populations relied on British support to suppress rebellion and to keep order.

Only the thirteen British mainland colonies, then, existed under conditions that could foster a separate political identity. Locally rooted elites, significant populations of free working people, fairly autonomous political institutions, and a degree of economic diversity all contributed to the possibility of independence from Europe. But in 1750 British Americans still had little sense of separateness. Over the next quarter century, that separation would be generated first by social and political conflicts within the colonies, and then by mounting conflicts with Britain as well.

Political and Social Tensions in the Thirteen Colonies

By the mid eighteenth century, each of the British American colonies had evolved its own distinctive pattern of tensions and political disputes. In New York, factions that formed around the rival DeLancey and Livingston families competed for preeminence in the provincial legislature and city governments. In Pennsylvania, different ethnic and religious groups began

"... Stones and Brickbats"

To supply men for its navy, the British government regularly employed "press gangs" to seize colonial merchant seamen. Boston was plagued by such impressment in the 1740s; trade suffered as colonial seamen fled the port. On November 16, 1747, several hundred Boston sailors and laborers, white and black, tried to halt an impressment by taking British officers hostage. The following account is taken from a December 1, 1747, letter written by Massachusetts governor William Shirley to the Lords of Trade.

The mob now increased and joined by some inhabitants came to the Town House (just after candle light) and armed as in the morning, assaulted the Council Chamber . . . by throwing stones and brickbats in at the windows, and having broke all the windows of the lower floor . . . forcibly entered into it. . . .

In this confusion . . . the Speaker of the House and others of the Assembly pressed me much to speak two or three words to the mob . . . ; and in this parley one of the mob, an inhabitant of the town, called upon me to deliver up the Lieutenant of the *Lark,* which I refused to do; after which among other things, he demanded of me why a boy, one Warren now under sentence of death in jail for being [involved] in a press gang which killed two sailors in this town in the act of impressing, was not executed; and I acquainted 'em his execution was suspended by his Majesty's order till his pleasure shall be known upon it; whereupon the same person, who was the mob's spokesman, asked me "if I did not remember Porteous's case who was hanged upon a sign post in Edinburgh." I told 'em very well, and that I hoped they remembered what the consequence of that proceeding was to the inhabitants of the city; after which I thought it high time to make an end of parleying with the mob, and retired into the Council Chamber. . . .

In the evening the mob forcibly searched the Navy Hospital upon the Town Common in order to let out what seamen they could find there belonging to the King's ships; and [searched] seven or eight private houses for [British] officers, and took four or five petty officers; but soon released 'em without any ill usage . . . their chief intent appearing to be, from the beginning, not to use the officers ill any otherwise than by detaining 'em, in hopes of obliging [British commodore Charles] Knowles to give up the impressed men.

Source: Charles Henry Lincoln, ed., *Correspondence of William Shirley* (1912).

to challenge the political dominance of Quakers and of the colony's proprietors. In Virginia, the popular evangelism of the Great Awakening produced social and political challenges to the Anglican gentry. In New England, too, the Great Awakening fueled controversy. New Light ministers and their congregations attacked established Old Light control of pulpits and town affairs, breaking the tradition of consensus in town government that had been built up since the seventeenth century.

In many port towns, disputes over markets and bread prices, the forced impressment of seamen into service with the Royal Navy, trade fluctuations, and relief for the poor provoked heated debate, even riots. The interests of town-based merchants clashed with those of the farmers and planters who formed the majority of colonial populations. Massachusetts, for instance, was divided in 1740–1741 by conflict over the establishment of a land bank, a scheme to issue paper currency backed by the mortgages on farmland. The proposal was favorable to many farmers and other working people because it promised to ease the payment of debts, and it had supporters in five out of six towns in the colony. Urban merchants, however, opposed the scheme because they preferred being paid in silver or gold, and they used their influence with the colonial governor to have the land bank defeated. Rural taverns across Massachusetts buzzed with pro-bank sentiments and rumors of protest, although no direct action to revive the land bank scheme materialized. Yet Massachusetts farmers remained wary of potential threats to their freehold system of property ownership, and protective of the local institutions, including town meetings, that guaranteed them a degree of self-government.

Land Rioters and Demands for Freehold Rights

The land bank dispute did not lead to violent confrontation, but various causes did spark protests and rioting across the countryside from northern New England to South Carolina in the last decades of the colonial period. Aspirations for freehold land and self-government were significant features of these movements. Because the colonies were predominantly rural, these upheavals often had broad political implications.

In several areas—for example, New Jersey and New York's Hudson River valley—conflict arose between large landholders and the claims of tenant farmers. Small farmers, who believed they had the right to freeholds of their own, confronted landowners who, as one protester put it, wanted to lord it over "amiable and innocent tenants." Landlords' claims to vast tracts of land enjoyed the authority of the Crown and the law. Against this, small farmers asserted a moral right to secure ownership of land they themselves had cleared and improved.

New Jersey witnessed a long-running campaign against the "East Jersey Proprietors," who, on the basis of a seventeenth-century grant from the Duke of York, claimed for themselves a huge area around present-day Newark. The proprietors tried to collect overdue rent from farmers on the land, and began evicting as squatters those who refused to pay up. Arguing that this land had been granted illegally, without the consent of the Indians who held title to it, protesting farmers released fellow squatters from jail. One prisoner, Samuel Baldwin, was rescued in 1746 by 150 men armed "with clubbs, Axes, and Crow barrs." Rioters tore down the fences and houses of people who had accepted titles from the proprietors. One Jerseyman, spoiling for a fight, was quoted in 1749 as saying he wished the authorities had "fired upon them the said Rioters, for if they

Conflicts Over Land in the Mid Eighteenth Century.

From northern New England to South Carolina, struggles over land and rights erupted between the 1740s and 1770s, as backcountry settlers fought with provincial governments, land speculators, or Indians.

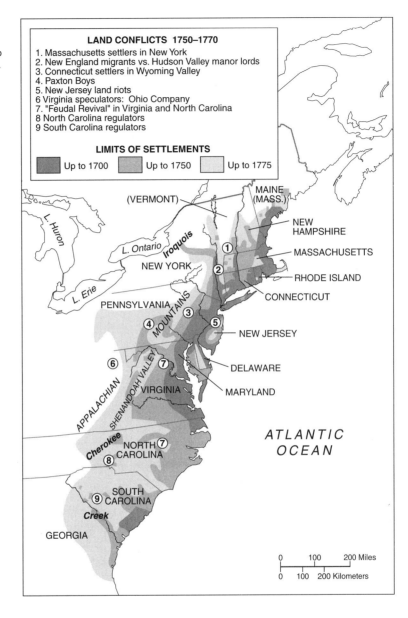

LAND CONFLICTS 1750–1770

1. Massachusetts settlers in New York
2. New England migrants vs. Hudson Valley manor lords
3. Connecticut settlers in Wyoming Valley
4. Paxton Boys
5. New Jersey land riots
6 Virginia speculators: Ohio Company
7. "Feudal Revival" in Virginia and North Carolina
8 North Carolina regulators
9 South Carolina regulators

LIMITS OF SETTLEMENTS

Up to 1700   Up to 1750   Up to 1775

had . . . [the rioters] would have destroy'd them all and drove them into the sea." Acting as though they were running their own government, land rioters collected taxes from their supporters, formed militia companies, opened courts of their own in which to try their enemies, and imprisoned those found guilty in their own jail "back in the woods."

In New York, protest focused on the great manors and estates of the Hudson River valley, some of whose landlords were raising rents and reducing tenants' entitlements. Angry tenants knew that the titles to some of these estates, most notably Livingston Manor, were fraudulent, and they challenged the very basis of landownership in the colony, seeking to demolish its quasi-feudal structure. In 1766, the valley erupted in an insurrection that spread from Manhattan to Albany, as tenants withheld rent payments, banded together against opponents, and claimed freehold title to the land that they farmed. Their leader, William Prendergast, declared that they "sought the good of the country" and that "it was hard they were not allowed to have any property." Tenants from Cortlandt Manor marched toward New York City, demanding that their landlord "give them a grant forever of his lands." Landlords, looking to their incomes from leases and rising land values, refused. "Selling," remarked Philip Livingston, "I am not fond of att all."

This Hudson Valley conflict also involved New England migrants who were settling on land adjacent to New York, including the Green Mountains. Most of these settlers took up land under titles from New Hampshire that, on the New England pattern, granted freehold ownership. But New York disputed New Hampshire's claim to the region. Settlers also knew that the boundary between New York and Massachusetts had never been fixed and that Hudson Valley landholders were eager to expand their estates eastward. They feared that if New York's claims were successful, proprietors would gain title to their farmland and turn them into tenants. In 1764, the king's Privy Council in London decided that the Green Mountains did indeed belong to New York, not New Hampshire. The holders of New Hampshire grants claimed that they had bought their land in good faith, with the intention of farming it themselves, whereas their New York rivals only sought gain by speculation.

From 1764 onward, these Green Mountain Boys waged sporadic guerrilla warfare against the New York authorities and settlers under the New York claim. Regarding New York's authority in the region as illegitimate, they declared themselves "out of the bounds of the law." Their leader, Ethan Allen, swore at a hostile New Yorker, "God Damn your Governour, Laws, King, Council, and Assembly." Like other land rioters, though, they created their own quasi-legal institutions. They established New England–style town governments and "appointed by their own authority" courts that could handle cases more equitably than those in proprietor-dominated regions. Agreeing with William Prendergast that "there was no law for poor men," they tried to provide one that would guarantee the rights of independent small farmers against the claims of the wealthy.

Conflict on the Frontier

Further south, demand for new farmland was prompted by immigration from Britain, Ireland, and Germany, as well as local population growth. Migration to the frontier produced conflict between new settlers and leaders in older regions. Settlers demanded both better political representation and government help to remove Indians from the land they wanted to occupy.

In Pennsylvania, frontier settlers—many of them Scots-Irish—encroached on the territory of tribes with whom the Quaker-dominated colonial government had usually managed to deal peacefully. Fraud and violence accompanied these encounters, making frontier life dangerous and precarious. Like Bacon's rebels in Virginia in 1676, settlers sought to kill or remove natives. In 1763, when the Pennsylvania government failed to protect them from Indian counterattacks, frontiersmen formed their own army, the Paxton Boys. Sixty men raided a settlement of Christianized Indians at Conestoga. They killed six inhabitants on the spot and later murdered fourteen more who had taken shelter in the jail at Lancaster. Two hundred and fifty of these armed frontiersmen then marched on Philadelphia, where assemblymen conceded many of their demands.

On South Carolina's frontier, farmers and slaveholding planters protested at the almost complete lack of governmental institutions in the backcountry. They were unrepresented and had no effective officers or courts to protect them, or to prosecute bandits who threatened life and property. They claimed equal rights with fellow-colonists, declaring "We are *Free-men*—British subjects—Not Born Slaves." But their appeals to the colonial assembly, which was dominated by coastal planters, fell on deaf ears. So frontiersmen took up arms, formed vigilante groups who called themselves Regulators, and seized control of the backcountry from 1767 to 1769. They hanged, whipped, or banished suspected thieves, and burned their homes. Although the leaders came from the small minority of ambitious, commercially oriented slave owners, thousands of small farmers supported them. At length the assembly responded to their grievances. In 1769 it provided for extra representatives and two new inland parishes (counties) with legal and political institutions, including the courts, jails, and sheriffs frontier settlers wanted. Having achieved their aims, the South Carolina Regulators disbanded.

In North Carolina, however, a separate Regulator movement faced a more hostile colonial government. A group of lawyers and land speculators had recently moved to the frontier, taking over local offices and accumulating large tracts of land, much as the then-new planter elite of Virginia had done a century earlier. Their arrival shut out middling and poor whites, who had previously been able to acquire land and hold political office in the backcountry, but now faced evictions, high taxes, and indebtedness, as well as excessive court fees charged by corrupt officials. From 1765 on, many of these farmers, tenants, and laborers rose in rebellion. But the government, dominated by the coastal elite, resisted them and their demands. In 1771, when hundreds of armed Regulators clashed with colonial militia at the Alamance River, twenty were killed, one hundred wounded, and the rest dispersed. Five Regulator leaders

"Have Not Your Purses Been Pillaged . . . ?"

Regulators of the North Carolina back country circulated open letters to their fellow citizens, setting forth their grievances against the ruling planters and the local men who were profiting at their expense. The following tract, written by an anonymous Regulator in September 1769, is addressed "to the INHABITANTS of the Province of North-Carolina." The tract appeals to farmers to vote for representatives of their own kind.

Dear Brethren,

Nothing is more common for Persons who look upon themselves to be injured than to resent and complain. These are sounded aloud, and plain in Proportion to the Apprehension of it. . . .

The late Commotions and crying Dissatisfactions among the common People of this Province, is not unknown nor unfelt by any thinking Person. No Person among you could be at a Loss to find out the true Cause. I dare venture to assert you all advised [as] to the Application of the Public Money; these you saw misapplied to the enriching of Individuals, or at least embezzled in some way without defraying the public Expenses. Have not your Purses been pillaged by the exorbitant and unlawful Fees taken by Officers, Clerks, &c? . . .

The Exorbitant, not to say unlawful Fees, required and assumed by Officers; the unnecessary, not to say destructive Abridgement of a Court's Jurisdiction; the enormous Encrease of the provincial Tax unnecessary; these are Evils of which no Person can be insensible, and which I doubt not has been lamented by each of you. . . .

I need not inform you that a Majority of our Assembly is composed of Lawyers, Clerks, and others in Connection with them, while by our own Voice we have excluded the Planter. . . . We have not the least Reason to expect the Good of the Farmer, and consequently of the Community, will be consulted by those who hang on Favour, or depend on the Intricacies of the Laws. . . .

But you will say, What is the Remedy against this malignant Disease?

I will venture to prescribe a sovereign one if duly applied; that is, as you have now a fit Opportunity, choose for your Representatives or Burgesses such Men as have given you the strongest Reason to believe they are truly honest: Such as are disinterested, publick spirited, who will not allow their private Advantage once to stand in Competition with the public Good. . . .

Source: William K. Boyd, ed., *Some Eighteenth Century Tracts Concerning North Carolina* (1927).

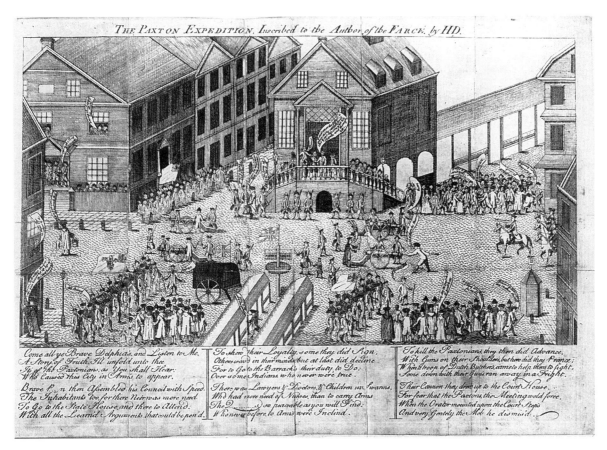

"The Paxton Expedition." A contemporary engraving satirized Quaker Philadelphia's military preparations as the Paxton Boys neared the city in 1763. An accompanying poem concluded:

To kill the Paxtonians, they then did Advance,
With Guns on their Shoulders, but how did they Prance;
When a troop of Dutch Butchers came to help them to fight,
Some down with their Guns, ran away in a Fright.

Their Cannon they drew up to the Court House,
For fear that the Paxtons the Meeting would force,
When the Orator mounted upon the Court Steps
And very Gently the Mob he dismis'd.

Source: Henry Dawkins, *The Paxton Expedition, Inscribed to the Author of the Farce, by HD,* line engraving, 1764, 13 11/16 × 7 5/16 inches—Library Company of Philadelphia.

were executed, including one summarily on the battlefield, and their movement collapsed.

Colonial governments usually directed tough measures against rural rioters, because rural rebellion posed a serious threat to them. As the Paxton Boys marched on Philadelphia, panic gripped the city and even pacifist Quakers trained to use muskets. New York's rulers sent British regular troops against the Hudson Valley rioters in 1766, suppressed their movement, and sentenced their leader, Prendergast, to death. North Carolina Regulators were enraged by a colonial law that allowed any rioter who failed to answer a court summons to be killed as an outlaw. The Green Mountain Boys similarly dubbed a New York law, which condemned eight of their leaders to death if they did not surrender, the Bloody Act, because it "destines men to awful fate, and hangs and damns without a trial."

Unlike most town riots, which were short-lived and sporadic affairs over the price of bread or similar matters, unrest and rebellion in rural and frontier areas concerned fundamental social and political issues: who would own land; how rights would be distributed and upheld; and whether society would tend toward hierarchy or equality. A recurrent theme was rural peoples' assertion of a right to self-government and to legal and political structures that would allow them to live without subservience to the wealthy and well-connected. During the 1750s and 1760s, these same themes would emerge in conflicts arising out of Britain's control over its empire. Questions of rights, freedom, and self-government would come to alter colonists' views of their relationship to Britain. When imperial and internal conflicts became entangled, and particularly when rural people became involved in disputes with Britain, the mix would prove explosive.

Britain's Imperial Triumph

During the first half of the eighteenth century, the British government rarely intervened actively in colonial business. It usually left governors and provincial assemblies to get on with things for themselves. Still, the continent's increasingly important role in overseas trade and in Britain's rivalries with other European powers meant that the British were by no means indifferent to North America. Commercial development and war caused Britain's interest in the colonies to grow.

Britain's trading regulations had, since the seventeenth century, directed colonial products in ways that best served British interests. In the eighteenth century, new regulations tried to ensure that colonial manufactured goods did not compete with those of Britain's burgeoning industrial producers. As the colonies expanded and matured, their economies became increasingly interdependent with Britain's. The southern and middle colonies exported agricultural goods, whereas the Northeast exported fish, ships, and forest products. Growing prosperity in the colonies meant increased demand for European manufactured items, as well as for capital goods to supply colonial manufacturers. Colonists with means, moreover, were purchasing increasing amounts of luxury or ornamental products: fashionable cloths and furnishings, tableware, and beverages such as tea. Indeed, such items were being consumed across a growing spectrum of colonial society.

British merchants were keen to meet colonial demand, but they were also wary of acquiring bad debts if payments were not forthcoming. Like the bigger colonial merchants, they looked askance at paper currency schemes, such as the Massachusetts Land Bank, or at currency issued by colonial governments. Twice, the British Parliament legislated against colonial paper money: a 1751 act prohibited it in New England, and the Currency Act of 1764 extended the ban to the rest of the colonies. Such laws produced little opposition by themselves, but as events unfolded, a growing number of colonists came to see them as signs that Britain was taking a dangerous interest in regulating colonial affairs.

American colonists also found themselves repeatedly embroiled in wars, not usually of their own making, for which they had to raise armies and pay taxes. Normally arising out of European concerns, these wars nevertheless involved North American territory. Because colonists took pride in their "liberties" as "freeborn Englishmen"—voting for representatives, protection from arbitrary power, common law rights such as that to trial by jury—they were often content enough to support wars against France or Spain, which they saw as "tyrannies" unblessed by such privileges. Their support for war was greatest when colonial and British ambitions coincided. New England's Protestants, for example, enthusiastically backed campaigns against the French Catholic colonists in Quebec. In 1745, during King George's War between Britain and France, Massachusetts soldiers and seamen captured the mighty French fortress of Louisbourg, on Cape Breton Island, that controlled the entrance to the St. Lawrence River. News of the victory caused great jubilation among New Englanders, because it promised an end to their long-standing fear of their Catholic neighbors.

New England's joy later turned to dismay, however, when Britain—pursuing its own interests at peace negotiations in 1748—returned Louisbourg to the French, exchanging it for a valuable Caribbean sugar island. A few colonists began to question their subordinate relationship to Britain. In a sermon of 1750, preached in Boston on the anniversary of Charles I's execution, Rev. Jonathan Mayhew argued that obedience to rulers was required only so long as they "perform the duty of rulers, by exercising a reasonable and just authority for the good of human society." Condemning as "slavish" the prevailing doctrine of unlimited submission to government, Mayhew suggested that the public good might "make us withhold from our rulers that obedience and subjection which it would, otherwise, be our duty to render."

The peace of 1748 between Britain and France was soon broken by American events. France saw Virginia settlers and Pennsylvania traders, who were pushing west across the Appalachian mountains, as a threat to its territorial interests. When the French tried to build forts in the Ohio Valley, the British and colonial governments warned them off. In western Pennsylvania in 1754, a Virginia militia unit under a young colonel named George Washington blundered into an engagement with French troops. This encounter set off a war that would spread to Europe, India, and the Caribbean, as well as North America. By the time peace came in 1763, France's position in North America had been thoroughly undermined.

At first, however, the French were successful. When the British general Edward Braddock led an expedition in 1755 to drive them from Fort Duquesne in western Pennsylvania, the French ambushed and killed him along with much of his force. They scored other victories, too. But the British were already securing their hold on Nova Scotia in eastern Canada, and in 1755 they forcibly deported thousands of Acadians, the region's French-speaking settlers. Some were dispersed to other British colonies, but after much hardship many made their way to Louisiana, forming the nucleus of its Cajun community. From 1757 onward, the British, with colonial help, made preparations to invade French Canada itself. They retook Louisbourg, captured Quebec in 1759, and seized Montreal the following year, shattering the French hold on North America. At the peace negotiations this time, Britain chose to hold on to Canada, and France's threat to New England and the western frontier was ended. Obtaining Florida from Spain as well, Britain gained control of the continent's entire east coast.

Though the war was successful for both Britain and its American colonies, it exposed some of the disagreements between them. Colonists, for instance, disliked having British troops "quartered" (compulsorily billeted) in their homes. Small incidents, such as an attempt by British regulars in 1759 to free two comrades jailed for law breaking in New Haven, Connecticut, provoked strong resentment at "their Insults."

The Death of General Wolfe. This 1770 painting by the American-born British painter Benjamin West, showing an incident that occurred during the Battle of Quebec in September 1759, transformed the way artists depicted historical events. West portrayed the death of the commander of the English forces, Major General James Wolfe, at the height of the battle that would end in a French defeat. When the painting was exhibited it stirred great controversy because its subjects wore contemporary dress instead of the ancient Greek and Roman costumes that were usually deemed appropriate for a history painting. West confronted his critics, declaring, "The same truth that guides the pen of the historian should govern the pencil of the artist . . . if instead of the facts . . . I represent classical fictions, how shall I be understood by posterity? I want to mark the date, the place, and the parties engaged in the event." However, West's painting included men who were not with Wolfe when he died, including the lone Indian figure. No Indians fought with British forces in Quebec.

Source: Benjamin West, *The Death of General Wolfe,* 1770, oil on canvas, 60 × 84 1/2 inches— National Gallery of Canada, Ottawa; transfer from the Canadian War Memorials, 1921 (gift of the Second Duke of Westminster, Eaton Hall, Cheshire, 1918).

197

The British never regarded colonists as equals; indeed, until a change was made in 1758, all British officers were formally superior to colonial officers, regardless of rank. The British looked down upon colonial militias as less effective than their own regular soldiers, because the militias did not embody what they believed to be proper social subordination. British regulars served for long terms, and were expected to regard their service as a duty. Militiamen, by contrast, saw military service as temporary, to last no longer than the term of enlistment. Most British officers were aristocrats and gentlemen who commanded soldiers drawn from among the poor and disadvantaged. Many militia units reflected the greater democracy of New World settlements, with much less social distance between officers and men. In 1758 Governor Thomas Pownall of Massachusetts claimed that "most of these soldiers . . . are Freeholders, who pay taxes, [or] are the sons of some of our Militia colonels, and the sons of many of our Field Officers, now doing duty as Privates." Colonial soldiers were often commanded by officers who were also their neighbors. In some units they even elected their company commanders. To incredulous British officers these practices signaled unreliability, and they treated American units as mere auxiliaries. The French and Indian War left them with a poor impression of colonists' fighting capabilities.

But prejudice blinded the British to colonial military achievements that were in fact boosting Americans' sense of self-confidence. The main survivors of Braddock's defeat in 1755 were members of a Virginia militia detachment commanded by the same George Washington whose mistake the previous year had ignited hostilities. The reputation Washington gained for saving his unit would stand him well twenty years later, when the colonies chose a commander to lead their own forces against the British. Colonial soldiers took pride in their contributions to British victories. The war began to alter colonists' sense of identity. They still saw themselves primarily as belonging to their own specific provinces, but many had served alongside units from other colonies, and this fostered a sense of unity in the colonial world. Some, for the first time, began to speak of themselves as "Americans."

The Costs of War

The war spurred British political interest in the colonies, and a shift toward greater intervention in colonial affairs. The war had also been costly, and Britain looked to the colonies to foot part of the bill. The war's end, meanwhile, brought a decline in demand for military goods and services, which in turn caused suffering for many working people in the ensuing economic depression. All these things, coupled with existing social tensions in the colonies, brought about a dramatic crisis in Anglo-American relations.

None were more affected by the French defeat in North America than Indians. The war's outcome opened the prospect of renewed American westward settlement, and hence renewed pressure on Indian lands. Previously able to secure their position by playing the French and British off against each other, many native groups feared the consequences of having a single dominant European power to deal with. During the war, Native Americans from Maine to Virginia had taken the opportunity to push back white settlements. From 1760 on, the Cherokees in South Carolina had also fought to resist new encroachments on their lands. Leaders such as the Chippewa chief Minevavana told the British that "although you have conquered the French, you have not yet conquered us. These lakes, these woods and mountains . . . are our inheritance; and we will part with them to no one." By 1763, former French allies in the Ohio Valley and Great Lakes regions were mounting a concerted effort to hold off Anglo-American expansion.

Several tribes, including the Ottawas, Hurons, Shawnees, and Delawares, had switched alliances from the French to the British in 1759, hoping that the British would withdraw from lands west of the Appalachians and leave them alone. When this did not happen, the Delaware prophet Neolin called for the expulsion of "the dogs clothed in red." The Ottawa chief Pontiac led an uprising aimed at dislodging British troops from forts spread across the Great Lakes region. A "nativist" belief in the common ancestry of Indian peoples underscored the concerted action of several tribes to hold off the white invasion. But Pontiac's forces became depleted by disease and were unable to subdue the garrisons in the bigger forts, so had to abandon their campaign in 1764. Still, Pontiac's rebellion helped create conditions for a serious breakdown in relations between Britain and its colonists.

Despite Pontiac's attack, frontier settlers and land speculators quickly moved through the mountains into what would become Ohio, Kentucky, and Tennessee. The British government wanted to impose order on this movement, to secure its own influence in the region, and to end conflict between white settlers and Indians. By a proclamation in 1763, the British prohibited settlement west of a line running along the Appalachian mountains. The ban would be enforced by troops permanently stationed for the purpose.

By itself, the Proclamation Line provoked some anger in America. Frontier settlers found their land titles in question. Speculative investors in land companies (who included men such as George Washington and Benjamin Franklin) found their hopes for profit jeopardized. Calling on the traditions of the English Civil War and the Glorious Revolution of

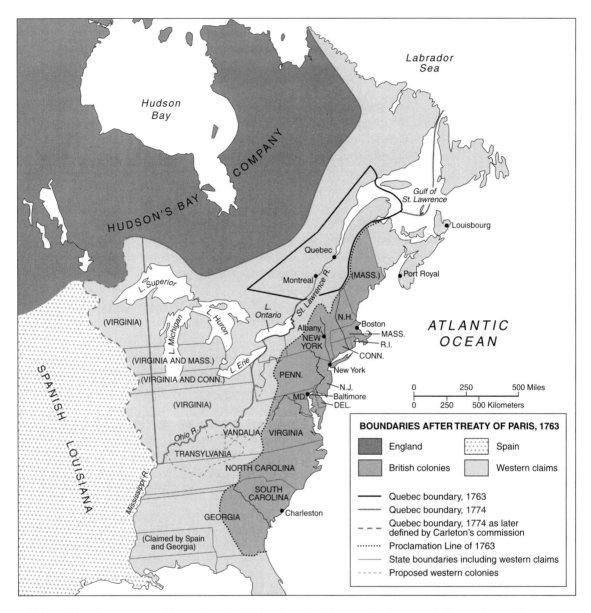

British North America, 1763–1774. This map illustrates British policy in North America after the conquest of French Canada. The Proclamation Line of 1763 limited colonial settlements west of the Appalachian Mountains, whereas the Quebec Act of 1774—passed at the same time as the Coercive Acts—fueled colonial anger by extinguishing several provinces' western land claims, extending the boundary of Quebec, and denying Quebec an elected assembly.

1688–1689, colonial pamphleteers denounced the specter of tyranny that arose from Britain's "standing army" in America. But more important, these writers saw Britain's new frontier policy as evidence that Parliament was embarking on a determined effort to make the colonies serve British interests.

The French and Indian War had benefited some colonists, particularly those in a position to profit from it. Colonial merchants who had won wartime government contracts grew very rich. In New York City, Britain's American military headquarters, Oliver DeLancey used his political connections to boost his fortune to well over 100,000 pounds, the equivalent of many millions today. Some lesser folk also prospered. Farmers found that the army needed their crops; gunsmiths made weapons; blacksmiths fashioned ironware; shipyard workers produced vessels; carpenters built barracks and fortresses; women brewers sold beer to soldiers; respectable widows provided bed and board for officers. Even wagoners and porters gained, for the army needed their carts and muscle to transport its supplies. But prosperity was not equally shared. Many saw no gain from the war, and the good fortune of some made the disparity between rich and poor more obvious. This aggravated social tensions.

As the war ended, so did the prosperity it had generated. The slump was worst in Boston, which had sunk into a period of economic stagnation that the war had only temporarily alleviated. Its population ceased to grow around 1750, and some of its trade was drawn away by other ports, especially the rapidly growing towns of Philadelphia and New York. Weakened to begin with, Boston was thrown into a severe postwar depression as work disappeared and people found themselves without ready employment. Among the worst hit were families who lost their men's wages through wartime death or injury. Almshouses filled up with new inmates, many of them women and children. Wages fell, but prices remained high, so even those who could find work were hardly better off.

Though less severely hit than Boston, New York, Philadelphia, and Charleston were also affected by the postwar slump. A New York rum seller regretted that "the Tipling Soldiery that used to help us out . . . are gone," and it was reported that the depression in the city had "reduced very many Families and poor People to great Distress." Charleston shipwrights and tanners found their work halved, while laborers faced irregular work and rising food prices. According to a verse in a 1767 New York newspaper:

> The times grow hard,
> poor people cry,
> for want of money,
> corn to buy.

The next year, journeymen tailors struck when their wages were cut. In all the port cities, the combination of inequality and hardship influenced the political events that were soon to unfold, although hard-hit Boston would play a particularly prominent role.

The French and Indian War also laid a heavy financial burden on Britain. The government of prime minister William Pitt had spent lavishly to conduct the fighting in the late 1750s. The new prime minister, George Grenville, faced enormous debts, as well as the need for more expenditures on the navy, army, and well-paid officials that were essential to keep Britain's newly expanded empire intact. Taxes in Britain had risen during the war, and Grenville's unstable administration was reluctant to raise them further. Accordingly, he looked to the American colonies to provide some of the necessary revenues.

Grenville was one of many British political leaders who reasoned that the colonists had gained most from the war. Their French enemy had been removed, and their access to furs and other trade was enhanced. Moreover, it seemed that the colonists had won these gains at little cost to themselves. The separate provinces had cooperated poorly during the war. Provincial assemblies had held back contributions of men and resources, or refused to pay governors' salaries unless they were given control of military appointments and supplies. Colonists had traded with the enemy, under flags of truce or by smuggling. The White Pine Act, intended to reserve America's best timber for the Royal Navy, had been ignored. In fact, trading regulations were so disregarded that the customs service in the colonies cost more money to run than it collected in revenue.

Unlike most other European monarchies, the British Crown could not tax or make laws without Parliament's consent. This principle lay at the heart of Britain's unwritten constitution and was celebrated as one of the safeguards of British liberties. In Grenville's view, the American colonists were, like all Britons, subject to Parliament's authority. Their own provincial assemblies were subordinate to Parliament, which alone could legislate for the general good. The general good now required that colonists start paying their own way within the empire.

Grenville and his successors discovered that colonists did not share this view, and were reluctant to comply. Parliamentary efforts to levy taxes in the colonies met with repeated resistance. Between 1765 and 1775, three major imperial crises, each more serious than the last, drew increasing numbers of people from all levels of American society into a struggle that would eventually lead to independence. Animating this struggle was a growing belief that the British intended to remove their "liberties" and subject them to the tyranny of arbitrary government — to "enslave" them, as many colonists started to say.

The Stamp Act and Townshend Duties Crises

George Grenville began his effort to increase revenues from the colonies with the Sugar Act of 1764, designed to end the notoriously inefficient enforcement of the navigation laws. Beginning in 1733 there had been a high duty imposed on molasses imported to North America from foreign colonies such as Guadeloupe or Santo Domingo, but no duty on molasses brought from British colonies such as Jamaica. Revenues suffered as merchants either smuggled foreign molasses into the colonies or bribed officials to levy only token duties. The Sugar Act imposed a new, low duty on imported molasses, making smuggling less lucrative, and provided for more customs officers to be sent to America to enforce the law. These officers would have the right to receive one-third of the value of every vessel and cargo they condemned for smuggling. Moreover, smuggling cases would be removed from local courts, whose juries were often full of the defendant's friends and neighbors, to "vice-admiralty" courts whose judge alone would render a verdict. Measures against smuggling caused some resentment, but the erosion of the entitlement to trial by jury was more serious to many colonists, who saw it as undermining their rights as "freeborn Englishmen."

Seeming to attack these rights more strongly, Grenville's next step ignited the first serious imperial crisis. In the Stamp Act of 1765 he extended to the colonies a revenue-raising measure already used in Britain: the requirement that a stamp be purchased for many documents and printed items (land titles, contracts, court documents, playing cards, books and newspapers, even advertisements). The tax had to be paid in hard currency. The money raised would remain in the colonies to pay for troops and administration, but it would be controlled by colonial governors, not the elected assemblies.

Trade laws and customs enforcement directly concerned relatively few people, but the Stamp Act provoked widespread anger because it affected almost everyone. Apprentices signing indentures, young couples getting married, merchants making contracts, old people making wills, anyone buying or selling land or slaves, newspaper readers, and gamblers—all would have to pay the new tax. The act also hit at the power of colonial political elites. For decades they had controlled the taxation and administration of their colonies, imitating in their assemblies the practices of the English House of Commons. They told themselves and their people that they were the guardians of British liberties. They had become used to acting as a ruling class and to arguing that their rule was in the common interest. The Stamp Act was Parliament's first attempt to levy a widespread colonial tax over the assemblies' heads. The assemblies began to resist parliamentary initiatives. As they were quick to point out, the

Stamp Act threatened to make colonists pay for their own subjection to British rule. By giving royal governors an independent revenue, it promised to cut them free from restraint by the assemblies that voted their salaries. The rest of the tax would go to pay for the soldiers and officials who were enforcing unpopular British laws.

Political instability in Britain led to the ousting of Grenville, and to the repeal of the Stamp Act early in 1766. Parliament, however, made clear that it would enforce its will in the colonies by passing a Declaratory Act that asserted its right to "make laws and statutes . . . to bind the colonies and people of America . . . in all cases whatsoever." Although this act contained no specific measures, its words paved the way for future imperial crises.

The next crisis arose in 1767, when Parliament and a new chancellor of the exchequer, Charles Townshend, tried to tax the colonies again in an effort both to raise money and to exercise parliamentary supremacy. Believing that colonists had rejected the Stamp Act because it was an "internal" tax, collected within the colonies themselves, Townshend set out to levy "external" taxes at the ports on goods brought into the colonies. The Revenue Act of 1767 (the so-called Townshend Duties) taxed paint, paper, lead, glass, and tea as they reached America. Colonists did not believe that the distinction between internal and external taxes was valid, so these new duties again provoked fierce opposition.

Colonists objected to British taxes because without representation in Parliament they had no say in levying them. They also opposed them because they saw these taxes as part of a broader British plan to curb their accustomed liberties. Further resentment arose when the British suspended the New York assembly after it refused to vote for supplies for British troops stationed in the province. Parliament then passed a Quartering Act obliging New Yorkers to board soldiers in their houses when required. The British also set up a special board of commissioners in Boston to run the colonial customs service, and in 1768 posted two regiments of troops to the town to protect the commissioners and their hirelings. This was the first time a garrison had been stationed outside New York or frontier outposts. The colonists' contention that standing armies were a dangerous threat to liberty appeared vindicated when

"The Colonies Reduced." Britannia, surrounded by her amputated limbs—marked Virginia, Pennsylvania, New York, and New England—contemplated the decline of her empire in this 1767 engraving published in Great Britain. The cartoon, attributed to Benjamin Franklin, warned of the consequences of alienating the colonies through enforcement of the Stamp Act. Franklin, who was in England representing the colonists' claims, arranged to have the image printed on cards that he distributed to members of Parliament.

Source: "The Colonies Reduced. Design'd and Engrav'd for the Political Register," 2 3/8 × 3 7/8 inches, 1767—Prints and Photographs Division, Library of Congress.

This is the Place to affix the STAMP.

"This Is The Place." This protest against the Stamp Act was printed in the bottom right-hand corner of the October 24, 1765, *Pennsylvania Journal and Weekly Advertiser.*

Source: *The Pennsylvania Journal and Weekly Advertiser,* October 24, 1765—Prints and Photographs Division, Library of Congress.

the army erected a guard-post at Boston Neck to catch deserters, putting everyone entering or leaving town under the sentries' scrutiny.

Meanwhile it seemed to colonists as if the customs service itself had declared war on the American economy. Tidewaiters, inspectors, and other minor officials charged with enforcing trade regulations regarded colonists as disloyal at best, criminal at worst. They worked for the large rewards they could earn by catching smugglers, using a set of laws so complex that virtually any vessel or traveler entering or leaving port violated some technicality. Even a minor discrepancy in a ship's papers could result in the seizure of the vessel and its entire contents. All involved in commerce, from great merchants such as John Hancock of Boston to the ordinary seamen who crewed the ships, fell foul of the laws.

Elite Protest

The crises of the 1760s over the Stamp Act and Townshend Duties provoked different kinds of protest and involved different parts of colonial society. Disparate groups of colonists with different desires and interests united to oppose British measures. They took the first steps toward forming themselves into a coalition that included not only merchants, slaveowners, lawyers, and clergymen, but also ordinary men and women—urban artisans and laborers, farmers, servants, and sailors.

Prominent in the arguments over British policy were colonial political leaders, who gathered in the provincial assemblies to debate what action to take. In 1765 the Stamp Act provoked prompt opposition. In June, the Virginia House of Burgesses passed strongly worded resolutions against the act, and over the next few months eight other colonial assemblies followed suit. In October, official delegations from nine colonies gathered in New York City for a Stamp Act Congress, which adopted fourteen resolutions condemning the measure, called for a boycott of British goods, and sent petitions to Parliament and an address to the king.

Concern about British policy was already propelling gentlemen, lawyers, clergymen, and merchants into their studies to write essays and treatises on constitutional rights. The imperial crisis unleashed a decade-long outpouring of such works. At first writers were hesitant, aware that they were toying with dangerous ideas. In response to the Stamp Act, the Townshend Duties, and other events of the 1760s, they debated Parliament's power to tax and to interfere with colonial assemblies. The conduct of these debates pushed them toward new conceptions of the colonies' relationship with Britain.

Colonists initially claimed that Parliament could not tax them for revenue because they were not represented in the House of Commons. The Virginia House of Burgesses argued at the time of the Stamp Act that "taxation of the People by themselves or by persons chosen by themselves . . . is the distinguishing Characteristick of British freedom." For the burgesses, the "persons chosen" by Virginians could only be the members of their own House, the only people for whom Virginians could vote. As pamphleteers developed the point, some came to suggest that Parliament might have no authority at all in the colonies, and that the colonial assemblies governed in its place in their own provinces, under the direct authority of the king. But this theory contradicted the British constitutional principle that the king ruled in and through Parliament and held no authority separate from it.

Working tirelessly through such issues, the pamphleteers gradually undermined virtually everything colonists had once believed about their relationship with Britain. They arrived at increasingly radical conclusions, so that by 1774, Thomas Jefferson could suggest that by migrating to the colonies settlers had placed themselves beyond the sovereignty of the British parliament. In *A Summary View of the Rights of British America,* Jefferson argued that the Navigation Acts were "void" because "the British Parliament has no right to exercise authority over us." The succession of recent British measures in the colonies were "acts of power, assumed by a body of men, foreign to our constitutions and unacknowledged by our laws." Taken one by one, these measures might appear "accidental," but together they "too plainly prove a deliberate and systematical plan of reducing us to slavery." Jefferson and like-minded colonial leaders were but a few steps short of regarding the American colonies as independent from Britain.

Popular Protest

Yet Jefferson and his fellow-pamphleteers did not conduct political argument in a vacuum. Attitudes toward Britain became radicalized in light of events acted out on the colonies' streets, wharves, farmlands, seaways, and households, as well as in the colonial assemblies. British taxes and the presence of British troops intruded on the daily lives of ordinary men and women. In Boston, Jane Mecom wrote to her brother Benjamin Franklin of the "confusion and distress those Opresive Actts have thrown us poor Americans into." As popular crowds joined political elites in the protests against British policy, they revealed the social tensions within the colonies, asserted their own sense of rights and justice, and helped turn protest into resistance.

Crowd action had long been an integral part of colonial life. Disguises, effigies, parades, bonfires, razings, and ritualized confrontations all had characterized popular political culture for decades. Targeting hoarders of scarce goods, price-gougers, or the press gangs that rounded up sailors for service in the navy, crowds had expressed popular concepts of justice. They enacted rituals that really or symbolically corrected perceived wrongs, or that asserted rights despite differences of wealth and position. Mock elections, mock trials, and hangings-in-effigy had parodied legal procedures while asserting the opinions of those, wealthy or poor, who viewed themselves as victims of injustice. Now women and men deployed these traditions against the symbols of British rule. In New York alone, fifty-seven crowd risings took place between 1764 and 1775, and there were numerous similar episodes elsewhere.

In Boston, a small group of men calling themselves the "Loyal Nine" initiated popular resistance to the Stamp Act in the summer of 1765. They decided to make August 14 a day of political theater to show Bostonians what the Stamp Act would mean when it went into effect that November. They hanged from a tree near Boston Neck effigies of George Grenville, of Lord Bute, a hated Scot who had been the king's tutor and briefly his prime minister, and who was popularly suspected as a behind-the-throne manipulator, and of Andrew Oliver, the Boston merchant who had accepted the office of stamp distributor. Naming this the Liberty Tree, one of the first of many that would appear across the colonies in the next decade, the Nine set up a mock stamp office where they ceremoniously stamped the goods of farmers and carters coming to town with produce, and of passers-by on foot and on horseback.

The Nine also drew on the tradition of Boston's popular Pope's Day celebrations, giving these new political content. They contacted Ebenezer MacIntosh, a shoemaker who led one of the town's two rival

Pope's Day crowds. In an act of popular unity, MacIntosh appeared with both crowds behind him; his fellow-shoemaker George Robert Twelves Hewes may have been among them. The crowd cut down the effigies, paraded them, and then burned them. When someone found a small building thought to be Oliver's stamp office, the crowd demolished it, and then marched to Oliver's house, where they broke some windows, tore down fencing, and built a bonfire. The following day, Oliver resigned his office.

The August 14 protesters confined themselves to denouncing the British ministry, the Stamp Act, and Andrew Oliver, its local agent. But Stamp Act protestors also touched on social divisions within the colonies. A second Stamp Act riot on August 26 revealed the class antagonism that underlay Boston life in the wake of war and depression. This riot targeted symbols of wealth, culminating in a furious attack on the home of Lieutenant Governor Thomas Hutchinson. The crowd ransacked the house, and with considerable effort demolished the cupola that had made it one of the town's grandest residences. The Massachusetts-born Hutchinson had risen to hold several prominent Crown offices in the province, and the destruction marked popular resentment, not just about British policy, but also at the power and privilege colonial rule gave to a few men.

Popular leaders were alarmed at the crowd's excesses on August 26, and tried to avoid further attacks on symbols of wealth. But they could not prevent social differences and tensions from emerging. In November, a fine mansion in New York was sacked by a crowd, and the governor's chariot, sedan chair, and sleighs "burnt in the Bowling Green with effigies and Gallows." The following May, another New York crowd, enraged by the ostentatious dress and carriages of a wealthy audience at the opening night of a new theater, razed the playhouse to the ground and then marched off in parade formation chanting "Liberty! Liberty!" In Charleston, a Stamp Act protest revealed not only opposition to British taxes, but also the fragility of the South's social fabric. As a white crowd paraded to the shout of "Liberty! Liberty! and [no] stamped paper," a group of African Americans provoked a panic when they took up the cry of "Liberty!" from the sidelines.

Resistance to the Stamp Act. A generation after the event, an etching in a 1784 German pocket almanac imaginatively celebrated the Boston crowd (including women, African Americans, and artisans wearing leather aprons) burning stamped papers.

Source: Daniel-Nicholas Chodowiecki, *Historisch-genealogischer Calender, oder Jahrbuch der merkwürdigsten neuen Welt* (1784)—Prints and Photographs Division, Library of Congress.

Opposition to the Stamp Act produced an unprecedented degree of political organization among colonists. Groups with names such as "Sons of Liberty" emerged in several towns and cities. The one in Albany, New York, began as a protest by Dutch descendants against British measures, but then broadened to include Anglo-Americans, too. Although as a formal organization the Sons of Liberty did not outlast the Stamp Act crisis, the name came to be used as a generic term in subsequent crises for similar groups that provided the nucleus of a revolutionary movement. The participants in these groups came from a variety of backgrounds. Many were artisans. For instance, when John Adams listed the names of Boston's Loyal Nine, he included "John Smith the Brazier [a maker of brasswork], Thomas Crofts the Painter, [Benjamin] Edes the Printer, Stephen Claverly the Brazier, . . . [and] George Trott [the] Jeweller." Wealthy merchants also protested, and made up an important segment of the revolutionary leadership. The most famous was the Boston merchant and smuggler John Hancock. Finally, there were men who were not wealthy, but who did not (as the artisans did) work with their hands for a living. They included Samuel Adams of Boston, Isaac Sears of New York, and Dr. Thomas Young, who turned up in Albany, Boston, Newport, and finally Philadelphia.

The men in this last category were a varied lot. Samuel Adams was a Harvard graduate who dreamed of turning America into a "Christian Sparta"—a rigorous republican commonwealth—and who courted a popular following in the Boston town meeting. Thomas Young was a religious freethinker, and a self-taught physician who treated mainly the poor. Isaac Sears was the son of a Cape Cod oysterman who, after going to sea early in life, worked his way up to command merchant vessels and privateers before settling down ashore as a trader in his own right, and marrying the daughter of a waterfront tavern keeper. His trade was with other colonies, not with Britain, and he was looked down on by grander merchants who addressed him as "Captain," rather than the more eminent "Mr." or "Esquire." Sears's social world was closer to the seamen in his father-in-law's tavern than to the wealthy of New York. As men such as Adams, Young, and Sears devoted themselves to building popular resistance to British authority, they started to transform American political life.

Colonists took Parliament's repeal of the Stamp Act early in 1766 as a sign that their protests had been successful. Thus, when the Townshend Duties were enacted in 1767, protest resumed, lasting this time for over two years. To combat the duties, protesters in the main ports organized nonimportation agreements binding merchants not to purchase goods from Britain. As the British general Thomas Gage reported, violators had to "undergo the Discipline of the Populace." They were denounced at public meetings as "Enemies to their Country," tarred and feathered, or had their houses daubed with the contents of cesspits (known as "Hillsborough paint" after the British minister for the colonies). Symbols of wealth were again targets. In Marlborough, Massachusetts, the merchant Henry Barnes had his carriage (one of the very few in town) vandalized when he refused to comply with nonimportation. Abstaining from European products or fashions became a mark of patriotism, and of a willingness to give up personal luxuries for the public good.

Women as well as men supported the boycotts, and women's support became an important patriotic act. In Philadelphia in 1768, Milcah Martha Moore copied down a verse published to urge women to join the cause:

> Let the Daughters of Liberty nobly arise
> And tho' we've no Voice but a negative here,
> The use of the Taxables let us forbear.

Women assembled at spinning bees to produce yarn for homespun cloth that would substitute for British textiles. They announced their refusal to purchase or drink the tea imported by British traders. A group of Rhode Island ladies "rejected the poisonous Bohea" (a black China tea) in favor of homemade herb tea; some New Hampshire women "made their breakfast upon Rye Coffee"; in Massachusetts, over three hundred agreed to "totally abstain" from drinking tea. Women at one spinning bee expressed the hope that they "may vie with the men in contributions to the preservation and prosperity of their country, and equally share the honor of it." For women usually barred from a formal public role, the patriotic cause offered an opening into political events, and some claimed that their support for it should earn them political rights.

At first nonimportation agreements formed a rallying point for popular political cohesion, but as the campaign dragged on it revealed the divisions in colonial society. Jane Mecom, who sold imported goods in her Boston store, wrote that it was "unlucky" for her "that our People have taken it into th[eir] Heads to be so Exsesive Frugal," and that "I should like to have those that do b[u]y . . . and can afford it should b[u]y . . . what Litle I have to sell." Unless their patriotism outweighed comfort and convenience, wealthier women sought renewed access to European luxuries and household items. Poorer women found support for the boycott easier because they had less and less money to spend on anything. Nonimportation was never popular with colonial merchants, and never fully enforceable. Bostonians loyal to Britain scored a propaganda victory against the radicals when they published lists of goods imported by supposedly "patriotic" merchants. By early 1770 merchants involved in the protest were jockeying for position, anxious not to break the boycott, but

"A Society of Patriotic Ladies." Cheap prints depicting current events were in great demand in both England and the colonies. This 1775 British print presented a scene in Edenton, North Carolina. Fifty-one women signed a declaration in support of nonimportation, swearing not to drink tea or purchase other British imports. The artist treated the women with scorn, portraying them as ugly, impressionable, and neglectful of their children.

Source: Philip Dawe(?), "A Society of Patriotic Ladies, at Edenton in North Carolina," mezzotint, 1775, 13 3/4 × 10 inches—Prints and Photographs Division, Library of Congress.

A SOCIETY of PATRIOTIC LADIES,

also eager to resume trade with England as soon as nonimportation ended. That year, by repealing all but one of the import duties (that on tea), the British government succeeded both in breaking the boycott and in exacerbating divisions within the radical movement.

Artisans were the most avid supporters of nonimportation, not least because it increased the demand for goods manufactured at home, a boon for craftspeople in a time of economic depression. In 1770, after the boycott collapsed and this demand diminished, the shoemakers George Hewes and Ebenezer MacIntosh were among many who ended up in debtor's prison. But artisans were doing more than protecting their material self-interest. They were also asserting a right to participate in political decisions. One New Yorker argued that nothing could be "more flagrantly wrong, than the assertion of some of our mercantile dons, that the Mechanics have no right to give their Sentiments."

Seamen and laborers viewed the resistance to Britain from a different vantage point. For them, nonimportation meant hardship: reduced trade meant fewer ships at sea and fewer jobs ashore. Some sailors tried to persuade merchants to support the resistance not by refusing to carry goods, but by evading the duties on them. Poorer colonists also developed their own perspective on the evils of a standing army. Among out-of-work seamen and laborers, competition for scarce waterfront jobs grew tougher, and the presence of poorly paid and idle British troops made matters even worse. In New York, as well as in Boston from 1768 on, friction between local workers and British soldiers hunting for jobs became commonplace.

In New York in January 1770, a two-day street fight, dubbed "the Battle of Golden Hill," broke out between soldiers and laborers. Events in Boston soon overshadowed this. There, social divisions and resentments came to a head as demonstrations against the Townshend Duties continued. On February 22, a customs official named Ebenezer Richardson tried to break up a picket line in front of an importer's store. Some boys pelted him with stones; Richardson retreated to his own house, where he fired his gun through a window, killing eleven-year-old Christopher Seider. The day of the boy's funeral was observed throughout the town. A few days later an off-duty British soldier, Patrick Walker, called at a ropemaker's looking for casual work, as was common for an ill-paid private trying to supplement his wages. Resentment was running high after the Seider shooting, and the ropemaker told Walker that if he wanted a job he could go and clean "my shithouse."

This insult sent Walker back to his barracks to fetch his friends, and a brawl broke out. A few nights later, on March 5, men from Walker's regiment guarding the customs house on King Street were confronted by a crowd, some of them ropemakers, who began to throw snowballs and brickbats at them. Frightened by what seemed to be a bloodthirsty mob, the soldiers retaliated. George Hewes, who was among the crowd, was struck by a private's gun. Then the troops opened fire. Within minutes four Bostonians were dead, and another fatally wounded. All five were laboring men: Crispus Attucks, a half-Indian, half-African sailor; Patrick Carr, an Irish journeyman leathermaker; Samuel Gray, a ropemaker; Samuel Maverick, an ivory turner's apprentice; and James Caldwell, a ship's mate. As Caldwell was shot in the back and fell, the injured Hewes — who knew him — caught him in his arms.

"The Bloody Massacre." Paul Revere issued his version of the Boston Massacre three weeks after the incident. The print (which Revere plagiarized from a fellow Boston engraver) was widely circulated and repeatedly copied (over twenty-four times). The print was the official Patriot version of the incident: British soldiers actually did not fire a well-disciplined volley; white men were not the sole actors in the incident; and the Bostonians provoked the soldiers with taunts and thrown objects.

Source: Paul Revere, "The Bloody Massacre perpetrated in King Street Boston on March 5th, 1770 . . . ," etching (handcolored), 1770, 7 3/4 × 8 3/4 inches—Prints and Photographs Division, Library of Congress.

Bostonians were outraged at what they quickly came to call the "Boston Massacre." Radical propaganda made sure that, unlike the Battle of Golden Hill, the Massacre would remain firmly lodged in public memory. Paul Revere made an engraving of the scene, widely copied and distributed, which became the most familiar depiction of the event. Showing an orderly rank of redcoats discharging their muskets into the crowd. Revere presented the massacre not as the result of panic, but as a deliberate act of murder by the British army.

In the short run the incident marked the end of a phase in the resistance to British policies. Within months Britain removed its troops from the town of Boston to Castle Island in Boston Harbor and also repealed most of the Townshend Duties. With the radicals already divided, the nonimportation movement collapsed. In time, though, the Boston Massacre came to seem a turning point in the conflict with Britain. For the next thirteen years, Boston observed March 5 as a day of public mourning. Radicals used the event to rebuild popular opposition to British rule. The Massacre's five victims came to be viewed as

The Boston Massacre, c. 1868. Artists continued to redraw, repaint, and reinterpret the Boston Massacre. This engraving based on a painting by Alonzo Chappel still omitted Crispus Attucks, but it showed the chaos of the confrontation and captured the horror of soldiers shooting down unarmed citizens.

Source: American Social History Project.

the first martyrs of a revolutionary cause. The fact that they were laborers built support for that cause among the poor. In this way, an event that had reflected divisions in Boston society became a basis for building a new, united coalition.

Resistance Becomes Revolution

After 1770, although concerted colonial opposition to Britain receded, sporadic attacks on customs officers and other officials continued up and down the coast. In 1772, when a government revenue vessel, the *Gaspée*, ran aground in Narragansett Bay, a crowd from Providence burned it, and erected liberty poles to mark the event. But these protests chiefly involved urban residents, not people in the countryside. This pattern changed during a third imperial crisis, which began in 1773 with Parliament's passage of the Tea Act. Once again, protest began in the towns, but this time resistance spread to rural regions, where the vast majority of colonists lived. When rural people became engaged in the struggle, resistance turned to revolution. Without them, American independence would not have been possible.

Ever since they had fled England in the seventeenth century and settled on American land they could call their own, rural New Englanders had been wary of any measure that might threaten their freeholds, return them to some form of feudalism or, as one writer put it, "reduce them to lordships." Urban radicals played upon this deeply rooted fear in the hope of igniting rural opposition to British taxes. In 1772 the Boston town meeting appointed a Committee of Correspondence to rouse the interior, warning that if "a British house of commons can originate an act for taking away our money, our lands will go next or be subject to rack rents from haughty and relentless landlords who will ride at ease, while we are trodden in the dirt." At first, these efforts met with apathy. Some of the people to whom the committee wrote thought that relations with Britain were not their business to interfere in. The people of Ashfield, Massachusetts, were more concerned about divisions in their church than about imperial politics. But the campaign over the Tea Act of 1773 prompted country people to respond, and they did so with vigor.

Ironically, the Tea Act was not primarily intended as a colonial taxation measure. Parliament was trying to solve the financial troubles of the British East India Company. The act permitted the company to raise money by selling tea directly to America through chosen agents in each colonial port. Its prices would be low enough that, even after paying the Townshend Duty on tea (which the act cut in half), the company could undercut other American merchants who had, as John Adams put it, "honestly smuggled" their tea from Holland. The Tea Act should have made everyone happy: Britain would get its taxes, the East India Company would get its revenue, and colonists would get cheap tea.

Instead, the act reignited American outrage at British policy, as colonists spurned the attempt to bribe them into accepting the tax on tea. Charleston landed its first cargo of tea, but Philadelphia and New York refused even to let tea ships enter their harbors. In Boston in November 1773, the first vessels carrying tea docked because Thomas Hutchinson, now governor (and whose sons were Boston agents for the East India Company), insisted that the cargo land and the tea duty be paid. But before this could be done, daylong protest meetings of "the whole Body of the People" convened, choosing leaders to negotiate with Hutchinson and persuade him to desist. The talks broke down. On the night of December 16, parties of patriot leaders and workingmen boarded the ships and dumped the tea overboard into the harbor. The shoemaker George Hewes was put in charge of one of the groups.

This "Boston Tea Party" became a powerful symbol of American resistance. The men who carried it out were disguised as "Mohawks." Hewes had blackened his face with a piece of charcoal and thrown a blanket around his shoulders. When another tea ship reached New York a few months later, another group of "Mohawks" prepared to reenact the event,

215

The able Doctor, or America Swallowing the Bitter Draught.

"The Able Doctor, or America Swallowing the Bitter Draught." Many British prints sympathized with the colonists' claims. In this engraving published in the April 1774 *London Magazine,* America (depicted as an Indian woman) was assaulted by several recognizable British statesmen—principally Lord North, the Prime Minister, who was shown forcing tea down her throat (only to have it spat back into his face). Meanwhile, France and Spain looked on and Britannia averted her eyes in shame. By June 1775, the engraving reached the colonies, where it was copied and reproduced by Paul Revere.

Source: *London Magazine,* April 1774—Rare Books and Manuscript Division, New York Public Library, Astor, Lenox and Tilden Foundations.

but were beaten to it by a quayside crowd that surged onto the ship, destroyed the tea themselves, and then paraded the empty tea chests to "the Fields" outside the city walls and burned them. In central Massachusetts, a "number of Indians" chased a peddler who was carrying a bag of tea, and burned the tea in front of a tavern. The crowds disguised themselves in Mohawk or Indian dress not for practical reasons (secrecy was unnecessary in a sympathetic neighborhood), but as a symbolic gesture. Rioters' Indian attire proclaimed their identity as Americans, rather than as Englishmen living in America. They were beginning a shift from being "freeborn Englishmen" to being "American freemen."

Britain's response to the Boston Tea Party was severe. Parliament passed four measures, which colonists called the Coercive or Intolerable Acts. The first closed Boston harbor until the town paid for the tea, cutting off Boston's main source of livelihood. The second altered Massachusetts government, revoking the 1691 royal charter that had given the colony the unique privilege of electing its own council, and limiting town meetings to one each year for the election of local officers. The third measure allowed British officials accused of wrongdoing to face trial in another province, or in Britain itself, away from Boston's charged atmosphere. The fourth made it easy for the British government to billet troops in colonial homes. Soon after the Coercive Acts were announced, in May 1774, Hutchinson was replaced as governor by Thomas Gage, the general in charge of Britain's army in America, and Gage's troops reoccupied Boston.

"Let Every Man Do His Duty . . ."

The Boston Tea Party is described by George Robert Twelves Hewes, a poor shoemaker who was a participant in the dramatic actions. Hewes had been at the scene of the Boston Massacre three years earlier. In this memoir, taken down by James Hawkes in 1834, Hewes describes the meeting of "the Whole body of the People" that deliberated on the action and then describes the disciplined destruction of the tea.

On the day preceding the seventeenth [of December], there was a meeting of the citizens of the county of Suffolk, convened at one of the churches in Boston, for the purpose of consulting on what measures might be considered expedient to prevent the landing of the tea, or secure the people from the collection of the duty. At that meeting a committee was appointed to wait on Governor Hutchinson, and [to ask] whether he would take any measures to satisfy the people on the object of the meeting. . . . When the committee returned and informed the meeting of the absence of the Governor, there was a confused murmur among the members, and the meeting was immediately dissolved, many of them crying out, "Let every man do his duty, and be true to his country"; and there was a general huzza for Griffin's wharf. . . .

When we arrived at the wharf, there were three of our number who assumed an authority to direct our operations, to which we readily submitted. They divided us into three parties, for the purpose of boarding the three [tea] ships. . . . We were immediately ordered by the respective commanders to board all the ships at the same time, which we promptly obeyed. The commander of the division to which I belonged, as soon as we were aboard the ship, appointed me boatswain, and ordered me to go the [ship's] captain and demand of him the keys to the hatches and a dozen candles. I made the demand accordingly, and the captain promptly . . . delivered the articles; but requested me at the same time to do no damage to the ship or rigging. We then were ordered by our commander to open the hatches and take out all the chests of tea and throw them overboard, and we immediately proceeded to execute his orders, first cutting and splitting the chests with our tomahawks, so as thoroughly to expose them to the effects of the water.

In about three hours from the time we went on board, we had thus broken and thrown overboard every tea chest to be found in the ship, while those on the other ships were disposing of the tea in the same way, at the same time. We were surrounded by British armed ships, but no attempt was made to resist us.

Source: James Hawkes, *A Retrospect of the Boston Tea Party* (1834).

Britain meant to show that it would retreat no further in the face of American protests, and that it would restore its authority in the colonies. But the Coercive Acts had exactly the opposite effect. They redoubled the radical movement in Boston, whose leaders signaled their defiance by harking back to England's own radical past. The "Captain" of a "Committee for Tarring and Feathering" called himself "Joyce, Jun.," after the young Cornet Joyce who had captured King Charles I and so assured his execution in 1649. Many Bostonians so far sympathetic to the Crown began to change their views. Among them was Benjamin Franklin's sister Jane Mecom, who a few years before had regarded Thomas Hutchinson as

The BOSTONIAN'S Paying the EXCISE-MAN, or TARRING & FEATHERING
Plate I.
London Printed for Rob.ᵗ Sayer & J.Bennett,Map & Printseller, N.º 53,Fleet Street as the Act directs 31 Oct.ʳ,1774.

"The Bostonians Paying the Excise-Man, or Tarring and Feathering." A 1774 British print depicted the tarring and feathering of Boston Commissioner of Customs John Malcolm. Tarring and feathering was a ritual of humiliation and public warning that stopped just short of serious injury. In this print, Malcolm was attacked under the Liberty Tree by several Patriots, including a leather-aproned artisan, while the Boston Tea Party occurred in the background; in fact, the Tea Party had taken place four weeks earlier. This anti-Patriot print may have been a response to the sympathetic "The Able Doctor" published earlier the same year.

Source: Philip Dawe(?), mezzotint, 1774, 14 × 9 1/2 inches—Prints and Photographs Division, Library of Congress.

"the Gratest ornement of our Country," but was now angered by "the town[']s being so full of Proflegate soulders [soldiers] . . . and "the[ir] Profane language."

More important still, the British measures spread colonial resistance from town to countryside to an extent that the Boston Committee of Correspondence had not been able to achieve. Requiring that ordinary people house British troops on demand, and particularly by interfering with town meetings and county courts, the Coercive Acts carried Britain's quarrel with Boston to every corner of Massachusetts. Rural people, many of whom had been reluctant to resist British policy, now acted decisively to prevent the new measures from taking effect. In doing so, they turned their province away from the path of submission to royal authority and onto the road to revolution.

The first court to convene under the provisions of the Coercive Acts was due to open in Worcester County in August 1774. Its judges held fresh commissions, issued under the acts by Governor Gage. Patriots throughout Massachusetts agreed that such courts were unconstitutional and that permitting even one of them to sit would set a dangerous precedent. When the judges arrived in the town of Worcester, they found virtually the whole male population of the county armed and assembled in their militia units near the courthouse. Orderly but determined, the crowd remained in place until each of the judges had undergone the humiliation of walking bareheaded through the throng to read a public statement resigning his post. The Worcester court never opened; nor did any of the other county courts in the province.

When prominent men were appointed to the new council that replaced the elected one, crowds again gathered to "persuade" them to resign. Those who refused were forced to change their minds. One of the Connecticut Valley "River Gods" resigned only after being locked up for the night in a smokehouse; another loyalist was confined to a livestock pound and fed on dried fish thrown over the wall. The methods drew on those of Stamp Act protesters in the 1760s, but the implications were far-reaching.

By late summer 1774, royal government in Massachusetts had virtually collapsed, and the governor's authority ran no farther than his troops could march. Defying the governor's order that it dissolve, the province's General Court met in Salem, and militia units drilled under officers who now acknowledged the authority, not of the governor, but of this extralegal provincial assembly. Extending the principles of self-government enacted by land rioters and Green Mountain Boys, Massachusetts people created their own political institutions and took over the province. Defying the British laws, town meetings and county conventions met to direct affairs, conducting their business no longer in the name of the king, but in the name of the "commonwealth" or "the people of Massachusetts." Farm families named newborn boys Oliver, after Oliver Cromwell, who had led Parliamentary forces against Charles I in the English Civil War. A revolution was under way.

The Coercive Acts and resistance to them prompted patriotic action in other colonies. By late 1774 much of New England was effectively united behind Massachusetts. So was white Virginia where, despite the evangelical challenge to its leadership, the planter class remained firmly in control. Having suffered from weak tobacco prices in the 1760s and indebtedness to British merchants, many Virginia planters were reconsidering the benefits of being part of the British empire and coming to see colonial status as a disadvantage. Meanwhile, the colony's popular leaders, such as Patrick Henry, forged links between the gentry and others in the population, denouncing "luxury" and proclaiming the "virtue" of the patriot cause. Whereas in the Carolinas frontier settlement had provoked an east-west split over the extension of government institutions, Virginia's rulers and frontiersmen had been able to form an alliance in protest over British refusal to permit the organization of new counties in their colony. From 1774 to mid-1776 the combination of New Englanders and Virginia gentlemen led a drive for strong measures against Britain that would forge a path to independence.

Virginia and New England leaders found their forum in two Continental Congresses, formed of representatives from the different colonies gathered to resist British policies. Although intercolonial cooperation had been attempted before—especially in response to the Stamp Act—none had been as widespread or as far-reaching as this. The first Continental Congress met in Philadelphia for six weeks in the autumn of 1774, and the second convened there in May 1775. Called to rally to the aid of Massachusetts, delegates came to the first congress from twelve, then thirteen colonies. Among them were participants in popular protests; South Carolina's delegation, for instance, included artisan members of the Charleston Sons of Liberty. Led by radicals keen to make the rest of America see that they shared Massachusetts' problems, this congress passed the Continental Association, a measure that decreed a complete boycott of European products and called for the creation of committees throughout the colonies to enforce it. In Boston, Jane Mecom regarded "the Uniteing of the Colonies" as "a token of God[']s design to deliver us out of all our tro[u]bles."

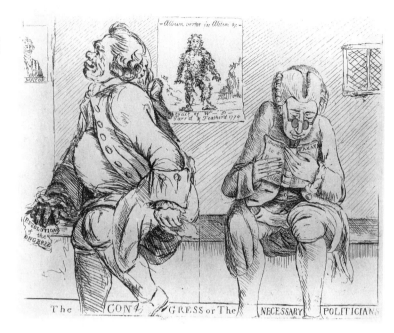

"The Necessary Politicians." A particularly derisive comment on colonial demands, this 1775 British etching showed two Tory politicians evaluating Patriot documents in a privy (or "necessary" house). A tarred-and-feathered figure decorated the outhouse wall.

Source: "The Congress or Necessary Politicians," etching, 1775?, 8 × 6 1/2 inches—Prints and Photographs Division, Library of Congress.

By linking the colonies together in a common cause and providing for support for that cause at a local level, the Continental Association harnessed popular action to the nucleus of a national movement. Sometimes acting against opposition, local patriot committees started to enforce the Association's provisions. Even more than in the boycotts against the Townshend Duties, support for the patriot cause entailed forgoing European goods and fashions, and adopting symbols of domestic frugality. At Edenton, North Carolina, a meeting of fifty-one women proclaimed its support for the Association and asserted a woman's right and duty to participate in political action. Other colonies began to follow Massachusetts and set up extralegal institutions to take over effective government.

War Begins

Before the Second Continental Congress could meet, fighting with Britain broke out in Massachusetts. During the fall and winter of 1774–1775, New Englanders had collected weapons and organized their town militias to uphold their closure of the county courts and defend their extralegal committees and conventions. Their resolve was made evident in September 1774, when a mere rumor that British troops had left Boston to capture a provincial powder store set thousands of rural Massachusetts men marching eastward until they could be recalled. According to one observer, women in their houses along the way were "making Cartridges, [and] running Bullets . . . animating their Husbands and Sons to fight for their Liberties." It was a sign of what would come. In occupied Boston a committee of artisans watched troop movements closely. The extralegal provincial congress began planning to raise an army of fifteen thousand men. But this army still did not exist when, on the night of April 18–19, 1775, General Gage finally dispatched troops to capture militia supplies hidden at Concord.

The Boston artisans' committee sent Paul Revere and other riders to warn the interior. When the British detachment arrived at Lexington, the town's militia was drawn up on the green to face it. They probably intended no more than a symbolic confrontation, but someone's gun went off, an exchange of fire began, and within minutes eight militiamen were dead. The British troops marched on, completed their task at Concord, and set out to march back to Boston. Their outward march had been easy, but the return was not. Farmers and workmen rallied from the surrounding towns and attacked the British units from the fields and woods along their route, scoring heavy casualties. Among the attackers, it was said, were women from the town of Groton, dressed in men's clothing. Once

"The Battle of Lexington."
This picture was one of a set of four prints based on drawings sketched shortly after the battle of Lexington by Amos Doolittle, a twenty-one-year-old engraver who visited the site as a member of the Connecticut militia. Although the location was rendered with accuracy, the drawing misrepresented the behavior of British troops, whose discipline was less than perfect. The four prints, on sale by December 1775, were the first American illustrations of warfare during the Revolution.

Source: Amos Doolittle, "The Battle of Lexington, April 19th, 1775," line engraving (hand-colored), 1775, 13 × 17 1/2 inches—Print Collection, Miriam and Ira Wallach Division of Art, Prints, and Photographs, New York Public Library, Astor, Lenox and Tilden Foundations.

the British had reached Boston, militia units—citizen-soldiers, poorly trained, and mostly without uniforms or good weapons—threw up siege lines around the city and kept the army penned up there. The British, commented Jane Mecom, "were much mistaken in the people they had to Deal with."

In June the colonial militia again showed that they could fight. Gage decided to dislodge them from Breed's (Bunker) Hill overlooking Charlestown. He did so, but only at great cost. Determined to demonstrate the superiority of regular soldiers over the provincial forces that he and his officers regarded as an ill-disciplined rabble, Gage launched a nearly suicidal uphill frontal assault on the defenses at the top. Before retreating to new positions, the militia killed or wounded nearly half of Gage's men. The British made no more such attacks, and when in the winter of 1775–1776 the provincials were reinforced by cannons captured from Ticonderoga, New York, Gage was obliged to withdraw from Boston altogether. The "ill-disciplined rabble" had driven the British away.

During the summer of 1775 the Continental Congress took steps to support the New England armies and to ready the colonies for war. It appointed George Washington to head a new Continental Army that would fight alongside the locally raised provincial militias. The choice of Washington was based partly on his reputation from the French and Indian

The Retreat

From Concord to Lexington of the Army of Wild Irish Asses Defeated by the Brave American Militia

M.ʳ Deacon M.ʳ Loeings M.ʳ Mulikens M.ʳ Bonds Houses and Barn all Plunderd and Burnt on April 19.ᵗʰ

According to Act June 14 1775.

"The Retreat." This print, possibly made in America, presented the plundering retreat of British troops on April 19, 1775. The unknown artist chose to portray the King's soldiers as donkeys, and the advancing Massachusetts troops in disciplined ranks (in fact, they fought as guerrillas, harassing the British from the shelter of houses, trees, and rocks).

Source: British Museum.

War, but it was also political. The appointment of a southerner such as Washington was essential if the war was to become more than a New England affair, and the creation of a continental force was necessary if the cause was not to be fragmented by individual provinces' own interests. Moreover, Washington was a wealthy member of Virginia's ruling class, and he would bring prestige to this new position.

The Second Continental Congress would remain in session for over a decade, until well after the war itself was over. In July 1775, it issued a "Declaration of the Causes and Necessity of Taking Up Arms," summarizing the succession of injuries that Britain had inflicted on the colonies, condemning the "cruel aggression . . . commenced by the British troops," and declaring that the "united colonies" faced a stark choice between "an unconditional submission to . . . tyranny" and "resistance by force." "The latter is our choice," it declared. Yet the advocates of strong action against Britain still faced considerable opposition within the colonies, and Congress took pains to assure these opponents that its intentions were moderate and purely defensive. "We have not raised armies with ambitious designs of separating from Great-Britain, and establishing independent states. . . . [W]e sincerely wish to see restored . . . that union which has so long and so happily subsisted between us." Although Virginia and New England were effectively united, much of the

"An Unprovoked Assault Upon the Inhabitants"

In early July 1775, the Second Continental Congress issued a declaration explaining why it had directed the colonies to fight the British. This included a description of the first hostilities, in Massachusetts on April 19, 1775, and of the subsequent condition of the people of Boston as colonial militias surrounded the city and kept the British army penned in there. Among those able to flee Boston to safety elsewhere was Benjamin Franklin's sister, Jane Mecom, who moved to Rhode Island.

. . . general Gage, who in the course of the last year had taken possession of the town of Boston, in the province of Massachusetts-Bay, and still occupied it a garrison, on the 19th day of April, sent out from that place a large detachment of his army, who made an unprovoked assault on the inhabitants of the said province, at the town of Lexington, as appears by the affidavits of a great number of persons, some of whom were officers and soldiers of that detachment, murdered eight of the inhabitants, and wounded many others. From thence the troops proceeded in warlike array to the town of Concord, where they set upon another party of the inhabitants of the same province, killing several and wounding more, until compelled to retreat by the country people suddenly assembled to repel this cruel aggression. Hostilities, thus commenced by the British troops, have been since prosecuted by them without regard to faith or reputation.—The inhabitants of Boston being confined within that town by the general their governor, and having, in order to procure their dismission, entered into a treaty with him, it was stipulated that the said inhabitants having deposited their arms with their own magistrate, should have liberty to depart, taking with them their other effects. They accordingly delivered up their arms, but in open violation of honour, in defiance of the obligation of treaties, which even savage nations esteemed sacred, the governor ordered the arms deposited as aforesaid, that they might be preserved for their owners, to be seized by a body of soldiers; detained the greatest part of the inhabitants in the town, and compelled the few who were permitted to retire, to leave their most valuable effects behind.

By this perfidy wives are separated from their husbands, children from their parents, the aged and the sick from their relations and friends, who wish to attend and comfort them; and those who have been used to live in plenty and even elegance, are reduced to deplorable distress.

Source: Continental Congress, *"Declaration of the Causes and Necessity of Taking Up Arms,"* July 6, 1775.

rest of America was not. Within a matter of months, however, events would bring Congress to face the issue of independence.

The People Take Sides

Between 1774 and 1776, as the dispute with Britain grew, many people in the colonies were forced to take sides. Americans entered the final crisis with Britain divided, not united. Among the merchants, slave holders, farmers, artisans, laborers, housewives, and seamstresses who formed the revolutionary coalition, there was a powerful feeling of belonging to a grand cause, and of having an opportunity to remake their world as they wanted it to be. But what some found exhilarating many others feared. Some of them decided to go along with revolution, "swimming with a stream," as one New Yorker put it, "it is impossible to stem." Others decided that life would be intolerable without a king and the social order he stood for. The ambivalence of many was expressed by a man named John Commons as he addressed a meeting of upcountry New York farmers. "Those who think the Congress is right should go," he said, "and those who think the king is right should stay." Commons himself admitted, "I do not know who is right."

Loyalism proved a stubborn problem for the revolutionaries. In a few places, such as the prosperous farming country around New York City, loyalists formed a strong majority. In the Hudson and Mohawk valleys, parts of New Jersey, Maryland's eastern shore, and much of the Carolina backcountry, loyalists were numerous enough to turn the struggle between Britain and the colonies into a civil war.

People chose sides according to circumstances, and in light of older social and political conflicts. Inhabitants in and around Manhattan knew

"The Destruction of the Royal Statue." An incident in New York City in 1776 inspired this German engraving. After a public reading of the Declaration of Independence, Patriots marched to a statue of George III standing in the city's Bowling Green and pulled it off its pedestal. The lead statue was reputedly melted down and used for ammunition.

Source: Francois Xavier Habermann—Prints and Photographs Division, Library of Congress.

LA DESTRUCTION DE LA STATUE ROYALE A NOUVELLE YORCK.

Die Zerstorung der Koniglichen Bild Saule zu Neu Yorck | La Destruction de la Statue royale a Nouvelle Yorck

that they were vulnerable to attack by the British army headquartered there. Some Hudson Valley tenants followed their loyalist landlords, whereas others became loyalist when landlords they hated chose the patriot cause. Poor white Marylanders were suspicious of the planter elite. One wheelwright asserted that "The gentlemen were intending to make us all fight [the British to protect] their land and Negroes. . . . If I had a few more white people to join me I could get all the Negroes to back us, and they would do more good in the night than the white people could do in the day." Some Virginia slaves rallied to the king because they were promised freedom in exchange for service in the army. A considerable number of whites in the North and South Carolina backcountry supported the Crown because their provinces' patriot leaders were the same men who had opposed the Regulator movements a few years before. Many Indians, too, backed Britain, because only British restraint stood between them and land-hungry Americans. Tens of thousands of loyalists would ultimately emigrate from their homes — some back to Britain, many more to Nova Scotia or New Brunswick, where they would remain British colonists.

Many who sided with the revolution did so only after long hesitation. Prior to independence, the greatest disunity and doubts about militancy existed in Pennsylvania and New York. In both these provinces, political leaders were sharply divided. Pennsylvania's Joseph Galloway, longtime political associate of Benjamin Franklin, led a sizable portion of the Philadelphia elite to oppose any effort by Congress to do more than petition the king for redress of grievances. New York's DeLancey family and the political faction associated with it quickly chose loyalism. These men, including wealthy import merchants, decided that the gathering revolutionary movement posed more danger than British policies. Much of the rest of New York's upper class, along with men such as Pennsylvania's John Dickinson, foremost of the pamphleteers against the Townshend Duties, hesitated on the brink long after Virginians such as Washington and Jefferson, and New Englanders such as John Hancock or John and Abigail Adams, had made up their minds for independence. After independence, these hesitant leaders did their best to obtain a new political order that would be secure for their own class.

Popular opinion in Pennsylvania and New York was also split. Both radicalism *and* strongly felt loyalism to the king were emerging. Philadelphia and New York City witnessed the development of a new political movement made up of artisans and the old Sons of Liberty. New York artisans started meetings "to concert matters" as early as 1773, and the next year they bought a building of their own and named it Liberty Hall. It was artisans who carried out New York's "tea party" in March 1774.

Gradually, popular organization pushed New York and Philadelphia in a radical direction. In 1774, as those at a New York City meeting debated how to respond to the Coercive Acts, an astute young gentleman named Gouverneur Morris looked on from a balcony. On one side of the debate were merchants and property owners, men like Morris himself. On the other side were "all the tradesmen, etc. who thought it worthwhile to leave daily labor for the good of the country. . . . The mob begin to think and to reason." He called them "poor reptiles," but "with fear and trembling" predicted that " 'ere noon they will bite." Morris tended to overdramatize, but he understood what he saw. Nine years of resistance to Britain had given working people a new political identity and a voice that would not be stilled.

Indeed, the notion of radicalism had two dimensions that often, but not necessarily, coincided. On one hand, it entailed firm opposition to British measures, and a willingness to take steps that would lead, by 1776, to a complete break with British rule. On the other, some radicals went further, advocating social and political change within America itself. Pennsylvania patriots, including rural Germans and Scots-Irish, and members of the urban popular movement, pressed for more equal political representation in the province, and for a reduction in the property qualifications for voting. In Virginia and the Carolinas, radical political leaders found that patriotism involved compromising with popular demands for equality. When gentry in Fairfax County, Virginia, first formed a volunteer militia company in September 1774, they adopted a gentlemen's uniform of blue coats, breeches, waistcoats, and white stockings. Five months later, now organized as the Fairfax county militia and "Embodying the people," they wore hunting shirts and trousers. When the provincial assembly met in June 1775, gentry members appeared wearing coarse linen or canvas shirts and carrying tomahawks—the clothes of ordinary frontiersmen. As the royal governor of South Carolina noted, "the People . . . have Discovered their own strength and importance," and would not be "so easily governed by their former Leaders."

Between 1774 and 1776 urban artisans found a new forum in the popular committee movement. They formed Committees of Correspondence even before the Continental Congress called for committees to enforce its Continental Association. These early committees were deliberately based as broadly as possible. New York City's Committee of Fifty-One contained both fiery radicals and men who would soon declare their loyalty to the Crown. But the election of new committees to enforce the Association, and then to coordinate the war effort once fighting started, shifted the membership. By early 1776 urban committees were dominated by the same types of patriotic men who had formed the Sons of Liberty ten years earlier. New York artisans formed a committee of their own. In Philadelphia there was a committee representing privates in the city's militia. Rural committees were controlled by obscure farmers. Women, too, became involved in popular action, helping committee searches, enforcing boycotts, raising funds, and making clothing and supplies. After a hard day's carding and spinning wool on her family's Connecticut farm, Betsy Foote wrote that she "felt Nationly." A young New Yorker, Charity Clarke, claimed that America, helped by a "fighting army of amazons . . . armed with spinning wheels," would be able to "retire beyond the reach of arbitrary power." These developments unleashed a greater militancy and radicalism, bringing new figures into public life and altering the way it was conducted.

Common Sense. The cover of Thomas Paine's 1776 pamphlet.

Source: Prints and Photographs Division, Library of Congress.

Philadelphia's popular movement gained particular importance because of the city's size and the fact that it was the seat of the Continental Congress. Among artisans and apprentices the resistance to Britain had fostered a lively radical political culture. As the city's elite retreated, divided and confused, radical committees secured support for the revolutionary cause. Philadelphia produced the revolution's most powerful pamphleteer, Thomas Paine, an English radical who had arrived in America only in 1774 but quickly immersed himself in political journalism. Early in 1776, as the Continental Congress was wavering over whether or not to pursue independence from Britain, Paine's pamphlet *Common Sense* struck a powerful blow in favor. "We have it in our power," Paine wrote, "to begin the world over again."

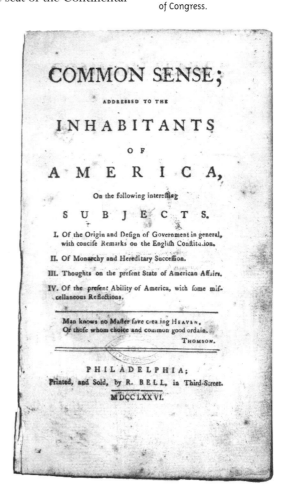

Paine used plain language. He addressed the political concerns of patriot elites, but he aimed his ideas in particular at artisans and farmers, whom he urged to join the political discussion and to sever the ties between themselves and Britain. He argued that Britain's military attacks on colonists had made reconciliation impossible, and that Americans' future would in any case be jeopardized by retaining their colonial dependency on Britain. Independence would not only be just ("a government of our own is our natural right"), but also expedient: America's prosperity would follow from having "the legislative powers in her own hands."

Above all, Paine ridiculed the idea of a monarchy and the principle of government by hereditary succession on which it rested. He laid out instead a plan for an independent America under republican government, in which annually elected provincial assemblies based on "more equal . . . representation" would be overseen by an elected congress governed by a Continental Charter. Paine's book won such acclaim that he immodestly called it "the greatest sale that any performance ever had since the use of letters." Up to 150,000 copies were printed. From Georgia to New Hampshire people read and applauded Paine's argument for independence and his vision of a great popular democracy freed from the ties of European monarchy.

Independence

As the war deepened, the case for independence made increasing sense. Loyalists and those urging moderation found their arguments weakening as fellow colonists faced not only political oppression but actual attack by the British army. The popularity of Tom Paine's argument and of other calls for independence helped move the cause forward, and the existence of the Continental Army gave Congress the political strength to contemplate such a step. In the early summer of 1776 the Continental Congress appointed Thomas Jefferson and others to draft a declaration of independence that, after making amendments, it adopted in early July.

The Declaration's chief purpose was to explain and justify the severing of ties with Britain. It catalogued a long list of grievances against the king that amounted to "a history of repeated injuries and usurpations, all having in direct object the establishment of an absolute Tyranny over these States." If a people were suffering under oppressive rule, the Declaration proclaimed, "It is their right, it is their duty, to throw off such Government," and to set up a new political system.

By declaring independence, and forming a new entity—the United States of America—Americans markedly raised the political and military stakes in their struggle with Britain. Britain, if it wanted to prevail, would no longer have to suppress a rebellion, it would have to reconquer what had become an independent people. With independence, American radicals took the final step in redefining themselves and their protest against Britain. They no longer saw themselves as "colonists," as rebels against British authority, or as protecting their "rights and privileges [as] freeborn Englishmen." They were now free Americans defending their independent states against an overseas power.

Independence did much more, however, than alter Americans' relationship to Britain. The Declaration of Independence proclaimed

"Remember the Ladies . . ."

Some American women were fired by the possibilities of the revolution, among them Abigail Adams, wife of John Adams, a Boston lawyer who was attending the Continental Congress in Philadelphia. Abigail Adams read Paine's *Common Sense* and agreed with its plea for independence; she wrote to her husband, raising the question of revising laws affecting the status of women. John Adams's response shows the fears of elite patriots that subordinate people of all sorts were throwing off their deference to their social "betters."

Abigail Adams to John Adams, Braintree [Mass.], March 31, 1776

I long to hear that you have declared an independency—and by the way in the new Code of Laws, which I suppose it will be necessary for you to make, I desire you would Remember the Ladies, and be more generous and favorable to them than your ancestors. Do not put such unlimited power into the hand of the Husbands. Remember all Men would be tyrants if they could. If particular care and attention is not paid to the Ladies we are determined to foment a Rebellion, and will not hold ourselves bound by any Laws in which we have no voice, or Representation.

That your Sex are Naturally Tyrannical is a Truth so thoroughly established as to admit of no dispute, but such of you as wish to be happy willingly give up the harsh title of Master for the more tender and endearing one of Friend. Why then, not put it out of the power of the vicious and the Lawless to use us with cruelty and indignity with impunity? Men of Sense in all Ages abhor those customs which treat us only as the vassals of your Sex. Regard us then as Beings placed by providence under your protection and in imitation of the Supreme Being make use of that power only for our happiness.

John Adams to Abigail Adams, Philadelphia, April 14, 1776

As to your extraordinary Code of Laws. I cannot but laugh. We have been told that our Struggle has loosened the bands of Government everywhere. That Children and Apprentices were disobedient—that schools and Colleges were grown turbulent—that Indians slighted their Guardians and Negroes grew insolent to their Masters. But your Letter was the first Intimation that another Tribe more numerous and powerful than all the rest were grown discontented. This is rather too coarse a Compliment but you are so saucy, I won't blot it out.

Depend upon it, We know better than to repeal our Masculine systems. . . . Rather than give up this, which would completely subject Us to the Despotism of the Petticoat, I hope General Washington, and all our brave Heroes would fight.

Source: L. H. Butterfield and Wendell D. Garrett, eds., *Adams Family Correspondence, Vol. I* (1963).

universal rights, rooted not in British precedents, but in the laws of nature. It suggested a radical vision of a new American society. It affirmed that the ultimate source of authority should lie not with kings or rulers, but with "the good People of these Colonies." Its bold statement "that all men are created equal" reflected the popular attempt to wrest self-government and self-determination from the hierarchical power of an imperial monarchy. Alongside liberty and political rights it placed the concept of equality. Tom Paine had written that "Whenever I use the words *freedom* or *rights,* I . . . mean a perfect equality of them. . . . The floor of Freedom is as level as water."

Yet Americans were not all agreed that equality or popular government should be the basis of their new nation. The citizen-militias of New England had brought them to war and revolution, but Americans were divided as to whether these should provide a model for continuing the war or for forming new governments. When Washington arrived in Massachusetts to take command of the Continental Army, he viewed his ragtag soldiers with as much disdain as any British officer would have. They were, he wrote, "generally speaking the most indifferent kind of people I ever saw . . . an exceedingly dirty and nasty people." New York patriot generals cursed at having New England soldiers to command. "It is extremely difficult," wrote Philip Schuyler, "to introduce a proper subordination among a people where so little distinction is kept up," and Richard Montgomery complained that "New England troops are the worst stuff imaginable. There is such an equality among them." He called for "*gentlemen* to serve, . . . [to] render the troops much more tractable."

George Washington's goal from the start was to build "a respectable army," and he gradually made conditions more and more like those of the British regulars his troops were fighting. The rough, often unruly democracy of the war's beginning was superseded by harsher discipline, and Washington's recipe for the Continental Army reflected the wishes of many members of Congress for an independent America. Once the British were finally removed, they hoped, they could build an ordered, disciplined society under the control of an American upper class. James Duane, a future mayor of New York, urged that leadership should be "in the hands of property and rank who . . . will preserve . . . authority over the minds of the people." The tension between popular and elite conceptions of the new United States would be a recurrent theme throughout the revolution and the events that were to follow.

The Years in Review

1744–1748

- New England Protestants enthusiastically support British campaigns against the French Catholic colonists in Quebec during King George's War between Britain and France.

1751

- Britain prohibits New England colonies from making paper currencies legal tender in payment of debts; some see the ban as a dangerous intrusion on colonial affairs.

1752

- Nineteen Days Have September: Britain and colonies adopt the Gregorian calendar and so Thursday, September 14, follows Wednesday, September 2.

1753

- Liberty Bell installed in Independence Hall; there is no evidence, however, that it was rung to mark the Declaration of Independence in 1776; it only began to be called the Liberty Bell by antislavery activists in 1839.

1754

- French and Indian War begins, lasting for seven years and not settled until the Peace of Paris, 1763. Spreading to Europe in 1756, the war is known there as the Seven Years' War.

1760

- Ben Franklin invents bifocals after tiring of carrying around two pairs of glasses.

1763

- At the Peace of Paris, Great Britain acquires Canada from France and Florida from Spain.
- Scots-Irish frontiersmen (the Paxton Boys) march on Philadelphia to force the government to remove Indians from the land they want.
- A French fur trader establishes St. Louis as a Mississippi trading post.

1764

- Green Mountain Boys from New Hampshire wage sporadic guerrilla warfare against New York land speculators.
- The Sugar Act, a revenue raising measure, is strongly opposed in the colonies.
- Currency Act demands that all American colonies cease printing paper money.

1765

- Stamp Act, which requires a stamp on printed materials ranging from wills and newspapers to playing cards, sparks colonial reaction. Boston protest against the Stamp Act results in a mob attack on Lieutenant Governor Thomas Hutchinson's house.

1766

- Stamp Act repealed, but in the Declaratory Act, Parliament declares its authority over the American colonies.

- First St. Patrick's Day Parade held in New York City by an Irish military unit recruited to serve in the colonies.

1767

- Revenue Act (Townshend Duties) places a duty on goods imported by the American colonies.

1770

- March 5: Boston Massacre.
- The Public Hospital for Persons of Insane and Disordered Minds, the first mental hospital in the colonies, opens in Williamsburg, Virginia.

1771

- Battle of the Alamance ends six-year conflict in the North Carolina backcountry between disenfranchised middling and poor whites and the provincial government dominated by the coastal elite.
- Umbrellas first appear in Philadelphia, and are widely derided.

1772

- Boston town meeting establishes Committee of Correspondence to build a coalition between town and country.
- Angry Rhode Islanders burn the British schooner *Gaspée*. The British government overrides the authority of the colonial courts by appointing a special commission to investigate.

1773

- The Tea Act gives the British East India Company a monopoly on tea imported to America.
- December 16: Boston Tea Party.

1774

- May: Parliament passes the Intolerable or Coercive Acts.
- September 5 to October 26: First Continental Congress meets in Philadelphia.

1775

- April 19: American War of Independence begins at the Battles of Lexington and Concord.
- May: Second Continental Congress convenes in Philadelphia.

1776

- Thomas Paine publishes the pamphlet *Common Sense,* which rapidly gains popularity among artisans and farmers.
- Continental Congress declares independence from Britain on July 2 (not July 4, as most people believe). The Declaration of Independence is adopted two days later, although most delegates do not sign it until August 2.
- Phi Beta Kappa at William and Mary becomes the first fraternity in the colonies; only in 1831 does it become a mark of academic distinction.

- Bartender Betsy Flanagan makes the first cocktail; the term comes from the fact that the bar is decorated with tail feathers.
- American Revolutionary soldier Nathan Hale is hanged by the British as a spy. His last words were not, however, "I only regret that I have but one life to lose for my country." He probably said, "It is the duty of every good officer to obey any orders given him by his commander-in-chief."

Suggested Readings

Anderson, Fred, *A People's Army: Massachusetts Soldiers and Society in the Seven Years' War* (1984).

Bailyn, Bernard, *The Ideological Origins of the American Revolution* (1967).

Brown, Richard D., *Revolutionary Politics in Massachusetts: The Boston Committee of Correspondence and the Towns, 1772–1774* (1970).

Countryman, Edward, *A People in Revolution: The American Revolution and Political Society in New York, 1760–1790* (1981).

Countryman, Edward, *The American Revolution* (1985).

Dayton, Cornelia H., *Women before the Bar: Gender, Law, and Society in Connecticut* (1995).

Deloria, Philip, *Playing Indian* (1998).

Foner, Eric, *Tom Paine and Revolutionary America* (1976).

Greene, Jack P., *Pursuits of Happiness: The Social Development of Early Modern British Colonies and the Formation of American Culture* (1988).

Gross, Robert, *The Minutemen and their World* (1976).

Hoerder, Dirk, *Crowd Action in Revolutionary Massachusetts* (1977).

Hoffman, Ronald, and Peter J. Albert, ed., *The Transforming Hand of Revolution: Reconsidering the American Revolution as a Social Movement* (1996).

Isaac, Rhys, *The Transformation of Virginia, 1740–1790* (1982).

Jennings, Francis, *Empire of Fortune: Crown, Colonies, and Tribes in the Seven Years' War* (1988).

Maier, Pauline, *From Resistance to Revolution: Colonial Radicals and the Development of American Opposition to Britain, 1765–1776* (1972).

Maier, Pauline, *American Scripture: The Making of the Declaration of Independence* (1997).

Marston, Jerrilyn Greene, *King and Congress: The Transfer of Political Legitimacy, 1774–1776* (1987).

Matson, Cathy, *Merchants and Empire: Trading in Colonial New York* (1998).

Nash, Gary B., *The Urban Crucible: Social Change, Political Consciousness, and the Origins of the American Revolution* (1979).

Nobles, Gregory H., *Divisions throughout the Whole: Politics and Society in Hampshire County, Massachusetts, 1740–1775* (1983).

Norton, Mary Beth, *Liberty's Daughters: The Revolutionary Experience of American Women, 1750–1800* (1980).

Purvis, Thomas L., *Proprietors, Patronage, and Money: New Jersey, 1703–1776* (1986).

Ryerson, Richard Alan, *The Revolution is Now Begun: The Radical Committees of Philadelphia, 1765–1776* (1978).

Shannon, Timothy J., *Indians and Colonists at the Crossroads of Empire: The Albany Congress of 1754* (1999).

Sung Bok Kim, *Landlord and Tenant in Colonial New York: Manorial Society, 1664–1775* (1978).

Thomas, P. D. G., *British Politics and the Stamp Act Crisis* (1975).

Thomas, P. D. G., *The Townshend Duties Crisis* (1987).

Thomas, P. D. G., *From Tea Party to Independence* (1991).

Tiedemann, Joseph S., *Reluctant Revolutionaries: New York City and the Road to Independence, 1763–1776* (1997).

Walsh, Richard, *Charleston's Sons of Liberty* (1959).

Young, Alfred F., *The American Revolution: Explorations in the History of American Radicalism* (1976).

And on the World Wide Web

Colonial Williamsburg Foundation, *Historical Almanack*
(http://www.history.org/almanack.htm)
Library of Congress, *The Thomas Jefferson Papers at the Library of Congress*
(http://memory.loc.gov/ammem/mtjhtml/mtjhome.html)
University of Groningen, *From Revolution to Reconstruction*
(http://odur.let.rug.nl/~usa)

chapter 5

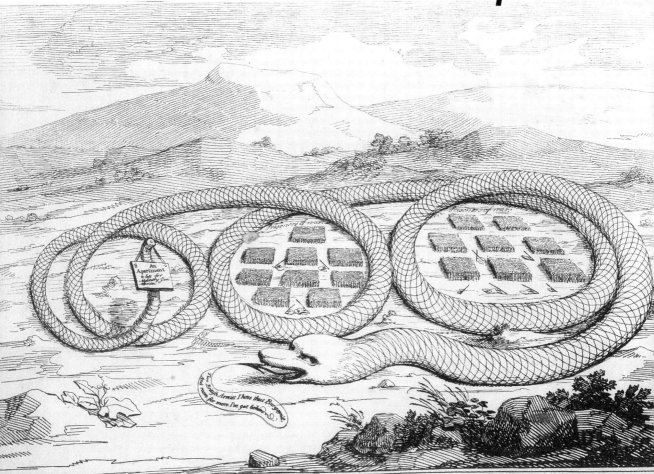

Britons within the Yankean Plains,
Mind how ye March & Trench,

| The AMERICAN RATTLE SNAKE. |

Pub.d April 12.th 1782. by W.Humphrey N.o 227 Strand.

The Serpent in the Congress reigns,
As well as in the French.

Revolution, Constitution, and the People
1776–1815

As war erupted between the American colonies and Britain, and as the colonies declared their independence, great numbers of working men and women took up the patriot cause. Boston shoemaker George Hewes was among them. He used his seafaring experience to fight as a seaman aboard Massachusetts warships. Serving the revolution shaped his growing sense of his place in a more democratic society. In 1778 or 1779 he signed up to join one vessel, but "not liking the manners of the Lieutenant very well" he left it, and enlisted on another. The officer had offended Hewes when he "ordered him one day in the streets to take his hat off to him—which he refused to do for any man." Hewes saw himself no longer as the subject of a colonial monarchy, but as a citizen in the new republic, and he rejected the deferential habits and expectations of colonial days. For him and for many others, America's revolution meant becoming equal participants in a new society.

From the first shots in the war to a decisive American victory in 1781 took six hard years; it was another two before Britain signed a peace agreement recognizing American independence. Ordinary people helped bring about the military successes that secured this independence, questioned older hierarchical assumptions, and claimed for themselves a stake in political sovereignty. The Latin motto on the new U.S. official seal proclaimed a *novus ordo seclorum*—a new order of the ages. For the first time ever, overseas colonies of a European power had achieved political independence from their mother country and the opportunity to set up their own form of society.

Americans had to make crucial decisions about how they were now to govern themselves, how they should act in relation to one another, who would get a say in public affairs, and how they should use the vast land area over which they now claimed control. Many among American elites disagreed with popular conceptions of republican society, and their views shaped the U.S. Constitution that would be drafted and ratified in the late 1780s. Large groups were excluded from the aspiration for equality. Economic conditions ensured that inequalities would persist. And the regional differences that had emerged in the colonial period, especially between North and South, not only persisted but grew. Yet America was changed by revolution, and new social and political attitudes ensured that the colonial world would not be re-created. Moreover, the creation of an

"The American Rattle Snake." The British political artist James Gillray's 1782 cartoon commented on the military situation the King's delegates faced at the start of peace negotiations with the United States. British forces commanded by Generals Burgoyne and Cornwallis are shown trapped within the snake's coils, while its rattle carries a placard stating, "An Apartment to Lett for Military Gentlemen."

Source: James Gillray, etching, London, April 12, 1782—Prints and Photographs Division, Library of Congress.

independent United States would permanently alter the balance of power on the North American continent, with profound consequences for American Indians, for the European powers, and for the inhabitants of Spain's American colonies, who would themselves seize political independence within the next fifty years.

The Toils of War

From the British evacuation of Boston early in 1776 to their surrender at Yorktown in 1781, armies campaigned in eastern New York, New Jersey and Pennsylvania, and the South, with numerous secondary actions and skirmishes elsewhere on the continent. Although the war started in New England, its center of activity shifted southward as the British increased their forces in an effort to recapture their rebellious colonies. The Americans were able to win a notable victory at Saratoga, New York, in 1777, when their forces trapped a British army marching down from Canada and captured over five thousand soldiers with their equipment. More important than its scale, the victory at Saratoga removed the threat of

"Surrender of the British Army." A French print depicted the 1781 victory of American and French armies over the British in Yorktown, Virginia. As shown here, French ships blocked the entrance of Chesapeake Bay, preventing British ships from resupplying their troops on the shore. But, having no knowledge of the locale, the French artist rendered Yorktown as a European walled city.

Source: Mondhare, "Reddition de l'Armée Angloises Commandée par Mylord Comte de Cornwallis," etching with watercolor, Paris, 1781—Chicago Historical Society.

238

invasion from the north and, above all, convinced the French government that eventual American success in the war was possible. France quickly joined the war on the American side, and was soon contributing military and naval support. Subsequently Spain and then Holland also declared war on Britain, forcing it to confront the combined threat of three of Europe's most significant powers as well as the American revolutionaries. French assistance proved critical in finally bringing the fighting to a close four years after Saratoga. In 1781, George Washington's Continentals, together with a sizable French army, were able to trap a large British force in the fortress at Yorktown, Virginia. At a critical moment, a French naval fleet evaded a British blockade of its ports, crossed the Atlantic, and prevented British supply ships entering Chesapeake Bay to relieve Yorktown. Surrounded and threatened with starvation, the 9,500 British troops surrendered, giving the Americans a decisive victory.

Yet such dramatic military gains had been rare for the Americans. An attempt in late 1775 to invade Canada and capture Quebec ended in disaster. In general, American success depended less on winning battles than on avoiding losing them—on keeping armies intact, and scoring minor victories when opportunity arose. Regrouping after their withdrawal from Boston, British forces returned in strength in the summer of 1776. They captured Long Island and then New York City, which they retained as their main military and naval base until 1783. Defeated on Long Island, Washington (aided by East River fishermen) escaped with the remains of his army and retreated, first to Manhattan, then to Westchester County, then again across the Hudson River into New Jersey. The people of eastern New York and New Jersey included many loyalists, and the British used the area to obtain supplies for their forces. By late 1776 they had driven Washington's army into Pennsylvania. Yet Washington's men avoided being crushed by the British. After months of dodging defeat, they returned to New Jersey and won small victories at Trenton and Princeton in the winter of 1776–1777. These led the British to withdraw from much of the state. The following summer, however, the British attacked again and, brushing aside Washington's attempts to stop them, captured Philadelphia, which they held until the following year.

The presence of the opposing forces imposed a great burden on the people of the mid-Atlantic states. The British in particular foraged for food and supplies, and they and their loyalist allies fought numerous skirmishes with patriots. As armies moved to and fro, families fled their homes and farms to take shelter in safer areas. One woman said later that "there was so much suffering, and so many alarms in our neighborhood . . . that it has always been painful for me to dwell upon them." Patriots and loyalists alike endured the suffering. Yet British depredations and the continued presence of an American army in New Jersey and Pennsylvania restrained the further growth of support for the loyalist cause there, and helped keep the mid-Atlantic states on the revolutionary side. Just as they had previously in New England, the British found that they could not secure control of the region. They held New York City, and occupied Philadelphia for a period, but they could not conquer the countryside, where the majority of the population lived.

Accordingly, in the late 1770s the British embarked on an extensive campaign in the South. Their plan was to draw on the support of the many loyalists in the backcountry to help bring the southern states back under British rule, to demonstrate royal authority, to weaken French resolve to support the Americans, and to undermine the patriots' resolve to fight. They took Savannah and Charleston, at the latter capturing five thousand American soldiers, and defeated another patriot army at Camden, South Carolina. These successes went some way to restoring royal control over Georgia and South Carolina. But the British efforts also fomented a civil war between patriots and loyalists, whose armed militias fought a grim guerrilla-style struggle across the countryside. In October 1780 at King's Mountain, North Carolina, patriot fighters won a battle in which almost all the participants on both sides were Americans. The following January a patriot force defeated a British detachment at Cowpens. The struggle was bitter. An American general reported that the patriot militia were "without discipline and addicted to plundering." One South Carolina fighter carved notches in his rifle for each of the loyalists he shot. Resentments ran high. More than one loyalist militia leader, captured by patriots, was seized by vigilantes and murdered. South Carolina's David Ramsay would remark that few people in his state "did not partake of the general distress."

The American war effort relied on two distinct kinds of military force. Each province or (after Independence) state raised its own militia from among its citizens, often for short enlistment periods. In addition, Congress raised the Continental Army for longer-term service. In all, about two hundred thousand men were enlisted for one period or another during the war.

The militias comprised the great majority of American soldiers. At first, most militia units were filled by the kinds of men who had started the fighting in Massachusetts in 1775. Farmers, artisans, their sons, and apprentices, with a scattering of merchants, lawyers, and clergymen, dropped their work to fight off the invaders of their countryside. Six thousand or so militiamen rallied to help defeat the British at Saratoga. But the early enthusiasm of these units quickly waned. Militiamen became more difficult to recruit, and often proved reluctant to serve for extended periods or at great distances from their homes. In a largely rural society, particularly outside plantation regions with their slave labor, young and able-bodied men were essential for planting and harvesting crops. As a

North Carolinian noted, "a soldier made is a farmer lost." The need to maintain an army capable of preventing the British from recapturing the colonies constantly conflicted with the basic requirement that labor be available for farming — without which the country would have starved. After Washington's defeat on Long Island in 1776, many of his militiamen returned home for the harvest. Even so, farm labor was scarce. A Connecticut woman recalled that "so many [men] were gone" that Fall, "that she, her aged Father in Law . . . and such little children as could be had, dug the potatoes and husked the corn." Virginians protested in 1781 when the state attempted to draft militiamen at planting time.

First the Continental Army and then, increasingly, state militias also, began to recruit from more marginal segments of society, such as the ranks of the young and the poor. Recruitment from these groups made possible the fighting of a defensive war in this largely rural society that had slender resources to call on. Most Continental soldiers were young men who had formerly been apprentices, laborers, landless farm boys, or slaves. Jeremiah Greenman of Rhode Island was seventeen when he marched to take part in the siege of Boston in the summer of 1775. Without a trade or prospect of land to inherit, he decided to enlist in the Continental service. Captured twice and wounded three times, he was an officer by the time he left the army in 1783.

Some men, like Greenman, enlisted voluntarily; some were draftees; others served as paid substitutes for richer men. Some African Americans fought in place of their masters, such as the Connecticut slave Gad Asher, who was wounded and lost his sight at Bunker Hill, but returned home to work to purchase his freedom. Many other slaves, North and South, ran away to enlist, expecting to gain their freedom by fighting. After the British surrender at Saratoga, revolutionary leaders even tried to recruit prisoners of war. These included some of the "Hessian" mercenary soldiers from minor German states, whose deployment by George III had been one of the grievances listed in the Declaration of Independence. Thousands of women, too, traveled with the

The Homefront. A detail from an English printed handkerchief presented the contributions of three American sisters to the struggle for independence: while their husbands fought, they ran the farm — milking, baking, and, shown here, plowing.

Source: Concord Museum, Concord, Massachusetts.

armies. Many were "on the ration" as cooks, nurses, laundresses, orderlies, or gravediggers. Their work was essential to the war effort. They endured all the hardships of soldiers except that of battle itself. A few women, usually disguised as men, did in fact fight.

Hardship was plentiful for the American forces and the people whose support they relied on. Continentals and militia alike often faced worse conditions than the British soldiers they were confronting, as acute shortages of supplies added to the discomforts and dangers of wartime service. During the winter of 1777–1778, when the British occupied Philadelphia and enjoyed all the comforts of town life and the produce of the surrounding countryside that their money could purchase, Washington's army endured severe privations in its camp at Valley Forge only twenty miles away. At Morristown, New Jersey, two winters later, on one-eighth rations and with pay five months in arrears, the army faced even worse conditions. The weather was so bitter that there were still twelve feet of snow on the ground in March. When Jeremiah Greenman's unit was finally issued with clothing, he wrote that it "altered their Condition they being almost naked for nigh two Months."

As the war ground on, morale almost broke. A private named Joseph Plumb Martin wrote in 1780 that soldiers cursed themselves for their "imbecility in staying there and starving . . . for an ungrateful people." Near the end of the ordeal at Morristown, two Connecticut militia regiments "paraded under arms" to demand better conditions, but were dispersed by Pennsylvania troops. The next January the Pennsylvanians themselves mutinied; fifteen hundred marched off toward Philadelphia to protest to Congress. A mutiny of New Jersey soldiers was crushed, and two leaders were shot by firing squads of fellow mutineers. Even after Yorktown, the agony continued. The Continental Army remained encamped at Newburgh, New York, for nearly two years awaiting the final payment of its wages. Washington had to talk disgruntled officers out of staging a coup against Congress, and soldiers finally disbanded with only a token settlement of what they were owed.

Yet the hopes of many Americans for independence and a new republic were strong enough to overcome hardships and low morale. From his defeat at Long Island to the British surrender at Yorktown, Washington knew that the most important military task was to keep the Continental Army together, however much suffering it faced. With the mix of poor whites, slaves, foreigners, and women who either composed or supported the armies in the field, he achieved this aim. Without them the British would have triumphed. The Continental Army was small; at its largest it numbered fewer than twenty thousand. But it was more than a military

Wishful Thinking. A British caricature portrayed the American soldier as disheveled and maladroit.

Source: Metropolitan Museum of Art.

"She Faithfully Performed the Duties of a Soldier"

After the Revolution several women petitioned Congress for compensation for disabilities inflicted in combat. Deborah Sampson Gannett was the only petitioner known to have fought disguised as a man. As Robert Shurtleff, she served with the Continental Army, and these excerpts, from the *Journals of the House of Representatives* in 1797–1798, record her unsuccessful attempt to obtain funds. Massachusetts, however, did provide her with some compensation.

The Petition of Deborah Gannett to the House of Representatives, Tuesday, November 28, 1797, recorded in *Journals of the House of Representatives,* vol. 3, p. 90.

A petition of Deborah Gannett of the town of Sharon in the state of Massachusetts, was presented to the house and read, stating that the petitioner, though a *female,* enlisted as a continental soldier, for the term of three years, in the Massachusetts line, of the late American Army, by the name of Robert Shurtleff; that she faithfully performed the duties of a soldier during the time above specified, and received a wound while in the actual service of the United States, in consequence of which she is subjected to pain and infirmities; and praying that she may receive the pay and emoluments granted to other wounded and disabled soldiers.

Ordered, that the said petitions . . . be referred to the Committee of Claims.

[March 9, 1798] Mr. Dwight Foster, from the committee of claims, to whom were referred the petitions of James Brown, of Deborah Gannett, of John Smuck, one of the heirs of Francis Koonz, deceased, and of John Henry Zimmerman, made a report, which was read and considered: Whereupon,

Resolved, that the prayer of the petitions of the said James Brown, Deborah Gannett, John Smuck and John Henry Zimmerman, cannot be granted.

Source: Carol Berkin and Leslie Horowitz, eds., *Women's Voices, Women's Lives: Documents in Early American History* (1998).

force: it symbolized the new American nation, and its preservation intact acted as a political guarantee of independence. Although in military terms the state militias were often uneven in performance, they too served a vital political role. Particularly in the former middle colonies and the South, where many loyalists entered the action when British armies came nearby, patriot militias worked, often violently, to restore American authority once the British had gone again.

". . . We Should Suffer Every Thing for Their Benefit"

Winters on campaign meant particular hardships for soldiers. Albigence Waldo, a surgeon serving with the Continental Army, wrote this graphic description of conditions at the encampment at Valley Forge, Pennsylvania, in his diary for December 14, 1777.

December 14. Prisoners and deserters are continually coming in. The army, which has been surprisingly healthy hitherto, now begins to grow sickly from the continued fatigues they have suffered this campaign. Yet they still show a spirit of alacrity and contentment not to be expected from so young troops. I am sick—discontented—and out of humour. Poor food—hard lodging—cold weather—fatigue—nasty cloathes—nasty cookery—vomit half my time—smoked out of my senses—the Devil's in't—I can't endure it—Why are we sent here to starve and freeze?—What sweet felicities have I left at home: A charming wife—pretty children—good bed—good food—good cooking—all agreeable—all harmonious! Here all confusion—smoke and cold—hunger and filthyness—a pox on my bad luck! People who live at home in luxury and ease, quietly possessing their habitations, enjoying their wives and families in peace, have but a very faint idea of the unpleasing sensations and continual anxiety the man endures who is in a camp, and is the husband and parent of an agreeable family. These same people are willing we should suffer every thing for their benefit and advantage and yet are the first to condemn us for not doing more!!

Source: Alden Vaughan, ed., *Eyewitness Accounts of the American Revolution.*

Support for American independence was strong enough, and the endurance of the Continental and militia forces sufficient, that Britain was never able to gain the balance of advantage in the war. Despite their great military and naval strength, the British were unable to reconquer and hold onto significant areas of their former colonies. As first France and then other European nations joined the war against them, the British had to expend resources defending other parts of their empire, and guarding against a French invasion of England itself. As these pressures mounted and serious riots in London in 1780 added the fear of domestic insurrection, the British government lost the will to fight in America. The surrender at Yorktown convinced many British officials that the war was lost, and soon led to peace negotiations.

War on the Frontier

The war was not confined to contests over the settled parts of the former colonies. It also concerned control of the whole eastern part of the continent. Colonists' desire for frontier land had been one of the underlying sources of antagonism to British policy. Part of Britain's purpose in establishing the unpopular Proclamation Line of 1763 had been to moderate settler-native conflict by seeking to regulate trans-Appalachian settlement. When war broke out in 1775, fighting rapidly flared up in the west, as patriots sought to dislodge British frontier garrisons and seize land to which they had been denied access. First in what is now Kentucky, then in other areas, armed settlers and militia forces pushed into fresh territory. Both British and American units responded by doing what they had done through the succession of previous colonial wars: they drew on alliances with Indians.

Indians, too, pursued the strategies they had developed in previous wars. This time, however, circumstances were different and the stakes were higher. With the removal of the French in the early 1760s, the Iroquois in particular had negotiated more and more closely with the British, their traditional allies, to protect their lands from incursions by colonial settlers and speculators. This had angered some other Native Americans. Shawnee leaders denounced the Iroquois as "Slaves of the White People," and such resentments foreshadowed schisms that occurred when the Revolutionary War broke out. Different Indian groups found themselves on opposite sides of the conflict. A few tribes chose to ally with the revolutionaries in the hope that this could spare them from the worst depredations of white settlers. Many, including most Iroquois, supported Britain as the most likely protector against the invasion of their lands. Others tried to remain neutral, but as conflict and murder took their toll, they were driven to resistance.

Along the frontier, patriots attacked Indian settlements, scattering the inhabitants, destroying crops, spreading starvation and disease. William Henry Drayton urged South Carolinians to "cut up every Indian cornfield and burn every Indian town and every Indian taken shall be the slave and property of the taker." Natives retaliated. In Kentucky in 1775, Cherokee warriors resisted an illegal land purchase by attacking settlers, but they were dispersed by white counterattacks the following year and their villages destroyed. Cherokees and Creeks again came under attack in 1781 and 1782 by southern patriot militias determined to prevent them from assisting the British. The Iroquois Confederacy broke apart. Many followed the Mohawk leader Joseph Brant in supporting the British, but a smaller number allied with the Americans, so that there were Iroquois fighters on both sides at the battle of Oriskany in 1777. Britain's Iroquois

Thayendanega. Guy Johnson, who succeeded his father-in-law Sir William Johnson as British superintendent of Indian affairs, was the ostensible subject of Benjamin West's painting, but it was the shadowy figure of Thayendanega, or Joseph Brant, that characterized the picture. This Mohawk chief, educated at New Hampshire's Indian School (later Dartmouth College), saw the war as an opportunity to gain Indian independence; he sided with the British in exchange for specific concessions. After a brief visit to Great Britain in 1775–1776 (where this picture was painted), Thayendanega returned to the colonies. Throughout the war, he led Iroquois raids on New York frontier settlements.

Source: Benjamin West, *Colonel Guy Johnson,* 1776, oil on canvas, 79 3/4 × 54 1/2 inches—National Gallery of Art, Washington, D.C.

allies faced repeated attacks in the years that followed. In 1779 patriot forces under General John Sullivan attacked and burned forty Iroquois settlements in western New York, destroying vast amounts of crops and driving the population away. Starvation and disease then ravaged the refugees.

Even neutral or patriot-supporting Indians came under vicious attack when whites wanted to clear them from the land. After occupying Kentucky, American forces pressed on into the Ohio country. In 1781 they raided their Delaware and Shawnee allies gathered around Coshocton on the Muskingum River, and the next year they attacked a settlement of pacifist Moravian converts at Gnadenhütten, killing ninety-six and causing many of the survivors to flee to Canada. However, such attacks also prompted natives to form increasingly effective alliances of their own against American incursions as the war drew to a close. The Shawnees and others launched counterattacks, and laid the ground for further resistance over the following three decades.

The Movement for a People's Government

As fighting flared across much of eastern North America, the ideology of revolution was being forged in the main coastal regions. The Declaration of Independence was its written expression. The Declaration rooted the colonies' claim to independence from Britain in theories about the nature of sovereignty and legitimate government. Americans were trying not just to free themselves from British rule, but also to build and codify a new social and political order. As British troops marched out to surrender at Yorktown in 1781, their band played a tune, "The World Turned Upside Down," that had been popular during the English Revolution over a century before. It symbolized their view of what the Americans were doing: overturning the established way of organizing government and society.

In its affirmation that "all men" were "created equal," and had "unalienable rights" to "life, liberty and the pursuit of happiness," the Declaration of Independence suggested that proper government rested on universal truths evident not just to an educated political elite, but to the common sense of all. This was not just an abstract statement, but designed to forge unity across the revolutionary political coalition of farmers, artisans, laborers, slaveholders, merchants, and professional men. It indicated that common folk as well as the wealthy and powerful could claim a role in their own self-government.

Most supporters of the revolution agreed that new American governments should be republican, resting on "the consent of the governed" rather than the sovereign authority of a monarch. But Americans had differing opinions about how democratic their republic should be, about how broadly or directly ordinary people should participate in political affairs. Conflict between elite and popular influences had been evident during the period from 1774 to 1776, when the patriot cause was in the hands of extralegal committees. These divisions persisted as the new states moved to establish their own permanent governments and constitutions.

In Philadelphia's increasingly radical atmosphere early in 1776, Tom Paine's pamphlet *Common Sense* put forward more than an attack on the legitimacy of monarchy and an urgent call for American independence. It also sketched a vision of democratic government for the new nation. Confident that people could govern themselves without the artificial distinctions of monarchy or aristocracy, Paine advocated a simple set of institutions based on direct democracy. States, and the nation as a whole, would each be governed by an annually elected assembly and headed by a president. Paine's popularity among the artisans and farmers whom the revolution had aroused ensured that his pamphlet would remain a symbol of this popular democracy. When Jeremiah Greenman's Rhode Island regiment celebrated the Fourth of July in 1783, its thirteen toasts included "the Congress of 1776 and *Common Sense*." Paine's was the clearest argument that, as another enthusiastic pamphleteer put it, "the people" would make "the best governors."

The men who came to power in Pennsylvania in 1776 fashioned a new state constitution that embodied many of Paine's ideas. There would be a state legislature with a single chamber, elected annually by all taxpaying adult males. There would be no property requirements for officeholders. Executive power would be lodged not in a powerful governor, but in a president and council who would serve the legislature.

". . . Common Sense and a Plain Understanding"

When a convention was called in 1776 to frame a constitution for the state of Pennsylvania, James Cannon, a radical patriot leader, advised ordinary Pennsylvanians to be certain to select delegates who would respect the rights and authority of the people. Cannon addressed the following broadside to the members of the Philadelphia militia, setting forth the qualities—including "common Sense and a plain Understanding"—he thought such delegates should possess.

A government made for the common Good should be framed by Men who can have no Interest besides the common Interest of Mankind. It is the Happiness of America that there is no Rank above that of Freeman existing in it; and much of our future welfare and Tranquillity will depend on its remaining so forever; for this Reason, great and over-grown rich Men will be improper to be trusted, they will be too apt to be framing Distinctions in Society, because they will reap the Benefits of all such Distinctions. . . . Honesty, common Sense, and a plain Understanding, when unbiased by sinister Motives, are fully equal to the Task—Men of like Passions and Interests with ourselves are most likely to frame us a good Constitution. . . . Some who have been very backward in declaring you a free People, will be very forward in offering themselves to frame your Constitution; but trust them not, however well recommended.

Source: Eric Foner, *Tom Paine and Revolutionary America* (1976).

"The Rights of Man: or Tommy Paine, the Little American Taylor, Taking the Measure of the Crown, for a New Pair of Revolution Breeches." British conservatives had little love for the author of *Common Sense* — especially after he returned to England in 1787 and pressed for radical republican goals in the land of his birth. Caricaturist James Gillray lampooned Paine in this 1791 cartoon, which appeared soon after the publication of his *The Rights of Man*. But the British establishment took Paine more seriously; within the year, Paine fled to revolutionary France to avoid imprisonment.

Source: James Gillray, engraving, 1791, 13 13/16 × 9 3/4 inches — American Philosophical Society Library.

THE RIGHTS OF MAN; — or TOMMY PAINE, the little American Taylor, taking the Measure of the CROWN, for a new Pair of Revolution-Breeches.

Except on "occasions of special necessity," every bill that came before the legislature would be "printed for the consideration of the people" before becoming law. Paine helped inspire patriots who were radical both in the sense that they supported independence and in the sense that they advocated a democratic, egalitarian society and political system. From 1776 to 1790 Pennsylvanians governed themselves on these democratic

YANKEE - DOODLE . or the American SATAN.

"Yankee Doodle, or the American Satan." This print, by an American-born engraver living in London, may have mocked British characterizations of the Patriot enemy by portraying the "evil" archetypal American as a plainly-dressed, serious-looking young man. After British soldiers started losing battles, their favorite song deriding colonists, "Yankee Doodle," was proudly appropriated by American forces.

Source: Joseph Wright, "Yankee Doodle, or the American Satan," engraving, c. 1778— Chicago Historical Society.

principles, designed to keep government close to the influence and scrutiny of the people.

The drafters of Pennsylvania's constitution included the radical physician Dr. Thomas Young, who regarded it "as near perfection as anything yet concerted by mankind." Among others, Young influenced the Green Mountain Boys, whose campaigns against New York landlords he had supported since the 1760s. As British rule collapsed and the British army suffered setbacks in New England, the Green Mountain Boys spearheaded their own local revolution, declaring independence from New York in 1777 and establishing Vermont as a separate republic. Drafting their own constitution, they accepted Young's advice to copy from Pennsylvania's,

Legislatures Become More Democratic, 1765–1790. State legislatures after the Revolution were considerably less dominated by men of wealth than the colonial assemblies had been in the decade before war with Britain began. In the North the rise in the proportion of legislators with less than £2,000 of property was particularly striking.

Source: James A. Henretta, et. al., *America's History* 2nd ed. (1993) vol I; adapted from Jackson Turner Main, "Government by the People: The American Revolution and the Democratization of the Legislatures," *William and Mary Quarterly,* 3rd ser. vol. 23 (1966).

Wealth of State Legislators Before and After the Revolution

Northern States / Southern States

1765–1775: Northern — 36%, 47%, 17%; Southern — 52%, 36%, 12%

1783–1790: Northern — 12%, 26%, 62%; Southern — 28%, 42%, 30%

Legend: Over £5,000 | £2,000–£5,000 | Under £2,000

and set up a direct democracy that would continue to operate in Vermont after it formally joined the United States in 1791.

Elsewhere, too, people felt exhilarated at the notion of abandoning the old ways. Again following Pennsylvania's example, Georgia adopted a single-chamber legislature, and Delaware, New Hampshire, and South Carolina all dropped the term "governor"—with its connotations of arbitrary, royal power—and adopted the more democratic title "president" for their chief executive. Increasing numbers of farmers and tradesmen replaced wealthy men in the legislatures. Before 1775, only one-sixth of New Hampshire, New Jersey, and New York assemblymen were of modest means; by the 1780s over three-fifths of them were. Even the Virginia legislature was, according to an observer, "composed of men not quite so well dressed, nor so politely educated, nor so highly born as . . . formerly."

The Limits to Democratization

But there were limits to this democratic thrust. Some Americans were horrified by the possibilities of democracy. The revolutionary coalition was deeply divided over how government should be formed, who should rule, and in whose interests policies should be conducted. When Jefferson—himself a slaveholder—included in an early draft of the Declaration of Independence a statement condemning the slave trade, members of the Continental Congress, mindful of their property and economic interests, had this deleted. Democracy, they felt, should be tempered by the claims of privilege.

John Adams of Massachusetts, for instance, was as keen as Paine for independence, but his vision of government was altogether more conservative. Published in 1776 as a counter to Paine's *Common Sense,* Adams's major pamphlet, *Thoughts on Government,* argued that it was impossible to govern without "balanced" institutions that gave elites a voice alongside that of the "people." Legislatures should have two chambers, not one, so that the members of the upper house could counter the influence of the citizenry represented in the lower. As Virginia's Charles Lee put it, the second chamber would hold "men of great worth . . . not possessing popular qualities." The question at issue was social as much as political. Who should rule: the "better sort," who had long held sway, or the artisans, farmers, and small traders for whom Paine had spoken? Adams was a republican, but he envisaged a republican society based on hierarchy and order. He wanted the country to "glide insensibly" in this direction, from the habits of a colonial society in which people "knew their place."

The new governments formed in Virginia, Maryland, New York, and Massachusetts were closer to Adams's vision than to Paine's. The Virginia gentry adopted a constitution that preserved their political control. Maryland's planter class, frightened by the democratic implications of the revolution, fashioned a new state constitution that put as much distance as possible between ordinary people and their rulers. It prescribed stiff property requirements for voting, stiffer ones for holding office, and long intervals between elections. In New York, unlike in Pennsylvania, opponents of democracy successfully used "well-timed delays, indefatigable industry, and minute . . . attention to every favorable circumstance" to hold their ground against democracy's advocates. The New York constitution created a state senate intended to represent property, not people, and a strong governor, who would be independent of the legislature, not its servant. Massachusetts followed suit.

For the period of the war and its aftermath, the states remained substantially independent of one another. Each sent representatives to the Continental Congress, which oversaw the conduct of the war and constructed a rudimentary government for the new United States. In 1777 Congress put forward a framework for a national government: the Articles of Confederation. Many states accepted this quickly, but others were skeptical of signing away powers to a government distant from them and from their people. Above all, there was disagreement on whether western lands should be assigned to the federal government. Only reluctantly did some states with land claims across the Appalachian mountains begin to give them up. As a result, it was 1781 before the Articles went into effect.

The Articles preserved the sovereignty of the individual states and held a tight rein on federal government. The states' annually elected delegations to Congress varied in size, but each state had only a single vote. Congress could create executive departments, but these remained under its direct control. To become law, its decisions required the support of a majority of states, but amendments to the Articles had to be unanimous. Above all, Congress had no independent power to levy taxes. For its expenditures—including financing the war—it had to rely on requisitions from the states, which might or might not provide them. To many Americans these provisions ensured that no federal government could exercise a tyranny of the sort that they had feared from Britain, and that power would lie with the states and their people. To some, however, the Articles of Confederation seemed weak and ineffectual. Advocates of stronger national government would soon challenge them.

Conflict Over Economic Issues

In addition to debating how democratic government should be, the revolutionary coalition was also divided over economic problems. The war brought inflation and shortages. War damage and loss of life, and the disruption of farming, trade, and manufacturing, produced severe difficulties. The war's end brought depression and glut, as goods that people could not afford went unsold. Production declined sharply. It would be a quarter century before America's output per head of population regained its pre-revolutionary level. Circumstances trapped many of the poor and middling in conditions that they could do little to control.

Having difficulty levying taxes, most state governments had financed their war contributions by printing ever-larger quantities of paper money. Congress was forced to do the same. The result was the worst inflation America had ever known. In 1779 Congress partly solved the problem by drastically devaluing its currency, but that did not deal with the huge demands created by the American, French, and British armies, or with the shortages of goods that resulted from the British blockade of American ports.

Many, especially those who had read Paine so avidly in 1776, turned to traditional concepts of social responsibility and justice, arguing that in a good society public interest should come before private gain. If supplies were scarce, they suspected "hoarders" of holding them back for profit. If prices rose, they blamed "speculators." Such circumstances had traditionally provoked people into action, and they did so again. Crowds, often made up of women, used the rituals of popular price setting to fight wartime inflation. For example, news that a trader had a supply of salt or sugar could lead to a visit from a crowd, who would offer a "just price" and then take what they needed. In Fishkill, New York, in August 1776, a group of women formed a committee to confront a prominent merchant who was refusing to sell from his stock of tea. Appointing a "clerk" and a "weigher," the women measured out the tea, announced that they would pay "the continental price" for it, and then gave the money to the local county committee. There were similar episodes in coastal and interior

New England, where the women were sometimes protected by Continental soldiers. In Boston "Joyce, Junior"—a figure symbolic of the republicans of the English Revolution—led crowds that drove monopolizers out of town.

By 1779, inflation was so severe that people across the North revived their revolutionary committees. A few had argued in 1776 that the committees should form a permanent part of government, and New York artisans and laborers had sent a strongly worded demand to the provincial congress that they be allowed to revive their committees whenever they wanted. But most people probably assumed that committees would disappear. New York's 1777 constitution referred to them as merely "temporary expedients . . . to exist no longer than the grievances of the people should remain without redress." In 1774 and 1775 the grievances had been with the British. Now committees were re-formed by people angry that state governments were failing to deal with the economic crisis, or with the "overbearing merchants, a swarm of monopolizers, an infernal gang of Tories" they blamed for it. When the price of bread rose

". . . We Cannot Live Without Bread"

In December 1778 a Philadelphia resident, styling himself "Mobility," wrote the following letter to a local newspaper, attacking monopolizers and calling, in no uncertain terms, for strong measures by crowds to guarantee the distribution of bread, "the Staff of Life."

This country has been reduced to the brink of ruin by the infamous practices of Monopolizers and Forestallers. Not satisfied with monopolizing European and West-Indian goods, they have lately monopolized the Staff of Life. Hence, the universal cry of the scarcity and high price of Flour. It has been found in Britain and France, that the People have always done themselves justice when the scarcity of bread has arisen from the avarice of forestallers. They have broken open magazines [warehouses]—appropriated stores to their own use without paying for them—and in some instances have hung up the culprits who have created their distress, without judge or jury. Hear this and tremble, ye enemies to the freedom and happiness of your country. We can live without sugar, molasses, and rum—but we cannot live without bread. Hunger will break through stone walls, and the resentment excited by it may end in your destruction.

Source: Eric Foner, *Tom Paine and Revolutionary America* (1976).

in Philadelphia during the winter of 1778–1779, an advocate of crowd action to regulate prices warned merchants and bakers that "Hunger will break through stone walls, and the resentment excited by it may end in your destruction."

Not everyone, however, favored price regulation by committee. Merchants had responded to the Continental Association by claiming "undoubted . . . liberty, in eating, drinking, buying, selling, communing, and acting what, with whom, and as we please." In 1776 the Scottish political economist Adam Smith had published *The Wealth of Nations,* his famous argument in favor of free markets. By 1779 American critics of regulation, including Tom Paine himself, suggested that free markets could be liberating and need not lead to the rich trampling the poor. Small traders joined great merchants such as Philadelphia's Robert Morris in criticizing the committees. At the height of the 1779 crisis in Philadelphia, a militia armed by merchants faced down crowds seeking price controls and broke the power of their movement. The city's tanners attacked the committee revival and declared that trade ought to be "as free as air, uninterrupted as the tide." Knowing that to get what they wanted they would need to be organized as a political force, Philadelphia merchants and artisans began to gather into a "Republican society" to oppose the state's radical constitution and promote free trade.

At first advocates of free markets accomplished little, because many states followed policies dictated by popular wishes. They issued paper currencies, making them legal tender for the payment of taxes and private debts, and they passed laws giving debtors relief from lawsuits by their creditors. New York, in particular, also confiscated the estates of loyalists and redistributed them. Even Maryland's elite, which virtually monopolized political office, was forced to recognize "the wisdom of sacrifice" and give in to popular demands.

In Massachusetts, however, the advocates of hard currency, free trade, and balanced political institutions did manage to hold sway, with disastrous results for farmers in the interior who faced heavy debts. It took the state until 1780 to adopt its constitution, and commercial men then dominated the new government. They ensured that Massachusetts adopted strict policies on money and debt. Paper currency would not be acknowledged as legal tender, and debtors would receive no protection from their creditors, regardless of whether the creditors were patriots, loyalists, or British.

Peace with Britain in 1783 led to worse problems. American ports reopened to British commerce, unleashing a burst of consumption as people with money craved goods that had been unavailable during the war. But this boom quickly led to a glut, and then, in 1784, to a trading slump that lasted for three years. As depression struck, British creditors called in debts from American merchants, who in turn demanded payment from rural traders and customers. In most states the law would have given debtors some protection, but not in Massachusetts. Here farmers, artisans, and small traders were expected to pay both their debts and their taxes in cash, which they did not have. They saw the public good sacrificed to privilege. As the people of Dracut protested, "Money . . . seems to have . . . hid itself in the secret confines of those who have a greater love to their own Interest than they have to that of their Neighbours." As in the late 1680s and the mid 1770s, they were haunted by the fear that they would lose their property and be reduced to the status of tenants or hired laborers. Outstanding debts went unpaid, lawsuits were brought, and as the courts and debtors' prisons began to crowd with defendants, popular fears began to turn into reality.

Once more, people took traditional steps to relieve their burden. The result, in 1786, was an uprising in western and central Massachusetts that became known as Shays's Rebellion after one of its leaders, a former captain in the Continental Army. Having formed committees and conventions to oppose the government's policies, farmers gathered under arms to close the courts and prevent lawsuits being heard. In concert with Boston radicals such as Samuel Adams, they had done the same in 1774 in response to the Coercive Acts. Now they found themselves pitted against some of these same radicals, including Adams, who controlled the state government in alliance with conservative merchants. Adams defended the law and the courts both as agents of a constitution adopted by the people and as necessary to preserve commerce.

To restore the courts and disperse the rebels, the Boston government sent General Benjamin Lincoln and a well-organized militia force to the west. When Shays and his armed farmers mounted an ill-coordinated assault on the federal armory at Springfield, local militia scattered them. Lincoln's army then chased them into the hills. Shays and others fled into exile in neighboring states. Four rebel leaders were captured, tried, and condemned to death for treason. To show Massachusetts farmers who was in control, the govern-

Shays's Rebellion. The portraits of Daniel Shays and Job Shattuck, leaders of the Massachusetts "Regulators," appeared on the cover of *Bickerstaff's Boston Almanack* in 1787.

Source: *Bickerstaff's Boston Almanack of 1787* (c. 1787)— National Portrait Gallery, Smithsonian Institution.

ment mounted a theatrical display of judicial terror. At the trial Chief Justice William Cushing berated the rebels for trying "to overturn all government and order, to shake off all restraints, human and divine," and give themselves up "wholly to the power of the most restless, malevolent, destructive, tormenting passions." Just as they were about to be hanged, the four were reprieved by the governor in a public show of mercy. These methods worked as intended. Individuals and whole towns begged forgiveness for rebelling. " 'Tis true that I have been a committee-man," wrote one, but "I am sincerely sorry . . . and hope it will be overlooked and pardoned."

This defeat at the hands of men who had been their revolutionary allies taught Shaysites and their sympathizers a basic lesson about the politics of the new republic. The old notion that small communities could defend themselves against outsiders no longer applied. To overturn policies that they resented, people with common interests would have to organize themselves and formally enter the political arena. Almost immediately Massachusetts farmers did just that. In the 1787 state elections, they unseated the hard-money governor James Bowdoin and replaced him with the popular John Hancock. New men, many from western towns that for years had not bothered to send delegates, flooded into the legislature. Although Hancock, like Bowdoin, was a Boston merchant, he was an experienced popular politician who recognized "the genius of the people." Symbolically, at least, the elite made concessions to ordinary peoples' demands. Never again would the state's government allow debtors to be hounded with the ruthlessness that had been evident in the mid 1780s.

Slaves and the American Revolution

The revolution raised more questions about equality and human rights than it answered. Among these was slavery. White colonists had proudly borne the status of "freeborn Englishmen" that distinguished them from slaves, and patriots' chief grievance against Britain was that the Crown seemed bent on reducing them to political slavery. To many of them there was no contradiction between the patriot cause and slave ownership; having property in other human beings was simply a fact of life. British and loyalist commentators were quick to condemn American revolutionaries who complained of enslavement but were complicit in slavery itself. For some slave owners, including Washington and Jefferson, slavery was a problem they agonized over, but could not resolve. To a few white Americans meanwhile—among them Quakers and evangelicals, including some Southerners—slavery became an abomination, a travesty of the principles for which Americans were fighting to secure their own freedom from British rule.

Slavery was an abomination, above all, to most slaves. "In every human Breast," wrote the African-born Boston slave Phillis Wheatley in 1774, "God has planted a principle which we call love of Freedom. It is impatient of Oppression, and pants for Deliverance." The inspiration of revolution and the confusion of war led thousands of slaves to seek freedom. Many simply ran away when opportunity arose. Runaways were often younger men without family ties, but some women also fled, sometimes taking children with them. A considerable number of runaways headed for Philadelphia, the city where antislavery sentiment was strongest.

Some slaves sought liberty by fighting for the British. In 1775, Lord Dunmore, Virginia's last royal governor, promised freedom to those who rallied to the King. In the Chesapeake, in New Jersey, and the Deep South, slaves escaped to British lines, and many served in British or loyalist units. A New Jersey slave named Titus became "Colonel Tye," leader of an irregular Black Brigade that made a "fearsome presence" harassing patriots. Several of George Washington's own slaves ran away to join the British in Virginia. During the southern campaign of 1779–1781, as many as twelve thousand slaves escaped in South Carolina alone. Among them was a man called Boston, who ran from a plantation at Tranquil Hill to the British lines around Charleston in 1779. The next year about one-third of the slaves on John Ball's Kensington plantation ran away.

Several thousand other slaves sought freedom by fighting with the American forces, or escaping to the French army that arrived to help them. When he saw "liberty poles and the people all engaged for the support of freedom," the New England slave Jehu Grant fled his master and enlisted in the Continental Army. "I could not but like and be pleased with such a thing," he said. A few states, especially Rhode Island, solved their military recruitment problems by promising freedom to slaves who would enlist. But in the South, slaveholders opposed recruiting slaves even when military necessity seemed to compel it. In 1780 South Carolina's leaders preferred to see Charleston captured by the British rather than arm slaves to assist in its defense.

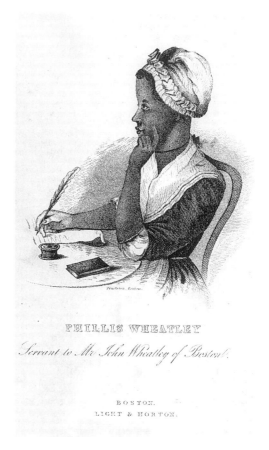

PHILLIS WHEATLEY

Servant to Mr John Wheatley of Boston.

BOSTON.
LIGHT & HORTON.

Phillis Wheatley. Born in 1754 in Africa, Wheatley was enslaved and transported to America, where she became the house servant of a Boston tailor. At the age of fourteen, she began to write poetry and, in 1773, she published a collection of her work in England. A year later, she was freed.

Source: *Memoir and Poems of Phillis Wheatley, A Native African and a Slave* (Boston 1835)—Chicago Historical Society.

". . . A Determined Resolution to Get Liberty . . ."

After Virginia's royal governor, Lord Dunmore, promised freedom to slaves who would escape and serve in the British forces, newspapers printed numerous advertisements for runaways whose owners suspected them of responding to Dunmore's proclamation.

Stafford County, Aquia, Nov 3, 1775.

Run off last night from the subscriber, a negro man named CHARLES, who is a very shrewd sensible fellow, and can both read and write; and as he has always waited upon me, he must be well known through most parts of *Virginia* and *Maryland*. He is very black, has a large nose, and is about 5 feet 8 or 10 inches high. He took a variety of clothes, which I cannot well particularise, stole several of my shirts, a pair of new saddle bags, and two mares, one a darkish, the other a light bay, with a blaze and white feet, and about 3 years old. From many circumstances, there is reason to believe he intends an attempt to get to lord *Dunmore;* and as I have reason to believe his design of going off was long premeditated, and that he has gone off with some accomplice, I am apprehensive he may prove daring and resolute, if endeavoured to be taken. His elopement was from no cause of complaint, or dread of a whipping (for he has always been remarkably indulged, indeed too much so) but from a determined resolution to get liberty, as he conceived, by flying to lord *Dunmore.* I will give 5l. to any person who secures him, and the mares, so that I get them again.

Robert Brent.

Source: *Virginia Gazette* (Dixon and Hunter), February 3, 1776.

Often enough the British or Americans kept the promises of emancipation made to slaves who fled to them. When the British evacuated New York City in 1783, over three thousand African Americans sailed with them to resettle in Nova Scotia. Boston, from South Carolina, was among them; he had married another runaway and renamed himself Boston King after his new sovereign. But in other instances promises were not kept. Besieged at Yorktown, the British expelled African Americans from the fort, leaving them to the mercy of the Americans camped outside. Recaptured slaves often faced violent punishment and the risk of being sold away. George Washington and other planters managed to negotiate the return of their escaped slaves from the British who had been harboring them.

Nevertheless, the Revolution did alter American slavery. In the North, an increasing number of people opposed slavery on principle. One New Yorker condemned it as "cruelty in the extreme" and "the severest reproach" to the new nation. Notables such as Alexander Hamilton

manumitted (released) slaves they had acquired, and helped found organizations such as the New York Manumission Society to promote the abandonment of slavery. In Massachusetts, several slaves brought lawsuits, and the case of Quok Walker struck a heavy blow against slavery. Walker had declared his own freedom in 1781, and then sued his master for wages, and for damages for the assault and imprisonment he had endured when the man recaptured and beat him. Chief Justice Cushing, the judge who would later condemn the Shays rebels, ruled that Walker's enslavement violated the declaration of Massachusetts' new constitution that "all men are born free and equal." This effectively abolished slavery in the state. New Hampshire and Vermont abolished it too.

However, abolition was embraced only where economic circumstances permitted. Although declining, slavery did remain important in other northern states, and was dismantled only slowly. Starting with Pennsylvania in 1780 and ending with New Jersey in 1804, these states passed abolition laws that bound the children of existing slaves to labor until they were adults. In the resulting "gradual" abolition, New Jersey's last slave was not freed until 1846, and Pennsylvania's not until 1847. After the Revolution the number of slaves throughout the North fell from the fifty thousand who had lived there in 1775, but in 1810 there were still twenty-seven thousand northern slaves.

In the upper South, a shift from tobacco to grain cultivation reduced the demand for plantation slave labor, and the number of manumissions rose. About ten thousand slaves obtained freedom in Virginia in the

". . . A Natural and Inalienable Right to . . . Freedom"

Throughout the revolutionary era, scores of slaves signed petitions that linked their demands for freedom with the cause of American independence. Below is the text of one such petition presented to the Massachusetts legislature.

To the honorable Counsel and House of Representatives for the State of Massachusetts in General Court Assembled, January 13, 1777:

The petition of a great number of blacks detained in a state of slavery in the bowels of a free and Christian country humbly show that your petitioners [state] that they have in common with all other men a natural and inalienable right to that freedom which the Great Parent of the heavens has bestowed equally on all mankind and which they have never forfeited by any compact or agreement whatever. They were unjustly dragged by the hand of cruel power from their dearest friends and some of them even torn from the embraces of their tender parents—from a populous, pleasant, and plentiful country, and in violation of laws of nature and of nations, and in defiance of all the tender feelings of humanity brought here to be sold like beasts of burden and like them condemned to slavery for life. . . .

Every principle from which America has acted in the course of their unhappy difficulties with Great Britain pleads stronger than a thousand arguments in favor of your petitioners, and they, therefore, humbly request that your honors give this petition its due weight and consideration and cause an act of the Legislature to be passed whereby they may be restored to the enjoyments of that which is the natural right of all men—and their children who were born in this land of liberty—not to be held as slaves.

Source: Herbert Aptheker, *A Documentory History of the Negro People in the United States,* Vol. 1 (1951).

decade after 1782, for example. Some owners freed their slaves on principle. A Maryland woman did so because slaveholding violated "the inalienable rights of mankind," and a man in Virginia because it was "contrary to the command of Christ to keep fellow creatures in bondage." But many slaves had to purchase their freedom with their own earnings or those of relatives. Graham Bell of Petersburg, Virginia, obtained his liberty in 1792, and then spent the next thirteen years working to buy the freedom of another nine slaves. Before independence free blacks were rare, but by 1820 their numbers exceeded two hundred thousand. Where plantation agriculture remained strong, however, freedom was hardest to

Slavery after the American Revolution: Emancipation and Expansion. This map illustrates the emerging contrasts between northern and southern states. Whereas the South continued to permit slavery, and carried the system into new territories in the Southwest, northern states took steps to ban slavery or gradually phase it out.

Source: Arwin D. Smallwood, *Atlas of African-American History and Politics* (1998).

achieve. In the lower South only four percent of African Americans were free by 1810, compared with ten percent in the upper South.

Revolutionary Rhetoric and New Possibilities

For women, too, the rhetoric and circumstances of revolution seemed to raise new possibilities for freedom and independence. A Rhode Island woman wrote that "The Women of this State are Animated with the Liveliest Sentiments of Liberty." Women were heavily involved in the war effort, ran farms, shops, and businesses when men went to fight or were killed, and undertook much of the extra manufacturing work that helped America to achieve a degree of economic autonomy from Britain. Prominent in protest movements and food riots, women carried forward the campaigns for price regulation that dominated wartime politics, especially in the towns. For perhaps the first time, women formed public organizations. A 1780 association of Philadelphia women to raise funds for soldiers was copied in Virginia, Maryland, and New Jersey. "America will not wear chains," wrote Abigail Adams, "while her daughters are virtuous."

Their important roles encouraged some women to question the subordination that their mothers and grandmothers had taken for granted. Elite women discussed politics and issued calls for improved education. In New England and some other parts of the North the proportion of women who could read and write rose to the same high level already attained by men. A small number of women used more liberal divorce statutes to free themselves from oppressive marriages. In 1788 Abigail Strong of Connecticut noted in her divorce petition that if "even Kings may forfeit . . . the allegiance of their subjects," husbands could not command unconditional control over their wives. The revolutionary language of republicanism and independence inspired a few, such as the Bostonian Judith Sargent Murray, toward new theories of women's independence.

In practice, however, the Revolution did not much alter women's social position. Many commentators argued that women's proper role in the new republic was to raise and educate children to be good republican citizens. Property and marriage laws affecting women remained unchanged. Abigail Adams could urge her husband and his colleagues to "remember the ladies" in their national deliberations, but men were not prepared to overturn institutions and assumptions that served their power and interests. "We know better," John Adams had replied to his wife, "than to repeal our masculine systems." Only in one state, New Jersey, did any women achieve political rights. Free, propertied women could vote in local elections there in the 1780s, and a 1790 state election law referred to voters as "he or she." These rights would soon be abolished, however.

FRONTISPIECE.

Thackara & Vallance sculp.

Publish'd at Philad.ª *Dec.r 1.st 1792.*

Opportunities and Limitations. In the frontispiece from a 1792 Philadelphia publication (above), *The Lady's Magazine and Repository of Entertaining Knowledge,* Columbia was presented with a petition for the "Rights of Woman." In contrast, an engraving published sometime after 1785 (right) prescribed the limits beyond which no virtuous woman's aspirations should go.

Source: (above) *The Lady's Magazine and Repository of Entertaining Knowledge* (December 1, 1792) — Library Company of Philadelphia. (right) "Keep Within Compass," c. 1785-1805, sepia engraving, 9 5/16 × 7 1/8 inches — Henry Francis duPont Winterthur Museum.

ENTER NOT INTO THE WAY OF THE WICKED, AND GO NOT IN THE PATH OF EVIL MEN.

Nevertheless, although the actual opportunities available to them varied enormously, many people—men and women; rich, middling, and poor; black and white—were encouraged by the Revolution to think that it was both possible and necessary to take greater control of their circumstances. Merchants and some farmers gained greater access to commercial markets. The confiscation of royal and loyalist property, and the opening of vast new western territories now in the public domain gave more farmers access to land that they could purchase or claim as their own. This vision of taking control further undermined older colonial concepts of deference. In 1788 an elderly New Hampshire congressman complained that now "young and old all mix together, & talk & joke alike so that you cannot discover any distinction made or any respect shewn to one more than to another." Some Americans saw the possibility of taking control of their societies, even at the risk of conflict with those whose interests and ideas differed from their own.

Constitution and Compromise

Members of the elite saw such concepts as dangerous. Amidst the upheavals of the end of the war and events such as Shays's Rebellion, they took action to resolve the question of what kind of place an independent America would be. In 1787, only months after the suppression of Shays's Rebellion, a group of delegates drawn from the elites of the thirteen states met in a special convention at Philadelphia. Its ostensible purpose was to revise the Articles of Confederation, but it quickly resolved to scrap them altogether and to draw up a new framework for government. The result was the Federal Constitution, a document that embodied elite concerns about the threat of "too much" democracy, and sought to put a conservative curb on America's political development. After special conventions in nine states had ratified it, this Constitution went into effect in 1788, and the remaining four states joined the union within two years. The adoption of the U.S. Constitution marked the completion of the political revolution. In many respects it was a step away from the Revolution's most radical possibilities.

Most members of the Philadelphia convention were merchants, lawyers, landholders, or southern planters. They included Robert Morris of Philadelphia, the "financier" of the Revolution; New York's Alexander Hamilton, who had risen from obscurity to fame as George Washington's aide-de-camp, to marriage into the New York landed elite, and to influence as a lawyer, essayist, and politician; and James Madison of Virginia, who had already written a private essay on "The Vices of the Political System of the United States," which outlined many of the changes that the

Constitution would make. George Washington himself chaired the convention. The convention's members have been remembered as the Founding Fathers, or framers of the Constitution, but as they campaigned for ratification they came to call themselves Federalists.

Almost all had been at the Revolution's center, as army officers, traders and suppliers, members of Congress, or ambassadors. They had experienced the difficulties of organizing the war, had been repeatedly embarrassed by America's inability to deal straightforwardly with foreign diplomats and generals, and had watched states ignore provisions in the peace treaty, such as its promise to end the harassment of loyalists. They had protested in vain when, to protect debtors, states passed laws that they saw as heedless of the interests of creditors and damaging to the international reputation of American traders. They had been horrified at the threat posed by Shays's Rebellion in the one state that had refused to pass such laws.

To most of these men, the radical democratic possibilities of the Revolution presented a threat to what they considered to be good government. They were republicans, committed to the belief that government must rest on the people's consent, but they were not democrats: they had little faith that ordinary people could run society wisely or well. Most believed that government should be conducted by "the best men"— those fitted by birth, education, and sober political principle to govern wisely. Since 1782 Hamilton and others who called themselves "nationalists" had been campaigning for a strong central government run by men "whose principles are not of the *leveling* sort." In his own state of New York, Hamilton had succeeded in forging an alliance of landlords and merchants to end the political dominance of a coalition of farmers and artisans. The Constitution that emerged from the Philadelphia convention strengthened national government and the position of propertied elites. However, it also reflected compromises between conflicting elite interests, and between the elite views of government and popular demands for participation that the revolutionary process had generated.

The convention was seeking a new understanding of republicanism, because in current thinking about republics, the American situation seemed unhopeful. The idea of a republic was an ancient one, but the examples of classical Greece and Rome suggested to virtually all thinkers that republics could succeed only in special circumstances. A republic would have to be small in size and population. Its people would have to be virtuous, putting the common good above private interests. They should be bound together by a single economic interest. The republic might be either commercial (like Renaissance Venice) or agrarian (like Switzerland) but many believed that putting two different interests together would lead to tyranny as each sought to dominate the other. Most re-

"The Looking Glass for 1787."

New Haven engraver Amos Doolittle's 1787 print commented on the political situation preceding the Constitutional Convention. While a wagon labeled "Connecticut" sinks in a mud pit, nationalists (left) and localists (right) are too divided to cooperate in its rescue.

Source: Prints and Photographs Division, Library of Congress.

publics had, in fact, collapsed. Now Americans were trying to sustain republican governments in large, varied societies that seemed the very opposite of ideal for the purpose. The rebellion in Massachusetts seemed to confirm to the men who met in Philadelphia that republicanism in America might prove another tragic failure.

But some Federalists took a new point of departure, which James Madison would express most clearly in the tenth and fifty-first of the *Federalist* papers that he, Hamilton, and John Jay would publish during the campaign to ratify the Constitution. Instead of a small republic, Madison saw the potential of a large one; instead of a single, virtuous public interest he envisaged the jostling and competing of many private interests. If the arena were large enough, he argued, no single interest would become so powerful as to oppress the others. "Extend the sphere," he wrote, "and you take in a greater variety of parties and interests; you make it less probable that a majority . . . will have a common motive to invade the rights of other citizens." This was a major breakthrough in political thought, and it guided the Philadelphia convention to its first solution to the American situation: create a large republic that would dwarf any previous attempt to live without a monarch.

The second solution was to give the republic a much stronger government than it had under the Articles of Confederation. Government under the Articles had succeeded to the extent that it won the war and negotiated a very favorable peace. Congress could make war, peace, and foreign policy; it could create an army, a navy, and an administration in the name of the United States; and it had obtained from the states control over the western lands ceded by Britain under the peace treaty. But the Confederation had been unable to pay its debts, enforce the terms of the peace treaty, or resolve disputes between states; it lacked the power to tax, and had no executive to do its will, or courts to enforce laws and treaties. Federal government relied entirely on the will of the states.

Although many Americans regarded these circumstances as acceptable in a republic, the delegates at Philadelphia saw them as weaknesses, and designed the new Constitution to rectify them. They erected a set of balances and compromises that would enable a new federal government to be built on top of the existing social and political institutions in the various states. One compromise was to leave the states themselves intact. Hamilton and Madison would have gladly reduced states to simple administrative units, but the system of "dual federalism" that emerged made both federal and state governments the legal creatures of the people, who were the real sovereign power. Resolving what Madison regarded as the greatest difficulty, that of representation, the convention adopted the proposal that Congress's single chamber be replaced by two houses: a Senate in which all states would be equally represented, and a House of Representatives in which representation would be based proportionally on population.

But more vexing questions remained concerning the relationships between the central government, the separate states, and American society as a whole. These issues arose in several forms at the convention, but none presented more difficulty than the divisions that emerged between northern and southern states over slavery. Though some Southerners, including Washington, had qualms about slavery, most planters did not question its legitimacy or the concept of human property. Still, the fact that slaves were both people and things presented unavoidable problems.

Above all, should slaves be counted as part of the southern states' populations for the purpose of deciding the size of delegations to the House of Representatives? Southern delegates, including Madison, wanted to have it both ways. Slaves would not, of course, be entitled to vote, but counting them as part of the population would significantly increase southern political influence; they were, after all, forty percent of Virginia's population and an even higher proportion of South Carolina's. Northerners saw through this ploy. Gouverneur Morris of Pennsylvania pointed out that slavery was just one special interest, and that if it won representation, other special interests should as well. Other delegates agreed.

The outcome was a compromise, the first of many between North and South. Slaves would be counted for political representation, but not fully. By the so-called "three-fifths clause" five slaves would count as three free persons. Compromises over slavery continued to be made. While the constitutional convention was sitting, the Continental Congress passed the Northwest Ordinance, including a clause banning slavery from the western territories north of the Ohio River. But the Constitution included two further concessions to Southerners: an agreement that there could be no consideration of banning the slave trade until 1808, and a clause that obliged states to return fugitive slaves to their owners. Although it did not use the word *slavery,* the Constitution gave slavery legal standing at a time when many Americans were questioning its legitimacy.

If the Constitution bowed to the requirements of southern planters, it also suited the needs of northern commerce. It created a vast common market, on the principle that uniform laws and the needs of long-distance trade were more important than local custom or the needs of particular communities. States would be restricted from erecting trade barriers against each others' goods. In addition to certain powers to tax, Congress would be able to regulate interstate and foreign commerce, establish a uniform bankruptcy law, mint coin, regulate money, "fix the standard of Weights and Measures," register patents and copyrights, and create a postal service. Each state would be obliged to give "full faith and credit" to court decisions made in other states. States were forbidden to "emit Bills of Credit, make anything but Gold or Silver Coin a Tender in Payment of Debts," or "pass any . . . Law impairing the obligation of Contracts." The problems of the mid 1780s, when many states protected insolvent debtors against their creditors, would not be allowed to recur.

Elites and the People: The Fight for Ratification

The Constitution was written by elites to address their own interests, but it also proved to have popular appeal, largely because it was grounded in the sovereignty of the people. Popular support for it was essential. If the Constitution was to go into effect, it would require the election of enough state convention delegates who favored it to ensure its ratification.

However, there was also a powerful opposition. Two states refused to ratify the Constitution, and in four others the contest was extremely close. Anti-Federalists included state politicians who feared loss of influence, and many popular radicals who distrusted the schemes of the those who had met in Philadelphia. The New York Anti-Federalist leader

Melancton Smith feared that it would create a government of "the few and the great," and exclude "those of the middling class of life" whom the revolution had brought into politics. The most strongly opposed were farmers in the interior, notably from areas with a history of rural unrest. In some states only clever political maneuvering surmounted their influence. The Pennsylvania ratification convention was called at short notice, preventing the backcountry from organizing its opposition. In the New York convention, Anti-Federalists won a massive majority, but strong support from New York City Federalists, and their threat that the city would secede and ratify the Constitution on its own, persuaded the rest of the state to consent.

In the major towns, indeed, support for the Constitution was overwhelming. Working people, especially artisans, saw in strong national government their best chance for securing prosperity, regular employment, and markets for their products. They had little hand in drafting the Constitution but played a key role in getting it ratified, not only in New York, but in Pennsylvania and Massachusetts too.

". . . They Will Swallow Up All Us Little Folks"

Many rural Americans opposed the ratification of the Constitution, contending that the new federal government would be controlled by "aristocrats" and wealthy men. In the debates at the convention held in Massachusetts in 1788 to consider how the state should vote on ratification, Amos Singletary, a farmer from the interior, who claimed never to have had a day of schooling in his life, expressed these fears.

Hon. Mr. Singletary: Mr. President, I should not have troubled the Convention again, if some gentlemen had not called on them that were on the stage in the beginning of our troubles, in the year 1775. I was one of them. I have had the honor to be a member of the court all the time, Mr. President, and I say that, if any body had proposed such a Constitution as this in that day, it would have been thrown away at once. It would not have been looked at. We contended with Great Britain, some said for a threepenny duty on tea; but it was not that; it was because they claimed a right to tax us and bind us in all cases whatever. And does not this Constitution do the same? Does it not take away all we have—all our property? Does it not lay *all* taxes, duties, imposts [import fees], and excises? And what more have we to give? They tell us Congress won't lay dry taxes upon us, but collect all the money they want by impost. . . . They won't be able to raise money enough by impost, and then they will lay it on the land, and take all we have got. These lawyers, and men of learning, and moneyed men, that talk so finely, and gloss over matters so smoothly, to make us poor illiterate people swallow down the pill, expect to get into Congress themselves; they expect to be the managers of this Constitution, and get all the power and all the money into their own hands, and then they will swallow up all us little folks, like the great *Leviathan*, Mr. President; yes, just as the whale swallowed up *Jonah*.

Source: *Massachusetts Gazette*, January 25, 1788.

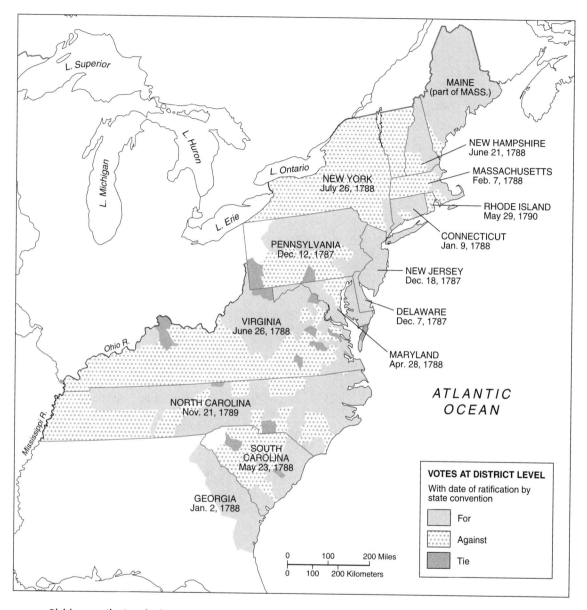

VOTES AT DISTRICT LEVEL

With date of ratification by state convention

☐ For

☐ Against

■ Tie

Division over the Constitution. In several of the most important states there was sharp division between the supporters and opponents of ratifying the U.S. Constitution. This map, which plots votes in state ratifying conventions, reflects the broad support for the Constitution in seaboard regions, and strong opposition in the backcountry. Note, for example, the small areas of support in Massachusetts and New York, and the split between the coast and the interior in South Carolina—a legacy of the Regulator movement of the 1760s.

In Pennsylvania the campaign for ratification coincided with the growing "Republican" movement to revise the democratic state constitution of 1776. The Philadelphia elite drew on increasing support from the city's artisans to achieve both these goals. This coalition first spearheaded the state's ratification of the U.S. Constitution, and then in 1790 ensured that the Pennsylvania constitution was rewritten in a more conservative form.

In Massachusetts the fight over ratification was critical, for failure to ratify there might defeat the Constitution altogether. When the ratifying convention met in January 1788, the state was still deeply divided after Shays's Rebellion. Delegates from central and western Massachusetts, aware that the Constitution would threaten the power of custom and community solidarity on which their rebellion had been based, strongly opposed ratification. Even some Boston radicals mistrusted the proposed new form of government. "I confess," said Samuel Adams, "as I enter the Building, I stumble at the threshold." But Adams's political base was among Boston artisans, and they wanted the Constitution. Paul Revere presided over a meeting of four hundred of them, gathered to persuade

Solid and Pure. This flag was carried by master, journeymen, and apprentice pewterers in the July 1788 parade in New York City celebrating ratification of the Constitution.

Source: New-York Historical Society.

Adams and other delegates to vote in favor of ratification. Adams came around in support, and the convention did vote to accept.

When the news was announced, Boston artisans celebrated with a parade in which forty different groups of tradesmen marched. One newspaper called it "an exhibition to which America has never witnessed an equal." Similar parades were held in other states as they too voted to ratify. The biggest, in Philadelphia on July 4, 1788, included eighty-six units in its line of march, and reflected the coalition of the city's elites and working men that had worked together to achieve ratification in Pennsylvania. At the center were two elaborate floats carrying symbols of what

"This Federal Ship Will Our Commerce Revive"

The following account of the New York City parade commemorating the ratification of the Constitution—taken from the New York *Packet,* August 5, 1788—includes descriptions of the floats constructed by each artisan group and the banners they carried. The slogans and mottoes reveal the reasons for their support of a stronger federal government.

About ten o'clock, 13 guns were fired from the Federal Ship, *Hamilton,* being the signal for the procession to move, the different bodies of which it was composed having already collected from their various places of meeting. It now set out from the Fields [a public park] proceeding down Broadway. . . .

First Division . . . A Band of Music. Tailors. A flag 10 by 11 feet, field sky blue, a fine landscape—Adam and Eve represented naked excepting fig leaves for aprons, nearly in full stature in a sitting posture—motto "And they sewed fig leaves together." . . .

Second Division . . . Tanners and Curriers . . . Skinners, Breeches Makers and Glovers . . . a flag of cream-colored silk . . . the motto, "Americans encourage your own manufacturing." . . .

Fourth Division. Carpenters . . . Representing under the standard of the United States a portraiture of his Excellency General Washington, the motto, "Freedom's favorite son!" . . . a motto on the frieze "The love of our country prevails" . . . 392 rank and file. . . .

Fifth Division . . . Windsor and Rush Chair Makers . . . 60 men with Green and Red cockades in their hats, emblematical of their business . . . the motto:

    The Federal States in union bound

    O'er all the world our chairs are found

Sixth Division. Black Smiths and Nailors . . . 120 in order . . . Ship joiners. Motto:

    Our Merchants may venture to ship without fear

    For Pilots of skill shall the Hamilton steer

    This federal ship will our commerce revive

    And merchants and ship wrights and joiners shall thrive. . . .

Source: *New York Packet,* August 5, 1788.

artisans thought the Revolution had achieved. One, showing the "New Roof" or "Grand Federal Edifice" that the Constitution would erect over the states, was followed by the city's construction trades: architects, carpenters, sawmakers, and filemakers. The other was the Federal Ship *Union,* with a crew of twenty-five, followed by pilots, boatbuilders, sailmakers, ship carpenters, ropemakers, merchants, and traders. Then came the rest of the tradesmen, on floats working at their crafts or carrying banners. Blacksmiths beat swords into sickles and plowshares beneath the motto "By Hammer and Hand All Arts Do Stand."

Securing a Bill of Rights

Although the coalition of urban and elite support was sufficient to ratify the Constitution, the margin of victory was narrow. Federalists knew that there remained widespread fear and distrust of the stronger, more centralized government among a people who had just fought a bitter war against "tyrannical" British rule. The ultimate key to popular acceptance of the Constitution would lie in the addition of a Bill of Rights to guarantee certain liberties as safeguards to balance government power.

George Mason of Virginia had called for a Bill of Rights at the Philadelphia convention, but most of the Founding Fathers had thought it unnecessary and delegates from every state voted against him. In state ratifying conventions, however, Anti-Federalists exerted strong pressure for a Bill of Rights. Rural delegates in particular were determined to prevent the creation of an excessively powerful federal government. Five states, including three of the most powerful (Massachusetts, New York, and Virginia) ratified the Constitution on the understanding that a Bill of Rights would quickly follow. Federalist leaders gave ground to popular demand. Congress, under Madison's leadership, drafted constitutional amendments suggested by the state conventions, ten of which were subsequently ratified and appended to the Constitution on December 15, 1791.

The Bill of Rights (as these first ten amendments are known) addressed issues that had been raised in the resistance to British policies from the 1760s onward, and in the experience of revolution. The first amendment guaranteed the freedoms of speech, the press, religion, and assembly. Others guaranteed the right to petition government for redress of grievances, to be protected from unwarranted searches and seizures, to trial by jury, and to the "due process of law." "Cruel or unusual" punishments were prohibited. To establish local militias, and so avoid the need for a standing army, the Second Amendment guaranteed Americans the right to bear arms. These were weak versions of the protections that Anti-Federalists wanted against strong government, and the Bill of Rights would in practice play little part in American politics for many decades to come. It did not settle the question of the relationship between federal and state governments, which would always remain at issue. Its provisions, moreover, concerned not only people. The right to "due process," in particular, referred to property as well. The new constitutional arrangements, in fact, fulfilled a double-edged purpose. They protected individuals, but they also protected the "privileges"—such as ownership of slaves—that accompanied wealth.

American Society: Competing Visions

The adoption of the Constitution and the Bill of Rights did not end the debates about who should rule and who should benefit from the new social and political order. The tension between elite presumptions and popular pressure that had marked the revolutionary struggle continued to shape the politics of the early American republic.

The Constitution meant many things to many people. To northern merchants and traders it was a necessary underpinning for commercial wealth and their own class advantage. For southern planters, it became a bulwark for the perpetuation of slavery. For urban artisans, the new powers of the federal government could encourage the commerce and manufacturing that would enable their crafts to flourish and grow. Even small farmers, initially opposed to the Constitution, soon learned that the federal system made possible a society in which people could organize around their own common interests. The first federal administration, with George Washington as president, took office in 1789, assuming that consensus over the Constitution could achieve political unity. Despite Madison's theoretical endorsement of competition between conflicting interests, most Americans still believed that republican government was best secured by political harmony, and that factional or party divisions would undermine it.

But the new republic was not politically harmonious. In fact, the 1790s saw increasing factional strife. Washington's own administration was divided between men such as Jefferson and Madison, who were suspicious of strong central power, and those such as Hamilton, who favored it. Differences over commercial policy and foreign affairs became focused on France, and on the French Revolution that had begun in 1789 and moved in an increasingly radical direction until 1794. Hamilton and commercial elites, who continued to identify themselves as Federalists, rejected France's radical democracy and instead advocated trading agreements with Britain. Jefferson, with support among planters, small farmers, and urban workingmen, stood at the center of a political opposition to the Federalists that had started to organize in "Democratic-Republican" clubs, and advocated alliance with France against Britain.

Although the two emerging political parties each had supporters from across American society, Federalists argued for rule by the "best men," Democratic-Republicans for a more popular democracy. This division led to great political drama and paranoia after war broke out between Britain and France in 1793. The United States declared its neutrality in the war, and its merchants and ship owners profited greatly because they could trade with both sides. But America's relative weakness also made it vulnerable. Debates over foreign alliances affected the very nature and future of the republic. To Federalists, the presence of a political opposition threatened the republic's existence.

Divisions over foreign policy accompanied continuing domestic conflict. Federalists and Democratic-Republicans divided particularly over financial policy. As secretary of the treasury, Hamilton brought forward plans to resolve the financial problems that remained from the Revolution and to tie the nation's wealthy elites more tightly to the new political system. The federal government would assume the debts of the states. It would also pay its debts at the full face value of the paper notes that had been issued to pay for war supplies or soldiers' wages. Both policies would mean levying federal taxes and import duties. However, Hamilton's plan was not to pay off the debts. By retaining a national debt, he would encourage those with means to invest in federal bonds and notes on which interest would be paid. The Federalist administration also organized a Bank of the United States to handle the government's transactions and so help influence the financial system.

The Federalists' opponents condemned these policies as socially unjust and an excessive extension of federal power. Many thousands of soldiers who had been paid in paper money or land certificates during and after the Revolution had been forced by necessity to sell them at heavily discounted prices, often to wealthy speculators. Under Hamilton's plan the government would pay the speculators the full value of the paper, using the tax revenues collected from ordinary Americans to give them great profits. Hamilton's opponents scorned the "large monied interest" that his funding scheme and the Bank of the United States would create.

Against this background, disputes over taxation provoked protest, especially in rural regions. A federal liquor tax led to riots by armed farmers in western Pennsylvania who had not forgotten their lost struggles over the state and federal constitutions. Protesters attacked revenue officers on the frontier, and a crowd of seven thousand set fire to the then-new town of Pittsburgh. In 1794, Washington dispatched an army of fifteen thousand men under Hamilton's command to hunt down these so-called "Whiskey Rebels," but most of them had melted into the countryside and could not be found.

A few years after the Whiskey Rebellion, again in Pennsylvania, discontent over a direct federal tax on houses and other property provoked another small uprising. These protests added to a sense of panic, both in Washington's administration and in the administration of John Adams, who succeeded him as president in 1797. Federalists so feared opposition that when a naval war broke out with France in 1798 they used their majority in Congress to pass the Alien and Sedition Acts, severely curtailing free political expression. Critics of the government were prosecuted for seditious speech or writings, but their trials mainly exposed the Federalists themselves to ridicule. A New Jersey man was tried for making a drunken rude remark about Adams. The republican congressman Matthew Lyon of Vermont, imprisoned for accusing the administration of incompetence, got the satisfaction of being re-elected while he was in jail. Resolutions in the Kentucky and Virginia legislatures, drafted by Jefferson and Madison respectively, asserted the rights of states and of the people against federal power. The Federalists' attempts at repression hastened the turning of the political tide against them, and led to a sound defeat in the 1800 elections, which secured Jefferson the presidency.

Washington Suppresses a Rebellion. Faced with a primitive transportation system, western Pennsylvania farmers distilled whiskey from grain as the best means to get their produce to eastern markets. In 1794, after a new federal liquor tax disrupted their livelihood, the farmers rebelled. In this painting President Washington is shown at Fort Cumberland, Maryland, reviewing the vanguard of the fifteen thousand troops he dispatched to suppress the Whiskey Rebellion.

Source: Frederick Kemmelmeyer, *General Washington, Reviewing the Western Army at Fort Cumberland the 18th of October, 1794,* c. 1794, oil on paper backed with linen, 18 1/8 × 23 1/8 inches—Henry Francis duPont Winterthur Museum.

GENERAL GEORGE WASHINGTON.
Reviewing the Western army at Fort Cumberland the 18th of Octobr 1794

The election of 1800 marked another step in the erosion of social deference that had begun in the 1760s during the protests against British rule. Jefferson saw his election as a victory in the battle between "the advocates of republican and those of kingly government." As British colonists, Americans had been subjects of a monarch who was the source of political authority and who sat at the apex of a social hierarchy. Now, because of the Revolution, working people could see themselves as equal participants in a new social order in which sovereignty lay with the people. People were increasingly reluctant to view the wealthy or well-born as their social betters, or as entitled to power or influence. No man, declared a Massachusetts farmer, deserves "any degree or spark of . . . a right of dominion, government, and jurisdiction over [an]other." Republican critics of "aristocracy" had vigorously condemned the proposal of former army officers to form the hereditary Society of the Cincinnati in 1783, and forced them to modify their plans. Among the banners carried in Philadelphia's great Fourth of July parade in 1788 was one belonging to a group of bricklayers, proudly asserting that "Both Buildings and Rulers Are the Work of Our Hands."

Thirty years earlier the suggestion that working people could "make" rulers would have been almost unthinkable. Until the 1760s elites had referred to artisans patronizingly as "mere mechanics." Now artisans themselves had adopted the term, proudly referring to themselves as "mechanics." Participating in Fourth of July celebrations every year across the country, farmers, artisans, and other workingmen could mark both their sense of identity as members of their group and trades, and their position as equal citizens of the republic. In New York, patriotic contingents paraded behind the banner of the General Society of Mechanics and Tradesmen. Like similar groups in Boston, Albany, Providence, Portsmouth, Charleston, and Savannah, New York's General Society was composed mainly of master craftsmen, but sought to promote the common interest of all artisans, and to foster "a general harmony . . . throughout the whole manufacturing interest of the country." Masters claimed responsibility for the journeymen and apprentices in their workshops, and at the end of the eighteenth century it was assumed that all younger craftsmen could one day become masters themselves. Artisans and others claimed equal rights and equal citizenship with the elites who dominated political affairs. Fourth of July speakers emphasized civic equality. "Every man looks with independent equality in the face of his neighbor," one proclaimed. "Those are exalted whose superior virtues entitle them to confidence; they are revered as legislators, obeyed as magistrates, but still considered as equals." As a Pennsylvanian put it, "no man has greater claim of special privilege for his hundred thousand dollars than I have for my five dollars."

"The Waggery and Humor of the Gallery"

Elite observers were upset at the unruly behavior of artisans, journeymen, and apprentices who joined them in attending early-nineteenth-century theaters. In 1802 Washington Irving, author of *Rip Van Winkle* and *The Legend of Sleepy Hollow,* published this account of his visit to a New York City theater in the New York *Morning Chronicle.* His comments on the treatment of "the honest folks" who sat in the pit, the floor of the theater near the stage, at the hands of the rowdies above them in the upper gallery (the "gods") echoed the views of those who wanted political rights restricted to "the best men."

My last communication mentioned my visit to the theatre; the remarks it contained were chiefly confined to the play and the actors: I shall now extend them to the audience, who, I assure you, furnished no inconsiderable part of the entertainment.

As I entered the house, some time before the curtain rose, I had sufficient leisure to make some observations. I was much amused with the waggery and humor of the gallery, which, by the way, is kept in *excellent* order by the constables who are stationed there. The noise in this part of the house is somewhat similar to that which prevailed in Noah's ark; for we have an imitation of the whistles and yells of every kind of animall. —This, in some measure, compensates for the want of music, (as the gentlemen of our orchestra are very economic of their favors). Somehow or another the anger of the gods seemed to be aroused all of a sudden, and they commenced a discharge of apples, nuts, and ginger-bread, on the heads of the honest folks in the pit, who had no possibility of retreating from this new kind of thunder-bolts. I can't say but I was a little irritated at being saluted aside of my head with a rotten pippin, and was going to shake my cane at them; but was prevented by a decent-looking man behind me, who informed me it was useless to threaten or expostulate. They are only *amusing themselves* a little at our expense, said he, sit down quietly and bend your back to it. My kind neighbor was interrupted by a hard green apple that hit him between the shoulders—he made a wry face, but knowing it was all in joke, bore the blow like a philosopher. I soon saw the wisdom of this deter-mination, —a stray thunder-bolt happened to light on the head of a little sharp-faced Frenchman, dress'd in a white coat and small cock'd hat, who sat two or three benches ahead of me, and seemed to be an irritable little animal: Monsieur was terribly exasper-ated; he jumped upon his seat, shook his fist at the gallery, and swore violently in bad English. This was all nuts to his merry persecutors, their attention was wholly turned on him, and he formed their *target* for the rest of the evening.

Source: Bruce I. Granger and Martha Hartzog, eds., *Letters of Jonathan Oldstyle* (1977).

Opportunity for Some, Exclusion for Others

Even so, according to republican theory full citizenship and access to politics by no means extended to everyone. These privileges were reserved for those deemed personally "independent," capable of acting without reliance on others, and whose "virtue" and "disinterestness" would guarantee the republic against corrupt manipulation. Most states after the Revolution restricted the right to vote to white men with property or taxable income. The great majority of people—eighty percent in 1783, according to one estimate—were excluded from participation in public life. Most poor laboring men were unable to vote. Their lack of property or status as servants disqualified them. Most women and people of color, similarly, found themselves excluded on the grounds of their gender, race, or status as wives or slaves. All were said to be "dependents," unable to exercise their own judgment. For these groups the revolutionary era raised possibilities of liberation or emancipation that were only very inadequately fulfilled.

Democratic-Republicans' attacks on Federalist privilege did to some degree continue the Revolution's democratizing tendencies into the nineteenth century. In office, the Jefferson administration abolished federal direct taxes, and took steps to open up access to western land. After 1800, state after state abolished property qualifications for voting, opening the franchise to all adult white men; by the late 1820s all but three had done so. Participation in elections soared. But the inclusion of all white men in politics still meant the exclusion of other groups. The electoral law of 1807 that abolished New Jersey's property qualification also abolished the limited voting rights of the state's women. Elsewhere laws specifically reserved political rights to white men.

For many African Americans, the Revolution and its aftermath produced only limited or temporary hope of liberty. The Declaration of Independence had proclaimed that "all men are created equal," and slaves, such as a group in New Hampshire, had subsequently asserted that freedom was "an inherent right of the human species, not to be surrendered but by consent." But to slaves and many free blacks the Constitution represented a major blow to their hopes of freedom. Leaving the franchise to be determined by the states, it did nothing to interfere with voting rules that excluded most free blacks on grounds of color or poverty. The three-fifths clause, the guarantee of property rights, and the fugitive-slave law lent renewed legitimacy to slavery. The protections of the Bill of Rights offered nothing to slaves, who were not regarded as citizens in the first place. Although the Revolution enabled some to emancipate themselves, it also paved the way for economic developments that would enslave many more. The expansion of cotton production in the South strongly re-

Toussaint L'Ouverture. This portrait of the leader of the St. Domingue revolution was published in a contemporary British history book.

Source: Marcus Rainsford, *An Historical Account of the Black Empire of Hayti* (1805)—New-York Historical Society.

vived slavery from the 1790s onward. By 1820, although the United States had an unprecedented number of free black people, it also had an unprecedented number of slaves—about one and a half million.

Nevertheless, the revolutionary period provided ideological markers for African Americans and their supporters as they struggled for emancipation. The possibility of revolution, itself a new ingredient, was especially charged by events in St. Domingue (Haiti) in 1791, when slaves rebelled, toppled the French colonial government, seized power, and defended their new republic against repeated efforts to destroy it. The insurrection in St. Domingue struck fear into the hearts of slaveholders across the New World. It may have emboldened some American slaves to attempt rebellion, for several slave revolts and conspiracies were uncovered in the early nineteenth century. At his trial for plotting insurrection in Richmond, Virginia, in 1800, the slave blacksmith Gabriel was said to have declared that "we have as good a right to be free from your oppression, as you had to be free from the tyranny of the King of England."

A surging evangelical movement, with its emphasis on the equal brotherhood of believers, added to the egalitarian and libertarian rhetoric of the Revolution. But it was tempered by a growing white racism. Churches that, in the late colonial period, had included white and black believers together, began in the 1790s to erect firmer racial barriers. Black Methodists in Philadelphia, for example, withdrew from a church they had just helped rebuild in 1792 when the elders insisted that they occupy segregated seating. Such episodes reinforced the efforts of African Americans, both slave and free, to organize social and cultural institutions of their own. In northern towns, freedpeople built families and neighborhoods, made their own styles of dress and deportment, founded their own churches and schools, and formed voluntary associations such as the African Union Society of Newport, Rhode Island, and the Free African Society of Philadelphia.

Even for whites who had the benefits of citizenship, the Revolution's legacy was mixed. Philadelphia's mammoth 1788 parade to celebrate the new federal Constitution expressed confidence that social harmony and republican virtue would produce commercial expansion from which all would benefit. Yet inequalities of wealth widened during the Revolution, and even in the economic revival of the 1790s the benefits of prosperity were unevenly distributed. Of Philadelphia's journeymen shoemakers,

281

only about half were able to set up as masters with shops of their own during the decade; among tailors the proportion was just one in ten. A young woman, Polly Nugent, had been a servant of the city's wealthy Drinker family before she married a blacksmith. By 1796 her husband was facing hard times, and Polly had to turn to her old employers for financial assistance. Revolution may have unleashed opportunity for many, but it also meant disappointment for others.

Much prosperity depended on seaborne trade, and hard times followed when this trade was disrupted. The port cities boomed in the 1790s, when the United States could trade as a neutral entity with various European nations. But the renewal of war yet again between Britain and France after 1803 put American shipping and seamen in increasing difficulties. This time, the combatants each tried to stop neutrals from dealing with the other. Britain began seizing ships and cargoes that it suspected of trading with France. After the French followed suit, Jefferson tried to put pressure on both sides by declaring an embargo in 1807. For two years the embargo legally prevented Americans trading with either power. The result was significant hardship for American ports, and for the men and women who lived and worked in them. In 1809, as James Madison was about to succeed Jefferson as president, the embargo restrictions were lifted.

As trade resumed, however, American seamen still faced another hazard: the British navy's long-standing practice of searching neutral vessels for alleged deserters, whom they "impressed" (forced to serve) aboard their warships. American ships, with their English-speaking crews, were especially vulnerable; the British even seized men from a U.S. warship near the American coast. The conflict over shipping and the impressment of seamen eventually drove the Madison administration to war with Britain in 1812. Americans celebrated their seamen as upholders of patriotism. Many thousands endured captivity in one of Britain's harshest prisons rather than be forced to fight for the Royal Navy against their own countrymen.

For ordinary soldiers and sailors, war service in the revolutionary period brought a measure of honor and recognition, but for many it did not bring economic security. Many of the Revolutionary War soldiers who had helped to win independence found themselves impoverished. They had been paid in depreciated currency or land warrants, which they needed to sell at much less than face value in order to live. Officers received pensions from the end of the war onward, but enlisted men did not. Not until 1818 did Congress provide pensions for them, and then only for those in "reduced circumstances." As testimony to the era's hardships, more than twenty thousand former soldiers sought assistance on the grounds of poverty. Among them was Jeremiah Greenman, who had enlisted as a youth in Rhode Island in 1775. Now in old age he wrote that he was facing "increasing poverty and loneliness" on a small farm in Ohio.

Revolution and Territory: Crisis in the Spanish Empire

Although many tensions and conflicts remained in American society, the effects of the Revolution were far-reaching. Creating an independent United States out of a disparate group of British colonies, and erecting a federal system of republican governments based on the people's sovereignty were in themselves massive changes. But the Revolution also altered the balance of power on the North American continent. This had profound implications for the future of the peoples in the territory to the west of the United States, and for the New World in general.

Previous colonial wars had altered the balance of power across the continent, but the Revolutionary War and the creation of an independent United States brought more sweeping and permanent change than ever before. The French and Indian War had banished the French and left North America divided between a strong Britain and its colonies and a relatively weak set of Spanish possessions. American independence defeated the British and curbed their power in North America. For the first time a unified nation with an interest in the rest of the continent was based in America itself, rather than in Europe. U.S. hegemony would consequently be stronger than that of any previous power, a fact that would affect the future of millions of people.

The revolutionary period altered the balance of power among Europeans interested in North America, generally to the advantage of the United States. British, French, and Spanish designs on North American territory all to a greater or lesser extent suffered setbacks. Spanish territories still girdled North America's southern and western margins after 1763, from Louisiana to Texas and New Mexico. After its defeat in the Revolutionary War, Britain also returned Florida to Spain, rather than ceding Gibraltar instead. A period of political reform in Spain produced new efforts to regulate its New World colonies; one consequence of this was the decision in 1768 to occupy present-day California, partly to check Russian activity on the Pacific coast.

Spanish settlement in California, spearheaded by the building of missions as well as military and civil institutions, quickly developed characteristics similar to earlier phases of conquest. Natives of California, organized mainly in small, decentralized groups unused to war, were at first in a poor position to resist Spanish encroachments. But the invaders' efforts to extract labor from them, their punishments for infractions, and the rape of Indian women in due course sparked retaliation. In 1775 local Ipais attacked and burned the mission at San Diego, killing its priest. Other rebellions followed. Even the Spanish governor declared the condition of Indians at the missions to be "worse than that of slaves."

Nevertheless, by making religious converts and using forced native labor, Spanish friars managed to raise sufficient foodstuffs to support the small but growing settlements. Increased prosperity, in turn, made it easier for the friars to convert natives. As in previous periods of settlement, though, California's Indians fell victim to European diseases. It is estimated that the coastal region's population of about sixty thousand in 1769 had been reduced to thirty-five thousand by 1800. Meanwhile, there had been no great rush of Hispanic settlers to California. There were fewer than one thousand in 1790, and about eighteen hundred ten years later. Distance from the larger population centers of Mexico, and California's function as a defensive outpost, kept migration there low.

In New Mexico the uneasy balance between Hispanic and Indian societies, established after the conflicts of the seventeenth century, continued to hold sway. Florida settlements remained small and interfered little with native groups in the interior. Altogether, Spanish society in North America's borderlands still remained marginal to the larger interests of Spain and its empire. This was evident after 1800, when it became known that Spain had secretly traded back to France the territory of Louisiana and its vast land holdings in the Mississippi valley. Control of the great river might have made Louisiana the nucleus of a North American commercial empire, but instead Spain found the region an encumbrance.

The United States quickly became the beneficiary of Spain's decision to relinquish Louisiana. France might once again have exploited the vast territory, but was now in too weak a position to do so. Its hold on the Caribbean had been shaken by the revolution in Haiti, and by the fact that disease had ravaged a large army sent to reconquer the island. The French ruler Napoleon, fighting wars in Europe and the Middle East, no longer had use for Louisiana, and in 1803 he sold the whole territory to the American government for fifteen million dollars. With the Louisiana Purchase, the United States at a single stroke acquired a claim to territory between the Mississippi and the Rocky Mountains that roughly doubled its land area.

The Spanish empire in America would soon be crippled by external events and internal rebellion. Many factors now fed aspirations for political independence in Central and South America: long-standing tensions between colonial-born *criollos* and Spanish-born *peninsulares;* the stresses of administrative reform; popular tax revolts; the burdens of war; and the

"Sale of the Deserts of Scioto by the Anglo-Americans." As this 1799 French engraving demonstrated, Americans were selling land to the French as well as purchasing it. The Scioto Company was one of many land companies that bought property from the federal government to resell at great profit to speculators and prospective settlers in the United States and abroad. Often the value of the land was not what the companies claimed. "Better to ensnare dupes," this print's caption commented, "they draw up geographical maps, convert the rocky wastes into fertile plains, show roads cut through impassable cliffs, and offer shares in lands which do not belong to them." The Scioto Company went bankrupt, but not before it had relieved many French investors of their francs.

Source: Chicago Historical Society.

Vente des deserts du Scioto par des Anglo-americains

example of successful anticolonial revolution to the north. Then, in 1808, Napoleon sent French armies to conquer Spain itself. As the empire's center tottered, rebellions erupted from Mexico to Argentina, setting off protracted revolutionary struggles between nationalists and royalists. As a result, most of mainland Spanish America seized independence from Spain in the years around 1820.

The republics that emerged modeled their constitutions substantially on the U.S. example, and North Americans welcomed this evidence of the advance of republicanism against monarchy. But Americans' intentions toward their new sister republics were not wholly benign. In 1819, after American settlers and fighters had entered the region, the United States took advantage of the chaos in the Spanish empire to annex Florida. When Mexico gained its independence in 1821, assuming control of the vast Spanish territories in California, Texas, and the Southwest, some Americans saw this too as an opportunity to gain yet more land for themselves. Struggles over Mexico's North American territories would become a prominent theme of the 1830s and 1840s.

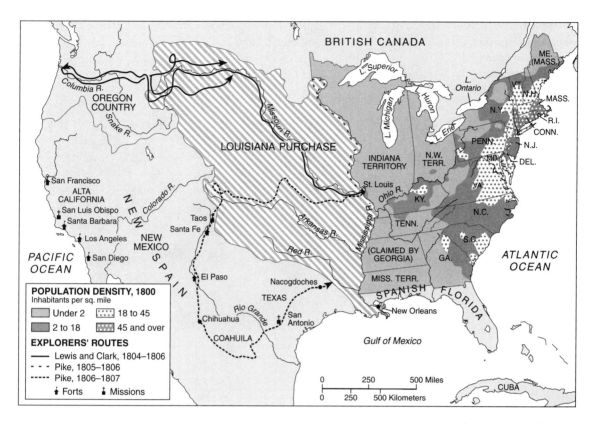

The United States after 1803.
The Louisiana Purchase of 1803 doubled U.S. land territory and helped confirm that the new nation's orientation in the nineteenth century would be westward, across the continent. Spain's grip on the South and West would be weakened within a few years by revolutions across the Spanish Empire.

Revolution and Territory: Indian Resistance

Meanwhile, in the area between the Appalachians and the Mississippi, the American Revolution had initiated a process that would make American Indians strangers in their own land. Groups that had sided with the Americans benefited little from their alliance. Settlers took their land anyway. Native Americans were virtually absent from the constitutional provisions and settlements that the people of the new United States made as they established their new governments. Unlike most indigenous peoples in Central and South America, who were regarded as subjects of Spain, and then citizens of newly independent republics, most native North Americans were specifically excluded from U.S. citizenship, and their tribes treated as separate foreign nations.

The 1783 peace with Britain ensured American dominion over the eastern part of the continent and opened up the access to lands across the Appalachians that settlers had been seeking for decades. As soon as the peace was signed, and well before the drafting of the Constitution, the American government assumed the right to control the distribution of

The Death of Jane McCrea.
John Vanderlyn's 1804 painting portrayed an incident that
may have occurred near
Saratoga, New York, during
the Revolutionary War, involving Indians who accompanied
British forces. The sexually
charged image left Americans
with the lasting impression
that Indians during the Revolution were (in the words of
the Declaration of Independence) "merciless savages"
and helped to build a rationale for dispossession.

Source: 1804, oil on canvas,
32 × 26 1/2 inches. — The
Wadsworth Atheneum,
Hartford, Connecticut.

land in the West. Congressional negotiations with states that claimed
western land of their own resulted in these claims being surrendered to
federal control. In 1785 and 1787 land ordinances laid the basis for the
creation of new states and the surveying and division of land for settlement, particularly in the region that would become known as the "old
Northwest," north of the Ohio River and stretching from Ohio to Wisconsin. By providing for the admission of newly settled land to the United
States on an equal basis with existing states, the ordinances both encouraged white settlement and underlined the exclusion of Indians from the
new political arrangements.

These measures assumed that Americans were entitled to the land of
Indians who lay in their path. Although the Northwest Ordinance of
1787 stated that land should not be taken without consent, treaties and
legal procedures frequently veiled fraud, extortion, and theft. Implicit,
too, was a notion that would frame more than a century of western expansion: although individuals and groups of pioneers would carry out
the settlement process, federal and state governments would support
and assist it.

Wartime plunder and destruction, population growth and clamor for
new land, contempt for Indians and their
ways of life, and European concepts of absolute property ownership all meant that
the immediate losers in post-revolutionary
America would be Indians. The exchanges
and understandings of past decades rapidly
collapsed under the pressure of a white invasion of the west. American Indians were
either divided and demoralized by this
new onslaught, or driven to attempt a
concerted resistance to it.

The Iroquois' location and their
wartime alliance with the British both contributed to the fragmentation of their
society. War and white settlement shattered their confederation and its strategy
for resisting European incursion. Some
Mohawks, led by Joseph Brant, removed
themselves to Canada. Other Iroquois
moved westward in retreat to preserve
their way of life. Those who remained,
largely in upstate New York, negotiated
away large parts of their land in return for
guaranteed settlements in reservations.

This averted their removal, but it did not prevent social collapse and demoralization. At the end of the 1790s, however, among Seneca Iroquois settled in new reservations, there arose a spiritual revival led by a former warrior, Sganyadai:yo, or Handsome Lake, to whom visions had appeared calling for a strict moral reform of Seneca society. Preaching the rejection of white notions of individualism, Handsome Lake sought to restore Iroquois society's communal traditions and persuaded many Indians to give up whiskey, gambling, and other evils associated with white Americans. Yet he also encouraged accommodation to "American" customs and values, welcoming Christian missionaries and seeking the transformation of Iroquois hunters into farmers, and female farmers into housewives. Hoping to form a united front among Iroquois committed to his vision, he was particularly critical of women who rejected demands to give up their traditional power and authority.

Indians further west resisted white settlers more vigorously. Peace in 1783 had meant that American migrants could settle in southern Ohio. There they encountered resistance from the Algonquian-speaking Shawnees, who had already been driven back and fragmented as they faced European encroachments in the seventeenth and early eighteenth centuries. To hold off these previous invasions the Shawnees had first supported the French in their losing war with Britain, and then the British against the colonists' war for independence. Now there could be no alliance with whites. American settlers sought land, not diplomacy, and the Shawnees' only recourse was to fight.

Shawnee efforts at first succeeded, in part because they engineered alliances with other Indian groups, forging a western confederacy of tribes that resisted incursions by American settlers. When the U.S. government sent military force against them, the Shawnees and their allies defeated them. In 1791 members of nine tribes attacked and killed, wounded, or captured nine hundred American soldiers out of an army of fifteen hundred. But at length the Shawnees were outnumbered. In 1794 a force of three thousand well-equipped U.S. soldiers defeated them at the Battle of Fallen Timbers, and by treaty the next year the Shawnees ceded most of their land east of the Mississippi. What was left was soon invaded by white hunters, trappers, and horse thieves, and the Shawnees were driven close to starvation. Their leaders pleaded with the federal government to "Hear the lamentations of our women and children" and "Stop your people from killing our game. At present they kill more than we do. . . . [T]hey would be very angry if we were to kill a cow or hog of theirs; the little game that remains is very dear to us." In response officials solemnly advised the Shawnees to take up agriculture instead of hunting, and to cede more land in return for cash.

Across the Middle West the federal government wrested land cessions from tribes, often with the help of pliant "government chiefs." The conduct of these chiefs drove many young warriors into rebellion. Among the Shawnees, social disintegration, growing dependence on trade with whites, and mounting frustration drove many to alcohol. Drunkenness and random violence deepened the sense of shame and decay. Kinship and family ties eroded; traditional rules of sexual conduct broke down. Even the pro–U.S. Shawnee chief Black Hoof noted that "The white people have spoiled us. They have been our ruin."

As among the Senecas, demoralization caused a major religious awakening. This time, between 1805 and 1808, it spread from the Shawnees to other northwestern tribes, and galvanized them to resist once more. The movement's inspiration was a prophet known as Tenskwatawa, or the Open Door, who promised to show his people the entrance to paradise, "a rich, fertile country, abounding in game, fish, pleasant hunting grounds, and fine cornfields," where spirits could follow the life they had once been used to "in all things unchanged." Demanding self-discipline and the rejection of alien and corrosive behavior, Tenskwatawa, a former alcoholic, denounced whiskey as "poison and accursed" and required strict temperance. Life should be conducted without use of goods, clothing, or techniques acquired from whites. Animals should be hunted, not domesticated, and hunted with bows and arrows, not guns. Only traditional crops should be raised, and no one should eat bread, "the food of the whites." Tenskwatawa condemned the accumulation of "wealth and ornaments," insisting that only those who shared what they had while they were alive would, after death "find their wigwam furnished with everything they had on earth." Debt incurred to whites should be repaid, but "no more than half, . . . because [the Americans] have cheated you."

This spiritual movement became increasingly political. In 1808 Tenskwatawa declared an intention to draw a clear "boundary line between Indians and white people" and forge the political unity among western tribes that would enable them to defend it. "If a white man put his foot over it . . . the warriors could easily put him back." Leadership shifted from Tenskwatawa toward his warrior brother Tecumseh. The only way to stop the whites' invasion of their lands, Tecumseh announced, was "for all the red men to unite in claiming a common and equal right in the land, as it was at first, and should be yet; for it never was divided, but belongs to all, for the use of each."

Unfortunately for the northwestern tribes, holding off white incursion required more advanced military technology and greater political unity than were compatible with the social structures and traditions they were striving to defend. Once more, the United States threw heavy military force against them. In November 1811, territorial governor William Henry Harrison led a thousand troops in an advance on Shawnee headquarters at Prophetstown in what later became Indiana. Six or seven hundred Shawnee warriors attacked Harrison's encampment on the Tippecanoe River, but were beaten off in a defeat that weakened Tenskwatawa's reputation and his efforts at tribal unification. Once more, Indians turned to European allies for help in resisting American whites. Tecumseh and Tenskwatawa supported the British against the United States in the War of 1812. But their hopes collapsed in October 1813, when the Americans defeated them at the Thames River in Canada. Among the dead was Tecumseh himself.

This defeat ended armed resistance against white settlement in the Old Northwest. It paved the way for the removal by the 1830s of the Shawnees and other tribes further to the west and for the cession to the United States of most Indian land in Ohio, southern Indiana, Michigan, and Illinois. Further south, Cherokees, Creeks, Choctaws, and other tribes also attempted various strategies to confront the invasion that threatened to overrun them. They mounted armed resistance; some voluntarily withdrew to the west; and many among the Cherokees and others became agriculturalists, turning their societies into miniature republics that claimed equal standing with whites on whites' own terms. But most, in the end, faced defeat and forced removal in the 1830s. Land-hungry settlers and planters brushed them aside with little compunction. Although battles like Tippecanoe marked defeat for Native Americans, they turned men such as William Henry Harrison into heroes in the United States. Even sympathetic whites came to regard Indian cultures as doomed and their decline and removal as inevitable. Yet Indian leaders resisted the white insistence that they were "savages" obstructing the advance of "civilization." The Chickasaw chief Shullushoma wrote to the federal government in 1824, "it has been a great many years since our white brothers came across the big waters and a great many of them has not got civilized yet."

Legacies of Revolution

The American Revolution and its aftermath secured the independence and political development of the United States and placed the new republic in a position to dominate the North American continent in the decades to come. Americans were divided in their views about who should rule their new society, and elite and popular conceptions of government clashed. On the one hand, state and federal constitutions tended to take political institutions in a conservative direction, erecting checks and balances against the exercise of direct democracy, while at the same time securing the rights of property and economic privilege. On the other hand, the principles of equality and popular sovereignty influenced both political rhetoric and behavior. Americans and visitors alike remarked on the egalitarianism and lack of formal hierarchy in U.S. society, and noted the decline of formality and deference in relationships between individuals. When Pennsylvania workingmen gave a toast in 1805 to "the independent mechanic, who nobly thinks for himself without giving fear to any," they were celebrating their own claim to equal standing with men who would once have assumed themselves to be superior. To a degree, the revolutionary period also extended the aspiration to equality to the many men and women who were still formally excluded from full participation in the life of the republic. Even as barriers of gender and race became firmer in the early nineteenth century, the possibilities of freedom and emancipation conjured up by the Revolution remained alive and would continue to shape events.

Revolution also unleashed a long period of economic expansion in the United States. In part this would entail the prolonged invasion and settlement of the territories west of the Appalachian Mountains that warfare and treaties with European powers and the Indians had secured for the new nation. But it would also involve the expansion and development of existing economic and social patterns in the rural and urban areas of the seaboard states. Despite the hopes of the republicans of the revolutionary generation, formal political equality for white men did not translate into economic equality. Prosperity and economic development would lead to sharper conflict between rich and poor, merchant and artisan, master and journeyman, planter and small farmer.

Above all, the different regional patterns established in colonial America would continue to shape the development of the United States, both in the older regions of the East, and in the settlement of the West. The distinctions between northern societies based on family and wage labor, and southern societies dominated by the presence and expansion of slavery, would assume increasing significance in the nineteenth century. The consolidation and growth of plantation slavery and its territorial expansion into the Southwest would come into increasing conflict with the development of wage labor in the North and the emergence there of an industrial society. These changes, and the role of workingpeople in them, would have the most profound effect on the future of the new United States.

The Years in Review

1775

- Ipai Indians attack and burn the mission at San Diego in response to Spanish expansion in California.

1776

- British troops evacuate Boston but then capture New York City and Long Island, which they hold until 1783; the following year, they capture Philadelphia.
- Radicals come to power in Philadelphia.

1777

- George Washington and his eleven thousand troops spend winter in Valley Forge, Pennsylvania; mythology aside, nobody froze or starved and morale was good.
- Congress adopts the Articles of Confederation, which go into effect in 1781.
- American victory at Saratoga, New York, convinces the French government to join the war against the British.

1779

- Patriot forces attack and burn forty Iroquois settlements in western New York.

1780

- Pennsylvania passes law providing for gradual abolition of slavery, as do Rhode Island and Connecticut in 1784; a court decision ends slavery in Massachusetts in 1783.

1781

- British surrender at Yorktown, Virginia.

1783

- Revolutionary War officially ended by Treaty of Paris, by which Britain recognizes American independence.
- Noah Webster publishes *The American Speller,* which begins the standardization of American spelling.

1785

- Virginia authorizes the construction of Little River Turnpike, the nation's first turnpike.

1786

- Shays's Rebellion: indebted farmers from central and western Massachusetts close the local courts to prevent lawsuits being heard and, taking up arms, attempt to seize the U.S. armory at Springfield, Massachusetts.

1787

- Constitutional Convention meets in Philadelphia.
- U.S. Constitution adopted on September 17.
- Northwest Ordinance lays the basis for the creation of new states, encourages white settlement, and excludes American Indians from the new political arrangements.

1788

- New Hampshire becomes ninth state to ratify Constitution, and by doing so officially puts it in effect as of March 4, 1789.

1789

- First federal administration with George Washington as president takes office.
- The nation's first road maps appear in *A Survey of the Roads of the United States of America.*

1791

- The Bill of Rights (the first ten amendments to the U.S. Constitution) is ratified.
- Toussaint L'Ouverture leads a Haitian slave revolt to secure independence from France and strikes fear into the hearts of slaveholders in the New World.
- First one-way street is introduced, in New York City.

1792

- Washington wins reelection for second term as president in unanimous vote of Electoral College; only contest is for the office of vice-president, which John Adams wins.
- Work on constructing White House and Capitol is begun.
- Black Methodists in Philadelphia withdraw from church when the elders insist on segregated seating, part of trend toward separate black churches.

1794

- Federal liquor tax leads to the Whiskey Rebellion in western Pennsylvania.
- English writer Mary Wollstonecraft publishes *Vindication of the Rights of Women,* which attacks the oppression of women and proves influential in the United States.

1795

- Treaty of Grenville: Shawnees cede most of their land east of the Mississippi to the U.S. government.

1796

- Federalist John Adams defeats Democratic-Republican Thomas Jefferson in first contested presidential race.

1798

- Congress passes the Alien and Sedition Acts, severely curtailing rights to free political expression.

1799

- Death of Washington leads to efforts to mythologize him; in 1800 Mason Locke Weems publishes the first of his biographies of Washington; he invents the story of the cherry tree for the 1806 edition (although Weems has him cutting off the bark rather than cutting the tree down).

1800

- Thomas Jefferson defeats federalist John Adams in bitter campaign for the presidency. Federalists whisper that Jefferson fathered a child with his slave Sally Hemings. DNA tests in 1998 prove this to be true.

1803

- The United States makes Louisiana Purchase (territory between the Mississippi and the Rocky Mountains) from France and roughly doubles its land area.

1805

- Tenskwatawa leads religious awakening among Northwest Indian tribes.

1807

- New Jersey abolishes property qualification for voting, one of many states to do so in this period, but in New Jersey it also ends the limited voting rights of women.
- Jefferson administration imposes trade embargo.

1812

- United States at war with Britain, until 1815.

1819

- United States takes advantage of the chaos in the Spanish empire to annex Florida.

1821

- Mexico declares its independence from the Spanish empire; independence movements spread throughout Latin America.

Suggested Readings

Beeman, Richard R., Stephen Botein, and Edward C. Carter II, eds., *Beyond Confederation: Origins of the Constitution and American National Identity* (1987).

Berlin, Ira, *Many Thousands Gone: The First Two Centuries of Slavery in North America* (1998).

Berlin, Ira, and Ronald Hoffman, eds., *Slavery and Freedom in the Age of the American Revolution* (1983).

Bolster, W. Jeffrey, *Black Jacks: African American Seamen in the Age of Sail* (1997).

Calloway, Colin, *The American Revolution in Indian Country: Crisis and Diversity in Native American Communities* (1995).

Countryman, Edward, *A People in Revolution: The American Revolution and Political Society in New York, 1760–1790* (1981).

Dann, John C., ed., *The Revolution Remembered: Eyewitness Accounts of the War for Independence* (1980).

Dowd, Gregory Evans, *A Spirited Resistance: The North American Indian Struggle for Unity, 1745–1815* (1992).

Durey, Michael, *Transatlantic Radicals and the Early American Republic* (1997).

Edmunds, R. David, *The Shawnee Prophet* (1983).

Edmunds, R. David, *Tecumseh and the Quest for Indian Leadership* (1984).

Frey, Sylvia, *Water from the Rock: Black Resistance in a Revolutionary Age* (1991).

Gross, Robert A., ed., *In Debt to Shays: The Bicentennial of an Agrarian Rebellion* (1993).

Hoffman, Ronald, and Peter J. Albert, eds., *Arms and Independence: The Military Character of the American Revolution* (1984).

Hoffman, Ronald, and Peter J. Albert, ed., *Launching the 'Extended Republic': The Federalist Era* (1996).

Hoffman, Ronald, Thad W. Tate, and Peter J. Albert, eds., *An Uncivil War: The Southern Backcountry during the American Revolution* (1985).

Juster, Susan, *Disorderly Women: Sexual Politics and Evangelicalism in Revolutionary New England* (1994).

Kerber, Linda K., *Women of the Republic: Intellect and Ideology in Revolutionary America* (1980).

Langley, Lester D., *The Americas in the Age of Revolution, 1750–1850* (1995).

Lee, Jean B., *The Price of Nationhood: The American Revolution in Charles County* (1994).

Morgan, Edmund S., *Inventing the People: The Rise of Popular Sovereignty in England and America* (1988).

Nash, Gary B., *Forging Freedom: The Making of Philadelphia's Black Community, 1720–1840* (1988).

Norton, Mary Beth, *Liberty's Daughters: The Revolutionary Experience of American Women, 1750–1800* (1980).

Rosswurm, Steven, *Arms, Country, and Class: The Philadelphia Militia and the 'Lower Sort' during the American Revolution* (1987).

Royster, Charles, *A Revolutionary People at War: The Continental Army and American Character, 1775–1783* (1979).

Shy, John, *A People Numerous and Armed: Reflections on the Military Struggle for Independence,* revised edition (1990).

Slaughter, Thomas P., *The Whiskey Rebellion: Frontier Epilogue to the American Revolution* (1986).

Smith, Billy G., *The 'Lower Sort': Philadelphia's Laboring People, 1750–1800* (1990).

Steffen, Charles G., *The Mechanics of Baltimore: Workers and Politics in the Age of Revolution, 1763–1812* (1984).

Storing, Herbert J., *The Antifederalists* (1985).

Tise, Larry E., *The American Counterrevolution: A Retreat from Liberty, 1783–1800* (1998).

Waldstreicher, David, *In the Midst of Perpetual Fetes: The Making of American Nationalism, 1776–1820* (1997).

Weber, David J., *The Spanish Frontier in North America* (1992).

White, Richard, *The Middle Ground: Indians, Empires, and Republics in the Great Lakes Region, 1650–1815* (1991).

White, Shane, *Somewhat More Independent: The End of Slavery in New York City, 1770–1810* (1991).

Wood, Gordon S., *The Creation of the American Republic, 1776–1787* (1969).

Wood, Gordon S., *The Radicalism of the American Revolution* (1992).

Young, Alfred F., *The Democratic-Republicans of New York* (1967).

Young, Alfred F., *Beyond the American Revolution: Studies in the History of American Radicalism* (1993).

Young, Alfred F., and Terry J. Fife, with Mary E. Janzen, *We the People: Voices and Images of the New Nation* (1993).

And on the World Wide Web

- Library of Congress, *George Washington Papers at the Library of Congress, 1741–1799*
  (http://memory.loc.gov/ammem/gwhtml/gwhome.html)
- Library of Congress, *The Thomas Jefferson Papers at the Library of Congress*
  (http://memory.loc.gov/ammem/mtjhtml/mtjhome.html)
- Library of Congress, *A Century of Lawmaking for a New Nation: U.S. Congressional Documents and Debates, 1774–1873*
  (http://memory.loc.gov/ammem/amlaw/lawhome.html)
- University of Groningen, *From Revolution to Reconstruction*
  (http://odur.let.rug.nl/~usa)

part two

Between roughly 1790 and 1850, America was transformed from a small agrarian society along the Atlantic Coastline into a wealthy, economically diverse country that stretched across the continent to the Pacific. Eighteen new states joined the original thirteen, and the nation's population swelled from four million to over twenty-three million. But this period of unparalleled growth and prosperity also produced deepening divisions related to class, race, gender, and nationality. The most divisive issue—whether America would be a society based on free labor or on slavery—was addressed at critical moments by legislative compromises. But no long-term solution was reached.

In 1790, the issue of slavery seemed of secondary importance to Americans of European descent. The new nation was confidently launching an unprecedented experiment in national republican government, backed by a seemingly limitless supply of land and natural resources. Most white Americans were optimistic about the nation's future. Even African Americans had some reason for hope as substantial numbers gained freedom and organized churches and mutual aid societies in the decade following the Revolution.

In the North, a market economy and a new system of industrial production took root. Here, revolutions in transportation, communication, and manufacturing undermined the old systems of local craft production and family farming. By the 1830s and 1840s, New England capitalists had brought workers—either women or entire families—together in the nation's first factories to weave cloth. Other workers labored in their homes to make shoes and clothing for market. An expanding network of roads,

Free Labor and Slavery

1790 – 1850

canals, and, later, railroads carried consumer goods from the Northeast to the new settlements in Ohio, Indiana, and Illinois and brought raw materials and foodstuffs from west to east.

The South remained predominantly agricultural, but there, too, Americans felt the profound changes wrought by an international industrial revolution. Cotton replaced tobacco as the South's principal cash crop and large quantities of the raw fiber fueled industrial development in England and New England. As a result, the region's plantation economy burgeoned, spreading from the upper South to Alabama, Mississippi, Louisiana, and, by the 1840s, to Texas. If the bonds of slavery loosened briefly in the revolutionary era, they were now tightened with renewed vigor. To keep pace with the demand for cotton, the slave labor force expanded both numerically and geographically. These changes resulted in harsh working conditions and devastating family separations for vast numbers of African Americans.

American Indians, in the North and the South, faced whites' insatiable desire for land. Many tribes were confronted again with either extermination or migration further westward. Some were forced out of their communities in the Southeast and onto reservations in the Indian Territory of present-day Oklahoma. Many Mexicans were also pushed out of their homes to make way for U.S. settlers in Texas and California. And in the aftermath of Texas statehood in 1845 and the Mexican-American War of 1846–1848, hundreds of thousands of Mexicans came under U.S. jurisdiction.

The United States was expanding economically as well as geographically. By midcentury, millions of Americans — including artisans, factory hands, domestic servants, day laborers, and even some slaves — had been drawn into a market economy where they sold their labor or their products. In the process, the ideal of the self-sufficient, independent farm or artisan family came under attack as large numbers of women and men became dependent upon wages. At several points in this era, wage workers (by now two out of every five American workers) experienced the full meaning of that dependency as manufacturing ground to a halt and tens of thousands were suddenly jobless.

Despite periodic recessions and depressions, northern employers were more concerned about a shortage of labor than an oversupply in the early nineteenth century. Beginning in the 1840s, a massive wave of immigrants from northern and western Europe entered the United States, supplying abundant workers for all kinds of manufacturing and agricultural enterprises. Most of these new immigrants—many of whom came to escape economic, social, and political injustices at home—became wage laborers, contributing to the formation of a growing and distinctly multinational working class. They also contributed to other changes initially inspired by the industrial revolution: the growth of cities, a new urban culture, and transformations in family structures and gender roles. In addition, some immigrants introduced radical theories and practices, including socialism, to American politics and broadened the base of American religion. These contributions were not always welcomed, however. In the 1840s and 1850s, many native-born Americans attacked new immigrants, blaming them for the wrenching changes that resulted from industrial and urban development.

Industrialization, and the demographic and cultural changes that accompanied it, profoundly affected the nation's political life. Americans engaged in intense debates over what kind of society they were creating. The commercial and industrial elite embraced a liberal capitalist interpretation of the revolutionary legacy, emphasizing the role of self-interest and the marketplace in governing social and economic relations. Many working people, especially those who did well in the new order, were attracted to the idea that liberty meant individual freedom to better themselves and improve their living standards. Others, including many of the working people dislocated by industrialization, criticized the emerging order as antithetical to revolutionary ideals and celebrated instead republican traditions of independence, mutuality, and citizen participation derived from the French and other European revolutions as well as the American Revolution.

Working Americans—men, women, and children; free-born, slave, and emancipated—resisted the dependent status that came with industrial and agricultural development. They insisted that the United States had not been created to make a few men rich and powerful at the expense of all others. They attacked the "tyranny" of their employers and masters, condemning them as "Tories in disguise," in the words of women textile workers in the 1830s. Others argued for liberty and equality by drawing upon new religious principles espoused by evangelical, Quaker, and Moravian believers. Poor whites, African Americans, and women were especially keen to claim their spiritual equality and to translate it into practical, divinely sanctioned rights whenever they could. Working people defended their interests in a variety of other ways as well, through local workingmen's parties, trade unions, cooperative workshops, utopian communities, strikes (engaged in by free and enslaved workers), and outright rebellion, most notably among slaves. Some working women demanded rights for their sex, as did their middle-class counterparts. Growing circles of women and men also denounced alcohol and prostitution and demanded the abolition of slavery.

Of all the diverse claims for social justice raised in these years, one—the end of slavery—became the central political issue of the day. Over the decades, the country divided between those who desired an America whose labor was legally free, as in the North, and those who believed that only a system based on slave labor could guarantee social order, as in the South. A basic question thus emerged as the United States expanded westward and new territories sought statehood: should these new states be free or slave? As we will see in Part Two, this question affected American politics, moral values, and the economy. Several political compromises from 1820 onward maintained an uneasy peace between the two systems. By 1850, however, the acquisition of new territories as a result of the U.S. war with Mexico intensified debates and steered the young nation toward civil war.

chapter 6

The Consolidation of Slavery
1790–1836

As the War of 1812 wreaked havoc along the northern and western borders of the United States, disruptions of a different kind helped transform the lives of the white and black residents of Virginia's long-settled agrarian communities. In the midst of the war, Fanny, a slave whose owner had recently died, was sold with two of her children to an up-and-coming young planter, John Cowper Cohoon, Jr. Fanny was forced to leave behind several other children (the records are not clear how many) and probably a husband and other relatives as well. She was sent to Cedar Vale plantation in Nansemond County, Virginia, located some fifty miles from the lower Chesapeake Bay. The slave community at Cedar Vale included thirty-eight men, women, and children acquired from at least a dozen different owners. Like Fanny, many of the Cedar Vale slaves had been separated from family and friends so that Cohoon and his young bride, Maria Louisa Everette, could stake their own claim to independence.

Cohoon's power over his property set the boundaries of his slaves' lives. Fanny, whether by choice or by force, set up house with another slave, Jacob, who Cohoon purchased around 1815. Over the next twenty years, Fanny worked in the fields and gave birth to at least seven children. And although Cohoon apparently never separated a husband and wife by sale when he owned them both, he did sell slaves, including Fanny's daughter Lucy, born in 1824. Cohoon also gave slaves as gifts to his sons; seventeen slaves in all were sent away to help younger Cohoons make their fortunes on newly established plantations. When Fanny died in 1857, at age 68, Cohoon noted, "She was a good and faithful servant, leaving many children and grandchildren to mourn her loss." Yet good and faithful as she was, Fanny could not make even the most fundamental decisions about her life—where she lived, whom she married, what kind of work she performed, and what happened to her children.

John Cowper Cohoon, Jr., and thousands like him grew rich by using slaves such as Fanny and her offspring to produce the raw materials, especially cotton, for burgeoning industries in the North and in Europe, or to grow the food needed to feed the rapidly expanding populations of cities in America and abroad. By 1830, a cotton kingdom had been established across the South, with millions of enslaved men, women, and children laboring to produce that crop. Most lived in a broad area that stretched like a belt from coastal South Carolina inland through central Georgia, Al-

"Five Generations on Smith's Plantation, Beaufort, South Carolina." This African-American family was photographed in 1862.

Source: Prints and Photographs Division, Library of Congress.

303

abama, and Mississippi and then bent southward down the lower Mississippi Valley to New Orleans. The creation of this cotton belt, and the consolidation and defense of slavery needed to support it, reshaped the lives of all Southerners. Whites and blacks, slaves and free people, men and women, wealthy planters, small farmers, and landless whites alike found themselves living in a new era that revolved around slavery and cotton cultivation. Over time, the great profits to be made in the slave trade and in cotton pushed up the price of slaves; retarded the growth of southern industry, towns, and cities; and affected all other aspects of economic life in the South.

Yet in the 1780s, the future of slavery had seemed uncertain as profits from traditional crops—especially tobacco and indigo—declined. Many white Southerners, frustrated by dwindling resources, were looking for new ways to support themselves and their families. They would find opportunities in territories opened to the south and west. Two new states entered the union in the 1790s—Kentucky (1792) and Tennessee (1796)—promising a better life for those white Americans willing to move across the mountains. Other new states—Ohio (1803), Louisiana (1812), Indiana (1816), Mississippi (1817), Illinois (1818), Alabama (1819), and Missouri (1821)—expanded that promise

The federal government had one strong incentive to encourage migration; the profits to be made from the sale of western lands. Of course, the sale of this acreage overlooked the fact that these territories were already home to tens of thousands of American Indians. Western expansion put whites, rich and poor alike, on a collision course with indigenous peoples. The war with Britain that raged from 1812 to 1815 provided one way for the government to determine which native peoples were loyal to the new United States. But loyal or not, as the nineteenth century unfolded, Indians were once again forced off their lands.

The greatest boon to western settlement in the South, and so the greatest danger to American Indian communities, was the revitalization of slave labor. Southern planters at the Constitutional Convention had secured the legal and institutional support necessary to maintain slavery, and assured both the continuation of the slave trade through 1807 and the power of the states rather than the federal government to determine the institution's ultimate fate. Although declining farm profits in the 1780s might have led to the gradual demise of slavery, the South experienced a dramatic economic recovery in the 1790s. Tobacco production shifted from nutritionally depleted Chesapeake lands to North Carolina, Kentucky, and Tennessee, where production eventually surpassed pre-revolutionary levels. Planters who grew rice in the Carolinas and Georgia did better than ever, helping to cement the need for slavery there. But most of all, a device invented by a New Englander in 1793—

the cotton gin—helped launch a revolution in the South's economy. Over the next thirty years that invention would lead to the consolidation and dramatic expansion of slavery in the region.

The Invention of the Cotton Gin

It was New England–born Eli Whitney who, while living on a Georgia plantation in 1793, invented the cotton gin, a simple device that changed the face of southern agriculture. Long-staple cotton, with its resistance to rot and characteristic long fibers and smooth seeds, was already profitable in the Sea Islands of the Carolinas and Georgia. By 1791, planters there, responding to demands from British factory owners, had produced some two million pounds. But long-staple cotton could be grown only in the mineral-rich alluvial soils of the South's coastal districts. Short-staple cotton, on the other hand, could be grown much more widely, but the time and effort it took slaves to pluck out its sticky seeds by hand were substantial, limiting the crop's profitability.

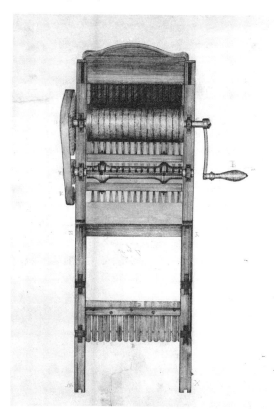

Cotton Gin. This sketch was submitted by Eli Whitney in 1793 when he applied for a patent for his new invention.

Source: Eli Whitney Papers, Yale University Library.

Whitney solved this problem with a simple device: a wooden box filled with a series of combs attached to a handle. As a worker (usually a slave) cranked the handle, the combs separated seeds from fiber. Using even the most primitive gin, a worker could clean ten times more than was possible when plucking seeds by hand. Whitney never profited from his invention because it was too easy to copy and too hard to patent. But others did, as larger and ever-cheaper cotton gins were produced and sold across the South. By the early 1800s, cotton could be produced profitably almost anywhere south of Virginia, Kentucky, and Missouri. It was produced not only on large plantations by bound labor, but also on small farms where families, sometimes assisted by one or two slaves, could hope to turn a profit.

The spread of short-staple cotton generated by the invention of the cotton gin coincided with two other developments that guaranteed cotton would be king throughout the region. The first happened just after 1750, when a population explosion in Europe created an enormous demand for food, clothing, and shelter. Woolen and linen cloth were already popular in Europe, but the demand for cotton skyrocketed with the increase in population. Further fueling the booming market were technological innovations that enabled English textile factories to increase production and lower the prices of cotton goods. By the mid eighteenth century, British craftsmen, utilizing the power of water and steam, had developed machines to drive textile looms and spin cloth. Entrepreneurs then built factories where workers, paced by machines, produced much greater quantities of cloth than ever before.

In the early nineteenth century, the domestic demand for cotton also began to grow. Britain and France, at war with one another, used naval blockades to keep U.S. goods from reaching enemy shores. In response, President Jefferson and the U.S. Congress instituted the Embargo Act of 1807. U.S. ships could no longer carry goods to any European nation until Britain and France stopped interfering with American trade. The act devastated the economy of the nation's young seaports. The end of export trade crippled merchants and threw sailors, dockworkers, and laborers of all sorts out of work. Some enterprises benefited, however. The Embargo Act proved a boon to nascent textile manufacturers in New England. They had managed to replicate some of the most important British inventions and now, for a short time at least, would have access to cheap southern cotton and protection from the flood of English cloth. This combination helped create a domestic market in raw cotton and manufactured cloth.

Cotton soon became not just the South's but the nation's leading export. That accomplishment, however, assured that a vast army of enslaved workers and huge expanses of fertile soil would be harnessed to cotton production. Realizing that the importation of slaves would come to an end in 1808 (as permitted by the U.S. Constitution), planters indulged first in frenzied purchases of Africans and then in an expanding internal slave trade. By the 1810s, that internal slave trade stretched across the Deep South, into the lands of Louisiana that the United States had purchased from France. Small farmers, large planters, and thousands of enslaved blacks followed this cotton trail.

The invention of the cotton gin, then, led to the expansion and consolidation of slavery in the South, encouraged the acquisition of new territories and the establishment

King Cotton. The South's staple, packed into bales and awaiting transport up the Mississippi River, filled a New Orleans wharf.

Source: Prints and Photographs Division, Library of Congress.

The Westward Spread of Cotton Production, 1790–1840. In 1793 the invention of the cotton gin made it profitable to grow short staple cotton in many parts of the South. Between 1820 and 1860, the most important areas of cotton production shifted from the Carolinas and Georgia into Alabama, Mississippi, Louisiana, and Texas. This also meant a massive shift in the slave labor force and the painful disruptions of slave life caused by an expanded internal slave trade.

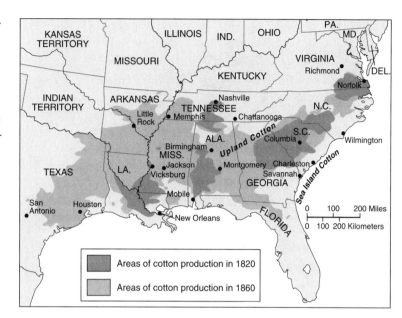

of new states, and fueled the birth of industry in England and the northern United States. Cotton's success also led to the forced removal of American Indians from southern soil and the sale of African Americans from the upper to the lower South. It inspired resistance and rebellion among the growing population of slaves, posed new challenges for non-slaveholding whites, and fed antislavery sentiments among wary whites, North and South. As the new republic took shape, it was influenced at every turn by the profits and problems associated with cotton.

Territorial Expansion and New Opportunities

Throughout the early 1800s, the United States acquired vast tracts of new territory, gaining lands through purchase, the repayment of debts, and military conquest. The Louisiana Purchase of 1803 was the most important in opening lands to small farmers. Indeed, the decision by Jefferson to purchase the Louisiana Territory had been a response in part to the needs of southern farmers and landless white laborers.

In the long run, geographical expansion assured political conflict as slavery became more entrenched in the South and free labor grew dominant in the North. In 1790, the populations of North and South were about equal, and so was their representation in Congress. But during the next few decades, the North's population grew faster, and the balance of

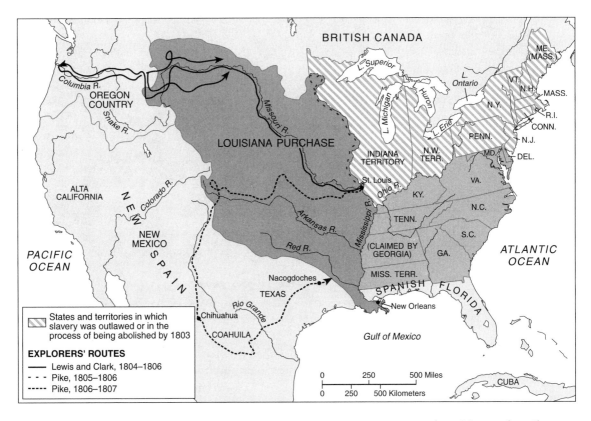

States and territories in which slavery was outlawed or in the process of being abolished by 1803

EXPLORERS' ROUTES
—— Lewis and Clark, 1804–1806
- - - Pike, 1805–1806
----- Pike, 1806–1807

power in Congress shifted accordingly. By 1820, the states that relied on slave labor found themselves with just forty-two percent of the votes in the House of Representatives; only in the U.S. Senate was parity maintained.

During these years of declining southern political power many white Southerners eagerly headed west. In droves they left the Piedmont region of the Carolinas and Georgia. Although planters along the eastern coast sought to stem this migration, more than one hundred thousand Southerners moved into Kentucky and Tennessee by 1790. After 1800, migrants flooded into these areas through the Cumberland Gap and along the Knoxville Road. About half of the North Carolina migrants headed for Kentucky, Tennessee, and Missouri, whereas the other half ventured further south. Still others went from eastern Tennessee into Arkansas and from Kentucky into Missouri. Some moved into Alabama, Mississippi, and eventually Texas.

Their migration was facilitated by an expanded network of roads and by the invention and subsequent improvement of the steamboat. In 1817,

The Louisiana Purchase. The Louisiana Purchase doubled the territory of the young United States, providing opportunities for many, mainly white, Americans to seek their fortunes on the new frontier. At the same time, the expansion of settlement into this region over the next forty years would spark conflicts with many Indian societies and intensify debates over the place of slavery in a democratic republic.

"A Regular Row in the Back-woods." The 1841 issue of the *Crockett Almanac,* named after the Tennessee back-woodsman made famous by his self-serving tall tales, por-trayed a rough rural "sport." Inexpensive comic almanacs combined illustrated jokes on topical subjects with astrolog-ical and weather predictions.

Source: *Crockett Almanac* (1841)—Prints and Pho-tographs Division, Library of Congress.

steamboats were already plying the western rivers, and that year the port of New Orleans welcomed some seventeen steam-boats, loaded with migrants and freight. Just three decades later, more than five hundred steam-boats arrived each year. A large proportion of the early migrants were single men, seeking adventure as well as economic opportu-nity. Often as practiced at drinking, gambling, and fighting as farming, they embraced frontier life.

Everyday existence in the region was characterized by a level of vio-lence shocking to many Americans. Eye-gouging contests, ear biting and teeth bashing, and arrests for stabbings and knifings all provided evidence of the rough-and-tumble quality of life on the southern frontier. The sto-ries of Davy Crockett and other legendary figures, who killed bears or Indian warriors with their bare hands, reflected the raw virility that de-fined and dominated much of frontier culture. Even those who later rose to political fame and social respectability, including Crockett, continued to impress their neighbors with tales of wild exploits in the untamed West.

The earliest migrants, whether they moved out into the Louisiana Territory or closer to home in western Georgia, Tennessee, or Kentucky, often chose to "squat" on land rather than to buy it. Squatters simply staked claims to what they considered empty acreage by selecting a spot, settling on it, and implementing "improvements"—building a rough cabin, clearing the land, and planting crops. In most newly opened fron-tier areas, north and south, squatters were as prevalent as owners. Over time, however, state and federal agents, land speculators, and large farm-ers and planters sought to regularize land ownership, demanding land titles and payments to assure continued occupancy.

The state of Georgia, which claimed lands reaching to the Mississippi River, instituted a lottery to distribute land in the sparsely settled western part of the state. Most winners, however, got cash for their land certifi-cates from speculators who then resold the land to small farmers. The federal government sold land in the West on credit. In 1800 and again in 1804, Congress, in order to assist cash-poor migrants, lowered both the minimum acreage that needed to be purchased and the price per acre.

309

Politics on the Tennessee Frontier, the Autobiography of Davy Crockett

Davy Crockett (1786–1836) was a frontiersman, soldier, and politician who used his autobiography to help create an image of himself as a larger-than-life American hero. The description of frontier politics presented here is based on his campaign for a seat in the Tennessee legislature in 1821. He suggests that humor, hunting skills, and male camraderie were as important to electoral success as a clear stance on the issues of the day.

I . . . set out electioneering, which was a bran-fire new business to me. It now became necessary that I should tell the people something about the government, and an eternal sight of other things that I knowed nothing more about than I did about Latin, and law, and such things as that. . . .

I went first into Heckman country to see what I could do among the people as a candidate. Here they told me that they wanted to move their town nearer to the centre of the county, and I must come out in favour of it. There's no devil if I knowed what this meant, or how the town was to be moved; and so I kept dark, going on the identical same plan that I now find is called "non-committal." About this time there was a great squirrel hunt on Duck river, which was among my people. They were to hunt two days: then to meet and count the scalps, and have a big barbecue, and what might be called a tip-top country frolic. The dinner, and a general treat, was all to be paid for by the party having taken the fewest scalps. I joined one side, taking the place of one of the hunters, and got a gun ready for the hunt. I killed a great many squirrels, and when we counted scalps, my party was victorious.

The company had every thing to eat and drink that could be furnished in so new a country, and much fun and good humor prevailed. But before the regular frolic commenced, I mean the dancing, I was called on to make a speech as a candidate. . . .

The thought of having to make a speech made my knees feel mighty weak, and set my heart to fluttering almost as bad as my first love scrape with the Quaker's niece. But as good luck would have it, these big candidates spoke nearly all day, and when they quit, the people were worn out with fatigue, which afforded me a good apology for not discussing the government. But I listened mighty close to them, and was learning pretty fast about political matters. When they were all done, I got up and told some laughable story, and quit. I found I was safe in those parts, and so I went home, and didn't go back again till after the election was over. But to cut this matter short, I was elected, doubling my competitor, and nine votes over.

Source: David Crockett, *A Narrative of the Life of David Crockett of the State of Tennessee* (1973).

"Woodcutter's Cabin on the Mississippi." French artist August Hervieu sketched a poor white family in 1827. The drawing later appeared as an illustration in British author Frances Trollope's acerbic and very popular account of a stay in the United States, *Domestic Manners of the Americans,* published in 1832.

Source: (August Hervieu) Frances Trollope, *Domestic Manners of the Americans* (1832)—Rare Books and Manuscripts Division, New York Public Library, Astor, Lenox and Tilden Foundations.

Again, however, most land ended up in the hands of speculators rather than individual owners.

By the 1810s, steamboats and improved roads made it possible for more southern men to bring their families west. They also facilitated the exchange of products with people back East and with other migrants settling the Northwest — Ohio, Indiana, and Illinois. With the aid of the steamboat, especially, Northwesterners could market their surplus grain and livestock in the new South, just as new planters in Louisiana, Mississippi, Arkansas, and Tennessee could sell some tobacco, sugar, rice, and cotton in the Northwest. Towns and cities along this route — including Pittsburgh and Cincinnati on the Ohio River, and New Orleans and St. Louis on the Mississippi — flourished. In this manner these newly settled western areas, north and south, became temporarily linked in an economic partnership that helped make them political allies during the 1820s and 1830s.

Unlike small farmers who lived in the cotton belt, those who lived further west were less likely to select crops demanded by the export economy. These Southerners prized economic and social independence as highly as their eighteenth-century forebears had. For most, staking everything on cotton was still too risky: a sudden drop in prices could land them in debt, even strip them of their land. Farm families concentrated instead on fishing, hunting, and farming to produce the food, tools, and clothing they needed.

If they produced more than they needed, they could sell or exchange the surplus locally for such necessities as sugar, coffee, molasses, nails, needles, tableware, and cooking utensils. Corn was the preferred crop, because it was useful regardless of its market price; it could be eaten by family members and by livestock, and it could easily be bartered for other goods. Fishing, particularly for shad, was also an important source of food and income. Only with a record rise in the price of cotton during the 1850s would large numbers of frontier and upcountry farm families finally change this strategy of subsistence farming.

For residents of the frontier, family labor and local exchange networks were the keys to success. Trade and barter among neighbors had important benefits, leading to the formation of social as well as economic ties and creating a community out of scattered households. In this context, the marriage market was as important as the cotton or produce market for those seeking a larger stake. Landless men hoped to marry the daughters of settled farmers, and farmers sought to marry the daughters of neighbors as a way of increasing their holdings. Wives and daughters enhanced a family's standing by selling domestic manufactures for cash or raising chickens, churning butter, and working in the fields. Expansion, then, shaped not only economic opportunities and choices but also family and community relations.

War in 1812, Compromise in 1820

Although these frontier communities seemed far removed from events in the nation's capital, they were in fact deeply affected by both domestic and foreign politics. The acquisition of territory and the building of roads into the trans-Appalachian region were of particular concern to small farmers. Threats from Indians, whose lands were repeatedly trespassed on by white settlers, led to frequent demands that the government provide protection to the settlers. Also, conflicts between the United States and Britain, culminating in the War of 1812, heightened tensions between migrants and local Indians who hoped that alliances with the British would end white encroachment.

Back east, concerns about the British impressment of American ships and seaman dominated political debates. Yet most merchants and politicians from New England and the Middle Atlantic states opposed the renewal of armed conflict with Britain because of the potentially devastating effects on maritime trade. It was instead farmers in the West and South who most enthusiastically advocated war. Angered by the effects of the British naval blockade on the price of cotton and other crops and by British support for Indians hostile to white settlers, frontier residents sought to defeat the nation's perennial foe once and for all. In addition, many dreamed of annexing additional British territories in Canada.

Although the hawks who persuaded President Madison to declare war believed the conflict would be short lived, they were badly mistaken. The strength of British troops staved off any chance that the United States might capture Canada. Instead, Madison found himself defending the nation's new capital, Washington, D.C., against British attack. British troops actually captured the city in 1814 and many U.S. government buildings were burned. Although American forces finally repelled the advancing

BROTHER JONATHAN *Administering a Salutary Cordial to* JOHN BULL.

"Brother Jonathan Administering a Salutary Cordial to John Bull." In a bellicose 1813 cartoon by Connecticut engraver Amos Doolittle, Brother Jonathan (a precursor to Uncle Sam) forces the personification of Great Britain, John Bull, to drink the bitter brew of U.S. Captain Oliver Hazzard Perry's naval victory in Lake Erie.

Source: October 21, 1813 — American Antiquarian Society.

British troops at Baltimore (in the battle that inspired Francis Scott Key to write "The Star Spangled Banner") the Royal Navy continued to control the Atlantic coastline. And many Indians joined the British cause in hopes of stemming U.S. expansion.

By 1814, the economic devastation caused by the war led New England states to threaten secession. Only Britain's defeat of Napoleon in France and its desire to end years of warfare on all fronts led to peace with the United States. The fighting ended but U.S. borders remained as they had before the war, and few of the original disputes between the two nations were resolved.

In fact, the most significant battle of the war occurred after the treaty of peace had been signed in Ghent, Belgium, in 1814. Before news of the accord reached the United States, British and American troops clashed at New Orleans. Under the leadership of General Andrew Jackson, a slave-owning planter from Tennessee, the U.S. Army crushed the invading forces. The Battle of New Orleans was won with regular troops, including the Corps d'Afrique, a contingent of French-speaking black troops, and the overwhelming power of cannon and artillery fire. Nonetheless, the battle became a symbol of the fierce determination of frontier fighters.

The efforts of Jackson at New Orleans, combined with his earlier exploits as an Indian fighter, made the general a national hero with particular appeal to southern small farmers and western settlers. His campaigns opened new lands and thereby expanded the opportunities available to landless sons and daughters, small farmers, and in the long run, large planters, like himself. The U.S. government, moreover, rewarded War of 1812 veterans with land warrants, increasing the pressure on western territories. And in 1820, Congress lowered the price per acre from $2.00 to $1.25 to make settlement even more appealing.

International developments soon provided opportunities for the United States to expand further still. In the 1800s, Spain claimed the territory of Florida, present-day Texas, and lands in the Pacific Northwest. In 1812, U.S. Marines invaded Florida, in hopes of capturing runaway slaves who had fled across its border. Seminole Indians joined with the fugitive blacks to repel the invaders. The Seminole War only reinforced planters' interest in gaining control over the region. Finally, on the heels of an 1817 military incursion into Florida led by Andrew Jackson, Spain agreed to sell the territory to the United States. According to the terms of the Adams-Onís Treaty, signed in 1819, Spain gave Florida to the United States along with its lands in the Northwest, and the United States gave up its claims to Texas.

That same year, one long-term implication of U.S. expansion became clear. The Missouri Territory applied in 1819 for admission to the Union as a slave state, and it promptly touched off a heated debate over the place of slave and free labor in the nation. New York congressman James Talmadge, Jr., confirmed planter fears that the North would apply its political power to weaken chattel slavery, proposing as a condition of Missouri statehood that no additional slaves be admitted within its borders and that all slave children born there following statehood be emancipated at age twenty-five. Such gradualist approaches to emancipation were popular among northern whites.

Despite the limited form of manumission proposed by Talmadge, it triggered a sectional battle. Most northern congressmen, 87 of 101, voted for the proposal, whereas the vast majority of Southerners opposed it. The U.S. Senate, where the slave owners held more power, voted to impose no restrictions on slavery in Missouri. But the Senate alone could not admit a state into the Union.

Henry Clay, the Speaker of the House, finally engineered a compromise. Missouri would be admitted with no restrictions on slavery. At the same time, the line of Missouri's southern border (at 36 degrees, 30 minutes latitude) would be extended westward through the rest of the Louisiana Purchase. Henceforth, no territory north of that line would be admitted to the Union as a slave state. The Missouri Compromise also opened the way for the statehood of Maine, blocked in the U.S. Senate until the Missouri issue was resolved.

Many in the North bitterly denounced the 1820 compromise as a slaveholder victory. But planters were unhappy, too; the entire affair confirmed their suspicions about the North's attitude toward their labor system. The freewheeling debate over the Missouri Compromise in Congress had also given a public forum to subversive ideas. Free blacks living in the capital had filled the House galleries during the debates and listened intently to the antislavery speeches. Who knew how far these words might travel and what their effects might be?

Still, the conflicts engendered by territorial expansion did not stop Southerners from seeking lands farther west. As early as the beginning of the century, some American whites had settled in the Mexican province of Coahuila-Texas. And despite the terms of the Adams-Onís Treaty, system-

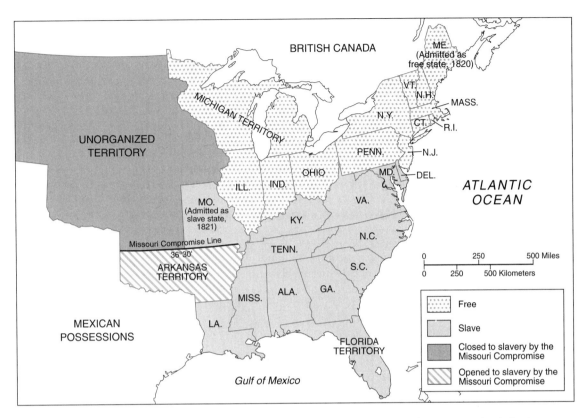

The Missouri Compromise. The Missouri Compromise, which provided for the nearly simultaneous admission to statehood of Maine and Missouri, established a pattern that would be followed for the next thirty years. To maintain equal representation of free and slave states in the U.S. Senate, each admission of a free state necessitated the admission of a slave state and vice versa. Although in the end the Missouri Compromise did not resolve the debates over slavery in western lands, it did produce a temporary truce that assured further expansion.

atic colonization of the area began in earnest during the 1820s, organized by Virginia-born Stephen Austin. Even after the now-independent Mexico outlawed slavery in 1829, Southerners continued to move into the region. In 1830, about a thousand slaves, owned by U.S. citizens, also lived in the province. Austin had secured a special provincial law permitting slavery to operate under a different name: "permanent indentured servitude."

Planters moved in much greater numbers into the rich and fertile U.S.-controlled lands along the Mississippi Delta and the Gulf of Mexico. The mixed population of poor whites, small farmers, free blacks, and Indians that had characterized the lower Mississippi was supplanted in the 1820s and 1830s by a vast plantation society in which small numbers of whites controlled the labor of thousands of slaves. Over time, these differences in access to land, to slaves, and to wealth would generate increasing antagonism among southern whites of different classes. In addition, for planters to make the greatest profits possible required the massive importation of slaves and more brutal work regimens, leading to increased fears of slave rebellions. These problems would not surface in their most acute forms for another generation, however. In the early 1800s, Indians provided the greatest resistance to white Americans' plans for westward expansion.

American Indians: Resistance and Retreat

The goals of King Cotton converged with those of General Andrew Jackson to set white settlers on a collision course with Indians. In 1790, Indians occupied villages throughout the twenty-five million acres of what would become the cotton-growing states. During the early 1800s, many were herded into reservations. Others moved west, voluntarily or not. Still others tried to survive by adopting the ways of white missionaries and farmers. Such efforts at integration ultimately failed, however, owing partly to resistance from Indians who sought to retain traditional customs but mainly to the desire among white Americans for land.

Among the largest tribes in the Southeast were the Cherokees and the Creeks, who occupied the western Carolinas, Georgia, eastern Alabama, and Tennessee. Their neighbors, the Choctaws and Chickasaws, occupied parts of western Alabama and northern Mississippi. The Seminoles resided in central Florida. Despite the fierce resistance offered by the Seminoles, who waged two wars against white invaders in Florida, these Indian tribes became known among white Americans as the "Five Civilized Tribes." They bought land, shifted property ownership from women to men, adapted to plows and spinning wheels, and sent their children to English-language schools and Christian churches. Some Indian farmers even adopted slavery. They also attempted to use the U.S. courts to salvage their political autonomy and their lands.

For many Native Americans, especially tribal leaders, conversion to Christianity seemed to offer one of the best hopes for peaceful coexistence with whites. Indians had a range of Protestant religions that they could embrace, because Moravians, Quakers, Baptists, Methodists, Presbyterians, and Congregationalists had all sent missionaries into southeastern Indian societies in the late eighteenth and early nineteenth centuries. Yet among the Choctaws, the greatest number of converts were African Americans enslaved by the Indians and the mixed-blood children of white traders and Indian wives. Even among the Cherokees, where missionaries enjoyed considerable success, many people who converted also continued to practice traditional burial and marriage rituals.

The educational and economic resources offered by Christian missions attracted as much attention as the faith itself. Moravian missionaries were welcomed by the Cherokees in 1799, for instance, because they offered to open a school. In the 1820s, the agent for the American Board of Commissioners for Foreign Missions, Daniel Butrick, introduced oxen in an attempt to convince the Cherokees that men should farm and women should sew. The Indians accepted the oxen, but women continued to perform the bulk of agricultural labor.

Government officials hoped to replace tribal institutions and values with those more appropriate to a market-oriented society. Communal land ownership was particularly a target. "Unless some system is marked out by which there shall be a separate allotment of land to each individual," a U.S. commissioner of Indian affairs reasoned, "you will look in vain for any general casting off of savagism." He concluded, "Common property and civilization cannot coexist." Yet replacing communal land ownership was not in the best interest of Indians. It meant weakening the ties connecting the individual Indian to the community and binding the community as a whole to its land. Dividing communal tribal land into private plots made it easier for whites to acquire legal title to that land. One method was already tried and true: merchants drew Indians into debt, often through questionable bookkeeping. This debt then became a tool with which to dispossess debtors.

By the early 1800s, as a result of government policy, missionary intervention, and trade relations, a new class of culturally assimilated Native Americans, many of mixed Indian and white parentage, emerged. Some, such as William Shorey, the son of a white man and a Cherokee woman, tried to impose U.S. rather than tribal rules of inheritance, depriving women in his family of the benefits of matrilineal descent. At the same time, because clan membership did pass through the mother's line, the sons of white men and Cherokee women could claim seats on tribal councils. The children of such marriages were often bilingual and familiar with white American as well as Indian ways, making them increasingly valuable in negotiating with U.S. officials. And with white backing, these acculturated men acquired growing political power within tribal councils and used it to promote the transformation of Indian society into an approximation of white male-dominated America.

Yet the decision to acculturate spurred resistance within many tribes. For instance, young Creek warriors, who had earlier fought against white Americans with the Shawnee leader Tecumseh, became increasingly es-

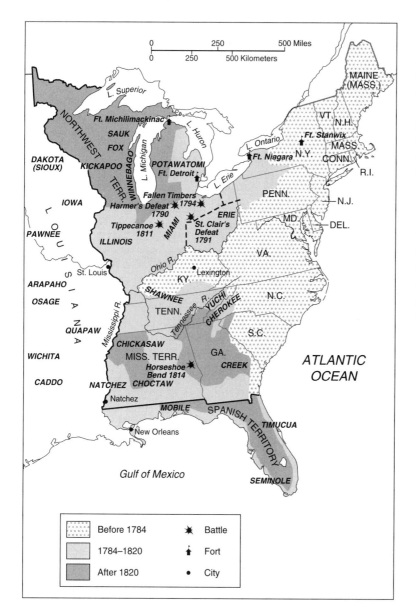

Indian Cessions, 1790–1820.
Between the end of the American Revolution and 1820, most Indian tribes living east of the Mississippi River were forced to cede their lands to the U.S. government. Battles between the U.S. Army and various confederations of Indians in the 1790s and 1810s assured U.S. control of most Indian territories that could not be obtained by purchase or treaties. Still, Cherokees and Seminoles continued to fight their removal from the Southeast to the Indian Territory in present-day Oklahoma into the 1830s.

tranged from Creek elders, who favored accommodating to U.S. authority and Christian missionaries. In 1813, a bloody war erupted, pitting these young "Red Sticks," as they were known, against thousands of white southern militiamen, as well as against Creek, Cherokee, Choctaw, and Chickasaw warriors who hoped for greater leniency from whites in ex-

318

. . . Beyond the Great River

In this 1832 petition to Congress, leaders of the Creek nation protested their forcible expulsion from the Gulf coast region onto lands beyond the Mississippi River, in present-day Oklahoma.

It has been . . . with alarm and consternation that we find ourselves assailed in these our last retreats. Though our possessions have shrunk to a narrow compass, they contain all that endears itself to our heart. Beneath the soil which we inhabit, lie the frail remnants of what heretofore composed the bodies of our fathers and of our children, our wives and our kindred. Their value was enhanced as their extent was curtailed. Yet we are now menaced with being driven from these narrow limits, and compelled to seek an asylum from the craving desires of the white man, beyond the great river. If the alternative offered us—if the lands offered us be, as we are told, of greater value than those which we derived from our ancestors, and they from God, we freely relinquish all the advantages which they possess, and will be satisfied with that which we already have. If they are inferior in value, we submit it to the justice of our white brethren, whether they will compel us to a disadvantageous exchange. If there be any particular inducements either to individuals or communities which render our lands particularly valuable, why should not we, the rightful proprietors, be suffered to enjoy them? Can any adventitious value enhance them more in the eyes of the white man, than the solemn associations to which we have adverted, do in our own?

We are assured that, beyond the Mississippi, we shall be exempted from further exaction; that no State authority can there reach us; that we shall be secure and happy in these distant abodes. Can we obtain, or can our white brethren give assurances more distinct and positive, than those we have already received and trusted? Can their power exempt us from intrusion in our promised borders, if they are incompetent to our protection where we are? Can we feel secure when farther removed from our father's [the president's] eye than now, when he hears our remonstrances and listens to our complaints? We have heretofore received every assurance and every guarantee that our imperfect knowledge could desire; we confided in it as ample for all our purposes; and we know not what to require which would obviate further embarrassments.

Source: House Document 102, 22nd Cong. 1st Sess. (1832).

---

change for this alliance. The fierce, but unequal, combat ended in March 1814 at the battle of Horseshoe Bend, where more than a thousand Indians died. Andrew Jackson, then commanding the Tennessee militia, was considered by white Americans the hero of this engagement.

Among the losers were those Creeks who allied with Jackson. The Treaty of Fort Jackson, which ended the fighting, transferred fourteen million acres (more than half the land in Alabama) from Creek to U.S. control. Moreover, the defeat at Horseshoe Bend opened the floodgates to southern white migrants, who soon wanted to complete the Indians' removal. By 1826, the Creek Indians of Georgia had been driven westward, setting a precedent that would eventually unseat almost the entire population of the Five Civilized Tribes.

Native Americans Seek Justice but Face Removal

In response to these threats of removal, some southeastern Indians turned to the U.S. courts. Over the course of the early nineteenth century, Indian tribes—although technically recognized as independent nations—were increasingly subject to federal and state laws. They now hoped to use federal and state courts, along with existing treaties, to save themselves from eradication.

Throughout the 1820s, white southerners sought to secure lands owned by Indians, setting off repeated jurisdictional disputes not only between sovereign tribes and state courts, but also between state courts and federal authorities. Georgia led the way, forcing the Creeks to cede land to the state in 1825 and 1827 and claiming in 1828 that the Cherokees were not a sovereign nation but simply a collection of individuals subject to state laws.

Cherokee leaders, hoping to avoid the fate of other tribes, had been especially active in adapting to the white society surrounding them. They had embarked on this path years earlier, and many in the tribe had followed the instructions of both Christian missionaries and government agents in embracing white gender roles, farming techniques, religious ceremonies, educational practices, and legal doctrines. In 1827, the Cherokees adopted a formal constitution modeled on that of the United States, complete with dis-

Removal of American Indians. Those American Indians who retained control of eastern lands after 1820 were forced to move to reservations west of the Mississippi River during the 1830s. The most famous of these forced migrations is that of the Cherokees along the Trail of Tears. Despite the adoption by many Cherokees of Anglo-American language, religion, and customs, southern planters insisted that they be removed west to open their lands for white settlement.

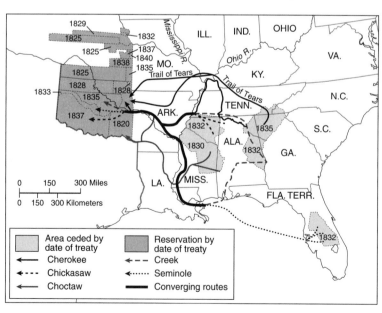

Area ceded by date of treaty		Reservation by date of treaty
← Cherokee		←--- Creek
←···· Chickasaw		←······ Seminole
← Choctaw		── Converging routes

tinct legislative, executive, and judicial branches. John Ross, who was born of a mixed marriage, was elected principal chief under this new constitution.

The whites soon made clear, however, that they were less interested in transforming the Indians than in removing them from the region altogether. Although Cherokee women repeatedly protested land cessions made by male leaders in the 1810s and 1820s, they no longer had the power to intervene effectively. Only when it became clear that removal was the ultimate goal of southern whites did a majority of Cherokees oppose further concessions.

The Cherokees fought their removal right up to the U.S. Supreme Court, which held responsibility for adjudicating cases between states and foreign governments. In *Cherokee Nation* v. *Georgia* (1831), the plaintiffs argued that their tribe was a sovereign, thereby "foreign," nation, requiring the intervention of the federal courts. Although Chief Justice John Marshall was generally sympathetic to the Indians' claims, he was unwilling to grant them independent political authority. Instead the Court ruled that Indian tribes had a special but still dependent status within the nation. Marshall used the analogy of "a ward to his guardian" to express this special status, and on that basis argued that the Cherokee tribe had no standing before the U.S. Supreme Court.

Just a year later, in *Worcester* v. *Georgia* (1832), the Marshall Court strengthened federal authority over American Indians, but this time it also strengthened tribal sovereignty. The Court invalidated a Georgia law that required any U.S. citizen wishing to enter Indian territory to obtain permission from the governor. Marshall argued for the majority that Indians were members of "domestic dependent nations" with a right to their own land, and "distinct political communities" with exclusive authority within their territorial boundaries. Only the federal government, not the states, could regulate commerce with tribes.

The Court's rulings proved largely meaningless, however. Andrew Jackson, elected president in 1828, had pushed through an Indian Removal Act in 1830, offering Indians reservations west of the Mississippi in exchange for their current lands. Under the pressure of federal agents and the threat of military intervention, many tribes, or at least tribal leaders, signed away most of their eastern territory. Then the federal government set out to relocate all southeastern tribes. Twenty-three thousand Choctaws and some Cherokees were pressured into moving west in 1831–1832. Most of the Seminole Nation was removed between 1832 and 1835. Others were transported by force—the Alabama Creeks in 1836, the Chickasaws the next year. In 1838, those Cherokees who had refused the government's offer of land in the West were uprooted by federal troops. The troops herded some fifteen thousand members of the tribe across the eight-hundred-mile "Trails of Tears" to present-day Oklahoma. One in four died on the way.

Cotton, Rice, Tobacco, and Sugar: Crops, Regions, and Labor Organization

The removal of the Five Civilized Tribes from lands that could be profitably cultivated in cotton and sugar opened the door to a new and expanded plantation economy. In the early 1800s, cotton's emergence as the economic foundation of the South halted any shift away from slave labor in that region. Indeed, in the two decades before the 1808 embargo on importing slaves, planters purchased some quarter million Africans, doubling the number who had been imported in the previous two centuries. In the following years, natural reproduction and the internal slave trade would take the place of importation from Africa in meeting the demand for workers.

The demand for labor was motivated in large part by the rapid expansion of cotton production. "To sell cotton in order to buy negroes," one Mississippian noted, "to make more cotton to buy more negroes, *ad infinitum,* is the aim and direct tendency of all the operations of the thoroughgoing cotton planter." Yet cotton was not the only source of profit for slave holders. Rice and sugar also underwrote the expansion of slave labor and, in the case of sugar, the movement westward as well. Following the fate of the Indians, tens of thousands of black workers from the Chesapeake and the Carolinas were forced to move to new homes and adapt to new work regimens.

The growing number of slaves trapped in bondage in the 1820s and 1830s labored under a variety of conditions. In 1830 a significant portion of slaves still worked on small farms, where a laborer might cook one day and hoe cotton the next. Here patterns of labor varied from season to season as owners tried to assure profits and, at the same time, cultivate sufficient food and raw materials to sustain their own families. In such situations, slaves had more direct interaction with owners and, as long as the farm was successful, could hope that an owner might purchase nearby family members. But African Americans who lived on small holdings also had less chance of developing kin and community ties within their own quarters, and they faced a greater danger that one bad season could cause them to be transferred as payment for debts.

On large plantations, the demands on laborers differed from place to place, from crop to crop, and from job to job. For instance, house slaves lived under quite different conditions from field hands. Frederick Douglass remembered that domestic slaves were "carefully selected, not only with a view to their capacity and adeptness, but with special regard to their personal appearance, their graceful agility, and pleasing address." These slaves, he wrote, "constituted a sort of black aristocracy" who "resembled the field hands in nothing except their color."

Yet house slaves, although privileged in certain ways, still worked hard. Moreover, female domestics lived in closer proximity to whites and were thus more vulnerable to sexual exploitation and abuse. Black women worked washing clothes, cleaning, caring for children, and cooking, tasks that were tedious and burdensome in the early nineteenth century. The white teacher Emily Burke considered cooking the most demanding of all. "After having cooked the supper and washed the dishes," Burke observed of one slave woman, "she goes about making preparations for the next morning's meal. In the first place she goes into the woods to gather sticks and dried limbs of trees, which she ties in bundles and brings to the kitchen on her head, with which to kindle the morning fire." The woman completed her night's work by grinding all the corn needed for the next day's hominy and bread. The next morning she had to rise early, "for she has every article of food that comes on to the table to cook."

Although the specific demands on field hands varied from crop to crop, the general conditions of agricultural labor were harsh indeed.

We Weren't Allowed to Sit Down

As young female slaves grew old enough, most went to work in the fields. But some became personal servants to their owners, an experience one of them later recalled.

When I was nine years old, they took me from my mother and sold me. Massa Tinsley made me the house girl. I had to make the beds, clean the house, and other things. After I finished my regular work, I would go to the mistress's room, bow to her, and stand there till she noticed me. Then she would say, "Martha, are you through with your work?" I'd say, "Yes, mam." She'd say, "No you ain't; you haven't lowered the shades." I'd then lower the shades, fill the water pitcher, arrange the towels on the washstand, and anything else mistress wanted me to do. Then she'd tell me that was about all to do in there. Then I would go to the other rooms in the house and do the same things. We weren't allowed to sit down. We had to be doing something all day. Whenever we were in the presence of any of the white folks, we had to stand up.

Source: Dorothy Sterling, ed., *We Are Your Sisters: Black Women in the Nineteenth Century* (1984).

From planting time through harvest season, dawn signaled the start of a working day that often extended far into the night. Most field-work ended at dusk, but there might be cotton to gin, sugar to mill, corn to grind, or any number of other tasks that could be done indoors by the light of a lantern. Even in winter there were miscellaneous chores: fences to build and mend, hogs to slaughter, and wood to chop, haul, and stack. Slaves also performed the carpentry and blacksmithing that kept a plantation productive and in good repair.

From Dawn to Dusk. An unknown photographer captured this scene of men, women, and children picking cotton under the watchful eye of an overseer.

Source: Prints and Photographs Division, Library of Congress.

Whatever the season, after laboring for the white master, slaves needed to prepare their own meals; feed and wash their children and put them to bed; clean their cabins; wash and mend their clothes; and do all the other chores of daily life. In addition, if slaves were fortunate enough to have their own gardens or access to hunting or fishing, late nights and early mornings were almost the only times they could take advantage of these opportunities to augment their diet.

The work that women and men performed in the slave quarters was essential to their survival, for most owners spent as little as they could on food, shelter, and clothing for their slaves. This led to what former slave Frederick Douglass remembered as "the close-fisted stinginess that fed the poor slave on coarse cornmeal and tainted meat, that clothed him in [coarse] tow-linen and hurried him on to toil through the fields in all weathers, with wind and rain beating through his tattered garments." Even more generous owners supplied slaves with inferior and inadequate clothing, shelter, and food. Planters typically supplied a weekly food ration of only three and a half pounds of salt pork or bacon and a quarter bushel of cornmeal. Although high in the calories needed for heavy labor, that diet was seriously deficient nutritionally.

Rice cultivation—of major importance in the South Carolina and Georgia low country and in Louisiana—required highly skilled but back-breaking labor. Women generally were responsible for March plantings. Rice was never just scattered about a plowed field like other crops; each grain had to be carefully placed in a single row along the deep trenches

"Ration Day." A master distributed provisions in an illustration from a weekly newspaper report on the operations of a plantation around 1860. The engraving suggested that this planter provided his slaves with a varied and nutritious diet, which was not typically the case. It failed to show the gardens and other methods slaves used to supplement often meager or boring fare.

Source: *Harper's Weekly* — American Social History Project.

that had been plowed and shaped earlier. Over the next five months, the fields had to be alternately flooded, left to dry in the sun, and hoed. Delay in any of these steps could ruin an entire crop. The harvest began in August and kept every able-bodied slave in the fields until October. Men cut the rice plants with sickles while women followed, bundling the plants. Later the plants had to be flailed by hand to separate the grain from the stalk. Rice cultivation involved intricate systems of dams and dikes to flood and drain the land; these were usually built or repaired after the harvest and before the spring planting.

Much of the work on rice plantations was organized according to the task system, in which each slave was assigned a particular task each day. Those who worked slowly might find themselves working longer hours than usual, but if the task was completed early, the rest of the day was free. This arrangement was intended to encourage slaves to do their work quickly even without close supervision. It also shifted responsibility for feeding the slaves onto themselves. Former slave George Gould remembered that his master "used to come in the field, and tell the overseers not to balk [us], if we got done soon to let us alone and do our own work as we pleased." The task system permitted a degree of personal autonomy and even modest economic well-being unknown under gang labor. Those finishing their tasks early might spend their free time producing or acquiring fish, game, handicrafts, crops, even livestock for personal use, barter, and sale.

But rice cultivation also involved special perils. Work in the fields exposed slaves to malaria, pneumonia, and tuberculosis. One visitor attributed the high number of deaths among slaves to the "constant moisture and heat of the atmosphere, together with the alternate floodings and dryings of the fields, on which the negroes are perpetually at work, often ankle-deep in mud, with their bare heads exposed to the fierce rays of the sun. . . . At such seasons every white man leaves the spot, as a matter of course, and proceeds inland to the high grounds; or, if he can afford it, he travels northward to the springs of Saratoga, or the lakes of Canada."

On tobacco plantations the largely unskilled work was performed by gangs of slaves. Plowing began in April. In May the tobacco plants that had

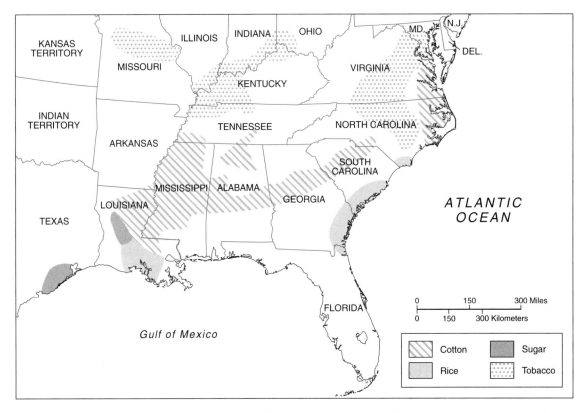

Rice, Cotton, Tobacco, and Sugar Production in 1839. Although cotton was considered the king of southern agricultural products by 1830, several other crops competed with cotton for labor and profits. Tobacco, rice, and sugar, although they could not be grown in as many parts of the South as cotton, were highly profitable in those sections where the climate and soil were favorable. These crops demanded different kinds of labor and were characterized by different growing seasons and cycles, which contributed to the distinct experiences of slaves on rice, tobacco, cotton, and sugar plantations.

Source: Lewis Cecil Gray, *History of Agriculture in the Southern United States to 1860* (1933).

been growing indoors since March were transplanted to the fields. For the next several months, gangs periodically worked in the fields, weeding, hoeing, and pruning the lower leaves of the tobacco plants. The plants were harvested in August and September, and hung to dry. Slaves then stripped the stalks and prepared the leaves for export or manufacturing. Charles Ball, a slave who had worked both rice and tobacco, recalled that in the winter, there was "some sort of respite from the toils of the year," as he and other slaves "repaired fences, split rails for new fences, slaughtered hogs, cleared new land, [and] raised tobacco plants for the next planting."

In the early 1800s sugar was just starting to be grown in Louisiana. Like tobacco, it was cultivated by gangs of slaves laboring together, but the seasonal rhythms varied somewhat. Slaves planted and hoed between January and April. During late spring and summer they tended the plants constantly. Harvesting began in October, with gangs of fifty to one hundred slaves wielding knives and machetes. By January they began preparing for another crop.

Cotton, too, was cultivated by large gangs, and planters could profit from the labor of the entire slave family — men, women, and children. In the interest of profit, cotton planters emphasized supervision and discipline, dividing most tasks by age and sex. In general, men plowed and women hoed, working side by side with members of their own sex. As schoolteacher Emily Burke observed, "During the greater part of the winter season, the negro women are busy in picking, ginning and packing cotton for market," while men repaired buildings and cleared land.

During the harvest season, men and women worked together as they

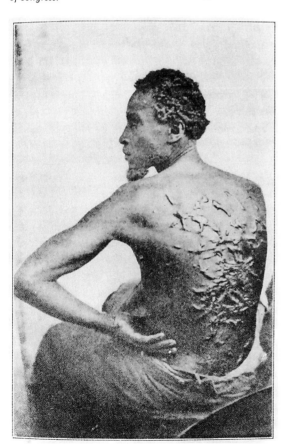

A Map of Servitude. The back of a Louisiana slave named Gordon, photographed in 1863 after he escaped to the Union forces.

Source: Prints and Photographs Division, Library of Congress.

swept across one field after another, picking at an unrelenting pace set by a leader. Solomon Northup, a free black man from New York, was kidnapped and sold to a Louisiana cotton planter. He recalled that the fastest worker took "the lead row," and anyone who fell behind or was "a moment idle [was] whipped." Through the heat of August, September, and October, all able-bodied men and women picked the cotton, stooping as they walked, pulling the bolls from the prickly pods, which cut their hands. This unrelenting labor kept them in the fields from sunrise until it was, Northup wrote, "too dark to see, and when the moon is full, they oftentimes labor till the middle of the night." No one would stop, "even at dinner time, nor return to the quarters, however late it be, until the order to halt" was heard. Each day ended at the scales where an overseer weighed the cotton each slave had picked. Those who fell short of their quota were whipped.

Punishment was used more often than reward to induce slaves to work harder, and whipping was the most common means. In the South Carolina rice-growing region, according to former slave Hagar Brown, "Don't do your

327

task, driver wave that whip, put you over a barrel, beat you so blood run down." An overseer employed by a prominent planter, Robert Allson, gave twelve lashes to eight women for "hoeing bad corn." On the Louisiana cotton plantation of Bennett Barrow, some three-quarters of the incidents that led to physical punishments were work-related: for "not picking cotton," "for not picking as well as he can," for picking "very trashy cotton," "for not bringing her cotton up," and so forth. On average, Barrow whipped one of his slaves every four days. Others were imprisoned, chained, beaten, shot, or maimed in other ways. And with all this, his biographer tells us, Barrow treated slaves better than did many of his neighbors. "Talk not about kind and Christian master," claimed James Pennington, a former slave. "They are not masters of the system. The system is master of them."

The Internal Slave Trade

The growing importance of slavery to southern agriculture was accompanied by rising prices for slaves. In the seventeenth and eighteenth centuries, competition from Caribbean sugar planters had begun to bid up slave prices. Congress's 1808 prohibition against the importation of Africans further constricted the supply, boosting prices even higher. These high prices led early nineteenth century owners to place a premium on the survival and natural reproduction of the slaves they already owned, sometimes limiting their cruelty and even inspiring them to more generous food and housing allotments.

The former Georgia planter John C. Reed reported that "the greatest profit of all was what the master thought of and talked of all the day long—the natural increase of his slaves as he called it," which required "keeping slaves healthy and rapidly multiplying." A South Carolina planter kept his slaves' cabins whitewashed because he believed doing so "makes the slave prolific," adding, "I have, at this time, a hundred and fifty of these people; and their annual increase may be estimated as adding as much to my income as arises from all other sources."

Yet the value of slaves and the movement of plantation agriculture into new areas also ensured the expansion of the interstate slave trade. Perhaps nothing symbolized the human cost of bondage so vividly as the wholesale destruction of slave families through this trade. Such destruction was the key to success for some masters, especially in the Chesapeake. They managed to adapt to the declining profits of tobacco production by turning to the sale of surplus labor. When sold to an Alabama cotton planter, a Kentucky tobacco farmer, a Louisiana sugar

Slave trader, Sold to Tennessee,

Arise! Arise! and weep no more dry up your tears, we shall part no more, come rose we go to Tennessee. that happy Shore, to old virginia never — never — return.

the Company going to Tennessee from Staunton. Augusta County, the law of virginia Suffered them to go on. I was Astonished at this boldness, the carrier Stopped a moment, then Ordered the march, I Saw the plan it is Commonly in this State, with the negro's in droves Sold,

"Sold to Tennessee." Lewis Miller, a sometime artist and carpenter whose work often took him to Virginia, observed this "cottle" of slaves en route to new owners in Tennessee. Miller sketched the scene and transcribed the words of the slaves' song.

Source: Lewis Miller, *Virginia Sketchbook*—Abby Aldrich Rockefeller Folk Art Center, Williamsburg, Virginia.

baron, or a Carolina rice grower, a slave born and raised in Maryland or Virginia fetched his or her master a handsome return on his investment.

Although some planters tried to sell slave families intact or at least to keep mothers and their children together, this practice declined over time. Increasingly, buyers sought younger and less expensive slaves, and sellers ultimately complied with the demands of the market. Of course, some white owners never recognized the existence of slave families at all. Of those who did, many felt no obligation to maintain kin connections when high prices promised otherwise unobtainable profits.

Particularly from the 1820s on, the market in slaves wreaked havoc on the families of southern African Americans, causing them enormous anguish. In March 1829, a Virginia resident wrote to the *Genius of Universal Emancipation,* an antislavery paper, describing "a most tragic occurrence . . . occasioned by those monsters who traffic in HUMAN FLESH." A planter in the town of Hillsborough had sold a group of slaves to a trader, who held the chattel in a room overnight. In the morning, a middle-aged woman among those sold was found dead, "choosing death rather than be dragged off by these tyrants." Henry Watson, another Virginia slave, recalled his agony when, as a small child, his mother was sold away. An older woman tried to comfort him, but Watson was inconsolable. "Every exertion was made on my part to find her, or hear some tidings of her, but all my efforts were unsuccessful; and from that day, I have never seen or heard from her. This cruel separation brought on a fit of sickness, from which they did not expect I would recover." Watson did recover, however, and as a young adult escaped slavery and wrote a narrative of his life, including the story of how he lost his mother.

Slave families were broken apart not only by the sale of slaves to the Deep South, but also by the death of owners, which led to the division of estates for inheritance or payment of debts. Slave families might be broken up through the marriage of white planters, which were often accompanied by "gifts" of young slaves to the new couple. Or a slave owner moving from one county to another might take his chattel with him, thereby severing connections between slave husbands and wives who lived on neighboring plan-

tations. Slaves, then, were dependent on their owners not just for food, clothing, and shelter, but also for the very existence of African-American families.

"The Slave Auction." Slavery, and particularly slave auctions, left an indelible impression on many visitors to the antebellum South. One of them was a British artist, Eyre Crowe, who sketched a Richmond slave sale in 1853. During the Civil War, he painted a series of pictures based on his earlier drawings and notes that delineated the auction and subsequent separation of slave families.

Source: Eyre Crowe, 1862, oil on canvas, 13 × 21 inches— Kennedy Galleries, Inc., New York.

The Planter Class

Planters were, of course, also dependent on their slaves. They needed African Americans for the labor that supported their lifestyles and their economic and political power. Yet planters responded in different ways to the black workers who served as the foundation of their world. Some planters were incredibly cruel, frequently employing the lash and the branding iron. Others, particularly those with close ties to the church, believed in a more benevolent style of authority. This might include teaching slaves to read, allowing them to attend Christian churches, and providing lighter workloads for pregnant women and nursing mothers. At the same time, many planters who embraced evangelical teachings, particularly Baptists, used religion to defend slavery as an institution and to reassert their authority in backcountry counties where protests from small farmers or racially integrated camp meetings and churches threatened to subvert the traditional order.

Plantation mistresses as well as masters varied in their responses to slaves. Although a few left all management concerns in the hands of men, most were responsible at least for directing the house slaves and often for organizing clothing, food, and health care for fieldhands as well. Many mistresses complained about the burden of such responsibilities, but few thought about eliminating the institution of slavery, which provided the basis for their own station in life. At most, they sought to improve slaves' living conditions and intervened to diminish harsh punishments. But some were as likely as their husbands to inflict the whip, scalding water, or the branding iron, particularly on slave women they viewed as recalcitrant.

The ranks of slave owners expanded steadily in the early nineteenth century. By 1830, some 225,000 white Southerners owned slaves. Still, although the absolute number of slave owners grew, the total white population grew faster. Slaves were becoming more expensive, and only a shrinking proportion of all southern whites could afford to own them. The thirty-six percent of white families who owned slaves in 1830 shrank to thirty-one percent in 1850, and to twenty-six percent by 1860. Nonetheless, because slavery was the source of economic, social, and political power in the pre–Civil War South, it was this segment of the white population that controlled the great bulk of the region's wealth and wielded most of its political power.

Of course, not all slaveholders were wealthy planters. The elite among plantation owners were those who held fifty or more slaves, and owned enough land to make such an investment in labor profitable. Next were the more numerous but less wealthy middling planters who owned between fifteen and fifty slaves. Even more numerous were the small farmers who owned five or six slaves and land valued at about three thousand dollars. Even that much property made the small southern farmer many times wealthier than the average Northerner. But dependence on the export economy left the southern farmer vulnerable to sharp decreases in crop prices or increases in the prices of slaves, land, and transport. Debt and economic uncertainty affected such people much more than they did the planter aristocracy.

We know the planter elite best from its self-descriptions and later from novels and films that romanticized their life as elegant, cultured, leisurely, and removed from the hectic pace and pressures of commerce or industry. Planters liked to see themselves in the role of stern but loving fathers guiding the lives of their plantation families — especially their slave "children" — with paternal wisdom and justice. The slave, wrote Virginian George Fitzhugh, "is but a grown-up child, and must be governed as a child. . . . The master occupies toward him the place of parent or guardian." Fitzhugh contrasted this supposed paternal guardianship with the reckless individualism he saw in the "free society" of the North. "Selfishness," he declared scornfully, "is almost the only motive of human conduct in free society, where every man is taught that it is his first duty to change and better his pecuniary situation."

Southern planters were distinguished from northern merchants and manufacturers by the experiences, expectations, and values that grew out of owning a laborer's body instead of hiring part of his time for wages. But both were deeply enmeshed in the international market economy.

Large-scale commercial production of cotton, sugar, rice, and tobacco were businesses run for profit. And slavery was first and foremost a way of controlling the labor that produced those profits. As North Carolina's Supreme Court observed approvingly in 1829, the purpose of slavery "is the profit of the Master," and the purpose of the slave is "to toil that another may reap the fruits."

THE OLD PLANTATION HOME.

The contribution of slave labor to profits affected both slaveholders and slaves. Because this labor yielded their wealth, power, and leisure, successful farmers and planters felt compelled to accumulate more slaves—not unlike northern industrialists accumulating machinery, but without the same increase in productivity. As eastern land in the South became depleted of nutrients, even elite planter families were compelled to uproot themselves, join the southwestern migration, and submit to the ruder life on the cotton frontier.

Indeed, the story of slave masters and mistresses seated on the porches of grand mansions sipping mint juleps and ordering others to do their bidding, although widely circulated in the late nineteenth century, was largely fictive and had little to do with life on most plantations in the 1820s and 1830s. Instead, many planters along the coast and on the frontier built modest homes on their lands, putting their wealth into city rather than country estates. Fanny Kemble, a British actress who married planter Pierce Butler in 1834, was shocked when she first saw his South Carolina Sea Islands rice plantations. Although she admits that she was "prejudiced against slavery" when she arrived, she was most concerned about her own plight. She considered her husband's plantation to be located "on the outer bounds of civilized creation," and described the Butler homestead in harsh terms:

> It consists of three small rooms and three still smaller, which would be more appropriately designated as closets, a wooden recess by way of pantry, and a kitchen detached from the dwelling—a mere wooden outhouse with no floor but the bare earth.

"The Old Plantation Home." This lithograph by the popular firm of Currier and Ives portrayed the slave quarters as a carefree world, basking in the glow of the planter's benevolence. The plantation as the perfect extended family was a common theme of pro-slavery prints before the Civil War—and after.

Source: Currier and Ives, 1872, lithograph, 9 × 12 1/2 inches—Prints and Photographs Division, Library of Congress.

332

"Family Amalgamation Among the Man-Stealers." An illustration from an 1834 anti-slavery tract depicted an unlikely domestic scene in a plantation household, with slave children joining their owners at the dinner table. Some antislavery advocates viewed the potential for inti-macy between whites and blacks as one of the demoral-izing effects of the "peculiar institution."

Source: George Bourne, *Pictures of Slavery in the United States of America* (1834)—Prints and Photographs Division, Library of Congress.

Mrs. Butler was equally concerned about the ease with which slaves gained access to her household. Doors were rare and did not always close. African-American women and men wandered into the parlor at all times of the day and night, and, much to Mrs. Butler's chagrin, felt no compunction about sitting close to her and touching her hair or dress. She may have been "prejudiced against slavery," but she was equally prejudiced against "the crowd of filthy Negroes, who lounge in and out of [the house] like hungry hounds . . . , picking up such scraps of food as they can find about."

At least through the 1830s, the augmentation of planters' power was seen mainly in cities and towns rather than in the more remote agricul-tural hinterlands where their wealth was produced. Urban centers offered the chance to inhabit fancier living quarters, participate in the best social and political circles, join in courting rituals and marriage arrangements with other planter families, buy new furniture and the latest fashions, and keep up with news on national and international markets and prices.

On election and court days, held in county seats and major cities, planters could mingle with non-slaveholding whites, small farmers, and lesser masters to cement ties of credit, kinship, and political clout. Mean-while militia musters, market days, and slave auctions provided regular opportunities for elite whites to demonstrate their mastery, authority, and largesse. The wives of wealthy planters did their part by assisting the sick and poor and planning church and social events. Such functions were par-ticularly important in the first three decades of the nineteenth century when the planter elite was buffeted by unstable markets, slave rebellions, antislavery campaigns, colonization schemes, evangelical revivals, and the constant pressure to move and expand.

Still, despite the upheavals of the post-revolutionary era and the un-certainties of the early nineteenth century, the planter class was increasingly in control of the South's economy and politics. Expansion into western lands had been achieved through the acquisition of new ter-ritories and the removal of various Indian tribes. Southern elites controlled political offices in their home states and maintained a powerful presence in the nation's capital. In towns and cities across the South, these elites had established banks and civic associations, founded churches and political parties, and built alliances with foreign merchants and northern factors. They stood on the cusp of a new era, in which cotton was king and the plantation owner its favored subject.

Poor Whites and Small Farmers Engulfed in a Slave Society

After about 1820, opportunities began to narrow for the South's small farmers, known as yeomen. The frontier no long offered them the chance for a better life, as large planters took over the most fertile areas. The removal of the Indians, however, did provide access to new lands in the Georgia upcountry, the western Carolinas, and northern sections of Louisiana and Mississippi. Here many independent farm families managed to secure a comfortable livelihood, while others at least succeeded in maintaining ownership of their fields and homesteads.

The South's small farmers had never been completely isolated from the plantation economy. But now they were becoming more enmeshed in its web as cotton, rice, and sugar became more central to the region's economic welfare from the 1820s onward. Small farmers often depended on planters for credit in hard times and members of yeoman families might be employed on plantations as overseers, skilled laborers, or in other jobs dominated by non-slaveholding whites. In addition, the extensive family networks that characterized southern life assured that some small farmers and even poor whites might claim kinship with their more well-to-do slaveholding neighbors. Others built connections with planters through church membership, attendance at county courts, and participation at the polls on election day.

But despite their ties to the planter elite, yeomen farmers did not always side with planters in their defense of slavery. By the 1820s and 1830s, throughout the upper South—in Missouri and Kentucky as well as Maryland and Virginia—residents came to doubt the financial profitability of slavery. Many farmers turned from tobacco to other crops, such as wheat, that did not require year-round labor. In 1831–1832, the Virginia state legislature considered resolutions that would have led to the gradual emancipation of slaves or their shipment back to Africa. These resolutions were supported mainly by representatives from the western part of the state (what is today West Virginia), where yeomen rather than planters dominated the population. The resolutions received a substantial number of votes but failed to pass. Their defeat was due in part to timing, for in 1831 a major slave rebellion (see pages 343–345), led by Nat Turner, erupted in Virginia. Nonetheless, the existence of such a debate suggests the problems upper-South planters faced in sustaining the "peculiar" institution.

Even in states with strong plantation economies in their coastal counties, residents who lived in more mountainous regions often questioned the wisdom of sustaining and expanding slavery. North Carolina and Georgia, for instance, harbored large populations of white farmers who owned few or no slaves. Some in these yeomen households hoped to make sufficient profits to rise into the planter class. A growing percentage had to be content with maintaining a respectable lifestyle despite a lack of slave labor, and many harbored deep ambivalence about the institution.

But slavery was not the issue about which small southern families most often launched protests. They generally considered more important the ways in which wealthy planters sometimes usurped their rights and privileges as landowners. In the post-revolutionary era, southern legislators had expanded the voting rights of white men and increased the representation from newly settled western counties, so yeomen now had new weapons to fight encroachments on their livelihood. As a result, they petitioned for better fence laws and payment for wartime damages, and they protested against hog thieves and against milldams and other obstructions to their fishing rights. In Georgia and the Carolinas in the early 1800s, for instance, upcountry farmers found their access to shad, a source of cheap and abundant food along frontier rivers, severely curtailed. Plantation owners who needed to feed and house ever-larger slave labor forces supported the construction of dams and millraces on the lower portions of numerous rivers by which they could be supplied with large quantities of flour and lumber at low prices. Arguing that "the allmity [sic] intended" the fish "for all man kind," petitioners complained, "We are rougued out of a part of our rights." These non-slave-owning yeomen still believed it was possible to contest the spread of slave-based agriculture with its implications for and limitations on small farmers.

Poor whites, on the other hand, who owned neither land nor slaves, were largely at the mercy of yeomen and planters for their sustenance. In frontier areas, they might still survive by hunting, fishing, and trapping, but in Georgia, the Carolinas, and the Chesapeake, women and men of this class generally sold their labor to more well-to-do neighbors. Some moved to the region's seaport cities, seeking work along the docks or as seamstresses or day laborers, but there they had to compete with free black as well as slave labor, making steady employment unlikely. And although some managed to remain in the same community for years, others drifted from place to place, seeking financial opportunity wherever it might be.

By the 1830s, then, from western Virginia and Carolina to upcountry Georgia and South Carolina, and even farther west, poor whites and small farmers found themselves simultaneously pushed to the margins and enmeshed in a slave-based market economy. The plantation economy rewarded single-crop agriculture and reinforced a clear social hierarchy. Of course, being white and male promised some measure of status and protection against dependency. But increasingly it was large slaveholders who ruled the South, politically and economically.

Evangelical Religion in Black and White

In the early 1800s, evangelical religion had questioned the sense of hierarchy favored by most large planters, but by the 1820s this challenge began to fade. Nationwide, those churches that embraced the new evangelical creed — Methodists, Baptists, and Presbyterians — saw their combined formal membership multiply more than thirteen times between 1800 and 1860. African Americans comprised nearly one-third of Baptist membership and perhaps one-quarter among Methodists. Yet a vision of a Christian community united across race and class lines did not materialize.

In the 1820s southern evangelical churches were still homes to diverse congregations, but increasingly such mixed bodies of worshippers reinforced rather than subverted social and political hierarchies. Although poor whites and slaves might pray alongside yeomen farmers and large planters, the minister to whom they listened was beholden to the wealthier and more economically secure parishioners. Those denominations and ministers who continued to preach a more radically egalitarian message — the Quakers and Wesleyan Methodists, for instance — found themselves marginalized, even silenced, or else they attracted only poor congregants and northern-born preachers. Religion still provided solace for those less fortunate, but, at least among southern whites, it no longer provided a powerful vehicle for resistance against planter domination.

From its emergence in the late 1700s, evangelical religion held a strong appeal for blacks as well as whites. Many African Americans sought to combine traditional African beliefs with elements of Christianity introduced by white preachers or by their owners. Although owners often used Christian beliefs to support the institution of slavery, claiming that it was God's will that Africans were in bondage and whites were free, slaves still found solace in religion.

By 1800, African Americans constituted about one out of every five Virginia Methodists, and one out of three Virginia Baptists. There were racially mixed congregations in the Carolinas, Georgia, and Maryland in which black members outnumbered white. African-American evangelicalism then

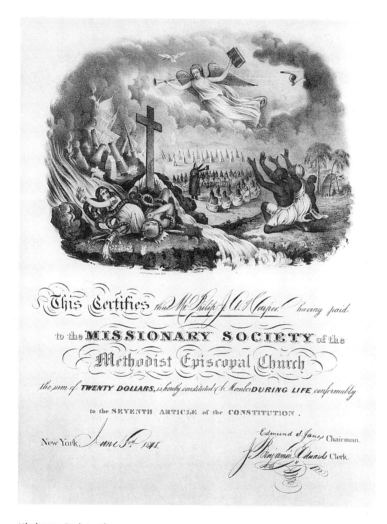

Missionary Society. The iconography on the certificate of the Methodist Episcopal Church's Missionary Society espoused the church's evangelical creed, but obscured growing division among its members over the issue of slavery.

Source: Smithsonian Institution.

spread across the South as cotton production grew. Slave sales combined with practices of itinerant ministry to spread the message into new areas. By accepting Christianity, slaves could claim membership in the same spiritual world as whites. And in that case, were they not God's children, too? If so, didn't they deserve the same rights as any other of His children?

In the early 1800s, some independent black congregations were allowed to form, principally in southern cities. They were often linked to free black denominations in the North, such as the African Methodist Episcopal Church. Although often sponsored and supervised by whites, these churches were the first and only community-wide institutions that allowed slaves membership. Their deacons and preachers (commonly free blacks) were some of the only African Americans whom whites permitted to play any kind of leadership role among slaves. Some black ministers even attracted a white following.

In Richmond, Virginia, the First Baptist Church attracted a substantial congregation, both black and white. Its membership multiplied nearly five times between 1809 and 1831, from 360 to 1,830 parishioners. In the 1840s, the church would be reorganized into an all-black institution, the African Baptist Church. Among black Methodists, the district surrounding Charleston, South Carolina, attracted the largest number of converts, tripling in size between 1811 and 1817. In 1817, the district's 5,699 Methodists formed the largest religious society black or white in North America.

In rural and frontier areas, ordained black ministers and established black or mixed-race congregations were harder to find. There, charismatic individuals gathered groups of believers around them, opening leadership roles to slaves and to African-American women, who were largely excluded from the ordained ministry. A traveler in the Georgia backcountry, near the Indian territory, witnessed a group of some two hundred slaves attending an open-air funeral service under the direction of a "preacher" from the local slave community.

Black women were especially active in the evangelical movement, both in established churches and in less formal gatherings. Evangelical practices could replace traditional African birth rituals as protection for their children. Evangelicalism could also be wielded as a weapon against sexual abuse, with women calling on church authorities to discipline owners, employers, and even ministers who exploited them or their daughters. Some women drew on African customs that recognized women as spiritual leaders. Although Methodists and Baptists refused to ordain women ministers, women comprised well over half of black evangelical converts throughout the early 1800s. Clarinda, a self-appointed preacher in Beaufort, South Carolina, attracted unrelenting hostility from white and black church leaders, but also welcomed a steady stream of followers to attend weekly meetings in her home.

Relying on African-American forms of evangelical Protestantism, slaves and free blacks were able to formulate their own standards of proper behavior. They used them not only to judge their treatment by whites but also, and just as important, to clarify mutual rights and obligations among themselves. For instance, the all-black Gillfield Baptist Church in Petersburg, Virginia, expelled a man named David for adultery and for slandering "every Sister in the Church." Through such means, southern blacks strengthened their sense of group identity and their ties to one another. At the same time they asserted an increased (if still very restricted) degree of self-regulation and self-rule.

"Plantation Burial." Funerals were sad occasions in the slave quarters, but they gave African Americans a chance to confirm their community identity. They were often held at night, so friends and family members from neighboring farms could attend.

Source: John Antrobus, 1860, oil on canvas, 53 × 81 1/2 inches (1960.46)—The Historic New Orleans Collection.

A Battle of Wills: Daily Resistance and Open Rebellion

Although some African Americans accommodated themselves to their owners' wishes in order to avoid sale, brutal beatings, or other forms of punishment, others demonstrated their opposition to bondage through everyday acts of resistance. Using whites' own prejudices about the laziness and irresponsibility of black labor, they broke tools, worked at a slow pace, damaged property, feigned illness or pregnancy, and engaged in other forms of sabotage. Some enslaved men and women also ran away, hiding out for days or weeks at a time. Many of them even found their way to freedom in the North.

Despite insuperable barriers, some slaves chose open revolt over daily resistance. These revolts revealed the feelings, values, aspirations, and abilities that slaves normally had to conceal from their masters. Although such open rebellions were rare, they were greatly feared by white Southerners of all classes, and their outbreak often resonated across the region no matter how limited the actual event.

In these direct challenges to planter authority, African Americans often wielded the values, language, and symbols of evangelical Prostestantism regularly invoked by the whites who held them captive. African Americans also made use of the nation's revolutionary and republican heritage to express their own ideals and demands. African Americans in the United States had another model of revolution available as well: that of their counterparts on the Caribbean island of Saint Domingue (present-day Haiti) where blacks had overthrown French rule in a bloody revolt in the 1790s.

Certainly the events in Saint Domingue worried southern planters. Most slaveholders were unaware of day-to-day resistance on their own plantations—both because it was concealed by the slaves' skilled performance and because their own social blindness led them to regard their slaves as childlike and docile, even as shiftless and clumsy "Sambos." Nonetheless, the image of the contented slave never fully managed to calm the slaveholders' deep-seated fear that, given capable leadership and the right circumstances, their slaves might rise up and cut their masters' throats. As Virginia congressman John Randolph reported, "the night bell never tolls for fire in Richmond, that the [white] mother does not hug the infant more closely to her bosom."

The fear of revolt became a reality in Richmond in 1800, immediately following the Saint Domingue uprising. A slave and blacksmith named Gabriel, believing that strained relations between France and the United States had finally given way to war, organized an insurrection in an attempt to seize the city. Gabriel and other urban African Americans were aware that conflicts among whites, within the United States or between the United States and its European competitors, promised rebels essential maneuvering room and perhaps even allies. In this case, the rumor of war was false, but Gabriel could still hope that the antislavery sentiments unleashed by the American Revolution would yield at least some white support for his cause. Moreover, Gabriel's brother was a black preacher, whose evangelical views may have reinforced the sense that at least some whites were sympathetic to the plight of slaves.

Gabriel and his followers, who were reported to number nearly one thousand African Americans, reportedly planned to begin the uprising when a group of slaves gathered to attend a child's funeral. They were apparently prepared to kill all whites in their path save those they deemed friendly: Quakers, Methodists, and Frenchmen. The insurrectionists would carry out their plans under a banner proclaiming "Death or Liberty," a slogan that fellow Virginian, and slaveholder, Patrick Henry would surely have recognized. The plot was revealed to white authorities, however, by two African Americans. The Virginia militia put down the revolt before it began, and Gabriel was executed, along with thirty-five others.

In the year of Gabriel's planned revolt, the slave Denmark Vesey purchased his liberty. In 1822, Vesey, now a free black carpenter in Charleston, South Carolina, organized one of the broadest and best-planned insurrectionary conspiracies in southern history. His wide travels as a merchant seaman left him not only literate but multilingual. He was inspired to rebel in part by his reading of antislavery materials, and he encouraged his comrades in arms by reading from an antislavery speech by New York senator Rufus King. His confederates, who may have numbered as many as nine thousand, included freedpeople and slaves: other craftsmen, house servants, and a slave foreman. Together they fashioned an arsenal including hundreds of bayonets, daggers, and pike heads. Had the uprising succeeded, Vesey and his lieutenants evidently planned to sail for the now self-governing black state of Haiti. Like Gabriel's, however, this conspiracy was betrayed before any action had taken place.

White authorities responded quickly and with brutal repression. They arrested 131 Charleston blacks. Testimony at the Vesey trials revealed the influence of both religious and political ideas among the plotters. To encourage his confederates, Vesey regularly read aloud from the Bible "about how the children of Israel were delivered out of Egyptian bondage." He also attended closely to news bearing on the future of slavery, such as the enduring independence of Haiti. Acknowledging Vesey's spiritual kinship to revolutionaries of other nations, one white Charlestonian concluded

Let it never be forgotten that our Negroes are truly the *Jacobins* of the country; that they are the *anarchists* and the *domestic enemy;* the *common enemy of civilized society,* and the barbarians who would, IF THEY COULD, become the DESTROYERS *of our race.*

In the summer of 1822, partly as a warning to other would-be rebels, Vesey and thirty-six others were hanged.

Discipline. During the Civil War, Wilson Chinn, a former Louisiana slave, exhibited instruments of punishment devised by masters.

Source: Prints and Photographs Division, Library of Congress.

Open rebellion against white domination did not end in 1822, however. Free blacks and skilled slaves, inspired by evangelical religion and northern antislavery sentiment, would continue to play central roles in slave rebellions until the Civil War. Yet by 1830, it was clear that armed resistance was unlikely to overcome white hunger for bound labor, just as American Indian resistance was unable to thwart white hunger for land. With the power of government regulation and military force behind them, southern whites seemed destined to defeat all who stood in their way.

The Failure of Gradual Emancipation in the South

In the aftermath of the American Revolution, many white Southerners, particularly in the upper South, had imagined that slavery would one day end. Ideas circulated regarding systems of gradual emancipation in which planters would be repaid for their investment in human flesh. Some, such as the wealthy white Virginians who founded the American Colonization Society in 1817, planned for that day by raising funds to ship African Americans back to their "homeland." The Colonization Society received funds from private donors, the U.S. Congress, and the Virginia and Maryland state legislatures, and did manage to send several boatloads of blacks out of the country. In 1830, the Society established the nation of Liberia on the west coast of Africa to receive those it brought out of bondage.

Southern antislavery societies, usually dominated by Quakers, Methodists, or Baptists, also continued to exist during the first third of the nineteenth century, especially in the upper South. Some white craftsmen and farmers may have supported them. There were certainly instances in which white artisans and tenant farmers encouraged and even helped individual slaves to escape from their masters.

Yet during the early 1800s the total number of slaves freed by colonization or antislavery societies was tiny compared to the rapid growth in the slave population. With the profits promised by cotton, sugar, and rice, the entrenchment of slavery was assured. More and more opponents of human bondage, South and North, abandoned hopes for the peaceful and gradual disappearance of the "peculiar institution."

As slavery became more central to the southern economy, some discontented small property owners moved from the South to southern Ohio, Indiana, and Illinois. One of these migrants, Thomas Lincoln, had been living in Kentucky, where he had owned a few slaves. There he came to repudiate bound labor, perhaps inspired by evangelical ideals, and joined an antislavery Baptist congregation. He moved his family, including his son Abraham, to Indiana, and then Illinois.

By the mid 1820s, some northern and midwestern states had abolished slavery, while others passed laws to ensure its eventual demise. New York was the last northern state to end slavery, passing its final gradual abolition act in 1817. In 1810, more than sixty percent of white households in Flatbush, on western Long Island (in what is today Brooklyn), contained slaves. Under the act of 1817, children born into slavery before July 4, 1827, would have to serve as indentured servants until the age of twenty-eight if male, and twenty-five if female. And blacks throughout the North and Midwest were still denied voting rights, the right to testify in court, equal access to public accommodations and public schools, and entrance into an array of occupations. They were confined to menial and low-paying jobs and were subject to racist abuse and physical attacks. Still, they were technically free, and they founded an array of churches, schools, and mutual aid and literary societies to improve the quality of their daily lives.

Northern free blacks also expressed their horror of slavery. In 1826, members of the Massachusetts General Colored Association advocated both abolition and the advancement of free blacks. One compelling spokesperson was David Walker, the free-born son of a slave father. Walker had left his native North Carolina for Boston as a youth and there earned a living by selling new and used clothing. He soon became a leading figure in the city's growing free black community and an agent and writer for the New York–based *Freedom's Journal,* the nation's first newspaper published by African Americans.

In 1829, Walker published a seventy-six page *Appeal.* It caused a sensation. Its militant tone and uncompromising message marked a fundamental breach with most earlier antislavery arguments. Its very form indicated its departure: it was a call to action by the slaves rather than a plea for mercy from their owners. "Brethren," Walker urged, "arise, arise! Strike for your lives and liberties. Now is the day and the hour." When he did address white readers, it was to hurl their own principles in their faces. He quoted to them: "ALL MEN ARE CREATED EQUAL, that they are endowed by their Creator with certain inalienable rights; that among these are life, liberty, and the pursuit of happiness." Walker claimed for slaves the rights proclaimed "in this Republican Land of Liberty," adding, "and tell us no more about colonization, for America is as much our country as it is yours."

On an oppressively hot August night in 1831, Walker's warning was written in blood in an uprising in Southampton County, Virginia. Nat Turner, a religious leader and self-styled Baptist minister, was also a skilled slave who had been forced into field work and then sold away from

Let No Man of Us Budge One Step . . .

In a work that soon came to be known as *Walker's Appeal,* David Walker in 1829 demanded the complete and immediate emancipation of slaves in the United States, challenging the prevailing beliefs among most white critics of slavery that emancipation should come gradually and that free blacks should be sent abroad to distant colonies.

Will any of us leave our homes and go to Africa? I hope not. Let them commence their attack upon us as they did on our brethren in Ohio, driving and beating us from our country, and my soul for theirs, they will have enough of it. Let no man of us budge one step, and let slaveholders come to beat us from our country. America is more our country, than it is the whites'—we have enriched it with our *blood and tears.* The greatest riches in all America have arisen from our blood and tears:—and will they drive us from our property and homes, which we have earned with our *blood?*

. . . Throw away your fears and prejudices then, and enlighten us and treat us like men, and we will like you more than we do now hate you; and tell us now no more about colonization, for America is as much our country, as it is yours.— Treat us like men, and there is no danger but we will all live in peace and happiness together. For we are not like you, hardhearted, unmerciful, and unforgiving. What a happy country this will be, if the whites will listen.

Source: David Walker, *Walker's Appeal* (1829).

---

his wife. Turner had received a vision while working in the fields, and he believed God had assigned him a mission. Although he was a polite, respectful, and seemingly eager-to-please servant when he was in the company of whites, he plotted with a close circle of friends and family to overthrow their masters. An eclipse of the sun in late August 1831 was the "sign" for which he had been waiting. On the night of August 21, Turner and a group of confederates killed all the members of the Travis family, his owners, beginning a bloody insurrection and a desperate, ultimately unsuccessful, bid for freedom that would end in the deaths of some sixty white men, women, and children.

Turner and all his coconspirators were captured and tried, but Turner refused to acknowledge that he had done anything wrong. In prison, his captors taunted him, "Do you not find yourself mistaken now?" But the armed prophet continued to draw strength from his Christian faith. "Was not Christ crucified?" he responded. Although Turner and sixteen of his compatriots were executed, the uprising continued to haunt southern whites. A letter published in the *Richmond Whig* a month after Turner's capture placed responsibility for his religious zealotry squarely in the hands of white evangelical preachers and their "canting about equality." It

The Scenes which the above Plate is designed to represent, are—Fig 1, a Mother intreating for the lives of her children.—2. Mr. Travis, cruelly murdered by his own Slaves.—3. Mr. Barrow, who bravely defended himself until his wife escaped.—4. A comp. of mounted Dragoons in pursuit of the Blacks.

Turner Rebellion. This woodcut was published in an 1831 account of the slave uprising.

Source: Samuel Warner, *Authentic and impartial narrative of the tragical scene which was witnessed in Southampton County (Virginia)* . . . (New York, 1831)—Prints and Photographs Division, Library of Congress.

was they, or perhaps the master's son, who had taught Turner to read, who had infected "an imagination like Nat's" with "the possibility of freeing himself and his race from bondage. . . . "

Whoever was responsible, slaves themselves paid dearly in the aftermath of the rebellion. They were randomly killed all over Southampton County. Some were beheaded, and the heads of some were put on poles and posted along the roads to serve as a warning to others. In nearby Richmond, the Virginia legislature was debating a proposal that would have instituted gradual emancipation and colonization. Defeated 73 to 58, the bill may have offered a final chance for a peaceful solution to slavery. Instead, southern planters tightened their grip on blacks, free and enslaved, and on anyone else, South or North, who challenged their right to hold humans in bondage.

These hard-nosed planter tactics had unexpected consequences in the North, where they allowed abolitionists to gain a more sympathetic audience for their cause. Although labor leader George Henry Evans published the only paper in New York City (the *Daily Sentinel*) that openly defended Turner's insurrection, his attack on slave owners may have resonated with many readers. Regretting the bloodshed, Evans noted that the rebels

> . . . no doubt thought that their only hope . . . was to put to death, indiscriminately the whole race of those who held them in bondage. If such were their impressions, were they not justifiable in doing so? Undoubtedly they were, if freedom is the birthright of man, as the declaration of independence tells us. . . . Those who kept them in slavery and ignorance alone are answerable for their conduct.

In the year of Turner's uprising, important new voices arose in the slaves' defense. William Lloyd Garrison, a journalist and reformer living in Boston, called on evangelical and republican principles to demand the immediate abolition of slavery and full civil equality for blacks. Such calls, however, only hardened resistance to the antislavery message among the planter class.

Although only a small minority of Northerners ever signed an anti-slavery petition or subscribed to abolitionist newspapers, those who did represented a serious threat to white Southerners, who became more actively proslavery after 1831. Virginia and North Carolina, fearing the influence of antislavery literature, made it illegal to teach slaves to read. Others outlawed black-controlled worship services. James Henry Hammond, a South Carolina planter, informed his journal in 1831, "Intend to break up negro preaching and negro churches. Refused to allow Ben Shubrick to join the Negro Church . . . but promised to have him taken in the church [that] I attended." And, "ordered night [prayer] meetings on the plantation to be discontinued."

Increasingly, the only preaching that was allowed by planters was that which bound slaves more tightly to their masters. In some places, any preaching to slaves seemed dangerous. Monroe County, Georgia, was the home of a large population of white yeomen who had once worshipped alongside their black neighbors. However, in 1835 plans for a slave revolt were uncovered. The instigator, a slave named George, was hanged. White farmers in the area then closed the Baptist church to black worshippers as a safeguard against future insurrections. One of the last hopes for racial cooperation in the South, the evangelical church with a mixed-race congregation, was lost.

The South's Free Blacks Face a Reign of Terror

By 1830, the growth of the free black population in the South had slowed considerably. Those who managed both to avoid the chains of enslavement and to remain in the region lived predominantly in urban areas. They supported themselves as manual laborers, domestics, petty traders, artisans, or small shopkeepers. Within these free black communities, women generally outnumbered men, making it difficult to form and sustain intact free black families. And the children of free mothers, especially when a father was not present, were subject to apprenticeship laws that placed them in virtual bondage to white employers.

Still, African Americans outside of bondage created institutions and social and familial networks to sustain their fragile freedom. In Natchez, Mississippi, sometime in the late 1820s or early 1830s, free black William Johnson opened a barber shop, catering to white as well as black clientele. He eventually owned three barbershops and a small plantation. His wife, Ann Battles, was a freed slave. When she married into the Johnson family, she quickly became part of a tight-knit circle of free black female kin, stretching from New Orleans to Natchez, who corresponded regularly, contributed to the family income through sewing and petty trading, and maintained the respectability required by both community mores and white anxieties. Black churches attracted large numbers of free blacks in the upper and lower South, and black men might find status not only through success in business but by an appointment as a preacher, exhorter, or class leader.

Yet in the aftermath of Nat Turner's rebellion, whites viewed the presence of free blacks among slaves as they might a match near a powder keg. The Virginia legislature immediately passed new restrictions on their activities, denying free blacks the right to own firearms, be ordained as ministers, or meet for worship without the sanction of local white officials.

Throughout most of the South, from the early nineteenth century onward, the mere presence of free blacks was viewed by whites as a source of danger and disruption. The modest emancipationist sentiment of the 1780s and 1790s gave way in the early 1800s to a state-by-state campaign

The Colored Man Has No Redress . . .

Uneasy about the existence of a free black population in the South, lawmakers passed strict measures restricting the rights of nonslave blacks in their states, as described below by a black Kentuckian named Washington Spaulding.

Our Principal Difficulty here grows out of the police laws, which are very stringent. For instance, a police officer may go [to] a house at night, without any search warrant, and, if the door is not opened when he knocks, force it in, and ransack the house, and the colored man has no redress. At other times, they come and say they are hunting for stolen goods or runaway slaves, and, some of them being great scoundrels, if they see a piece of goods, which may have been purchased, they will take it and carry it off. If I go out of the state, I cannot come back to it again. The penalty is imprisonment in the penitentiary. . . . If a freeman comes here (perhaps he may have been born free), he cannot get free papers, and if the police find out that he has got no free papers, they snap him up, and put him in jail. Sometimes they remain in jail three, four, and five months before they are brought to trial. My children are just tied down here. If they go to Louisiana, there is no chance for them, unless I can get some white man to go to New Orleans and swear they belong to him, and claim them as his slaves. . . . There are many cases of assault and battery in which we can have no redress. I have known a case here where a man bought himself three times. The last time, he was chained on board a boat, to be sent South, when a gentleman who now lives in New York saw him, and bought him, and gave him his free papers.

Source: John W. Blassingame, ed., *Slave Testimony* (1977).

to make even individual emancipation more and more difficult. By the 1830s, free blacks found themselves hounded and had their rights limited, their movements restricted, and their very presence in southern states assailed and sometimes banned.

Whites assumed that the freedom of some blacks would stimulate dangerous notions among slaves. An 1831 petition to Virginia's legislature explained whites' fears. Once "indulged with the hope of freedom," otherwise "submissive and easily controlled" slaves "reject restraint and become almost wholly unmanageable." The petition added, "It is by the expectation of liberty, and by that alone, that they can be rendered a dangerous population." The mere presence of free blacks, then, offered slaves a goal to which they might aspire.

The laws that restricted the mobility, employment, education, and residence of African Americans assured that the free black population would remain small across the South. Only in a few areas—mainly cities such as Baltimore, Washington, D.C., Savannah, and New Orleans—did significant populations of free blacks congregate. To survive in this setting, they formed support networks among themselves, founded their own churches and clubs, and demonstrated, at least in public, deference to those whites who paid their wages, bought their goods and services, and tolerated their presence.

The Planter Class Consolidates Power

Having further restricted the rights and movements of slaves and free blacks, state and local governments also suppressed nearly all opposition to, and even doubts about, chattel slavery, whether voiced by whites or blacks, Northerners or Southerners. They banned antislavery messages conveyed in books, newspapers, schools, politics, or any other public forum. And they fought back directly against northern abolitionists. Georgia offered a $5,000 reward for the trial and conviction "under the laws of this state" of abolitionist editor William Lloyd Garrison. A reward of $1,000 was offered for the delivery of David Walker's corpse, $10,000 if he was captured and returned to the South alive. In Charleston in July 1835, a mob broke into the local post office, seized stacks of antislavery literature, and publicly set them on fire. State

The Whipping of Amos Dresser. A Theology student traveling through Nashville, Tennessee, in 1835 was one of the many abolitionist victims of proslavery repression. Dresser was discovered to be carrying antislavery literature in his luggage. He was abducted during the night, brought to a public square, and whipped before a cheering crowd.

Source: Amos Dresser, *The Narrative of Amos Dresser . . .* (1836)—American Antiquarian Society.

"New Method of Assorting the Mail, As Practised by Southern Slave-Holders." This print depicted a July 1835 nighttime raid on the Charleston, South Carolina, Post Office. An antiabolitionist crowd broke into the building, removed antislavery mail, and burned it in the street.

Source: Library Company of Philadelphia.

officials endorsed the action, and Andrew Jackson's postmaster general, Amos Kendall, refused to interfere.

In his annual message to Congress that year, President Jackson called for legislation to prohibit, "under severe penalties, the circulation in the Southern States, through the mail, of incendiary publications intended to instigate the slaves to insurrection." Recognizing their support in the White House, southern congressmen insisted that the House of Representatives reject antislavery petitions without consideration. By May 1836, the House instituted a regular "gag rule" according to which "all petitions, memorials, resolutions, propositions, or papers relating in any way or to any extent whatever to the subject of slavery" were tabled and "no further action taken thereon."

By 1836, northern abolitionists had printed and distributed more than one million pieces of antislavery literature, sent mostly through the mails. Some ended up in the South. Over the next few years, slavery's northern opponents, according to one estimate, collected more than two million signatures on petitions. These petitions were forwarded to Congress, where they were tabled and filed away. But the issues they raised and the challenge they posed to the South's economic, social, and political systems could not be so easily dismissed.

Aware of the dangers posed both by antislavery advocates and by the North's greater representation in the U.S. Congress, southern planters no longer believed that federal power was sufficient to quell their concerns. Instead, they argued with renewed force that the Constitution had given only certain powers to the federal government; the rest were reserved for the states. Determined to assert the primacy of these state's rights, South Carolina seized the political initiative in the early 1830s. The tariff of 1828, known to southern critics as the "tariff of abominations," provided the pretext. Before the northern and southern economies had begun to diverge sharply, slave owners such as South Carolina senator John C. Calhoun had supported protectionism. By the early

1830s, however, they despised tariffs on imported, manufactured goods as an arbitrary tax levied by the industrializing North on the agricultural South. In November 1832, the state's planter leadership met in special convention and declared the tariff "null, void, no law, nor binding upon this state, its officers or citizens." Sounding surprisingly like the Cherokee Nation in declaring its sovereignty, South Carolina forbade the collection of the tariff by federal agents and refused its enforcement within state boundaries.

This stance was backed by sentiments stronger and calculations deeper than those connected simply with the tariff. By nullifying this federal law, South Carolina meant to serve notice that it would not allow the federal government to impose laws harmful to planter interests. Thus, even as government agents and troops were welcomed in Georgia and the Carolinas to help in the removal of Indians, planters were asserting their freedom from unwanted federal interference. As Robert Turnbull, a South Carolina planter, explained of his opposition to the tariff of 1828:

> [G]reat as is this evil, it is perhaps the least of the evils which attend an abandonment of one iota of the principle of controversy. Our dispute involves questions of the most fearful import to the institutions and tranquility of South Carolina. I fear to name them. The bare thought of these is enough to rouse resistance were there no other motive.

Although sympathetic toward his fellow planters, Andrew Jackson considered Carolinians' fears exaggerated and responded angrily to their attack on the federal government, of which he was after all the chief executive. He promptly reinforced the federal fort in Charleston Harbor and obtained a "force bill" from Congress authorizing the use of the military to implement federal law. Once again, Henry Clay and others managed to fashion a compromise. Congress agreed to reduce tariffs over the next nine years, and in early 1833 South Carolina repealed its nullification act. But to demonstrate its continued belief in the right of states to veto federal law, South Carolina also nullified Jackson's force bill. The defiant gesture kept the states-rights claim alive, but it could not conceal the defeat of the nullification strategy at this stage.

Despite southern planters' attempts to isolate themselves from northern antislavery advocates and unpopular federal mandates, the expansion of agricultural production continued to link them with merchants, manufacturers, cotton factors (entrepreneurs involved in the cotton trade), and industrial and maritime workers in the North and in England. Although other goods were important in the South's economy, cotton was the one that formed the strongest ties to those outside the region. It also served as the main thread that connected poor whites, small farmers, and slaves with plantation owners and was thus crucial in allowing planters to close ranks in the South even as they expanded their ties to a wider world.

Within the web of southern labor and economic relations, growing distinctions appeared between blacks and whites, between free people and slaves, and between wealthy planters and yeoman farmers. By the mid 1830s, as the plantation system consolidated and expanded, differences among these diverse groups crystallized, and it became more and more difficult to move from one to another. Yet one consequence of the growing differentiation of Southerners along race and class lines was the increasing dependence of slaves, free blacks, and yeomen on the resources and largesse of large planters. Plantation owners considered the growing classes of dependents as evidence of their success. Those lower down the ladder chafed at the restrictions placed upon them, but few could seriously contest the new order.

At the same time, planters themselves were caught up in a larger web of regional, national, and global connections, where they might find themselves dependent on others for their own success. In fact, protecting the southern way of life depended in part on the ability of planters to ensure that the strength of a cotton economy would bind together whites of all classes across the South, as well as affluent whites across the nation and across the sea who shipped goods to and from the South and served as the planters' trading partners.

Moreover, even as northern and midwestern states gradually abolished slavery within their own borders, many residents of those areas continued to rely on the products and profits of slave labor to support the industry and commerce that fueled their economic growth. Manufacturers, for instance, who supplied the South with textiles, shoes, plows, and other finished products, were deeply committed to the cotton economy. Such economic ties assured that, even as those in the free states saw themselves as increasingly distinct from their southern neighbors, they were still intimately connected to the success of slavery. In this sense, king cotton spun a web that spread to the free states as well.

The Years in Review

1793
- Eli Whitney invents the cotton gin.
- Fugitive Slave Act passed.

1798
- XYZ Affair: French demand a $250,000 bribe from American delegation to begin negotiations, which outrages Americans. Charles

Pinckney reportedly responds, "Millions for defense but not one cent for tribute"; actually he says, "No, no, not a sixpence."

1800

- A Virginia slave and blacksmith named Gabriel organizes an insurrection aimed at seizing Richmond.

1803

- French government sells the Louisiana Territory to the United States, which Lewis and Clark set out to map the next year.

1804

- Thomas Jefferson re-elected over Federalist Charles C. Pinckney.

1807

- Embargo Act forbids U.S. ships to sail for foreign ports.

1808

- Ban on slave importation leads to growth in internal slave trade.
- Republican James Madison defeats Federalist Charles C. Pinckney for presidency; he is re-elected four years later.

1811

- Massive New Madrid, Missouri, earthquakes change course of Mississippi River and raise and lower parts of Mississippi Valley region by as much as fifteen feet.

1812

- First Seminole War: U.S. Marines invade Florida to recapture runaway slaves and meet resistance from black fugitives and Seminole Indians.
- The United States declares war on Great Britain.

1814

- Red Sticks defeated at Battle of Horseshoe Bend. Treaty of Fort Jackson transfers fourteen million acres of Creek territory to U.S. control.
- Washington, D.C., captured and burned by British troops; New Englanders threaten secession over war.
- Treaty of Ghent ends War of 1812, but news doesn't arrive in time to stop Battle of New Orleans (1815), in which the United States under Andrew Jackson defeats the British.

1816

- James Monroe elected president in landslide; this inaugurates the "Era of Good Feeling"; four years later he is re-elected without organized opposition.

1817

- American Colonization Society founded to resettle slaves in Africa.

1818

- Sir Walter Scott's *Rob Roy* is a bestseller; U.S. publishers routinely pirate English novels, because there is no copyright protection in the United States.

1820

- Missouri Compromise: The line of Missouri's southern border is extended westward. No territory north of that line will be admitted to the union as a slave state.

1822

- Free black carpenter Denmark Vesey organizes insurrectionary conspiracy in Charleston, 131 blacks arrested and 37 hanged.

1824

- No candidate receives majority in the presidential election; House of Representatives selects John Quincy Adams over Andrew Jackson, who had received the largest number of popular and electoral votes.

1828

- New tariff law passed, which southern critics label "Tariff of Abominations"; four years later South Carolina declares it "null" and "void."
- Andrew Jackson elected president over John Quincy Adams in dirty campaign.

1829

- Mexico outlaws slavery in Texas, but settlement by Southerners led by Stephen Austin continues.
- David Walker publishes his *Appeal,* a seventy-six-page call to action by slaves.

1830

- Indian Removal Act offers Indians land west of the Mississippi in exchange for their current territorial holdings; under pressure and threats, many tribes sign away land; tens of thousands are pressured to move west.
- American Colonization Society establishes Liberia on the west coast of Africa to resettle free blacks.

1831

- In the case *Cherokee Nation* v. *Georgia,* the Supreme Court rules that Cherokees, who are trying to fight removal, do not have independent political authority.

- The first issue of the abolition journal the *Liberator* is published by William Lloyd Garrison.
- Religious leader Nat Turner leads slave insurrection in Virginia; Turner and sixteen of his allies caught, tried, and executed.

1832

- Andrew Jackson wins re-election over Henry Clay.

1833

- South Carolina repeals nullification act after Congress agrees to reduce tariffs over the next nine years.

1836

- U.S. House of Representatives institutes a gag rule that covers all future discussion of slavery.

1838

- Fifteen-thousand Cherokees who had earlier refused the U.S. government's offer of land in the west are uprooted by federal troops and led across the eight-hundred-mile "Trail of Tears" to present-day Oklahoma; four-thousand die from starvation and exposure to the cold.

Suggested Readings

Berlin, Ira, *Slaves Without Masters: The Free Negro in the Antebellum South* (1974).

Bolton, Charles, *Poor Whites of the Antebellum South: Tenants and Laborers in Central North Carolina and Northeastern Mississippi* (1994).

Bruchey, Stuart, ed., *Cotton and the Growth of the American Economy, 1790–1860* (1967).

Curry, Leonard P., *The Free Black in American Society, 1800–1850* (1981).

Douglass, Frederick, *The Life and Times of Frederick Douglass* (1969).

Fields, Barbara Jeanne, *Slavery and Freedom on the Middle Ground: Maryland During the Nineteenth Century* (1985).

Frey, Sylvia, and Betty Wood, *Come Shouting to Zion: African American Protestantism in the American South and the British Caribbean to 1830* (1998).

Genovese, Eugene D., *The Political Economy of Slavery: Studies in the Economy and Society of the Slave South* (1965).

Gould, Virginia Meacham, ed., *Chained to the Rock of Adversity: To Be Free, Black and Female in the Old South* (1998).

Hahn, Steven, and Jonathan Prude, eds., *The Countryside in the Age of Capitalist Transformation: Essays in the Social History of Rural America* (1985).

Joyner, Charles, *Down By the Riverside: A South Carolina Slave Community* (1984).

Kemble, Frances Anne, *Journal of a Residence on a Georgia Plantation, 1838–1839,* edited with an introduction by John A. Scott (1984).

Kulikoff, Allan, *The Agrarian Origins of American Capitalism* (1992).

Matthews, Donald, *Religion in the Old South* (1977).

McCurry, Stephanie, *Masters of Small Worlds: Yeomen Households, Gender Relations, and the Political Culture of the Antebellum South Carolina Low Country* (1995).

Meier, August, and Elliott Rudwick, *From Plantation to Ghetto,* 3rd ed. (1976).

Mullin, Gerald W., *Flight and Rebellion: Slave Resistance in Eighteenth-Century Virginia* (1972).

Oakes, James, *The Ruling Race: A History of American Slaveholders* (1982).

Oates, Stephen B., *The Fires of Jubilee: Nat Turner's Fierce Rebellion* (1975).

Osofsky, Gilbert, ed., *Puttin' On Ole Massa: The Slave Narratives of Henry Bibb, William Wells Brown, and Solomon Northrup* (1969).

Perdue, Theda, *Cherokee Women: Gender and Culture Change, 1700–1835* (1998).

Quarles, Benjamin, *Black Abolitionists* (1969).

Raboteau, Albert J., *Slave Religion: The 'Invisible Institution' in the Antebellum South* (1978).

Reidy, Joseph P., *From Slavery to Agrarian Capitalism in the Cotton Plantation South* (1992).

Rose, Willie Lee, ed., *A Documentary History of Slavery in North America* (1976).

Stevenson, Brenda E., *Life in Black and White: Family and Community in the Slave South* (1996).

Tushnet, Mark V. *The American Law of Slavery* (1981).

White, Deborah Gray, *Ar'n't I A Woman? Female Slaves in the Plantation South* (1985).

White, Richard, *The Roots of Dependency: Subsistence, Environment and Social Change among the Choctaws, Pawnees, and Navajos* (1983).

And on the World Wide Web

Harry W. Fritz, *Discovering Lewis and Clark*
(http://www.lewis-clark.org/)

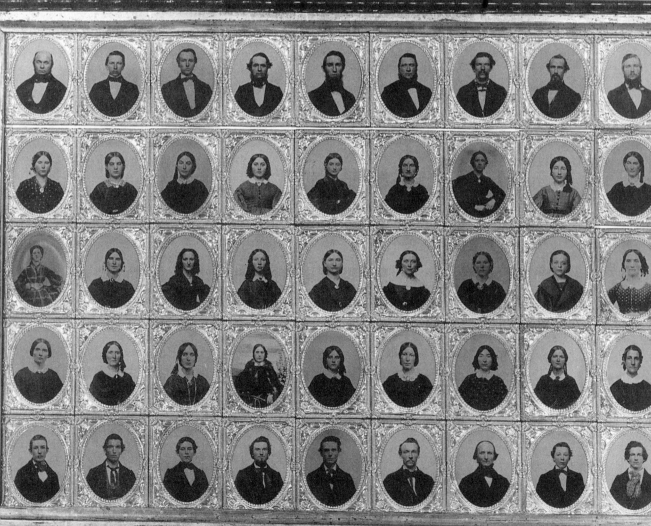

chapter 7

Northern Society and the Growth of Wage Labor
1790–1837

Like one in three Massachusetts women of her generation, Abigail McIntire was pregnant when, in 1788, she married Mayo Greenleaf Patch in Reading, not far from Boston. Patch was the tenth child of a farmer who had lost his land to his creditors. He brought no property to the marriage so the couple lived in a small house built by Abigail's father and earned money by making shoes. When his father-in-law died in the 1790s, Patch tried to grab his property, but instead had to leave town, taking Abigail and their children with him, to evade neighbors' and relatives' anger. For several years the Patches struggled to make a living from rented farms and shoemaking shops in various towns, but they ended up deep in debt. In 1807 they moved to the growing manufacturing town of Pawtucket, Rhode Island, where spinning mills turned slave-grown cotton from the South into yarn for making cloth. Abigail and her children worked at home, cleaning cotton and weaving cloth for local mill owners. Patch took to drink, stole Abigail's and the children's wages, and in 1812 walked out on them. Six years later Abigail divorced him. She and the children continued to support themselves by working for wages in Pawtucket.

The lives of Abigail and Greenleaf Patch illustrate the struggle of thousands of northern families to sustain their economic independence in the years after the American Revolution. Many experienced the scarce resources of settled rural regions such as eastern Massachusetts, and were obliged to move or change their occupations to make ends meet. Many would leave for the newly opening West, hoping to establish successful farms on frontier land. Others would find work at sea or in the growing port cities. Abigail Patch and her children were among the first generation to become wage workers in the North's new manufacturing industries. Men and women who remained in the rural towns that they had grown up in also became increasingly involved in producing goods for market sale, or in working for other people in return for wages. Such changes rapidly altered the social and political character of the newly formed United States.

One of the legacies of the American Revolution was the belief that the republic would best be preserved if voters were politically "independent," not subject to coercion by others. At first it was assumed that this was best guaranteed if voters were economically "independent," too. They should own property so that they would have a stake in society and be

New Hampshire Textile-Mill Workers. Framed portraits of workers of the Amoskeag Manufacturing Company in Manchester, c. 1854.

Source: Manchester Historic Association.

357

free to act on their own, without fear of influence by people with some hold over them. By contrast, those without property — including women, children, the poor, servants, and slaves — were seen as "dependent" on others, and deemed incapable of exercising political rights. They were to be excluded from voting, officeholding, or public debate. Even elite women were assigned the subsidiary role of "republican mothers," who were expected to raise their children to be moral, virtuous citizens, but who would not themselves obtain the full benefits of citizenship.

This "republican" set of assumptions was widely shared, both North and South, in the late eighteenth and early nineteenth centuries, when an overwhelming majority of Americans were engaged in agriculture, many on small freehold farms, and a significant proportion of men owned land. Indeed, most people expected the United States to have an agrarian future. Their expectation was to some extent borne out in the nineteenth century. Rural America, North and South, expanded rapidly. By 1840, in the North as a whole, over eighty percent of people still lived in rural areas; in the South, the proportion was over ninety percent. Most people continued to work in agriculture, and agricultural goods such as cotton, grain, lumber, and leather were among the United States' most important products.

But the success of the Revolution, the opening of the continent, and the establishment of new state and federal governments also sowed the seeds of new political traditions and massive economic change. Even in the first half of the nineteenth century, political culture was transformed, turning republicanism in a more democratic direction, although restricting participation to white males only. It also became clear that the United States would not remain simply an agrarian society. Particularly in the North, economic development altered the agrarian vision. By 1840 an industrial revolution was under way in the Northeast. Cities were growing rapidly both in size and influence. Population growth and commercial expansion were creating new divisions, both between North and South and within northern society itself.

Many Northerners hoped that economic expansion and prosperity would guarantee their ownership of property and material independence. Whereas in the plantation South the consolidation and expansion of slavery created a growing propertyless and dependent workforce, it seemed possible that the North, where slavery was disappearing, would become a society of independent proprietors. Instead, however, northern towns, industries, and farms came to rely increasingly on the labor of wage workers. In 1800 about twelve percent of the U.S. labor force worked for wages. By 1860, the proportion was around forty percent, and the majority of wage employees were concentrated in the North. This social change both undermined the vision of property-owning independence for a great many Americans and laid the roots of a widening divergence between the northern and southern economies. It also gave rise to a working peoples' movement. By the 1830s, wage earners were asserting their right to equal respect with their more prosperous fellow-citizens, and seeking to defend their economic position.

Early Nineteenth-Century Ideology: An Agrarian Republic and "Natural Aristocracy"

Belief in the virtues of a rural way of life was deeply engrained in early American culture. Suspicious of cities with their large crowds and potential disorder, Thomas Jefferson wrote in 1785 that rural people were "the chosen people of God," and implied that city growth would threaten the republic's future. When he arranged the Louisiana Purchase of 1803, doubling the territory of the United States, Jefferson proclaimed the acquisition of an "empire for liberty," a vast reserve of land that could ensure the future stability of a property-owning republic. In this agrarian vision of the future, the United States would grow crops to feed its own population and for export to Europe, exchanging them for industrial

"Venerate the Plough." The independent farmer plowed the path to prosperity for the Republic on this seal of the Philadelphia Society for Promoting Agriculture.

Source: "The Plan of a Farm Yard," *Columbian Magazine,* October 1786—American Philosophical Society Library.

goods produced in more unequal and socially divided countries such as Britain. In 1780 John Adams had predicted that the United States would not supply its own manufactures for a thousand years because its social structure and values inhibited manufacturing. As late as 1810, Treasury Secretary Albert Gallatin noted that obstacles to manufacturing included "the superior attractions of agricultural pursuits, the abundance of land compared with the population, the high price of labor, and the want of sufficient capital."

Other conditions in the 1790s also seemed to favor an agrarian pattern of development. The invention of the cotton gin boosted exports of cotton from the South, and circumstances favored the commercial expansion overseas that could supply America's need for manufactures and other goods. Wars in Europe following the French Revolution of 1789 helped American merchants to trade successfully in foreign markets. Contacts with Western Europe and the Mediterranean grew, and new trade with Asia opened up.

However, although Jefferson and others extolled rural America's republican virtues, they did not suggest that all rural people were fit to exercise political leadership. Beneath the fierce partisan strife of the 1790s and 1800s between the Federalists and Jefferson's Democratic-Republicans lay shared expectations about who should rule. Federalists were explicitly elitist. Government should be guided by "the best men," who by birth, education, or wealth had attributes guaranteeing their virtue and independence; lesser property owners should defer to these leaders and accept their authority. Democratic-Republicans attacked the most hierarchical of their opponents' assumptions, but leaders such as Jefferson also assumed that power was best exercised by a "natural aristocracy," whose talents made them suited to lead.

The Rural North in the Early Nineteenth Century

Although North and South were both mainly rural in 1800, they differed from each other in fundamental ways. Southern planters had built an economy that used large enslaved workforces to produce exportable commodities. Most northern whites, in contrast, lived in small-farm regions that consumed much of what they produced. Family-based farming, supported by cooperation between neighbors, sustained a republican vision of economic independence.

The typical northern farm was modest in size, between 40 and 120 acres, and worked by the family that owned it. Temporary employment as

The Residence of David Twining, 1787. Edward Hicks, a Quaker painter of coaches and signs, completed this painting in the late 1840s. Hicks's idealized representation of a "well-ordered" eighteenth-century farm was based on memories of his childhood in Bucks County, Pennsylvania.

Source: Edward Hicks, 1845–1848—Abby Aldrich Rockefeller Folk Art Center, Williamsburg, Virginia.

a laborer or tenant often served as a steppingstone to acquiring one's own farm. Certainly, rural inequality was widespread. Tenancy blighted parts of New York and other states. In the Middle Atlantic states, too, some farmers still used the labor of slaves who were not yet freed under gradual emancipation laws. Landless farm laborers could be found everywhere, and a majority of free blacks in the rural North had little or no land of their own. Still, the ideal of land ownership remained within reach for many. Journeying through New York and New England in the early nineteenth century, the Yankee clergyman Timothy Dwight was convinced that "[n]o man here begins life with the expectation of being a mere laborer. All intend to possess, and almost all actually possess, a comfortable degree of prosperity and independence." For white farmers at least, property ownership conferred the right to be treated by others as an equal. "Every man," boasted the *New England Farmer,* "is a free, independent landlord, thinks himself, while pursuing a virtuous course, as good as his neighbor, and asks none but his Maker's leave to live and thrive."

Realizing this ideal of economic independence required the labor of all family members. Husbands and sons, by and large, worked the fields. Most other tasks, including the manufacture of household goods, fell to wives and daughters. One contemporary farm journal reported that women's work amounted to fully half of all farm labor:

> Women . . . picked their own wool, . . . spun their own yarn, drove their own looms, made and mended their own chairs, braided their own baskets, wove their own carpets, quilts, and coverlets, picked [the feathers of] their own geese, milked their own cows, fed their own calves. . . .

In southern Maine in the 1790s, Martha Ballard and her daughters produced cloth, raised garden produce, preserved vegetables, and did household chores on their family's farm, while Ballard herself served as a midwife throughout her neighborhood. Women raised children, nursed the sick, and cared for the elderly. Men celebrated an economic independence that rested heavily on the varied skills and exertions of their sisters, wives, and daughters.

Farm families lived in small communities, often linked by ties of kinship, religion, and ethnicity. Most settlements included a church, a general store, and a few artisans, such as carpenters and blacksmiths, who often plied their trades only part-time. Proper schoolhouses and the services of doctors and lawyers were scarce. Farm families aided one another, sharing tools or lending a hand when a task such as harvesting or barn raising required extra help. In return they might receive cash, but payment was frequently in the form of produce, homemade goods, or labor.

"There Is No Want of Meat and Drink Here"

America's extraordinary material abundance was a recurring theme in letters recent European immigrants wrote home in the early nineteenth century. In the following letter, written in August 1818 from Germantown, Pennsylvania, Alice Barlow describes in detail the bounty of available food and drink. Letters such as this helped lure other Northern Europeans to migrate to America in the decades that followed.

Dear Mother:

I write to say we are all in good health, and hope this will find you so. . . . Tell my brother John I think he would do very well here; my husband can go out and catch a bucket of fish in a few minutes; and John brings as many apples as he can carry, when he comes from school; also cherries, grapes, and peaches, we get as much bread as we can all eat in a day for seven pence; altho' it is now called dear [expensive]. Dear mother, I wish you were all as well off as we now are: there is no want of meat and drink here. We have a gallon of spirits every week; and I have a bottle of porter per day myself, in short I have everything I could wish. . . . Tell little Adam, if he was here, he would get puddings and pies every day. Tell my old friends I shall be looking for them next spring; and also tell my brother John and sister Ann, if they were here, they would know nothing of poverty. I live like an Indian Queen. . . .

Your affectionate daughter,
Alice Barlow

Source: Edith Abott, ed., *Historical Aspects of the Immigration Problem* (1926).

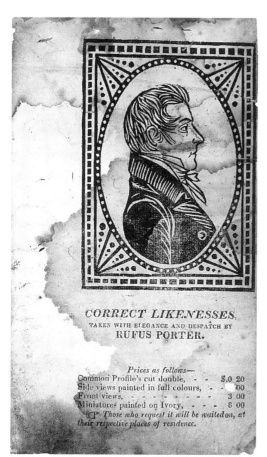

CORRECT LIKENESSES,
TAKEN WITH ELEGANCE AND DESPATCH BY
RUFUS PORTER.

Prices as follows—
Common Profile's cut double, - - $.0 20
Side views painted in full colours, - - 00
Front views, - - - - - - 3 00
Miniatures painted on Ivory, - - 8 00
☞ Those who request it will be waited on, at
their respective places of residence.

Correct Likenesses, c. 1820.
Itinerant portrait artists offered rural people reasonably priced portraits, using simplified techniques to render enough of a "correct likeness" to satisfy a client. Portraitists and other traveling tradesmen served as scouts for capital, introducing attractive goods and services to the countryside.

Source: American Antiquarian Society.

Beyond these family and community ties, rural independence also rested on crucial links to the outside market. These links were most significant in grain-exporting regions such as Pennsylvania, but everywhere even minimal comfort required contact with traders. Salt, sugar, molasses, coffee, tea, tobacco, gunpowder, guns, knives, and axes could not be produced at home. To pay for them, farm families had to produce sufficient crops or home manufactures to exchange for them. Yet as late as 1820, only a fifth of the North's farm crop found its way beyond local communities into the nation's urban markets. Farm families also purchased modestly: about two-thirds of the clothing rural Americans wore between 1810 and 1820 was homemade. Near Burlington, Vermont, Hannah Matthews Stone "wove all the cloth for the family's wearing," while in Creekvale, New York, in 1822, Mary Ann Archbald sewed or knitted twenty-six linen and woolen shirts for her family, using yarn spun at home by her daughters.

Poor transportation hindered inland trade and protected those producing for limited local markets from distant competitors. Few rivers connected coast and hinterland. Roads and bridges were few, poorly built, and not well maintained. It cost as much to ship a ton of goods thirty miles overland as it did to bring it by sea the three thousand miles from Europe.

Towns and Commerce in the Early Nineteenth Century

In 1800 the wealthy and powerful northern merchant elite lived and conducted business largely at the country's physical and social periphery, in the cities and smaller port towns of the coast. Unlike southern planters, they generally did not concern themselves directly with production. Much of their wealth came from trade—the profits from "buying cheap and selling dear"—that brought them into contact primarily with the small fraction of the population who lived in or near towns and seaport cities.

In 1800 fewer than one in twelve Americans lived in "urban" centers, places with populations of twenty-five hundred or more. Urban markets were small. The biggest mercantile profits went to traders involved in the transatlantic and coastal trade, carrying European manufactures to the Americas, and U.S. and Caribbean plantation produce to Europe. By remaining neutral in the wars that preoccupied Europe in the 1790s and early 1800s, American's northeastern merchants virtually monopolized trade routes closed to others. Trade with China also offered substantial rewards. Mercantile success brought great wealth to some and gave employment to many others, especially smaller merchants and the artisans connected with shipping, such as sailmakers, ropemakers, carpenters, caulkers, and barrelmakers.

But the benefits of mercantile success were not equally shared. Seamen formed the nation's largest group of workers after farmers, and they often labored on long voyages for modest wages in dangerous conditions. In port towns, large numbers of women lived in poverty or struggled to make a living while their husbands were at sea. In Salem, Massachusetts, while her husband was away on a voyage, Lydia Almy wove cloth, tanned leather, made cider, looked after livestock, worked in the fields, carted wood, and cooked for boarders at her house. In Boston, mariners' wives worked for the city's ropemakers and other employers. Wherever vessels put to sea there lived the widows and families of men who never returned.

Maritime trade did not substantially improve the North's position in world production. "Our catalogue of merchants," wrote Adam Seybert, a Philadelphia congressman and statistician, "was swelled much beyond what it was entitled to from the state of our population. . . . The brilliant prospects held out by commerce caused our citizens to neglect the mechanical and manufacturing branches of industry." Between 1795 and 1815, the United States imported twenty percent more than it exported, spending $350 million more for foreign goods than it received for exports. Indeed, nearly half of U.S. exports were really re-exports—goods produced abroad, purchased by American merchants, and resold to other countries. Although this kind of trade amassed profits, it did not directly stimulate the growth of domestic commercial agriculture or industry.

Start of a Transformation: Manufacturing, Urbanization, and Westward Expansion

Pressure for social and economic change arose from several directions. One was international. Immigration, especially to the Middle Atlantic region, raised levels of urban poverty and dependence and increased the supply of urban labor. In 1795 Peter and Hannah Carle reached Philadelphia from Holland. Peter worked as a laborer, finding jobs on the docks, or at casual work around the city. The Carles rented a small frame house where they could take in boarders, for whom Hannah cooked and cleaned to help make ends meet. But their position was precarious. A yellow fever epidemic in 1799 interrupted trade. Peter could find no work, and boarders were scarce. By November the Carles were facing great hardship. Their small child fell ill and died, and Peter and Hannah had to apply to the poorhouse for financial assistance.

Then new trade patterns forced many U.S. merchants out of maritime commerce. Jefferson's embargo policy from 1807 to 1809, and the War of 1812, severely disrupted American trade. After the European peace settlement of 1815, England, France, and other major powers quickly resumed their overseas trading roles. Competition was fierce, and cargo rates fell by half. Northern merchants retained only a declining share of Atlantic and Pacific commerce. A prominent Bostonian, John M. Forbes, steadily forced out of the China trade and into retirement by 1837, explained: "Competition is so sharp . . . that money must be made by the most penurious saving in fitting or storing goods . . ., or by being constantly on the lookout and giving up body and soul to managing business." Faced with diminishing opportunities in overseas trade, urban merchants and artisans sought new activities and markets.

Other pressures for change came from within rural society. To some farmers, maintaining independence required the aggressive accumulation of wealth. But for most, it meant cultivating enough fertile land to feed one's family decently, to acquire any necessary items that could not be made at home, and eventually to buy enough land for grown sons to establish their own homesteads. Yet population growth and land scarcity in older rural regions made these things more difficult to achieve. Many southern New England farms were too small to support all the offspring of large families, and ran short of essential resources such as wood for fuel. One son might be given a farm of his own upon coming of age, but if a father had several sons, division of his homestead among them would create small, unprofitable holdings. Seeking to avoid this, farmers took various steps according to their wealth and means. They turned increasingly to the marketplace to raise the cash (at least six hundred dollars in the 1830s) needed to buy new farms for their sons. They tried new crops and raised more livestock for sale. In some regions farm women increased their output of dairy produce.

In search of more land and greater opportunity, many rural people also migrated westward. Starting in the 1780s, but in increasing numbers after 1815, men, women, and families moved out of older farming districts in New England, New York, and Pennsylvania, heading for "new" land in western New York, the Ohio Valley, and other parts of the "old Northwest." As always, expansion involved the destruction of pre-existing American Indian societies, the seizure of their lands, and the removal of their populations. By 1800, the white population of Ohio had reached 45,000; twenty years later it was 581,000. This opening of new land enlarged the range of choices open to family members, and many new settlers found renewed prosperity by moving west. Four Thomson brothers from Bellingham, Massachusetts, migrated to Ohio in the 1810s and 1820s, leaving a fifth brother behind on the family farm. Two of them moved on to Indiana, a third was said to be "doing very well," but the youngest, Dan, was only "mak[ing] a Living in Ohio and that is about all." Although many migrants encouraged others to follow them, some advised caution. John Stillman Wright sold his farm in New York state in 1818 and went to Ohio, but later published *Letters from the West* to warn others of

". . . The Truth About This Country"

For some European immigrants, American society in the 1830s proved a profound disappointment. In this 1834 letter to his mother back home, David Davies, a Welsh immigrant in the coal town of Carbondale, Pennsylvania, suggests how unhappy his prospects had become in America, less than a year after his arrival.

IT IS SOME comfort to me that hundreds of my fellow countrymen are as unfortunate as I am or else I do not know what would become of me. I cannot blame anyone but myself because nothing would do but that I should come to America. It is coal work here and that very stagnant at present and the outlook is poor that any improvement will take place for a long time. Also the news that we get from newspapers and letters makes things worse and, consequently, the more dissatisfied with our situation. . . . This makes everyone here want to return home. I wish that I could persuade Welsh people to believe the truth about this country.

There is no acre to be had under ten shillings, and that covered by trees and wilderness. If a young man lived for fifty years he could not gather all the stones from off it even if he worked every day. If you spent a year here seeing nothing but poor cottages in the woods with the chimneys smoking so that Welsh people could not breathe in them and the jolly Welsh women here losing their rosy cheeks and smiling eyes—what would your feelings be? You would sigh for the lovely land that you had left.

Source: Alan Lonway, ed., *The Welsh in America* (1961).

"the cruel disappointment and vain regret, which so many thousands are now enduring." Some could not abide the harshness and loneliness of the rural frontier. Livvat Knapke Böke, a German woman who reached Ohio in the 1830s, wrote of people "locked in the solitude of their own hearts and minds," and acting "silent and sulky, sullen and pouty."

As an alternative to migration westward, some sons (as well as daughters) without land or others means of their own stayed in the East, but moved to the towns or port cities, tried new occupations, or became laborers. Along with new immigrants from Europe, they swelled urban populations, helping turn small market centers into bustling towns, and the larger ports such as New York, Philadelphia, and Baltimore into teeming metropolises. And whether they stayed in the countryside or moved to towns, more people became engaged in manufacturing activities, forming the basis of America's first industrial workforce.

Improvements in Communication

Merchants with money to invest reinforced these changes as they turned their attention from international trade toward the American continent. They put money into urban property or speculated in western land. A handful invested directly in manufacturing, especially of textiles. But in the first decades of the nineteenth century, most investors chose to concentrate on internal commerce and improvements in transportation, especially the construction and maintenance of roads, turnpikes, bridges, and canals, and later of steamboats and railroads.

Keen to share in the prosperity anticipated from rising commerce, state and local governments encouraged such investments. By 1812, Massachusetts alone had authorized the construction of 105 turnpike roads, and New York had authorized 57. Much labor for road building was recruited from local farm families, but larger projects required greater numbers of workers. Some states poured public funds directly into these projects. Others rewarded private investors with subsidies, tax exemptions, government backing for privately issued bonds, special banking and lottery franchises, and exclusive corporate charters conferring lucrative monopoly privileges.

Expenditures increased steadily, resulting in great improvements in internal travel and communication. New York State's Erie Canal had the most remarkable effects. Built at public expense by thousands of laborers between 1817 and 1825, the canal stretched 364 miles from Albany to Buffalo, linking the Great Lakes and Ohio Valley with the Hudson River, New York City, and transatlantic trade. Freight rates to the interior fell sharply, boosting trade. In 1817 it cost nineteen cents a mile to take a ton

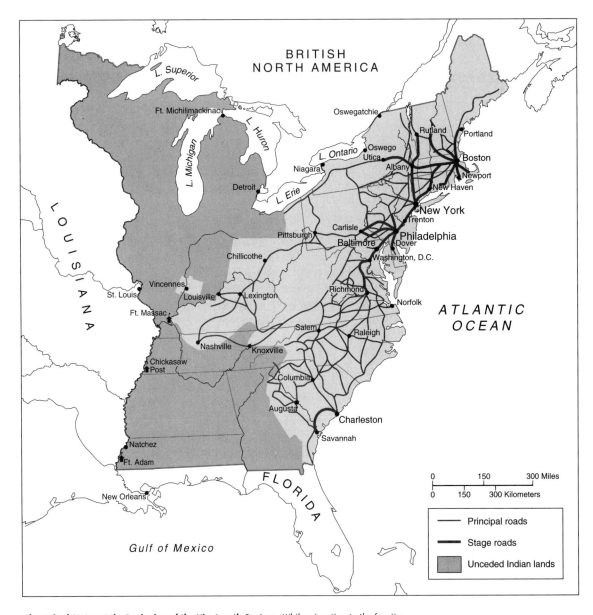

The United States at the Beginning of the Nineteenth Century. While migration to the frontier pushed the settled areas of the United States westward and southward, the northeastern states were already emerging as a region of denser population, larger urban centers, and better roads than in the rest of the nation.

Source: D. W. Meinig, *The Shaping of America: A Geographical Perspective on 500 Years of History,* vol. 2, *Continental America, 1800 – 1867* (1993).

Building the Erie Canal.
Building the canal took heavy physical labor. A contemporary lithograph by Anthony Imbert shows the excavation at Lockport, New York.

Source: Cadwallader Colden, *Memoir on the Celebration of the Completion of the New York Canals* (1825)—Metropolitan Museum of Art.

of goods from New York to Buffalo; by the 1830s it cost less than one-tenth of that. Other northern states sought to emulate the Erie's success by building their own canals. Railroad developments soon followed. Promoters in Baltimore started a line to the Ohio River in 1828, although it took a quarter century to complete. By 1840 shorter railroads connected Boston and other cities with manufacturing and commercial towns in the hinterlands.

Transportation improvements helped end local self-sufficiency by knitting together regional and national markets. Household manufacture for home use died out as early as 1820 in parts of rural New England, and in most other places within the next forty years. Although upstate New York households were still making an average of more than ten yards of cloth per person per year in 1825, this output dropped to less than half a yard thirty years later as farm families switched to buying factory-made cloth. Falling freight costs made internal trade more profitable for merchants and made store-bought items of decent quality available to rural families at declining prices. For example, between 1809 and 1836 the prices of soap and candles fell by about a third. A coffee mill costing five dollars in 1813 sold for only two in 1836. The prices of glassware, cotton mattresses, buttons, pins, hooks-and-eyes, and a host of other goods all fell. "Formerly," noted a Pennsylvanian in 1836, "no man thought of going to a tailor for a sheet. Now everybody goes to one even for a handkerchief."

However, the need for cash to buy these goods meant that farm families had to devote more of their time to producing for market whatever crops would command the highest price. Instead of providing for many of their own basic food needs, they purchased foodstuffs from others. Some farmers flourished as commercial producers. They added to their property, hired less-fortunate neighbors as laborers and servants, and supported further measures to increase commerce. To them, independence and commerce seemed to complement one another. "Our sons," said the *New England Farmer* in 1835, "from the very cradle, breathe the air of independence—and we teach them to owe no man. It is to gratify this love of independence that they rake the ocean and the earth for money."

But commerce further altered the fabric of rural society. Competition began to replace cooperation. The *New England Farmer* warned

> The cultivator who does not keep pace with his neighbors as regards agricultural improvements and information will soon find himself the poorer in consequence of the prosperity that surrounds him. . . . He will be like a stunted oak in the forest, which is deprived of light and air, by its "towering neighbors."

Farmers who lost out in the new competition often found their independence threatened by debt or poverty. Middlemen, who connected the inland farmer and the urban consumer, added to the difficulties of these marginal farmers. In order to increase their own profits, they could force down the prices they paid for agricultural goods, and resell those goods at higher prices. Farm families faced ruin if they were caught between rising costs and dwindling incomes, and could no longer produce much of their own food and clothing. They mortgaged property to stay afloat but, unless they used the loans to increase productivity and output, the debt became just another burden. By 1832, one farmer claimed, "[t]his business of mortgage has already dispossessed a large portion of the best farmers in New England, and it constantly increases." He feared that "the independent yeomanry of our country" would soon "give place to wretched tenantry," and that "a very few rich men . . . will own the whole soil." Another voiced the fears of many in 1831: "We are willing to work, our wives are willing to work—but spare us . . . the humiliation of performing the servile offices and living in the kitchens of our more fortunate neighbors."

Competition from the West also posed a strong challenge to eastern farmers. Improved transport brought produce from newly cultivated lands into market with crops grown on rocky, nearly exhausted New England soils. Commerce through the Erie Canal virtually ended wheat production in much of the East and put heavy pressure on hog and cattle raising, too.

At the same time, western expansion fostered commerce and manufacturing. Although little merchandise had moved westward from the seaports in 1810, by 1835 the value of goods westbound on the Erie Canal alone approached $10 million a year. Located at key points along now-bustling east–west trade routes, cities such as Buffalo, Pittsburgh, and Cincinnati boomed. By the 1830s, Cincinnati was the leading center of pork packing, and the foundations were being laid for some of the industries that would later dominate the Midwest: grain-milling;

meat-packing; distilling and brewing; lumbering; iron smelting; and the production of farm equipment and consumer goods for local markets.

The Beginnings of an Industrial Revolution

The earliest development of a manufacturing sector occurred in the East, however. Before 1850, three-quarters of America's manufacturing employment was concentrated in the New England and Middle Atlantic states. Many people who stayed in the East sought new occupations to supplement or replace their reliance on the land. Growing urban populations and immigrants from Europe provided the workforce needed to sustain an industrial revolution.

Many opposed the development of large-scale industry. Advocates of an agrarian America urged that the expansion of manufactures take place at the household level. A Massachusetts Democratic-Republican, Benjamin Austin, wrote Thomas Jefferson in 1815 that *"Domestic* manufacture is the object contemplated[,] instead of establishments under the sole control of capitalists." At first, this is what happened. Apart from shipbuilding and ironworking, which were conducted on a larger scale, most early manufacturing was performed in households. From the late eighteenth century onward, rural artisans and farmers complemented their work on the land with seasonal manufacturing — making tools, pumps, wagons, barrels, and other items for local and regional sale. Other families supplemented meager farm earnings by producing household manufactures for sale. Women worked on shoes, wove straw hats, and sewed shirts for merchants, who paid them by the piece. In cities, artisans ran shops at their homes, assisted by live-in apprentices. Those who expanded their businesses to meet the rising demand from growing commercial and rural populations often did so by putting work out to others. For instance, large numbers of Philadelphia weavers took in work from merchant tailors and textile masters, producing cloth on a piecework basis in their homes in Kensington, Northern Liberties, or Moyamensing.

During the early nineteenth century, however, rising demand and investment began to move a range of industrial activities out of households and into larger units. In the skilled crafts (producing consumer goods such as clothing and hats, boots and shoes, leather, furniture, barrels, soap and candles, books and newspapers), some masters enlarged their shops, employing more apprentices or journeymen, and in doing so increased the numbers of urban wage workers. Master craftsmen also began to change the character of work by dividing skilled tasks into separate stages, for which they could employ cheaper, less-skilled labor. In southwestern

Connecticut, master clockmakers such as Eli Terry and Seth Thomas organized networks of farmers and artisans to produce different parts of wooden clock movements and cases for final assembly in their workshops. Elsewhere, rural wagon-, tool-, and furniture-making, which had also started by drawing on the part-time labor of farm families, similarly expanded, and different stages of production became divided, first among different households, then in some cases consolidated in shops employing tens or even scores of wage workers.

Meanwhile, yarn, cloth, and thread production largely moved from homes into factories. Using profits from overseas trade, merchants began investing in textile operations that used machinery developed in late-eighteenth-century Europe. "The time spent in a factory," explained a Massachusetts observer, "will produce at least ten times as much as it will in household manufactures." In 1790, Samuel Slater, an immigrant who had worked as an overseer for one of England's largest cotton manufacturers, succeeded in mechanizing the spinning of cotton yarn for the first time in the United States. In an old clothier's shop at Pawtucket Falls, Rhode Island, he set up his machines, using the Blackstone River to power them. Slater's capital came from the wealthy Brown family, a Rhode Island mercantile dynasty that had made its fortune in the colonial rum and slave trades and helped make Providence one of New England's chief commercial and manufacturing centers. Slater's early success encouraged the firm of Almy, Brown, and Slater to erect the country's first textile factory in 1793. A modest, two-and-a-half-story spinning mill just upstream from the clothier's shop, the factory depended largely upon children to run its spinning machines. Adults, often the parents of child employees, were paid to weave the yarn into cloth in their own homes. It was for these mills that Abigail Patch and her children worked in Pawtucket from 1807 onward.

By 1815, southern New England boasted several yarn-spinning factories based on the Rhode Island model. By 1840 they dotted the Blackstone Valley in Rhode Island and Massachusetts, and the nearby valleys of eastern Connecticut. Philadelphia merchants also invested in mills in the city's manufacturing districts and the river valleys of nearby Chester and Delaware Counties.

During the War of 1812 another distinctive textile factory system arose near Boston. Initiated by a mechanic named Paul Moody, it was owned and controlled by Francis Cabot Lowell and a circle of merchants eventually known as the Boston Associates. Its first mill was at Waltham, Massachusetts, and in the 1820s additional mills were built at a site on the Merrimack River that would become the town of Lowell.

The Waltham system differed from the Rhode Island system in important ways. It involved a far greater financial investment and operated

View of Lowell, Massachusetts. In this illustration, which was printed in a Merrimack Company folder containing fabric samples, the Lowell mills nestled peacefully amidst the countryside.

Source: American Textile History Museum.

on a larger scale. The first Waltham factory cost $400,000, more than ten times the average investment in a Rhode Island mill. Incorporating power looms as well as power-driven spinning frames, the system mechanized each stage of cloth production. Unlike many proprietors who managed their own mills, the owners of the Waltham–Lowell mills were absentees who hired agents to oversee operations. The Waltham–Lowell system also used a different kind of labor force. Most of its workers were young, single women from rural New England families, attracted to the mills after the decline of household textile production, and called "operatives" because they worked powered machinery. Because factory work drew them away from their families' homes, the companies constructed special boarding houses for them.

All these developments marked a shift away from household-based production. Although the tradition by no means died out, by 1830 a decreasing number of workers lived in the households of their employers. Factory workers inhabited their own rented houses or tenements, or — as in the Lowell system — lived with their fellow operatives in the company-owned boarding houses. Even in craft trades where the scale of production remained smaller, residential separation of workers and bosses became common. Almost all New York City artisans had workshops attached to their homes in 1790, but by 1840 two-thirds of them lived and worked in separate places. In Rochester, New York, by 1827 less than one journeyman in four lived in a household owned by an employer. Among shoemakers in the same city, the proportion fell to one in twenty by 1834. Residential separation between bosses and workers was just one part of a trend toward greater social division.

Industrialization and Social Stratification

Many among the generation born around 1800 found greater prosperity and opportunity than their parents had. But they also faced a society of increasing disparities between rich and poor, of greater reliance on wage workers, and in which trade and manufacture were increasingly competitive. Periodic economic slumps created hardship and uncertainty. The first severe downturn occurred in 1819, at the end of an import boom following the War of 1812. Many people found themselves in debt and without work. Other slumps would follow, particularly in the late 1830s. Amidst prosperity, there was also poverty and insecurity.

Yet for some the growth of manufacturing brought great economic success. Chauncey Jerome was the son of a modest Connecticut blacksmith and nailmaker who died when Chauncey was eleven. He started work as a maker of clock dials for Eli Terry, but then built his own business and by 1840 was owner of one of America's largest clock manufacturing firms. Another Connecticut-born artisan, Thomas Rogers, began as a house carpenter. He moved to Paterson, New Jersey, where he became a loom-builder and machinist before, in 1831, he helped to establish what would become one of the nation's largest locomotive builders. Successful master manufacturers and factory owners such as Jerome and Rogers could view themselves as beneficiaries of the republican ideal of a property-owning citizenry. Rogers even named his factory the "Jefferson Works" to commemorate the ideal's political hero. For them, industrialization brought opportunities for "independence."

The success of men such as Jerome and Rogers contrasted with the lives of those who struggled to make ends meet. Industrial growth created larger numbers of people whose manual labor was essential, but whose access to property and wealth was precarious or nonexistent. Although slavery and indentured servitude disappeared from the North, reliance on wage labor increased. The result was greater social stratification: the division of society into layers of people with unequal access to resources.

The growth of cities, driven by the surge in commerce and industry, added to the disparities between rich and poor. By 1840, thirty-eight percent of the Massachusetts population lived in settlements of over 2,500 inhabitants. Although much manufacturing took place in small towns, large industrial centers also developed, of which Philadelphia and New York City were the biggest. New York's population, over 312,000 in 1840, had almost tripled in just two decades, and the city's manufacturing workforce—already over 25,000 strong—would more than triple in the next ten years. Much of this growth was the result of migration from the countryside and from Europe. Many poorer workers who arrived in the cities were obliged to take unskilled or casual labor at very low wages. Their meager incomes were a fraction of those of urban elites.

Both in the established port cities of Philadelphia, New York, Boston, and Baltimore, and in newer centers such as Pittsburgh and Cincinnati, conditions for the poor were often bleak. Thousands of women labored in the clothing and millinery trades for extremely low wages. A report in 1830 noted that women earned as little as $55 a year at sewing, and had to pay $26 of this for rent alone. A missionary wrote that he had visited many homes whose "entire furnishings" were "one bed, one chair, and the half of another, one table, one candlestick, one cup, an old pot, and a piece of a frying pan."

Middle-class reformers began to protest these conditions. Poverty, they feared, would lead to prostitution, crime, and social disorder, yet they had no practical solutions to propose. Some urged country folk to stop moving to town in search of work; others urged employers to be kinder. Poor men and women themselves faced not moral dilemmas but a struggle for survival. When they could, they sought out better-paid work or better conditions, but circumstances were often against them.

The gap between rich and poor was apparent not only at home and in the workplace, but in leisure activities as well. Seating in urban theaters, segregated by price, placed different social classes in distinct sections. Artisans and shopkeepers perched on backless benches in the pit. Above and behind them merchants, professionals, and their ladies occupied expensive box seats. Above everything was the gallery, where apprentices, servants, and African Americans (if admitted at all) mingled with prostitutes and other members of the laboring poor. The presence, tastes, and behavior of lower-class audiences displeased some. Men and women strolled, ate, and chatted during performances. Noises from the gallery, noted English visitor Frances Trollope in the 1830s, "were perpetual and of the most unpleasant kind."

On the streets, too, middle- and upper-class citizens expressed affront at lower-class behavior. Taverns and grog shops were staples of lower-class socializing. Inexpensive spirits helped wash away the day's cares, and the company was familiar and congenial. Cards, billiards, and bowling absorbed much time, energy, and cash. Other diversions included carousing and brawling among rival militia companies, volunteer fire brigades, and neighborhood street gangs, and raucous celebrations on July Fourth and other holidays or the weekly Sabbath work break. And although respectable society expressed disdain, excited crowds gathered to watch and wager on cockfights, bullfights, dogfights, and bull and bear matches. A Philadelphia newspaper in 1833 denounced the "riot, noise and uproar" visited upon "many of our central and most orderly streets."

Jacksonian Democracy

Struggles over popular behavior and amusement paralleled significant changes in political culture. The rivalry in the 1790s and 1800s between Federalist and Democratic-Republican political visions had generated increasing popular involvement in electoral politics. The post-revolutionary conception that republican citizenship should be based on possession of property gave way under pressure to reform. State after state modified its electoral rules to reduce or abolish property qualifications for voting, and to widen popular access to political activity. Among northern states, by the 1820s only Rhode Island had not taken steps that effectively granted the vote to all adult white males. This equality was still circumscribed, however. No state permitted women to vote, and many states barred African-American men from voting on grounds of race. Only white men could share in the privileges of political "independence."

Increased participation helped to promote new, more democratic political styles. Astute politicians grasped that the genteel methods appropriate to government by a "natural aristocracy" were inadequate to channel the votes of an expanding electorate, and that new forms of political organization were necessary. In New York State in the 1820s, the Democratic Party led by Martin Van Buren pioneered local party organizations and campaigning tactics that emphasized popular inclusiveness and recruited support at elections. Soon these methods would spread across the nation. Committees drummed up support at the local level, and elections were dominated by public meetings, picnics, parades, and popular entertainments that became part of the fabric of social life in town and country alike. A new breed of professional politician appeared. These men, like Van Buren, devoted their whole time to politics, building their careers and vote-getting organizations on appeals to voters and on the ability to dispense state or federal government patronage. They returned favors and cemented alliances in part by distributing government jobs among those outside the political elite. Campaign speeches, banners, and handbills bristled with effusive vows of loyalty to "the working man" and "the producing classes."

This emerging political culture was symbolized at the national level by the figure of Andrew Jackson, who narrowly lost the presidential election in 1824 under controversial circumstances, and whose electoral victory in 1828 helped consolidate the new era of popular politics. In a message to Congress, Jackson spelled out what he called "the first principle of our system—*that the majority is to govern.*" The first president not to be drawn from either the Virginia gentry or the New England elite, Jackson represented an attack on social and political "privilege" and on the apparent threat of "aristocracy" to republican institutions. He headed a

Democratic Party that aimed to minimize the power of government to grant "special privileges and monopolies," which the wealthy could exploit to their own advantage.

Jackson's Democrats criticized banks as financial monopolies that threatened "Republican Government." As president, Jackson vetoed a bill that would have rechartered the Second Bank of the United States. He and his followers urged the prevention of "the undue aggregation of capital in the hands of a . . . few" and the protection of "the people in the enjoyment of the fruits of their labor." They opposed incorporation laws because, as one Democrat put it, corporations concentrated "large masses of property" and impeded "the natural tendency of capital to an equal distribution among the people." Jacksonian Democrats also resisted bankruptcy statutes, which they suspected of sheltering the rich from their poorer creditors. Above all, they attacked federal expenditure for internal improvements such as roads and canals, and attempted to break what they saw as "aristocratic" monopolies allegedly sought by a national elite.

The Democrats' policies were enacted in the name of equality and popular interests. A New Hampshire Democrat explained that he supported the party that "gives to all an equal share." Yet avoiding the use of government to create privilege did not always benefit working people. Since 1816, the federal government had enacted protective import tariffs to encourage manufacturing. By the 1830s, under pressure from southern members of the party, many northern Democrats were criticizing tariffs and working for their reduction, even though many northern workers supported them. Democrats' preference for leaving the economy unregulated also made it very hard for workers to obtain laws that could protect them from the abuses and exploitation of long working hours and poor working conditions.

The growth of political participation accompanied a rapid expansion of the press. Local and regional newspapers, many with strong political loyalties or party connections, multiplied. So did journals and magazines, some of which started to enjoy a national circulation. Improvements in printing—particularly the use of steam presses after 1830—slashed the price of newspapers and led to the start of a mass-circulation "penny press." By 1836, nearly one in four New York City residents bought daily papers, a dramatic increase over earlier periods. "These papers are to be found in every street, lane, alley," noted one observer, and "in every hotel, tavern, and counting house. . . . Almost every porter and drayman, while not engaging in his occupation, may be seen with a paper in his hands."

In one sense, the expansion of the press marked the growing inclusion of all white men in the political process. Any literate person could follow political events and so be an informed citizen. As more and more free white males gained the right to vote, the press helped to underpin

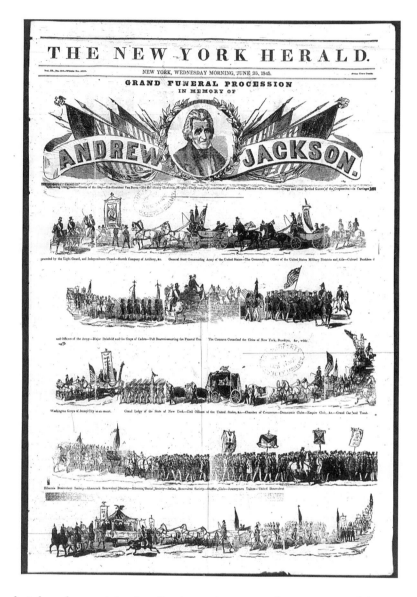

their broader participation. But in another sense, the expansion of the press signaled new forms of differentiation. Women's magazines, the labor press, African-American papers, and antislavery papers were all initiated during the 1820s and early 1830s.

The Jacksonian era also saw new political alignments emerge. Jackson's Democratic Party drew on the support of rural planters and proprietors, especially in the South and Southwest, and on the urban poor, some craftsmen, and some businessmen in the North. The opposition to

Jackson, represented first by the National Republican Party and, in the mid 1830s, by the new Whig Party, had supporters in the South, but drew especially on northern farmers engaged in commercial agriculture, on financiers, and on industrial craftsmen and proprietors. Party politics became a complex mix of regional and class-based schisms and alliances. In the North, the Whigs became strongly associated with a middle-class ideal rooted in the interests and assumptions of urban and rural property holders.

The New Middle Class and Family Ideals

Commercial prosperity and industrial development swelled the ranks of property-owning farmers, merchants, professionals, and master manufacturers. During the 1820s and 1830s many such people came to view themselves as members of a distinct "middling class" whose interests, as Boston publisher Joseph T. Buckingham wrote, differed from those of the "unprofitable poor and the unproductive rich." The decline of household manufacturing, the separation of home and business, and the increased availability of consumer goods altered the lives of these people and their families. Around them, writers and moralists constructed a new ideal of family life, centered upon a home sheltered from the anxieties of work and business, in which age and gender roles were subtly altered from the patriarchal and hierarchical assumptions of an earlier period.

In such families, fathers increasingly conducted their business in offices, shops, workshops, and factories separate from their homes. Involvement in this public sphere diverted their energies from household matters. Their wives remained in the home, now freed and excluded from most income-earning activities. In the shops of rising master craftsmen, the efforts of wage-earning employees replaced the efforts of family members. In shoemaking, for example, the responsibility for stitching shoe uppers shifted from the master's wife to the daughters of poorer families, employed as outworkers.

Middle-class women contributed to the family economy by performing household work and shrewdly planning their purchases. From around 1830, the increasing availability of stoves and, in some cities, a public water supply eased some of the burdens of housework. For women who could afford to hire them there were domestic servants, whose numbers, since 1800, had grown twice as fast as the number of white families and whose ranks in northeastern cities by the 1830s were starting to be dominated by immigrant women, particularly from Ireland. Servants, typically working for sixteen to eighteen hours a day, relieved middle-class women of strenuous or unpleasant household tasks. In 1841, the writer Lydia Maria Child claimed that genteel women no longer washed or dressed

The American Woman's Home. This was the frontispiece and title page of a popular 1869 guide to the "formation and Maintenance of Economical, Healthful, Beautiful, and Christian Homes." Intended to instruct young women on their proper role in the middle-class home, this book was continually expanded and reprinted after its first publication in 1841. Its lessons about Domestic Science ranged from the correct way to raise children to the appropriate type of picture to hang in the parlor.

Source: Catherine E. Beecher and Harriet Beecher Stowe, *The American Woman's Home or, Principles of Domestic Science . . .* (1869)—General Research Division, New York Public Library, Astor, Lenox and Tilden Foundations.

their children, made their own clothing, made fires, scrubbed floors, or emptied out slops.

Writers idealized the family and home life as largely separated from business and politics, and as a refuge from the driving economic pressures and personal frictions of a man's working life. Sarah Josepha Hale, editor of *Godey's Lady's Book,* one of the most popular magazines of the 1830s, told her middle-class female readers, "Our men are sufficiently money-making; let us keep our women and children free from the contagion as long as possible." Women's role, in this view, was to preserve the home as a domestic haven and to instill in their children the habits and standards of behavior deemed essential to republican government and personal prosperity. These included the importance of hard work, perseverance, and diligence; frugality, saving, and accumulation; and personal reserve, self-discipline, restraint of the emotions, and steady and temperate habits.

Childrearing came to rely less on intimidation and physical punishment and more on affection and patient instruction. Instead of simply bending before authority, children were now expected to understand and internalize their parents' values. Machinist Morton Poole encouraged his sister to strengthen in her son "the liberties which are essential to the formation of a free and independent spirit," relying on "superior understanding" instead of fear. "A child that is afraid of its parents," he wrote, "can never feel that confidence which is necessary to the receiving of information in conversations with its parents."

But this new concept of women's role as domestic haven maker and teacher of middle-class values did not challenge the husband's ultimate power over his wife and household, or bring women into political life. Wives, Sarah Josepha Hale advised, must remain "pure, pious, domestic, and submissive." They performed their domestic roles at the pleasure of their husbands, and could improve the society's moral temper by participating in church affairs and setting an example for other family members. Wives of respectable artisans were expected to follow the same precepts. A book addressed to "the American mechanic" in 1840 explained that the proper mate was "patient, resolute, loves her home." Her place, it added, "is eminently at the fireside."

As the center of youthful instruction, shielded from the public sphere, the mother-supervised home became equated with proper Christian values. Indeed, middle-class women now assumed greater responsibility for overseeing the morals not only of their own households, but also, by extension, of society as a whole. While men saw to the nation's material needs, women would see to its spiritual ones.

"Mose and Lize on the Third Avenue, New York." This 1848 sketch showed the exuberant style of dress and behavior favored by many young working-class women. Although Lize (like her boyfriend, Mose) was a fictional character, her popularity in the press and theater suggested that the principles of Domestic Science did not represent the ideal for all young women.

Source: James Baillie, 1848, lithograph—New-York Historical Society.

MOSE AND LIZE ON THE 3ᴿᴰ AVENUE N.Y.

Mose - Well, d-n my buttons if Is aint sport - now we pass ur Red House - do yer pettiest now Ole Gal; ere's ur lot ur Soo-foo's lookin at us, an if they kin beat is ore Team, ile give Corneil Anderson leaf ter hit me over de gourd mid de Trumpet more'n once - if I dont; d-n me !

Published by James Baillie, 87th St. near 3rd Avenue New-York.

Evangelical Revivals and Social Reform

The emergence of these middle-class, domestic ideals was shaped by, and in turn reinforced, a strong renewal of evangelical Protestantism across early nineteenth-century America. This Second Great Awakening began in the South at the turn of the century, but in the 1820s and 1830s it swept northward to take root in new farming regions such as upstate New York, and among the middle classes of the cities and smaller commercial towns.

Revivals drew strength from many sources — from democratic thought and economic development, as well as from changes in culture and family life. As the revivals spread, more Americans than ever before entered active religious life. The emotional scenes that marked southern revival meetings were repeated across the North, most of all in western New York State, where constant revivals caused the region to be dubbed the "Burned-Over District." The powerful emotions aroused at camp meetings and mass prayer meetings knocked converts off their seats. "If I had had a sword in my hand," reminisced evangelist Charles Grandison Finney, "I could not have cut them off . . . as fast as they fell." The movement embraced many, often opposing, doctrines, but affirmed that anyone experiencing a profound religious rebirth or conversion and then living an upright Christian life would be saved from eternal damnation. Most believed that this salvation was an act of free will, not — as Calvinists had maintained — predestined by God. If so, men and women had the power to choose for themselves the path to eternal life. Self-discipline and self-control could save them just as, they believed, it could gain them material comfort and prosperity on Earth. The confidence that, with self-discipline and effort, people could influence their afterlives complemented their belief in personal initiative, hard work, and individual advancement.

The evangelical movement sought to bridge the social divisions that were opening up, and it em-

Evangelist Meeting. A camp-meeting in the woods painted by Pennsylvania artist Jeremiah Paul.

Source: Jeremiah Paul, n.d., oil on board, 19 × 28 inches — Spanierman Gallery, New York.

braced people from every social class. Merchants, masters, and journeymen who now lived and worked separately might still worship together. Everywhere women formed a clear majority of congregations and church membership. In one sense evangelicalism endorsed women's separation from the business world, stressing their moral and spiritual authority as teachers and examples for their families and society at large. However, because of their importance to the churches, and because evangelicalism had a social as well as a purely spiritual dimension, many women found that the movement gave them the opportunity to develop a new type of semipublic role as well.

Rather than accepting society as it was, evangelicals believed in changing it by reforming ("perfecting") the individuals who composed it. "To the universal reformation of the world [we] stand committed," wrote Finney. Evangelicals would accomplish change through personal example and by spreading the word of Christ. Most shared the view that social ills grew out of "the ungoverned appetites, bad habits, and vices" of individuals rather than the workings of society itself. Their activism generated an imposing network of church-linked voluntary organizations pledged to pursue moral reform, to fight alcohol and prostitution, to enforce a strict Sabbath, to encourage public and religious education, and to support charitable institutions of all kinds. Men usually headed these organizations, but women composed much of the membership and also played prominent roles as organizers and activists.

The evangelical revivals were an important spur to the antislavery movement, which grew rapidly in many northern towns and agricultural districts in the 1830s and would sharpen the distinctions and antagonism between North and South in the decades that followed. The American Anti-Slavery Society, founded by Arthur Tappan, William Lloyd Garrison and others in 1833, particularly benefited from evangelical enthusiasm. Like revivalist churches, Garrisonian abolitionists used itinerant lecturers, emotional oratory, and printed periodicals and tracts to spur the abolitionist appeal and condemn slavery as a sin.

Despite evangelicals' attempts at social inclusiveness, they by no means attracted universal support. Even many Christians rejected their doctrines and their efforts to become "their brothers' keepers." Class distinctions, especially, shaped evangelical activism. Families of the successful master craftsmen, merchants, and farmers who had adapted best to the new, competitive economy were among the strongest supporters of a reformist revivalism that became closely associated with the Whig Party in politics. Although commercial and industrial change brought them prosperity, businessmen worried about the threats to order that change seemed to bring with it. In his private journal in 1834, minister Henry Clark Wright expressed the fear that faster transport and communication, "while increasing the business and moneyed interests of the Nation . . . will by spreading vice and irreligion prove its ruin. Those very things which all regard as improvements will be our destruction." Reform often meant converting the poor to evangelical ideas about proper family life and personal behavior. Drinking alcoholic beverages, the Presbyterian minister Albert Barnes argued, "produces idleness and loss of property . . . . [T]he man who will not work . . . is the enemy of his country." Other Whig evangelicals warned against "the ascendancy of the rabble, . . . the filth and offscouring of all things," and advocated the influence of "the mass of intelligence and property of the country."

As well as endorsing their personal convictions, evangelicalism offered reformers a means to convert others—including their employees—to their own values. Hoping to secure docile workers, many employers, including Samuel Slater and the owners of the Waltham–Lowell mills, encouraged church attendance by their operatives to foster regularity of habits and acceptance of discipline. Mill owners were also among the sponsors of evangelical churches built in the Rockdale district of Pennsylvania in the 1830s.

But religious involvement was not just imposed on workers by employers. Itinerant preachers—workingmen and -women themselves—evangelized in factory villages, and young workers found spiritual and social companionship in church activities. Nor did religion necessarily make them more docile. Camp meetings and prolonged revivals sometimes disrupted work, causing frustrated factory agents or owners to combat local churches or evangelists. In one Massachusetts textile district, revivals were followed by increased labor turnover in the mills.

Radically minded working people also identified with evangelicalism because it emphasized spiritual equality and sincere belief rather than elitism and formality. They opposed the privileges of the wealthy in church (such as their purchase of choice pews) and denounced them for flaunting their finery there. They sought a religion that would help workers defend and extend their rights. They shared the demand for personal self-discipline, viewing alcohol, gambling, and prostitution as snares set by a corrupt society to trap people or at the very least to distract them from exercising their liberties. Although, in the longer run, evangelicalism fostered acceptance of the wage system, it also promoted self-assurance and a strong sense of equal rights. As it grew in importance during the 1830s, evangelicalism helped fuel, as much as diminish, the determination of labor leaders and activists to secure justice for working people.

A concern with equal rights and justice gave evangelicals some common ground with radical freethinkers whose religious views they vigorously denounced. Champions of human reason instead of faith, in the tradition of Thomas Paine and Vermont's Ethan Allen, freethinkers were suspicious of organized religion as the promoter of superstition, privilege, and tyranny. Although never a large group, prominent freethinkers such as George Henry Evans, Frances Wright, and Robert Dale Owen served as labor journalists and as leaders and activists in early trade unions and workingmen's parties. Radical free thought found much of its support among urban craftsmen, especially those (like shoemakers and tailors) affected most by industrial development, the division of labor, and poorer working conditions. It also found support among printers, who regarded themselves as the intellectuals of the working classes.

Paths to Wage Labor: Artisans and Outworkers

The early-nineteenth-century expansion of industry involved different types of labor, different forms of economic organization, and people of different social (and sometimes national) backgrounds. Both the changing organization of work and the growing numbers of wage-earners challenged the post-revolutionary ideal of a republic of property owners. Wage workers were drawn from a variety of sources, each with a different experience of the transition to industrial work. Two important wage-earning groups were artisans and "outworkers" — people paid by the piece to perform manufacturing tasks in their homes. The circumstances of each of these two groups evolved from older patterns of craft and household production.

Traditional craft production centered on independent master artisans, their journeymen, and apprentice helpers who worked together in small shops. Apprentices were boys contracted to work for the master during their youth in return for instruction in the master's trade. Journeymen were trained workers who earned wages by the day. Although their relationship with the master was not an equal one, most apprentices and journeymen could look forward to becoming proprietors in their own right once they had acquired skill and capital. Looking back in 1857, the antiquarian John Fanning Watson recalled that in late-eighteenth-century Philadelphia

> No masters were seen exempted from personal labor in any branch of business — living on the profits derived from many journeymen. . . .
> Then almost every apprentice, when of age, ran his equal chance for his share of business in his neighborhood, by setting himself up for himself, and, with an apprentice or two, getting into a cheap location, and by dint of application and good work, recommending himself to his neighborhood. . . . Thus every shoemaker or tailor was a man for himself.

Though he idealized this older system, Watson witnessed its collapse during his lifetime, as market forces redefined the skilled artisan's work and social position.

Commercial growth and transportation improve   nts destroyed craftsmen's independence and increased competitic   between them. Enlarged markets meant a shift from the custom-made production of a few items to larger-scale production of ready-made goods. Boston, New York, Newark, and Philadelphia shoemakers, for example, soon competed not only with one another but also with Lynn, Massachusetts, the nation's rising center of shoe production. By 1820, especially in trades supplying goods to southern and other nonlocal markets—where quantity and price, rather than quality, counted—shops had grown in size, and craftsmen's tasks were subdivided into more specific and often less skilled segments of work. Some New York shoe manufacturers each employed from twenty to thirty-five men and women.

Although many artisans prospered in these new conditions, more were forced either to migrate to more promising areas or to stay put and face decline, debt, and eventual dispossession, losing their shops and perhaps even their tools to more successful neighbors. Deprived of independent means of support, they became employees, working up materials supplied to them by merchants or working in an employer's shop for wages. In New York and other cities, many shoemakers, tailors, hatters, and others employed in production for a big market were reduced to living in cramped, squalid conditions on low pay.

Working patterns in many trades were irregular. On one hand, this relieved the monotony and intensity of work. New Jersey ironworkers left the job to go hunting, get drunk, go to the beach, or take in the harvest. One ironmaster threatened to fine men who brought liquor to work, only to be told that one of them had "got drunk on cheese." On the other hand, many men and women suffered from irregular hours and periods of idleness. Even when, in theory, a skilled workman could make $600 a year, many had difficulty earning half this amount because there were days or seasons when there was no work for them to do.

As more artisans were forced into permanent wage work, master craftsmen faced a dilemma. Some remained loyal to tradition, and to their journeymen and apprentices, resisting pressure for change. In 1830 a New York master, urged to divide the work in his shop according to skill, refused because it would violate republican principles: "this Sir is a free country[;] we want no one person over another which would be the case if you divided the labour." But this stance usually led to economic ruin.

Other masters responded to market changes by pressing their own employees to produce more and more goods. As their shops grew in size,

"Cookies and Cakes . . . One Cent Apiece"

In the early nineteenth century, traditional work patterns still limited the pace and intensity of labor in many industries. Below, a ship carpenter recalls the frequent breaks for food and drink that punctuated a typical day in a New York shipyard. Employers increasingly regarded such practices as intolerable obstacles to efficiency and profit.

IN OUR YARD, at half-past eight A.M., Aunt Arlie McVane, a clever kind-hearted woman but awfully uncouth . . . would make her welcome appearance in the yard with her two great baskets, stowed and checked off with crullers, doughnuts, ginger-bread, turnovers, pies, and a variety of sweet cookies and cakes; and from the time Aunt Arlie's baskets came in sight until every man and boy, bosses and all, in the yard, had been supplied, always at one cent a piece for any article on the cargo, the pie, cake, and cookie trade was a brisk one. Aunt Arlie would usually make the rounds of the yard and supply all the hands in about an hour, bringing the forenoon up to half-past nine, and giving us from ten to fifteen minutes' "breathing spell" during lunch; no one ever hurried during "cake-time."

After this was over we would fall to [work] again, until interrupted by Johnnie Gogean, the English candyman, who came in always at half-past ten, with his great board, the size of a medium extension dining table, slung before him, covered with all sorts of "stick," and several of sticky candy, in one-cent lots. Bosses, boys, and men—all hands, everybody—invested one to three cents in Johnnie's sweet wares, and another ten to fifteen minutes is spent in consuming it. Johnnie usually sailed out with a bare board until eleven o'clock, at which time there was a general sailing out of the yard and into convenient grog-ships after whiskey. . . .

In the afternoon, about half-past three, we had a cake-lunch, supplied by Uncle Jack Gridder, an old, crippled, super-annuated ship carpenter. No one else was ever allowed to come in competition with our caterers. Let a foreign candyboard or cake basket make their appearance inside the gates of the yard, and they would get shipped out of that directly.

At about five o'clock P.M., always Johnnie used to put in his second appearance; and then, having expended money in another stick or two of candy, and ten minutes in its consumption, we were ready to drive away again until sundown; then home to supper.

Source: Herbert G. Gutman, *Work, Culture and Society in Industrializing America* (1976).

some owners ceased to be directly engaged in production and instead employed agents or foremen to supervise and discipline workmen. In 1825, when Thomas Babcock was made foreman of his family's printing office in New Haven, Connecticut, he was expected to hire and fire workmen as needed, to set their hours of work, to oversee production, and to "keep . . . [workmen] . . . still, sober and peaceable, and attentive to their business." "Capitalists," objected the *New York State Mechanic* in 1842, "have taken to bossing all the mechanical trades, while the practical mechanic

"Job Visited by a Master Tailor from Broadway." An illustration from the 1841 novel *The Career of Puffer Hopkins* caricatured the growing distinction between masters and journeymen. The master tailor's prosperous outfit, stance, and fancy business address (New York's Broadway) sharply contrasted with the journeyman's wretched appearance and workshop-home.

Source: Cornelius Mathews, *The Career of Puffer Hopkins* (1841)—American Social History Project.

has become a journeyman, subject to be discharged at every pretended 'miff' of his purse-proud employer."

Workers did what they could to resist what they saw as encroachments on their rights and working conditions. When the owners of a Catskill, New York, machine works with twenty-eight employees installed a bell in 1836 to mark the beginning and end of the workday, the workers

Shoemakers in a "Ten-Footer" Shop. A master cordwainer and his journeymen made shoes in a workshop attached to the master's home. By the time this engraving was published in 1880, the shoemaker's "ten-footer" was only a memory.

Source: (M. Newhall) David N. Johnson, *Sketches of Lynn, or the Changes of Fifty Years* (1880)—U.S. History, Local History, and Genealogy Division, New York Public Library, Astor, Lenox and Tilden Foundations.

threatened to strike. The dispute was settled with a compromise. Workers promised to work steadily, and to cease drinking and storytelling on the job, but they insisted on regulating the beginning and end of the day for themselves. Such victories, though, did not stem the tide of changes sweeping over many craft industries.

The transformation of shoe production in Lynn, Massachusetts, illustrates the general pattern of change. In the eighteenth century, most shoemakers worked in their own homes or small workshops (called ten-footers), cutting and sewing leather pieces and joining soles and uppers. There was minimal division of labor. Masters had a journeyman or two and a couple of apprentices, whom they trained to carry out all the tasks of production. Around the turn of the nineteenth century, however, increasing demand for cheap shoes for the growing southern slave population began to alter the way shoemaking was conducted. Shops multiplied, the division of labor increased, and some masters moved into large central shops, where they concentrated on cutting the leather, leaving other tasks to journeymen. In time the job of cutting was delegated to workers called clickers, and masters now became bosses (supervising the labor of others) or merchants (selling finished shoes). Journeymen resented masters' changing attitudes toward them. One complained that

> They seem to think it is a disgrace to labor; that the laborer is not as good as other people. These little stuck-up, self-conceited individuals who have a little second-hand credit. . . . You must do as they wish . . . or you are off their books; they have no more employment for you.

Production was further subdivided as the new system took root. Simplified tasks made it possible to replace skilled journeymen with less-fully-trained workers, including women and children. Journeymen's wives and daughters often assumed the less-skilled work of binding — stitching together the uppers and linings of the shoes. Journeymen were left only two tasks: lasting (fitting the uppers over a foot-shaped wooden last) and bottoming (attaching the uppers to the soles). A influx of part-time rural craftsmen displaced from the land added to journeymen's problems, competing for their work and enabling employers to hold down wages and lengthen working hours.

The division of labor and reduction of skill levels worsened most journeymen's prospects. Few now became masters. Apprenticeship declined. Journeymen protested the "anti-republican" distinctions emerging between them and the masters, which were like "those existing between the aristocracy and the laboring classes in Europe." As shoe bosses prospered, they scoured the New England countryside for new workers. Families that had fallen on hard times came forward eagerly. Thousands of farmers and fishermen supplemented their incomes by lasting and bottoming shoes at home, and increasing numbers of women took up shoe binding as outwork, at one-third to one-half the wages paid to male shoemakers in the central shops.

Indeed, from the 1820s on, work in more and more industries was "put out." When outworkers are included, women in 1840 made up almost half of all American manufacturing workers and about two-thirds of those in New England. Rural families and the urban poor alike took in work from merchants for piece-rate wages. Eighteen thousand Massachusetts women,

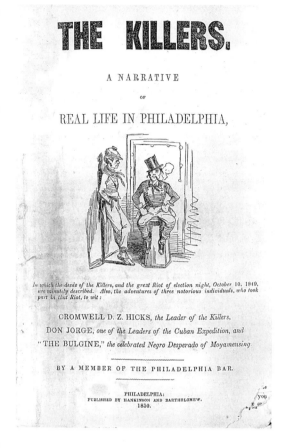

THE KILLERS.

A NARRATIVE

OF

REAL LIFE IN PHILADELPHIA,

In which the deeds of the Killers, and the great Riot of election night, October 10, 1849, are minutely described. Also, the adventures of three notorious individuals, who took part in that Riot, to wit:

CROMWELL D. Z. HICKS, the Leader of the Killers,

DON JORGE, one of the Leaders of the Cuban Expedition, and

"THE BULGINE," the celebrated Negro Desperado of Moyamensing.

BY A MEMBER OF THE PHILADELPHIA BAR.

PHILADELPHIA:
PUBLISHED BY HANKINSON AND BARTHOLOMEW.
1850.

Killers. As master artisans' control over their journeymen and apprentices dwindled, their former charges were freer to choose how to spend time away from the workshop. Some, like these two "Killers," joined proliferating urban gangs. This is the cover from an 1850 novel that was based on the violent activities of a notorious Philadelphia gang of journeymen, laborers, and apprentices.

Source: George Lippard, *The Killers. A Narrative of Real Life in Philadelphia . . .* (1850)—Library Company of Philadelphia.

for example, braided straw hats at home in the 1830s; others made buttons, socks, mittens, suspenders, and palm-leaf hats. At first rural outwork was a strategy for household independence, mainly among farm families with daughters in their teens or early twenties who had previously undertaken home textile production. As wage rates fell, however, outwork was taken up by poorer rural families—often by women with young children who used it to fill in the gaps left by their other work. Mary Bullard Graham of Buckland, Massachusetts, helped her husband at his shoemaking during busy periods, but when that work was slack she took in work making button molds for a local merchant.

Homeworking was also a staple for poor urban dwellers. In 1831, businessman and philanthropist Mathew Carey estimated that in the country's four largest cities twelve or thirteen thousand women worked at home making paper boxes, hoopskirts, shirts and collars, artificial flowers, cloaks, and similar goods. This outwork was often essential to their survival, or that of their families.

Like shoemaking, men's clothing manufacture followed broader changes in patterns of work. In New York, until the early 1800s, the clothing trade was dominated by skilled male tailors who catered to upper-class demand for custom-made garments, and by seamstresses and female dressmakers who worked largely on shirts, dresses, children's clothing, and mending. But after the federal government enacted a protective tariff in 1816, the U.S. clothing trades expanded, as city merchants, using cheap cloth from the new textile mills, captured the market in clothing for southern slaves from English suppliers. Later, the trade of these merchants grew to include clothing for plantation owners, while the completion of the Erie Canal added upstate New York and western markets. New York merchants' profits were handsome. In the early 1830s, ready-made clothing sold for five times what it cost to produce. By mid-decade, there were several clothing firms with over three hundred employees each.

Profits rested on low wages and low overhead costs. The outwork system allowed manufacturers to replace skilled tailors with less-skilled women homeworkers. Some were wives and daughters of poor day laborers, declining craftsmen, and men seeking work in the West. But most women clothing workers headed their own households; many had been widowed or abandoned, and many had children to support. A swelling stream of poor women and families, especially immigrants, increased competition for work, depressing already low piece rates and forcing outworkers to work longer hours to maintain their incomes. Isolated in their homes, outworkers had difficulty banding together to defend their common interests. They remained poorly housed and ill fed, making clothing for others but often unable to afford comfortable clothing of their own.

Paths to Wage Labor: Manual Laborers and Factory Operatives

The demand for manual laborers also grew during the early nineteenth century. The building of canals, roads, and railroads furnished employment to thousands of men. So did the unparalleled rate of construction in towns and cities. Expanding populations needed more streets, houses, shops, and factories. Carters, porters, warehousemen, dockworkers, sailors, and boatmen loaded, transported, unloaded, and stored the commodities that created rising mercantile fortunes.

Although the labor for all these tasks was considered unskilled, in an age before power-driven machinery it entailed heavy exertion, often under harsh conditions. As Erie Canal construction workers sang,

Free Labor and Slavery

We are digging the ditch through the mire;
Through the mud and the slime and the mire, by heck!
And the mud is our principal hire;
Up our pants, in our shirts, down our neck, by heck!

In winter, canal laborers "had to work in the water, and sometimes in the ice." In summer, digging through swamps and marshes exposed them to leeches, mosquitoes, and disease. Living conditions were wretched. Workers lived in tents or rough shanties, which one observer described as "more like dog-kennels than the habitations of men"—poorly built, scantily furnished, and little protection against harsh weather.

After 1820 unskilled day laborers' wage rates rose about twelve percent each decade in real terms, but for many reasons this rise often failed to produce incomes much above bare subsistence. Streams of migrants from rural districts and from Europe fed the pool of available workers. By the 1830s most canal laborers were Irish. Wage payments were often irregular, or in the form of "truck"—goods or credit at an overpriced company store. Many unskilled jobs were irregular or seasonal. The aver-

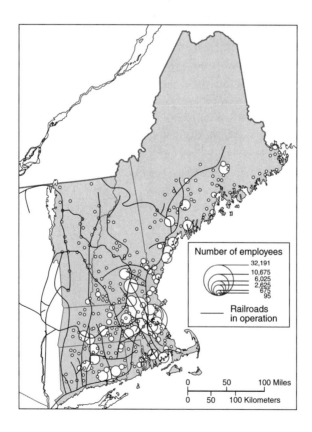

Industrial Workers in New England, 1850. The map shows the widespread distribution of factories and workshops across New England, and their presence in small rural centers as well as large towns and cities. The circles represent concentrations (large and small) of workers, female and male, from machine operatives to skilled craftsmen

Source: D. W. Meinig, *The Shaping of America: A Geographical Perspective on 500 Years of History,* vol. 2, *Continental America, 1800–1867* (1993).

Number of employees

— 32,191
— 10,675
— 6,025
— 2,625
— 675
— 95

—— Railroads in operation

0   50   100 Miles
0   50   100 Kilometers

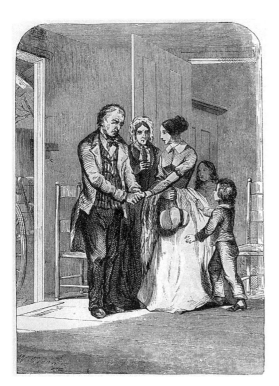

"Starting for Lowell." An illustration from T. S. Arthur's reform tract *Illustrated Temperance Tales* (1850) presented a young woman leaving her farm family to work in a cotton mill. This picture was accurate in showing that New England farm families often had to rely on income from factory labor. But reformers blamed economic hardship on personal weaknesses—in the case of Arthur's story, the father's alcoholism.

Source: Timothy Shay Arthur, "The Factory Girl," *Illustrated Temperance Tales* (1850)—American Social History Project.

age day laborer found work only two hundred days a year. Large construction projects were handled by contractors who bid for jobs "as low as labor and capital can afford," and hired workers for as little as they could. Not infrequently, contractors went bankrupt and fled without paying workers the wages they had earned.

Irregular employment and low wages for unskilled laborers put a premium on increasing family income. Laborers' wives and children worked to help fill minimal everyday needs. Many women labored as outworkers or took in boarders. Small children sought jobs in factories, as errand runners, and in casual work of all kinds. In towns and cities, daughters hired out as live-in domestic servants for money wages averaging a dollar a week or less besides room and board.

As factories grew in number and size, they became another major source of wage work. Large, heavily capitalized mills, such as those of the Waltham–Lowell system, had to attract workers in sizable numbers. Many of Lowell's first women workers were the daughters of farmers. Rural economic change both pushed them out of their parents' homes and attracted them to factory work, typically for periods from a few months to a few years. By the 1830s most were from northern New England, where farming households were hardest pressed. Although not drawn from the poorest families, mill women had nonetheless experienced hard times at home. Often sisters would follow one another to work for periods in the mills. The Fowler family, who owned a small farm in Boscawen, New Hampshire, had five daughters, four of whom worked in a Lowell mill at different times between 1831 and 1842.

Women hoped that a stint of factory work would give them cultural opportunities and the chance to earn a dowry that impoverished farm life denied them. Although early wages for the young, unmarried Yankee women who came from the countryside to Lowell's mills and boarding houses were lower than those for male laborers, they were better than those available to women workers in any other industry. Mary Paul of Barnard, Vermont, worked in her early teens as a domestic servant and boarded with nearby relatives before seeking her father's consent for her to work in Lowell. "I think it would be better for me than to stay out here," she wrote him. "I am in need of clothes which I cannot get about

"... I Am a Factory Girl"

This letter, written in April 1839 by Malenda M. Edwards to her niece Sabrina Bennett, illustrates several aspects of factory work for young New England women. Malenda Edwards was twenty-nine years old, but still referred to herself as a "factory girl." She came from the rural town of Bristol, New Hampshire, where she had done farm and household work, and had recently joined her sister to work in a textile mill seventy miles away in Nashua. Family and acquaintanceship structured many women's factory experience, and may—as in this case—have helped reconcile them to the work. Friends and relatives played an important role in finding both employment and places to live. Malenda Edwards worked in Nashua for about seven years, alternating spells in the mills with looking after her aging parents at home in Bristol.

Dear Sabrina,

I have nothing special to write you but Persis has commenced a letter [and] I will try and think of something [even] if it is not so very interesting. You have been informed I supose that I am a factory girl and that I am at Nashua and I have wished you were here too but I suppose your mother would think it far beneith your dignity to be a factory girl. Their are very many young Ladies at work in the factories that have given up milinary d[r]essmaking & s[c]hool keeping for to work in the mill. But I would not advise any one to do it for I was so sick of it at first I wished a factory had never been thought of. But the longer I stay the better I like [it] and I think if nothing unforesene calls me away I shall stay here till fall. Persis has told you that the folks at Bristol were all well but sister Bryant and I fear if she does not get help soon she never will be any better. Your uncle Frisbies folks have moved to New York where his Brother lives. Your uncle [Daniel] Sandborn has buried his father he died the 4 of March. Give my respects to your fathers folks and except [sic] much love your self from me. Write soon and write me all the news you can think. I want to hear from Haverhill. Write too where you are and what you are doing and what you intend to do this summer. My health is very poor indeed but it is better than it was when I left home. If you should have any idea of working in the factory I will do the best I can to get you a place with us. We have an excelent boarding place. We board with a family with whome I was acquainted with when I lived at Haverhill. Pleas to write as soon and believe your affectionate Aunt

M[alenda] M. Edwards

Source: Thomas Dublin, ed., *Farm to Factory: Women's Letters, 1830–1860* (1981).

394

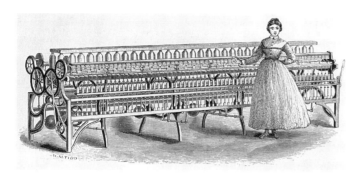

The Latest Model. A mill woman stands in unlikely repose beside a Fale and Jenks spinning frame in this promotional engraving. The benign relationship of the figure to the machine may have served to reassure nineteenth-century observers that factory work would not debase "virtuous womanhood."

Source: James Geldard, *Handbook on Cotton Manufacture . . .* (New York, 1867)—Rare Books and Manuscript Division, New York Public Library, Astor, Lenox and Tilden Foundations.

here and for that reason I want to go to Lowell or some other place." Some young women felt that factory work offered them a degree of independence that they had not previously enjoyed. Sally Rice of Somerset, Vermont, had hired out as a farm worker in New York State, but found farm life exhausting and isolating. She wrote to her parents that she wanted to find work in a Connecticut textile mill: "I am most 19 years old. I must of course have something of my own before many more years have passed over my head. And where is that something coming from if I go home and earn nothing?"

Work in the Lowell mills, never easy, grew harder over time. In the 1820s, the average operative worked twelve hours a day, six days a week. Holidays were few and short: July Fourth, Thanksgiving, and the first day of spring. Still, the need to ensure that women would stay in the mills for four or five years required tolerable working and housing conditions. Fair conditions were affordable because the first large mills earned substantial profits. From 1814 to 1825, the Boston Manufacturing Company (owners of the Waltham mill) paid its shareholders dividends of twenty percent each year. However, the opening of new firms meant increasing competition in textiles. By the mid 1830s Lowell operatives found conditions worsening, as wages were cut, boarding-house rents raised, or workloads increased. Twice, in 1834 and again in 1836, women took strike action to resist the changes.

Working People Resist Capitalism

With the growth of wage labor, controversies arose from the very principles underlying republicanism. Workers of all sorts—male journeymen and laborers, as well as female factory operatives and outworkers—resisted the subordinate positions assigned to them. From the mid 1820s to the late 1830s there was a tide of protest and political action by working people, who asserted their rights and equal participation as citizens under circumstances in which economic power was unequally distributed. New political parties, a new network of labor journals and newspapers, trade unions, and spontaneous actions by workers all carried forward campaigns against the emerging capitalist economic arrangements.

"No. 5 & 7 Looms Stopped — No Weavers. . ."

Finding and disciplining an adequate supply of competent weavers plagued early textile-mill managers. N. B. Gordon managed a small woolen mill in rural Massachusetts. The daily entries in his 1829 diary reveal recurring problems of absenteeism, unpredictable natural conditions, and poor production standards.

January

  5: One weaver sick, four looms stopped. Water wheel froze up this morning. Took until 8 o'clock to start it.

  6: One weaver still sick. Four looms stopped. Water failed some about 4 o'clock.

  8: Last night and yesterday warm, which gave plenty of water this day for all hands. One weaver sick. Four looms stopped.

  13: 6 weavers—2 looms stopped. One weaver sick. Sally and Mary Ann Leonard out $^3/_4$ of the day by permission.

  14: Looms all in operation.

  16: Fine warm day. Almira Lowell absent this day and also to be tomorrow, to bury her grandmother. P.M. went to Mr. Carver's to get harness made.

March

  23: No. 4 weaver absent $^1/_2$ day. No 5 and 6—$^1/_4$ day each. Extreme cold. Lovell's children did not get in until $^1/_2$ past 7 A.M. on account of water on the road.

  24: Mr. Thayer's party last night broke up 3 o'clock. Morning hands in consequence come in late, and one, No. 6 weaver, not until noon. H. Kingman commenced repairing the old looms.

April

  18: No. 6 loom stopped, no weaver. No. 5 weaver quit.

  19: Went to Norton after weavers.

  21: No. 5 & 7 looms stopped—no weavers. New spinning badly tended.

Source: Gary Kulik, Roger Parks, and Theodore Z. Penn, eds., *The New England Mill Village, 1790–1860* (1982).

These efforts took two main forms. First, working people sought political measures to restrain the accumulation of power and wealth by a few capitalists, and to keep alive the republican vision of a society in which all could aspire to economic independence. They won some tangible gains through the political system that enhanced their political and economic rights. When the main parties declined to make concessions to them,

Bells, Bells, Bells. The mill workers' day in 1853, as dictated by the managers of the Lowell Mills.

Source: American Textile History Museum.

TIME TABLE OF THE LOWELL MILLS,

Arranged to make the working time throughout the year average 11 hours per day.

TO TAKE EFFECT SEPTEMBER 21st., 1853.

The Standard time being that of the meridian of Lowell, as shown by the Regulator Clock of AMOS SANBORN, Post Office Corner, Central Street.

From March 20th to September 19th, inclusive.

COMMENCE WORK, at 6.30 A. M.   LEAVE OFF WORK, at 6.30 P. M., except on Saturday Evenings.
BREAKFAST at 6 A. M.   DINNER, at 12 M.   Commence Work, after dinner, 12.45 P. M.

From September 20th to March 19th, inclusive.

COMMENCE WORK at 7.00 A. M.   LEAVE OFF WORK, at 7.00 P. M., except on Saturday Evenings.
BREAKFAST at 6.30 A. M.   DINNER, at 12.30 P.M.   Commence Work, after dinner, 1.15 P. M.

BELLS.

From March 20th to September 19th, inclusive.

Morning Bells.	Dinner Bells.	Evening Bells.
First bell,..........4.30 A. M.	Ring out,..........12.00 M.	Ring out,..........6.30 P. M.
Second, 5.30 A. M. ; Third, 6.20.	Ring in,..........12 35 P. M.	Except on Saturday Evenings.

From September 20th to March 19th, inclusive.

Morning Bells.	Dinner Bells.	Evening Bells.
First bell,..........5.00 A. M.	Ring out,..........12.30 P. M.	Ring out at..........7.00 P. M.
Second, 6.00 A. M. ; Third, 6.50.	Ring in,..........1.05 P. M.	Except on Saturday Evenings.

SATURDAY EVENING BELLS.

During APRIL, MAY, JUNE, JULY, and AUGUST, Ring Out, at 6.00 P. M.
The remaining Saturday Evenings in the year, ring out as follows :

SEPTEMBER.	NOVEMBER.	JANUARY.
First Saturday, ring out 6.00 P. M.	Third Saturday ring out 4.00 P. M.	Third Saturday, ring out 4.25 P. M.
Second " " 5.45 "	Fourth " " 3.55 "	Fourth " " 4.35 "
Third " " 5.30 "		
Fourth " " 5.20 "	**DECEMBER.**	**FEBRUARY.**
	First Saturday, ring out 3.50 P. M.	First Saturday, ring out 4.45 P. M.
OCTOBER.	Second " " 3.55 "	Second " " 4.55 "
First Saturday, ring out 5.05 P. M.	Third " " 3.55 "	Third " " 5.00 "
Second " " 4.55 "	Fourth " " 4.00 "	Fourth " " 5.10 "
Third " " 4.45 "	Fifth " " 4.00 "	
Fourth " " 4.35 "		**MARCH.**
Fifth " " 4.25 "		First Saturday, ring out 5.25 P. M.
NOVEMBER.	**JANUARY.**	Second " " 5.30 "
First Saturday, ring out 4.15 P. M.	First Saturday, ring out 4.10 P. M.	Third " " 5.35 "
Second " · " 4.05 "	Second " " 4.15 "	Fourth " " 5.45 "

YARD GATES will be opened at the first stroke of the bells for entering or leaving the Mills.

SPEED GATES commence hoisting three minutes before commencing work.

Penhallow, Printer, Wyman's Exchange, 28 Merrimack St.

working people organized parties, formulated programs, and ran candidates of their own. Secondly, journeymen and workers in large workshops or factories took steps outside party-political channels to defend or improve their wages, conditions, and working hours. They marched, protested, and made demands on their employers that they often backed by strikes.

These two strands of action embodied different forms of consciousness. When they took political action, workers often allied with small masters or proprietors, implying that the groups had common interests.

PROCESSION OF VICTUALLERS

"Procession of Victuallers." A commemorative lithograph shows butchers parading in the streets of Philadelphia in 1821. Their costumes, floats, and banners (including one in the center with the motto "We Feed the Hungry") displayed symbols of the butchers' trade.
Source: Joseph Yeager (after John Lewis Krimmel), 1821, aquatint and etching with watercolor, 14 3/8 × 23 3/4 inches—Gift of the Estate of Charles M. B. Cadwallader, Philadelphia Museum of Art.

In industrial protests, workers were pitted against their employers, suggesting an emerging struggle between labor and capital. But in both cases the republican vision of equality generated by the Revolution served as a reference point for working people seeking to assert their rights.

The Workingmen's Movement

The movement to create Workingmen's parties arose in Philadelphia around 1827 out of a short-lived union of mechanics' associations. It spread quickly to other major cities, including Boston and New York, and to scores of rural districts and smaller towns. The *Albany Advocate* declared, "Throughout this vast republic, the farmers, mechanics, and workingmen are assembling . . . to impart to its laws and administration those principles of liberty and equality unfolded in the Declaration of our Independence." Thomas Skidmore, a self-educated New York City machinist, wrote a radical prescription for a Workingmen's policy. In *The Rights of Man to Property,* published in 1829, he argued that the poor and

". . . This Monopoly Should Be Broken Up"

Workingmen's parties attacked monopolies. Like the Philadelphia Working-men's Committee which published this report in 1830, many condemned the in-equality between the education available to those who could afford it, and the lack of provision for the poor. They advocated the adoption of free public schooling in their states, as a means of promoting "general and equal educa-tion" and "equal knowledge" as a step toward achieving "equal liberty."

THE ORIGINAL ELEMENT of despotism is a monopoly of talent, which consigns the multi-tude to comparative ignorance, and secures the balance of knowledge on the side of the rich and the rulers. If then the healthy existence of a free government be, as the commit-tee believe, rooted in the will of the American people, it follows as a necessary conse-quence, of a government based upon that will, that this monopoly should be broken up, and that the means of equal knowledge (the only security for equal liberty) should be rendered, by legal provision, the common property of all classes. . . .

It appears, therefore, to the committee that there can be no real liberty without a wide diffusion of real intelligence; that the members of a republic should all be alike in-structed in the nature and character of their equal rights and duties, as human beings and as citizens; and that education, instead of being limited, as in our public poor schools, to a simple acquaintance with words and cyphers, should tend, as far as possi-ble, to the production of a just disposition, virtuous habits, and a rational self-governing character.

When the committee contemplate their own condition, and that of the great mass of their fellow laborers, when they look around on the glaring inequality of society, they are constrained to believe that until the means of equal instruction shall be equally secured to all, liberty is but an unmeaning word, and equality an empty shadow, whose sub-stance to be realized must first be planted by an equal education and proper training in the minds, in the habits, in the manners, and in the feelings of the community.

Source: *Working Men's Advocate*, March 6, 1830.

other "friends of equal rights" should win control of government and re-distribute property equally among all adults, including women and slaves. If inheritance were abolished, equality could be maintained over genera-tions. Society would have "no lenders, no borrowers; no landlords, no tenants; no masters, no journeymen; no Wealth, no Want," and indepen-dent self-employment would become general.

"No More Grinding the POOR—But Liberty and the Rights of Man." An engraving printed around 1830 depicted the forces of monopoly attempting to undermine the workingman's vote. While the devil offered an aristocrat the support of his "favourite" newspapers "to grind the WORKIES," a mechanic placed his faith in the suffrage.

Source: Kilroe Collection, Butler Library, Columbia University.

Although Skidmore helped launch it, the New York Workingmen's movement adopted much more modest proposals, typical of Workingmen's party platforms elsewhere. These included the abolition of paper money, the passage of a homestead law to provide free land in the West, and some of the earliest calls for publicly funded schooling. By the early 1830s, groups in New England, New York, and Pennsylvania were fielding candidates who pledged to abolish imprisonment for debt, to give mechanics the means to enforce payment for their work, and to resist the encroachment of banks and corporations on economic activity. Workingmen condemned legislation that granted "exclusive privileges" to a wealthy elite, and acted to oppose "exclusive monopolies" that could undermine the independence of farmers and artisans. Their electoral success was modest, but sufficient to jolt the major parties into adopting many of their policies. Unable to withstand this competition, most of the Workingmen's parties dissolved during the 1830s, many of their leaders affiliating with the Democrats and a few with the Whigs. But the end of their electoral challenge by no means erased the economic conflicts or the hopes that had given rise to it.

Strikes and Protests

In 1838 fifty-one journeymen carriage-makers from small Massachusetts workshops protested a proposed law that would have incorporated a large carriage-building firm. They argued that this would block their aspirations to become proprietors in their own right. Although they currently worked for others, "We . . . do look forward with anticipation to a time when we shall be able to conduct the business upon our own responsibility and receive the profits of our labor, which we now relinquish to others." Large incorporated businesses, they argued, would destroy the republican ideal: "we believe that incorporated bodies tend to crush all feeble enterprise and compel us to work out our days in the Service of others."

As the petitioners knew, a growing number of journeymen and other wage workers had little or no chance of achieving propertied independence. To gain any benefits from republican citizenship they needed reasonable wages and working conditions. Philadelphia journeymen house carpenters noted that "in this favored nation we enjoy the inestimable blessing of 'universal suffrage,' and constituting, as we everywhere do, a very great majority, we have the power to choose our own legislators." However "this blessing . . . can be of no further benefit to us" unless "we possess sufficient knowledge to make proper use of it." To acquire knowledge, workers needed more time to read, think, and discuss—and less time chained to the workbench. In 1827 they struck in support of a demand that their working day be shortened from twelve hours to ten. Antagonism between masters and journeymen, employers and employees continued to deepen during the 1830s, causing an unprecedented mobilization of trade unions and labor protest.

The issue of working hours sparked heated conflict. To protect their profits in 1824, Pawtucket mill owners tried to extend the workday and cut piece rates. Led by women weavers and supported by neighbors and townsfolk, workers went on strike to resist the changes. When, in 1828 and 1829, it was rumored that New York employers were about to extend the workday from ten hours to eleven, mass meetings of journeymen and their supporters denounced the proposal as a selfish assault on the rights of republican citizens. A crowd of five or six thousand workers threatened to strike against any boss insisting on more than ten hours, and the employers backed down.

Wages were a more frequent source of friction, and often the basis on which labor unions could organize. Despite their relative isolation in the

outwork system, sixteen hundred women joined the New York Tailoresses' Society, founded in 1831, to fight a series of wage cuts imposed by
merchants and contractors. In 1833 journeymen carpenters in the city
struck for higher wages, winning a month-long campaign.

Wage issues also enabled otherwise divided workers to cooperate
with one another. The New York carpenters obtained the support of organizations in fifteen other trades, and the printers' union president John
Finch noted that their success underscored the "necessity of combined efforts for the purpose of self-protection." Finch's union issued a call for all
organized trades to unite in a citywide federation of craft unions. Journeymen's organizations in nine trades attended the first convention of
New York's General Trades Union (GTU), and three more sent messages
of support. In 1834, a GTU parade that also included associations from
Newark, New Jersey, stretched for a mile and a half. The GTU aided
strikes over wages or conditions among bakers, hatters, ropemakers, sailmakers, weavers, and leatherworkers, not only in New York, but in
Newark, Poughkeepsie, Boston, and Philadelphia as well.

Radical printer and former Workingmen's Party leader George
Henry Evans urged that such mutual support should become general, so
that "[t]he rights of each individual would then be sustained by every
workingman in the country, whose aggregate wealth and power would be
able to resist the most formidable oppression." A convention in August
1834 formed the National Trades Union (NTU), with delegates representing over 25,000 workers. Although never truly national in extent and
limited in its influence, the NTU nevertheless aided a labor upsurge in the
next few years that spawned at least sixty new unions and called more
than a hundred strikes.

Such organization across trades and regions was largely restricted to
male workers in skilled occupations. But militancy was not limited to
these groups. Women workers, as we have seen, took strike action in their
own behalf. When competition drove Lowell mill owners to cut wages in
1834, hundreds of women struck in protest, in a "turn-out" that involved
one-sixth of the Lowell workforce. Their action failed: the companies recruited other rural women to tend the machines and within a week most
mills were operating near capacity. But two years later the Lowell employers raised rents in their boarding houses, provoking a more
widespread and better-organized response from women operatives, who
stayed out on strike until the increases were cancelled or reduced.

Female strikers asserted, almost two decades before the birth of a
formal women's rights movement, the right of women to defend their interests in a society that denied them political participation or a public
voice. New York Tailoresses' leader Sarah Monroe asked "if it is unfashionable for the men to bear oppression in silence, why should it not also

become unfashionable with the women?" In 1833 women shoebinders from Lynn and neighboring towns formed their own protective organization. They drew on the Declaration of Independence and the Constitution to proclaim that "Women as well as men have certain inalienable rights, among which is the right at all times of 'peaceably assembling to consult upon the common good,'" Lowell women asserted their own independence. They warned that the mill owners' "oppressive hand of avarice would enslave us," and rebuffed the owners' assurances that those in need could turn to charity. "We prefer to have the disposing of our charities in our own hands; and as we are free, we would remain in possession of what kind Providence has bestowed upon us; and remain daughters of freemen still."

Although some male unions supported women workers' campaigns, the labor movement generally remained hostile to women. The NTU's committee on female labor held that "the physical organization, the natural responsibilities, and the moral sensibility of women prove conclusively that their labors should be only of a domestic nature." Most men regarded women's employment as an attack on their own independence and dignity as providers, as weakening the family by leading women away from their proper domestic roles, and as threatening to undercut their own wages rates.

Craft workers had little interest in supporting laborers either, but unskilled workers, like women, organized on their own behalf, initially with little trade union support. Canal laborers struck on at least four occasions in the 1820s and another fourteen times in the 1830s. Irish laborers on the Chesapeake and Ohio and other canals formed secret societies to defend wages and conditions, fighting off men who refused to join, or who were hired by the companies to break the societies' influence. A pitched battle on the C and O in January 1834 was suppressed by a detachment of federal troops. But four years later, when the company failed to pay wages and laborers destroyed the work they had not been paid for, militiamen called out to quell them refused to march, declaring their sympathy with the workers. Urban laborers, such as dockers in New York in 1828, and various maritime workers there in 1834, stopped work in response to layoffs and wage cuts.

Further strikes by New York laborers, riggers, and dockworkers in 1836 took place against the background of a tailors' strike and were suppressed by police and militia. This initiated collaboration between laborers and craftsmen, even to talk of a general strike. The previous year Philadelphia coalheavers had brought about the first general strike in American history when they walked off the docks to demand shorter hours; shoemakers and other craftsmen joined their march through the city

"By Hammer and Hand All Arts Do Stand." The artisan's symbol adorned an announcement in New York's General Trades' Union newspaper, *The Union,* calling for a demonstration to support union tailors convicted of conspiracy in 1836.

Source: *The Union,* June 14, 1836—Rare Books and Manuscript Division, New York Public Library, Astor, Lenox and Tilden Foundations.

A Voice from the People!

"When We for Freedom Strike at Length . . ."

This song, "The Temperance Strike," was printed for a Fourth of July celebration during the Philadelphia general strike of 1835, the first citywide general strike in American history. Workers were seeking to limit the length of the working day, but their song reflects their commitment to freeing themselves from the effects of "demon rum," as well as oppressive working conditions. This combination of social rebellion and self-reform would remain a feature of working people's movements. Here they are explicitly linked to the revolutionary tradition.

His chains the tyrant rum, too long
Has tried to cast around us.
Shall not Mechanics prove too strong,
When any would confound us?
We shall! we shall! we feel our strength
And who no sword will draw,
When we for freedom strike at length?
Hurrah! hurrah! hurrah!

Our Fathers—who may see their like?—
When trodden down as cattle,
For liberty knew how to strike,
And win the righteous battle!
And shall their sons be slaves to drink?
O never! never! Nor
Will Working Men like cowards shrink,
No, boys!—hurrah! hurrah!

The pledge to Temperance we renew
For she is Freedom's Daughter—
In generous draughts of mountain dew,
In cold and limpid water!
Strike hands with us!—for wine like this
The toper never saw;
E'en Woman's lip such cup may kiss
Unstained, hurrah! hurrah!

Some strike for wages, some for hours,
Shall we refuse—O never!
For time and cash we pledge our powers,
And strike for both for ever!
Then strike who will for "6 to 6,"
We flinch not in the war;
For Temperance and for '76
We strike—hurrah! hurrah!

Source: Bruce Laurie, *Working People of Philadelphia, 1800—1850* (1980).

streets. The strike quickly spread to other trades, even to textile workers and outworkers, before employers conceded shorter hours, the laborers gained a wage increase, and a city ordinance made ten hours the legal working day on public projects. Cooperation between skilled and unskilled workers continued, and in 1836 the Philadelphia General Trades Union, which had previously refused admission to the laborers' union, voted to allow laborers into its ranks — the first time skilled workers reached across the gap that had separated them from the unskilled.

Two Outlooks: Morality or the Market?

In supporting striking workers, the NTU insisted that in a republican society a citizen's conduct and the "value of all social institutions" had to be judged by standards of "moral justice" rather than according to profitability, supply, and demand. Pursuit of private profit, the NTU argued, had undermined "the social, civil, and intellectual condition of the laboring classes," and resulted in "the most unequal and unjustifiable distribution of the wealth of society in the hands of a few individuals." That, in turn, imposed upon working people "a humiliating, servile dependency, incompatible with . . . natural equality" and "subversive of the rights of man."

The claims and actions of organized workers outraged many merchants and employers. They retaliated, citing an alternative view of republican order that identified moral justice with the free play of the market — a market in which labor was merely a commodity like any other. "The true regulator of prices," held the New York *Journal of Commerce,* "whether of labor, goods, real estate, or anything else, is demand." Certainly, the editor agreed, "we wish to see all men, mechanics as well as others, receive an adequate compensation for their labor." But collective action was "at war with the order of things which the Creator has established for the general good." In trade unions and strikes, he advised, the best and most skilled workingmen — "whose wages would go up . . . if they would but go on their own merits" — suffered needlessly because they aided in "lifting up the unworthy, [even] though they sink themselves."

These outlooks — one demanding that economic life conform to republican principles, the other insisting that life in the republic be regulated by the marketplace — clashed head-on in New York in 1836. Over the previous two years, price inflation had proven catastrophic for working people, driving shoemakers, carpenters, cabinetmakers, weavers, and others to strike for higher wages. New York employers decided to make an example of the journeymen tailors' association, in part because it was one of the strongest unions in the city. Early in the year, masters and merchant tailors repudiated the pay scale previously negoti-

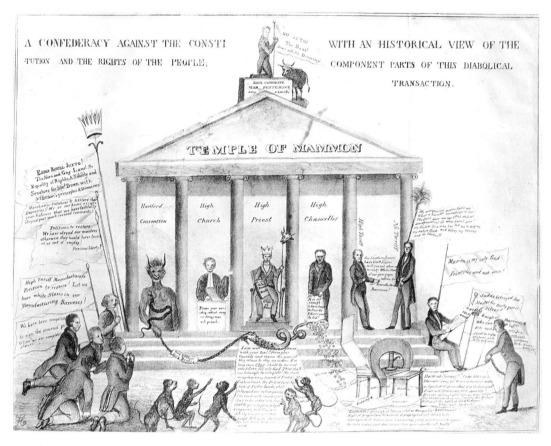

"A Confederacy Against the Constitution and the Rights of the People."

ated, and agreed with each other not to hire union members. Journeymen picketed the shops of the masters and sought to discourage other journeymen from taking their places. A grand jury, however, labeled this conduct "conspiracy"—a criminal offense under a state law of 1829 prohibiting collective action "to commit any act injurious to public morals or to trade and commerce."

At trial in May, twenty of the indicted tailors were found guilty. Judge Ogden Edwards imposed stiff fines and lectured them on the error of their ways, echoing the opinions of the city's employers and antilabor newspapers. In this "favored land of law and liberty, the road to advancement is open to all," Edwards explained, "and the journeymen may by their skill and industry and moral worth soon become flourishing master mechanics." Unions, he claimed, were by nature alien to American society "and . . . mainly upheld by foreigners." This attack on the right to organize and strike provoked massive protest. Twenty-seven thousand people—more than one tenth of New York's entire population—

"A Confederacy Against the Constitution and the Rights of the People." A typically busy 1830s cartoon denounced monopoly and privilege. On the right side of the "Temple of Mammon," a northern manufacturer conspired with a southern planter: "You Southern Barons have black Slaves; will you not allow us to make white Slaves of our poor population in our Manufacturing Baronies?"

Source: Anonymous, 1833, lithograph—Library Company of Philadelphia.

"The Rich Against the Poor!"

Shortly after the striking tailors were convicted, a placard appeared in various parts of New York City. Its text was printed within the outline of a coffin, signifying the "coffin of equality." Below are excerpts from that text. The Common Council promptly offered a reward for the apprehension of the anonymous author of this "Coffin Handbill."

THE RICH AGAINST the Poor! Judge Edwards, the tool of the Aristocracy, against the People! Mechanics and Workingmen! A deadly blow has been struck at your Liberty! The prize for which your fathers fought has been robbed from you! The Freemen of the North are now on a level with the Slaves of the South! with no other privileges than laboring that drones may fatten on your lifeblood! Twenty of your brethren have been found guilty for presuming to resist a reduction of their wages! and Judge Edwards has charged an American jury, and agreeably to that charge, they have established the precedent, that workingmen have no right to regulate the price of labor! or, in other words, the Rich are the only judges of the wants of the Poor Man!

Source: New York *Courier and Enquirer,* June 8, 1836.

attended a rally endorsed by the GTU. The crowd burned Judge Edwards in effigy, invoked the traditions of 1776, and branded the trial "a concerted plan of the aristocracy to take from them that Liberty which was bequeathed to them as a sacred inheritance by their revolutionary sires." The court's principles were "utterly at variance with the spirit and genius of our Republican government." Although Judge Edwards claimed that in a republic workers were free to advance themselves, workers argued that their ability to organize would restore republican rights undermined by class division and social inequality.

This conception of workingmen's rights, however, was increasingly confined to white men. There was a small prosperous black middle class in the Northeast, but most African Americans faced segregation and job discrimination that held them in relative poverty. By the 1820s they were excluded from many occupations, even those with long traditions of black participation. In Philadelphia the number of black artisans fell by more than one quarter between 1832 and 1837 alone, and even black seamen declined in number. An observer claimed that there were no black workmen in many New York City trades, and that Boston had only a handful. Whites hostile to black workers rioted in Providence in 1831,

"A Militia Drill Thirty Years Ago." Congress authorized universal military duty for all males, but inequalities in the system led to calls for reform. The Workingmen's Party in Pennsylvania and New York attacked privately organized elite units whose members' costly uniforms and elaborate ceremonies displayed their wealth and connections. The aristocratic pretensions of "private" units contrasted with the ragtag appearance of "public," neighborhood militias (remembered here in an 1862 lithograph). Public militia service was a financial burden: members lost wages to attend drills and risked fines if they were absent or violated dress codes.

Source: David Claypoole Johnston, 1862, lithograph, 10 7/8 × 16 inches—American Antiquarian Society.

and in Philadelphia in 1834, driving many African Americans out of their homes. Black workers of both sexes were increasingly confined to service or heavy laboring jobs, but even domestic servants found themselves displaced by European immigrant women. In Philadelphia, for instance, over half of black women workers by 1837 were washerwomen. Few black workmen joined labor organizations because they rarely worked in organized trades, and would often have been met with hostility.

Depression and Crisis in Northern Society

A severe economic slump, starting with a financial crisis in 1837, wiped out much of the organized labor movement and marked a deeper crisis in the North's emerging wage labor economy. As with the slump of 1819, its roots were partly international. A fall in the price of cotton in Europe caused some brokerage firms to fail and prompted the Bank of England to call in American loans. This sparked a panic in New York and other eastern cities. Banks collapsed and thousands of businesses and individuals were ruined. Recovery proved difficult. By 1839, the northern economy was sliding into a depression that would last into the mid 1840s. Commerce and transportation declined, most construction ceased, and goods went unsold. Countless businesses folded, including many manufacturing operations, both large and small, scattered across the rural and urban

Northeast. Most of New York City's large clothing firms and many of its metal foundries were wiped out. Even firms whose products were in high demand, such as the printing press manufacturer R. Hoe and Company, were caught out by the financial disruption, failed, and laid off their employees. In all the main centers of industry and commerce, many workingmen and -women abruptly found themselves without work or income of any kind.

In Lynn thousands of shoemakers were jobless, and the wages of those still employed were cut in half. The poor in Philadelphia were reported to be "dying of want." A committee of Boston citizens tried to drive the unemployed out of the city. In New York City, an estimated fifty thousand people — more than a third of the total labor force — were thrown out of work. At least as many again were reduced to working part-time or at drastically reduced wages. When a notice appeared offering rural employment for twenty laborers at four dollars a month plus board (one-quarter of the usual wage), five hundred men applied. As conditions worsened, growing numbers of the poor were forced to live in cramped buildings, as one report put it, "crowded beneath mouldering, water-rotted roofs, or burrowed among rats in clammy cellars." More than seven thousand people were living in New York City cellars by 1842 and their numbers were rising fast.

The labor movement plunged into crisis. In contrast to their resistance in 1834 and 1836, Lowell factory women put up no organized protest against wage cuts between 1837 and 1843. With so many jobs lost and so many people desperate for work at any pay, strike threats quickly lost their effect, and most unions dissolved. For employers, this was the depression's silver lining. A hat manufacturer boasted that his workers were now free of "the moral gangrene of Trades Union principles" and "the inconveniences" and "injustice" of "regular combinations and periodical strikes." The *Journal of Commerce* urged proprietors to "employ no men who do not forever abjure the unions." The opportunity had now arrived, the editor noted, to eradicate labor organizations, and "it should be done thoroughly."

Hardship helped employers extinguish the new labor organizations, but it also fanned the flames of antibusiness sentiment. In 1837 a flour riot in New York reflected popular conceptions of justice handed down from the revolutionary period. A meeting of four to five thousand angry, hungry people heard speakers denounce landlords and high rents, along with merchants holding back food from starving neighbors. One speaker announced that the commission merchants Hart and Co. had many thousands of barrels of flour at their store, and suggested that the crowd "go and offer him eight dollars a barrel for it" — a figure below the market rate, but deemed just by the public. As crowds had done in the

The Theater of Artisan Republicanism. After the depression and collapse of the Workingmen's Party, insurgent "shirtless" Democrats in New York City challenged their political party's conservative leadership. Laborers, journeymen, and small master-craftsmen gathered around the charismatic figure of Mike Walsh, an Irish immigrant artisan and newspaper editor, who combined rough street tactics with provocative calls for social reform. Part of Walsh's appeal derived from a calculated public image that owed a lot to styles of performance in working-class theater. In this engraving from a collection of his speeches, Walsh struck a standard actor's pose.

Source: (S. H. Gimber), Michael Walsh, *Sketches of the Speeches and Writings of Mike Walsh . . . Compiled by a Committee of the Spartan Association* (1843)—New-York Historical Society.

eighteenth-century, the New Yorkers went to extract economic justice from an individual more powerful than they.

Rioters were met at the store by police and by the mayor with an appeal to disperse, but they chased the authorities away, broke into the store, and seized the flour barrels. After the police returned with state militia and made arrests, the crowd regrouped to rescue the prisoners. Rioters were eventually broken up, but had made their point: a depression might undermine labor organizations, but it would not reconcile working people to the absolute rule of the marketplace. Alternative conceptions of popular rights and community justice retained their strength.

"Whoever looks at the world as it is now," Thomas Skidmore had written in 1829, "will see it divided into two distinct classes: proprietors, and non-proprietors; those who own the world, and those who own no part of it. If we take a closer view of these two classes, we shall find that a

"The Times." The ravages of the depression were cataloged and blamed on the Jackson administration in this 1837 lithograph by a Whig printmaker. In the foreground, a family descended into alcoholism, a mother and child begged for charity, and unemployed workers stood about. In the background, citizens lined up outside a pawnbroker's establishment, while others made a run on a bank. Signs all around announced the devaluation of currency and lack of credit. Above the dismal scene shone Andrew Jackson's well-known beaver hat, spectacles, and clay pipe.

Source: Henry R. Robinson (after a drawing by Edward W. Clay), 1837, lithograph, 19 × 12 inches — J. Clarence Davies Collection, Museum of the City of New York.

very great proportion even of the proprietors are only nominally so; they possess so little that in strict regard to truth they ought to be classed among the non-proprietors." Growth in commerce, productivity, and total output seemed only to deepen the chasm between rich and poor and further erode values of mutual assistance and community rights. Depression and the hardship to which it led further undermined working peoples' ability to share in the products of their own labor.

Depression brought the wage system itself under critical scrutiny. "No one can observe the signs of the times with much care," wrote

Bostonian Orestes Brownson, "without perceiving that a crisis as to the relation of wealth and labor is approaching." The source of the social conflict Brownson anticipated was the whole "system of labor at wages." If America were truly to become a society grounded in equality, he concluded, "there must be no class of our fellow men doomed to toil through life as mere workmen at wages."

The North in the 1820s and 1830s had witnessed a crucial modification of the post-revolutionary republican conception of personal "independence" and its role in citizenship. Laboring men continued to uphold their claim to the respect due independent citizens, but they rejected the old idea that political participation should be restricted to those with property. As supporters of Workingmen's parties or the mainstream parties, they asserted the dignity of labor and condemned the notion that power should belong to an "aristocracy" of wealthy or professional men. Some laboring women in the 1830s claimed the same rights to respect and independence that laboring men did. Their criticism of "aristocracy" led some working people to become increasingly suspicious of the rapidly growing slave society in the South, where a planter class lived off the labor of unfree men and women. As union members and as strikers, they asserted their right as poor laborers to live in dignity. Yet many others, identifying themselves as white males, asserted the priority of manhood and race over women and people of color whom they sought to exclude.

The Years in Review

1793

- First U.S. textile factory built in Pawtucket Falls, Rhode Island.

1800

- Second Great Awakening: Evangelical movement, emphasizing the need to perfect the individual, sweeps the nation and involves people from every social class.

1804

- First shipment of bananas to United States, but the fruit does not become commonly available until later in the century.

1812

- War of 1812: Congress declares war against the British on June 14.

1814

- Boston Associates build textile mill in Waltham.
- British attack and burn public buildings in Washington, D.C.

412

1815

- Treaty of Ghent ends war with the British.

1816

- Second Bank of the United States is chartered.
- "The year without a summer": snow covers New England on June 6; there is still ice in August in Vermont and New Hampshire.
- Jacob Hyer becomes the nation's first boxing champion after beating Tom Beasey in a bare-knuckles bout.

1817–1825

- Construction of the 364-mile Erie Canal links the Great Lakes and Ohio Valley to the Hudson River, New York City, and transatlantic trade.

1817

- Thomas Gallaudet founds first public school for the deaf.

1818

- President's residence reopens after being burned out by British in 1814; now called "White House" because of new coat of white paint.

1821

- Troy Female Seminary begins higher education for women in the United States.

1822

- Yale College President Timothy Dwight prohibits the playing of football.

1823

- President Monroe says the United States will not tolerate European interference in internal affairs of Western Hemisphere—what comes to be called "Monroe Doctrine."

1824

- Pawtucket weavers strike to resist a reduction of piece rates and an extension of their workday.
- Robert Owen creates a cooperative community in New Harmony, Indiana, which influences the many communitarian experiments of the period.

1825

- Charles Beck, disciple of German gymnastics, sets up nation's first gymnasium in Northampton, Massachusetts.

1826

- Samuel Morey gets patent for two-cylinder internal combustion engine.

1827

- Movement to create Workingmen's parties spreads from Philadelphia to other major cities, as well as small towns and rural districts.
- Philadelphia journeymen house carpenters strike in support of a demand that their workday be shortened from twelve hours to ten.

1828

- Construction of the Baltimore and Ohio Railroad begins.

1829

- Inauguration of Andrew Jackson as president includes thousands of his supporters trampling through White House — an action symbolic of the era of the "common man."
- Sam Patch (the Evel Knievel of his day) dies in an attempt to leap over Genessee Falls. He had previously made many successful jumps over cliffs, gorges, and bridges.
- Peter Cooper's *Tom Thumb* is the first U.S.-built locomotive.

1830

- Invention of the steam press, which will lead to a drastic reduction in the cost of printing.
- Robert Dale Owen publishes the first American book on birth control.
- *Godey's Lady's Book* is the first U.S. magazine directed at women.

1831

- New York Tailoresses' Society founded.

1832

- Jackson vetoes rechartering of Second Bank of the United States and removes federal deposits from the bank.
- U.S. Army ends daily liquor ration.

1833

- New York journeymen carpenters strike for higher wages and gain support of fifteen other trade organizations.

1834

- Lowell, Massachusetts, workers strike to protest worsening working conditions.
- National Trades Union representing twenty-five thousand workers is founded.
- C & O canal workers' strike suppressed by federal troops.
- The U.S. Senate censures President Jackson for removing deposits from the Bank of the United States — the only censure of a president in U.S. history.

1835

■ P. T. Barnum begins his career as a showman by displaying Joice Heth, a slave who is claimed to be George Washington's 160-year-old former nurse.

1836

■ Democrat Martin Van Buren elected over candidates of new Whig Party. Twenty journeymen tailors on strike are convicted of conspiracy by a New York state judge, who denies them the legal right to organize and strike.

1837

■ Flour riot: angry New Yorkers protest high rents and food prices.

1838

■ Oberlin becomes the first co-educational college in the nation.

1839

■ Sylvester Graham (father of the Graham cracker) urges Americans to give up fried meat and alcohol and to eat fruits, vegetables, and whole wheat flour. He promises improved health and diminished sexual urges.

Suggested Readings

Appleby, Joyce, ed., *Recollections of the Early Republic: Selected Autobiographies* (1997).

Ashworth, John, *'Agrarians' & 'Aristocrats': Party Political Ideology in the United States, 1837–1846* (1983).

Blewett, Mary P., *Men, Women, and Work: Class, Gender, and Protest in the New England Shoe Industry, 1780–1910* (1988).

Boydston, Jeanne, *Home and Work: Housework, Wages, and Ideology in the Early Republic* (1990).

Burroughs, Edwin, and Mike Wallace, *Gotham: A History of New York City to 1898* (1999).

Butler, Jon, *Awash in a Sea of Faith: Christianizing the American People* (1990).

Carwardine, Richard, *Evangelicals and Politics in Antebellum America* (1993).

Clark, Christopher, *The Roots of Rural Capitalism: Western Massachusetts, 1780–1860* (1990).

Dublin, Thomas, *Women and Work: The Transformation of Work and Community in Lowell, Massachusetts, 1826–1860* (1979).

————ed., *Farm to Factory: Women's Letters, 1830–1860* (1981).

————*Transforming Women's Work: New England Lives in the Industrial Revolution* (1994).

Faragher, John Mack, *Sugar Creek: Life on the Illinois Prairie* (1986).

Gilje, Paul, and Howard B. Rock, eds., *Keepers of the Revolution: New Yorkers at Work in the Early Republic* (1992).

Gutman, Herbert G., *Work, Culture and Society in Industrializing America: Essays in American Working-Class and Social History* (1976).

Hahn, Steven, and Jonathan Prude, eds., *The Countryside in the Age of Capitalist Transformation: Essays in the Social History of Rural America* (1985).

Halttunen, Karen, *Confidence Men and Painted Women: A Study of Middle-Class Culture in America, 1830–1870* (1982).

Hewitt, Nancy A., *Women's Activism and Social Change: Rochester, New York, 1822–1872* (1984).

Hirsch, Susan E., *Roots of the American Working Class: The Industrialization of Crafts in Newark, 1800–1860* (1978).

Jensen, Joan M., *Loosening the Bonds: Mid-Atlantic Farm Women, 1750–1850* (1986).

Johnson, Paul, *A Shopkeeper's Millennium: Society and Revivals in Rochester, New York, 1815–1837* (1978).

Kelly, Catherine E., *In the New England Fashion: Reshaping Women's Lives in the Nineteenth Century* (1999).

Laurie, Bruce, *Artisans into Workers: Labor in Nineteenth-Century America*, rev. ed. (1997).

Lazerow, Jama, *Religion and the Working Class in Antebellum America* (1995).

Osterud, Nancy Grey, *Bonds of Community: The Lives of Farm Women in Nineteenth-Century New York* (1991).

Prude, Jonathan, *The Coming of Industrial Order: Town and Factory Life in Rural Massachusetts, 1810–1860* (1983).

Rock, Howard B., Paul A. Gilje, and Robert Asher, eds., *American Artisans: Crafting Social Identity, 1750–1850* (1995).

Ross, Steven J., *Workers on the Edge: Work, Leisure, and Politics in Industrializing Cincinnati, 1788–1890* (1985).

Ryan, Mary, *Cradle of the Middle Class: The Family in Oneida County, New York, 1790–1865* (1981).

Sellers, Charles, *The Market Revolution: Jacksonian America, 1815–1846* (1991).

Sheriff, Carol, *The Artificial River: The Erie Canal and the Paradox of Progress, 1817–1862* (1996).

Stansell, Christine, *City of Women: Sex and Class in New York, 1789–1860* (1986).

Taylor, Alan, *William Cooper's Town: Power and Persuasion on the Frontier of the Early American Republic* (1995).

Ulrich, Laurel Thatcher, *A Midwife's Tale: The Life of Martha Ballard, based on her Diary, 1785–1812* (1991).

Wallace, Anthony F. C., *Rockdale: The Growth of an American Village in the Early Industrial Revolution* (1978).

Watson, Harry L., *Liberty and Power: The Politics of Jacksonian America* (1990).

Way, Peter, *Common Labour: Workers and the Digging of North American Canals, 1780–1860* (1993).

Wilentz, Sean, *Chants Democratic: New York City and the Rise of the American Working Class, 1788–1850* (1984).

And on the World Wide Web

Kate Pullano, *Early American History: A Midwife's Tale*
(http://www.pbs.org/wgbh/pages/amex/midwife/)

Hal Morris, *Tales of the Early Republic*
(http://www.panix.com/~hal/)

Library of Congress, *A Century of Lawmaking for a New Nation: U.S. Congressional Documents and Debates, 1774–1873*
(http://memory.loc.gov/ammem/amlaw/lawhome.html)

University of Groningen, *From Revolution to Reconstruction*
(http://odur.let.rug.nl/~usa)

chapter 8

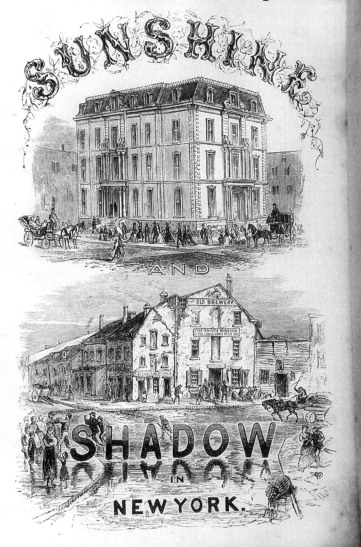

Immigration, Urban Life, and Social Reform in the Free Labor North

1838–1855

Early in 1849, two Irish travelers, Bridget Murphy and Patrick Kennedy, landed in Boston harbor after a storm-tossed Atlantic crossing. They had met on the ship bringing them to America, and a few months after their arrival they were married. Both were fleeing the potato blight that had devastated Irish agriculture and had left millions of men, women, and children on the brink of starvation. The young couple settled into a corrugated shack on Noddle's Island in Boston Harbor. They had few resources with which to start a new life, but they were willing to work hard, which meant a good deal in a country that was eager for labor. Patrick found a job as a cooper, crafting wooden barrels and Conestoga wagon wheels. Like many newly arrived Irish women, Bridget may have sewed or performed domestic work to help build a nest egg.

These non-English arrivals were considered the nation's first immigrants. Patrick and Bridget Kennedy lived within the growing Irish community in Boston where they struggled to create a home and start a family. The Boston Irish formed the first immigrant ghetto in the United States. They coped with overcrowded and dilapidated housing, epidemics of cholera and consumption, inadequate water supplies and abundant raw sewage, and the suspicion and prejudice that New England's more prosperous Protestant majority heaped on impoverished Catholic newcomers. Conditions were grim and mortality rates higher than those in any major European city.

A decade after their arrival, good fortune seemed to smile on the Kennedys. Patrick's skill as a cooper sustained them economically, and Bridget was pregnant with their first child. Then catastrophe struck. Shortly after his son P. J. was born in 1858, Patrick Kennedy, then in his early thirties, died, probably of cholera or consumption. In 1860, the widowed Bridget was eking out a living for herself and her son P. J. by running a notions shop.

Although P. J. Kennedy would eventually become the patriarch of a wealthy and powerful political clan that, two generations hence, would produce a president of the United States, his humble origins were typical of millions of immigrants in the mid nineteenth century. Forming a mas-

Sunshine and Shadow.
Regular mid nineteenth-century publications presented the East's industrializing cities—New York, Philadelphia, and Baltimore—as fractured societies. According to articles, novels, and city guides, each was really two cities: one orderly, prosperous, and bathed in "sunlight," the other menacing, poor, and steeped in "darkness" (or "gaslight"). In this frontispiece from the 1868 *Sunshine and Shadow in New York,* the symbolic extremes of day and night were represented by a Fifth Avenue mansion and the Old Brewery, an infamous "thieves' den."

Source: Matthew Hale Smith, *Sunshine and Shadow in New York* (1868)—American Social History Project.

419

sive movement from western and northern Europe, these immigrants were pushed out of their homelands by famine, political upheaval, and economic crisis. They were drawn to the United States by the availability of land, the high demand for labor, and the promise of a better life.

In 1847, just two years before Patrick Kennedy and Bridget Murphy arrived in Boston, Daniel Webster, the senator from Massachusetts, declared his enthusiasm for the changes that attracted immigrants to the United States. American cities were growing, the West was attracting more settlers, new technologies were springing up yearly, commerce and industry were booming, and agricultural production was increasing rapidly. "It is an extraordinary era in which we live," Webster exulted, an era "remarkable for scientific research into the heavens, the earth, and what is beneath the earth" and its application "to the pursuits of life."

But the economic and technological transformations that marked the new era required a radical reorganization of the relations between labor and capital. A smaller and smaller percentage of people were able to rise from common laborers to skilled artisans to master craftsmen, or from agricultural workers to land owners. Instead, more and more American workers, whether immigrant or native born, spent their lives earning a wage. Many still earned those wages working on farms or at sea or constructing roads, canals, commercial buildings, and homes. However, a growing number of workers were recruited to industrial labor, manufacturing goods either in their households or in newfangled factories that housed the machines that so enthralled Webster.

These workers were free in the sense that they were not legally enslaved like the African-American labor force in the South, but they were no longer independent in the sense that Thomas Jefferson or even Alexander Hamilton had intended when the nation was new. Free labor increasingly came to include people who were employees of others as well as independent farmers, shopkeepers, and artisans. In prosperous times, such as the late 1840s, jobs were relatively plentiful and wages generally sufficient to support a family. But in periods of economic crisis, such as the depressions that hit in the 1830s and the 1850s, unemployment skyrocketed, wages plummeted, workers struggled to survive, and once-affluent businessmen went bankrupt.

Yet there were some merchants, industrialists, professionals, and commercial farmers who took advantage of others' misfortunes. They bought land, labor, and goods at low prices, consolidating their capital until good times returned. Their shrewd business deals spawned a widening gap between rich and poor in American society, a gap that was exacerbated by the massive influx of impoverished immigrants from Europe.

Immigration transformed the meaning of color as well as class in the United States. Some native-born white Protestants viewed Irish Catholics in particular as racially inferior and religiously threatening. Lumping them together with blacks at the bottom of the social hierarchy and denigrating their loyalty to the Catholic Church and the Pope in Rome, they forged nativist societies to defend the white, Protestant world they valued. At the same time, relegated to the least skilled jobs and the least desirable neighborhoods, many Irish immigrants found themselves in fierce competition with African Americans.

The growth of cities and industry, the periodic upheavals created by financial panics, and the development of immigrant and poor communities assured that traditional ways of living and working had to be abandoned. Old values and assumptions were either redefined or replaced. For many Americans, the transformations of the 1830s and 1840s fostered a moral crisis. The North was characterized not only by changes in the relations between workers and employers, blacks and whites, and native-born and immigrant residents, but also by increases in poverty and crime; challenges to religious and family authority; and the spread of prostitution, alcohol use, and disease.

Many Americans believed that these social ills had to be addressed. A few, such as Lewis Tappan of New York City, donated substantial sums to charitable and missionary efforts. Others, steeped in the spiritual lessons of the Second Great Awakening, organized societies to save prostitutes, end drunkenness, and abolish slavery. By the 1840s, smaller groups of Americans, including workers, women, and African Americans, were inspired by radical forms of evangelicalism, Quaker principles, or revolutionary upheavals in Europe to advocate more dramatic changes in society, such as land reform, utopian communities, racial equality, and the rights of workers and women. These movements for social change brought new groups of Americans into the public sphere and helped to redefine the parameters and meaning of politics.

The women and men who engaged in reform efforts did ameliorate some of the worst effects of the expanding capitalist and industrial system. However, they also contributed to its consolidation. In doing so, they assured that the transformations in work, ethnic and race relations, and political culture that occurred in the mid-nineteenth-century North had far-reaching effects on the region and the nation.

An Era of Technological and Economic Expansion

When prosperity returned in the early 1840s, opportunities existed for people even of modest means to enjoy the fruits of technological advancement and economic expansion. By the mid 1840s, the pace of business was brisker than ever. Slumps would recur in 1854–1855 and in 1857, but overall, the period between 1842 and 1860 saw commerce and industry expand at an unprecedented rate. Particularly in cities, the general store gave way to specialty shops that offered wider selections of specific goods—hardware, dry goods, groceries, and so on. Owners, relying on state incorporation laws passed in the 1830s, moved from individual and family-based businesses to selling shares that would combine the resources of a larger number of people while limiting each investor's liability. Banks, although still risky ventures, increased in number to create the credit required by merchants who now traded large quantities of goods over long distances. A growing number of capitalists also turned from investing in trade to investing in factories in order to feed Americans' voracious demand for manufactured goods.

Technology led to impressive gains in productivity. Compared to a worker in 1800, a worker in 1860 could produce twice as much wheat, twice as much pig iron, and more than four times as much cotton cloth. New power-driven machines—looms, sewing machines, reapers, lathes, and steam boilers—fueled this soaring productivity. Refinements in production processes contributed too, with each worker now completing smaller and more simplified tasks. Combined with a growing population, increased productivity led to a staggering increase in national wealth. For instance, between 1840 and 1860 alone, the nation's agricultural output more than doubled in value, and that of its construction, mining, and manufacturing industries grew four times or more. In 1840, the value of manufactured goods produced in the United States equaled $483 million. By 1850, the figure had more than doubled to just over $1 billion.

New means of transportation also transformed the economic landscape. As the canal era gave way to the railroad age, the region beyond the Appalachian Mountains was accessible to Easterners and European immigrants as never

"The Lackawanna Valley". George Inness's panoramic painting, commissioned by the Delaware, Lackawanna, and Western Railroad in 1855, placed the symbol of industrialization in a bucolic setting. The railroad's president paid Inness $75 to paint a scene showing three locomotives. The artist gave him only one train, but obliged the president's zeal for advertising by painting three tracks leading into the new Scranton roundhouse, instead of the one that actually existed.

Source: George Inness, oil on canvas, 1855, 33 7/8 × 50 1/4 inches—Gift of Mrs. Huttleston Rogers, National Gallery of Art, Washington, D.C.

before. Ten thousand miles of railroad track laid in the 1850s helped link western farmers to older railroad lines — the New York Central, the Pennsylvania, the Erie, and the Baltimore & Ohio — and to eastern markets. People and goods now moved at far lower cost, with freight rates dropping by about ninety-five percent between 1820 and 1860. And the speed of travel increased almost as dramatically. In 1817, the fastest freight shipments from New York to Cincinnati took almost two months. By the early 1850s, shipping freight by railroad between these two cities took only about a week.

At the same time, technological advances allowed Americans to communicate with each other more readily, even across great distances. During the 1840s, the telegraph made it possible for the first time to send information (including commodity prices and election results) instantaneously across the country. Cheap newspapers made possible by the steam press and itinerant lecturers traveling by railroad spread new ideas that sparked ongoing debates throughout the free states. The pleasures of city life, as well as its dangers, were broadcast to small towns and farming communities. The benefits of frontier life, the possibilities for industrial jobs, the horrors of racial, sexual, and wage slavery, the threat of mass immigration, the saving grace of evangelical conversion or utopian lifestyles — all were proclaimed far and wide across the United States.

The new communication links combined with improvements in transportation to knit together local markets and scattered communities into regional and interregional networks. As canals and then railroads replaced rivers as the primary link between regions in the 1840s and 1850s, the Northwest exchanged more goods and people with the Northeast than it did with the South. As a result, the free-labor North stood in increasingly sharp contrast to the slave-labor South. Later debates over the extension of slavery and

Freeze. Frenchman Louis Daguerre's improvements in photography reached America in the 1840s. Personal portraits were soon the craze, and "daguerreotype" studios sprang up in every city, while traveling daguerreotypists served the countryside. This picture presents the controlled environment of the early studios. It took so long to properly expose a photographic plate that the subject needed a head brace to hold a pose.

Source: A. H. Wheeler, 1893 — Prints and Photographs Division, Library of Congress.

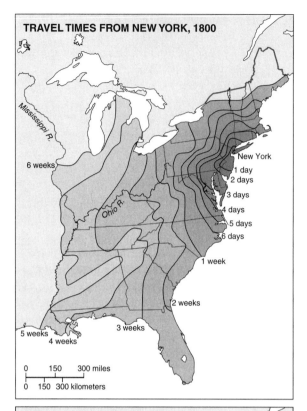

TRAVEL TIMES FROM NEW YORK, 1800

Mississippi R.

6 weeks

Ohio R.

New York
1 day
2 days
3 days
4 days
5 days
6 days

1 week

2 weeks

3 weeks

5 weeks
4 weeks

| 0 | 150 | 300 miles |
| 0 | 150 | 300 kilometers |

The Mobility of Goods and People, 1800—1857. Advances in technology made the movement of goods and people across the United States faster and more reliable. In 1800, a traveller from New York City required a full week to reach western New York, an area that was still largely settled by American Indians. By the late 1850s, western New York cities such as Buffalo served as hubs for the transhipment of goods and people between the eastern seaboard and the western frontier of white settlement. It took only one day to reach Buffalo from Chicago and another day to travel on to New York City.

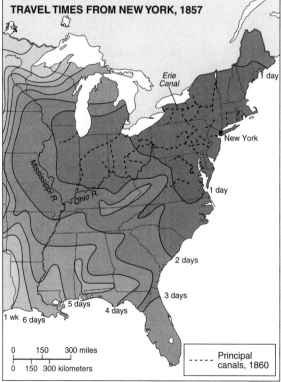

TRAVEL TIMES FROM NEW YORK, 1857

Erie
Canal
1 day

New York

Mississippi R.

Ohio R.

1 day

2 days

3 days

5 days

4 days

1 wk 6 days

| 0 | 150 | 300 miles |
| 0 | 150 | 300 kilometers |

- - - - Principal
canals, 1860

free labor into western territories would transform these commercial links into political fault lines.

A Changing World for Northern Working People

Economic and technological changes reshaped the daily lives of Americans in the mid nineteenth century. Among the important transformations was the emergence of a new category of professionals and managers, many of whom were willing to forego the ownership of land or businesses for the relative security of a salary. The members of this group, who embraced the values and ideals of the emerging middle class, sought to stave off the risks associated with boom-and-bust cycles by investing their savings wisely in new financial institutions such as state banks. At the same time, they bought a growing number of mass-produced consumer products—pianos, chairs, rugs, glass mirrors, silverware, and carriages—to show off their newfound wealth and status.

Wage workers also hoped to mute the effects of economic downturns. But during hard times they had to rely primarily on good luck and extensive family and friendship networks. Both were risky supports in bad times. Moreover, workers hit by economic recession could no longer hope to eke out survival by relying on goods produced in their local communities. A consumer society was emerging in which workers increasingly exchanged their wages for the goods they required in order to live. This entailed a large dose of dependency for them and a further decline in the local self-sufficiency that

"Dumping Ground at the Foot of Beach Street." This engraving showed people scavenging on garbage barges, searching for coal, rags, and other discarded items that might be used or sold to junk dealers. The picture, according to a *Harper's Weekly* editor, showed how some people in New York were forced to "live upon the refuse of respectable folk."

Source: Stanley Fox, *Harper's Weekly,* September 26, 1866—American Social History Project.

had characterized rural areas and small towns until the early nineteenth century.

Farmers were also caught up in the new cash economy. By the 1840s and 1850s, steadily declining prices for manufactured goods expanded the items that farmers bought to include stoves, furniture, rugs, kitchenware, churns, corn shellers, harnesses, and carriages. To get the cash needed to purchase all these goods, farm families devoted more of their time to producing marketable crops that would command high prices in expanding urban markets. As a result, farmers were soon buying large quantities of their own food. The New York State Agricultural Society's president wrote in 1851:

> At an early period "production for consumption" was the leading purpose; now no farmer would find it profitable "to do everything within himself." He now sells for money, and it is in his interest to pay for every article that he cannot produce cheaper than he can buy.

Ironically, then, the "free" northern farmer, like the northern factory worker, was becoming more dependent on others for basic needs.

Production for the market also prompted significant social changes in rural communities. Sellers had to fight to maintain their market position, and competition began to replace cooperation, pitting farmer against farmer. The *New England Farmer* warned

> The cultivator who does not keep pace with his neighbors as regards agricultural improvements and information will soon find himself the poorer in consequence of the prosperity that surrounds him. . . . He will be like a stunted oak in the forest, which is deprived of light and air, by its "towering neighbors."

And farmers were also competing with others far away. Improved transportation brought produce from the West into competition with crops grown on rocky and nearly exhausted New England soil. Commerce through the Erie Canal alone virtually ended grain production in much of the East and brought heavy pressure to bear on hog and cattle farming there. For example, during 1840, only ten thousand bushels of grain and flour left Chicago for the East. Twenty years later, over fifty million bushels followed that route. Much of this increased yield went to feed the people of New England and the Middle Atlantic states, but some also went to feed the South, Ireland, and other parts of Europe. Between 1840 and 1860, western competition made possible by the railroads also effectively wiped out sheep raising in New England. As a result of this increasing competition, by 1860 fully one-third of all those born in Connecticut and New Hampshire had left their home states in search of a second chance, mostly out West. Four of every ten Vermonters did the same. The center of northern agriculture had moved West, and so too did the farming population.

There were other attractions to western migration as well. Gold, discovered in California in 1848, provided one powerful magnet. So did a boom in western construction and manufacturing, especially mining (lead, copper, iron) and smelting, lumbering, farm equipment, and food processing (milling, meatpacking, distilling, and brewing). The demand for labor thus drew industrial workers as well as farmers to the West. This westward movement would reshape political as well as economic relations by the late 1840s and 1850s.

The surge in commerce and industry also swelled the number and size of cities. In 1790, the entire country claimed only twenty-four towns or cities with populations greater than twenty-five hundred, and none greater than fifty thousand. Fewer than one Northeasterner in ten lived in a town. But by 1860, there were nearly four hundred towns and cities, and more than a third of all Northeasterners lived in them. Although much of the Northeast's manufacturing took place in small cities and towns, there were also several major centers of industry and commerce. New York City (with more than one million residents by 1860) and Philadelphia (with over one-half million) became the dominant manufacturing cities in the nation. Western urban centers were important, too. Located at key points along the now-bustling East–West trade routes, cities such as Rochester, Buffalo, Pittsburgh, and Chicago boomed.

Urban and industrial growth brought another momentous change. More and more people were now making their living in ways that challenged the values of the revolutionary generation. The absolute size of the nation's farm population grew steadily through 1910. But the number of people working outside of agriculture grew considerably faster. Almost seven in every ten working residents of the North had tilled the soil in the days when Thomas Jefferson sang the praises of the independent American farmer. By 1860, the figure was only four in every ten.

Not all of these former farmers simply became cogs in the new industrial machine. Some benefited from the expansion of commerce and the growth in wholesale and retail establishments by rising into the new ranks of white-collar workers. Clerks and bookkeepers, for instance, were in greater demand than ever before. The expansion of transportation and communication created such midlevel occupations as insurance agents, railroad dispatchers, and telegraphers. These were workers who were paid in wages or commissions, but they had hopes of rising one day to positions as managers or independent entrepreneurs.

More ominously, however, these economic shifts marked another form of growing dependence for "free" workers. Although indentured servitude all but vanished among whites in the early nineteenth century, those dependent for their survival upon wage labor moved from the fringes of northern society to its center. In 1800, according to one rough estimate, those who worked primarily for wages accounted for only twelve percent of the country's total working population. By 1860, however, such people represented forty percent of the working population. The great majority of these wage-earners worked in the free-labor North, which grew increasingly distinct from the slave-labor South. Neither system conformed to the ideal of a nation of independent landowners.

Immigrants Swell the Wage Labor Ranks

The changing world of northern workers was accompanied and in part created by the arrival of large numbers of immigrants such as Patrick Kennedy and Bridget Murphy. With the growth of industry and commercial agriculture and the rise of cities where day laborers and domestic servants were in high demand, the North faced a serious labor shortage. Large numbers of women and men continued to arrive in the United States from England. But for those who owned property and the means of production, it was the influx of hundreds of thousands of new residents from Ireland and Germany in the 1830s, 1840s, and 1850s that assured a steady and often cheap supply of labor.

Events in Europe created the circumstances that led millions of people to settle in the United States. Drought, famine, revolution, and political persecution all contributed to the wave of emigrants, which peaked in the mid 1840s to mid 1850s. For instance, in 1845, a potato blight hit Ireland, causing acres of the island's most basic foodstuff to blacken and die. The blight continued for five years. Men, women, and children starved to death; the faces of the young were "bloated yet wrinkled and of a pale greenish hue." Landlords evicted over a half million tenant farmers who could no longer pay their rent. At the same time, Ireland's traditional small industries declined un-

"The Irish Harvest." "In many districts of Ireland," read the caption accompanying this 1852 illustration in a Boston weekly, "there are scenes like this which give unmistakable evidence of prosperity, notwithstanding the reports that are constantly reaching us of want and misery in that unfortunate land." Although the British press depicted the ravages of the Irish potato famine, American publications seemed reluctant to unsettle their readers with disturbing images.

Source: *Gleason's Pictorial and Drawing-room Companion,* December 11, 1852— American Social History Project.

" . . . The Pestilent Air of the Steerage"

Herman Melville, the author of *Moby Dick,* was a cabin boy on a packet ship sailing between New York and Liverpool, England, in the 1830s. In his novel *Redburn,* Melville describes the conditions of work and life on board the sailing ship *Highlander.* The following selection describes the horrifying conditions experienced by Irish immigrants traveling below decks in steerage. Hundreds of thousands of Irish immigrants died onboard ship while traveling from Ireland to the United States in the 1840s and 1850s.

During the frequent *hard blows* we experienced, the hatchways on the steerage were, at intervals, hermetically closed; sealing down in their noisome den, those scores of human beings. [It] was beyond question, this noisome confinement in so close, unventilated, and crowded a den: joined to the deprivation of sufficient food, from which many were suffering; which, helped by their personal uncleanliness, brought on a malignant fever. . . .

The cases [soon] increased: the utmost alarm spread through the ship. . . . Many of the panic-stricken emigrants would fain now [to be] domiciled on deck; but being so scantily clothed, the wretched weather—wet, cold, and tempestuous—drove the best part of them again below. Yet any other human beings, perhaps, would rather have faced the most outrageous storm, than continued to breathe the pestilent air of the steerage. . . .

The sight that greeted us, upon entering [steerage], was wretched indeed. It was like entering a crowded jail. From the rows of rude bunks, hundreds of meager, begrimed faces were turned upon us; while seated upon the chests were scores of unshaven men, smoking tea-leaves, and creating a suffocating vapor. But this vapor was better than the native air of the place, which from almost unbelievable causes, was fetid in the extreme. In every corner, the females were huddled together, weeping and lamenting; children were asking bread from their mothers, who had none to give. . . .

About four o'clock that morning, the first four died. They were all men; and the scenes which ensued were frantic in the extreme. . . . By their own countrymen, they were torn from the clasp of their wives, rolled in their own bedding, with ballast-stones, and with hurried rites, were dropped into the ocean.

At this time, ten more men had caught the disease. . . .

On land, a pestilence is fearful enough; but there, many can flee from an infected city; whereas, in a ship, you are locked and bolted in the very hospital itself. Nor is there any possibility of escape from it; and in so small and crowded a place, no precaution can effectually guard against contagion. . . .

However this narrative of the circumstances attending the fever among the emigrants on the *Highlander* may appear . . . the only account you obtain of such events, is generally contained in a newspaper paragraph, under the shipping-head. *There* is the obituary of the destitute dead, who die on the sea. They die, like the billows that break on the shore, and no more are heard or seen. . . . What a world of life and death, what a world of humanity and its woes, lies shrunk into a three-worded sentence!

You see no plague-ship driving through a stormy sea; you hear no groans of despair; you see no corpses thrown over the bulwarks; you mark not the wringing hands and torn hair of widows and orphans:—all is a blank. . . .

Source: Herman Melville, *Redburn* (1849).

der the weight of English competition. Those who were lucky found their way onboard ships whose bottom decks were crammed with their countrymen. Although about one in ten died on the journey, some two million Irish arrived on American shores between 1820 and 1860.

Arriving in the same period were some one and one-half million Germans. German peasants, too, faced the devastation of the potato blight. Those who could, made their way to Bremen to board ships to the United States. Small farmers in Germany were also forced off their lands by the agricultural depression, and skilled laborers were losing their jobs as English textiles flooded German markets. At the same time, shoemakers, furniture makers, and other artisans faced the deskilling of their crafts as mass production broke the manufacturing process into a larger number of discrete tasks, each of which required less and less skill to perform. Economic stagnation was reinforced by political upheaval, as the short-lived revolution of 1848 failed to overturn Prussian rule. In its aftermath, shopkeepers, artisans, and professionals who supported the revolution fled their homeland.

Other countries experienced similar exoduses. In England, government repression of workers who advocated democratic reforms such as universal manhood suffrage, annual meetings of Parliament, and the secret ballot led many to seek asylum in the United States. Italian radicals, who were defeated in their attempt to win independence from Austria in 1849, also sought asylum. Scandinavians, too, faced agricultural stagnation and repressive landlords; they came to the United States seeking economic opportunity on America's vast western farmlands. Chinese migrants began arriving as well. Almost all of them were men seeking employment in the cities and mines of the West. The greatest number of immigrants came between 1840 and 1859, when over four million arrived. By 1860, nearly one-third of adult white men in the free states were immigrants. A few were well-to-do merchants, manufacturers, and professionals who established themselves as respectable residents of their new nation. A far larger number, many from impoverished rural areas, ended up working as unskilled or low-skilled laborers in industry, con-

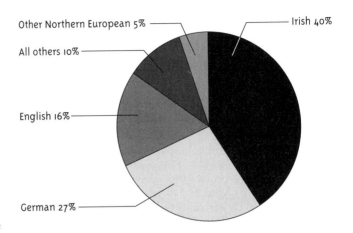

Sources of Immigration, 1840–1860

Other Northern European 5%
All others 10%
English 16%
German 27%
Irish 40%

Sources of Immigration, 1840–1860. The largest group of immigrants to arrive in the United States between 1840 and 1860 came from Ireland, followed by those from Germany and England. Most were driven out by famine, political upheaval, and religious persecution and drawn to America by democratic promises and economic opportunities. Immigrants provided a critical source of skilled and unskilled labor to fuel industrial, commercial, and agricultural development in the northern and western United States.

Immigration to the United States, 1820–1860. The most dramatic increase in immigration to the United States occurred between 1845 and 1855. In that decade, hundreds of thousands of people left Ireland, Germany, and other parts of northern Europe in hopes of finding a better life in America. With improved economic conditions in Ireland and Germany and the onset of depression and then the Civil War in the United States, immigration declined significantly in the late 1850s and early 1860s.

Source: U.S. Bureau of the Census. *Historical Statistics of the United States, Colonial Times to 1970* (1975).

struction, or the maritime trades, or as domestic servants or casual workers paid by the day.

The largest concentration of immigrants arrived in the Northeast and settled in seacoast and inland cities in that region. Three-quarters entered the United States through the Port of New York. Although most of these immigrants eventually moved on, those who stayed drove the population of New York City (comprised only of Manhattan in this period) from 313,000 to 814,000 between 1840 and 1860, and that of Brooklyn from 11,000 to 267,000 in the same period.

Immigrants changed the economic landscape of the North. The lower wages they were paid increased profits for employers and contributed greatly to economic growth. At the same time, having so many workers from different cultures speaking different languages made it hard for labor to organize collectively on its own behalf. Some immigrants, particularly exiled German revolutionaries, held more radical views than their American counterparts. Others, including many impoverished Irish and German peasants, hoped for little more than a steady job and a bare-subsistence lifestyle when they first arrived. Native-born white workers often resented the competition for work from immigrants. This resentment assured that ethnicity would become a new source of division in American society.

As both the kinds of work to be done and the kinds of workers seeking jobs multiplied, employers created a more elaborate division of labor. The vast majority of wage workers before 1840 were native-born white men who were ranked primarily by their skills: artisans, outworkers, laborers, and factory operatives. White women, who entered textile mills in the 1820s, and African Americans, who most often worked as domestic servants or manual laborers, occupied their own well-defined niches near the bottom of this occupational hierarchy. After about 1840, however, the kind of jobs a person could obtain was dictated by national origin as well as by the traditional criteria of skill, sex and race. This transformed the face of America's labor force and further complicated the ability of workers to unite around common grievances.

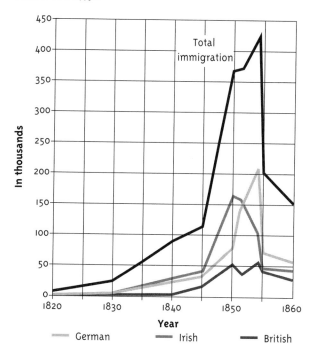

Total immigration

In thousands

Year

German   Irish   British

Irish Americans Trade Famine for Unskilled Labor

Eight out of ten Irish emigrants fleeing the famine were bound for the United States, and two-thirds of these settled in New York, Pennsylvania, and New Jersey, overwhelmingly in manufacturing towns and cities. A few managed to buy farms. Others (including those who had gained skills and experience working in England) found employment as craftsmen, miners, and construction workers. But the vast majority arrived virtually penniless and without any industrial training. Ireland's stunted agricultural economy had denied them anything but the most primitive farming experience.

In general, the only work in the New World open to Irish men was unskilled, temporary, and often heavy. After the mid 1840s, Irish immigrants dominated day labor in most coastal towns and cities and formed the majority of workers on canals, railroads, and other construction projects. A visiting Irish journalist remarked in 1860, "There are several sorts of power working at the fabric of this Republic: water-power, steam-power, horse-power, Irish-power. The last works hardest of all."

Young Irish women did more than their share of heavy work. With more Irish women than men arriving in the United States and most families needing the labor of all their members, few women arriving from Ireland could afford the luxury of leisure. The largest number labored as domestic servants. Beginning in the 1830s and throughout the next two decades, prosperous urban families hired Irish women in swiftly rising numbers. Wealthier employers might divide the household tasks among a cook, a maid, and a butler, but most families employed only one woman to do all the chores. It was her responsibility to cook, clean, prepare and serve meals, care for the children, mend the family's clothing, and haul all the wood, coal, and water that was needed.

Significant numbers of Irish women were also recruited by New England textile factories. In 1836, less than four percent of the workers in a typical Lowell factory were foreign-born. But that proportion rose to nearly forty percent by 1850; most of these were women. At first the factory bosses treated foreign-born workers even worse than they did the native-born, forcing the Irish to bear the brunt of increasing workloads and declining wage rates designed to lower labor costs. This temporarily took some of the pressure off Yankee women but created deep divisions within the workforce. So did the company policy of segregating native-born and immigrant housing, with the worst facilities going to the Irish. But by the 1850s, the workload of the average Lowell spinner and weaver—immigrant and native born alike—had more than doubled, and the heavy work and low wages that had been initially reserved for immigrants became the standard for all textile operatives.

Economic hardship was widespread among Irish immigrants. Even though real wages for unskilled day laborers rose about twelve percent per decade between 1820 and 1860, several factors conspired to keep Irish immigrants in poverty. First, most unskilled jobs were of short duration, lasting only a few weeks, sometimes only a day or two, and competition from a growing pool of the unemployed, including many immigrants, made finding work difficult. As a result, the average day laborer worked only about two hundred days a year. Second, the real wages of the unskilled in 1820 were very low indeed. So subsequent wage increases failed to pull the incomes of many Irish immigrants much above bare subsistence. Under these circumstances, temporary unemployment, illness, or the death of a wage-earner could quickly lead to economic crisis for a family.

Extreme poverty sometimes forced immigrants to turn to petty crime to survive. For instance, in January 1850, John McFealing was arrested for stealing wood from the docks in Newburyport, Massachusetts. He had been unable to find work, and a court investigation described his family as being in dire need: "The children were all scantily supplied with clothing, and not one had a shoe to the feet. There was not a stick of firewood nor scarcely a morsel of food in the house."

"Let the Public Look at These Plague-Spots." An illustration from an 1860 edition of the *New York Illustrated News* showed a reporter and artist working on a story about the Glennan family, residents of a shanty district near the city's East River called Dutch Hill. Although newspapers and magazines failed to recognize the causes of urban poverty, by mid century editors consistently dispatched reporters to cover the "dark background of our civilization."

Source: *New York Illustrated News,* February 11, 1860—General Research Division, New York Public Library, Astor, Lenox and Tilden Foundations.

Families such as the McFealings lived in increasingly crowded and decaying neighborhoods. Boston's North End was one such place. Slightly more than ten thousand of its seventeen thousand residents in 1855 were of Irish birth, and these were mostly unskilled laborers and their families. The area no longer housed the prosperous merchants and master artisans whose substantial homes had by now been subdivided, as

433

had the North End's warehouses. Shoddy frame dwellings rose on empty land. The North End's 3,441 families crowded into about one thousand three-story dwellings. "Houses, once fashionable," noted a contemporary, have "become neglected, dreary tenement houses into which the low-paid and poverty-smitten . . . crowd by the dozens." Cholera and other infectious diseases thrived in such neighborhoods, and, according to the Boston physician and pioneer public health worker Josiah Curtis, mortality rates there equaled "anything we have been able to discover in European cities." This was a shocking observation in a society that prided itself precisely on avoiding the social ills of the Old World.

Yet for many Irish, life in the New World was still preferable to that in the Old. In the United States, the Irish were at least no longer subject to the tyranny of their English overlords. England had worked for centuries to concentrate land, wealth, religious privilege, and political power in the hands of Ireland's pro-English Protestant minority at the expense of the Catholic majority. In pursuit of increased revenue, the largely Protestant landlord class steadily squeezed the already impoverished Catholic tenants and landless laborers. In the midst of the potato famine, corn, cattle, and dairy products were all being produced in Ireland, but landlords sold them abroad for profit rather than give these foodstuffs to the starving people at home. "God sent the blight," went an Irish saying, "but the English landlords sent the famine!" For those seeking a living off the land, Irish nationalist leader Thomas Francis Meagher made the following observation: "One business alone survives! That fortunate business, . . . that favored, privileged, and patronized business is the Irish coffin-maker's."

Irish immigrants, such as Patrick Dunny of Philadelphia, praised America's more democratic atmosphere. He wrote to family and friends back in Ireland that

> People that cuts a great dash at home, when they come here they think it strange for the humble class of people to get as much respect as themselves. For when they come here it won't do to say I had such-and-such and was such-and-such back at home. But strangers here they must gain respect by their conduct and not by their tongue.

For Irish Catholics, the growth of the Catholic Church in the United States was also something to applaud. The church provided immigrants with a broad array of services—not only spiritual but social, economic, educational, and charitable as well—and offered solace in the face of hard work, homesickness, and discrimination. Finally, however difficult their plight, the Irish in the United States stood a better chance of survival than their friends and relatives back home.

Germans Migrate Toward Crafts and Farms

In some ways, Germany's emigration resembled Ireland's. In Germany, as in Ireland, industrial and agricultural changes had undermined the position of farmers and craftsmen. Crop failures devastated the lives of many German tenants and small landholders, forcing them off their land, and onto ships bound for America. Both peasants and artisans also chafed at the tax burdens, social restrictions, and political repression imposed by the German nobility, its armies, its bureaucracies, and its state churches. Efforts at reform by merchants and industrialists often deepened the economic insecurities of the less well-to-do. The new economic order, complained one petition from master craftsmen, forced independent producers "into the abyss of the proletariat."

But the German experience differed from the Irish in several important respects. For one thing, skilled craftsmen made up a larger proportion of those leaving Germany. For another, Germany's national crisis produced full-scale revolution in 1848–1849. Craftsmen, imbued with values similar to those of Thomas Paine, provided much of the driving force and popular following for the revolution. Some of these activists sought a new "organization of labor . . . recognizing the equal rights of all producers." They demanded narrower differences in personal wealth, limits on the length of the working day, free universal education, producers' and consumers' cooperatives, and a guaranteed right to employment. Although they represented only a small percentage of immigrants to the United States, these exiled revolutionaries made their voices heard through German mutual aid societies, newspapers, and labor organizations.

By the 1850s, one-third of German immigrants lived in New York, Pennsylvania, and New Jersey, the three states favored by the Irish. Even more ventured farther west, into Ohio, Indiana, Illinois, Missouri, Michigan, Iowa, and Wisconsin. Germans were more likely than the Irish to become farmers, shopkeepers, and skilled tradesmen, and less likely to become unskilled laborers, factory workers, or domestic servants. Given the higher wages garnered by German men, a far smaller percentage of German than Irish women worked for wages.

Large numbers of German immigrants entered the traditional urban, skilled crafts, especially those producing consumer goods. They won these jobs not only because of their skills, but also because of the expansion of the North's light industry, although the pay and working conditions for these positions continually declined. Having fewer alternatives than the native-born artisans, immigrants were more easily induced to accept the limited opportunities left to them. The *Chicago Daily Tribune* was delighted to find that "our German population" was "fitted to do the cheap and ingenious labor of the country." They "will live as cheaply and work infinitely more intelligently than the negro," a racist *Tribune* editor wrote.

Germans excelled in brewing, piano and furniture making, the printing trades, cigar making, baking, and butchering. German-Jewish bakers provided their *landsmen* with matzohs, bagels, and other specialty foods. Brewers such as Adolph Busch transformed American tastes by offering a more highly carbonated, lighter, and less intoxicating beer—lager—that kept better and longer than English ales, porters, and stouts. In New York City in the 1850s, next to the Schaefer's Brewery, Heinrich Steinwig and his sons opened a piano factory that combined Old World skills with New World mechanization. The factory employed three hundred workers, mostly German, by 1860. In deference to middle-class Americans' demand for English pianos, he named his company Steinway and Sons. German printers produced cigar labels and other early forms of advertising for U.S. companies, and German-language newspapers for their countrymen and women in the United States.

Of course, large numbers of, perhaps most, German immigrants ended up in semi-skilled jobs as construction workers or employees in breweries, piano factories, furniture shops, and shoe factories. Yet the entrance of a significant segment of German immigrants into skilled crafts, farming, and the professions assured that they, far more than their Irish counterparts, would be accepted as fully white by Anglo-Americans, despite the differences in their language and culture.

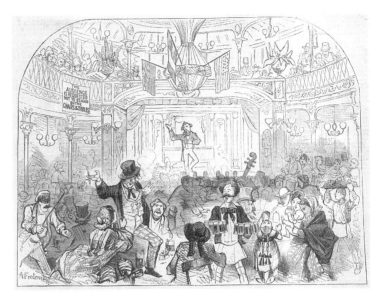

"A German Beer Garden on Sunday Evening." Although German immigrants did not mix politics and liquor, reformers were disconcerted by the atmosphere of their social establishments. Unlike the bars in Irish neighborhoods, the beer gardens catered to whole families. As this 1859 engraving showed, public drinking was only one attraction at a beer garden; but to reformers the presence of women and children suggested immorality.

Source: *Harper's Weekly,* October 15, 1858—American Social History Project.

Scandinavian, British, and Canadian Immigrants Find Opportunity

From Europe's northern tier, nearly forty thousand Swedes and Norwegians made their way to the United States in the 1840s and 1850s. Like other Europeans during this period, Scandinavia's small farmers, tenants,

" . . . Rough Work is Performed Here by Machinery"

Large cabinetmaking (furniture) firms—especially in the Midwest—began to mechanize production earlier than did most other craft-based industries. In 1851, Cincinnati booster Charles Cist proudly described the big new Mitchell and Rammelsberg factory as follows. Note that although machines were used to do the "rough work," skilled craftsmen remained central to the work process.

This, which is one of the heaviest of our furniture establishments, does not, as is generally the case with others, confine its operations to two or three staple articles, but comprehends in its [products] almost every description of cabinet ware and chairs. . . . The main building . . . is six stories high, and filled with workmen and material to its utmost capacity. . . . In the manufacture of furniture, the rough work is performed here by machinery, with great celerity and exactness—the finishing being, as in other shops, executed by competent and skillful workmen. This concern employs, directly and indirectly, two hundred and fifty persons, and manufactures to the value of two hundred and twenty thousand dollars annually.

   The various articles made are cut into lengths and shapes . . . by the agency of a series of circular saws. Every process here, from the ripping out and crosscutting of rough boards, to the finest slitting, progresses with inconceivable rapidity; the saws performing at the rate of from two thousand five hundred to three thousand revolutions in a minute; a speed which renders the teeth of the saw absolutely invisible to the eye.

   As many as two hundred pieces of furniture, and the various parts in the same series, prepared and adjusted to fit, as fast as they progress, at a time, are taken from story to story, until on the upper floors they receive their final dressing and finish for the market. . . . This is but one of the many cabinet ware establishments in Cincinnati, which supply the South, West, and Southwest with materials for housekeeping of all sorts on an extensive scale.

Source: Charles Cist, *Sketches and Statistics of Cincinnati in 1851* (1851).

and laborers were plagued by agrarian crisis, semifeudal class relations, and political inequality. Johan Reierson, a leading Scandinavian writer, warned that those of "the producing and working class" who remained in their homeland faced a future of "slavish dependence." The downtrodden groups were soon driven to religious dissent, mass protest movements, and emigrant fever.

   In the United States, most Scandinavians settled in the Northwest, starting in Illinois and Wisconsin, then spreading into northern Iowa, the Minnesota Territory, and Kansas. About half became farmers, a proportion three times that of the Irish and twice that of either the Germans or the British. Other Scandinavian immigrants gravitated toward agriculture-related industries such as lumbering, furniture making, and the manufacture of farm implements. Many women became domestic servants, although more often in rural or small town areas than in large cities. Although warned by skeptics at home that migration would just mean becoming "a foreign slave abroad," a popular Norwegian emigrant's song replied, "America is free. Work is not slavery. . . . In the free land of the West every man is a free-born citizen."

English, Scottish, and Welsh settlers also found opportunity in America. The government in Britain actively encouraged the expansion and mechanization of industry at the expense of both farmers and traditional craftspeople. The results included mass protest movements and large-scale migration across the Atlantic. Once in the United States, these immigrants spread out across the free states. About one-fourth became farmers and many others became industrial workers. British workers brought with them more skills and greater experience with modern machinery than any other national group. They were also more at home with U.S. language and customs. These two factors helped them move quickly into some of the most desirable jobs, especially in construction, in the manufacture of machines and tools, and in the production of textiles, coal, iron, cutlery, glass, and paper.

More than one hundred thousand people also migrated from Canada to the United States between 1840 and 1860. Some were refugees, fleeing the aftermath of unsuccessful nationalist revolts in the provinces during 1837–1838. Others were victims of British trade policies in the lumber, shipbuilding, and provisioning industries of the Maritime Provinces. Especially numerous were French-Canadian farmers fleeing from land speculation and British repression. Some sought farms in Illinois, Michigan, and Wisconsin. Others obtained wage labor in New England or northern New York State, commonly in textile mills and brickyards or as lumberjacks and farm hands.

Whatever the particular circumstances that drove English, Scottish, Canadian, and Scandinavian peoples to the United States, they were generally more skilled, better educated, and more culturally assimilable than Irish immigrants or African Americans and were assumed to share the values and characteristics of native-born whites. This assured many of them entry into better jobs and better schools and provided them with the political influence that would enhance their position in the future.

African Americans in the Free-Labor North

No group of native-born workers in the North was more affected by the mass immigration of the mid nineteenth century than African Americans. Although freed from slavery in the late eighteenth and early nineteenth

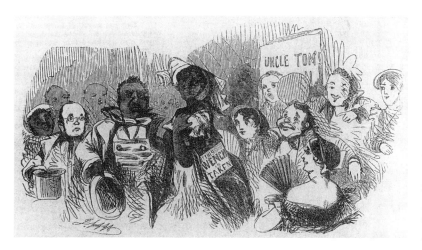

"A Black Joke." A racist cartoon in an 1854 edition of the humor magazine *Yankee Notions* inadvertently illustrated the everyday harassment and cruelty to which northern free African Americans were subjected. At a performance of a play based on Harriet Beecher Stowe's antislavery novel, *Uncle Tom's Cabin,* some white members altered a seat reservation card and, to the derisive laughter of the rest of the audience, pinned it on a black woman's shawl.

Source: *Yankee Notions* (September 1854)—General Research Division, New York Public Library, Astor, Lenox and Tilden Foundations.

centuries by state legislative action in the Northeast and by Congressional mandate in the states carved out of the Old Northwest Territory, blacks still suffered enormous disadvantages and discriminations. In most northern states, African Americans had to meet higher standards of residency and property qualifications than did whites in order to vote. Educational facilities were often segregated, with schools for blacks underfunded and more crowded. Theaters, public conveyances, and even most white-controlled churches forced African Americans to sit in separate and inferior sections. African Americans were also forced to live in the most delapidated housing in the least desirable sections of a city. In addition, white trade unions excluded black workers from their ranks; white employers refused to hire them for any but the most unskilled and lowest-paying jobs; and newly arrived immigrants pushed them out of the few more lucrative occupations— construction, the maritime trades, and carpentry—where they had earlier gained a foothold.

African Americans in the North vigorously responded to these insults to their free status. They also actively opposed colonization, a plan developed by whites to remove blacks from American society by resettling them in lands outside the United States. In meeting after meeting, they asserted, "This is our home, and this is our country. Beneath its sod lie the bones of our fathers; for it, some of them fought, bled, and died. Here we were born, and here we will die." Many of these anticolonization gatherings were held in churches founded by African Americans earlier in the century, including Philadelphia's Bethel Baptist Church, New Haven's African Congregational Church, and New York's Liberty Street Negro Presbyterian Church.

Churches formed the centerpiece of community life for many northern African Americans. Black ministers, moreover, often served as political as well as spiritual leaders. Men such as Theodore Wright, Amos G. Beman, Henry Highland Garnet, Samuel R. Ward, J. W. C. Pennington, and Samuel Cornish combined anticolonizationist and abolitionist efforts with religious and educational uplift. In the 1830s, Reverend Cornish served as editor of the *Colored American,* one of the most widely circulated black newspapers at that time. Reverend Beman, who presided over New Haven, Connecticut's, African Congregational Church, helped build a network of free black organizations in his city and state, including a benevolent association, library club, temperance society, employment office, and schools. Not all black ministers were as progressive as these, however. Some saw their role as helping parishioners accept discrimination in this life by focusing on the joys of the next. But despite the different approaches of their ministers, most black churches in the mid-nineteenth-century North offered solace, hope, and a place for community engagement outside the control of whites.

The small number of African Americans who had achieved success in business and the professions also served as spokespersons for their communities. Several, including editor Frederick Douglass, sailmaker James Forten, and teacher Sarah Douglass, were in the forefront of public efforts to improve the lives of freed blacks and to eradicate the institution of slavery. Yet they, too, were subject to discrimination and humiliation at the hands of whites. Frederick Douglass, for instance, was a skilled caulker when he escaped slavery. But upon reaching the North and freedom, he was refused employment in his trade because his presence would drive white workers away. He struggled as a common laborer, coachman, and waiter until, in 1847, he had collected enough funds to establish himself as an abolitionist editor in Rochester, New York. Even as a leading light of the antislavery cause, he was often dependent for financial support on the proceeds of women's antislavery fairs and the largesse of the predominantly white audiences who came to hear him lecture, many viewing him as an aberration from rather than a model for his race. Such prejudices were deeply rooted in native-born white Americans and were quickly embraced by many immigrants.

Wage-Earning Women Expand Their Sphere But Not Their Rights

All wage-earning women in the mid nineteenth century faced a small circle of options, most of them low paying and low status. In 1840, if outworkers — those who manufactured goods in their homes — are included, women held almost half of all manufacturing jobs in the nation, and about two-thirds of those in New England. These workers included large numbers of immigrants, but also a growing cohort of native-born women. The irregular employment and low wages of men put a premium on increasing the family income through the labors of women and children.

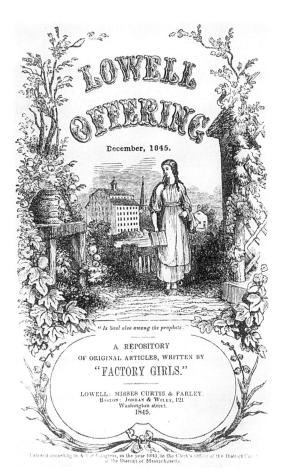

African-American women faced a double bind when seeking employment. They were discriminated against both because they were black and because they were female. Teaching and producing and selling homemade goods remained almost the only means by which black women could achieve a modicum of economic independence. Their opportunities were even more restricted than those available to immigrant or native-born white women because manufacturers were eager to hire whites but not blacks. Moreover, in the 1840s, as Irish immigrants entered domestic service in growing numbers, the demand for black servants declined markedly, further limiting one of the few occupations available to African-American women.

Technological advances sometimes improved the opportunities available to workers, but the invention of the sewing machine in 1846 did not work to women's advantage. The machine did reduce the labor required to make each garment, but employers reaped the benefits. For each completed piece they dropped the rates paid so low that women often worked fifteen to eighteen hours a day on the new machines just to sustain themselves. Furthermore, their social subordination as women, their isolation from one another, and their poverty made these women easy victims of other abuses such as the arbitrary withholding of wages or sexual harassment.

Female outworkers in large urban areas found themselves in the most destitute circumstances. In 1845 the *New York Daily Tribune* described housing conditions among these workers. Most rented "a single room, perhaps two small rooms, in the upper story of some poor, ill-constructed, unventilated house in a filthy street. . . . In these rooms all the processes of cooking, eating, sleeping, washing, and living are indiscriminately performed." These women, the *Tribune* reported, spent "every cent" of their wages on necessities but still often lacked cash to "buy any other food than a scanty supply of potatoes and Indian meal and molasses for the family." The winter cold brought freezing temperatures to their garrets. "They are destitute of the means not only of adding comfortable clothing to their wretched wardrobes," the account concluded, "but of procuring an ounce of fuel."

Some female clothing workers were the wives and daughters of poor day laborers, declining craftsmen, and men seeking work in the West, but most headed their own households. Many had children to support. Thousands labored for Brooks Brothers and other big companies or for contractors and subcontractors. Supplying their own work space, fuel, light, needles, and thread, they received orders and cloth from a merchant or tailor and returned the completed work to him. The competion from new immigrants and desperate older workers caused pitifully low piece rates to continue falling. And working in the home made it difficult for the outworkers to band together to defend their common interests.

Isolation also affected the lives of domestic servants. In the 1850s, more than half of all female wage-earners were domestics whose wages averaged just over a dollar a week, plus room and board. These women were often on call twenty-four hours a day, six days a week, and under the constant surveillance of their employers. Room and board were only as generous as the employer allowed, and most found themselves stuck in attics or cellars with little heat or light, eating cold leftovers. Moreover, young women on their own might find themselves subject to sexual advances by male

"The Intelligence Office". This 1849 painting depicted an interview in an employment agency for domestic servants. While these agencies were ostensibly organized to shield young women from exploitation, they operated more as a reference service to prospective employers to ensure against the hiring of women deemed as unreliable or criminal.

Source: William Henry Burr, 1849, oil on canvas, 22 × 27 inches—New-York Historical Society.

employers or their sons, with little recourse short of leaving their position. Servants were a mobile lot, and they could generally leave a miserable situation for one slightly better as the demand for servants increased in the 1840s and 1850s. However, few situations offered more than minimal benefits, and most white servants left the occupation after a few years.

Teaching was one of the few occupations that offered women some real economic independence, yet it, too, was underpaid. As compulsory public education at the elementary level became mandatory in states across the North, local officials and school boards saw the advantage of hiring women at one-third to one-half the salary demanded by men. This was a profession open to black as well as white women, although the latter were hired only to teach black children and so generally worked under more difficult conditions and for less pay than their white counterparts. Female teachers were constrained by a variety of rules and regulations — they generally had to remain single, attend church regularly, provide their own wood, water, and school supplies, and avoid even the hint of scandal. Still, they were the lucky ones — women who earned both wages and respect at the same time.

Attacks on Immigrants, African Americans, and Workers

Men often considered working women a separate and inferior group, whose low wages and limited occupational choices were appropriate to their sex. Similarly, native-born whites often disparaged immigrant laborers, claiming that the newcomers belonged in the low-paying jobs they held. Massachusetts educator and politician Edward Everett, for example, argued that the Irish should be welcomed to America because "their inferiority as a race compels them to go to the bottom" of the occupational scale "and the consequence is that we are all, all of us, the higher lifted because they are here." The Irish, he continued, "do the manual labor. They do it most cheaply, and so they leave those whom they find" in those jobs "free to do other and more agreeable walks of duty."

Such prejudices spawned a national movement. An army of anti-immigrant writers, educators, ministers, and politicians, known as nativists, overlooked the contributions of immigrant laborers and argued that most of the nation's ills were the result of the newcomers' rejection of "American" work habits, culture, and religion. Immigrants' consumption of liquor and beer deeply offended these pious nativists, who linked temperance to republican morality. Even temperate and devout immigrants angered nativists if they were Catholic.

"The Voting-Place." Evangelical reformers objected to the undisciplined and sometimes violent atmosphere of working-class saloons. But, as indicated in this 1858 engraving of a bar in the Irish "Five Points" section of New York, reformers' concern involved more than the excesses of public drinking. The saloons were the organizing centers for the reformers' rivals, urban political machines like New York's Tammany Hall.

Source: *Harper's Weekly,* November 13, 1858—American Social History Project.

Immigration also bolstered the number of Roman Catholics in the United States in the 1840s and 1850s. Their ideals and beliefs contrasted sharply with those of evangelical Protestants. Where evangelicals pursued human perfection, Catholics adhered to an older and more lenient point of view: human beings were conceived in sin and were incapable of perfection on Earth. Although the church demanded moral conduct from Catholics, it granted that human frailty would inevitably, and repeatedly, lead them astray. The way back from sin could be found not in a single conversion, but in regular confession, repentance, and priestly absolution. Many Protestants also mistakenly believed that the Catholic Church required a kind of loyalty from its congregants that undermined democratic political practices.

In 1850, scattered clusters of secret anti-immigrant and anti-Catholic societies banded together into a national organization, and a year later into a new political party. Officially named the American Party, its followers were popularly labeled "Know-Nothings" because members often responded, "I know nothing," when questioned by outsiders. These Know-Nothings sought to disfranchise immigrant voters through literacy tests and to unite northern and southern whites against the "alien menace." They believed that a Catholic conspiracy was threatening America's republican institutions. One important goal, which they shared with some antislavery advocates, was keeping the West open for free settlement, although in this case, they explicitly meant free native-born white settlement.

"Look at the Hordes of Dutch and Irish Thieves and Vagabonds . . . "

Nativist—anti-immigrant—appeals to American-born workers and merchants were common throughout the 1840s and 1850s. The following election circular, printed in the *New York Daily Plebeian* on April 20, 1844, conveys a sense of how fear of immigrants was manipulated by politicians in search of votes and by businessmen looking to further divide the urban working class.

Look at the hordes of Dutch and Irish thieves and vagabonds, roaming about our streets, picking up rags and bones, pilfering sugar and coffee along our wharves and slips, and whatever our native citizens happen to leave in their way. Look at the English and Scotch pick-pockets and burglars, crowding our places of amusement, steam-boat landings, and hotels. Look at the Italian and French mountebanks, roaming the streets of every city in the Union with their dancing monkeys and hand-organs, all as an excuse for the purpose of robbing us of our property the first favorable opportunity. Look at the wandering Jews, crowding our business streets with their shops as receptacles for stolen goods, encouraging thievery and dishonesty among our citizens. Look at the Irish and Dutch grocers and rum-sellers monopolizing the business which properly belongs to our own native and true-born citizens.

Source: *New York Daily Plebian,* April 20, 1844.

". . . We Are Strong and Getting Stronger"

Immigrants responded to nativist attacks in various ways. In this 1847 letter to the New York *Champion of American Labor,* one foreign-born worker warned of the effects of nativism on mutual support between American- and foreign-born workers in the United States.

You intend to shut out the foreigners or naturalized citizens of this country from any benefit that will arise from your plans to get better wages. . . . You use the word *American* very often and nothing at all is said about *naturalized citizens,* but if you think to succeed without the aid of foreigners you will find yourself mistaken; for we are strong and are getting stronger every day, and though we feel the effects of competition from these men who are sent here from the poorhouses of Europe, yet if you don't include us to get better wages by shutting off such men, why, you needn't expect our help.

Source: *Champion of American Labor,* April 17, 1847.

Now feller citizens don't forget that we are the bones & brustles of this here republic, remember we are the sovereign people & the best judges of law & gospel. Remember this is called the age of intellect 'cause we the people know more than we used to did, & can't be imposed on as we used to could. Remember that the greatest blessing secured to us by the constitution is Religious liberty, which means as I understand it (& I flatter myself my understand is by no means contemptible — that if you dont approve of the religion of your neighbour, you are at liberty to burn his house down & thereby advance the true faith. I see that you understand the law as I do which proves you to be what your appearance indicates, whole souled, high minded, intelligent citizens, worthy of the cause in which you are engaged, a bright example to the world at large to theUnited states in general; & to our own state in particular The wolfish expression of piety in the countenances of some of our allies; the holy meat are physiognomy of others together with the natural unequivocal, whole-hog expression of our own townmen assure me that the heroes of mount Benedict will be remembered when those of Bunker's hill shall be forgotten

Support and orname
Behald the

"I say Down with the rum-rum-ruman catholics!
& hoora for the gin, gin-oaine faith

I'm sniggered if I dont vote
for our captain for next
congress

Defenders of the true Faith

Plain unceremonious human beings
Of all but moral character bereaved Pollok

Buri

In some cases nativist actions resulted in violence. In May 1844, shots emanating from an Irish firehouse scattered participants in a nativist rally in Philadelphia. Three nativists were killed in the opening skirmish, ten more along with one Irishman as the hostilities dragged on. The following night a full-scale riot erupted as nativist residents went on the attack, burning and looting Irish establishments and homes and attacking churches and other community institutions. A decade later in Brooklyn, immigrants and Know-Nothings clashed during the fall elections. Know-Nothings challenged the citizenship papers of Irish voters, inspiring an Irish mob to beat to death an election official. The mob, which included women, also drove off the nine deputies sent to protect the polls. Some of the women threw stones and flatirons, and a Mrs. Murphy urged the crowd to "kill them bloody Know-Nothings."

"Defenders of the True Faith." Cartoonist David Claypoole Johnston condemned the nativist rioters who burned down the Ursuline Convent in Charlestown, Massachusetts, on August 11, 1834.

Source: *Scraps* (1835)—Boston Athenaeum.

Competition for jobs provided another volatile arena for native-born and foreign-born groups. The ethnic transformation of the nation's labor force was far from immediate or total. Many native-born workers did find more desirable positions in these years, but many others—women and men, blacks and whites—were displaced by lower-paid immigrants. Others stayed in their old jobs, resentfully sharing the burdens of the industrial revolution with new foreign-born coworkers. Employers frequently encouraged nativist attitudes, partly out of genuine conviction, partly to deflect workers' anger away from themselves, and partly to undermine their employees' capacity to organize across ethnic lines. During the 1840s and 1850s, bloody brawls repeatedly broke out as groups of workers of different origins pitted themselves against one another.

The most brutal battles occurred between newly arrived immigrants and native-born blacks. Irish immigrants had been forced to the bottom of the occupational hierarchy by native-born whites and there they vied for jobs with African Americans. Conflict between free blacks and Irish was further encouraged by some employers, who preferred what they perceived as "docile Negroes" to "rowdy Irish." An ad in the *New York Herald* in the 1840s read, "Wanted, A Cook, Washer, and Ironer; who perfectly understands her business; any color or country except Irish." In response to such prejudice, Irish immigrants often laid claim to the "wages of whiteness," ridiculing, demeaning, and attacking the African Americans with whom they competed simply because they were black. In 1842, Irish coal miners in Pennsylvania attacked blacks who competed for their jobs; in 1853, armed African Americans replaced striking Irishmen on the Erie Railroad; and in 1855, Irish and black dockworkers battled along the New York City waterfront. Over and over again, those on the bottom rungs of the economic ladder struggled to keep one step above their nearest competition.

Leisure Activities in an Industrial Age

Despite the class and ethnic conflicts of this era, most people found ways to enjoy their leisure time, which offered respite from hard work and social upheaval. Alongside militias, volunteer fire companies, and fraternal associations, other organizations were formed that brought structure and regularity to leisure activities such as team sports and choral singing. Some of the most durable and best known were the societies founded at midcentury by German immigrants striving to preserve their own distinctive cultural and political traditions in an unfamiliar setting. Other leisure time activities (such as boxing matches and plays) brought together workers from diverse ethnic backgrounds or different social classes. Theater, for instance, once the province of the wealthy, was now open to working people, too. Reduced ticket prices made this possible. In the late 1700s, tickets at New York's Park Theater had cost $2.00 for the boxes, $1.50 in the pit, and $1.00 in the gallery. One-half century later, these prices had fallen to 75¢, 50¢, and $37\frac{1}{2}$¢, respectively. Another popular form of entertainment was P. T. Barnum's American Museum, which

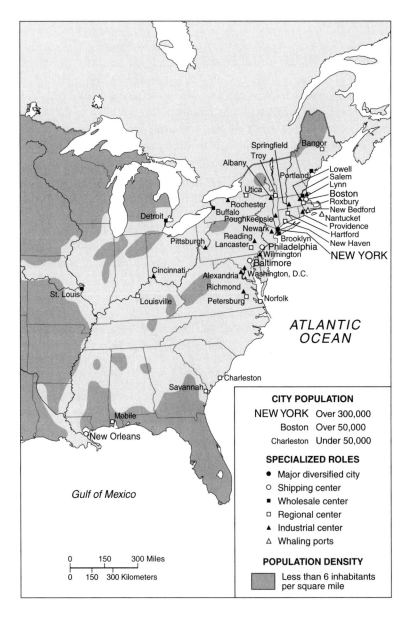

The Nation's Major Cities in 1840. In 1840, the eastern seaboard was still the site of the nation's largest cities, including New York, Boston, Philadelphia, and Baltimore. New urban areas were developing, however, to the west and south. These included industrial centers such as Rochester, Pittsburgh, Cincinnati, and Richmond, and regional centers such as Petersburg, Virginia, St. Louis, Missouri, and Louisville, Kentucky. Port cities such as Norfolk, Charleston, Savannah, and New Orleans were also growing rapidly in the early 1800s.

CITY POPULATION

NEW YORK Over 300,000
Boston Over 50,000
Charleston Under 50,000

SPECIALIZED ROLES

- ● Major diversified city
- ○ Shipping center
- ■ Wholesale center
- □ Regional center
- ▲ Industrial center
- △ Whaling ports

POPULATION DENSITY

Less than 6 inhabitants per square mile

offered visitors dwarfs, wax figures, jugglers, snake-charmers, bearded ladies, and fortunetellers. Over time, still other diversions arrived. In the 1840s, racetracks opened; and in the 1850s, baseball parks and music halls welcomed spectators.

The evolution of the theater clearly reveals the main forces shaping popular leisure and culture in this period. Theaters grew in size and attracted a more diverse audience. Less self-consciously highbrow than in earlier periods, theaters now offered many kinds of dramas (including temperance plays such as *The Drunkard* and so-called "equestrian dramas" featuring horses onstage) as well as comedies, musical revues, and specialty acts. Blackface minstrel shows (in which white actors crudely portrayed African Americans) that mixed antitemperance, anticapitalist, and racist themes were especially popular with white audiences. But Shakespeare also remained popular, owing to Americans' great love of melodramas with strong moral themes and larger-than-life heroes who took their fate into their own hands.

Democratic and patriotic themes especially pleased the crowds. Most popular were those plays in which a rough-and-ready American told off (and often knocked down) a pompous aristocratic Englishman. Audiences cheered such confrontations enthusiastically, and even Irish immigrants joined in. All might then climb onto the stage to join the battle. "When a patriotic fit seized them," British observer Frances Trollope noted, "and Yankee Doodle was called for, every man seemed to think his reputation as a citizen depended on the noise he made."

In May 1849, English actor William Charles Macready, popular with elite theatergoers, appeared in New York City at the same time as the American actor Edwin Forrest, who was a favorite of the working people. Anti-Macready protestors posted handbills all over the city demanding, "WORKING MEN, SHALL AMERICANS OR ENGLISH RULE IN THIS CITY?" On Macready's opening night, hostile audience members hurled everything handy (including their chairs), shouting,

Young Democracy at the Theater. As this 1852 lithograph indicated, it was often hard to tell where the performance really was situated in popular urban theaters. The raucous audience in this print included an aggressively critical German immigrant (in the center wearing a hat) and an artisan fire "laddie" preoccupied with a hasty meal (on the left).

Source: *The Old Soldier* (1852)—American Antiquarian Society.

"Down with the codfish aristocracy!" Two nights later, an angry crowd of thousands, led by young journeymen, gathered outside the Astor Place Opera House where Macready was scheduled to perform. The mob hurled paving stones through the windows. Police and the Seventh Regiment responded by shooting directly into the crowd, killing at least twenty-two and wounding more than one hundred forty others. The city was placed under martial law for three days. As one reporter wrote, the riot revealed "an opposition of classes—the rich and poor, . . . a feeling that there is now in our country, what every good patriot hitherto has considered it his duty to deny—a high and a low class."

Similar divisions between "high" and "low" culture shaped other forms of popular entertainment. Baseball and horse racing, for instance, offered respectable gentlemen a chance to enjoy the sporting life, whereas boxing matches and cockfights attracted working-class crowds. The middle classes praised the pure and sentimental ballads of Swedish singer Jenny Lind; spontaneous outbursts at neighborhood saloons or the racist tunes offered at minstrel shows were more common fare among the poor. This does not mean that workers might not have enjoyed the chance to hear Jenny Lind, or that respectable gentlemen were averse to "slumming" in working-class taverns. Rather, the differences in access to various forms of social life were, like access to jobs, determined by class, and often by sex and race as well.

Most of the diversions that lent excitement to the humdrum lives of the working class were dominated by men. These included boxing, baseball, and other sports and competitions among rival militia companies, volunteer fire brigades, and neighborhood street gangs as well as games at neighborhood taverns. The Bowery in New York City provided entertainment for both women and men, although only young, single women, freed from family responsibilities, could enjoy its assortment of saloons, sideshows, oyster houses, and gambling rooms. For men on the Bowery, betting added a special spice to all sorts of contests. Professional boxing was

"The Soaplocks, or Bowery Boys". This 1847 watercolor depicted the young men who habituated New York's working-class entertainment area, the Bowery. They wore the fashionable long sideburns that gave them the nickname. Around them, posters advertised some of the Bowery attractions the "B'hoys" attended after their workday ended.

Source: Nicolino Calyo, c. 1847, watercolor on paper, 10 7/16 × 14 7/8 inches—New-York Historical Society.

especially popular. Irish immigrants—many of them veterans of bloody "faction fights" in their homeland—produced both fighters for large purses and a growing number of fans in the 1840s. And although respectable society looked on with disdain, excited crowds gathered to watch and wager on traditional and violent animal sports such as cockfights, bullfights, dogfights, and bull and bear matches.

Boisterous entertainment could also turn violent, however. During the 1830s, 1840s, and 1850s, Philadelphia mummers—bands of youths (often mockingly made up as women or blacks)—marched through the city at Christmastime, assaulted members of various ethnic or racial groups, and filled the air with fireworks, gunfire, and raucous music. These demonstrations clearly reflected real hostilities between groups of working people, but they also ridiculed, annoyed, and harassed individuals higher up the social ladder, evoking an outraged response. In 1843, a newspaper decried the "riotous spirit raging" among the mummers that had turned Philadelphia into a "theater of disorders which practically nullify civil government." In cities throughout the North, raucous public celebrations of July Fourth and other holidays—including the weekly Sabbath work break—elicited similar expressions of outrage.

Much about these rough-and-tumble amusements was very old indeed. The noisy theater audiences were like those in Shakespeare's day. For centuries, crowds at leisure activities had protested actions and attacked people to whom they objected. Newer, at least in North America, was the chasm that now opened between this world and that of the respectable middle class. This chasm helped to give much of popular street life its anti-elite character.

Urban Disorder and Class Conflict

No doubt middle-class critics found boisterous entertainments particularly galling because they often took place right under their noses. The city was only just beginning to divide into distinct neighborhoods defined by income, and in older cities, this change would be very gradual. As late as 1863, according to one resident, New York's fashionable Washington Square area still encompassed lives of "every variety from luxury to poverty, and almost every branch of industry is represented." So the brawling was inescapable. Philadelphia's Christmas Eve revelers made sure that the middle class was aware of them by bringing their season's greetings downtown to the main business and theater district.

Disorderly public conduct, whether on the streets or in a theater, deeply affronted affluent urbanites. Their developing notions of propriety prized dignity, decorum, and strict self-control above most other virtues.

ST. PATRICK'S DAY 1867.

RUM   BRUTAL ATTACK ON THE POLICE. "THE DAY WE CELEBRATE" IRISH RIOT. Th Nast. BLOOD.

To watch a city's public spaces being dominated by the boisterous behavior of workers, immigrants, and the poor repelled them and challenged their right to dictate society's moral standards. Consequently, in city after city, taxpayers and the officials they elected decided it was time to curb such disruptions by investing in a paid police force. Boston established a police force in 1837 and New York in 1844, both in response to the riots, strikes, and growing crime and prostitution that now plagued large cities.

In the late 1840s, New York's chief of police cited another "deplorable and growing evil, the constantly increasing number of vagrant, idle, and vicious children . . . who infest our public thoroughfares." To most middle-class journalists and reformers, these children roamed the streets because their parents were morally bankrupt. An 1856 report by the New York City Children's Aid Society on a mother of such roaming children declared, "In such a woman there is little confidence to be put." Indulging "some cursed vice," the agent assumed, had reduced her to poverty in the first place, and "if her children be not separated from her, she will drag them down, too."

In fact, however, these children were a byproduct of the social changes of the era and the enormous pressures their impoverished parents faced. Rural American and immigrant families flowed to the cities, filling them with children. Although some hard-pressed parents did neglect or abandon their children, most needed their children's help to survive. Sons

"The Day We Celebrate."
Harper's Weekly cartoonist Thomas Nast portrayed a riot on St. Patrick's Day as a violent urban "sport." Nast's portrayal of the Irish, baring their teeth along with other weaponry, was typical of nineteenth-century cartoonists who gave each immigrant working-class group the physical traits supposedly characteristic of its "race" and place in a social hierarchy.

Source: *Harper's Weekly,* April 6, 1867 — American Social History Project.

452

". . . Vagrant, Idle, and Vicious Children"

In this 1850 letter, New York chief of police George W. Matsell deplored the growth of "juvenile vagrancy" and placed the responsibility on the youngsters' parents.

I deem it my duty to call the attention of your Honor to a deplorable and growing evil which [exists] amid this community, and which is spread over the principal business parts of the city. It is an evil and a reproach to our municipality for which the laws and ordinances afford no adequate remedy.

I allude to the constantly increasing numbers of vagrant, idle, and vicious children of both sexes, who infest our public thoroughfares, hotels, docks, &c. Children who are growing up in ignorance and profligacy, only destined to a life of misery, shame, and crime, and ultimately to a felon's doom. Their numbers are almost incredible, and to those whose business and habits do not permit them a searching scrutiny, the degrading and disgusting practices of these almost infants in the schools of vice, prostitution, and rowdyism, would certainly be beyond belief. The offspring of always careless, generally intemperate, and oftentimes immoral and dishonest parents, they never see the inside of a school-room, and so far as our excellent system of public education (which may be truly said to be the foundation stone of our free institutions) [is concerned], it is to them an entire nullity. Left, in many instances, to roam day and night wherever their inclination leads them, a large proportion of these juvenile vagrants are in the daily practice of pilfering wherever opportunity offers, and begging where they cannot steal. . . . Astounding as it may seem, there are many hundreds of parents in this City who absolutely drive their offspring forth to practices of theft and semi-bestiality, that they themselves may live lazily on the means thus secured,—selling the very bodiies and souls of those in whom their own blood circulates, for the means of dissipation and debauchery.

Source: George W. Matsell, Appendix, New York City Board of Aldermen Documents (1850).

and daughters might do household chores, run errands, look after younger sisters and brothers, buy provisions or borrow them from neighbors—even beg and scavenge for food, wood, and coal, or for items that could be sold to junk dealers. Boys as young as eight or nine earned money by peddling hot corn, sweet potatoes, string, pins, or newspapers. Girls worked alongside mothers doing outwork or helped out in more affluent households for a few pennies. Although most working-class parents regretted the uglier aspects of their children's lives, they simply found it impossible to live by middle-class standards.

The middle class was also appalled by the growing incidence of crime and prostitution, reported in lurid detail in the mass-circulation "penny press." In 1836, the press had had a field day covering the brutal murder of Helen Jewett, an attractive young woman from Maine working as a prostitute in Manhattan. She had been slashed and burned in her bed in the early morning hours of April 10. Prostitution was the danger most closely associated with impoverished women, and one that aroused intense concern in the early nineteenth century. In 1832, John McDowell, agent for the evangelical Magdalen Society, which sought to banish prostitution from New York City, proclaimed, "We have satisfactorily ascertained the fact the number of females in this city, who abandon themselves to prostitution is not less than TEN THOUSAND!!!!!" Although accurate statistics on the incidence of prostitution in the nineteenth century are nearly impossible to obtain, it is likely that the numbers did indeed rise steadily as urban populations rose.

Like so many other aspects of working-class street life in the 1840s and 1850s, prostitution was a product of changing economic relations and occupational opportunities. With more women than ever before needing to earn wages and with few chances for them to find full-time, year-round work at a living wage, women fell into prostitution during times of economic crisis. Some turned to it only temporarily or episodically, but others became trapped in this life. Many may have decided that prostitution was not the worst choice a workingwoman could make, offering better wages and hours than the more respectable jobs available to them.

"Hooking a Victim." This lithograph printed around 1850 depicted three prostitutes soliciting on a gas-lit city street. Some women chose prostitution as an alternative to (or to supplement) low-wage domestic or sewing work. Reformers (and artists) sentimentalized and demonized prostitutes, viewing them either as betrayed innocents, victimized by poverty or deceitful seducers, or as "abandoned women" craving sex and liquor.

Source: Serrell and Perkins, *New York by Gas-Light. Hooking a Victim,* c. 1850, lithograph—Museum of the City of New York.

As prostitution increased in large cities such as New York, Boston, Philadelphia, and Chicago, certain areas became known for their "houses of ill repute," and these areas themselves had distinct reputations based on the quality of both their prostitutes and their clientele. In New York, for example, the notorious Five Points district was inhabited, according to the *New York Evening Post* "by a race of beings of all colours, ages, sexes, and nations."

Lith & Pub by Serrell & Perkins.

A center of poor black and poor Irish settlement, it was home to numerous bars, gambling dens, and brothels. Although wealthy and middle-class white men might go slumming there, the level of drunkenness, crime, and disease in the district assured that it would remain off-limits to most genteel customers, and to those women who sought to attract a better class of clients.

Guides printed in such papers as *The Sporting Whip* helped visitors and locals find a better class of brothel. In the early 1840s, they ranked "Princess Julia's" house as one of the best in New York. It was located on 55 Leonard Street, in a block of three- and four-story private residences. A full-time police officer lived across the street; an opera house was down the block; a former mayor, Edward P. Livingston, lived at 73 Leonard; and in between the brothel and the Livingston mansion sat the Zion Methodist Church, whose black congregants included some of the city's most respectable families. No longer confined to the bawdy houses in poor neighborhoods, prostitution, claimed social investigator William Sanger, "boldly strikes through our most thronged and elegant thoroughfares." Elegant furnishings and genteel surroundings characterized Princess Julia's brothel. But this elegance did not save the women who worked for her from disease, assaults, or the inevitable decline in wages that occurred with age. It was at Princess Julia's that Helen Jewett was murdered.

Middle-Class Efforts at Moral Reform

Prostitution became a growing concern among middle-class Americans not only in cosmopolitan centers such as New York City. In Rochester, New York, a canal town of fewer than fifteen thousand in 1836, the wives of upwardly mobile bankers, merchants, and professionals formed a local Female Moral Reform Society and discussed such questions as "Ought licentious men be exposed?" Throughout the late 1830s and early 1840s, they prayed for the salvation of prostitutes, condemned the men who bought their services, and circulated religious tracts and *The Advocate of Moral Reform*. In 1849, they institutionalized their rescue efforts by founding a Home for Friendless and Virtuous Females to offer refuge to young women at risk of becoming prostitutes (although not to those already fallen). Many of these reform-minded women were also active in the city's temperance society; several helped to found the Rochester Orphan Asylum; and dozens signed petitions on behalf of the abolition of slavery. Although their efforts were temporarily frustrated by the depression of the late 1830s and early 1840s, the return to prosperity led to larger and more varied campaigns to uplift the poor, rescue the fallen, and purify society.

Earlier reformers had often argued that social ills were the fault of individuals rather than society and that only personal conversions and salvations could transform the world. Female moral reformers, however, took a different tack, blaming men, usually well-to-do and native-born, for ruining young women and driving them into a life of prostitution. These reformers believed that solutions could be found in the dissemination of middle-class Protestant values. In the 1850s, for instance, New York's Children's Aid Society placed poor urban (often Catholic) youngsters with rural Protestant foster parents as the best means of "saving" them from dangerous influences. At times they "rescued" such young people without the parents' approval. The Society's industrial schools and lodging houses also taught street girls that "nothing was so honorable as industrious *house-work*," thereby preparing them for the kind of domestic service jobs that made the lives of middle-class housewives easier without significantly improving the lot of working-class families.

House of Refuge. Reformers blamed poverty on the moral failure of working-class households. Giving up on adults, many "missionaries" focused on the children of the poor. This emblem of the Philadelphia House of Refuge declared the reformers' belief in their capacity to convert children into model citizens.

Source: C. G. Childs, Philadelphia House of Refuge—Print Collection, Miriam and Ira Wallach Division of Art, Prints, and Photographs, New York Public Library, Astor, Lenox and Tilden Foundations.

Moral reform campaigns appealed not just to well-to-do women but also to people of lesser means who had high hopes for themselves. The promise of personal advancement in the future, if only one lived right and worked hard, spoke to the dreams of many small shopkeepers, farmers, and craftsmen. Among this group, religious concerns with social disorder struck a sympathetic chord. They disapproved of the growing ranks of propertyless craft workers and laborers below them, with their boisterous and irreverent behavior and the radical ideas some of them voiced. This disapproval mounted in the 1840s and 1850s as more and more Irish and German immigrants flowed into these low-income occupations. Continuing to blame the poor for their poverty, these reform-minded Americans, many inspired by evangelical beliefs, provided support to nativist movements in the 1840s and 1850s.

Radical Evangelicalism, Communal Experiments, and Cooperative Enterprises

Other more radical-minded working people identified with less conservative forms of evangelicalism, rejecting an elitist ministry and coldly formal church services where the wealthy flaunted their power and privilege. "Is it strange?" asked labor leader Sarah Bagley, a worker in the Lowell textile mills, "that the operatives should stay away from the

"Can This be the Sabbath . . . ?"

Troubled by evidence of extreme poverty in the nation's industrializing cities, many Protestant reformers set up mission houses in poor, immigrant neighborhoods to minister to the needs of the largely Catholic residents. But a cultural abyss divided reformers from the people they wanted to help. In the House of Industry's 1857 *Monthly Record,* a shocked Protestant missionary, Louis M. Pease, describes the Sunday activity in the Five Points, a working-class immigrant neighborhood in New York City.

"Can this be the Sabbath—God's holy day?" I involuntarily exclaimed, as I stood for a moment at the entrance of one of the avenues leading to the Five Points, and beheld the crowd of people pressing up and down Chatham street, while the heavily laden cars passed by, crowded with pleasure-seekers bound for the country, on their weekly holiday excursion. And then, as I walked slowly up Baxter street, to see the rum-shops, the junk-shops, the pawn-shops, the groceries, and the low Jewish clothing-stalls all open, the side-walks lined with apple-stands, and juvenile traffickers in papers and peanuts, while here and there were groups of night-thieves, vagabond boys, and loathsome, shameless girls prematurely ripened into infamous womanhood. Oh! who would suppose that this was the sabbath of the Metropolis of this great and Heaven-blessed country!

Source: *Five Points Monthly Record,* May 1857.

churches where they see the men [their employers] filling the 'chief seats' who are taking every means to grind them into the very dust?" Radical evangelicals also denounced personal greed and the threat it posed to community rights and older values of mutual support and cooperation. God intended, wrote evangelical labor journalist William Young in 1845, that humanity "should be bound together by nature's golden chain . . . into one harmonious whole—no slaves—no servants—no masters—no oppressed and no oppressors—but in the language of Christ—'For one is your master, and all ye are brethren.'"

Less firmly based in the churches than the conservatives, radical evangelicals were drawn toward several religiously inspired social reform campaigns, such as those advocating temperance, public education, and the end of slavery. But they approached these issues in a distinctive spirit. Whereas conservative reformers hoped that public schools would help tame the lower classes and create more conscientious and disciplined wives and workers, radicals wanted them to help working people learn and defend their rights as citizens and producers. The same point of view influenced them to form separate reform groups such as the Washingtonian Temperance Society, through which reformed drunkards worked to uplift themselves and convert other workingmen to their cause. The result was a tug-of-war between radical and conservative evangelicals over the nature and goals of reform, with one side stressing popular participation and democratic rights, and the other emphasizing social order.

A few radical movements of the mid nineteenth century sought to bridge the traditional social divisions of class and gender. Some established entirely new communities based on collective ownership of property and infused with the spirit of cooperation instead of competition. Viewing North America as a new world still in the making, European emigrants had begun erecting model utopian societies early in the eighteenth century. The largest of these was a religious movement called the Shakers; by the 1830s, it claimed more than six thousand members. Smaller cooperative communities such as Brook Farm in Massachusetts also took seriously the need to change society. Founded in 1841, Brook Farm expressed Christian disenchantment with commercializing and industrializing America. The colony's founder, Unitarian minister George Ripley, decried

> the glaring inequalities of conditions, the hollow pretensions of pride, the scornful apathy with which many urge the prostration of man, the burning zeal with which they run the race of selfish competition with no thought for the elevation of their brethren.

Several communal experiments in the 1830s and 1840s, including some of the most long lived, were founded on religious principles. German Mennonites, for instance, who had first settled in North America in the eighteenth century, formed several communities in Pennsylvania.

"The Change from Error and Misery, to Truth and Happiness." Robert Owen and the design of his New Harmony utopian community in Indiana appeared on the title page of *The Crisis,* written by Owen and his son in 1833.

Source: Robert Owen and Robert Dale Owen, *The Crisis, or the Change from Error and Misery, to Truth and Happiness* (1833)—Rare Books and Manuscripts Division, New York Public Library, Astor, Lenox and Tilden Foundations.

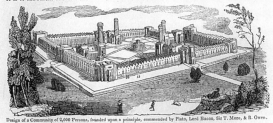

THE CRISIS,

OR THE CHANGE FROM ERROR AND MISERY, TO TRUTH AND HAPPINESS.

1832.

IF WE CANNOT YET LET US ENDEAVOUR — RECONCILE ALL OPINIONS, TO UNITE ALL HEARTS.

IT IS OF ALL TRUTHS THE MOST IMPORTANT, THAT THE CHARACTER OF MAN IS FORMED FOR—NOT BY HIMSELF.

Design of a Community of 2,000 Persons, founded upon a principle, commended by Plato, Lord Bacon, Sir T. More, & R. Owen.

EDITED BY
ROBERT OWEN AND ROBERT DALE OWEN.

London:
PRINTED AND PUBLISHED BY J. EAMONSON, 15, CHICHESTER PLACE, GRAY'S INN ROAD.
STRANGE, PATERNOSTER ROW. PURKISS, OLD COMPTON STREET, AND MAY BE HAD OF ALL BOOKSELLERS.
1833.

"Nashoba, April 19, 1828." Influenced by Robert Owen and New Harmony, Frances Wright established an interracial utopian community, Nashoba, near Memphis, Tennessee. Its white and black residents (including slaves purchased by Wright) worked and lived together. Believing that racism could be defeated only by the "amalgamation of the races," Wright permitted interracial sexual relationships in the Nashoba community. Even abolitionists condemned the experiment. This is a sketch by Charles-Alexandre Lesueur, a French artist-naturalist who spent ten years at New Harmony.

Source: Charles-Alexandre Lesueur, April 19, 1828, pencil drawing—No. 43122, Musée d'Histoire Naturelle du Havre.

Other utopian experiments based their ideas on those introduced in the 1820s at New Harmony, Indiana, and elsewhere by the Irish-born industrialist Robert Owen. Owen sought to apply ideas about social reform that he had first developed in Scotland. Some of these ideas fit particularly well in the new world. Like many Americans, for example, Owen was excited by the possibilities that the development of industry and technology opened up. Rising productivity made it possible to produce more and more goods and services while expending less and less human labor. But for all to reap the benefits of industrial development, Owen believed, humankind must replace the competitive economic system with one based on cooperation. In such a society there would be "no personal inequality, or gradation of rank and station; all will be equal in their condition." Like many other communitarians, Owen also sought equal rights for women. His ideas attracted business people, professionals, farmers, mechanics, and laborers to his communities.

Associationism, a kindred movement based on the ideas of French visionary Charles Fourier, gained popularity in the United States during the 1840s and 1850s. Nearly thirty phalanxes (as such communities were called) arose in these decades, appearing as far west as Michigan, Iowa, and Wisconsin. One of those drawn to them was Mary Paul, the daughter of a Vermont farmer and a textile-mill operative. In 1853–1854, her Lowell stint and a term of domestic service behind her, Paul entered the North American Phalanx in Red Bank, New Jersey. Her enthusiastic letters home extol the doctrines of sexual and economic equality. At the

phalanx, Mary Paul wrote, she would "not be confined to one kind of work but could do almost anything." Equally exciting was the prospect of receiving pay equal to that of a man. "You know," she reminded her father, in society at large "men often get more than double the pay for doing the same work that women do." Such discrimination was forbidden among Associationists. "*All* work there, and all are paid alike. Both men and women have the *same pay* for the *same* work."

". . . Crushing the Producers of Wealth to the Very Dust"

In 1845, the Boston Mechanics' and Laborers' Association founded a cooperative society. A committee of that association drafted the statement excerpted below to explain the purpose and methods of cooperation.

It is our belief that the same causes of evil and suffering are operative in this country, that, in the Old World, are developed to giant magnitude, and are crushing the producers of wealth to the very dust, and that unless a speedy change can be effected in our social condition the time is not far distant when the laborers of the United States will be as dependent, as oppressed, and as wretched as are their brethren in Europe. Here, as there, the soil, motive power, and machinery are monopolized by the idle few; all the sources of wealth, all the instrumentalities of life, and even the right and privilege of industry are taken away from the people. Monopoly has laid its ruthless hands upon labor itself, and forced the sale of the muscles and skill of the toiling many, and under the specious name of "wages" is robbing them of the fruits of their industry. Universal monopoly is the bane of labor not less in America than in Europe. . . .

The remedy lies in a radical change of principle and policy. Our isolated position and interests, and our antisocial habits, must be abandoned. The Money-power must be superseded by the Man-power. Universal Monopoly must give place to Societary ownership, occupancy, and use. . . . The direction and profits of industry must be kept in the hands of the producers. Laborers must own their own shops and factories, work their own stock, sell their own merchandise, and enjoy the fruits of their own toil. Our Lowells must be owned by the artisans who build them, and [by] the operatives who run the machinery and do all the work. And the dividend, instead of being given to the idle parasites of a distant city, should be shared among those who perform the labor. Our Lynns must give the fortunes made by the [shoe] dealer and employer, to those who use the awl and work the material.

Source: *The Awl,* January 18, 1845.

Between the American Revolution and the Civil War, more than one hundred experimental communities appeared. But great obstacles beset the communitarian experiments from the start. With their limited resources, most found it difficult to match the enticements offered by the competitive world outside. Moreover, even modest economic setbacks could spell disaster for communities already operating close to the financial edge. Critics cited these failures as proof that the whole attempt had been futile. Mary Paul felt differently. "I know," she added, "many will exult in the downfall of this place, but [they] are shortsighted." In just one year at the phalanx, she had "already seen enough to convince me that Association is the true life. And although all the attempts that have ever yet been made towards it have been failures . . . my faith in the principle is as strong as ever, stronger if possible."

Cooperative enterprises embodied some of the same values as cooperative communities, but on a smaller scale. They challenged the wage-labor system in one industry at a time. For instance, Lynn shoemakers as well as Lowell textile operatives organized cooperative workshops. Under the leadership of exiled English radical B. S. Treanor, Irish tailors in Boston did the same. So did German women tailors in Cleveland. Indeed, working people established cooperative enterprises in virtually every major town and city of the North and West. Sometimes workers on strike established cooperatives as temporary measures to help sustain themselves. Striking journeymen printers launched Cincinnati's *Daily Unionist* as well as New York's German-language *Abendzeitung*. Some cooperatives founded as temporary measures eventually became permanent institutions.

Movements for Land Reform

Land reform offered another means of improving the plight of Americans, especially of American workers. Since the beginning of European settlement in the New World, the promise of abundant land had lured millions across the Atlantic. It still beckoned in the 1840s and 1850s. The federal government owned huge tracts of unimproved soil in the West, but much of this was unavailable to small farmers. Most was given in subsidy to private railroad companies or sold in large tracts on the open market. Big land companies, banks, and wealthy individual speculators bought up enormous quantities of public land. By 1860, speculators owned over twenty million acres in Illinois and Iowa alone—nearly a quarter of the land in those states—and nearly half of all the privately held land in Minnesota. They then jacked up the price and resold the land in smaller plots to homesteaders. Those who could not afford land on these terms became

461

farm laborers or tenants of large landowners. Those who did buy their own farms frequently went into debt to do so. Later, unable to meet their payments, many lost both their homesteads and their life savings.

Reformers protested these government land policies and the speculation and landlordism they encouraged. Demanding that public lands be distributed to the needy, reformers hoped to slow the growth of wage labor and tenancy. The best-known and most energetic land reformer in the 1830s and 1840s was George Henry Evans, a Welsh-born printer and a leader of the Workingmen's Party. Evans and his allies denounced the concentration of land in the hands of a minority, branding it "the king monopoly, the cause of the greatest evils." Evans insisted, "If any man has a right . . . to live, he has a right to land enough for his subsistence. Deprive anyone of these rights, and you place him at the mercy of those who possess them." Without free soil, he concluded, trade unions were futile. Public land must be made available free of charge, and only to those who would actually settle and till it.

The National Trades Union (NTU), which was organized as a labor union in 1834, also linked "the interests and independence of the laboring class" to the land question. Its members believed that if "public lands were left open to actual settlers," surplus workers would be "drained off" from the cities into agriculture, relieving urban unemployment and job competition. Lowell's labor newspaper, the *Voice of Industry,* warmly endorsed demands for "free soil," as did Lynn's shoe workers. As one shoemaker, anguished by the prospect of permanent wage labor, demanded, "Where shall we go but on to the land? Deprive us of this and you reduce us to the condition of the serfs of Europe."

German immigrants were also enthusiastic about land reform. The best-known German-American land reform advocate was Hermann Kriege, who in the mid 1840s took up the argument made a decade earlier by the NTU. By easing urban overcrowding, Kriege argued, land reform would eliminate the principal cause of antiforeign sentiment in the United States. "Once the soil is free," he wrote, "then every honest workingman," regardless of birthplace, would be treated by all Americans as a "blessing to our republic."

At its inception, the land-reform movement in the United States had no direct connection with antislavery sentiment. Indeed, by the end of his life, George Henry Evans—once the champion of Nat Turner and a fierce critic of slavery—was explicitly advocating participation in the land reform movement instead of the abolitionist campaign. In later years, however, the seemingly separate threads of westward expansion, free labor, free land, and the future of slavery would all become tightly interwoven.

Women Reformers Seek Rights for Themselves

Women were active in many of the reform and radical movements of the 1830s and 1840s. Although the sphere defined for women varied dramatically by class, race, ethnicity, and region, almost all women lacked the right to keep their wages, retain custody over their children, or protect their bodies from assault. Free black women, many of whom were active in the antislavery movement, were often faced with having to support their families, to fend off attacks by white employers and neighbors, and to assist fugitives from slavery. Newly arrived immigrant women—Irish, German, Scandanavian, and Canadian—required adequate wages, decent housing, and access to education in order to maintain their families. Although few of these women joined the formal women's rights movement in this period, many recognized the need for wider opportunities and collective action.

Marriage was often the first lesson in the need for female autonomy. The diary kept by Massachusetts worker Sarah Trask during the 1840s and 1850s reveals one workingwoman's deep concern about male drunkenness and male domination of the household. A bride "must go just where her husband says," Trask observed, adding that "marriage to me seems a great responsibility . . . and almost all the care comes upon the wife." At the same time, her diary registers the wrenching impact on women when their men died or went off to seek their fortunes in the West.

The domestic lives of impoverished women did not fit the new middle-class ideals of domesticity. Middle-class observers viewed the divergence between their own homes and those of the poor with mounting alarm. Indeed, Elizabeth Cady Stanton, one of the founders of the women's rights movement in the United States, claimed that the plight of Irish women in her hometown of Seneca Falls, New York, helped inspire her interest in the cause. Recalling many years later the events that led her to call a women's rights convention in 1848, she wrote of her Irish neighbors with a mix of concern and condescension:

> Alas! Alas! who can measure the mountains of sorrow and suffering endured in unwelcome motherhood in the abodes of ignorance, poverty, and vice, where terror-stricken women and children are the victims of strong men frenzied with passion and intoxicating drink?

Other women were prompted to analyze the position of women in society because of their involvement in other social causes, such as the abolition of slavery. As Quaker abolitionist Angelina Grimke noted, "The investigation of the rights of the slave has led me to a better understand-

Yᴱ MAY SESSION OF Yᴱ WOMAN'S RIGHTS CONVENTION—Yᴱ ORATOR OF Yᴱ DAY DENOUNCING Yᴱ LORDS OF CREATION.

"The Amazonian Convention." The proceedings of a women's-rights meeting were disrupted by hecklers in an 1859 cartoon published in *Harper's Weekly*.

Source: J. M'Nevin, *Harper's Weekly*, June 11, 1859—General Research Division, New York Public Library, Astor, Lenox and Tilden Foundations.

ing of my own" rights. It was a Quaker contingent, in fact, that provided the core of the movement for women's rights in the mid nineteenth century. Led by Lucretia Mott of Philadelphia, Mary Ann McClintock of Waterloo, New York, and Amy Post of Rochester, these feminist Friends claimed a decade of experience in social movements. They advocated abolition, Indian rights, land reform, and other causes before joining the ranks of women's rights advocates. For these women, the campaign for equality of the sexes was important as part of a larger effort that included the achievement of racial and economic justice.

Four Quaker activists joined Elizabeth Cady Stanton in organizing the first women's rights convention in the United States, held in July 1848 at Seneca Falls, New York. Attended by some two to three hundred people, the convention issued a manifesto modeled on the Declaration of Independence, declaring that "all men *and women* are created equal." Demands for greater social and economic rights for American women had been voiced before this. But only now did an organized movement arise, led by women and dedicated to winning for women a wider sphere and equal rights. For a few leaders, including Stanton, the most crucial demand to assure women's first-class citizenship was the right to vote. Yet the resolution on behalf of female suffrage that she introduced at Seneca Falls raised

"... A Dependent and Abject Life"

The resolutions passed at the first women's rights convention, at Seneca Falls in 1848, parts of which are presented below, demanded that women be given their full political and civil rights as citizens of the United States.

The history of mankind is a history of repeated injuries and usurpations on the part of man toward woman, having in direct object the establishment of a absolute tyranny over her. To prove this, let facts be submitted to a candid world:

He has never permitted her to exercise her inalienable right to the elective franchise.

He has compelled her to submit to laws, in the formation of which she had no voice.

He has made her, if married, in the eye of the law, civilly dead.

He has taken from her all right in property, even to the wages she earns.

... In the covenant of marriage, she is compelled to promise obedience to her husband, he becoming, to all intents and purposes, her master—the law giving him power to deprive her of her liberty, and to administer chastisement.

He has monopolized nearly all the profitable employments, and from those she is permitted to follow, she receives but a scanty remuneration. He closes against her all the avenues to wealth and distinction which he considers most honorable to himself. As a teacher of theology, medicine, or law, she is not known.

He has created a false public sentiment by giving to the world a different code of morals for men and women, by which moral delinquencies which exclude women from society, are not only tolerated, but deemed of little account in man.

He has endeavored, in every way that he could, to destroy her confidence in her own powers, to lessen her self-respect, and to make her willing to lead a dependent and abject life.

Source: Philip S. Foner, ed., *We the Other People* (1976).

the most heated debate. Supported by Frederick Douglass, who was deeply concerned with votes for free blacks, the resolution passed, although not unanimously as the other resolutions did. For most women's rights advocates, an enlarged sphere of action for women in the home, the church, education, and work was as important as political rights. This was a platform on which many immigrant, African-American, and working-class women could have easily stood alongside their native-born, middle-class, reform-minded counterparts.

Abolitionists Fight Slavery and Each Other

For many reform-minded women and men, the eradication of slavery was the most important movement of the day. Led by people such as William Lloyd Garrison, Frederick Douglass, and Abby Kelley, who advocated immediate emancipation, radical abolitionists argued that other forms of bondage—wage slavery and prostitution, for instance—paled in comparison with the millions held in servitude by southern planters. Seeking to create a movement that reflected democratic and egalitarian ideals, radical abolitionists demanded that antislavery groups, including the American Anti-Slavery Society (AASS), be open to women as well as to men and to African Americans as well as to whites.

The commitment of radical abolitionists to principles of both racial and sexual equality ensured that some who agreed with the abolition of slavery but not equal rights for women would disagree over the means to achieve emancipation. By the late 1830s and 1840s the result was factionalism and infighting among abolitionists. But such disagreements also multiplied the number and range of antislavery movements, forcing more and more of those who lived in the free-labor North to confront their complicity with slavery in the South.

In 1837 the tensions mounted in response to a controversial lecture tour by Sarah and Angelina Grimke. Southern-born daughters of a slaveholder, the Grimkes rejected the values of their family and region, moved to Philadelphia, and joined the Society of Friends. They were quickly adopted by the Garrisonians, who organized the tour for them. Noting, among other issues, the links between the plight of slaves and their own plight as women, they were condemned by the Congregational ministers of New England. Although the Grimkes were supported by the AASS, some in the organization were not eager to embrace their pioneering call for women's rights, fearing that it would undermine the power of the antislavery message.

In 1840, all of these issues came to a head at the organization's annual meeting. After a bitter fight over Abby Kelley's election to the AASS executive committee, more conservative abolitionists walked out. One politically oriented group formed the Liberty Party, hoping to achieve through the electoral system what seemed impossible using merely the power of moral persuasion. Another religiously oriented faction, led by Lewis Tappan, founded the American and Foreign Anti-Slavery Society, which urged participants to work within the evangelical churches. Those who remained in the AASS formed an even more tightly knit and radical

"Am I Not a Woman and a Sister?" This engraving appeared in abolitionist George Bourne's *Slavery Illustrated in Its Effects upon Women,* published in 1837.

Source: George Bourne, *Slavery Illustrated in Its Effects upon Women* (1837)—Prints and Photographs Division, Library of Congress.

group than before. Women and free blacks played increasingly prominent roles in the organization, which attacked the churches and the government even more severely as props of southern slavery. Among this contingent, many opposed war and capital punishment, refused to buy slave-produced products, embraced health reforms such as high-fiber diets and water cures, rejected traditional forms of religious worship, participated in utopian experiments, and campaigned for women's rights, Indian rights, and land reform. Most free black and some white radical abolitionists also provided assistance to fugitive slaves, fought segregation in northern schools and jobs, and advocated black voting rights.

Throughout the 1840s and early 1850s, the battle to abolish slavery moved along several tracks at once. One of the most important new paths was followed by political abolitionists who rejected the tactics of the AASS and instead sought to end slavery through congressional intervention. This politically oriented segment of the antislavery movement entered electoral contests just as the influx of immigrants was beginning to change the face of American politics. Together these two new forces would redraw the political system in the United States.

Political Parties Compete for the Electorate

In 1848, a new political party, the Free Soil Party, was born. The founders included free black abolitionists such as Frederick Douglass, Samuel Ringwold Ward, Henry Highland Garnet, Charles Remond, and Henry Bibb. The party drew heavily on former Liberty Party supporters, such as the wealthy reformer Gerrit Smith, and it attracted the attention of more religiously inclined radical abolitionists, such as Thomas Wentworth Higginson and Theodore Parker. But the new Free Soil Party extended beyond these older circles of antislavery sentiment to attract disaffected Whigs and Democrats. In the 1848 presidential election, ex-Democrat Martin Van Buren headed the Free Soil ticket and former Whig Charles Francis Adams, the son of John Quincy Adams, was selected as his running mate. This was a party that could have broad appeal to diverse sectors of the electorate.

The rise of the Free Soil Party was a response in large part to the poor showing of the Liberty Party four years earlier. Political abolitionists had then been too narrowly focused on the abolition of slavery to compete successfully at the national level. Now they de-emphasized moral and political rights of blacks and instead aimed their efforts at defeating the "Slave Power" conspiracy. The Free Soilers claimed that the "Slave Power" endangered the rights of free speech and free press as well as free labor.

Party leaders argued that the critical issue was excluding slavery from the West to keep it open for white settlement. By 1848, then, the goals of political abolitionism had shifted dramatically, away from ending slavery in the South and toward promoting the settlement of free men, particularly free white men, in the West.

The Free Soil campaign angered many people. Radical abolitionists such as Garrison denounced the party platform, and many saw the nomination of Van Buren, who had earlier allied himself with slaveholders, as a travesty. Slave owners were also infuriated by the emergence of Free Soilers, who threatened to undermine the two major political parties and the federal union. Northern business and political leaders likewise feared that this third party might dangerously polarize the nation.

Nonetheless, the Free Soil platform proved sufficiently broad to attract widespread support. Van Buren received almost three hundred thousand votes in the 1848 election. This was nearly five times as many as Liberty Party candidate James G. Birney had received four years earlier. It represented nearly one in every seven ballots cast in the free states. Especially successful among small farmers, the Free Soil Party also found support among certain industrial workers. Lynn shoemakers proved quite receptive, and the party carried that city. Leading land reformers were attracted to the party, too. Many participated in its founding convention. German Free Soilers vowed to "carry out land reform measures in the most radical manner" and announced themselves "strictly opposed to Slavery in whatever shape it might be seen."

As the antislavery claims of the Germans suggest, the Free Soil Party gained the support of many ardent abolitionists despite the critiques of radicals. In the midwestern states, antislavery women formed dozens of societies to support the Free Soil campaign. In St. Cloud, Minnesota, reformer Jane Swisshelm founded a newspaper, the *Visitor,* that advocated Free Soil principles and won, she claimed, thousands of votes for the party. Perhaps even more significantly, free black abolitionists embraced the Free Soil platform, despite the antiblack sentiments of some party leaders. "It is nothing against the actors in this new movement," wrote Frederick Douglass later, "that they did not see the end from the beginning — that they did not at first take the high ground that further on in the conflict their successors felt themselves called upon to take. . . . In all this and more it illustrates the experience of reform in all ages, and conforms to the laws of human progress." Douglass and many black abolitionists saw the party as an opening wedge in the larger fight against slavery, and believed that events themselves would eventually force Free Soilers to reexamine their prejudices.

Yet the Free Soil Party was not strong enough in 1848 to transform the existing two-party system. The Whigs were dedicated to expanding the federal government, encouraging industrial and commercial development, and promoting reforms such as temperance and education that would ensure a sober and intelligent working class. They appealed especially to substantial merchants and manufacturers in the North, wealthy planters in the South (who sought to strengthen their ties with northern commercial interests), and successful farmers in the West who needed government-funded roads, canals, and railroads to advance their commercial ambitions. The Democrats were convinced they could defeat both Free Soilers and Whigs by appealing to the rapidly increasing wage-earning and immigrant populations. They favored the use of state power to expand economic opportunities, opposed great wealth and industrial and commercial monopolies, and supported western expansion in the interest of small farmers and workers. The party's ranks included smaller merchants, less-wealthy planters, workingmen, and small farmers.

Whereas evangelical Protestants generally favored Whig policies, the Democrats were far more successful than their opponents in attracting Irish and German Catholics to their banner. In 1840, the Whigs had won the White House, but when the newly elected president William Henry Harrison died in office after one month, they were left with ex-Democrat John Tyler in his place. Although Tyler had brought the party much-needed southern votes, he was not a successful advocate of the Whig Party platform. By 1844, Tyler and other conservative southern Whigs were ready to rejoin the Democratic Party.

In 1844, the Democrats, who had built powerful political machines in several cities with large immigrant populations, nominated James K. Polk for president, who ran on a strongly expansionist platform. Seeking to secure Texas and the disputed Oregon Territory for the United States, Polk won a significant victory, although he outpolled the Whig candidate Henry Clay by fewer than forty thousand popular votes. The Liberty Party candidate James G. Birney received sixty-two thousand votes, most from disaffected antislavery Whigs. Over the following four years, Polk was very successful in implementing his expansionist program, but in doing so he alienated a substantial number of northern Democrats.

By 1848, both Whigs and Democrats were trying to avoid the most divisive issues of the day, particularly the conflicts over slavery raised by the nation's westward expansion. Although the Whigs won, they did so with a candidate, General Zachary Taylor, who gained his national stature by serving as a leader in Polk's war against Mexico. And Taylor's lackluster reputation among abolitionists assured that the newly established Free Soil Party would pick up votes from Whigs as well as former Liberty Party men and disaffected Democrats.

At midcentury, then, the political scene was in flux. The Whigs were in decline, the Democrats disagreed about how to expand without antagonizing either their northern or southern constituencies, and the Free Soilers were a growing but as yet small force on the national scene. Only a small segment of the northern population held radical views that challenged the very order of the existing free-labor society. Particularly after 1840, when the antislavery movement split, it seemed that none of these movements or parties would be powerful enough to eradicate slavery in the South.

The assistance that abolitionists needed would come from an unlikely source — Southerners themselves. At the same time that northerners were struggling to adjust to an expanded commercial, capitalist, and industrial society, Southerners were confronted with economic and political challenges of their own. The contradictions posed by slave labor in a supposedly democratic society led more and more Northerners — white as well as black — to see in the South a threat to all they held dear. But only when those contradictions began to create conflicts among poor whites and slave owners did the institution of slavery become precarious enough to lead to its downfall.

The Years in Review

1837

- Boston establishes a regular police force in response to riots and strikes; New York City does the same seven years later.
- The Panic of 1837 lasts five years and devastates the nation.

1839

- Myth has it that Abner Doubleday invented baseball in this year, but, in fact, many similar games had long been played. Organized baseball does emerge in the 1840s.

1840

- Horse racing is the nation's most popular spectator sport in the 1840s.
- Whig William Henry Harrison is elected president over Democrat Van Buren, but Harrison dies one month after taking office and is replaced by ex-Democrat John Tyler.

1841

- Brook Farm, a cooperative community, is founded in New England.

1842

- During the Dorr Rebellion, disenfranchised Rhode Islanders form a special convention and elect Thomas Dorr governor in protest of the state constitution's property qualifications for voters.

1843

- North American Phalanx is established at Red Bank, New Jersey, on Fourierist principles, which enjoy popularity in this period.

1844

- Bloody Philadelphia riot reflects growing tensions between nativists and Catholic immigrants.
- Irving House hotel in New York City introduces the first bridal suite.
- Democrat James K. Polk defeats Whig Henry Clay on a strongly expansionist platform.

1845

- During the Irish potato famine, one-third of the Irish population dies and another 1.75 million leave Ireland for the United States and Canada.
- *Police Gazette,* a scandal sheet that is precursor of today's tabloids, begins publication.

1846

- Sewing machine is invented; it reduces the amount of labor it takes to make garments, but employers reap the benefits by dropping the rates they pay.

1847

- Escaped slave Frederick Douglass establishes himself as an abolitionist editor in Rochester.
- When a Maine baker's apprentice knocks the center out of a fried cake, the modern doughnut is born.

1848

- Unsuccessful German revolution leads many Germans to emigrate to the United States.
- Gold is discovered in California and lures people westward.
- First American women's rights convention held in Seneca Falls, New York; resolutions declare that all people are equal and that women should have the right to vote.
- Mexican War Hero General Zachary Taylor, a Whig, defeats General Lewis Cass for the presidency.
- Martin Van Buren (Free Soil candidate and former president) aids Taylor's victory by capturing Democratic votes.
- Associated Press is established to take advantage of the telegraph's ability to transmit news across the country.
- First commercially sold chewing gum in the United States is manufactured in Bangor, Maine.
- Frederick Douglass's daughter is granted admission to a girls' seminary in Rochester, New York, and then denied access to classes with white students.

1849

- An angry crowd of thousands riots outside of Astor Place Opera House; riot reflects class conflict over access to leisure.
- Elizabeth Blackwell, first woman doctor, graduates at the head of her class at Geneva Medical College in New York, where she had been shunned by male students.

1850

- Anti-immigrant and anti-Catholic societies come together as the American Party, usually called the Know-Nothings.
- Swedish singer Jenny Lind tours the United States to packed halls — part of the emergent popular culture.
- President Taylor dies (apparently from an illness brought on by cherries and ice milk he consumed at the laying of the cornerstone for the Washington Monument); Millard Fillmore becomes president.

1852

- Democrat Franklin Pierce elected president in an election that marks the death of the Whig Party.

1853

- Chef George Crum creates the potato chip after a customer complains that his french fries are too thick; Crum's response is to cut some potatoes razor thin.

1855

- Irish and black dockworkers battle on the New York City waterfront — one of many conflicts between Irish and African Americans over jobs.
- Walt Whitman publishes the first edition of *Leaves of Grass* to indifferent reviews and slow sales.
- Frederick Miller buys the Best Brothers Brewery in Milwaukee; its product will later be known as Miller's Beer. Meanwhile, prohibition sentiment grows and prohibition laws are passed in Delaware, Indiana, Iowa, and other states.

1857

- Economic slump.

1858

- Atlantic cable is laid connecting England and the United States by telegraph.

Suggested Readings

Andrews, William L., *To Tell a Free Story: The First Century of Afro-American Autobiography, 1760–1865* (1986).

Basch, Norma, *In the Eyes of the Law: Women, Marriage, and Property in Nineteenth Century New York* (1982).

Burrows, Edwin G., and Mike Wallace, *Gotham: A History of New York City to 1898* (1998).

Clark, Christopher, *The Roots of Rural Capitalism: Western Massachusetts, 1780–1860* (1990).

Cohen, Patricia Cline, *The Murder of Helen Jewett: The Life and Death of a Prostitute in Nineteenth-Century New York* (1998).

Conzen, Kathleen, *Immigrant Milwaukee, 1836–1860: Accommodation and Community in a Frontier City* (1976).

Cott, Nancy, *The Bonds of Womanhood: "Woman's Sphere" in New England, 1780–1835* (1977).

Davis, Susan G., *Parades and Power: Street Theatre in Nineteenth-Century Philadelphia* (1986).

Diner, Hasia, *Erin's Daughters in America: Irish Immigrant Women in the Nineteenth Century* (1983).

Dolan, Jay P., *The Immigrant Church: New York's German and Irish Catholics, 1815–1865* (1975).

Dublin, Thomas, *Transforming Women's Work: New England Lives in the Industrial Revolution* (1994).

Dudden, Faye, *Serving Women: Household Service in Nineteenth-Century America* (1983).

Grimsted, David, *Melodrama Unveiled: American Theatre and Culture, 1800–1850* (1968).

————, *American Mobbing, 1828–1861* (1998).

Haltunen, Karen, *Confidence Men and Painted Women: A Study of Middle-Class Culture in America, 1830–1870* (1982).

Hansen, Maurice Lee, *The Atlantic Migration, 1607–1860* (1961).

Henkin, David M., *City Reading: Written Words and Public Spaces in Antebellum New York* (1998).

Hewitt, Nancy A., *Women's Activism and Social Change: Rochester, New York, 1822–1872* (1984).

Horton, James Oliver, and Lois Horton, *Black Bostonians: Family Life and Community Struggle in the Antebellum North* (1979).

Hounshell, David A., *From the American System to Mass Production, 1800–1932: The Development of Manufacturing Technology in the United States* (1984).

Jeffrey, Julie Roy, *The Great Silent Army of Abolitionism: Ordinary Women in the Antislavery Movement* (1998).

Laurie, Bruce, *The Working People of Philadelphia, 1800–1850* (1980).

Levine, Bruce, *The Spirit of 1848: German Immigrants, Labor Conflict, and the Coming of the Civil War* (1992).

Levine, Lawrence, *Highbrow/Lowbrow: The Emergence of Cultural Hierarchy in America* (1988).

Litwack, Leon, *North of Slavery: The Negro in the Free States, 1790–1860* (1961).

Miller, Kirby A., *Emigrants and Exiles: Ireland and the Irish Exodus to North America* (1985).

Prude, Jonathan, *The Coming of Industrial Order: Town and Factory Life in Rural Massachusetts, 1810–1860* (1983).

Rosenblum, Gerald, *Immigrant Workers: Their Impact on American Labor Radicalism* (1973).

Rosenzweig, Roy, and Elizabeth Blackmar, *The Park and the People: A History of Central Park* (1992).

Ross, Steven J., *Workers on the Edge: Work, Leisure, and Politics in Industrializing Cincinnati, 1788–1890* (1985).

Schiller, Dan, *Objectivity and the News: The Public and the Rise of Commercial Journalism* (1981).

Sellers, Charles, *The Market Revolution: Jacksonian America, 1815–1846* (1991).

Stansell, Christine, *City of Women: Sex and Class in New York, 1789–1860* (1986).

Sterling, Dorothy, ed., *We Are Your Sisters: Black Women in the Nineteenth Century* (1984).

Von Frank, Albert J., *The Trials of Anthony Burns: Freedom and Slavery in Emerson's Boston* (1998).

Walters, Ronald, *American Reformers, 1815–1860* (1997).

Wilentz, Sean, *Chants Democratic: New York City & the Rise of the American Working Class, 1788–1850* (1984).

And on the World Wide Web

Worcester Women's History Project, Assumption College, *Historical Resources* (http://www.assumption.edu/WWHP/hr.html)

chapter 9

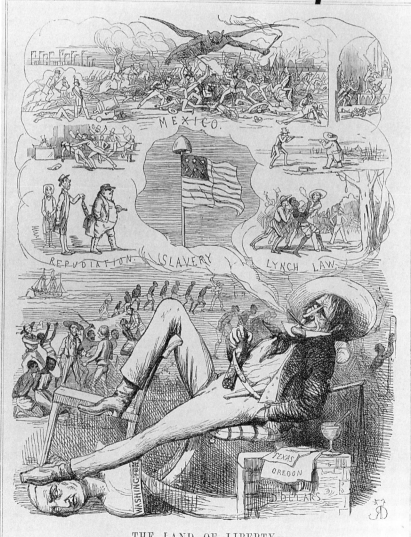

THE LAND OF LIBERTY.

RECOMMENDED TO THE CONSIDERATION OF "BROTHER JONATHAN."

Crises Over Slavery
1836–1848

In the 1830s, Charleston, South Carolina, was home to many wealthy whites who owned slaves. In one such slave-owning family the wife was a deeply religious woman. She regularly assembled her children for family prayer and was known in the community for her charity and her work among the poor. Yet the young African-American woman who worked for her as a seamstress and maid experienced little of this kindness. Perhaps it was because she was a mulatto (raising fears in her mistress that the master was sexually exploiting slave women) or perhaps it was because the young woman maintained an independent spirit despite being enslaved for all of her eighteen years. The seamstress ran away several times and when captured was sent to the Charleston workhouse to be whipped. When the brutal whippings, which left finger-deep scars along her back, did not deter the woman's desire for freedom, her owners placed a heavy iron collar around her neck. Three prongs projected from it to hold the collar tight. Her owners also yanked out her front tooth to make it easier for them to describe her in case she ran again. The supposedly charitable mistress watched the seamstress work, with her deeply lacerated back, her mutilated mouth, and her bowed neck. Still, the white woman could never be sure that she had shackled the young African American's heart and soul as well as her body.

Although the seamstress may have persisted in her resistance to bondage longer than most slaves and labored under closer scrutiny within an urban household, she was certainly not alone in challenging planters' authority. A black field hand from South Carolina, looking back on his days in bondage, claimed that when slaves gazed upon the soil of the South, they saw "land that is rich with the sweat of our faces and the blood of our back." When planters noted the richness of that same land, they focused on the wealth it produced for them, not on the pain and anguish it created for the workers. It was this irrepressible conflict between slaves and masters that generated repeated crises in plantation society during the 1830s and 1840s. The resulting upheavals affected not only masters and slaves but a range of other residents as well. Some were non-slave-holding white farmers who envied the profits made on plantations and fought to reap some of their abundance without the benefit of either the best land or bound labor. Others were whites with no land, who struggled to sustain body, soul, and family as they moved from place to

Actions Speak Louder than Words. "The Land of Liberty" was the ironic title of this cartoon published in an 1847 edition of the British satirical weekly *Punch*.

Source: *Punch* (1847)—General Research Division, New York Public Library, Astor, Lenox and Tilden Foundations.

477

place and job to job. They alternately engaged in common causes and open conflicts with free blacks with whom they often competed for jobs, housing, and the patronage of well-to-do whites. These groups vied with each other for respect, authority, and some degree of independence throughout the early nineteenth century. The conflicts generated by their competing economic, social, and political visions escalated in the years between the establishment of Texas as an independent republic in 1836 and the end of the U.S. war against Mexico in 1848. As the number of African Americans held in slavery grew, the number of resistant or rebellious slaves also increased, creating crises among southern whites as well as between whites and blacks.

Planters held most of the advantages in this competition, but they needed the labor of slaves and free blacks and the support, or at least the acquiescence, of non-slaveholding whites. Moreover, at the same time that they sought to consolidate their authority in the region, they were also eager to expand their reach. Planters wanted to push further west and to capture new lands in Florida and the Caribbean, both of which required the removal or pacification of those already living there: Indians, Spanish and French settlers, free blacks, and escaped slaves. These two goals — to consolidate power and to expand the lands under their control — often worked at cross-purposes, because the extension of slavery raised new conflicts and controversies both within and outside the South.

Still, as the Christmas holidays approached in 1836, most planters were satisfied with the progress being made toward their dual goals. Texas, with its vast and fertile cotton fields, had declared its independence from Mexico. The new republic would soon be a state, it was hoped, increasing Southerners' chances for both economic profits and dominance in national politics. Although neither slaves nor Indians were completely subjugated, the repression that followed Nat Turner's rebellion in 1831 and the passage of the Indian Removal Act of 1830 had given planters greater control over the South's destiny. Threats of class conflict had also diminished, because Indian removal and westward expansion promised less well-to-do whites access to better land.

Although planters believed they had conquered their greatest obstacles to economic and political ascendancy, this optimistic vision was challenged time and again over the next decade. The challenges came from slaves as individuals and in groups, from non-slaveholding whites, from organized churches and underground religious meetings, and from within the confines of planter families themselves. The conflicts surrounding racial slavery eventually absorbed or overshadowed all others in the young American republic. The crux of the slavery issue was the right of white planters to own their workers, enriching themselves through the blood and sweat beaten out of blacks.

In different ways, planters and slaves made clear their position on the issue. To planters, the need for slavery was obvious. Their whole way of life depended on it. As one South Carolina plantation owner bluntly explained, "Slavery with us is no abstraction but a great and vital fact. Without it our every comfort would be taken from us. Our wives, our children made unhappy . . . all, all lost and our people ruined forever." Virginian Thomas R. Dew agreed. "It is, in truth, the slave labor in Virginia which gives value to her soil and her habitations," Dew wrote. Slaves, even after Nat Turner's rebellion made clear the brutal consequences of revolt, refused to accept their lot passively. Periodically, groups of slaves turned to collective force, attempting against all odds to rise in revolt against their masters. Some slaves sought their freedom through escape. But most resisted slavery in less dramatic but still persistent ways—by praying for deliverance and covertly frustrating their owner's plans, thereby setting limits on his power and profits.

Revolts, escapes, day-to-day resistance, and the activities and organizations of free blacks disturbed the peace of white society and challenged claims that slaves were happy in their oppression. In response, planters defended the institution more aggressively. By the late 1840s, their proslavery arguments seemed to many Northerners to threaten free labor and defy moral logic. By then, the consequences of extending slave labor into new western territories had become clearer not only to planters but also to slaves, non-slaveholding white farmers, poor whites, free blacks, northern abolitionists, Indians, western settlers, and wage laborers. The crises borne of such expansion promoted regional, racial, and class conflicts that shattered party alignments and presaged the Civil War. And the planters, long masters of their domain, found themselves facing challenges from both inside and outside the South. Although they managed to retain their power, they were forced to make concessions, especially to non-slaveholding whites, in order to assure their continued control. It was in the years preceding the final confrontations over slavery in the western territories—from roughly 1836 to 1848—that planters were forced by African Americans and poorer whites to confront systematically, for the first time since the American Revolution, the limits on their power and authority.

The Master's Domain

Realizing the heady economic dreams that followed Texas independence from Mexico in 1836 was delayed, but not destroyed, by the onset of depression the following year. The Panic of 1837, triggered when the Bank of England called in many American loans, spread rapidly throughout the country. Banks failed and thousands of businesses went bankrupt, crippling American trade, manufacturing, and farming. When sharp declines in British demand for cotton coincided with abundant crops, precipitous drops in cotton prices resulted. These low prices assured that not just merchants and manufacturers, but southern planters too would be among the depression's victims. Among the first banks to fail were those in Natchez, Mississippi, and Tallahassee, Florida. When the panic hit Georgia, John Cobb owned a plantation with one hundred fifty slaves in Johnston County and an impressive mansion in Athens. He also held investments in goldmines, railroads, and banking enterprises, the value of which plummeted along with cotton prices. By 1840 he was deeply in debt and unable to sell his plantation, and he no longer owned sufficient slaves to work the land.

Even though prices fell by almost half between 1837 and 1843, those who survived the crash were rewarded when British and U.S. banks began extending credit on more favorable terms in the early 1840s. By that time, the failure of farms and businesses had lessened competition, and the demand for many goods, including cotton, once again rose. In fact, pent-up demand assured a steady market for both agricultural and manufactured items for the next several years.

Southern gentlemen who weathered the financial storm and took advantage of the devastation it wreaked on more vulnerable neighbors expanded their holdings significantly, emerging as the undisputed superiors of the master class. The percentage of white families who owned large plantations was now smaller, but their power was growing along with their desire to make their wealth and social prominence more visible. As cotton prices rose, these affluent planters began to replace the rough and unpretentious farmhouses that were commonplace through the 1830s with newer, more ostentatious mansions. Across the South, but especially in Alabama, Louisiana, and the Mississippi Delta—the areas along the Gulf Coast into which slavery was expanding—the new plantation houses were decorated with expensive, often imported, furnishings and filled with fine wines, fancy clothes, numerous guests, and a domestic labor force large enough to care for the new amenities.

This new aristocracy and opulent lifestyle was typified in Mississippi by the Natchez "nabobs," a group composed of the forty wealthiest families in the region, who had begun to buy up lands in the 1820s. During the late 1830s and early 1840s, members of this elite circle added both slaves and acreage at depression-era prices, and then took advantage of rising cotton prices in the mid 1840s to complete their climb to the top. Nabob Stephen Duncan, for instance, was a Pennsylvania-born physician who had moved to Mississippi in 1808. In the early 1830s, he was a successful planter and banker with close ties to the Whig Party and the

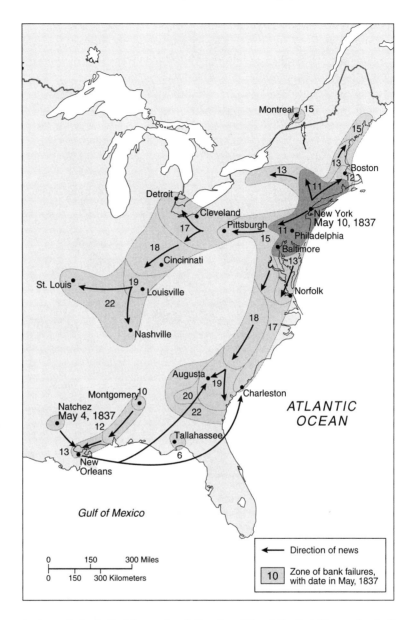

Anatomy of a Panic: Bank Suspensions in May 1837. Although New York City served as the financial center of the United States, the Panic of 1837 began in the South but soon spread to all regions of the country. Bank failures in Natchez, Mississippi, and Tallahassee, Florida, produced the first alarms on May 4 and 6, 1837. By May 22, northeastern financial centers as well as key western and southern cities were engulfed in the Panic.

American Colonization Society. Two decades later, Duncan owned six cotton and two sugar cane plantations spread across three counties in two states, along with more than one thousand slaves, twenty-three of whom labored as domestic servants at Auburn, his Natchez mansion. He still supported Whig politics and colonization for blacks, and he urged his peers to diversify and industrialize. His own road to wealth was built on

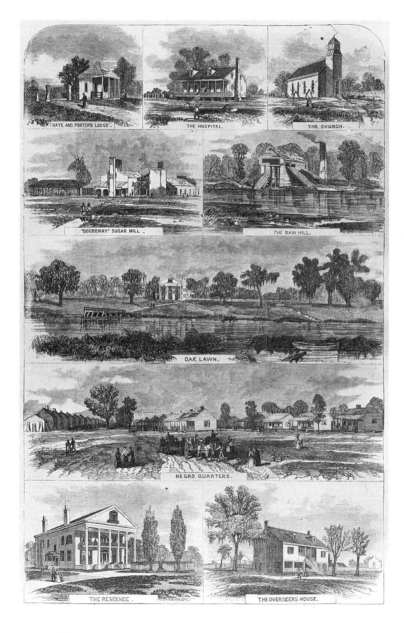

A "Model" Plantation. This pictorial survey of Oak Lawn, a large Louisiana sugar plantation on the Bayou Teche, included a view of its slave quarters, which included forty-two cabins.

Source: C. E. H. Bonwill, *Frank Leslie's Illustrated Newspaper,* February 6, 1864—General Research Division, New York Public Library, Astor, Lenox and Tilden Foundations.

his medical practice, shrewd land speculation, effective slave management practices, and a well-placed marriage. Indeed, upon the death of his socially prominent first wife, he married into another of the South's wealthiest families.

Duncan and his fellow nabobs threw elaborate parties and balls, traveled extensively, bred and raced horses, and planted boxed gardens in the manner that was fashionable in England decades earlier. William Johnson, a free black barber in Natchez who kept a close eye on the local aristocrats, detailed their comings and goings in his diary. In 1840, in the midst of the depression, he commented on the marriage of nabob Louis Bingaman, Duncan's brother-in-law, to a New York socialite. "The N.P. [newspaper] speaks of the wedding Dress Costing $2000. And of the marriage Contract or Settlement $100,000 — Not bad to take," he concluded.

Marriage played a critical role in the economic strategies of planters in Mississippi and elsewhere. For men, a good marriage required obtaining both a large financial settlement and a wife who understood her place. Planter society celebrated strongly patriarchal families. The father supervised the plantation's production of the staple crop and the financial transactions directly linked to it, including the purchase and sale of slaves. His wife was assigned the domestic sphere and denied access to most aspects of public life. "The proper place for a woman is at home," declared the *Southern Quarterly Review.* "One of her highest privileges [is] to be politically merged in the existence of her husband."

But a wealthy Southerner's business dealings often took him away from home, requiring his wife to assume many duties in running the plantation. This created enormous strains on many plantation mistresses. Catherine Hammond, wife of prominent South Carolina planter and politician James Henry Hammond, found herself in charge of affairs at Silver Bluff during her husband's frequent and extensive travels. The plantation was located on Beech Island, across the river from Augusta, Georgia. Catherine had inherited Silver Bluff at age eleven, when her father died. Six years later, Hammond, a dashing young lawyer of twenty-three, swept the shy teenager off her feet. Despite misgivings by the bride's family, in 1831 he married the young heiress and took control of her estate. In the summer of 1840, Catherine was pregnant for the seventh time in nine years. Yet she was suddenly forced to preside over the plantation when James decided that he needed "to go somewhere" to recover from the strain of his ongoing campaign for the governorship.

James spent the next six weeks in New York City, purchasing silver, linens, and furniture for a newly constructed residence in Columbia, while Catherine endured the hot and humid weather at Silver Bluff, overseeing the crops and slaves, caring for the sick, and entertaining a full house of family members and guests. She may not have welcomed a letter from her husband in late July, in which he noted reassuringly that "I expect too that you have found yourself excellent at plantation matters." James Hammond returned to the plantation in September, just three days before Catherine gave birth. Women such as Catherine Hammond, although enjoying all the benefits of wealth and position that the South had to offer, led lives restricted by the masculine authority that prevailed in the South's planter class.

Southern society's dependence on slaves rather than on free workers strengthened traditional beliefs in the sanctity of social order and the strict subordination of the members of one (supposedly inferior) social group to those of another (supposedly superior). Planters viewed their children, their wives, their poorer neighbors, their white employees, and their slaves as being, to one degree or another, inferior to themselves in social standing, independence, and personal rights. The master's power over his slaves was merely an extension of his power over his wife and children. "Do you say that the slave is held to *involuntary service?*" one spokesman asked rhetorically, before offering his justification. "So is the wife. Her relation to her husband, in the immense majority of cases, is made for her, not by her." This linking of slavery with white family relations did not prevent the forcible breakup of slave families or keep planters from enslaving or selling children whom they conceived with female slaves. It did, however, reinforce the patriarch's supremacy within his own home and emphasize still more than in the North the wife's subordinate position.

The Ties That Bind: Religion and Slavery

Despite the apparent triumph of the planter class, across the South seeds of conflict and dissension were being planted alongside cotton, rice, and sugar cane. Yet given the unlikely prospect of achieving freedom, slaves had to find ways to adapt to their circumstances, to accommodate themselves to brutal conditions without losing their sense of hope. Religion offered one means for slaves to challenge indirectly their subordinate place within southern society while building a sense of community with other African Americans and sustaining a vision of a better life in another world.

But religion remained a double-edged sword, providing planters with another means of controlling their slaves. The surge of slave conversions after 1820 made it clear that slave owners could not prevent the growth of evangelicalism among African Americans. So, many big planters decided to join the evangelical movement and use it for their own ends: to gain yet another means of controlling their slaves and warding off rebellion. As relations improved between the evangelical churches and the slaveholding elite, black attendance at churches sanctioned by white owners grew. For the most part, church leaders welcomed the approval and sponsorship of the planters and all the benefits their wealth and influence brought to the church.

One result of this union between slaveholders and evangelical leaders was a change in both groups' attitudes toward slaves and slavery. Southern evangelicalism shed its sympathy for emancipation, eliminating one more source of support for the enslaved. Antislavery preachers were either silenced or forced to leave the South, and some lay sympathizers, such as Sarah and Angelina Grimke of South Carolina, chose political exile in the North rather than social ostracism at home. In return, many slave owners dropped their objections to the practice of Christianity by slaves even as most refused to tolerate separate black churches and black preachers. Although many African-American preachers gained the respect of whites *and* blacks in the eighteenth century, they were often linked to slave uprisings in the nineteenth century, and suffered in the repressions that followed.

From the 1830s on, planters tried to use religion to bind slaves more tightly to the southern system and were somewhat successful. During his years as a slave, Frederick Douglass was frustrated by the "many good, religious colored people who were under the delusion that God required them to submit to slavery and to wear their chains in meekness and humility." But other blacks resisted the message of servility from white preachers as the experience of one white pastor, Robert Ryland of Virginia, illustrates. He began preaching in Richmond's First African Baptist Church in the 1840s. A defender of slavery, he extolled the merits of white

"Family Worship in a Plantation in South Carolina." An engraving from a British illustrated weekly depicted the scene in a "rude chapel" of a Port Royal, South Carolina, plantation, where the master and mistress were "engaged in Divine worship, surrounded by [their] slaves, in a state of almost patriarchal simplicity." Before the Civil War, virtually all published illustrations of slavery were either apologist images of planter benevolence such as this, or critical views of slavery's brutality.

Source: Frank Vizetelly, *Illustrated London News,* December 5, 1863—American Social History Project.

supremacy, sermonizing (as one free black man recalled) "that God had given all this continent to the white man, and that it was our duty to submit." (To that message one black congregant replied, "I'll be damned! God is not such a fool!") Groups of blacks would linger after regular services at the Richmond church, and other blacks would preach to them. Ryland himself admitted that one of these black preachers "was heard with far more interest than I was." Another witness noticed that at these informal services the "most active were those who had slept during [Ryland's] sermon."

In a few cities, independent black churches thrived. Membership in Baltimore's African Methodist Episcopal conference more than doubled between 1836 and 1856, and other southern cities experienced a similar upsurge in religious enthusiasm. In rural districts, however, separate black churches were rare, and slaves were forced to convene secret "night meetings," which continued despite their being prohibited. When interviewed in the 1930s Charles Grandy recalled his experiences as a young slave in Norfolk, Virginia:

> Whites in our section used to have a service for us slaves every fourth
> Sunday, but it wasn't enough for them who wanted to talk with Jesus.
> Used to go across the fields nights to a old tobacco barn on the side of a
> hill. . . . Had a old pot hid there to catch the sound. Sometimes
> would stick your head down in the pot if you got to shout awful loud. I
> remember ole Sister Millie Jeffries. Would stick her head in the pot and
> shout and pray all night while the others was bustin' to take their turn.

The tradition of a sound-catching pot used at these services originated in West Africa and reflected the continued importance of African culture in nineteenth-century Christian ceremonies. Those slaves who were able to participate in their own religious services found not only solace in them for their present condition, but a means of sustaining traditional customs and the hope of salvation.

Even notions of achieving ultimate freedom from bondage through death were considered highly dangerous by whites. It was such fears that led whites to force blacks to join white congregations and listen to white-sanctioned preachers. Yet even there, slaves might pick up dangerous ideas. Many white Southerners worried that prayers, songs, and sermons intended for their ears (and so filled with references to human freedom and universal brotherhood) might be "misinterpreted" by slaves and free blacks. Given the different meanings of salvation to blacks and whites, Christian appeals to blacks and the development of uniquely African-American forms of Christianity remained sources of conflict for decades.

The alliance between southern evangelicals and planters was also tested by the growing concerns over slavery among northern Christians. In the mid 1840s, northern Methodists and Baptists tried to convince their southern counterparts to oppose slavery on Christian grounds. The struggle intensified when slavery was extended into new territories, which heightened northern opposition to the institution and prompted many northern churches finally to take a stand on issues they had long tried to ignore. With waves of slave owners and slaves moving into western lands in the 1840s, national conventions of Methodists and Baptists, dominated by ministers and elders from the free states, felt it was time to speak out.

When southern congregations resisted northern entreaties, the national organization of these denominations split. Southern whites, particularly planters, found the antislavery stand of northern ministers treasonous. The founders of a southern Methodist congregation published a pamphlet after the separation in which they argued that

> The Northern Methodist Church . . . is so mixed up with the whole machinery of abolition and anti-slavery agitation and invasion, by its recent proclamation of hostility to the South, in so many forms of bitter and malignant assault, that its own chosen colors will not allow us any longer to distinguish it from the common enemy. It has become a pander to political agitation. It is an *Abolition* church.

The division between northern and southern churches no doubt reinforced the belief among slaves that the messages they received from southern white preachers were not the only ones to be learned from the Bible.

Forms of Slave Resistance and Community

Unable to break free of bondage, slaves nonetheless strove to assert their humanity and resist in whatever ways they could. They evolved an elaborate code of conduct that permitted them to limit their burdens without the masters fully understanding what was afoot. They pretended to be stupid, forcing masters and overseers to explain the simplest task time and time again. By destroying tools and injuring livestock (seemingly by accident), they convinced masters of their genuine inability to work too hard or to undertake certain tasks at all. Slaves sometimes feigned temporary illness to avoid some of the heavier work in the fields. Some women managed to avoid heavy labor by claiming to be pregnant, although the benefits they gained were rarely sufficient to offset the severe punishments that resulted when the deception was discovered. Through theft, slaves could improve their diet or add to their meager personal posses-sions. Domestic slaves, many of them women, had access to the greatest variety of moveable goods. They also had access to the surest means for poisoning a master or mistress, and were often suspects in cases of arson.

By slipping away from the farm or plantation and escaping to the northern United States, to Canada, or, more rarely, to Mexico, slaves could not only emancipate themselves but also raise the morale and as-sertiveness of those who remained in bondage. Most runaways were young men and most were eventually caught. But when one found the way to freedom, those left behind cheered the success, and a few must have considered copying it. One field hands' song ran,

> Go 'way Ol' Man,
> Go 'way Ol' Man
> Where you been all day?
> If you treat me good
> I'll stay till Judgment Day,
> But if you treat me bad,
> I'll sho' to run away.

Unable to recognize their slaves as human beings like themselves, who shared their desires for freedom and material possessions, owners generally interpreted slave behavior as proof of innate inferiority. African Americans, they argued, were by nature stupid, lazy, and dishonest. "They break and destroy more farming utensils," complained one planter, "ruin more carts, break more gates, spoil more cattle and horses, and commit more waste than five times their number of white laborers do. They are under instruction relative to labor from their childhood, and still when they are gray-headed they are the same heedless botches; the negro traits predomi-nate over all artificial training." Another planter remarked about slaves' untrustworthiness, "To keep a diary of their conduct would be to record nothing short of a series of violations of the laws of God and man." Those laws, however, looked different to the slave. "They always tell us it's wrong to lie and steal," recalled former slave Josephine Howard, "but why did the white folks steal my mammy and her mammy? . . . That's the sinfullest stealing there is."

Resistance was reflected not only in slaves' ef-forts to survive as individuals, but also in their

Escape. This icon, or symbol, appeared on notices about fugitive slaves in the classified section of the Mobile, Al-abama, *Commercial Register* in the 1830s.

Source: Richard Brough, *Com-mercial Advertiser,* June 16, 1832—Prints and Photographs Division, Library of Congress.

Death of Capt. Ferrer, the Captain of the Amistad, July, 1839.

Don Jose Ruiz and Don Pedro Montez, of the Island of Cuba, having purchased fifty-three slaves at Havana, recently imported from Africa, put them on board the Amistad, Capt. Ferrer, in order to transport them to Principe, another port on the Island of Cuba. After being out from Havana about four days, the African captives on board, in order to obtain their freedom, and return to Africa, armed themselves with cane knives, and rose upon the Captain and crew of the vessel. Capt. Ferrer and the cook of the vessel were killed; two of the crew escaped; Ruiz and Montez were made prisoners.

The *Amistad* Rebellion. In July 1839, captive West Africans rebelled and took over the Spanish slaveship *Amistad*. They ordered the owners to Africa but, instead, the *Amistad* was taken on a meandering course, finally waylaid by a U.S. Navy brig. The Africans were charged with the murder of the captain and jailed in New Haven, Connecticut. Abolitionists came to their support; ex-President John Quincy Adams represented them in court. After a long legal battle, the Supreme Court freed the "mutineers" in 1841. The following year they returned to Africa.

Source: John W. Barber, *A History of the Amistad Captives* (1840)—Prints and Photographs Division, Library of Congress.

determination to sustain a community despite hardship and separations from their loved ones. When slave men were married to women on neighboring plantations, they used their one day of rest to travel to visit family, bringing with them whatever surpluses of food and clothing they could produce or collect. Slave women helped sustain community life by working as cooks, midwives, healers, seamstresses, and quilters to provide the slave quarters with essential goods and services that owners either neglected or refused to give them. In addition, it was most often women who taught daughters coming of age to avoid sexual abuse by limiting contact with white owners and overseers whenever possible. And in the aftermath of assaults, it was female kin and neighbors who most often attempted to heal any physical and psychic wounds the assault had caused.

From the 1830s onward, as more and more adult slaves were sold to new territories in the South and West, those left behind in older areas such as the Chesapeake were forced to create ever more extended and innovative family forms. Women and older men cared for the children of other slaves as well as their own, sometimes taking into an already cramped household the sons and daughters of those who had been sold or killed, or who had escaped. In the midst of these severe challenges to familial and communal ties, men and women still found effective ways to teach the young. Slaves who excelled at preaching, singing, playing instruments, weaving, repairing shoes, clothing, or furniture, braiding hair, or other highly prized skills provided not only resources but also role models for those with whom they shared their bondage.

Native and African-American Rebellion on the Frontier

Most slaves were forced to find ways of surviving within the confines of bondage. Whites made up the great majority of the southern population, and their rapid settlement of the countryside from the early 1800s onward deprived potential black insurrectionists of a safe refuge where they might escape capture. African Americans still attempted to liberate themselves, but after Nat Turner's rebellion of 1831, most such revolts occurred in frontier areas where slaves mingled with free blacks, mixed-race populations, and Indians.

During the 1830s, one of the most successful and sustained battles against the white majority took place in Florida, which had long served as a haven for runaway slaves (known as "maroons"). Here, the swampy terrain provided protection for isolated groups of fugitives, the rich lands provided food and shelter, and the Seminole nation provided allies.

Although some Seminoles held African Americans as slaves, the Seminole society was not rigidly racist. Among the Seminoles, bondage resembled the traditional slavery of Africa more than it did the commercially oriented slavery fashioned by European settlers and their descendants. Slaves often lived on small farms with their own families and enjoyed many of the rights and liberties of full members of the tribe. Many married into the tribe, creating a mixed-race culture that drew on African, American, and Seminole traditions.

The Seminoles and the maroons who lived among them fought two wars against the United States. The First Seminole War broke out in 1812 when U.S. marines invaded Florida, hoping to wrest control of the region from Spain, or at least to return fugitive slaves to their American masters. The Seminoles and maroons repelled the invaders, with the black fugitives resisting most fiercely. After Spain ceded Florida to the United States in 1819, the removal of the Seminoles became a priority; between 1832 and 1835, the American government resettled most in Oklahoma and other western territories. A minority, however, refused to leave. Under the direction of a charismatic leader named Osceola, they fought a guerrilla action against the U.S. Army, and for seven years successfully resisted attempts to uproot them. Once again, maroons played a central role in Seminole resistance.

Joseph Cinque. "Our hands are now clean for we have striven to regain the precious heritage we received from our fathers." A portrait of the leader of the *Amistad* rebellion painted by Nathaniel Jocelyn.

Source: New Haven Colony Historical Society.

490

"Richard III." Andrew Jackson's role in the First Seminole War was resurrected in this anti-Democrat cartoon published during the 1828 presidential campaign. Whig caricaturist David Claypoole Johnston fashioned the Democratic candidate's head and shoulders out of a military tent, cannons, swords, and the bodies of dead Indians. The cartoon was captioned with a line from Shakespeare's play about the treacherous, despotic king: "Methought the souls of all that I had murder'd, came to my tent."

Source: David Claypoole Johnston, 1828, engraving with stipple, 6 1/8 × 4 3/8 inches—American Antiquarian Society.

Methought the souls of all that I had murder'd, came to my tent. Act 5 Sc. 3.

RICHARD III.

The Second Seminole War erupted partly because of efforts by the federal government to drive all southeastern Indian tribes beyond the Mississippi. However, the war had the support of slave traders, slave owners, and would-be slave owners who hoped to get their hands on fugitive slaves. The fighting, which began in 1835, was expected to last only a few months. It actually lasted years and cost the lives of some sixteen hundred U.S. troops as well as $30 to $40 million. According to a contemporary account, "The negroes, from the commencement of the Florida war, have, for their numbers, been the most formidable foe, more bloodthirsty, active, and revengeful than the Indian." The most militant of the Indian leaders, Osceola, counted many maroons and mixed-race warriors among his supporters. Even more alarming to whites was the active collaboration of slaves on nearby white-owned plantations. Hundreds escaped servitude and joined the Seminole ranks. American General Thomas Sidney Jessup wrote in late 1836, "This, you may be assured, is a negro, not an Indian war."

The war dragged on largely because white Southerners were bent on reenslaving recent plantation runaways living among the Seminoles. Finally stalemated, General Jessup considered offering milder terms, hoping to separate the mixed-race fighters from the full-blooded Seminoles. He would, he claimed, send those with African-American blood to the Indian (Oklahoma) Territory while allowing the Seminoles to remain in southern Florida. "Separating the negroes from the Indians," he wrote in 1838, would "weaken the latter more than they would be weakened by the loss of the same number of their own people." Other white military commanders developed their own reasons for wanting to exile rather than recapture the black warriors. They felt that, having tasted comparative freedom and proven themselves in battle, reenslaved black warriors would prove more dangerous than ever. "Ten resolute negroes," warned one officer, "with a knowledge of the country, are sufficient to desolate the frontier, from one extent to the other."

Seminolee

Seminoles. George Catlin's 1838 sketch showed seven of the 250 Seminoles imprisoned at Fort Moultrie, Charleston, South Carolina. They were captured with Seminole leader Osceola near St. Augustine, Florida, after U.S. troops violated a truce agreement.

Source: George Catlin, *Seminolee,* 1838, pencil drawing—New York Historical Society.

Ultimately the Second Seminole War ended in a U.S. victory, but only through a well-planned deception. Luring Osceola into their camp by means of a false treaty, the U.S. Army took him captive, landing a devastating blow to the exhausted Seminole and maroon forces. Even then the victory was by no means an unconditional one. In 1842, the victors agreed to allow the fugitive slaves among the Seminoles to accompany the Indians westward rather than be returned to their white former owners.

The fierce resistance by the former slaves and the Seminole warriors speaks eloquently of the courage, determination, and military capacity that existed among blacks and Indians in this area of the South, where a strong alliance between them was possible. Unfortunately for slaves, such allies were extremely rare. Even other Indian groups, such as the Cherokee, practiced a form of slavery from the 1830s on that was closer to that of whites than of Seminoles.

In the Indian Territory of Oklahoma, where the Five Civilized Tribes were resettled in the 1830s, slaves held by Cherokee, Creek, Chickasaw, and Choctaw masters fled to the Seminoles, just as those owned by Georgia whites had done decades before. Others fled north to find freedom. The slave Henry Bibb, for instance, escaped to Michigan and published his story, *The Life and Adventures of Henry Bibb,* which was widely read among Northerners. In 1842, two dozen slaves in the Cherokee settlement attempted a mass escape, fleeing southward in hopes of reaching Mexico. Slaves among the Creeks joined the group, which later liberated eight more blacks held by Choctaw slave catchers. Eventually, however, Cherokee militiamen overtook the fugitives, only two of whom escaped.

Although the Mexican border was a great distance from most plantations, it did offer a safe haven much like that provided by sparsely settled and Spanish-influenced Florida in the early nineteenth century. In the 1850s, the Seminole Indian Chief Wildcat led a band of some two hundred Indians and African Americans from the Indian Territory into Mexico. The Mexican government allowed the group to establish a settlement in the Santa Rosa Mountains, eighty miles southwest of the Rio Grande. Wildcat welcomed other fugitives fleeing enslavement in Texas or punishment by Plains Indians. Like their forebearers in Florida, when the community was attacked by American forces, now under the leadership of Texas Rangers, they fought back. This time, however, they forced the intruders to retreat and maintained their mixed-race colony south of the border.

Free Blacks Threaten Planter Control

Free blacks as well as slaves threatened planters' authority. In fact, by the 1830s, free blacks were often seen as a more serious threat to white supremacy than rebellious slaves. The chances for a mass uprising of slaves declined precipitously after Nat Turner's rebellion, but the mere existence of free blacks in the South challenged any simple connection between race and enslavement.

Fearing the influence that the existence of free blacks exerted on slaves, the Virginia General Assembly in 1837 reaffirmed an 1806 statute that allowed county courts to determine whether free blacks would be allowed to remain in residence permanently. To stay in Virginia, the petitioner had to demonstrate that he or she was "of good character, peaceable, orderly and industrious, and not addicted to drunkenness, gaming or other vice." African-American men had a more difficult time than women persuading courts to let them remain in the state as free persons. It was hard for them to be industrious without being viewed as competitors with white workingmen, and they were more likely to be considered disorderly by their mere presence in the population.

Free black women posed less of a threat to white male laborers because their most marketable skills were in areas—for example, laundry, domestic work, petty trades, and sewing—largely reserved for their sex and race. Harriet Cook, a washerwoman in Leesburg, Virginia, worked for twelve years after her 1838 emancipation to build an impressive and supportive clientele among that city's white residents. When she petitioned to gain permanent residence status, leading citizens swore that "It

In Chesterfield County Court Clerk's Office, *Sept 14th* 18*58*

Richard Thos Coghill a free *man* of color, who has been heretofore registered in the said office, this day delivered up to me *his* former certificate of registration, and applied for a renewal of the same, which is granted *him* ; and *he* is now of the following description, to wit: age *20* years, color *mulatto*, stature *five* feet *4 3/4 Inches*, *Has a scar on the right temple & was born free in Chesterfield County*

N°. *3217*

In Testimony Whereof, I have hereunto set my hand and affixed the Seal of the said County Court, this *14th* day of *September* A. D., one thousand, eight hundred and *fifty eight* and in the *83rd* year of our Independence.

Silas Cheatham C

Former N°. *1767*, date *13 Feb 1849*

A Free Man of Color. A form issued by a Virginia county court in 1858 to Richard Cogbill certified his claim to be a free-born African American.

Source: Mary O'H. Williamson Collection, Prints and Photographs Department, Moorland-Spingarn Research Center, Howard University.

would be a serious inconvenience to a number of the citizens of Leesburg to be deprived of her services as a washerwoman and in other capacities in which in consequence of her gentility, trustworthiness, and skill, she is exceedingly useful." Her petition was granted.

The larger numbers of women who were emancipated, the job opportunities afforded them in cities, and the greater leniency of courts and legislatures in granting them permanent residency resulted in a skewed sex ratio in the South's urban areas. As a result, free black women often had to support themselves and their families and to fend off economic and sexual exploitation by whites without the assistance of husbands, fathers, or brothers. Nonetheless, they were able to build and sustain communities in many of the South's cities, from Richmond and Norfolk to Charleston and Savannah to New Orleans and Natchez, Mississippi.

The number of free blacks in the South remained small throughout the mid nineteenth century, and most lived in towns and cities rather than plantation areas. Yet their presence still created considerable anxiety among whites in the region. By 1840 the state of Mississippi had passed laws expressly prohibiting free blacks from testifying against whites, serving in the militia, voting, or holding office. A year later, a group of Natchez whites called a meeting at City Hall to consider "imposing a fine on the owners of slaves who permit them to go at large and hire their time; and also . . . requiring free persons of color to remove from [Mississippi] and to prevent their emigration into the state."

Non-slaveholding whites often supported planter opposition to the presence of free blacks in the South. They tended to see free black workers as unwanted competition for jobs. But not all southern whites

" . . . He Had Been Too Free With the Niggers"

Frederick Law Olmsted, later known as the codesigner of New York's Central Park, made several extended tours of the South for the *New York Times* in the 1850s. Here Olmsted describes a coal mine operated by a workforce composed of slaves and white immigrants. His description suggests that although slaves doing industrial work in cities were granted a certain amount of autonomy, social relationships between blacks and whites remained severely regimented.

Yesterday I visited a coal-pit: the majority of the mining laborers are slaves, and commonly athletic and fine-looking Negroes; but a considerable number of white hands are also employed, and they occupy all the responsible posts. The slaves are, some of them, owned by the Mining Company; but the most are hired of their owners, at from $120 to $200 a year, the company boarding and clothing them. (I have the impression that I heard it was customary to give them a certain allowance of money and let them find their own board.)

The whites are mostly English or Welshmen. One of them, with whom I conversed, told me that he had been here several years; he had previously lived some years at the North. He got better wages here than he had earned at the North, but he was not contented, and did not intend to remain. On pressing him for the reason of his discontent, he said, after some hesitation, that he had rather live where he could be more free; a man had to be too *"discreet"* here: if one happened to say anything that gave offense, they thought no more of drawing a pistol or a knife upon him, than they would of kicking a dog that was in their way. Not long since, a young English fellow came to the pit, and was put to work along with a gang of Negroes. One morning, about a week afterwards, twenty or thirty men called on him, and told him that they would allow him fifteen minutes to get out of sight, and if they ever saw him in those parts again, they would "give him hell." They were all armed, and there was nothing for the young fellow to do but to move "right off."

"What reason did they give him for it?"

"They did not give him any reason."

"But what had he done?"

Why I believe they thought he had been too free with the niggers; he wasn't used to them, you see, sir, and he talked to 'em free like, and they thought he'd make 'em think too much of themselves."

Source: Frederick Law Olmsted, *A Journey in the Seaboard Slave States* (1856).

resented free blacks. A minority of them believed that exemplary free blacks should be allowed to reside in southern communities and some supported the petitions of free blacks who sought to remain in the region.

Most of the white women and men who supported the presence of free blacks lived in small towns and rural areas of the upper South. Many belonged to small religious denominations such as the Quakers and German Moravians. In Loudoun County, Virginia, for instance, some three dozen citizens, mostly Quakers and Germans, argued in 1843 that "every man [sic], *not convicted of a crime,* has a natural right, to reside in the community where he was born. . . ." Although such sentiments were expressed more and more rarely after 1840, they did not entirely disap-

---

" . . . So Cheapened the White Man's Labor"

Far from viewing black workers as allies, most southern white workers saw them as competitors to be excluded from their trades. Below is an open letter from a white Georgia artisan complaining in 1838 about black competition and demanding preferential treatment for white workers.

Gentlemen:
. . . I am aware that most of you have [such a] strong antipathy to encouraging the masonry and carpentry trades of your poor white brothers, that your predilections for giving employment in your line of business to ebony workers have either so cheapened the white man's labor, or expatriated hence with but a few solitary exceptions, all the white masons and carpenters of this town.

The white man is the only real, legal, moral, and civil proprietor of this country and state. . . . By white men alone was this continent discovered; by the prowess of white men alone (though not always properly or humanely exercised), were the fierce and active Indians driven occidentally: and if swarms and hordes of infuriated red men pour down from the Northwest, like the wintry blast thereof, the white men alone, aye, those to whom you decline to give money for bread and clothes, for their famishing families . . . would bare their breasts to the keen and whizzing shafts of the savage crusaders—defending negroes too in the bargain, for if left to themselves without our aid, the Indians would or can sweep the negroes hence, "as dewdrops are shaken from the lion's mane."

The right, then, gentlemen, you will no doubt candidly admit, of the white man to employment in preference to negroes, who *must* defer to us since they live well enough on plantations, cannot be considered impeachable by contractors. . . . As masters of the polls in a majority, carrying all before them, I am surprised the poor do not elect faithful members to the Legislature, who will make it penal to prefer negro mechanic labor to white men's. . . .

Yours respectfully,
J. J. Flournoy

Source: Athens (Georgia) *Southern Banner,* January 13, 1838.

pear, particularly in areas where the slave-labor system no longer promised the profits it had once delivered.

In cities, however, where white workers competed directly with free black laborers, tensions between the two groups often ran high. There many whites, like those in Natchez, wanted to assure that restrictive laws passed at the behest of planters were enforced. Throughout the 1830s, 1840s, and 1850s, southern white workers strove to force blacks, slave and free alike, out of their neighborhoods and out of their occupations. Frederick Douglass remembered a white ship's carpenter in Maryland named Thomas Lanman who had murdered two slaves. Regularly boasting of the crime, Lanman added that "when others would do as much as he had done, they would be rid of the d——d niggers." Douglass himself experienced this attitude more directly in 1836. Hired out by his owner as a caulker in a Baltimore shipyard, white workers severely beat Douglass because they resented his presence among them. Such scare tactics occasionally achieved limited results. Douglass's master pulled him out of the shipyard just as the white workers wanted. To deal with free blacks, however, white workers were largely dependent on legislation to remove them from the region and from the laborforce. Some politicians expressed sympathy for demands to limit certain occupations to whites only. But to write such provisions into law and enforce them would have limited the freedom of the planters to make use of the blacks they held in bondage in whatever way they saw fit. No southern legislature was prepared to do that. Angered by such legislative failures but unwilling to champion emancipation, white workers generally blamed their woes on the helpless black population.

Can Western Expansion Ease the Conflicts?

Many southern whites hoped that the opening of western lands to white settlement would ease conflicts created by differences of wealth, such as those between white workers and planters over the employment of slaves and free blacks. The availability of lands once occupied by American Indians or controlled by Mexico provided a temporary safety valve, especially for white yeomen hoping to join the plantation elite. There were other western areas, most notably the Appalachian foothills and highlands that ran from northwestern Virginia through Georgia, where slavery would never be profitable. These regions offered non-slaveholding whites the chance to carve out a living with only tenuous ties to the economic, political, and social system built on slave labor.

The vast majority of southern white workers and farmers betrayed no sympathy for slaves. Those who lived on the margins of the rich plantation lands were closely tied to external cotton markets and large planters. Their counterparts who settled in the foothills and highlands relied on diversified farming and benefited little from policies that enhanced the power of the big slave owners. Yet most wanted simply to be left to their own devices, and many still believed that slavery was the best way to maintain proper order in a society populated by both whites and blacks. Meanwhile, white workers in the state's urban areas, particularly those along the coast, benefited from the slave-produced cotton boom because it improved the general business climate.

Most whites evidently believed that the enslavement of blacks bolstered the prosperity and liberties of all whites, slave-owning or not. Others felt threatened by the slave system but tried to coexist with it while limiting its direct impact on themselves. All hoped that expansion to the West would help alleviate whatever tensions existed among whites by providing greater opportunities for every group—planters, small slaveholders, non-slaveholding farmers, urban workers, and poor whites.

Throughout the 1840s, the South continued to expand in both population and areas settled and planted. In the mid 1840s, moreover, a rise in cotton prices increased the optimism and the profits of small farmers, rural merchants, and large planters alike. Between 1840 and 1860, the South's total population grew by half (from seven to eleven million). In the wake of the removal of the Cherokees during the late 1830s, whites flooded into former Indian lands, and the railroad soon followed. The cotton kingdom, which in 1845 already extended from the Carolinas southwestward to eastern Texas and from Tennessee down to Florida, now pushed further, into Arkansas and the Texas plains. Frontier settlements in western Missouri and Arkansas, which contained but a tiny number of settlers in 1840, experienced the most rapid growth.

Life on the frontier was difficult, and for whites who had become used to living in more settled eastern regions, the move westward often required substantial adjustments. This was true both for small farmers, who once again had to carve fields out of forests without the aid of slaves, and for well-to-do planters, who enjoyed many luxuries back East. But as the overworked farmland in the East became less productive, some wealthy planters were compelled to join the southwestern migration and subject their families to the ruder life on the cotton frontier. Having moved from North Carolina to Alabama with her slaveholder husband, May Drake expressed her discontent in letters to her family: "To a female who has once been blest with every comfort, and even every luxury, blest with the society of a large and respectable circle of relations and friends . . . to such people Mississippi and Alabama are but a dreary waste." Another wrote, "The farmers in this country [Alabama] live in a miserable manner. They think only of making money, and their houses are hardly fit to live in." Although some planters, like the Natchez nabobs, tried to bring luxury and refinement to the frontier, many white families found themselves struggling to rebuild homes, communities, and social networks in the southwestern territories.

Yet even in these new territories where people of all social classes faced some hardships, small farmers and others of moderate means developed resentments against wealthy planters. For instance, the *Mississippi Free Trader,* published in Natchez, editorialized in April 1842 on the relative value of small farmers and larger planters to the city's economy. The small farmers, it noted,

> would crowd our streets with fresh and healthy supplies of home productions, and the proceeds would be expended *here* among our merchants, grocers, and artisans. The large planters . . . for the most part, sell their cotton in Liverpool; buy their wines in London or Havre; their negro clothing in Boston; their plantation implements and supplies in Cincinnati; and their groceries and fancy articles in New Orleans. . . .

The conflicts among whites in the southwestern territories centered on several issues, such as political representation, taxation, debt, and common rights to land and waterways. Planters, for instance, successfully supported legislation that limited the tax liability of slaveholders by putting a ceiling on the taxation of slaves. This meant fewer state funds available for projects—such as roads, railroads, and canals—that might benefit the citizens at large, including farmers in the western areas of Virginia, the Carolinas, and Georgia. Non-slaveholding whites had a difficult time changing such laws because many southern states continued to use property qualifications to restrict voting rights and holding office. Moreover, in the seaboard states, the eastern counties where large planters held sway were accorded much greater representation than were the western counties, which initially had been sparsely settled. As those western counties became more populated, the planter-dominated legislatures failed to reapportion representation.

Virginians complained loudly of the Tidewater grip on state politics, and Carolinians from the Piedmont west were equally vocal about their lack of representation. In addition, the property limits on voting lessened the electoral leverage of small farmers and working-class whites throughout each state. In North Carolina, which had some of the most restrictive requirements in the South into the 1850s, only adult white males who owned at least fifty acres could cast a ballot in the state senate election. This requirement disenfranchised about one-half of the state's potential voters. To run for the state senate a man had to own at least three hundred acres, whereas election to the House of Commons of North Carolina required a one hundred-acre holding. The governor was required to own land worth $2,000 and was not chosen by popular election until after 1850.

Not all southern states imposed such severe restrictions on political participation. In Mississippi, for instance, property qualifications for office were eliminated much

"The Verdict of the People." A clerk announced the results of a Missouri election in a mid 1850s painting by George Caleb Bingham. An enthusiastic supporter of the Whig party, states' rights, and slavery, Bingham was praised for his pictures that celebrated the boisterous, "pioneer" roots of America's democracy—and obscured the sectional tensions that increasingly characterized the nation's politics.

Source: George Caleb Bingham, 1854—55, oil on canvas, 46 × 65 inches—Boatmen's National Bank of St. Louis.

earlier than elsewhere in the South. Most white adult male Mississippians could vote for local, county, and state offices by 1850. Still, the vast majority of those who held office were planters, slave owners, or prosperous non-slaveholding yeomen. This was in part because party leaders were prominent and privileged men, such as the Natchez nabobs, and they set the agenda as well as the election slates for local, county, and state elections. In addition, elections were public events, presided over by local planters or merchants. The secret ballot was not yet utilized, assuring that most non-slaveholding whites, who depended on their economic superiors for credit, employment, or other forms of assistance, would support the planter candidate.

Yet non-slaveholding whites did not simply defer to the planter elite. Despite their limited electoral power, they did make demands on legislators and through the courts. During the 1840s and 1850s, for instance, property qualifications for voting were eliminated in nearly all the southern states, and the number and proportion of representatives from western regions in state legislatures was increased. Moreover, like their counterparts in the early nineteenth century, less well-to-do whites continued to protest the confiscation of property for debts, the construction of dams that interfered with fishing rights, and the fencing of supposedly communal lands by individual farmers and planters. Sometimes the protests were orderly affairs, involving petitions to legislatures and claims made at court. At other times, near riots erupted as mobs of dispossessed or indebted whites railed against their treatment at the hands of wealthier neighbors or high-handed judges.

There were, however, significant barriers to creating a united and sustained opposition to planter policies among non-slaveholding whites. First, many poor and working-class whites were as deeply racist as their elite counterparts. When planters claimed that challenges to their authority would increase the chances of slave uprisings or an expansion of free black rights, most southern whites chose to back down from their grievances. Just as importantly, non-slaveholding whites were themselves a varied group. Yeomen farmers who owned land and made a good living joined planters in confiscating the goods of indebted landless whites. Even those at the very bottom of white society, who moved from job to job and town to town, did not always share a common cause. Some lived as man and wife without benefit of marriage and found their only allies among petty criminals, free blacks, and other marginal groups. These were ostracized by their more respectable counterparts who, although landless, maintained steady work habits, stable families, and a proper distance from blacks and criminals.

Edward Isham, born in the late 1820s, grew up in the poorest and least respectable sectors of southern white society. He tried to take advantage of new opportunities, including westward migration, to improve his standing, but he failed time and again. Pinetown, in Carroll County, Georgia, where the Ishams settled in the 1830s, offered limited schooling, little religious training, and numerous outlets for men with violent tempers. Edward, in fact, fled the area in the mid 1840s after being jailed for assaulting a man in front of the justice of the peace. Over the next decade and a half, he moved back and forth between Georgia, Alabama,

Geographic and Economic Mobility of Poor Household Heads in North Carolina and Mississippi, 1840–1860. Poor whites moved frequently in search of better opportunities. As the southern frontier pushed westward, so did poor whites and at least some acquired land in these frontier areas. Nonetheless, the vast majority of poor whites remained landless whether they stayed in one place or resettled farther west. This chart illustrates the geographic mobility and the difficulties obtaining land for poor whites in Davidson County in central North Carolina from 1840 to 1860 and in the newly opened settlements of Pontotoc County and Tishomingo County in northeast Mississippi from 1850 to 1860.

Source: Charles C. Bolton, *Poor Whites of the Antebellum South: Tenants and Laborers in Central North Carolina and Northeast Mississippi* (1994).

	Davidson Co. 1840–1850[a]	Davidson Co. 1850–1860[a]	Pontotoc Co. 1850–1860[a]	Tishomingo Co. 1850–1860[a]
Left the county[b]	86 (48%)	116 (64%)	143 (80%)	134 (75%)
Stayed in the same county and acquired land	51 (28%)	18 (11%)	20 (11%)	22 (12%)
Stayed in the same county and remained landless	44 (24%)	47 (26%)	15 (8%)	22 (12%)
Total number of household heads	181	181	178	178

[a]Source: Tax Lists, 1840, Davidson County Records, NCDAH; 1840 Federal Census for Davidson County, Schedule I; 1850 and 1860 Federal Censuses for Davidson county, Schedules I and IV. 1850 and 1860 Federal Censuses for Pontotoc and Tishomingo counties, Schedules I and IV. A determination of household heads for Davidson County in 1840 was made by matching people from Tax Lists with the household heads listed on the 1840 Federal Census.
[b]Includes individuals who died during the period.

Arkansas, Tennessee, and western North Carolina. He worked at various jobs — splitting rails, tenant farming, mining, herding cattle, logging, hunting deer, collecting bees, performing odd jobs, and working on the railroad and river boats. He married three times, at least once without divorcing his previous wife, and had a series of affairs, some with married women. He gambled, stole goods and money, fought, and caroused with free blacks as well as other poor whites. He often moved to avoid the law, but his last stop was Catawba County, North Carolina, where he was convicted of killing a slave owner over a seven dollar debt and was hanged on May 25, 1860.

Stories such as that of Edward Isham reinforced images of "poor white trash" among more well-do-do Southerners, and certainly his kind existed in larger numbers than most southern whites cared to admit. Yet landless whites were not all like Isham. Probably numbering some thirty to fifty percent of all whites in the South in the mid nineteenth century, they comprised a large and diverse population at the bottom of the white social hierarchy. Most managed to create more stable and more prosperous lives than did Edward Isham. It was these very differences among the South's non-slaveholding whites that limited their ability, and desire, to forge a meaningful opposition to planter control. Yet various groups of whites outside the planter class continued to assert their own rights and interests, thereby complicating the lives of planters who hoped to achieve absolute authority over their inferiors, white as well as black.

The Ravages of the Internal Slave Trade

Until about 1850, as slavery expanded south- and westward, declining profits characterized older areas of cultivation, such as Virginia, Maryland, and North Carolina. The resulting losses were offset in part by monies made on the internal slave trade. Planters in the upper South could reap a significant return on early investments by selling the best field hands and most fertile mothers among their slaves to planters in South Carolina, Georgia, Alabama, and lands west. But without new slaves coming into the upper South, the prospects for future income were limited and the ability to leave one's heirs a planter lifestyle subverted.

The internal slave trade was one of the cruelest aspects of a harsh system. Although slaves had always been subject to sale, the possibility of being sold to a plantation hundreds of miles from one's family increased dramatically in the 1840s with the extension of slavery into Alabama,

The Spread of Cotton, 1820–1860. In 1820, cotton production was centered in the eastern seaboard states. Its spread to the South and West in the 1830s, 1840s, and 1850s ensured that the internal slave trade would expand throughout this period. The sale of slaves from the upper South to the lower South provided profits for slave owners in both regions but produced painful separations for African-American families and introduced harsher working conditions for those African Americans sold into the Deep South.

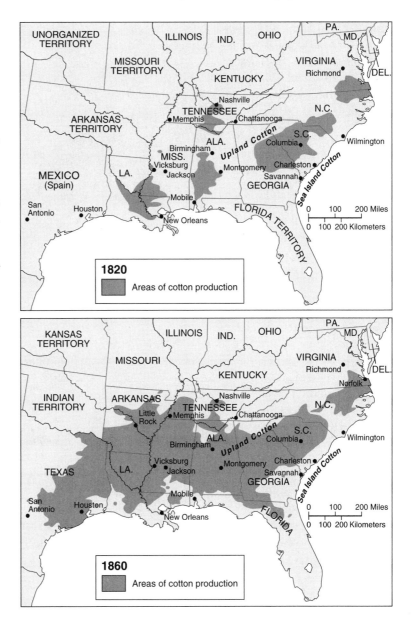

Louisiana, Mississippi, Missouri, Arkansas, and Texas. Because the slaves in greatest demand were between the ages of twenty and fifty, a high percentage of those sold further south left spouses and children behind. As slavery's heartland moved southwestward, the forced migration of hundreds of thousands of African Americans caused the massive destruction of families. When Fannie Berry, who had been a slave in Virginia, was interviewed in 1937, she recalled the horrors of the slave trade from her childhood. She told of a day when

> There was a great crying and carrying on among the slaves who had been sold. Two or three of them gals had young babies they were taking with them. . . . As soon as they got on the train this ol' new master had the train stopped and made them poor gal mothers take babies off and laid them precious things on the ground and left them to live or die.

At other times it was the mothers who were left behind and the children who were sold away. After 1840, with the boom in cotton in Texas, Mississippi, and other areas in the Southwest, planters in the upper South found a ready market for children aged ten or younger. Whether adults or children, slaves sold into the Deep South faced even hotter and less hospitable climates, more demanding work schedules, and harsher punishments than those they had experienced in the upper South.

Even when masters migrated and took all of their slaves with them, slave families were still broken apart because slave marriages often joined people belonging to different masters, especially on the smaller farms most common in the upper South. The migration of one master's chattel, then, meant separation of family members belonging to other masters. It is estimated that somewhere between a fifth and

"I Will Come Back." Having purchased his freedom, an Alabama ex-slave named Peter Still bade farewell to his enslaved wife, Vina. Still's self-purchased manumission in 1850—an opportunity few masters offered their slaves—had no effect on his wife, who was owned by a different individual.

Source: Kate E. R. Pickard, *The Kidnapped and the Ransomed, Being the Personal Recollection of Peter Still and His Wife "Vina," after Forty Years of Slavery* (1856)—General Research Division, New York Public Library, Astor, Lenox and Tilden Foundations.

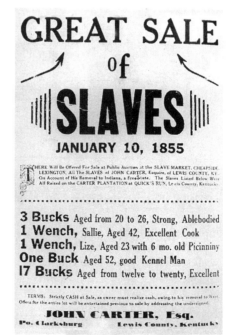

GREAT SALE
of
SLAVES
JANUARY 10, 1855

THERE Will Be Offered For Sale at Public Auction at the SLAVE MARKET, CHEAPSIDE, LEXINGTON, All The SLAVES of JOHN CARTER, Esquire, of LEWIS COUNTY, KY. On Account of His Removal to Indiana, a Free State. The Slaves Listed Below Were All Raised on the CARTER PLANTATION at QUICK'S RUN, Lewis County, Kentucky.

· ·

3 Bucks Aged from 20 to 26, Strong, Ablebodied
1 Wench, Sallie, Aged 42, Excellent Cook
1 Wench, Lize, Aged 23 with 6 mo. old Picinniny
One Buck Aged 52, good Kennel Man
17 Bucks Aged from twelve to twenty, Excellent

· ·

TERMS: Strictly CASH at Sale, as owner must realize cash, owing to his removal to West. Offers for the entire lot will be entertained previous to sale by addressing the undersigned.

JOHN CARTER, Esq.
Po. Clarksburg   Lewis County, Kentucky

Slaves for Sale. The twenty-three slaves to be sold belonged to a Kentucky planter, John Carter, who decided to "liquidate his assets" before moving to the free state of Indiana.

Source: John Winston Coleman, *Slavery Times in Kentucky* (1940).

"My Master Has Sold Albert to a Trader . . ."

In the following letter, a slave woman named Maria Perkins writes to her husband, Richard, about the sale of their children and the possibility of being sold herself.

Charlottesville, Oct. 8th, 1852

Dear Husband

I write you a letter to let you know my distress. My master has sold Albert to a trader on Monday court day and myself and [our] other child is for sale also and I want [to] . . . hear from you very soon before next court [day] if you can. . . . I don't want you to wait till Christmas. I want you to tell Dr. Hamelton and your master if either will buy me they can attend to it now and then I can go afterwards. I don't want a trader to get me. They asked me if I had got any person to buy me and I told them no. They took me to the courthouse too [but] they never put me up [for sale]. A man [by] the name of Brady bought Albert and [he] is gone. I don't know where. They say he lives in Scottesville. My things is in several places some is in Staunton and if I should be sold I don't know what will become of them. I don't expect to meet with the luck to get that way till I am quite heartsick. Nothing more.

I am and ever will be your kind wife,
Maria Perkins.

Source: Ulrich B. Phillips, ed., *Life and Labor in the Old South* (1929).

a third of all slave marriages were broken through sale or forced migration, or by willing slaves to relatives in distant regions of the South.

The internal slave trade destroyed families and brought misery to both individual African Americans and the larger communities in which they lived. Over time, it also created problems for whites who resided in what had once been profitable plantation regions. The sale of slaves to other regions increased owners' fears that slaves would retaliate against slaveholders and their families and sometimes assured that those left behind would be more recalcitrant and resistant than ever. In certain areas of Virginia and Maryland, the loss of large numbers of slaves increased the relative proportion of free blacks in the population. This development raised further anxieties about free blacks' influence on those left in bondage and their competition for jobs with poor whites, more of whom were now forced to seek work in urban areas. Some whites in the upper South wondered if the advantages of slavery still outweighed its costs. For a time at least, until proslavery ideologues claimed the cultural and political high ground in the late 1840s, Chesapeake planters who saw their way of life eroding discussed the potential benefits of colonization for blacks.

A few even arranged to have some slaves freed so that they could be shipped back to Africa.

The Tensions of Plantation Life among Whites

Throughout the 1830s and 1840s, despite the doubts of some slave owners (especially in the upper South), planters successfully fended off public challenges to their political and economic authority from those whites who received fewer benefits from a slave-based economy. Yet even in their staunch defense of slavery, planters found that the "peculiar institution" was not without its tensions and conflicts. Using overseers to supervise slave labor caused some of these tensions. Overseers were the most important paid laborers on most large plantations, and often the most problematic as well. They were expected to keep slaves employed to their utmost capacity, keep them healthy and relatively content, and keep the funds expended on their care to a minimum. Owners were demanding, but so too were the slaves, who recognized overseers as a potentially weak link in the chain of command and withheld their labor power from or protested to owners against especially brutal overseers.

Many planters hired a new overseer every year, hoping to find one with the perfect mix of agricultural expertise, personal authority, and managerial integrity. In the diaries and letters of planters, problems with overseers loomed large: they were too harsh or too lenient; they were more interested in sexual exploitation than agricultural production; they were unhappy with their wages, or housing, or chances for becoming a planter themselves; they had gained too much control in the absence of the owner; they were out of control. This catalogue of complaints penned by slave owners certainly must have had its counterpart among discontented overseers, although few had the leisure time or the education to leave much of a written record. Occupying a difficult middle ground between black laborers and their white owners, overseers provided a constant reminder that even economic success had its price.

A planter might find refuge from conflicts with overseers in the bosom of his family, but here too lurked tensions and contradictions. First and foremost, the planter's sexual access to female slaves strained marital bonds and undermined the mistress's self-respect and moral authority on the plantation. A proper lady would, of course, try to ignore evidence of sexual indiscretion. Mary Boykin Chesnut, in an oft-quoted passage, observed that "the Mulattoes one sees in every family exactly resemble the white children — and every lady tells you who is the father of all the Mulatto children in everybody's household, but those in her own she seems to think drop from the clouds or pretends so to think."

The Price of Blood. Thomas Satterwhite Noble's painting reflected on the ways property overwhelmed any ties of affection in the plantation "family." His picture portrayed the sale of a plantation master's Mulatto son to a slave trader.

Source: 1868, oil, 39 1/4 × 49 1/2 inches — The Morris Museum of Art, Augusta, Georgia.

Sometimes the evidence was so overwhelming that it could not be ignored. Catherine Hammond left her husband over his sexual relationship with the slave Louisa, but only after having overlooked earlier liaisons with Louisa's mother, Sally Johnson, and with four of Catherine's own nieces. The absence of testimony from Louisa, Sally Johnson, or Hammond's nieces about the agonies they experienced as a result of this abuse makes it impossible to understand the full horror of the man's actions. However, his flagrant infidelity, which eventually forced Catherine to act in order to save her own reputation, illuminates the dark underside of domestic relations that was often concealed to preserve the family honor. That Catherine eventually reconciled with her husband suggests the limited options available to even the most well-positioned southern women. Moreover, that Catherine apparently did nothing to stop the sexual exploitation of Louisa, other slave women, and even her own nieces also indicates the ease with which plantation mistresses became accomplices in the abusive system.

Prevailing attitudes not only minimized the private "indiscretions" of masters, they also denied the master's wife most public credit for the plantation's upkeep. On a plantation, the wife's domestic sphere could be huge. She supervised not only a broad range of essential tasks in her family's living quarters (often known as the Big House) but also in the separate kitchen, dairy, smokehouse, and storehouse. Managing the household budget and negotiating with local merchants might also fall within her sphere. If the husband was deceased or temporarily absent, she usually administered the plantation alone or with the aid of an overseer. But chattel slavery discredited menial labor, associating those who performed it with the slave's lowly status. Unlike industrious northern businessmen, planters generally prided themselves on being men of

507

leisure and culture, freed from hard work and financial concerns. The popular image of the plantation mistress reflected those values. She must be the very embodiment of grace, gentility, and refinement. "Maidenly delicacy," affirmed the president of one southern university in 1810, was the very foundation of society. These strictures became more rigid as slavery became more entrenched.

Strict adherence to these ideals placed the plantation mistress in the contradictory position of having to appear to be a delicate woman of leisure while performing hard work on a daily basis. At least one plantation visitor felt awkward when he inadvertently broke through the facade. Strolling the grounds, he came upon the mistress, disheveled and toiling over a salting barrel. Rather than greet her—and thereby accost her in a role deemed unseemly for a southern lady—he could only pretend not to see her and walk on. The incident highlights the extremes to which Southerners went to exile the reality of labor from the image of the Big House.

Plantation mistresses, like northern women, were encouraged to find solace in religion; but they discovered fewer opportunities there for self-expression and social initiative. In the late eighteenth and early nineteenth centuries, southern women, at least in more densely settled areas, had formed prayer, missionary, and benevolent associations. A scattering of temperance societies flourished in southern cities beginning in the 1820s. Soon, however, northern women's increasing visibility in antislavery agitation, much of it linked to religious awakenings, triggered a backlash in the South that curbed women's participation in voluntary associations, whether church-based or secular. By the late 1840s, such restrictions severely limited women's ability to launch collective and public protests against the abuses linked to male domination. However, this may have assured the continuation of a more intimate form of guerrilla warfare in southern households where wives believed that their planter husbands had overstepped the boundaries of patriarchal authority.

The Proslavery Movement

During the 1830s and 1840s, the power of planters was challenged in several ways, including revolts and escapes by slaves, the growth of the free black community, demands by non-slaveholding whites, and conflicts with overseers and wives. The British abolition of West Indian slavery in 1833, the Panic of 1837, and the emancipation of slaves in the French West Indies in 1848 intensified concerns over the future of the South's increasingly peculiar institution. Attacks from northern opponents—a growing abolitionist movement, the defection of the Grimke sisters and fugitive slaves, the condemnation of church leaders, and massive petition campaigns—all heightened slave owners' concerns as well.

The defenders of slavery did not retreat, however. Believing that expansion into western lands presaged a new day for planters, they developed an aggressive defense of their way of life and further restricted possibilities for change. Previously referred to apologetically as a necessary but temporary evil, black bondage was now described as the natural

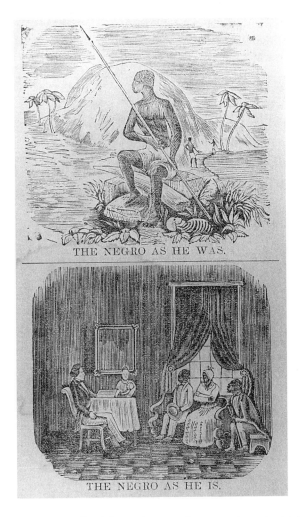

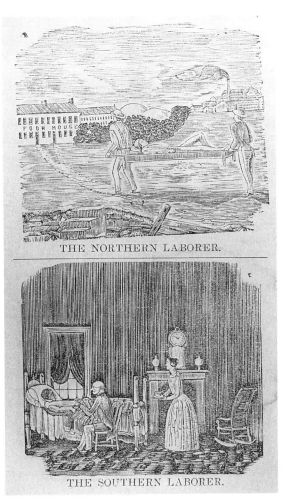

The Benefits of Slavery. Two pages from a pro-slavery tract published around 1860 presented the contrasting fates of unfree and free labor: while fortunate slaves were civilized and, in old age, cared for by benevolent masters, the northern wage worker faced only exhaustion and destitution.

Source: From the private collection of Larry E. Tise, Harrisburg, Pennsylvania.

order of things. In the words of South Carolina Senator John C. Calhoun, slavery was "a positive good," an institution beneficial alike to planters, slaves, and to all other social groups.

Defenders of the new creed developed their arguments along several different lines, but the most popular themes in the 1830s and 1840s were expressed by men such as Senator Calhoun, Professor Thomas Dew, and South Carolina Governor George Duffie. Calhoun held up slave labor as in all respects superior to wage labor. The sharpening of social conflicts in the North, he claimed, testified to the superiority of outright bondage. "There is and has always been, in an advanced stage of wealth and civilization," Calhoun told the U.S. Senate, "a conflict between labor and capital. The condition of society in the South exempts us from the disorders and dangers resulting from this conflict." This fact, he asserted, demonstrates "how vastly more favorable our condition of society is to that of other sections for free and stable institutions." In addition, planters did not cut loose their slaves when sick or aged. And, according to Calhoun and like-minded planters, the food, shelter, and clothing provided slaves was superior to that available to free laborers of the North.

Thomas Dew, a young professor at the College of William and Mary in Virginia, crafted the first significant proslavery document. His *Review of the Debates in the Virginia Legislature of 1831 and 1832* offered an argument on behalf of slavery in the guise of commentaries on the legislature's debates. Dew rejected on purely practical grounds the colonizationists' plans for the purchase and resettlement of slaves. He then argued that if blacks were to remain in Virginia, it was best that they do so as slaves. Drawing on historical examples from Greek, Hebrew, and Roman civilizations and on Biblical justifications from the Old and New Testaments, Dew claimed that slavery was best both for the South and for the slaves. Planters, in this scenario, were both the instruments of God and the upholders of classical traditions and values. Indeed, Biblical support for slavery may have been the most widely cited rationale for maintaining the institution because scripture offered the most effective response to northern abolitionists and ministers who claimed to have right and righteousness on their side.

Governor Duffie was one of many politicians who embraced Biblical justifications for slavery. He elaborated on Dew's themes when he spoke before the South Carolina legislature in 1835. He clearly distinguished between the character and rights of whites and of blacks, justifying slavery only for those of African ancestry. Blacks, he proclaimed, were "destined by providence" for bondage. They were "in all respects, physical, moral, and political, inferior to millions of the human race" and therefore "unfit for self-government of any kind."

"Guarded From Want, From Beggary Secure . . ."

The following poem, entitled "The Hireling and the Slave," argues that slavery not only guaranteed a stable labor force but also benefited blacks by providing them with a secure life. The poem was written in 1856 by southerner William J. Grayson.

Taught by the master's efforts, by his care
Fed, clothed, protected many a patient year,
From trivial numbers now to millions grown,
With all the white man's useful arts their own,
Industrious, docile, skilled in wood and field,
To guide the plow, the sturdy axe to wield,
The Negroes schooled by slavery embrace
The highest portion of the Negro race;
And none the savage native will compare,
Of barbarous Guinea, with its offspring here.

If bound to daily labor while he lives,
His is the daily bread that labor gives;
Guarded from want, from beggary secure,
He never feels what hireling crowds endure,
Nor know, like them, in hopeless want to crave,
For wife and child, the comforts of the slave,
Or the sad thought that, when about to die,
He leaves them to the cold world's charity,
And sees them slowly seek the poor-house door—
The last, vile, hated refuge of the poor. . . .

The master's lighter rule insures
More order than the sternest code secures;
No mobs of factious workmen gather here,
No strikes we dread, no lawless riots fear; . . .

Seditious schemes in bloody tumults end,
Parsons incite, and senators defend,
But not where slaves their easy labors ply,
Safe from the snare, beneath a master's eye;
In useful tasks engaged, employed their time,
Untempted by the demagogue to crime,
Secure they toil, uncursed their peaceful life,
With labor's hungry broils and wasteful strife.
No want to good, no faction to deplore,
The slaves escape the perils of the poor.

Source: Eric McKitrick, ed., *Slavery Defended: The Views of the Old South* (1963).

"Free Negroes in the North."
Apologists for slavery often constructed a grotesque picture of free blacks in the North. According to this etching published during the Civil War, without the supervision of benevolent masters, northern African Americans descended into violence and degradation.

Source: V. Blada (A. J. Volck), *Sketches from the Civil War in North America, 1861, '62, '63* (1863)—Print Collection, Miriam and Ira Wallach Division of Art, Prints, and Photographs, New York Public Library, Astor, Lenox and Tilden Foundations.

During the next twenty-five years, proslavery politicians, professors, physicians, and publicists dutifully elaborated the racist argument, offering a stream of scientific as well as religious evidence in slavery's defense. Racist doctrine was scientific nonsense, but it served three important purposes for the slave owners. First, it justified the bondage of African Americans by ruling out all arguments based on universal human rights. Second, it undermined the status and claims of free blacks. Third, it accomplished both of these objectives without explicitly threatening the rights of poor southern whites, whose support (or at least toleration) the slaveholders required.

The development of the proslavery argument both reflected and reinforced an increasingly rigid southern political and social structure at precisely the moment when reform and innovation were most necessary. The expansion of plantations into new geographical areas turned labor abundance into labor scarcity for many planters and exacerbated their financial dependence on single-crop, export-driven agriculture. As the Panic of 1837 had shown, such dependence on a single crop and on foreign markets, such as England, made white Southerners vulnerable to economic developments over which they had little control. The spread of slavery also intensified challenges from Northerners who opposed the system on moral, political, and economic grounds, from slaves whose family and community networks were shattered by the internal slave trade, and from southern whites who feared competition from blacks or resented the tyranny of planters.

The Limits of Economic Diversification

Although fewer and fewer planters questioned the institution of slavery itself, some began considering the advantages of economic diversification in the South. But during the mid 1840s, despite serious fluctuations in the prices paid for cotton, tobacco, and rice, the profitability of plantation agriculture allowed those who supported the status quo to gain the upper hand. Advocates of diversification, such as Stephen Duncan of Mississippi, found it difficult to gain adherents when both agricultural production and the demand for plantation crops was on the increase. Even Duncan himself, although extolling the advantages of multicrop agriculture, expanded his plantation holdings, nearly all of which revolved around the production of two crops: sugar cane and cotton. The market price for sugar cane remained stable during the late 1830s and early 1840s, helping large planters who grew this crop in Mississippi and Louisiana to ride out the depression. Prices for other staple crops rebounded in the mid and late 1840s. With the wealthiest residents of the South investing larger and larger sums in land and slaves, nonstaple food crops remained marginal to the region's economy.

Some investors, particularly in the cities and towns of the Southeast, began to diversify in another way: by investing in industry. In the 1840s, William Gregg's textile factory in Graniteville, South Carolina, and Joseph Reid Anderson's Tredegar Iron Works in Richmond, Virginia, were among the most profitable southern industrial ventures. Whereas the textile labor force was composed primarily of poor white women and children, the iron industry recruited African Americans, enslaved and free, in large numbers. Although these employment patterns demonstrated the capacity of women and blacks for industrial labor, they limited the potential for industrial growth. Only the poorest white women could work for wages without damaging their family's reputation; the increased employment of free blacks raised anxieties among skilled white men; and slaves were generally more valuable in agriculture than in industry. Factories, then, could flourish only on the periphery of plantation society.

Even though industrialization was marginal to the southern economy, some planters still saw it as a threat to the institution of slavery. Urban work brought a slave into close contact with free blacks and with the world outside the plantation and even outside the South. That exposure encouraged and assisted attempts to escape slavery. Frederick Douglass's experiences provide a good example. Hostile southern white workers had once forced Douglass to return to his plantation from the docks of Baltimore, where his owner had hired him out. Later, however, he found himself back on the docks, thankfully in friendlier surroundings. There, according to Douglass, two Irish longshoremen "expressed the deepest sympathy for me, and the most dedicated hatred of slavery. They went so far as to tell me that I ought to run away and go to the North, that I should find friends there, and that I should then be as free as anybody." Douglass "remembered their words and their advice, and looked forward to an escape to the North as a possible means of gaining the liberty for which my heart panted." By passing as a free black sailor, an impersonation aided by his experience in the shipyard and the assistance of real free blacks, Douglass did escape to the North a few years later. Other slaves simply took advantage of the relative anonymity that large cities provided and disappeared into the South's urban free black population.

In this case it was urban life more than industrial labor that led to Douglass's escape. In fact, in some areas, such as Richmond and Lynchburg, Virginia, slaves worked in factories without any weakening of the system of bondage. Moreover, industrial slavery was one way to breathe new life into the southern economy without challenging the basic racial and labor relations of the region. Still, many planters assumed that industry and urbanization were synonymous and that both threatened the southern way of life.

For the cities' detractors, slave flight was by no means the only problem. The greater freedom (especially freedom of movement) that generally went with urban employment tended to erode the slave owners' power and ability to demand unquestioned deference from blacks. "The ties which bound together the master and the slave," the New Orleans *Daily Picayune* complained, were being "gradually severed" in that city, as slave workers "become intemperate, disorderly, and lose the respect which the servant should entertain for the master."

The behavior of free blacks, fugitives, and resistant slaves in cities was considered "contagious upon those who do not possess these dangerous privileges." Industrial slaves, warned South Carolina Senator James Hammond, "were more than half freed" and destined to become "the most corrupt and turbulent" sector of the slave labor force. "It is not to be denied," determined a Savannah grand jury in 1845, that such freedoms were "striking directly at the existence of our institutions, and unless broken up in time, will result in the total prostration of existing relations." "The cities," another white Southerner concluded, "is no place for niggers! They get strange notions into their heads and grow discontented. They ought, every one of them, [to] be sent back onto the plantations."

In addition, in cities, slave owners were in close proximity of watchful neighbors and some felt more constrained in their behavior, including

514

their treatment of slaves. For instance, in the town of Edenton, North Carolina, the slave Harriet Ann Jacobs found some protection from abuse because she lived in a neighborhood where non-slaveholding whites and free blacks resided alongside slaves and their owners. In a provocative and painful memoir written after her escape to the North, she described the excruciating choices open to her at age fifteen when Dr. Flint, her master, began to demand sexual favors. Her grandmother, a free black, lived nearby, as did "a white unmarried gentleman" who "knew my grand-mother and often spoke to me in the street." In recalling this period of her life, Jacobs wrote of the importance of her grandmother's presence:

> I felt shamefaced about telling her such impure things. Though I did not confide in my grandmother, her presence in the neighborhood was some protection. . . . Dr. Flint dreaded her scorching rebukes — and he did not wish his villainy made public. It was lucky for me that I did not live on a distant plantation, but in a town not so large that the inhabitants were ignorant of each other's affairs.

Probably Dr. Flint had a different view of town life — seeing it as something that eroded his "rights" as a slave owner.

Most slave owners, then, feared and despised the possibility of increased industrialization and the growth of cities in the South. "We have no cities. We don't want them," exclaimed one white Alabaman, who no doubt expressed the feelings of many of his neighbors. "We want no manufactures; we desire no trading, no mechanical or manufacturing classes. As long as we have our rice, our sugar, our tobacco, and our cotton, we can command wealth to purchase all we want."

Above all, slave owners worried that free wage-earners and their employers would seek first to limit the use of slave labor and eventually collide with the whole slave-labor system. The small circle of southern leaders who advocated economic development and diversification agreed. One of their leading spokesmen, Senator George Mason of Virginia, complained that "slavery discourages arts and manufactures. The poor despise labor when performed by slaves." To distinguish white from black urban workers, white artisans demanded preferential hiring and voting rights based on their race, justifying planters' fears that industrialization and urbanization was the beginning of a slippery slope that would lead to the disruption of their traditional power and privilege.

It was even more frightening to slave owners, however, that white and black workers might make common cause, a situation more likely to occur in places with high rates of immigration from Europe. In cities such as New Orleans, Charleston, and Richmond, the South's urban working class population increasingly included immigrants, who seemed to have little loyalty to or even respect for the region's deeply rooted system of

chattel slavery. A Richmond newspaper assured its white subscribers that a major advantage of slave labor was its tendency to exclude "a populace made up of the dregs of Europe." But some African Americans viewed those "dregs" as potential allies and tried to assist them. For instance, in 1847, the members of Richmond's First African American Baptist Church sent forty dollars to Ireland to help victims of the famine. Later they donated smaller sums to assist the Irish poor in their hometown. The *Charleston Standard* no doubt spoke for many slave owners when it branded foreign-born workers as "a curse rather than a blessing to our peculiar institution."

The South might have sustained a plantation system based on slavery and staple-crop agriculture and, simultaneously, developed an extensive industrial base by encouraging immigrants to settle in the region. In fact, many Southerners who advocated economic diversification insisted that commerce and manufacturing would complement, not threaten, agriculture. James D. B. DeBow, who was inspired by the Memphis commercial convention of 1845, established a journal, the *Commercial Review of the South and the West,* that proclaimed in print, "Commerce is King." DeBow was also an ardent proslavery advocate who believed that only by creating southern commercial and industrial enterprises could the region maintain its existing traditions and institutions. This approach was rendered impossible, however, by planters' fears of foreign workers and their refusal to recognize manufacturing or wage labor as more than unworthy stepchildren in the southern economy. Indeed, planters tended to regard free labor as subversive and actively disruptive of the benefits of bound labor.

"Old Virginia Labor-saving Machine." A cartoon in an 1857 edition of *Harper's New Monthly Magazine* satirized the planting techniques espoused by "Squire Broadacre," a Virginia farmer. With access to slave labor, many southern planters resisted technical innovations, mechanical and otherwise, that would improve agricultural output.

Source: "A Winter in the South," *Harper's New Monthly Magazine* (September 1857)—American Social History Project.

By the time *Debow's Review* gained a significant readership at midcentury, the opportunity to reshape the South's economic structure had passed. Although complaints about planters' dependency on northern capital and commerce persisted, and although some white Southerners still spoke of the advantages of industrial development, when it came to practical action, most planters chose to invest in land and slaves. By the late 1840s, as prices and profits for cotton, rice, sugar, and tobacco rose, ventures that would extend the geographical boundaries of plantation slavery generated more interest than those that would diversify the economy.

The Lure of New Territories

Southern whites had long dreamed of extending their dominion into tropical climates. Congressmen and presidents cast greedy glances at Cuba and Central America throughout the early and mid nineteenth century. In New Orleans, the large number of French, free blacks, and slaves who arrived from St. Domingue (present-day Haiti) after the revolution there in the 1790s gave the city a Caribbean flair that made planters in the area think of the possibilities of exploiting the West Indies. Proslavery adventurers actually mounted invasions of Mexico, Cuba, and Nicaragua in this period. And the successful settlement and "emancipation" of Texas in the 1830s revitalized dreams of a slave empire that stretched into Mexico and the Caribbean.

Cuba was perhaps the most appealing prospect for annexation. In 1823, Secretary of State John Quincy Adams claimed, "There are laws of political as well as physical gravitation, and if an apple, severed by a tempest from its native tree, cannot choose but fall to the ground, Cuba, forcibly disjoined from its own unnatural connection with Spain, and incapable of self-support, can gravitate only towards the North American Union. . . ." In 1848, President James K. Polk tried, unsuccessfully, to help this "natural" gravitation along by offering Spain $100 million for the island. Similar offers, supported by circles of Cubans dissatisfied with Spanish rule, were made several more times over the next decade, although without success.

Southern planters also investigated economic possibilities in California during the 1840s. To encourage larger numbers of U.S. residents to settle the region, Anglo-American immigrants to the West Coast described the rich lands of the Sacramento and San Joaquin valleys and the docile population of Indian workers. Initially, these pioneers cared little about the origins of the new settlers, so long as the United States gained

Free Labor and Slavery

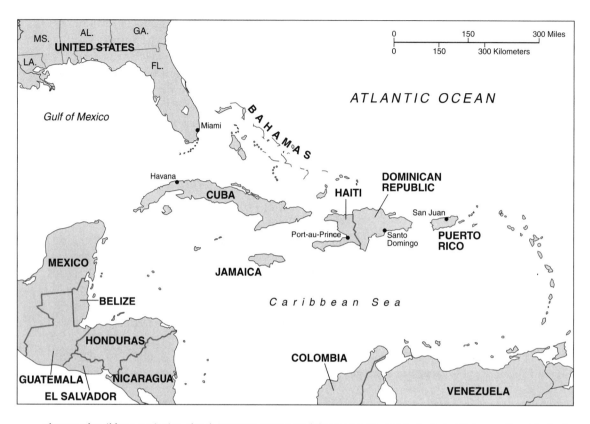

The Lure of Caribbean Territories. After the Louisiana Territory and Florida were acquired by the United States, wealthy white South-erners began looking for new areas in which to expand their plantation economy. Some set their sights on the Caribbean. Easily accessible from Florida and with a long history of slave-produced sugar, rum, tobacco, and coffee, Cuba seemed particularly attrac-tive. And even Haiti, the site in 1800 of a successful slave rebellion led by Toussaint L'Ouverture, was considered a possibility for future development of the plantation system. Although plans to add Caribbean islands to the United States did not progress much in the mid nineteenth century, when the United States engaged in its first imperial adventures in the 1890s, Cuba and Puerto Rico were the first areas to come under U.S. control.

Source: Louis A. Pérez, Jr., *Cuba and the U.S.: Ties of Singular Intimacy* (1994).

control of the region from Mexico. But planters, such as Richard Fulton of Missouri, wanted to know, "Is California a slave state and could our cit-izens bring their slaves with them?"

Those already established in the area tried to reassure potential southern émigrés. Rancher John Marsh, who had gained significant expe-rience in Indian affairs, admitted that Mexico did have laws against slavery, but he assured prospective migrants that the native peoples were willing workers. He even claimed that they submitted to "flagellation with more humility than negroes." Pierson B. Reading, a former New Orleans cotton broker who resettled in California, wrote to a friend back home in 1844, "The Indians of California make as obedient and humble slaves as the negroes in the south," and "for a mere trifle, you can secure their services for life." Although the indigenous peoples proved more resistant than these descriptions suggest, southern whites, encouraged by increased demand for agricultural products, eagerly envisioned plantations, stretching from the Atlantic to the Pacific, worked by dark-skinned slaves.

The Lone Star Republic of Texas formed a major part of this vision. It had sought U.S. statehood from the moment it achieved independence, but northern hostility to admitting this immense slaveholding republic into the Union had postponed action for several years. In 1844, however, the Democratic Party platform tied support for Texas statehood to the demand—popular among northern farmers—for the annexation of all of Oregon (a region claimed by both England and the United States). Farmers from the Old Northwest had been eyeing Oregon's Willamette Valley for years. By 1843, thousands of wagons were already following the Oregon Trail west from Missouri. Southern planters and politicians began to believe that the North's appetite for new lands might at last provide the basis for Texas statehood. The election the following year turned on the issue of admitting Texas and annexing Oregon.

The Democrats chose James K. Polk as their party standard-bearer, overlooking both President Tyler, who was considered ineffective, and Martin Van Buren, who was less enthusiastic about the admission of Texas. Andrew Jackson was a great fan of Polk who, like him, was a Tennessee Democrat with a vision of America as an expansive nation. The Whigs nominated Henry Clay, but the party was divided over the wisdom of westward growth. Southern Whigs were particularly angered at Clay's failure to support the admission of Texas with enthusiasm, whereas northern Whigs were annoyed that Clay even considered taking such a stand.

Although the popular vote was close—49.6 percent for Polk, 48.1 percent for Clay, and 2.3 percent for Liberty Party candidate James G. Birney—Polk's election was viewed as a mandate for expansion. The new administration did not annex all of Oregon, however. Instead, it agreed with Britain, which controlled Canada to the north, to define the 49th parallel as the northern boundary of the United States, simply extending the eastern border with Canada westward. But even before this boundary dispute was settled, the U.S. Congress approved the annexation of the Lone Star Republic of Texas in December 1845.

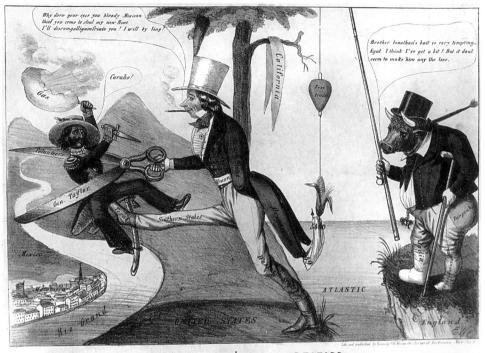

UNCLE SAM'S TAYLORIFICS

"Uncle Sam's Taylorifics." A beardless Uncle Sam sliced and booted Mexico across the Rio Grande in this bellicose 1846 lithograph cartoon.

Source: Henry R. Robinson (after a drawing by Edward W. Clay), 1846, lithograph—New York Historical Society.

The War with Mexico

President Polk had even grander plans for expansion. During his one term in office, he oversaw the acquisition of more territory by the United States than any other president. The annexation of Texas was completed under his predecessor, President John Tyler, but Polk presided over the settlement of the disputed Oregon Territory and then turned his attention to wresting more land from Mexico. Knowing that this plan would necessitate war, he promptly provoked one in 1846. The provocations were so blatantly false that a majority of Whigs voted against the resolution affirming the declaration of war. The newly elected Whig representative from Illinois, Abraham Lincoln, even demanded evidence about the precise spot where Mexicans had supposedly shed American blood. But the Democratic majority carried the day. "As war exists," the president then told Congress, "we are called upon by every consideration of duty and patriotism to vindicate with decision the honor, the rights, and the interests of our country." Many, probably most, Americans, North and South, agreed. Another Illinois representative, for instance, Democrat Stephen A. Douglas, was a fervent champion of westward expansion. He helped boost the war spirit in Congress and branded critics such as Lincoln as "traitors."

Most slaveholders eagerly looked forward to creating new slave states from these hoped-for territories. "Every battle fought in Mexico," cheered the Charleston, South Carolina, *Courier,* "and every dollar spent there, but insures the acquisition of territory which must widen the field of Southern enterprise and power in the future. And the final result will be to readjust the power of the [southern] confederacy, so as to give us control over the operation of government in all time to come."

For proslavery forces, the chance to acquire additional lands in the Southwest offered numerous benefits. The spread of slavery would aid planters in the upper South by creating an even greater demand and higher price for their excess slaves. The friction that dogged relations among different sectors of the white agricultural population might be relieved by new opportunities in the West. Small farmers who owned no slaves (a group that would constitute three-fourths of southern white families by 1860) could hope for a better chance on the new western lands, thereby alleviating the pressures on the planter class to respond to their needs by redistributing existing wealth. And finally, the rapid growth of a non-slaveholding and increasingly antislavery North endangered the political autonomy of the slaveholding South. Geographical expansion would help ensure planters equal representation in the Senate through the admission of one slave state to the Union for every new free state. This would prevent the North from using the federal government to block the interests of slaveholders.

In some parts of the country, however, the enthusiasm of slaveholders for war and their vision of a slave confederacy inspired vigorous opposition. Despite the passage of a resolution supporting the president's declaration of war, a majority in the House of Representatives also voted in favor of a Whig proposal that declared that the war had been "unnecessarily and unconstitutionally begun by the President of the United States." And while a prowar demonstration on May 20, 1846, occupied one part of New York's City Hall Park, George Henry Evans and John Commerford addressed an antiwar rally in another. Having "great reason to believe" that the Mexican War was the work of Texans and their business allies, the rally organizers urged "the Commander in Chief of the army to withdraw his forces, now on the Rio Grande, to some undisputed land belonging to the United States." And if war proved finally unavoidable, then the American sponsors of prowar meetings and messages "ought to be the first to volunteer, and the first to leave for the seat of war."

Opposition to the war was strong among northern farmers as well as some businessmen. The Massachusetts state legislature denounced the war and its "triple object of extending slavery, of strengthening the 'Slave

Power,' and of obtaining control of the Free States" by gaining a slave-state majority in the Senate. The *Cleveland Plain Dealer* carried a speech by an Ohio Democrat who argued that the administration's willingness to compromise with Britain on the Oregon boundary while going to war with Mexico over the Texas boundary demonstrated that "the administration is Southern! Southern! Southern! . . . Since the South have [sic] fixed boundaries for free territory, let the North fix boundaries for slave territories." And Connecticut Congressman Gideon Welles probably spoke for a majority of his constituents when he declared, we must "satisfy the northern people . . . that we are not to extend the institution of slavery as a result of this war."

War News from Mexico. In Richard Caton Woodville's 1848 painting, guests at the "American Hotel" (who represented a cross-section of the nation's citizenry) demonstratively reacted to news about the Mexican War. Their almost comical behavior was in marked contrast to the subdued response of the black man and child in the picture's foreground.

Source: 1848, oil on canvas, 27 × 24 3/4 inches—National Gallery of Art.

Abolitionists helped foment and then reinforce northern fears that the war was a planter conspiracy to assure southern control over the nation. During the 1830s, nearly every acquisition of territory in the South inspired abolitionist outcries against the extension of slavery. Announcement of the outbreak of war with Mexico was received at the 1846 meeting of the American Anti-Slavery Society by means of the new magnetic telegraph. Abby Kelley, an abolitionist who had not planned to speak at the New York gathering, impulsively rose in indignation to express her opposition to the war. "Our fathers were successful in the Revolution, because they were engaged in a holy cause, and had right on their side. But in this case we have not. This nation is doomed," she proclaimed. She prayed for defeat, but envisioned instead a U.S. victory, followed by the day of reckoning, when southern slaves would join forces with western Indians, "who are only waiting to plant their tomahawks in the white man's skull." And antislavery clergyman Theodore Parker intoned that although it would "be a gain to mankind if we could spread over Mexico the Idea of America—that all men are born free and equal in rights, we must first make those ideas real at home."

"Resistance to Civil Government"

In 1848, Henry David Thoreau gave a lecture entitled "Resistance to Civil Government," which was later published as the essay "Civil Disobedience." Thoreau had earlier argued that social constraints forced individuals into "lives of quiet desperation." Only by resistance to society's conventions could Americans realize their full potential. Refusal to pay taxes to the government was one such form of resistance that Thoreau embraced. He claimed that such "civil disobedience" was necessary when tax dollars were being used to support slavery in the South and war against Mexico. Thoreau's writings inspired such later advocates of nonviolent resistance as Mohandas (Mahatma) Ghandi and Martin Luther King, Jr.

It is not desirable to cultivate a respect for the law, so much as for the right. . . . Law never made men a whit more just; and, by means of their respect for it, even the well-disposed are daily made the agents of injustice. A common and natural result of an undue respect for law is, that you may see a file of soldiers . . . marching in admirable order over hill and dale to the wars, against their wills, ay, against their common sense and consciences, which makes it very steep marching indeed, and produces a palpitation of the heart.

Source: Henry David Thoreau, "Resistance to Civil Government" (1849).

As abolitionists engaged in acts of civil disobedience to protest the war, pacifists sometimes joined them. A young Henry David Thoreau refused to pay his taxes in protest against the war, and was jailed in July 1846. The brief imprisonment inspired his classic essay, "Resistance to Civil Government." Other antislavery advocates, however, followed Abby Kelley in taking a more belligerent pro-Mexico stance. Abolitionists across the country signed antiwar pledges and advocated military victory for Mexico. William Lloyd Garrison spoke for many abolitionists when he declared

> I desire to see human life at all times held sacred; but in a struggle like this, so horribly unjust and offensive on our part, so purely of self-defence against lawless invaders on the part of the Mexicans, I feel as a matter of justice, to desire the overwhelming defeat of the American troops, and the success of the injured Mexicans.

The abolitionist campaign bolstered opposition to the war, and may have helped moderate the peace terms, though it did little to dampen popular enthusiasm for the idea of westward expansion.

Manifest Destiny and Conflict over Slavery in the New Territories

Most white Americans, and certainly most Whigs, were not opposed to expansion. They might oppose expansion by force of arms or in the interest of slave owners, but even antiwar Northerners generally agreed that the conquest of western lands was beneficial to the nation. Journalist John O'Sullivan rallied support for westward expansion, declaring, "Yes, more, more more! . . . till our national destiny is fulfilled and . . . the whole boundless continent is ours." Although O'Sullivan's New York colleague Horace Greeley cautioned that a "nation cannot simultaneously devote its energies to the absorption of others' territories and the improvement of its own," recent settlers in the disputed western territories were enthusiastic about expansion and relatively unconcerned about contradictions between American principles and practice. John C. Frémont, who worked with the U.S. Army's topographical corps in California, was happy to oblige when Polk indicated that a settler uprising along the West Coast would be supported by the Pacific fleet. In 1846, he helped organize a rebellion among U.S. citizens living in California, and the "Bear Republic" soon declared its independence from Mexico. Frémont was certain that annexation would soon follow, counting on his brother-in-law, Senator Thomas Hart Benton of Missouri, to carry the banner of California statehood in Congress.

With war underway and further expansion seeming inevitable, politicians turned their attention to the fate of slavery in the territories that were now sure to be acquired. Congressman David Wilmot, a Pennsylvania Democrat, opened the debate almost immediately. In 1846, at Wilmot's initiative, the House of Representatives voted to prohibit slavery in any territory acquired through the war with Mexico. Although defeated in the Senate, the Wilmot Proviso by 1849 had nonetheless received the endorsement of all but one northern state legislature.

Wilmot never considered his proposal a move "designed especially for the benefit of the black race." Nevertheless, it won fervent support among people in the free states who opposed slavery. This sentiment was strongest in New England, where clergymen, followers of Garrison, Liberty Party adherents, and free blacks were among the numerous contingents of antislavery advocates by the late 1840s. In 1846, a convention of working people protested the fact that "there are at the present time three millions of our brethren and sisters groaning in chains on the Southern plantations." Delegates to the convention declared their refusal

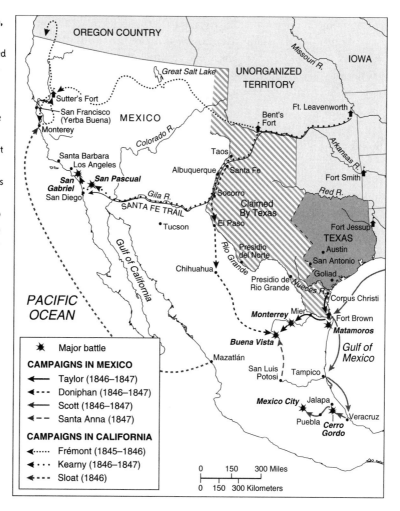

The U.S. War against Mexico, 1846–1848. During the war with Mexico, U.S. troops seized the northern sections of Mexico, and John C. Frémont led an uprising of U.S. settlers in present-day California. At the same time, under the leadership of Generals Winfield Scott and Zachary Taylor, the U.S. Army repulsed Mexican troops led by General Santa Anna. Defeated on all fronts, Mexico surrendered vast territories to the United States, comprising all or parts of present-day Texas, Arizona, New Mexico, Colorado, Utah, Nevada, and Wyoming. California became an independent republic but was soon annexed by the United States as well.

to do anything "to keep three millions of our brethren and sisters in bondage" and called upon other labor groups "to speak out in thunder tones" to secure for "all others those rights and privileges for which we are contending for ourselves."

But the majority of working people in the North were more cautious about abolishing slavery throughout the nation. Some no doubt recognized the economic contradictions highlighted in the Richmond, Virginia, *Enquirer*'s attack on working-class abolitionists. Referring to shoemakers in Lynn, Massachusetts, an editorial noted that they are "a people working all day on brogan shoes for the negroes at the South," but "who go to Abolition prayer meetings at night." Others feared that concerns over abolition were taking attention away from the needs of free white workers. George Henry Evans, once an outspoken enemy of slavery, became convinced that the fight for the emancipation of blacks must be postponed until the war against the exploitation of wage labor was won.

Still, if most Northerners were wary about the effects of abolishing slavery, they also hotly opposed its extension beyond what then constituted the borders of the South. Northern farmers wanted western lands held free for settlement as homesteads. These would-be western farmers did not want those lands preempted by slave plantations. Many urban workers and small producers also hoped eventually to populate the West's towns and cities. Even those workers and farmers who expected to remain in the East wanted the West kept free for their children and grandchildren. Immigrants, too, saw the West as a land of opportunity, and many eastern residents hoped that immigrants would settle there. If Europeans from agrarian regions could have their own western farms, there would be less competition for industrial and commercial employment in the East. Finally, free blacks in the North were appalled at the thought that slavery would spread beyond its present borders. They rightly feared that their own liberties would be jeopardized by such an expansion.

None of these groups wanted to live among slaves and slave owners nor to compete with slave labor. They believed that slavery had imposed multiple indignities, political restrictions, depressed wages, and harsh conditions on free workers in the South, and at the same time it had encouraged industrial stagnation. To all these people, slavery signified the death of everything they cherished or aspired to — personal independence, mutual respect, political equality, the right to enjoy the fruits of their own labor. In attacks on their employers, Lynn shoemakers, Lowell mill operatives, and many other workers compared factory owners with slave owners, and proclaimed the degrading conditions of their own labor by calling themselves "wage slaves." By accusing their employers of treating them like blacks, they hoped to horrify other white Americans and thereby gain their support.

With so negative a view of slavery, northern workers, farmers, merchants, and manufacturers could hardly relish having the institution gain new vigor by spreading farther west. Only a minority of them were abolitionists; most simply wanted slavery to remain restricted to the South. The vast majority of northern whites, including many abolitionists, believed that blacks were innately inferior and thus supported state laws that limited the economic, social, and political rights of free African Americans. They envisioned the western territories as a place

WANTED!

3,000 LABORERS

On the 12th Division of the

ILLINOIS CENTRAL RAILROAD

Wages, $1.25 per Day.

Fare, from New-York, only - - $4)5

By Railroad and Steamboat, to the work in the
State of Illinois.

Constant employment for two years or more
given. Good board can be obtained at two
dollars per week.
This is a rare chance for persons to go
West, being sure of permanent employment
in a healthy climate, where land can be
bought cheap, and for fertility is not surpassed
in any part of the Union.
Men with families preferred.
For further information in regard to it, call
at the Central Railroad Office,

173 BROADWAY,

CORNER OF COURTLANDT ST.

NEW-YORK.

R. B. MASON, Chief Engineer.

H. PHELPS, Agent.

July, 1853.

Go West, Young Man! An Illinois Central Railroad advertisement, probably directed to immigrants, posted in New York City in 1853.

Source: American Museum of Immigration, National Park Service, U.S. Department of the Interior.

where free white men could gain access to cheap and abundant land. Even though far more free whites were now wage laborers than independent farmers or artisans, they were proud that they could sell their labor as free persons. Although in the midst of strikes and protests, they might wield the rhetoric of wage slavery, most would have agreed with the abolitionist who distinguished between slaves and free workers by saying, "Does he not own himself?" Moreover, whatever their circumstances at that point, many northern workers still hoped one day to own their own home, land, or business, a hope that the image of wide-open spaces and new opportunities in the West kept alive.

This antipathy to slavery, and in many cases to African Americans, explains why the Wilmot Proviso was so appealing to northern whites. Local Free Soil clubs, which opposed the spread of slavery, sprang up quickly throughout the Northeast and upper Midwest at the start of the war with Mexico. By joining these clubs, workers, farmers, and shopkeepers—native-born and immigrant alike—announced that they would not tolerate chattel slavery in the territories acquired from Mexico.

This vocal opposition probably cut the war short, but it could not prevent Mexico's further dismemberment. In March 1848, the Senate approved a peace treaty granting the United States control over the provinces of California and New Mexico and moving the Texas-Mexican border southward from the Nueces River to the Rio Grande. The nation had reached a turning point. By waging and winning the Mexican War, Polk fused the issues of land reform ("free soil") and opposition to the spread of chattel slavery ("free labor"). In the process, he confounded all those who considered these issues to be distinct from one another.

The Conflict over Slavery Intensifies

The dispute over the spread of slavery became more and more important in American politics as the war with Mexico ended. This issue would remain central for the next decade and a half, splintering the two main political parties, the Whigs and Democrats. Even before 1848, abolitionists had run for political office. In 1840, abolitionists had formed the

MARRIAGE OF THE FREE SOIL AND LIBERTY PARTIES.

Liberty Party, and in 1844, their presidential candidate, James G. Birney, had received 62,300 votes. But it was four years later, when ex-president Martin Van Buren bolted from Democratic ranks to become the candidate of the new Free Soil Party that the tension mounted. Although not an abolitionist, Van Buren ran on a platform that coupled opposition to the westward spread of slavery with support for "the free grant [of land] to actual settlers." The Free Soil Party had been founded by leaders of the Liberty Party and by disaffected antislavery proponents from both the Whigs and the Democrats, thereby threatening the existing two-party system. And it attracted support from many free black and white abolitionists and more moderate northern voters concerned with keeping slavery out of the western territories.

In 1848, however, the Free Soil Party was still not strong enough to oust the Whigs or Democrats from national power, in part because it inspired fierce opposition. William Lloyd Garrison and other radical abolitionists dismissed the Free Soilers for supporting "whitemanism" (that is, keeping the West open to white men only). Most of the northern economic elite, also denounced the Free Soil Party. Although in most cases they morally opposed slavery, they opposed even more strongly the organized antislavery movement. Their reasons were many: A mass campaign against slavery would dangerously polarize the nation. It would

"Marriage of the Free Soil and Liberty Parties." This 1848 lithograph cartoon commented on the formation of the Free Soil Party in 1848. Free Soil presidential candidate Martin Van Buren, whose political career included alliances with slaveholding interests, was shown entering a "marriage of convenience" with the forces of the antislavery Liberty Party. The racial stereotypes were typical of the visual representation of African Americans in the antebellum period.

Source: National Museum of American History, Smithsonian Institution.

infuriate slave owners, whom the northern elite counted on as business and political partners. It would undermine the two major political parties and threaten the federal union itself. For instance, Whig leader and financier Philip Hone denounced Free Soilers as "Ishmaelites" who were against everybody and as "firebrands" who were ready to tear down the edifice of government to erect "altars for the worship of their own idols." And southern slaveholders were adamant in their opposition. As a result, Free Soil candidate Van Buren lost his bid for a second chance as president.

Despite this defeat, the issues raised by the Free Soil Party did not die. Instead, debates over land and labor grew more heated after 1848. Between 1845 and 1848, the United States had acquired 1.2 million square miles of territory. The victory over Mexico transferred California and the vast New Mexico territory to the United States and assured that the Rio Grande would be recognized as the Texas border. Nearly eighty thousand Spanish-speaking people, mostly of mixed Mexican-Indian descent, lived in the annexed areas. These people would perform much of the low-paid labor needed to make agriculture, ranching, mining, and industry profitable in the region. In addition, there were other racial and ethnic groups already settled in the western territories: Indians who had long inhabited the West, slaves carried there by their owners, immigrants and free blacks migrating westward to gain land and a better chance for an independent livelihood, and Chinese arriving in increasing numbers to work on railroads and in mining camps. These various groups increased the labor force, the competition for land, and the difficulties of resolving questions about the nation's social, racial, economic, and political order.

In 1848, however, Anglo-Americans focused more on their victory over Mexico than on the problems it spawned. Such vast territorial expansion in such a short time exhilarated many Americans. Didn't the war demonstrate the country's growing military prowess and finally seal its "manifest destiny" to dominate the continent from sea to sea? As it turned out, winning the war against Mexico greatly sharpened the internal conflict in the United States. The debate over what to do with the new land — specifically, whether to permit slavery there — aroused emotions that ultimately exploded in the Civil War.

The Years in Review

1812

- First Seminole War occurs, in which U.S. Marines invade Florida to recapture runaway slaves and meet resistance from black fugitives and Seminole Indians.

Free Labor and Slavery

1832

- The majority of Seminole Indians leave Florida.
- The College of William and Mary professor Thomas Dew crafts an influential proslavery document, which claims that slavery is best both for the South and for the slaves.

1833

- British government abolishes slave trade in the West Indies.

1835

- Second Seminole War occurs, in which fugitive slaves join Seminole Indians in their fight against the United States. Peace agreement forces the Seminoles to leave Florida, but allows maroons to accompany them to Oklahoma rather than to return to their masters.

1836

- Republic of Texas declares its independence from Mexico; outnumbered Texans lose at the Battle of the Alamo but then defeat Mexicans six weeks later at the Battle of San Jacinto, crying "Remember the Alamo!" Contrary to legend that has them fighting to the death, Davy Crockett and the other Texans were captured and executed.

1837

- Panic of 1837 lasts five years and devastates the nation.
- Virginia General Assembly reaffirms the 1806 statute that allows individual counties to determine whether free blacks could remain in residence.
- First Anti-Slavery Convention of American Women meets in Philadelphia.

1840

- Liberty Party founded by abolitionists.
- World's first dental school opens in Baltimore.
- Edgar Allen Poe introduces the detective story with "The Murders in the Rue Morgue."

1841

- Oil is first sold for any purpose—it is marketed as a medical cure-all.
- Supreme Court rules that Cinque and other slave mutineers on the Spanish ship *Amistad* should be free because international slave trade is illegal.

1842

- A Florida doctor, desperate to lower the temperature in his ailing wife's room, develops an artificial ice-making machine that is the precursor of air conditioning and refrigeration.

1844

- Democrat James K. Polk defeats Whig Henry Clay on a strongly expansionist platform.

- First telegraphic message is sent by Samuel Morse: "What hath God wrought."

1845

- Methodist Episcopal Church splits into northern and southern branches over slavery; Baptists also split in this same period.
- Congress approves the annexation of the Lone Star Republic (Texas).

1846

- Compromise with Britain establishes the northwestern border of the United States at the forty-ninth parallel despite cries of expansionists for "54°40′ or Fight!"
- War is declared against Mexico.
- Henry David Thoreau is jailed for refusing to pay taxes in protest of the Mexican war; his subsequent essay, "Civil Disobedience," will later influence Mohandas (Mahatma) Ghandi and Martin Luther King, Jr.
- The Wilmot Proviso prohibiting slavery in any territory acquired through the Mexican War is passed by the House of Representatives, but defeated in the Senate.

1848

- President Polk tries unsuccessfully to buy Cuba from Spain for $100 million.
- Treaty of Guadalupe Hidalgo ends Mexican War, gives California and New Mexico to the United States, and moves the Texas-Mexico border south to the Rio Grande.
- Free Soil Party formed to oppose slavery in the West; it runs ex-Democrat Martin Van Buren for president.
- Seneca Indians write their own constitution.
- Spiritualism, a religion based on the ability to communicate with the spirits of the dead, gains a popular following, especially among advocates of abolition, women's rights, and utopian communities.
- Stephen Foster's "Oh! Susanna!" is one of the year's most popular songs, performed in minstrel shows and sung by those heading westward in the California Gold Rush.
- Minie bullet (a conical bullet with a hollow base that expands when fired) is perfected; it will prove extremely deadly in the Civil War.
- Slavery is abolished in French West Indies colonies.
- First women's rights conventions in the United States are held in Seneca Falls and Rochester, New York.
- The first French feminist daily, *La Voix des Femmes,* advocates woman suffrage.

1849

- Walter Hunt patents the safety pin; seventeen years earlier Hunt had invented a sewing machine but didn't bother getting a patent.

1851

- Herman Melville publishes *Moby Dick,* which contemporaries find opaque; only in the twentieth century will it be regarded as a great work of literature.

Suggested Readings

Bleser, Carol, ed., *Secret and Sacred: The Diaries of James Henry Hammond, a Southern Slaveholder* (1988).

Bolton, Charles, and Scott P. Culclasure, eds., *The Confessions of Edward Isham: A Poor White Life of the Old South* (1998).

Clinton, Catherine, *The Plantation Mistress: Woman's World in the Old South* (1982).

Cooper, William J., Jr., and Thomas E. Terrill, *The American South: A History* (1990).

Faust, Drew, *A Sacred Circle: The Dilemma of the Intellectual in the Old South, 1840–1860* (1977).

Foner, Eric, *Free Soil, Free Labor, Free Men: The Ideology of the Republican Party before the Civil War* (1970).

Franklin, John Hope, and Alfred J. Moss, Jr., *From Slavery to Freedom: A History of Negro Americans,* 7th ed. (1994).

Friedman, Lawrence, *Gregarious Saints: Self and Community in American Abolitionism, 1830–1870* (1982).

Gould, Virginia Meacham, *Chained to the Rock of Adversity: To Be Free, Black and Female in the Old South* (1998).

Hahn, Steven, *The Roots of Southern Populism: Yeoman Farmers and the Transformation of the Georgia Upcountry, 1850–1890* (1983).

Hunt, Alfred N., *Haiti's Influence on Antebellum America: Slumbering Volcano in the Caribbean* (1988).

Hurtado, Albert L., *Indian Survival on the California Frontier* (1988).

Jacobs, Harriet A., *Incidents in the Life of a Slave Girl* (1861).

McDonald, Archie P., ed., *The Mexican War: Crisis for Democracy* (1969).

McMillen, Sally G., *Southern Women: Black and White in the Old South* (1992).

Perdue, Charles L., Jr., Thomas E. Barden, and Robert K. Phillips, eds., *Weevils in the Wheat: Interviews with Virginia's Ex-Slaves* (1976).

Raboteau, Albert J., *Slave Religion: The 'Invisible Institution' in the Antebellum South* (1978).

Sterling, Dorothy, ed., *We Are Your Sisters: Black Women in the Nineteenth Century* (1984).

Stevenson, Brenda, *Life in Black and White: Family and Community in the Slave South* (1996).

Taylor, Quintard, *In Search of the Racial Frontier: African Americans in the American West, 1528–1990* (1998).

Wyatt-Brown, Bertram, *Southern Honor: Ethics and Behavior in the Old South* (1982).

And on the World Wide Web

Exploring Amistad at Mystic Seaport
   (http://amistad.mysticseaport.org)

War, Reconstruction, and Labor

1848 – 1877

The dramatic events that unfold in Part Three constitute America's second revolution. Like the first revolution, the second was the bloody culmination of decades of conflict over what kind of society America should be. Between 1848 and 1860, societal changes created by immigration, industrialization, western expansion, and the growth of slavery led to repeated confrontations. Political compromises, such as the Compromise of 1850 and the Kansas-Nebraska Act, resolved the most bitter issues for a time. But it was not until the North defeated the South in the Civil War that the most volatile issue—slavery—was finally settled and the future development of the United States under industrial capitalism assured.

This second revolution also resulted in a fundamental expansion of constitutional guarantees of citizenship and political equality, just as the colonists' victory in the first revolution and the new citizens' persistent demands had resulted in the Bill of Rights. But the Civil War and its aftermath demonstrated, as well, that differences of class, race, and sex still limited the practical implementation of these constitutional claims for equality.

During this period, as earlier, working people were essential in fueling national growth and determining the outcome of momentous events. From the end of the Mexican-American War in 1848 up through the 1870s, women and men—including African Americans, Mexican Americans, Indians, Chinese and European immigrants, and native-born whites—constructed towns and railroads, managed farms, and extracted minerals in the West, furthered industrial and commercial growth in the

North, and contributed mightily to agricultural production in the South and Midwest.

Workers also participated in the important social and political movements of the period, joining both antislavery and antiabolitionist groups, forming unions and staging strikes, participating in political rallies and electoral campaigns, arming themselves for battle in Indian territory, or on behalf of Confederate independence or the salvation of the Union. Men and women of the laboring classes engaged in the increasingly heated debates over the place of slave versus free labor in newly acquired western lands, helped slaves escape along the Underground Railroad, argued over whether John Brown was an antislavery hero or a fanatical terrorist, and chose sides in arguments over Chinese immigration, African-American political rights, and women's demands for social equality.

Yet even as the struggle over slavery grew increasingly heated, few Americans imagined engaging in a civil war. But when war finally broke out in April 1861, nearly all Americans' lives were affected in profound ways. The South seceded from the Union to maintain the system of racial slavery upon which the region's very identity was based. Northern whites went to war, for the most part, not to free the slaves, but to limit slavery's expansion westward and to prevent the South's secession from the Union. And during the South's departure from the federal Congress, legislators from the free states reshaped western development by funding the transcontinental railroad and passing the Homestead Act. This legislation would gradually transform western society, further limiting the ability of American Indians to maintain traditional lifeways. Nonetheless, many Indians joined forces in support of Union goals while others supported the Confederate cause, all in hopes of gaining leverage in the postwar settlement.

For the Union in particular, these goals changed over the course of the war. This was largely the result of unexpected military defeats and the unanticipated actions of slaves. African Americans escaped from slavery in huge numbers. Many of them, along with northern free blacks, demanded the right to fight for the Union, and ultimately, nearly 200,000 African Americans served in the Union Army, helping turn the tide in the war's final two years and convincing Northerners to fight for the end of slavery as well as the preservation of the Union.

Neither side in this conflict was completely united. Clashes erupted within the South and the North over the personal, economic, and political costs of the war. In the North, however, a broad coalition—farmers, workers (including recent immigrants), businessmen, and politicians—emerged to support the Republican Party's policy of massive military action against the South. This wartime coalition then formed the core of support for Republican policies toward the South after the war.

The Confederacy's defeat raised as many questions as it answered. Slavery was now destroyed, but what kind of labor system would replace it? African Americans were now free, but what would they do with their new freedom? How would their former masters react? Who would lead the new South now? The policies of the period called Reconstruction were the attempt to answer these questions.

The freedpeople knew exactly how they wanted those questions answered. To them, emancipation meant the right to speak and act as free people, to reunite their families, and to end their automatic deference toward whites. And freed men and women acted decisively to guarantee these freedoms; their claims of individual rights quickly grew into collective demands for education, the ownership of land, and full political participation.

Southern whites had a very different notion of what Reconstruction should mean. Former slave owners wanted a rapid return to stability and a continuation of their rule. White farmers and workers did not want to face economic or political competition from millions of former slaves. And few whites could abide the freedpeople's demands for political and social equality.

Although most northern whites also abhorred the idea of racial equality, few wanted the South to return to its prewar ways. Most industrialists were committed to rebuilding the ravaged South as quickly as possible on free-labor principles, transforming slaves into wage laborers. Most of the North's white workers, though they did not want to compete with African Americans for jobs, were unwilling to accept the continued domination of slave owners over the freedpeople. And Republican Party leaders, intent on blunting the political power of the Democrats and former slaveholders, needed the votes of newly enfranchised African Americans to build their party in the South.

As we shall see, the diverse objectives of blacks and whites, North and South, resulted in sharp conflict and a growing sense of crisis. No group won all of its demands—least of all the freedpeople. They did win important victories, especially citizenship and the right to vote. But the freedpeople's quest for land of their own remained unfulfilled.

Nonetheless, even these gains, and the increasingly radical policies of the Republican Party, engendered intense opposition among southern whites. The rise of the Ku Klux Klan after 1867 and the use of violence to subvert constitutional guarantees soon halted the freedpeople's progress. Within a decade, the southern elite had reestablished its control, thanks in part to tacit support from moderate Republicans who came to dominate the northern party after 1870. Reconstruction ended tragically for the freedpeople, who saw their traditional antagonists returned to economic and political power.

Meanwhile, the North and West were also being transformed. Developments that began in the midst of the war accelerated after 1865. A transcontinental railroad system soon linked northern cities to western towns, mines, and farms. Industrial manufacturing multiplied as access to raw materials increased. Unprecedented numbers of immigrants filled the growing ranks of America's postwar industrial working class. Economic growth and immigration further fueled the westward expansion, creating new problems as well as increased conflict between settlers and Indians and among various native societies.

The wartime political coalition that had linked farmers, workers, and businessmen in the North broke apart in the face of these changes. The severe industrial depression that began in 1873 forced Americans to realize that their nation, too, was suffering the wrenching dislocations and class divisions already evident in Europe: increasingly, great wealth and opulence coexisted with grinding poverty and human misery. This widening gulf helped revive the labor movement.

Many sought to obscure this gulf during the celebration of the nation's centennial in 1876, yet the following year America experienced its first nationwide industrial rebellion: hundreds of thousands of railroad strikers and their supporters brought the nation to a standstill. The end of Reconstruction and the nationwide railroad strike in 1877 closed out an era. Decades of conflict over slavery had ended, but the drama in which capital was pitted against labor continued, as did the struggles over the place of women and men, whites, blacks, and Indians, and native-born Americans and immigrants in the society, economy, and polity.

chapter 10

Manifest Destiny and the Deepening Rift over Slavery
1848–1860

In 1845, John L. O'Sullivan, editor of the *Democratic Review* and the *New York Morning News,* claimed that it was Americans' "manifest destiny to overspread the continent allotted by Providence for the free development of our yearly multiplying millions." By the mid nineteenth century, even if they agreed on little else, most Americans shared with O'Sullivan an interest in fostering rapid settlement of the western territories. Speculators, merchants, and manufacturers enthused over business prospects there. Small proprietors and working people valued the greater economic independence and security that life in the West seemed to offer. Yeoman farmers, from both North and South, hoped to expand their holdings and their profits by moving to the more fertile lands of the plains. And slaveholders envisioned the region as the salvation of plantation agriculture, by which overworked areas of the Southeast could be abandoned for fresh lands to the West.

President James K. Polk's military approach to the expansion of U.S. territory was not popular with some Americans, who saw it as a blatant effort to extend slavery. Nevertheless, when the expansion was complete and 1.2 million square miles of new territory had been added to the nation, the country's mood, with rare exceptions, was jubilant. In 1848, the discovery of gold in California gave a boost to the U.S. economy and swelled the already high tide of westward migration.

Before long, however, competing visions of a new American West clashed with one another, and sectional rivalries spilled over into the region. Settlers from the North, including the old Northwest Territory, and the South brought with them different customs and values, and irreconcilably opposed systems of labor, social relations, and politics. Postponed for decades by Democratic and Whig politicians alike, the decisive confrontation between free labor and slave labor finally erupted into full-scale war during the contest for the West.

The standoff between northern and southern beliefs about race and labor had far-reaching implications, not just for the people who held them but for all who found themselves caught up in the dispute. Diverse populations already inhabited the West, and over the years others arrived from Asia and Europe, along with Americans from the eastern United States. These included, first, many Indian and Mexican communities with already deep roots in the region, then slaves taken west by their owners,

European immigrants and free blacks migrating west to gain land and a better chance for an independent livelihood, and Chinese who arrived in growing numbers to work on the railroads and in the mining camps.

The convergence of these groups in a single region increased the labor force, the competition for land, and ultimately the difficulties of resolving questions about the nation's social, racial, economic, and political order. In particular, the visions the South and the North had for the region clashed. In the eyes of southern planters, western expansion was the salvation of slavery. As one Georgia politician told Congress in the 1850s, "There is not a slaveholder in this House or out of it, but who knows perfectly well that whenever slavery is confined within certain specified limits, its future existence is doomed." For Northerners, the West offered a different kind of safety valve, one that would alleviate the economic pressures caused by the Panic of 1837, the heightened class divisions in American society, the growing number of propertyless workers, and the massive wave of immigrants from Germany, Ireland, and other areas of northern and western Europe. Whether the West was perceived as a refuge for slavery or a haven for free labor, however, white Americans back East imagined it as a vast and empty space awaiting settlement and civilization.

Western Lands, Western Peoples

People native to the western territories had suffered significant changes well before the United States took control of California and the vast New Mexico territory. An influx of Spanish soldiers and missionaries and Mexican settlers to California beginning in the late eighteenth century affected the Indians dramatically. Between the time of the first Spanish settlements in 1769 and 1849, disease, death, and labor exploitation devastated the native population, which dropped from some 300,000 down to 150,000 over those eight decades. Efforts to convert native peoples to Christianity disrupted their traditional culture and kinship patterns. Indians also became the primary labor force for the missions, which quickly gained control of the agricultural economy of California. Indians who remained in their villages had to compete with the invaders for the use of their traditional hunting, gathering, and farm lands. Rape and sexual abuse of native women by Spanish soldiers and Mexican settlers were widespread. Syphilis, which was disseminated to the native population through sexual contact, was especially devastating to the Indians, leaving victims more vulnerable to other diseases and also killing large numbers. The Spaniards' introduction of trade goods intensified competition and conflict among Indian societies and further altered their patterns of work and family life.

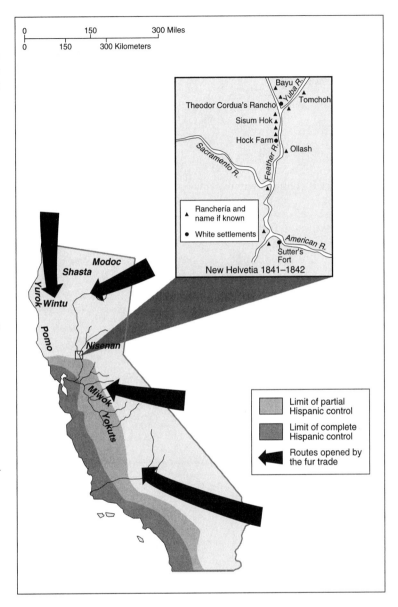

Hispanic and Anglo Influences on California Indians, 1820–1840. The diverse Indian tribes living in California came into contact with many groups of European missionaries, soldiers, traders, and settlers. Spanish, Russian, British, and French conquerors and colonists competed for control of the rich resources in the area. When Anglo-Americans and Mexicans gained independence from their colonial rulers, they, too, headed to California. Between 1820 and the early 1840s, the most important influences on the California Indians were the Spanish and Mexican residents who had moved to the region from the south, and the Anglo-Americans who had arrived from the north and east. One of the most important Anglo settlements, New Helvetia, was founded in 1841–1842 by John Sutter on whose land gold would be discovered in 1848.

Source: Albert L. Hurtado, *Indian Survival on the California Frontier* (1988).

Some of the most profound changes in Indian societies followed the spread of horses and guns across the West in the late eighteenth and early nineteenth centuries. Horses and guns changed Native Americans' relations to the land, to hunting, and to their neighbors. The availability of these innovations to Indians made nomadic tribes more mobile, settled villages more vulnerable, the hunting of big game more wasteful, and the conflicts among neighboring groups more deadly.

541

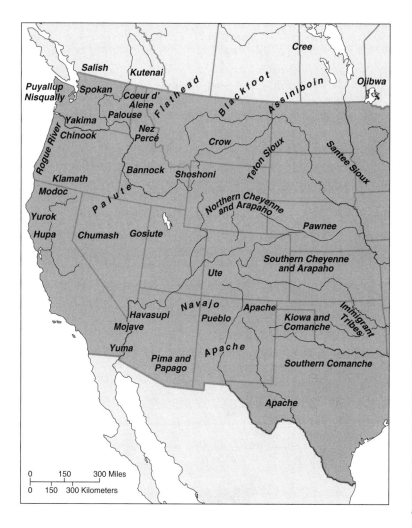

Major Indian Tribes in the American West in 1850. Before the arrival of vast numbers of Europeans and white Americans in the West, hundreds of Indian tribes coexisted on the land. The abundance of land, game, and edible plants compared to the relatively small size of the population assured that these diverse tribes could survive despite differences in political and economic systems, military capabilities, and religious beliefs. Though conflicts among some native peoples had always existed, the conflicts increased substantially when the native groups were forced by the pressure of white settlement to share ever-smaller territories. By 1850, these intertribal conflicts were exacerbated by growing tensions between the various Indian tribes and the large numbers of white Americans arriving from the eastern United States.

Source: Robert Utley, *The Indian Frontier of the American West, 1846–1890* (1984).

Though warfare among groups had existed long before Europeans and Americans settled the West, intertribal conflict on the Plains increased under the pressure of forced tribal movement. The Sioux, for example, were pushed out of the Minnesota territory by the Chippewas in the 1830s and by midcentury had themselves seized land from the Poncas, Pawnees, Hidatsas, Assiniboines, Crows, Mandans, Arikaras, and Iowas. In the 1840s and 1850s, the Navajos, who were skilled horsemen, staged more destructive attacks once they possessed guns, not only against Spanish and American soldiers and settlers but also against their traditional enemies, the Utes and Pueblos.

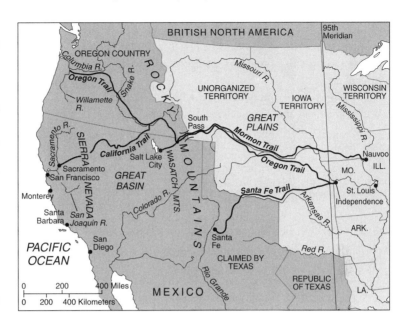

Settlement of the Trans-Missouri West, 1840s. The Oregon and Sante Fe Trails opened up the western plains, the Rocky Mountains, and the Pacific Coast to thousands of pioneers and settlers from the eastern and midwestern United States. In 1842, the first party of over one hundred people left Independence, Missouri, and headed across the Oregon Trail. Over the next eighteen years, some 350,000 men, women, and children headed out on this overland route to the Pacific Coast. Nearly one-tenth died along the way. One of the largest groups of migrants were the Mormons. Driven out of western New York in the 1830s and out of Illinois in the early 1840s by mobs who protested the Mormon practice of polygamy, the Mormons built an agrarian empire in the Great Salt Lake basin in present-day Utah.

The differences among Indian societies — in size, language, and religion as well as subsistence, political, and kinship systems — were great. Yet, there was common ground as well. Most groups depended on a precarious subsistence economy that was easily disrupted by war and trade. Most worshipped deities that resided in nature and most believed that the land was sacred. Most tribes considered territory and material goods to be collectively rather than individually owned, and most governed themselves by consensus and persuasion. Most accepted conflict as inevitable and expected to go to war over injuries done to them.

In the late 1840s, at the time the United States took possession of the western Plains, California, and Oregon, some 360,000 Indians occupied the West. There were probably some 75,000 native peoples on the Great Plains, including the Cheyennes, Blackfeet, and Sioux. It was these buffalo-hunting and warring tribes that fed European and American stereotypes of tipis, painted warriors, and chiefs in headdresses. Close to 85,000 Creeks, Cherokees, Seminoles, and others who had earlier been forced out of their eastern homes, now also inhabited western lands. Another 25,000, mostly Comanches and Apaches, resided in Texas. The Mexican Cession brought another 150,000 Native Americans into the United States, swelling the Navajo and Apache populations and placing the Utes, Pueblos, and a number of smaller California groups under Anglo-American laws and customs. Finally, some 25,000 Nez Perce, Yakimas,

543

Walla Wallas, and Coeur d'Alenes occupied the Oregon Territory, whose northern boundary had been fixed by the treaty with Great Britain just as the Mexican-American War broke out.

These indigenous peoples coexisted with significant numbers of Spaniards and Mexicans, and a growing number of U.S. residents. Still, they could not have imagined the density of population that characterized the eastern states, where 20 million Americans inhabited a considerably smaller territory. Between 1845 and 1869, some 1.4 million of those Americans moved west.

Some Indians were quick to recognize the significance of the arrival of large numbers of Americans. In 1846, as thousands of U.S. soldiers swarmed into the West on their way to wage war with Mexico, a Cheyenne leader named Yellow Wolf noted the "diminishing numbers of his people, and the decrease of the once abundant buffalo" and asserted that Indians would "have to adopt the habits of the white people, using such measures to produce subsistence as will render them independent of the precarious reliance afforded by the game." Though many Indians would have agreed with their aging Cheyenne brother, others, especially the younger ones, were not yet ready to make that concession. Resistance by Plains Indians ended only after decades of bloody warfare, which greatly decimated their numbers. Yellow Wolf himself was killed in a massacre by U.S. soldiers in 1864 at Sand Creek.

In California, native resistance was limited by the smaller size of existing Indian societies, the outbreak of deadly epidemics, and the efforts of U.S. pioneers to gain control over land, labor, and other resources. In the early 1840s, men like U.S. Army Captain John Sutter, stationed in California, confiscated tribal lands in the central part of the state. This process was made easier by a smallpox epidemic that claimed thousands of native lives in the 1830s. Sutter recruited and coerced the Nisenan people who lived in the area to work his land, alternating material incentives with corporal punishment to control them. When California declared independence from Mexico in 1846, the U.S. government began playing a more important role in the region, and Sutter became the local Indian agent, in charge of land grants, labor contracts, and the distribution of supplies. At the same time, more and more Americans began moving into California, most coming south from Oregon or across the Plains from the east. But the discovery of gold near Sutter's Mill unleashed a floodtide of migration.

Yellow Wolf. This 1846 sketch of the Cheyenne chief by Lt. J. W. Abert was included in the officer's official report.

Source: "Report of Lieutenant J. W. Abert, of His Examination of New Mexico, in the Years 1846-'47," Senate Executive Documents, 30th Congress, 1st session, no. 23 (1848)—Western History Collections, University of Oklahoma Library.

The Gold Rush

On January 24, 1848, James Marshall discovered gold in a millrace along the American River. Word of the event quickly circulated through the local area. In May, the San Francisco *Californian* reported that "the whole country from San Francisco to Los Angeles, and from the sea shore to the base of the Sierra Nevadas, resounds with the sordid cry of 'gold, GOLD, GOLD!' while the field is left half planted, the house half built, and everything neglected but the manufacture of shovels and pickaxes." By the end of the year, the news had spread across the nation. In December, President Polk himself declared that though accounts of the abundance of gold in California seemed "extraordinary," they were "corroborated by authentic reports of officers in the public service."

The 700 or so scattered settlers who had arrived in 1848 were joined by the thousands and then tens of thousands of Americans who headed to California in 1849 and 1850. These later pioneers cared little about farming, trading, or building settlements. They came to stake a claim. Mining camps turned into boomtowns literally overnight. A typical mining camp, Nevada City, emerged at the intersection of two creeks in the Sierra foothills in the fall of 1849. A few cabins, a general store, and hundreds of tents appeared along the creek beds during the winter. In the spring, thousands of men streamed into the area seeking their fortunes. A few decided to pursue wealth not by panning for gold, but by providing the necessities of life for those who did. Stores and saloons sprang up on the small flat along Deer Creek. New roads, carved out to assure a steady supply of goods, brought more merchants and miners into the town. In spring 1850, miner William Swain described the area's astonishing growth:

Sam Pit. Pit was one of the many Californian Indians who labored in the gold fields.
Source: California State Library, Sacramento.

> The speculators, traders, gamblers, women and thieves keep their eyes on the mines and when the miners move, they all move. This spring there was but one house in Nevada City, now there is said to be 17,000 men in and about it. . . . Everything is in a state of fermentation, rolling and tumbling about.

545

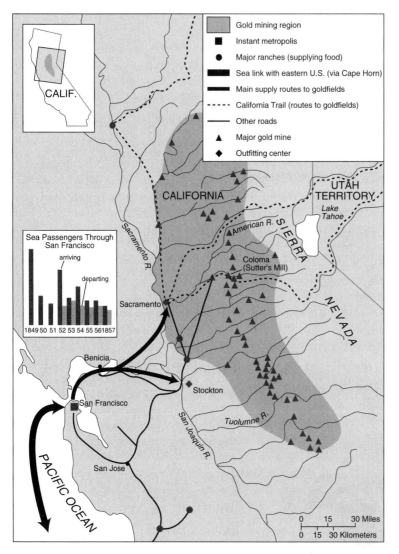

The California Gold Rush. Beginning in 1849, hundreds of thousands of people from the eastern United States, Canada, Mexico, South America, and other parts of the world converged on California. Because of the rapid rise in population and because so many of the newcomers were young men seeking gold rather than farmers, merchants, or manufacturers, an enormous demand for food, clothing, equipment, and housing was created. San Francisco, the main port of entry for those who arrived by sea, became a booming metropolis, and smaller trading outposts like Sacramento and Stockton were transformed into important commercial centers. Agricultural production increased in the rich interior river valleys, and new jobs were created by miners' demands for clean clothes, home-cooked meals, and adequate housing.

Source: James A. Henretta, W. Elliot Brownlee, David Brody, and Susan Ware, *America's History* (1993).

The fermentation that Swain observed had adverse implications for the region's long-time native residents. For the Nisenans, the gold rush ended the fragile hold on their lifestyle that they had maintained through the intrusions of the Spaniards, the Mexicans and the first American settlers. The miners and others rushing in razed the forests to make way for camps, towns, and roads. Timber was used for sluices, dams, houses, shops, and fuel. Food was imported from afar, since the miners considered nutritionally inadequate the seeds and acorns that the Nisenans harvested. Deer and other animals were killed off, fish habitats were de-

In the image: CALIFORNIA — A PROSPECT OF THOMAS TIDDLER HYS GROUND. WITH A SYGHTE OF TH YANKEE PICKYNGE VP GOLD AND SYLVER.

"A Few Days in the Diggins."
An 1849 cartoon in the satirical British magazine *Punch* portrayed the California "gold fever" frenzy and the illusion many prospectors held about easy access to riches.

Source: *Punch,* 1849—General Research Division, New York Public Library, Astor, Lenox and Tilden Foundations.

stroyed, devastating fires swept the Sierra mining towns, and water remained in short supply. The Nisenans nearly disappeared.

Over the next decade, the mining camps spread. Although new methods made the process of mining more profitable for a few, these changes were detrimental to the land and to native communities. Spaniards and Mexicans long settled in California found themselves exploited in the same ways in which they had once mistreated the Indians: the newcomers expropriated their land, imposed new forms of labor, and sexually abused local women. In California during the 1850s, the Indian population plummeted to between 30,000 and 35,000. Even those native peoples who had served the American cause—fighting with U.S. troops against Mexico in 1846 or aiding American forces in putting down a rebellion led by the Cupeno tribe in 1851—failed to receive the same rights to citizenship, suffrage, and property that were guaranteed to whites.

Workers in the West

To most white Americans, California remained a land of promise. For workers in particular, the promise of quick riches in the gold mines, or at least steady employment in a booming economy offered attractions hard to resist. The realities, however, proved more complicated. For most people, labor in California was no more rewarding than labor back East. For some, the situations of the Spaniards, Mexicans, and Indians offered a more accurate measure of what they could expect than did the lives of the small number of white pioneers who gained wealth and power.

By 1850, growing numbers of workers, whatever their race or ethnic background, found themselves in miserable conditions. The brutality of such conditions, however, did not drive the workers to band together. In an effort to keep California's wealth for whites only, white workers and employers who had migrated to the region from the eastern United States often cooperated in excluding those they defined as "intruders"—Indi-

Domesticated Indians in California by Mining District and County in 1852

County	Non-Indians	Indians	Indians as percentage of total population
Northern District			
Klamath	523	0	0
Shasta	3,855	73	1.8
Siskiyou	2,214	26	1.2
Trinity	1,933	4	0.2
Subtotal	8,525	103	1.2
Central District			
Butte	8,542	30	0.3
Calaveras	28,936	1,982	6.4
El Dorado*	40,000	—	—
Nevada	18,139	3,226	15.1
Placer	10,867	730	6.3
Sierra	4,808	0	0
Tuolumne	25,730	590	2.2
Yuba	20,593	120	0.6
Subtotal	157,615	6,678	4.1
Subtotal w/o El Dorado	117,615	6,678	5.4
Southern District			
Mariposa	4,231	4,533	51.7
Tulare	175	8,407	98.0
Subtotal	4,406	12,940	74.6
TOTAL	170,546	19,721	10.4
TOTAL w/o El Dorado	130,546	19,721	13.1

*El Dorado County returned a population estimate of 40,000 that was not broken down by age, race, or sex.
Source: 1852 California Special Census, California State Archives.

California's Indian Population, 1852. Though California Indians had confronted Spanish and American soldiers and settlers for nearly eighty years before the discovery of gold, the rapid influx of non-Indians to the area after 1848 disrupted their ways of life in new and profound ways. By 1852, in those northern and central districts of California where mining was most important, the percentage of Indians in the total population had dropped precipitously. Only on the southern edge of the main mining districts, in Mariposa and Tulares counties, did Indians still constitute a significant portion of the population.

Source: Albert L. Hurtado, *Indian Survival on the California Frontier* (1988).

ans, African Americans, Mexicans and Spaniards, and Asians. Yet it became increasingly difficult to sort out who was to be excluded from rights and privileges as the population of California became more and more diverse.

That diversity was the result of gold fever, which had spread to communities in Central and South America, Europe, and Asia. It drew Irish, Scottish, French, and German miners to California along with Chileans, Mexicans, Peruvians, and Americans. In 1849 alone, some eighty thousand immigrants—most of them men—poured into the area. This mass of gold-hungry adventurers ensured the complete decimation of the re-

Forty-niner. With the aid of a shoulder pole, which derived from his homeland, a Chinese immigrant carried the prospector's primary implement, a "rocker."

Source: Historical Society of Nevada.

gion's native communities. The scalping of Indians in northern California was perceived as more of a sport than a means of suppressing any actual threat — disease and the destruction of native habitats had already accomplished that end. Armed Americans also assaulted Chileans, Peruvians, Mexicans, and French miners, driving them off their claims. After California attained statehood in 1850, such physical coercion was reinforced by the passage of laws that taxed "foreigners" working in mining areas, including the Mexicans, who had lived in the region longer than many of the lawmakers.

Another series of regulations restricted the rights of those residents considered to be nonwhite. Even though California entered the Union as a free state, a significant number of early settlers came from the slave South and many of the northern migrants were concerned only with keeping the state's wealth in white hands. African Americans were denied the right to vote, claim a homestead, hold public office, serve on a jury, or attend school with white children. In San Francisco in the 1850s, it was even illegal for blacks to ride streetcars. In addition, "no black or mulatto person or Indian" was "permitted to give evidence in favor of or against a white person" in court. In 1854, the state Supreme Court affirmed, in the case of *People* v. *George Hall,* that Indians could not testify against whites in court and — incredibly — that Asians were Indians. Therefore, Chinese also were prohibited from giving testimony in court. The following year, the court clarified its stance, arguing that the Chinese were "a race of people whom nature has marked as inferior . . . incapable of progress or intellectual development beyond a certain point."

Embracing the logic of the state's legislators and jurists, white miners attacked Chinese settlements. In 1849, they drove out a group of sixty Chinese immigrants who had been hired by a British mining company. Whites knew that, amid the general violence and lawlessness that characterized life along the Mother Lode, assaults on Asians or Hispanics, even deadly assaults, were unlikely to lead to arrest, much less conviction. Still, the Chinese population in California increased—numbering some twenty-five thousand by the mid-1850s—and spread into other western states, like Nevada and Idaho. Though these immigrants performed critical services for mine owners and other miners—cooking, cleaning, and doing the most arduous manual labor—they were never accepted as part of the new western working class.

Life on the western mining frontier was difficult even for white workers, who had the privileges accorded their race. Most did not strike it rich, and after using up their original stake searching for gold, they had nothing with which to purchase land, tools, or supplies. Many were thus forced to become wage laborers in mines or railroads, or to find jobs as seasonal workers or tenants on large farms owned by wealthy whites. Others moved to the region's widely scattered cities, seeking jobs on the docks in San Francisco or in Sacramento's food processing plants. Many found themselves working shoulder-to-shoulder with those Chinese, Mexican, and African American men they had hoped to rise above. Although the white workers probably would have a slightly better job or a higher rate of pay than their nonwhite counterparts, the differences were often too narrow for the whites' comfort.

In the Southwest and along the frontier trails, Indians were seen as the most dangerous obstacle confronting white American settlers. Terrible tales of savage massacres haunted white families traveling in wagon trains. Although there were instances of deadly confrontation between Indians and pioneers, most white Americans never encountered Indians during the trip west. At times, this proved to be a problem. Some of those making the westward crossing had to seek out local tribes in order to replenish food supplies, find water, or trade surplus goods for fresh horses. Women pioneers, who supposedly had the most to fear from the "savages," often proved the most willing to set aside prejudices and seek assistance from Indian wives and mothers for themselves and their children.

The popular stereotypes that white women held of Mexican women were also reshaped during the first encounters in the Southwest. Susan Magoffin, the wife of a trader, was one of the first U.S.-born women to travel in the "New" Mexico territory, in

"Bloomer-ism and Bloomer-fus'em." A cartoon from an 1853 comic almanac took a swipe at Bloomers, loose-fitting trousers that were advocated by Amelia Jenks Bloomer and other women reformers as a relief from the inhibiting, uncomfortable, but standard corsets, petticoats, and crinoline gowns. Accosted by a police officer for wearing a dress in public, a hapless husband replied: "Oh, it's all owing to my wife, who is a Bloomer, and wears my breeches, and having walked out with my only pair, I could do nothing but put on her petticoats."

Source: *Fisher's Comic Almanac* (1853)—Historical Society of Pennsylvania.

1846. In her diary, she noted with shock that Mexican women wore loose blouses, flowing skirts, and no corsets, which to her suggested they had loose sexual morals. Yet she also appreciated their personal warmth and hospitality. Magoffin was surprised to discover that Mexican law granted married women property rights that were denied women under U.S. law. When the region was annexed by the United States in 1848, Mexican women lost not only the right to control their own property after marriage, but also the right to custody of their children and the right to sue in court without the consent of fathers or husbands.

The lack of such rights among American women, especially married women, shaped patterns of western settlement. Without rights to property or custody, or the ability to take independent legal action, pioneer wives generally had to accede to their husbands' wishes, including the man's desire to uproot their households and head to the frontier. Of course, some women eagerly embraced the opportunity and adventure of the frontier, but those who did not had little choice but to acquiesce.

Most migrants along the overland trails, especially in the years after the gold rush, traveled in wagon trains in which family groups predominated. Many were recently married couples with young children, infants, or babies on the way. During the long and difficult journey, families were often forced to abandon some of their possessions in order to lighten the wagons, with family heirlooms and other items of "merely sentimental" value being the first to go. Women and children were typically assigned the tasks of gathering fuel and hauling water. During the crises that all too frequently confronted such pioneers, women also had to take on normally masculine roles of driving the wagons, caring for the horses, or burying the dead. But men rarely reciprocated, and their wives and daughters had to perform the necessary domestic chores of washing clothes, preparing meals, and caring for children amid the chaos of constant movement.

For those families who settled in mining camps or in the new western boomtowns, life could be even more difficult than it was along the trail. Men's employment was erratic, and work for women, though plentiful, rarely paid well. Moreover, many of the opportunities for female employment — in dance halls and brothels, for instance — were not considered appropriate for respectable married women.

Those who followed the more conventional pattern of staking a homestead and starting a farm likewise faced hardship. Enormous labor was required to build a house, construct basic furnishings, break the ground, plant the first crops, keep a cow and chickens, do the milking, collect the eggs, churn the butter, make the clothes and bedding, complete the harvest, haul the water, chop the wood, and keep the household clean and the family fed.

Although men, women, and children all did their share, women's work was particularly taxing. For young wives, childbearing and caring for infants added to the physical burdens of frontier life. Women had far fewer opportunities than their husbands and sons to travel to nearby farms, trading posts, or towns and, as a result, had limited contact with one another. Churches were few and far between, and doctors and midwives were often too far away to attend births or provide assistance in emergencies. This placed the major burden of caring for the needy and sick on women.

To most women and men on the western frontier, events in eastern cities, including the nation's capital, seemed very far away. Even after the invention of the telegraph and the construction of railroads, many households remained isolated and did not receive regular mail deliveries and newspaper reports. Western political leaders, however, were often anxious to gain access to federal support and most hoped one day to apply for statehood for their territories. When statehood was gained, western residents, especially politicians, quickly became swept up in the political dramas unfolding back East.

An Uneasy Compromise

In California, the number of U.S. residents had grown so rapidly that in 1849 political leaders there sought statehood without having ever applied for territorial status. This made California the focal point of debates over slave labor and free labor that continued to dominate eastern political life. Just before California applied for statehood, the Free Soil Party had been founded to challenge the Whigs and Democrats for leadership in resolving conflicts over slavery. The new political party sought to address the concerns of Northerners by arguing that the West should be left open for settlement by free men. This would alleviate the pressures created by immigration and provide a fresh start for those families who were unable to find prosperity in increasingly crowded eastern cities. Nonetheless, Free Soilers did not advocate abolition. They were willing to leave slavery alone where it already existed, thereby hoping to assuage the concerns of Southerners.

The strengths and limits of free-soil sentiment were tested by the events unfolding around California. President Zachary Taylor, a Whig slave owner, encouraged California's application for statehood as a means of strengthening the Whig Party nationally. Here, thought Taylor, was an opportunity to defuse Free Soil Party support by demonstrating that a southern Whig could advocate the entrance of free states to the Union.

The president's success in this endeavor depended on his ability to convince other southern Whigs that slavery could be protected in the South without expanding the institution into every western territory.

When the issue reached Congress, however, Taylor's plan to demonstrate national unity through Whig leadership ran into several obstacles. Congressional Democrats, Whigs, and Free Soilers all wanted reassurances that the interests of their constituents would be protected. And no one seemed convinced that the simple admission of California as a free state could ensure those interests. After lengthy and contentious arguments, Congress rejected the idea of either allowing or forbidding slavery in the West by federal law and, instead, stitched together a compromise.

The process by which this compromise was constructed and passed involved some of the most charismatic figures and some of the most dramatic oratory in the history of the American Senate. Henry Clay, who had forged the Missouri Compromise thirty years earlier, spearheaded this effort at national reconciliation even though he was ill and in his seventies now. His bill called for passage of five measures: (1) California would be admitted as a free state; (2) territorial governments would be formed without restrictions on slavery in the rest of the land acquired from Mexico; (3) the federal government would assume Texas's public debt in exchange for Texas yielding in its border dispute with New Mexico; (4) the slave trade, but not slavery itself, would be abolished in Washington, D.C.; and (5) a new and more effective fugitive slave law would go into effect. But Clay could not get the bill passed, despite his appeals to shared national principles.

Among his most forceful opponents was John C. Calhoun, sixty-six years old and in worse health than Clay. Since Calhoun was unable to rise from his seat, his speech was read by a colleague. Clearly presenting Calhoun's sentiments, the speech demanded that the South be granted equal rights in the territories, that the North obey all fugitive slave laws, and that the North cease its attacks on the institution of slavery. He even suggested that the country be ruled by two presidents, one representing the North and one the South, each with veto power. Though he claimed that he, like Clay, wanted to save the Union, his blueprint for sectional reconciliation would have required the North to acquiesce to the South.

The North was reassured, however, by the Massachusetts elder statesman, Senator Daniel Webster, that this would not happen. Older than Calhoun by two years but still healthy, and hopeful of gaining the White House one day, Webster rallied support to Clay's cause. In a brilliant speech, he urged calm, advocated idealism, and praised patriotism. But even Webster could not convince a majority of his colleagues to vote for

Clay's compromise bill. He was perhaps glad when his appointment as secretary of state removed him from the Senate and the acrimonious debate. Death removed Calhoun, in July 1850. And although Clay remained in the Senate until his death two years later, he retreated from its leadership.

After six months of debate, then, the California issue remained unsettled. But at this point a younger and more pragmatic group of Senators took over the negotiations. These men—including William H. Seward of New York, Jefferson Davis of Mississippi, and Stephen A. Douglas of Illinois—initially seemed less willing to compromise to achieve sectional reconciliation. Seward was adamantly opposed to Clay's bill; Davis was just as adamantly in favor of slavery and its expansion; and Douglas was staunchly in favor of western growth and development. Yet despite this the three managed to move the legislation forward. Douglas provided the critical breakthrough when he broke Clay's bill apart, allowing Senators to vote for the sections they favored without accepting the sections they opposed.

CAUTION!!

COLORED PEOPLE OF BOSTON, ONE & ALL,

You are hereby respectfully CAUTIONED and advised, to avoid conversing with the **Watchmen and Police Officers of Boston,**

For since the recent ORDER OF THE MAYOR & ALDERMEN, they are empowered to act as **KIDNAPPERS AND Slave Catchers,**

And they have already been actually employed in KIDNAPPING, CATCHING, AND KEEPING SLAVES. Therefore, if you value your LIBERTY, and the *Welfare of the Fugitives* among you, *Shun* them in every possible manner, as so many *HOUNDS* on the track of the most unfortunate of your race.

Keep a Sharp Look Out for KIDNAPPERS, and have TOP EYE open.
APRIL 24, 1851.

The Fugitive Slave Law. A notice posted by Boston abolitionist Theodore Parker in 1851.

Source: Boston Public Library.

Ultimately, the Compromise of 1850 consisted of a series of separate bills passed by different, and sometimes competing, coalitions. Northeasterners and Midwesterners, for instance, nearly all supported the admission of California as a free state and the abolition of the slave trade in the District of Columbia. Southerners, on the other hand, voted overwhelmingly for the new Fugitive Slave Law, which denied jury trials to accused runaway slaves and empowered any marshal pursuing them to force local citizens to join the hunt. On each issue, just enough party loyalists crossed sectional lines to assure passage. In addition, the sudden death of President Zachary Taylor, who despite his support for California's admission had threatened to veto the larger compromise of which it was a part, paved the way for the bill's passage. The new president, Millard Fillmore, not only supported the compromise but used his powers as president to convince northern Whigs to support it as well.

Freedom or Death. Soon after passage of the Fugitive Slave Law, Margaret Garner fled from her Kentucky master with her four children. Slave patrollers followed her to Ohio. Faced with capture, Garner killed two of her children rather than have them return to slavery. The surviving children were taken from her and, on the return trip to Kentucky, Garner drowned herself in the Ohio River. Her story inspired an acclaimed nineteenth-century painting by Thomas S. Noble (on which this engraving was based) and Toni Morrison's Pulitzer Prize novel, *Beloved*.

Source: *Harper's Weekly,* May 18, 1867—American Social History Project.

Though Douglas, Seward, and Davis could take credit for completing the work Clay had begun, they failed to embrace the elder statesman's concern about national reconciliation. Achieving compromise only through the appeasement of separate and antagonistic interests created hostilities that soon became apparent. And the most controversial section of the 1850 Compromise—the Fugitive Slave Law—served as the lightning rod for a new round of sectional debate.

One of the major targets of the Fugitive Slave Law was the "underground railroad," a network of thousands of free blacks and white sympathizers who concealed, sheltered, clothed, and guided runaway slaves in the course of their northward flight. The best known of the "conductors" who served this railroad was Harriet Tubman, who escaped from slavery in Maryland in 1849. Over the next decade, Tubman returned to the South nineteen times, repeatedly risking recapture and death in order to liberate more than three hundred others. In the North, local vigilance committees—composed largely of free blacks and white Quakers—kept the railroad going. Free blacks provided most of the labor and funds required by the cause despite their long hours of work and limited economic opportunities. African-American members of the New York support committee were able to pledge only fifty cents a month; those in Philadelphia contributed even less. Fortunately, a few wealthy families, like the Motts (white Quakers) and the Fortens (free blacks), were also deeply committed to keeping the railroad running.

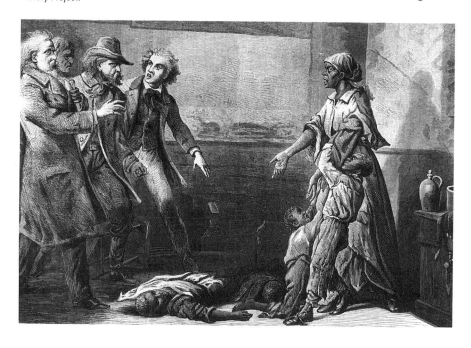

During the 1840s, slave owners grew more anxious about the underground railroad, even though the number of successful slave escapes may not have increased. Escapes affected far more than the few thousand who actually fled. News traveled through the slaves' "grapevine telegraph," emboldening many still in bondage. At the same time, successful fugitives such as Frederick Douglass, and William and Ellen Craft, who had escaped from Georgia in December 1848, became powerful and effective antislavery speakers in the United States and Britain. The Fugitive Slave Law, its proponents hoped, would not only reduce the number of escapes but also drive earlier runaways such as Tubman, Douglass, and the Crafts back into hiding.

Leaders of both major parties congratulated themselves on the 1850 compromise. They believed they had finally buried the dangerous slavery issue and thereby rescued the Union from conflict and division. "Much . . . . may be effected by a conciliatory temper and discreet measures," declared Philip Hone. "All praise to the defenders of the Union!" Former Democratic presidential candidate Lewis Cass, whose defeat in 1848 owed much to competition from the Free Soil Party, now declared confidently, "I do not believe any party could now be built in relation to this question of slavery. I think the question is settled in the public mind." Political and business leaders organized rallies in New York, Philadelphia, Boston, Pittsburgh, and Cincinnati, in support of the compromise.

Many workers and farmers also approved the new agreement in hopes that it would prevent the disruption of the Union and improve their chances for upward mobility. For large numbers of working folk, slavery was synonymous with degradation, and cries of "wage slavery" were used to condemn capitalists who oppressed their employees. But equating wage labor with slavery did not lead to sympathy for slaves themselves. Native-born and immigrant white workers were just as likely to define their own status as free men by distinguishing themselves from slaves. In addition, many white workers harbored racist attitudes not only toward slaves, but toward free blacks as well. Fugitive slaves who had escaped to the North were often viewed with suspicion: as competition for scarce jobs and as diminishing, by their race alone, the wages and status of free white workers. This led once again to a desire to keep slavery and African Americans out of the western territories, where white workers assumed the African Americans would necessarily undermine the value of free labor.

Not all working people embraced the Compromise of 1850, however. Some disavowed it, not only for failing to outlaw slavery in the West but also for endorsing the Fugitive Slave Law. In June, the land reformers of the National Industrial Congress held a mass meeting at which they denounced slavery as a "moral, social, and political evil." Participants decried "the idea that to satisfy the South, and to secure the perpetuation of the

"A Bold Stroke for Freedom."
On Christmas Eve, 1855, patrollers finally caught up with a group of teenaged slaves who had escaped by wagon from Loudon County, Virginia. But the posse was driven off when Ann Wood, leader of the group, brandished weapons and dared the pursuers to fire. The fugitives continued on to Philadelphia.

Source: William Still, *The Underground Rail Road* (1872)— American Social History Project.

Federal Union, the people of the United States must agree that the Slave as well as the Free Area shall be extended." They were joined in their denunciations by long-time abolitionists who found new allies now that western land as well as southern sovereignty was at stake.

At a large anticompromise meeting in Allegheny City, near Pittsburgh, land reformer John Ferral, a veteran of the Workingmen's movement of the 1820s and 1830s, attacked the Fugitive Slave Law in strong terms. Speaking for the free soil movement's most democratic wing, Ferral proposed a state constitutional amendment that gave black males the right to vote, and the meeting approved his proposal. This was at a time when only five northern states enfranchised African Americans on an equal basis with whites. A number of antislavery Whigs rode into Congress on the crest of this popular reaction.

Other dissenters took direct action. In Boston, Philadelphia, Syracuse, Chicago, and elsewhere, black and white opponents of slavery used force to protect fugitives from their hunters, sometimes attacking and even killing the pursuers. In October of 1850, Boston abolitionists helped two slaves escape to freedom and drove the Georgia slave-catcher pursuing them out of town. A year later, in Syracuse, New York, a crowd of two thousand broke into the courthouse to free a fugitive slave. And that same fall, a group of free blacks and fugitive slaves in the Quaker community of Christiana, Pennsylvania, arming themselves with guns against a group of slave-catchers, killed a Maryland slave owner and severely wounded his son. In this case, despite the willingness of federal officials to intervene on the slave owners' behalf, public outrage forced the government to drop charges against those who had defied the Fugitive Slave Act by force of arms.

Popular opposition to the Fugitive Slave Law was enhanced by the publication of *Uncle Tom's Cabin* in 1852. Harriet Beecher Stowe, who wrote this tragic tale of slavery and slave-hunters, first published the story in serial form in the *National Era,* an abolitionist newspaper. When it was published in book form, it sold three-hundred thousand copies in one year. It electrified northern readers and infused opposition to the Fugitive Slave Law with a powerful emotional appeal.

"What a Disgrace to a City Calling Itself Free . . . "

Harriet A. Jacobs's *Incidents in the Life of a Slave Girl,* published in 1861, was one of the few narratives of slavery written by a woman. Having escaped from her master in 1845, Jacobs—along with other fugitive slaves—found herself once more imperiled when Congress passed the Fugitive Slave Law. She here describes the impact of the 1850 law on the African-American community of New York City.

About the time that I reentered the Bruce family, an event occurred of disastrous import to the colored people. The slave Hamlin [James Hamlet], the first fugitive that came under the new law, was given up by the bloodhounds of the north to the bloodhounds of the south. It was the beginning of a reign of terror to the colored population. The great city rushed on in its whirl of excitement, taking no note of the "short and simple annals of the poor." But while fashionables were listening to the thrilling voice of Jenny Lind in Metropolitan Hall, the thrilling voices of poor hunted colored people went up, in an agony of supplication, to the Lord, from Zion's church. Many families, who had lived in the city for twenty years, fled from it now. Many a poor washerwoman, who, by hard labor, had made herself a comfortable home, was obliged to sacrifice her furniture, bid a hurried farewell to friends, and seek her fortune among strangers in Canada. Many a wife discovered a secret she had never known before—that her husband was a fugitive, and must leave her to insure his own safety. Worse still, many a husband discovered that his wife had fled from slavery years ago, and as "the child follows the condition of its mother," the children of his love were liable to be seized and carried to slavery. Everywhere, in those humble homes, there was consternation and anguish. But what cared the legislators of the "dominant race" for the blood they were crushing out of trampled hearts?

. . . . I was subject to it; and so were hundreds of intelligent and industrious people all around us. I seldom ventured into the streets; and when it was necessary to do an errand for Mrs. Bruce, or any of the family, I went as much as possible through back streets and by-ways. What a disgrace to a city calling itself free, that inhabitants, guiltless of offence, and seeking to perform their duties conscientiously, should be condemned to live in such incessant fear, and have nowhere to turn for protection! This state of things, of course, gave rise to many impromptu vigilance committees. Every colored person, and every friend of their persecuted race, kept their eyes wide open.

Source: Harriet A. Jacobs, *Incidents in the Life of a Slave Girl* (1861).

It was against this background that the Free Soil Party expanded its ranks. Contradicting Lewis Cass's claim that the Compromise of 1850 would forestall the growth of parties focused on slavery, the legislation created stronger bonds between established antislavery forces and growing contingents of free-soil advocates. Support for the Free Soil Party also came from some immigrant groups, particularly those who were forced to leave their homeland to escape political persecution. Many of the German land reformers and labor leaders who embraced free-soil politics had been deeply influenced and highly politicized by their experience in European revolutions in 1848–1849. Other immigrants were becoming increasingly aware that America was not the land of equality that it

Unveiled. After passage of the Fugitive Slave Law, escaped slave women living in the North sometimes wore veils when they appeared in public to avoid identification by slave-catchers.

Source: William Still, *The Underground Rail Road* (1872)—American Social History Project.

claimed to be. "The rich and distinguished here stand higher above the law than in any country," exclaimed one German-born Pittsburgher. In America, he went on, "in the land that boasts of its humanity, that claims to be at the very top of civilization . . . the laboring classes are treated in as shameful a manner as in Europe, with all its ancient prejudices." The existence of slave labor and the passage of the Fugitive Slave Act only reinforced the sense among many immigrants that the fight for free labor and free soil must be won if the move to America was truly going to improve their lives.

Contrary to the hopes of its sponsors, then, the Compromise of 1850 inflamed antislavery feeling in the North. As long as slavery seemed geographically contained and remote, free-state residents could try to ignore it, considering it someone else's worry and someone else's sin. But by refusing to outlaw slavery in the West and then welcoming slave-hunters into the free states and requiring all citizens to aid them, the new law put an end to those illusions. Like the Mexican War, the Fugitive Slave Law seemed to bear out the abolitionist claim that chattel slavery endangered freedom everywhere, not merely in the South.

The Plight of Free Labor

The economic depression following the Panic of 1837 had effectively destroyed most of the labor organizations constructed during earlier decades. And the slowness of the economic recovery left many workers unemployed into the early 1840s. The continual breakdown of skilled into unskilled labor reduced the bargaining power of other workers, while the cultural diversity within the new working class created by immigration further weakened its power.

The reduced combativeness of labor could be seen in the factories of Lowell. There the number of relatively independent young women origi-

"Bell Time." A cross-section of the Lawrence, Massachusetts, workforce as presented to the readers of *Harper's Weekly*. Winslow Homer sketched women, men, and children as they emerged from the city's textile factories at the end of a workday.

Source: Winslow Homer, *Harper's Weekly*, July 25, 1868— American Social History Project.

nally employed steadily lessened, to be replaced by Irish immigrants. Having fled famine in Ireland, these new workers were more preoccupied with supporting themselves and their dependents both in America and back home. As a result, they at first showed little enthusiasm for unions or strikes, even when mill owners repeatedly slashed pay rates while increasing the hours and the number of machines worked by each operative. The Lowell experience was repeated in many other places.

By the late 1840s, however, many workers were beginning to grow restive. A brisk business pace now strengthened their hands; and the years of long hours, low wages, and deteriorating working conditions hardened their resolve. The opening of new western lands seemed to offer workers some alternative to exploitation by eastern industrialists, although few laborers could afford the journey to the frontier. Perhaps more importantly, earlier-arriving immigrants set an activist example for those arriving later. A group of Boston Irishmen put the situation bluntly, denouncing "the petty domineering of would-be tyrants" who profited from their poverty. Irish tailors in the city resolved that a "fundamental change must take place in our social and industrial relations" or labor would be crushed under the "despotic weight of capital."

By midcentury, the efforts to improve wages and working conditions and to organize working people had picked up. The old ten-hour move-

A Dead Rabbit. Also entitled "Study of an Irishman," George Henry Hall's 1858 painting was rendered shortly after the July 1857 Dead Rabbit-Bowery Boy Riot, a conflict in New York's Five Points between rival Irish and nativist working-class street gangs. The painting subtly conveyed a sense of the fear and fascination that poor Irish immigrants provoked in many native-born, middle-class Americans—including, unusually straightforward for the era, a note of homoeroticism.

Source: George Henry Hall, 1858, oil on canvas, 32 × 40 1/2 inches—National Academy of Design.

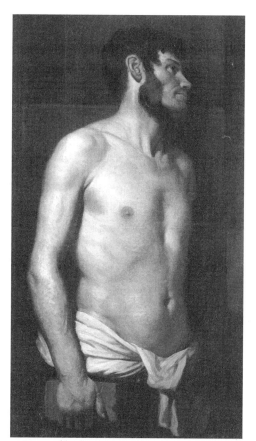

ment, weakened in the aftermath of the Panic, grew. Groups of immigrant and native-born workers began reaching out for mutual support, though mostly along national lines. Irish craftsmen in eastern cities organized unions of tailors, carpenters, shoemakers, bakers, cabinetmakers, blacksmiths, printers, and masons and stonecutters, among others. As the great mass of unskilled Irish laborers began to unite, the secret societies of the 1830s increasingly gave way to larger public, legal organizations. The New York Laborers' Union Benevolent Association, formed in 1843, embraced many different kinds of native-born white laborers and claimed six thousand members by 1850. The association focused mainly on demands for higher wages and an end to competition from convict labor. In Brooklyn and Boston, predominantly Irish longshoremen built organizations with similar aims. In October 1850, the first national congress of German and German-American craftworkers convened in Philadelphia. Delegates representing more than four thousand working people founded the Allgemeine Arbeiterbund [General Workers' League]. Through this organization, workers maintained close ties with a broad range of German and German-American cultural and political societies.

Groups of immigrant workers had long stood aloof from and even opposed to those of different nationalities, and many had found themselves excluded from organizations of native-born workers as well. At midcentury, religion remained one of the most profound barriers to labor solidarity. Though many of the Irish who settled in the United States were more Catholic in name than in practice, as foreigners with different beliefs and customs they were disdained by many native-born white workers. Raised to hate the Protestantism of their English conquerors and provided with an array of social services by Roman Catholic churches in America, Irish immigrants seemed to live in a world apart. In addition, their patterns of sociability, their wakes and other ritual practices, and a cultural fondness for alcohol seemed both un-American and un-Christian to the dominant Protestant population.

German immigrants, on the other hand, were more likely to be condemned for being altogether antireligious. Like Newark's immigrant journalist Fritz Anneke, they fought an ongoing war against attempts to write into law evangelical views about alcohol and Sabbath observance. In 1853, an angry Anneke criticized the hypocrisy of those who begrudged working people a few worldly pleasures on Sunday, their only day of rest:

> This money aristocracy, which has the time and means to take care of its body through the whole week, and which in spite of its hypocritical laws, knows how to serve all worldly desires on the holy Sabbath, strives zealously to deprive the working man of every means of escape from his drudgery.

The difficulty of building coalitions among workers from such different cultural and religious backgrounds was daunting. But as employers repeatedly used one national group to depress the pay and conditions of another, workers gradually learned a hard lesson. To defend themselves effectively, they would have to overcome mutual distaste and suspicion, or at least temper it. The growth of cross-national labor solidarity from the late 1840s on occurred mainly in the Northeast and Midwest, even as racist diatribes against free black workers and nativist attacks on new immigrant workers continued. Cincinnati's General Trades Union, formed in 1853, expressed the new awareness that drove labor unity forward. "All trades," declared the GTU's founders, "have an equal and identical interest" and "if united . . . could better resist the encroachments of capital" in the struggle "of right against might."

"The Great Meeting of Foreigners in the Park." An illustration from an 1855 nativist tract, *The Crisis; or, the Enemies of America Unmasked,* depicted a labor demonstration in New York's City Hall Park demanding relief for the unemployed during the 1854-55 panic. This wood engraving was one of the few images of organized working-class action published before the Civil War.

Source: (Cunnington) J. Wayne Laurens, *The Crisis, or the Enemies of America Unmasked* (1855)—American Social History Project.

It was German craftworkers who first sought to bridge the gap separating them from native-born and Irish workers. New York's German cabinetmakers, for instance, resolved to reorganize their union "for the accommodation of all nations." And German blacksmiths and wheelwrights likewise declared, "We all belong to one great family — the Workingmen's family." Some mainly Irish organizations also came to stress the importance of multinational unity. The banner of the New York longshoremen's organization featured the national flags of eight different European nations and the Stars and Stripes, together with the word "Unity." Above this display were the words "We know no distinction but that of merit."

Although continued immigration aggravated ethnic frictions within the swiftly expanding working class, there were growing numbers of instances of cooperation across ethnic lines. During an economic downturn in 1854–1855, large crowds of jobless workers of various nationalities held angry meetings to protest inflated prices and staggering unemployment. In New York City in January 1855, eight thousand native-born, Irish, and German workers demanded laws banning the eviction of ten-

Immigration to the United States, 1820–1860. Germans and the Irish constituted the largest groups of immigrants to the United States between 1820 and 1860. Most of both groups came in the 1840s and early 1850s, following agricultural crises and political upheaval in their homelands. By the late 1850s, improved conditions in Europe, combined with the onset of an economic depression in the United States, slowed immigration considerably.

Source: U.S. Bureau of the Census. *Historical Statistics of the United States, Colonial Times to 1970* (1975).

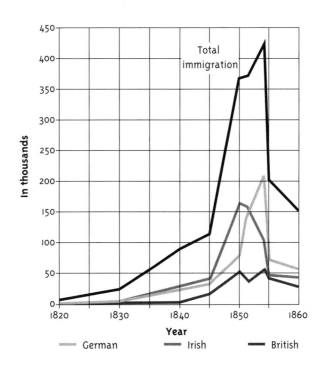

"A Billion of Acres of Unsold Lands"

This 1855 poem laments governmental policies allowing huge areas of the public domain to go to railroads and land speculators. A supporter of land reform, the poet Augustine Duganne insists on giving the soil to the landless.

A billion of acres of unsold land
Are lying in grievous dearth;
And millions of men in the image of God
Are starving all over the earth!
Oh! tell me, ye sons of America!
How much men's lives are worth! . . .

To whom do these acres of land belong?
And why do they thriftless lie?
And why is the widow's lament unheard —
And stifled the orphan's cry?
And why are the poor-house and jail so full —
And the gallows-tree built high? . . .

Those millions of acres belong to Man!
And his claim is — that he *needs!*
And his title is sealed by the hand of God —
Our God! who the raven feeds:
And the starving soul of each famished man
At the throne of justice pleads! . . .

Who hath ordained that the few should hoard
Their millions of useless gold? —
And rob the earth of its fruits and flowers,
While profitless soil they hold?
Who hath ordained that a parchment scroll
Shall fence round miles of lands, —
When millions of hands want acres
And millions of acres want hands.

'Tis a glaring *lie* on the face of day . . .
This robbery of men's rights!
'Tis a lie, that the word of the Lord disowns —
'Tis a curse that burns and blights!
And 'twill burn and blight till the people rise,
And swear, while they break their bands —
That the hands shall henceforth have acres
And the acres henceforth have hands!

Source: Augustine Duganne, *Poetical Works* (1855).

ants who could not pay their rent, providing large-scale employment of the jobless on public works, and giving free land to the landless. John Commerford, a former leader of the Workingmen's Party, drew cheers from the crowd by proposing that the city government employ jobless workers to build low-rent public housing. Upper-class critics, both native and foreign-born, scorned such calls for government action as "foreign" or "European." But "this has been the policy of the aristocracy at all times," Commerford argued. "They wish to separate the American mechanics from the German, and the German from the Irish; they want to keep you in a divided condition so that you cannot concentrate your action for the benefit of yourselves and fellow workingmen." Furthermore, he pointed out, the same people who oppose government aid to the poor are happy to accept it themselves. "Shall those," he asked, "who have received the millions that have been appropriated to individuals, states, railroads, and the various companies who confederate for the purpose of swelling the army of accumulating plunderers"—shall such people "tell us to [lie] down and wallow in the inferiority of the condition with which they have provided us?"

Broken Covenant: The Kansas-Nebraska Act

At the same time that economic crises heightened class conflicts in the East, political crises brought sectional conflicts to the fore along the western frontier. The struggle over slavery now erupted in the Great Plains and soon overshadowed all other concerns. Proslavery and antislavery forces vied for power in an effort to ensure that the territories and states carved out in the West would provide economic opportunity for the form of labor each side supported. The battles that engulfed the area raged in the national political arena as well for much of the 1850s. The focal point of the political battle was the Kansas-Nebraska bill, submitted to Congress in January 1854. The bill was proposed by Democratic Senator Stephen A. Douglas of Illinois, who had speculated heavily in western lands and who hoped that by attracting settlers to the region he could persuade Congress to route a planned transcontinental railroad through the area he had designated the Territory of Nebraska. Since many southern Senators preferred a more southern route, Douglas offered them an incentive to vote for his bill by including a clause that allowed residents of the territory to decide by popular vote whether or not they would permit slavery. This would effectively annul the Missouri Compromise, since the Nebraska Territory lay north of the 30° 30′ line set in 1820. All federal barriers to the spread of slavery would thereby be removed throughout the entire West.

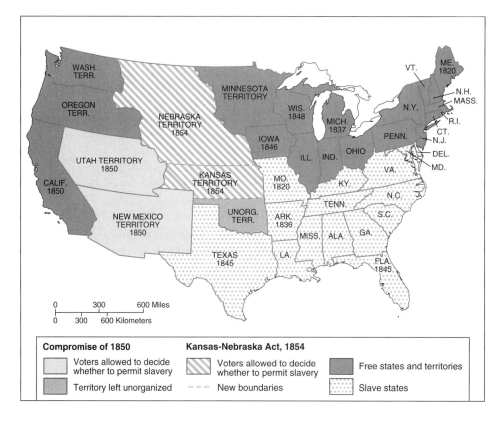

The Compromise of 1850 and the Kansas-Nebraska Act, 1854. By the early 1850s, vast new lands in the West had come under U.S. control. The desire of both northerners and southerners to settle those lands renewed the conflict between the advocates of free and slave labor systems. In the Compromise of 1850 and the Kansas-Nebraska Act, politicians attempted to settle these disputes through legislative action. However, leaving the final decision on slavery in large parts of the West to popular sovereignty assured that the battle over slave and free labor would only intensify in coming years.

In its final version, Douglas's bill not only explicitly annulled the terms of the Missouri Compromise, but also divided the Great Plains into two territories—Kansas and Nebraska—in order to assuage the concerns of free-state Iowans and slave-state Missourians. New antislavery and proslavery forces could each hope to win control over one of the new territories. Then, to replace the Missouri Compromise line, Douglas proposed a doctrine he called "popular sovereignty." This doctrine left the future of slavery to be decided by registered voters in each territory seeking admission as a state.

Reaction was almost instantaneous. A group of antislavery congressmen issued an impassioned and widely circulated manifesto calling the new law "a criminal betrayal of precious rights." In the West, they said, "it has been expected, freedom-loving emigrants from Europe, and energetic and intelligent laborers from our own land, will find homes of comfort and fields of useful enterprise." But Douglas's law would turn this great expanse "into a dreary region of despotism, inhabited by masters and slaves." Free labor would be excluded because "freemen, unless pressed by a hard and cruel necessity, will not, and should not, work beside slaves. Labor cannot be respected where any class of laborers is held in abject bondage."

Widely reprinted and translated, this appeal realized its intended effect. A wave of anger that dwarfed opposition to the 1850 compromise swept the North and West. In the months that followed, more than three hundred rallies mobilized tens of thousands of people of all social backgrounds who espoused a broad range of free-soil sentiments. Some were leading merchants and bankers in major northern cities, long-time advocates of compromise and friendly relations with slave owners. They now pleaded with the South to withdraw the bill in order to avoid inflaming the already dangerous antislavery sentiment in the North. Whig leader Amos Lawrence, a Boston merchant, begged them to "pause before they proceed further to disturb the peace which we hoped the Compromise of 1850 would have made perpetual." Others opposed to Douglas's bill were staunchly against slavery on principle. They denounced the bill not for causing bad sectional feelings, but because (as one group declared) it "authorizes the further extension of slavery," while "we have, do now, and shall continue to protest most emphatically against both white and black slavery."

Still others rejected the Kansas-Nebraska plan because they wanted the West reserved for whites only. A resolution adopted at a free-soil meeting in Pittsburgh in 1854 conveyed this sentiment:

> If the Douglas Nebraska bill should ever go into peaceful operation, which we doubt, it would completely Africanize the heart of the North American continent and divide the Free States of the Atlantic from the Free States of the Pacific by colonies of African boundmen and thereby exclude the free white race of the North from lands purchased by the whole nation from France. . . .

Despite these strong opposing views, the Senate passed the Kansas-Nebraska Act on March 3, 1854. The majority that favored the legislation included many southern Senators, who viewed "popular sovereignty" as the best hope for expanding slavery into the West. Senator Dixon of Kentucky praised Douglas for his leadership on the bill. Acknowledging that "I once recognized you as a demagogue, a mere manager, selfish and intriguing," he claimed, "I now find you a warm-hearted and sterling patriot." To achieve victory, Dixon and his supporters combined with northern Democrats who hoped this bill would provide the basis for expanding their party's support North and South. On May 22, the House added its assent by a narrow margin, and Democratic president Franklin Pierce signed it into law a week later. In elections that fall, candidates of the so-called Know Nothing Party claimed that they, too, wanted to protect the white race. They gained ground in local and state contests and temporarily controlled the governments of Massachusetts and Pennsylvania. In these same states, Free Soilers were also elected to office in significant numbers.

Bleeding Kansas

During the next two years, political passions burned fiercely as free-soil and proslavery forces alike began moving into Kansas. Missourians poured across the border, hoping to claim the Kansas Territory for themselves. But even more settlers arrived from the free states. Thousands were aided by abolitionists back east who formed the Kansas Emigrant Aid Society to assure the territory would remain a haven for free labor. Confronted by a free-soil majority, the proslavery forces quickly resorted to armed intimidation and violence. When antislavery forces responded, undeclared guerrilla war followed.

One especially passionate antagonist in this battle was John Brown. Standard accounts commonly portray Brown as a solitary and bizarre individual. And there is some truth in that portrait. Brown was unusual in many ways—for one thing, he felt things more deeply and acted more decisively than most others. But Brown was also very much a product of his time and place, and both his feelings and actions—if more extreme than those of his neighbors—reveal much about the world that produced him.

John Brown was born in 1800 into a white family of New England stock, deeply attached to the country's revolutionary traditions and stirred by the great religious awakenings of the age. Over the years, he tried his hand at various occupations to support himself and, after his marriage, his growing family. He sometimes achieved a modest prosperity, but Brown prized other things above commercial success. "To get a little property together," he once wrote his son, "is really a low mark to be firing at through life." Personal independence, democracy, equal rights, self-discipline, and self-respect—the traditional republican values of the North's small producers—meant more to

John Brown. This recently discovered portrait of the abolitionist (before he grew his famous beard) was taken in Hartford, Connecticut, in 1847 by an African-American daguerreotypist.

Source: Augustus Washington, 1847—National Portrait Gallery, Smithsonian Institution.

him. The quickening commercialization of American life disturbed
Brown, for he perceived it as a threat both to his world and to his moral
code. And the Panic of 1837, which ruined him along with so many others, confirmed his worst fears. As the years went by, Brown's views about
society and its ills grew clearer. He "thought that society ought to be organized on a less selfish basis," one of his associates recalled.

> He said that all great reforms, like the Christian religion, were based on
> broad, generous, self-sacrificing principles. He condemned the sale of
> land as chattel and thought that there was an indefinite number of
> wrongs to right before society would be what it should be.

Of all society's wrongs, none repelled Brown so thoroughly as human
bondage. Here was truly the "sum of all villainies," the starkest challenge
to all the social and religious beliefs that shaped his outlook. Like his father before him, Brown aided fugitive slaves. In 1831, he and his
neighbors cheered at the news of Nat Turner's insurrection. "The slaves
have risen down in Virginia," cried one community elder, "and are fighting
for their freedom as we did for ours. I pray God that they may get it." In
1851, Brown worked with free blacks to bolster resistance to the Fugitive
Slave Law.

In the mid-1850s, five of John Brown's sons moved west to Kansas as
free-soil homesteaders. Encountering armed groups of Southerners determined to force slavery upon the territory, they called on their father
for aid, and he soon joined them. In the often brutal fighting that followed
in "Bleeding Kansas," John Brown earned a reputation for ferocity, tenac-
ity, and an uncompromising hostility to slavery and racism generally.
Especially obnoxious to Brown, remembered one of his allies, was "that
class of persons whose opposition to slavery was founded on expediency,"
those who were "desirous that Kansas should be consecrated to free white
labor only, not to freedom for all and above all." Brown "soon alarmed and
disgusted" such people "by asserting the manhood of the Negro race, and
expressing his earnest antislavery convictions with a force and vehe-
mence" alien even to many free soilers.

Confrontations in the West soon found their echo back east. Senator
Charles Sumner of Massachusetts, an eloquent spokesman for African-
American rights, denounced the efforts of Democrats in the White House
and the Congress to force slavery into a free Kansas. He was particularly
vehement in a speech he gave in May 1856, in which he attacked his Senate colleague, Andrew P. Butler of South Carolina, for having taken "the
harlot slavery" as his mistress. He called the efforts of proslavery forces to
establish their own government in the territory the "Crime Against
Kansas." In retaliation for Sumner's inflammatory remarks, a distant
cousin of Butler, the young congressman Preston Brooks, attacked Sum-

ner with his walking cane. Brooks beat Sumner unconscious, landing some thirty blows while the Senator sat at his desk, unable to defend himself.

In Kansas, such brutality had become commonplace. Hannah Anderson Ropes, a young mother of two had moved to Lawrence, Kansas, in the fall of 1855 to join her husband. She wrote heart-wrenching letters to her mother back in Brookline, Massachusetts, including one on November 21, in which she described the dangers that surrounded her family.

> My dear mother, this is Saturday evening. . . . How strange it will
> seem to you to hear that I have loaded pistols and a bowie knife upon my
> table at night, three of Sharp's rifles, loaded, standing in the room. . . .
> All the week every preparation has been made for our defense; and
> everybody is worn with want of sleep.

Her fear, and that of her neighbors, was that proslavery Missourians who crossed the border to attack individual Yankees would soon launch an all-out attack on the abolitionist stronghold of Lawrence. Not long after, Hannah Ropes returned east with her children, feeling she had "been robbed of a large estate" during her six months in Kansas—"my faith in human nature."

That faith would be sorely tried in Kansas over the following year. In the summer of 1856, proslavery forces did attack Lawrence, sacking the town, destroying two newspaper offices, burning buildings, looting stores, and beating residents. Hearing the news, John Brown, accompa-

Rescued. In 1859 the Kansas abolitionist Dr. John Doy, called a slave-stealer by his enemies for his forays into Missouri to free slaves, was kidnapped by proslavery partisans and imprisoned in Missouri. This photograph showed Doy surrounded by the friends who subsequently rescued him.

Source: Kansas State Historical Society.

nied by four sons and two antislavery supporters, sought revenge by replicating the damage imposed on Lawrence in a small settlement of proslavery families along Pottawatamie Creek. Using broadswords, Brown and his followers rousted five families out of their beds in the middle of the night, murdered and mutilated five of the men, and left their wives and children to spread the tale of terror. The sack of Lawrence and the so-called "Pottawatamie Massacre" provoked a guerrilla war that raged in Kansas for months and cost some two hundred lives.

Free-state forces finally prevailed in Kansas in mid-1858, despite the partisan interference of a Democratic president and his appointed representatives. That victory, however, ended neither the broader dispute over slavery nor John Brown's role in it. The battle in Kansas, in fact, only stoked the flames of national conflict and convinced Brown that a final reckoning was near. And if it was only violence that had kept Kansas free, he asked, how could peaceful methods alone secure the same ends throughout the country? His brother Jeremiah reported unhappily that "since the trouble growing out of the settlement of the Kansas Territory, I have observed a marked changed in brother John." He "has abandoned all business, and has become wholly absorbed by the subject of slavery." When Jeremiah urged moderation, John replied

> that he was sorry that I did not sympathize with him [but] that he knew that he was in the line of his duty, and he must pursue it, though it should destroy him and his family. He . . . was satisfied that he was the chosen instrument in the hands of God to war against slavery.

The country would hear from this single-minded man again.

Birth of the Republican Party

For decades, the concerted efforts of politicians North and South had staved off a direct confrontation between the slave-labor and wage-labor systems. Geographical separation of the two systems had made compromise easier, but in "Bleeding Kansas," the systems met head to head. A peaceful end to slavery no longer seemed likely. As Congressman Abraham Lincoln wrote a Kentucky friend a year before the bloody attacks and reprisals in Kansas:

> You spoke [in 1819] of "the peaceful extinction of slavery" and used other expressions to indicate your belief that the thing was, at some time, to have an end. Since then we have had thirty-six years of experience, and this experience has demonstrated, I think, that there is no peaceful extinction of slavery in prospect for us. . . . Our political problem now is "Can we, as a nation, continue together *permanently*—*forever*—half slave and half free?"

During the 1850s, the issue of slavery broke apart the country's two major political parties and gave rise to a new one, the Republican Party, dedicated to barring slavery from the western territories. The Whigs' disintegration began with the Compromise of 1850. By opposing the Compromise, President Zachary Taylor alienated ardently proslavery voters, dooming the Whig Party's future prospects in the South. The remaining Whigs were deeply divided—into procompromise "Cotton Whigs" and anticompromise "Conscience Whigs." Some Whigs attempted to overshadow the antislavery movement altogether by combining forces with the nativist American (or Know Nothing) Party. Anti-immigrant riots in Baltimore and other east coast cities suggested that this strategy might be successful, but after making quick gains, the movement soon collapsed. The slavery question had simply become unavoidable. In mid-1855, the Know-Nothing Party itself split into proslavery and antislavery factions.

Democrats, meanwhile, suffered a series of splits and defections, beginning with the founding of the Free Soil Party in 1848. By 1854 and 1855, massive numbers of midwestern free-soil Democrats had left the party, alienated by Democratic support for popular sovereignty in Kansas and Nebraska. The formation of a national Republican Party in 1856 cut deeply into northern Democratic support.

The Republican Party coalesced out of the large but amorphous opposition to the Kansas-Nebraska bill of 1854. The Republican platform of 1856 denounced slavery as immoral, insisted on halting the further west-

A SKETCH, from *The New Tragic Farce*, of "AMERICANS SHALL RULE AMERICA." as enacted by Mayor SWANN of Baltimore, and his wonderful "STAR" Company.

"If I Don't Kill Something Else Soon, I'll Spile!" An 1856 drawing commented on Know-Nothing violence in Baltimore. The scene was populated by members of nativist gangs with names like "Blood-Tubs," "Cut-Throats," and "Plug-Uglies."

Source: Maryland Historical Society.

ward expansion of slavery, and rejected the politics of nativism. The new party attracted support from many formerly competing interests, including antislavery Whigs, Democrats, former Free Soilers, and Know-Nothings. One of its earliest organizers, Alvan Bovay, was a veteran land reformer and former Whig. Labor leader and land reformer John Commerford became a Republican spokesman in New York. But party leaders also included some prosperous northern businessmen, such as Thaddeus Stevens of Pennsylvania and Zachariah Chandler of Michigan. Prominent among them were rising manufacturers, often from relatively humble backgrounds, who had been competing against the established mercantile elite for many years. Meanwhile, many of the North's largest merchants and some manufacturers with important southern ties threw their political support to the Know-Nothings or to northern Democrats. Leading Republicans were more commonly middle-class men (especially lawyers, professional politicians, editors, and journalists) who accepted the values of the North's free-labor industrial system and were ready to fight for it—more so than much of the elite.

Yet the great majority of those who rallied to the Republican Party's banner during the 1850s were small farmers, small shopkeepers, and skilled urban working people, most of them native-born. Significant numbers of ordinary laborers also voted Republican. And the Republicans gained the support of many reform-minded Northerners, some of whom were themselves denied the right to vote. Large numbers of free blacks, for instance, who were disfranchised in northern states by literacy, residency, or monetary requirements, supported the Republicans, as they had the Free Soilers. They believed this was the best way to advance the larger fight to uproot slavery and secure full democratic rights for all African Americans. And many women, white and black, who had earlier formed societies to aid abolition and Free Soil efforts, now threw their resources behind the Republican Party.

Among the foreign-born, the response to the Republican agenda was mixed. Republican strength grew steadily among immigrant farmers and workers from Britain and Scandinavia during the 1850s, but Germans were divided, and most Irish remained loyal to the Democratic Party. Some of the wealthiest German-American businessmen, like so many of their native-born colleagues, clung to the Democratic Party for fear of angering southern customers, losing southern markets, and encouraging social and political conflict in the country. German-born small proprietors, liberal and radical democratic intellectuals, and craftworkers might have formed one of the pillars of the Republican organization had it not been for the nativist orientation and evangelical Protestant leadership of many state-level Republican organizations. Some Irish-Americans, too, were suspicious of nativist elements among the Republicans. Moreover, their own grievances against the "free-labor system," fear of splitting their beloved American republic, loyalty to a Democratic Party that had accepted them when others would not, and concern about job competition from an expected flood of low-wage ex-slaves helped to keep the vast majority of Irish and Irish-Americans in the Democratic column.

The Democrats were victorious in the 1856 presidential election, but the election of their candidate, James Buchanan, did little to allay fears of sectional conflict. Buchanan had sought the presidential nomination before. He succeeded this time because his party could not afford to renominate the sitting President, Franklin Pierce, who was too closely linked to the bloody events in Kansas. In addition, the Democrats hoped to gain favor among northern voters by nominating a candidate from their region. Buchanan was perfect: a dignified elder statesman from Pennsylvania who had been minister to Great Britain in the years that the Kansas-Nebraska conflict flared. He may have been uninspiring and unimaginative, but Buchanan was also uncontroversial and uncommitted on popular sovereignty and the extension of slavery.

The Republicans chose John C. Frémont, who had gained his reputation as a celebrated army explorer and leader in the conquest of California. He embodied the free-soil vision of America's manifest destiny. Compared with the mere ten percent of the vote that the Free Soil candidate, Martin Van Buren, had won just eight years earlier, Frémont's thirty-three percent of the total polling reflected a major transformation in public thinking. Debates over western territories, especially the Kansas-Nebraska question, had inspired this change. Frémont carried eleven of the sixteen free states and forty-five percent of all ballots cast in the North. The Republican campaign slogan—"Free soil, free labor, free men"—summarized the goals and ideals that drove millions into its ranks, almost overnight. Clearly, the new party was here to stay.

Though the Democrats had won the election, the Republican Party's dramatic gains accelerated the drive toward national conflict. Observing the deepening isolation of their political allies in the North, southern planters began to see the majority in the free states as entirely hostile to slavery. To them it was only a matter of time before Republicans gained control of the national government and used its power to undermine slavery everywhere—first in the West, then in the old South. These specific fears grew out of other, more general worries about southern society and its internal frictions and conflicts. Most immediately, what impact would a Republican national government have upon the slave population?

Throughout the South, blacks were paying close attention to national politics, pondering the significance of this new division of the white population, and hoping for liberation through a Republican victory. The 1856 election brought with it stories of plans for slave insurrections in at least six southern states. Though no such uprising occurred in the 1850s, slaves' everyday resistance and attempts to escape to freedom kept planters anxious. The rise of the Republicans only made matters worse. "The recent Presidential canvass has had a deleterious effect on the slave population," reported a Nashville, Tennessee, editor in alarm. "The negroes manifested an unusual interest in the result and attended the political meetings of the whites in large numbers. This is dangerous." A Memphis colleague agreed: "If this eternal agitation of the slavery question does not cease we may expect servile insurrections in dead earnest."

In the meantime, some Republican leaders (such as the Blair family in Maryland and Missouri) as well as some writers who supported the new party (such as Cassius Clay of Kentucky and Hinton Helper of the North Carolina hill country) began courting the non-slaveholding whites of the South. Francis P. Blair, Jr., was elected to Congress from St. Louis in 1856, suggesting that Republicans could gain popular support, at least in the border states. The *National Era,* an antislavery paper since the 1840s, responded to Blair's election by declaring, "We no longer stand upon the defensive. We have crossed the line, and are upon slaveholding ground." Helper's book, *The Impending Crisis of the South,* published in 1857, aided Republicans among southern-born residents of the Midwest. Helper argued that slavery was a political and economic curse on the South, driving non-slaveholding whites into poverty, forcing their wives and daughters to labor in the fields, and encouraging many to abandon the South altogether. Although others had made these claims before, here was a "son of the South," as Horace Greeley noted, "who speaks with an authority and a weight which no outsider can have." So impressed were Republicans with Helper's appeal to non-slaveholders, whom he encouraged to use their votes to overturn slavery and the southern aristocracy, that they printed an abridged version of the book in 1859 and circulated it widely in the North.

The immediate impact of Hinton Helper's book in the South was minor. Helper was no abolitionist. In fact, the necessity for poor whites to mingle with southern blacks was one of the effects of the slave system that he abhorred. Nonetheless, planters feared the long-term effects of his work and severely punished those caught circulating it. For them, it was another sign of the dangers that the Republican Party posed to slave owners in the South and nationally. So it was with growing seriousness that southern politicians threatened to pull their states out of the federal union and beyond the reach of the Republicans in order to preserve their social power and human property.

Defending the Rights of Labor

In the battle between North and South, Republicans touted the superiority of free labor, portraying northern workers as independent and responsible citizens who contributed mightily to both economic prosperity and western expansion. But northern workers themselves, especially those employed in the burgeoning cities and factory towns along the Atlantic coast, often expressed biting criticisms of the existing free-labor system. Though the growing sectional crisis tended to overshadow the grievances of free workers, their exploitation continued to divide northerners against each other.

The 1850s saw a significant advance for the labor movement—the beginnings of nationwide organization. Such efforts would ultimately gain advocates in those southern cities—including Baltimore, Richmond, St. Louis, and New Orleans—where free labor had gained a foothold, raising new fears among planters about the rise of Republicanism on their own soil. Initially, however, attempts to build "nationwide" unions were confined to the free states. Such efforts had begun in the labor crisis of the 1830s, but the impulse became much stronger after 1850, as national unions sprang up among hatfinishers, cigarmakers, typesetters, plumbers, painters, stone cutters, shoemakers, and iron molders. Some disappeared almost as fast as they arose, and in most cases, the national organizations merely dispensed advice to local branches. Moreover, rarely did the national organizations show leadership on controversial issues, such as the admission of African American, Mexican, or Asian workers to member unions. Nonetheless, in laying the groundwork for later, larger, and more successful efforts at labor organizing, these early national unions suggested the power of free workers to develop their own agenda and the need for both northern Republicans and southern slave owners to respond to workers' concerns.

As proslavery and antislavery forces vied for dominance in Kansas and in Congress, northern workers attempted to assert control in several key industries, including iron, textile, and shoe manufacturing. In the process, they challenged manufacturers and merchants to share the wealth that free labor produced and chastised them by comparing northern workers to southern slaves.

The case of the national union of iron molders—founded largely at the instigation of William H. Sylvis—illustrates the development of national labor organizations. Born in 1828, William Sylvis sought training and work as an iron molder in the 1840s, as the iron industry was mushrooming to meet demands for industrial tools and machinery. At first the wages were good for the few skilled iron workers. But the lure of higher pay steadily increased the number of molders, eventually allowing foundry owners to reduce wages and impose harsh working conditions. Simultaneously, iron production was becoming concentrated in the hands of a small number of large companies able to afford newer and more expensive equipment. The cost of opening an independent foundry soared, so that when Sylvis tried to open his own foundry, the venture ended in disaster. Sylvis soon found himself trudging Pennsylvania's roads in search of wage work.

Many men in Sylvis's situation chose to try their luck out west, but Sylvis settled in Philadelphia in 1853. There he attempted to support his new wife and a growing family on the meager wages of a journeyman molder. During the 1830s and 1840s, journeymen molders had formed several local unions around the country, most of which were temporary, typically organized to negotiate a single agreement or to call a single strike. The Philadelphia molders were among the first workers to move toward a larger and more permanent organization. Their 1855 constitution declared, "In the present organization of society, laborers single-handed are powerless . . . but combined there is no power of wrong they may not openly defy." Two years later, when some of Sylvis's coworkers struck over a twelve percent wage cut, Sylvis joined the strike as well as the picket committee.

The Philadelphia molders' action failed when a depression set in in 1857, cutting the ground from under them. This time, however, defeat failed to destroy the union itself. Sylvis, the union secretary, threw him-

"A Panic in Wall Street." A "truthful and vivid account" in *Harper's Weekly* of the 1857 financial panic. This wood engraving portrayed the "essential personages of a Wall Street scene," including a penny-pinching "Jewish capitalist" (second from left in foreground), a smiling loan-shark (center), and "the victim of an unexpected failure" (seated right). As in most nineteenth-century illustrations, this wood engraving served as a diagram of social "types" that appeared in literature and theater, if not in actuality.

Source: Thwaites, *Harper's Weekly,* October 10, 1857—American Social History Project.

"An Empty Pocket's the Worst of Crimes!"

The Hutchinson family was one of the country's most popular singing groups in the nineteenth century. Their successful stage performances combined entertainment with a social reform message; Hutchinson songs often took up the causes of abolitionism and woman's suffrage. As natives of Lynn, Massachusetts, the Hutchinsons were particularly aware of the plight of the city's shoeworkers. "The Popular Creed," first sung at shoeworkers' meetings, later became a standard song of the labor movement.

Dimes and dollars! Dollars and dimes!
An empty pocket's the worst of crimes!
If a man's down, give him a thrust!
Trample the beggar into the dust!
Presumptuous poverty, quite appalling!
Knock him over! Kick him for falling!
If a man's up, oh, lift him higher!
Your soul's for sale, and he's the buyer!
Dimes and dollars! Dollars and dimes!
An empty pocket's the worst of crimes!

I know a poor but worthy youth,
Whose hopes are built on a maiden's truth;
But the maiden will break her vow with ease,
For a wooer whose charms are these:
A hollow heart and an empty head,
A face well tinged with the brandy's red,
A soul well trained in villainy's school,
And cash, sweet cash!—he knoweth the rule.
Dimes and dollars! Dollars and dimes!
An empty pocket's the worst of crimes!

I know a bold and honest man,
Who strives to live on the Christian plan.
He struggles against fearful odds—
Who will not bow to the people's gods?
Dimes and dollars! Dollars and dimes!
An empty pocket's the worst of crimes!

So get ye wealth, no matter how!
No question's asked of the rich, I trow!
Steal by night, and steal by day
(Doing it all in a legal way!)
Dimes and dollars! Dollars and dimes!
An empty pocket's the worst of crimes!

Source: *The Awl,* 1844.

self into the job of strengthening the organization and its ties to other molders' associations around the country. The rise of a national market convinced Sylvis that molders had to organize nationally as well, and he played a central role in founding the National Molders' Union in 1859. Largely through Sylvis's efforts, this early national union more than doubled in size during its first year in existence.

That same year, in Lowell, Massachusetts, between three and five hundred female mill operatives walked off their jobs. The striking women made up only about six percent of the city's total workforce, and the strike was ultimately lost. But, significantly, most of the strikers were Irish. This was the first time that this group of immigrants participated collectively in an organized labor protest. At the same time, Lynn shoemakers also stepped up their protest activity. Declining wages, repeated layoffs, and disruptions caused by the introduction of the sewing machine finally exploded in 1860 in the largest strike the nation had ever seen. Over twenty thousand men and women laid down their tools—more than a third of all shoe workers in Massachusetts.

The Lynn strikers said they were defending individual dignity and freedom. To emphasize that point, they linked their struggle to symbols of national independence, launching the strike on George Washington's birthday. And they persuaded strikers to defend their rights with the ral-

"American Ladies Will Not Be Slaves." Preceded by the local militia, women shoemakers demonstrated in the streets of Lynn, Massachusetts, on March 7, 1860. In contrast to their failure to cover previous labor actions, illustrated newspapers published a number of images of the 1860 strike.

Source: *Frank Leslie's Illustrated Newspaper,* March 17, 1860—Prints and Photographs Division, Library of Congress.

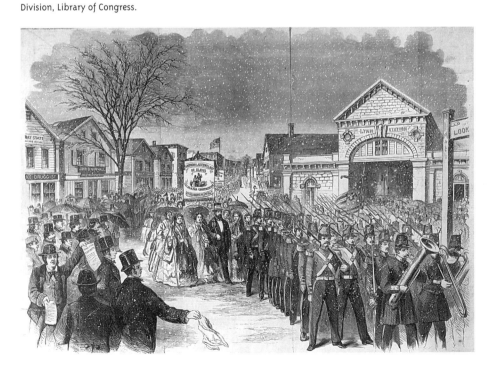

lying cry, "sink not to the state of a slave." On March 7, eight hundred female strikers marched through the wintry streets of Lynn behind a banner proclaiming, "American ladies will not be slaves: Give us a fair compensation and we labor cheerfully." The Lynn strikers turned out in huge street demonstrations, fought the use of scab labor, and battled the town marshal when he and his deputies intervened on the side of the bosses. Bolstered by additional police, the employers won the day. Nevertheless, the determined Lynn strikers became a symbol for other laborers seeking better treatment. And their repeated invocation of the slavery theme carried great significance in the context of heightened sectional tensions.

White Southerners Respond to Free Labor's Claims

Southern planters responded to the Lynn shoemakers' claims that their condition was similar to that of slaves. Many agreed with George Fitzhugh, a spokesman of Virginia's tidewater planters, that so-called "free" labor was more exploitative than slavery. Southern blacks, they maintained, although enslaved, were better off than industrial workers and peasants in England, Europe, and the United States when it came to food, clothing, and housing. Even Hinton Helper admitted, after visiting Chile, that the housing of peasants near Valparaiso was probably worse than that of southern slaves. Arguing that "the subjection of man to man" occurs in every country and every region of the country, proslavery advocates contrasted the "hunger and cold" and the daily suffering of impoverished "free" laborers with what they considered the humanitarian Christian arrangements of slavery. Using such reasoning in conjunction with older Biblical justifications for bondage, more and more southern planters argued that the South must stand firm behind its "peculiar institution."

In 1858, James Henry Hammond, former governor of South Carolina and later a U.S. senator, recalled that in the days of Washington and Jefferson, the South had "believed slavery to be an evil — weakness — disgrace — nay a sin." Fortunately, he went on, "a few bold spirits took the question up; they compelled the South to investigate it anew and thoroughly, and what is the result? Why, it would be difficult to find a southern man who feels the system to be the slightest burden on his conscience."

Hammond's remarks came after the Supreme Court's 1857 decision rejecting the claim of a Missouri slave named Dred Scott that he had become free when his master took him out of the South and into a free state (Illinois) and a free territory (Wisconsin). The Court, filled with Southerners and Democrats, and led by aging Chief Justice Roger B. Taney, a former slaveholder, pronounced unconstitutional all laws restricting the free movement of property, including human property. Indeed, Taney asserted further, Scott had no right to bring suit at all because since the founding of the American republic no black person in the United States had enjoyed any "rights which the white man was bound to respect." Although Taney had already freed his own slaves, he was committed to defending his beloved South against Republican threats to its time-honored institutions. Referring to the growing power of northern politicians, Taney and his slaveholding colleagues on the Court believed that their

William Walker's "Filibusters" Relax after the Battle of Granada. Slaveholders went to great extremes to expand slavery, turning to Mexico, western territories, and even Central America. Supported by fifty-eight mercenaries, the Tennessee-born William Walker "invaded" Nicaragua in May 1855. Within six months he succeeded in exploiting civil unrest in the country and declared himself president. Walker's government, which opened the country to slavery, was recognized by the United States in 1856. But he was overthrown a year later by forces financed by his former sponsor, the railroad entrepreneur Cornelius Vanderbilt.

Source: J. W. Orr, *Frank Leslie's Illustrated Newspaper,* May 3, 1856—American Social History Project.

"southern countrymen" were in great danger, "the knife of the assassin is at their throats."

Northerners were horrified. Feeling less like assassins than victims, they argued that the Dred Scott decision, followed to its logical conclusion, could lead to legalizing slave ownership not only in the territories but in the free states as well. The *New York Tribune* declared the decision was the work of "five slaveholders and two doughfaces," the latter referring to the two northern justices, both Democrats, who supported the majority decision. The "*dictum,*" it claimed, was "entitled to just as much moral weight as would be the judgement of a majority of those congregated in any Washington bar-room." The remedy, according to the *Chicago Tribune,* was "the ballot box" and the election of a Republican President in 1860.

For proslavery firebrands, the Dred Scott decision was just the kind of guarantee for slave labor they sought. Some went so far as to demand the resumption of the Atlantic slave trade. More called for an automatic southern veto over all federal legislation affecting southern interests. Southern politicians also tried to limit the rights of the foreign-born in their midst, fearing that they were less enthusiastic about the region's "peculiar institution." Southern congressmen also blocked homestead legislation that would have made western land more available to small farmers. A law turning western land over to independent farmers, exclaimed the Charleston *Mercury,* would be "the most dangerous abolition bill which has ever been directly passed by Congress." That land was to be

The Distribution of Slave Population, 1790–1860. The spread of slavery into the sugar and cotton lands of the lower Mississippi Valley and along the fertile "black belt" that stretched from Georgia through Mississippi increased the profitability of the "peculiar institution" in the first half of the nineteenth century. At the same time, the percentage of the population who could afford to own slaves declined, creating the large plantations and wealthy slave owners that have come to dominate our images of southern life in the decades before the Civil War. Life on the western frontier of slavery was anything but bucolic, however, with harsh work discipline, an active slave trade, and the constant threat of disease, debt, and rebellion.

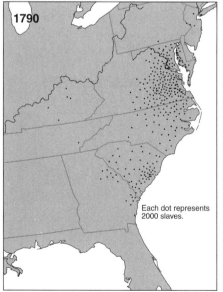

1790

Each dot represents 2000 slaves.

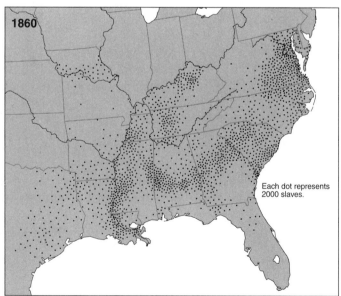

1860

Each dot represents 2000 slaves.

the salvation of the plantation system, which slave owners long believed could only remain profitable by expanding.

The "Worst Oppressed"

Expansion of the plantation system exacerbated the brutality of slavery. More black families were torn apart by the sale of slaves to new plantations in the west. On the frontier, slaves were increasingly subject to abuses as a consequence of absentee ownership. Black women, denied the minimal protections offered by extended families, suffered increased sexual abuse in frontier regions where men once again dominated the population. There, too, slaves were often deprived of necessities because the expansion of settlement outstripped the extension of railroads, banks, and other agents of commercial development. It was thus more difficult to supply slaves with sufficient food, clothing, and housing. In the West, as well, more slaves worked in gangs, which resulted in the harshest conditions of labor in the South.

The most oppressive conditions existed in the states of Alabama, Arkansas, Mississippi, Louisiana, and Texas. In Louisiana, where gang labor was first introduced, the difficulties of continuous ditching and draining of marshlands and the difficult and dangerous work of harvesting sugar cane allowed overseers to set a new standard of labor exploitation. Tom Wilson, who escaped from New Orleans in 1858 aboard an American cotton ship bound for Liverpool, explained why he chose to run after forty-five years in slavery:

> I was sold by auction . . . and was taken down to New Orleans, away from my wife and children, and I haven't seen them since. Shortly after I got there, Mr. Fastman's overseer, Burks, commenced to ill-use me. . . . They used to tie me down across a cotton bale and give me 200 or 300 lashes with a leather strap. I am marked with the whip from the ankle bone to the crown of my head.

In his first escape attempt, Wilson was hunted down by bloodhounds, who tore his limbs and bones with their teeth, and then he was shot in the hip by Burks. Later the overseer ordered him to be branded with a red hot iron and placed in irons for eight months. As soon as another opportunity presented itself, however, Wilson ran again. This time, with the aid of black sailors aboard the *Metropolis,* he reached freedom.

The brutal conditions of work, harsh discipline, and scorching temperatures that Tom Wilson faced affected growing numbers of enslaved African Americans as the planter frontier pushed west. In 1840, some 500,000 slaves lived in the southwestern states, comprising about a fifth of the total enslaved population. By 1860, they numbered 1.5 million, accounting for more than a third of the country's four million slaves.

Life on the frontier could be particularly harsh for isolated slave women. Celia, a thirteen-year-old African American, learned the horrors of isolation as soon as her new master, Robert Newsom, picked her up in his wagon. On the trip to his Missouri farm, Newsom, a widower, raped the girl. Once settled, he repeated his sexual assaults whenever he chose. When Celia sought protection by taking up with one of the two male slaves on Newsom's farm, her owner ignored her pleas to be left alone. Celia refused to accept her fate, and set a trap for her master. Apparently acting alone, she killed Newsom with a hatchet the night of June 23, 1855, after he had assaulted her. She then cut up and burned his body in her fireplace. Celia was eventually charged with murder and found some sympathy among whites appalled by her tale of abuse. But in the midst of the conflicts over slavery in neighboring Kansas, such an act of open defiance by a slave could not go unpunished. Celia was ultimately found guilty by an all-white jury and was hanged.

How do you like this — You d——d Negro Stealer

LOOK OUT.

The undersigned would announce to the public generally, that he has a splendid lot of well broke

NEGRO DOGS,

And will attend at any reasonable distance, to the catching of runaways, at the lowest possible rates. All those having slaves in the woods will do well to address
W. D. GILBERT,
Jan. 29, 1856.   Franklin, Simpson co. Ky.
[N. B.   Please post this up in a conspicuous place.]

"Negro Dogs." An 1856 advertisement for track dogs.

Source: Abraham Chapman, comp., *Steal Away: Stories of the Runaway Slaves* (1971).

Toward a Showdown: The Raid on Harpers Ferry

Individual acts of resistance by blacks could disrupt but never end the system of slavery. Allies were needed, though probably few slaves imagined finding them among white men. Then, in the late 1850s, as the nation lurched toward a final showdown, John Brown reappeared on the national stage and made clear that at least some white men would risk their lives to end the brutal institution.

On October 16, 1859, John Brown, three of his sons, and nineteen associates—black and white—launched a raid on the federal arsenal at

Harpers Ferry, Virginia. Trained in Kansas, the men planned to seize the arms stored at the arsenal, liberate slaves from Virginia plantations, and then retreat into the Allegheny Mountains. There they hoped to fortify a base from which to encourage, assist, and defend additional insurrections and escapes. The constitution that Brown drafted for this projected haven envisioned a utopian society in which "All captured or confiscated property, and all property [that is] the product of the labor of those belonging to this organization and their families, shall be held as the property of the whole, equally, without distinction."

Though Brown had gained substantial financial support from a group of six respected abolitionists, all white, he could not convince Frederick Douglass or other prominent black abolitionists to join his ranks. Though impressed by Brown's commitment, Douglass was convinced the project was suicidal. He was right. The plan pitted a handful of poorly armed men against virtually the entire white population of Virginia—and the South—plus the armed forces of the U.S. government. Though Brown and his men did capture the arsenal in the middle of the night, they never managed to free any slaves and they failed to make good on their escape plan. A detachment of U.S. Marines under Colonel Robert E. Lee and Lieutenant J.E.B. Stuart quickly surrounded the insurgents, subjected them to withering fire, and finally captured most of the survivors. By the afternoon, eight of Brown's men, among them two of his sons, were dead. Three townsmen had also died, and two more raiders were killed in the final battle. Brown, who remained with the survivors and prisoners to the end, was captured by the marines. He was promptly indicted and tried for treason, murder, and fomenting insurrection. On November 2, he was convicted, and one month later he was hanged. In one of his last letters, he wrote, "Men cannot imprison, or chain, or hang the soul. I go joyfully in behalf of millions that 'have no rights' that this great and glorious, this Christian republic, 'is bound to respect.'"

Though unsuccessful, the Harpers Ferry raid reverber-

"The Arraignment." A *Harper's Weekly* artist sketched John Brown and his co-conspirators as they were charged with treason and murder in a Charlestown, Virginia, courtroom.

Source: Porte Crayon, (David Hunter Strother) *Harper's Weekly,* November 12, 1859—American Social History Project.

"You Have Been Brave Enough to Reach Out Your Hands . . . "

In the days before his execution, John Brown received many letters of support from free blacks throughout the North. A black woman in Kendalville, Indiana, wrote Brown offering her thanks and speculating on the steps America would have to take to erase the "national sin" of slavery.

Kendalville, Indiana, Nov. 25

Dear Friend:

Although the hands of Slavery throw a barrier between you and me, and it may not be my privilege to see you in your prison-house, Virginia has no bolts or bars [that can stop me from sending you] my sympathy. In the name of the young girl sold from the warm clasp of a mother's arms to the clutches of a libertine or a profligate, in the name of the slave mother, her heart rocked to and fro by the agony of her mournful separations, I thank you, that you have been brave enough to reach out your hands to the crushed and blighted of my race. You have rocked the bloody Bastille; and I hope that from your sad fate great good may arise to the cause of freedom. . . . I would prefer to see Slavery go down peaceably by men breaking off their sins by righteousness and their inequities by showing justice and mercy to the poor; but we cannot tell what the future may bring forth. God writes national judgments upon national sins; and what may be slumbering in the storehouse of divine justice we do not know. We may earnestly hope that your fate will not be a vain lesson, that it will intensify our hatred of Slavery and love of freedom, and that your martyr grave will be a sacred altar upon which men will record their vows of undying hatred to that system which tramples on man and bids defiance to God. . . .

Source: Carter G. Woodson, ed., *The Mind of The Negro as Reflected in Letters Written During The Crisis, 1800–1860* (1926).

ated through the country. Southern leaders pointed to it as the final proof of the North's violent intentions. Republican moderates like Abraham Lincoln hastily condemned Brown's deed. Others rejected Brown's tactics but nonetheless saluted his values and goals. White abolitionists, southern slaves, and free blacks nationwide grieved at Brown's execution and proclaimed him a martyr in the American revolutionary pantheon. Church bells throughout the North pealed in mourning. In December 1859, Baltimore police, concerned about the activities of local African Americans, broke into an annual ball held by free blacks in the city. Their fears were no doubt heightened by what they saw: the hall was draped in banners bearing John Brown's likeness and a bust of him was inscribed: "The martyr — God bless him." The struggles so long waged in terms of western territory had finally come home to the South.

A House Divided

Undercover. An 1860 anti-Lincoln cartoon portrayed the presidential candidate trying to conceal the antislavery essence of the Republican platform.

Source: Currier and Ives, 1860, lithograph, 12 × 11 7/8 inches — Museum of the City of New York.

In 1860 matters came to a head. The Democratic Party — the last major national bastion of the compromise forces — could not agree on a single platform and candidate. The slavery issue had simply become too explosive. Democrats divided their party and their electoral strength in half as northern Democrats nominated Stephen Douglas and their southern counterparts, desperate to gain federal protection for slavery, chose Buchanan's Vice-President John C. Breckenridge of Kentucky as their standard-bearer. A weak echo of the old Whig and Know-Nothing forces dubbed itself the Constitutional Unionist Party and made a futile attempt to delay action on the slavery issue a while longer. Their ticket

was composed of John Bell of Tennessee and Edward Everett of Massachusetts.

The Republicans, however, stood united. They were determined to win and then to resolve the nation's sectional crisis once and for all. Looking past better-known party leaders—like Senator William Seward of New York and Governor Salmon P. Chase of Ohio—the Republican delegates selected Abraham Lincoln as their presidential candidate. The choice of Lincoln had several advantages. Lincoln was more moderate on slavery than Seward or Chase; he had demonstrated his skills as a debater during the 1858 Illinois congressional campaign; he had represented small farmers and workers throughout his career; and he lived in an area of the Midwest where voter support was critical to winning the presidency.

Both the North and the West went heavily Republican in the election, with Douglas, supported by northern Democrats, picking up most of the rest of the vote. At the local level, class divisions may have limited workers' support for the Republican party. For instance, in the wake of their defeated strike in 1860, the shoe workers of Lynn refused to vote for Republican candidates for local office because the shoe bosses controlled the local party organization. On national questions, however, workers had no doubt that their interests lay with the party of Lincoln. The workers of Lynn gave stunning majorities to Republicans at the state level and to the slate of Republican electors committed to Abraham Lincoln for president.

In the North, only New Jersey resisted Lincoln's triumphal sweep of the free states. In the South, the small urban vote generally went to the Constitutional Union Party, while the rural majority went heavily to Breckinridge and his proslavery southern Democrats. Lincoln's majority in the North and West proved sufficient to ensure his election as president. Though he received only forty percent of the popular vote nationwide, he earned the necessary majority of electoral votes by winning in the most populous states. His election, in turn, opened one of the most important and dramatic chapters in the nation's history. It signaled, as one observer noted, "the beginning of the Second American Revolution."

The Republican victory in 1860 grew out of the social, economic, cultural, and political changes that had taken place in the United States during the preceding half-century. By preserving slave labor, the first American Revolution stopped far short of the Declaration of Independence's stated goal—a society based on the principle that "all men are created equal." For a number of decades, national leaders worked long, hard, and successfully to hold together a nation increasingly divided into two different societies based on two distinct labor systems. But as the slave-labor South and the free-labor North matured, they developed needs, interests, and values that each region found to be increasingly dangerous and ultimately unacceptable in the other. Slave owners and their supporters became more and more committed to chattel slavery, viewing it as the essential prop to their own independence, while to them the North's vaunted "free society" became an object of fear and loathing. And although Northerners hotly disagreed among themselves about the meaning of "free labor," most came to view the expansion of slavery as the most direct challenge — and threat — to the American republic and Northerners' own rights, freedoms, and aspirations within it. The ongoing resistance to slavery and the response it evoked from slaveholders kept the issue alive and the stakes high. The dispute over the future of the West manifested and exacerbated the growing sectional clash, destroyed the old two-party system, and gave life to Republicanism. "Bleeding Kansas" and Harpers Ferry revealed how sharp the conflict had become and anticipated the way in which it would at last be resolved.

Even in death, John Brown continued to symbolize the powerful currents that drove North and South toward war. In late 1859, Brown died a traitor's death, brought to the gallows by U.S. troops led by Colonel Robert E. Lee. Two short years later, U.S. troops marched into battle against Lee. On their lips was a fighting song that began "John Brown's Body lies a moldering in the grave," but "his soul goes marching on."

The Years in Review

1843

- New York Laborers' Union Benevolent Association forms; it reflects the growth of organizing efforts at midcentury.

1845

- Editor John O'Sullivan writes of America's "Manifest Destiny to overspread the continent."

1846

- California declares its independence from Mexico.

1846–1847

- Donner party is trapped by snow in Sierra Nevada mountains; part of group survives by eating those who died.

1848

- Gold discovered in California; about 80,000 people arrive in California the next year to seek gold.
- Mormon farmers, who are plowing the shores of the Great Salt Lake, introduce irrigation to U.S. agriculture.
- The nation's first Chinese immigrants arrive in San Francisco; by 1852, an estimated 18,000 Chinese are in the United States.
- Free Soil Party organized; it favors prohibition of slavery in the new territories added as result of Mexican War.

1849

- Harriet Tubman escapes from slavery in Maryland and becomes a "conductor" on the Underground Railway, which got its start about a decade earlier.

1850

- Compromise of 1850—a series of bills passed by Congress to appease proslavery and antislavery groups—admits California to the Union as a free state, allows New Mexico and Utah territories to choose their status, abolishes the slave trade in the District of Columbia, and passes a tough new fugitive slave law.
- German-American craftsmen establish General Worker's League—reflection of upsurge of labor activism and influence of European democratic revolutions of 1848.
- Levi Strauss starts selling "bibless overalls" in San Francisco. Soon he will switch from using canvas to make the pants to using denim and to dying them a deep indigo blue that will give the pants the name "blue jeans."
- Congress ends flogging in the Navy.

1851

- "Go west, young man," declares John L. B. Soule in an editorial in the *Terre Haute Express,* although Horace Greeley is mistakenly credited with the line. Between 1845 and 1869, 1.4 million follow this advice.

1852

- Harriet Beecher Stowe publishes *Uncle Tom's Cabin,* which sells 300,000 copies in a year.

1854

- *People* v. *George Hall:* California Supreme Court rules that American Indians are prohibited from testifying against whites in court and, then, defines Asians as "Indians."
- Kansas-Nebraska Bill, which nullifies the Missouri Compromise and allows each individual territory or state to decide their slave status, becomes law.

- "Bleeding Kansas": What the war along the Kansas and Nebraska border between proslavery and antislavery landowners becomes known as.

1855

- Know Nothing Party splits into proslavery and antislavery factions.

1856

- Antislavery Senator Charles Sumner caned and severely injured by proslavery congressman Preston Brooks on the Senate floor.
- Democrat James Buchanan elected President over Know-Nothing Millard Fillmore and Republican John C. Frémont; newly formed Republican Party makes impressive showing in their first election.

1857

- U.S. Supreme Court's proslavery Dred Scott decision horrifies Northerners.
- First elevator installed in New York City.

1858

- Lincoln-Douglas debates during the Illinois senate race draw national attention to Abraham Lincoln.
- Antislavery forces triumph in Kansas.

1859

- National Molders' Union founded; in this decade national unions spring up among hatfinishers, cigarmakers, and others.
- John Brown leads two dozen people on a raid on the federal arsenal at Harpers Ferry, Virginia, to seize arms and liberate slaves in the area. He is caught after a bloody battle, tried, and hanged.
- "Dixie's Land," which made the word "Dixie" a synonym for the South and later a battle hymn for the Confederacy, is written by Ohio native Dan Emmett. First performed in New York and first popular in the North.

1860

- Twenty thousand men and women go on strike in Massachusetts to protest declining wages and repeated layoffs.
- Democratic party divides over the issue of slavery; Northerners nominate Stephen Douglas as presidential candidate; Southerners run John C. Breckenridge; Republican Abraham Lincoln defeats both of them and Constitutional Unionist John Bell.

1864

- Cheyenne leader Yellow Wolf dies at the massacre at Sand Creek; decades of bloody warfare decimate the Plains Indians.

Suggested Readings

Berwanger, Eugene H., *The Frontier Against Slavery: Western Anti-Negro Prejudices and the Slavery Extension Controversy* (1967).

Campbell, Stanley, *The Slave Catchers* (1970).

Chen, Jack, *The Chinese of America* (1980).

Dublin, Thomas, *Women at Work: The Transformation of Work and Community in Lowell, Massachusetts, 1826–1860* (1979).

DuBois, W.E.B., *John Brown* (1919).

Faragher, John Mack, *Women and Men on the Overland Trail* (1979).

Faust, Drew, *A Sacred Circle: The Dilemma of the Intellectual in the Old South, 1840–1860* (1977).

Foner, Eric, *Free Soil, Free Labor, Free Men* (1970).

Hurtado, Albert, *Indian Survival on the California Frontier* (1988).

Limerick, Patricia Nelson, *The Legacy of Conquest: The Unbroken Past of the American West* (1987).

Litwack, Leon, *North of Slavery: The Negro in the Free States, 1790–1860* (1961).

McClaurin, Melton, *Celia, A Slave* (1991).

McPherson, James, *The Battle Cry of Freedom: The Civil War Era* (1988).

Oates, Stephen, *To Purge This Land with Blood: A Biography of John Brown* (1970).

Peterson, Merrill, *The Great Triumvirate: Webster, Clay and Calhoun* (1987).

Potter, David, *The Impending Crisis: 1848–1861* (1976).

Quarles, Benjamin, *Allies for Freedom* (1974).

Riley, Glenda, *Women and Indians on the Frontier, 1825–1915* (1984).

Ripley, C. Peter, et al., eds., *Witness for Freedom: African American Voices on Race, Slavery, and Emancipation* (1993).

Sewell, Richard H., *Ballots for Freedom: Antislavery Politics in the United States, 1837–1860* (1976).

Slaughter, Thomas P., *Bloody Dawn: The Christiana Riot and Racial Violence in the Antebellum North* (1991).

Stampp, Kenneth, *The Imperiled Union* (1980).

Thorton, J. Mills, *Politics and Power in a Slave Society: Alabama, 1800–1860* (1978).

Utley, Robert, *The Indian Frontier of the American West, 1846–1890* (1984).

And on the World Wide Web

Library of Congress, *"California As I Saw It": First-Person Narratives of California's Early Years, 1849–1900*
(http://memory.loc.gov/ammem/cbhtml/cbhome.html).

chapter 11

SEQUEL TO
"KINGDOM COMING."

BABYLON
IS FALLEN!

SONG AND CHORUS.

WORDS AND MUSIC BY
HENRY C. WORK.

CHICAGO:
PUBLISHED BY ROOT & CADY, 95 CLARK STREET.

The Civil War: America's Second Revolution

1861–1865

Within three months of the November 1860 election in which American voters chose Abraham Lincoln as their sixteenth president, slaveholders led seven states of the lower South out of the Union. These states formed an independent nation, the Confederate States of America. Secession set off a crisis that rocked America, prompting some northerners to seek a compromise between the secessionists and the victorious Republicans. But the slaveholders demanded far more than most Republicans could accept, and in April 1861 the nation was plunged into war.

Lincoln's election had forced the hand of the slaveholders. The new president promised not to interfere with slavery where it already existed. But he had also pledged to stop its further expansion, and southern leaders believed that slavery's expansion was necessary to the South's survival. Moreover, many southern whites were convinced that the Republican Party would not hesitate to ignore the Constitution and trample states' rights in order to implement its program. Finally, they feared that the Republican victory would lead inevitably to slave rebellion. The southern slaveholding class thus proclaimed their unwillingness to accept becoming a permanent minority in the nation, a status that would inevitably undermine not only the institution of slavery but also the society upon which it was based.

When Northerners went to war to keep the South in the Union, they, like their southern counterparts, were fighting to preserve their vision of what American society should be. The Northerners' deeply felt, if somewhat idealized, beliefs about their nation were rooted in the traditions of the American Revolution. They included the ideal of opportunity for freeborn workers and farmers to attain economic independence, to end life higher on the social scale than they had started. This free-labor ideal, Northerners believed, was profoundly threatened by slavery's spread throughout the western territories. Like Southerners, then, most Northerners went to war to defend rather than change the world they knew.

To the surprise of the vast majority of whites on both sides, the Civil War became a massive venture, a brutal ordeal in which over six hundred thousand Americans—white, black, and American Indian—gave their lives. As the battles fought, soldiers killed, and years embroiled in conflict multiplied, the war inspired a revolution. Slaves became freed people, and

"Babylon is Fallen!" An illustrated sheet-music cover published in 1863.

Source: Lilly Library, Indiana University.

595

free blacks and their white abolitionist allies demanded not only emancipation but equality. White women, North and South, entered the labor force and the political arena in numbers never before imagined. Working people increasingly developed concerns and connections that reached beyond their local communities. And government extended its reach into more and more areas of daily life. The very course of the war dramatically accelerated the pace of economic, political, and social change, transforming American society in its midst and in its aftermath.

Most revolutionary of all was the Civil War's effect on the status of the nation's four million African Americans in bondage, an effect shaped in large part by the efforts of blacks, both slave and free. As white Southerners drew on the symbols and rhetoric of the American Revolution to support their rights as an oppressed minority against the tyranny of Yankee rule, enslaved women and men claimed the legacy of the Revolution as *theirs* and proved to be the real daughters and sons of liberty.

Famous legal documents, particularly the Emancipation Proclamation and the Thirteenth Amendment to the U.S. Constitution, registered the legal abolition of slavery. But it was the actions of slaves themselves that were central to the long and uneven process of uprooting the institution. Hundreds of thousands fled slavery and offered their labor and their lives to put an end to America's "peculiar institution." In the North, free blacks, supported by small circles of white allies, demanded the right to fight, to vote, to receive an education, and to work on an equal basis with whites. African-American women and men, serving as laborers, spies, nurses, cooks, teachers, seamstresses, and soldiers, fought to transform—not just to re-form—the Union.

The Forces Driving Secession

South Carolina led the secession movement, declaring its independence from the Union on December 20, 1860, just over a month after Lincoln's election. In the early weeks of 1861, the other Deep South states of Mississippi, Florida, Alabama, Georgia, Louisiana, and Texas, which were most dependent on slavery and farthest from the seat of federal power, followed suit. On February 9, a month before Lincoln had even taken office, representatives from these seven states met in Montgomery, Alabama, to establish the Confederate States of America. They adopted a provisional constitution and elected a Mississippi slave owner and former U.S. senator, Jefferson Davis, as their president.

Large slaveholders like Davis believed that Lincoln's victory blocked the growth of slavery and therefore placed its future in doubt. As one planter at Alabama's secession convention argued, "Expansion seems to be

"The First Flag of Independence Raised in the South, by the Citizens of Savannah, Ga. November 8, 1860." According to this lithograph, the earliest symbol of secession was the "Don't Tread on Me" snake—an image familiar to many Americans, having appeared on numerous flags and banners during the American Revolution.

Source: R. H. Howell (after Henry Cleenewercke), 1861, lithograph with tint-stone, 13 × 14 inches—Boston Athenaeum.

the law and destiny and necessity of our institutions. To remain healthful and prosperous within . . . it seems essential that we should grow without." For men who believed this, independence seemed the only way out. On the surface, this belief might have seemed unfounded. Shortly after his election, Lincoln had asked a southern acquaintance, Congressman Alexander H. Stephens, "Do the people of the South really entertain fears that a Republican administration would, *directly* or *indirectly,* interfere with their slaves, or with them, about their slaves? If they do, I wish to assure you . . . that there is no cause for such fears." But as far as the expansion of slavery was concerned, white Southerners' fears of interference were realistic. Republicans, true to their free-soil principles, did plan to keep slavery from being allowed in new territories. Lincoln summed up the issue to Stephens: "You think slavery is right and ought to be extended; while we think it is wrong and ought to be restricted. That I suppose is the rub." Stephens became vice-president of the Confederacy.

There were also grave concerns that the Republican Party would continue to ignore the laws of the land so long as it suited their political interests. From the perspective of southern slaveholders, the federal government had already failed to implement fully both the Fugitive Slave Law of 1850 and the Dred Scott decision of 1857. These concerns would intensify once southern states began to secede. Then, to keep border states like Maryland in the Union, President Lincoln would waive the right of habeas corpus, put secessionists in jail, arrest state legislators, and limit freedom of the press.

Slaveholders had an even more immediate reason for supporting secession—the fear that a Republican government in Washington would inevitably lead to a massive uprising of slaves. They remembered John Brown's raid on Harpers Ferry in 1859 and the intensified fears of insurrection that had lingered long after. One southern newspaper had warned at the time that the region was "slumbering over a volcano, whose smoldering fires may, at any quiet starry midnight, blacken the social sky with the smoke of desolation and death." Some white Southerners even believed that abolitionists were infiltrating the region and "tampering with our slaves, and furnishing them with arms and poisons to accomplish their hellish designs." In the wake of Brown's raid, "vigilance committees" of slaveholders and their supporters had sprung up all over the South. One such committee in Mississippi lynched twenty-three suspected slave rebels in a single three-week period. Coming on the heels of that hysteria, the Republican victory sparked new fears that "subversive" ideas would spread throughout the South and would eventually "infect" the slave quarters, inciting slaves to revolt. "Now that the black radical Republicans have the power I suppose they will [John] Brown us all," punned one South Carolinian.

Compounding the slaveholders' fears of uprisings and their frustration over the limits placed on slavery's expansion were their ongoing concerns about the sentiments of white Southerners who did not own slaves, a full three-quarters of the southern white population. "I mistrust our own people more than I fear all of the efforts of the Abolitionists," a politician in South Carolina had admitted in 1859. The Republicans, they thought, would highlight the social and economic inequalities among southern whites to recruit nonslaveholders to their party. A southern newspaper warned, "The contest for slavery will no longer be one between the North and the South. It will be in the South between people of the South." Only southern independence, many planters believed, could effectively isolate southern yeomen from their potential Republican allies in the North and thus protect the institution of slavery.

Southerners Debate Secession

The views of these southern yeomen, who had long lived on the margins of plantation society, reinforced planters' concern. Most nonslaveholding whites disparaged slaves for what they considered their abject dependency and apparent powerlessness, but they also disliked the haughty pretensions and prerogatives of planters. In the South, as in the North, small farmers and landless whites were drawn to the ideas of free labor and free soil. They resented having the more restrictive policies of planters imposed on them. One farmer from Floyd County, Georgia, expressed this resentment in a letter of protest to the Rome *Weekly Courier*. He and other militiamen had been called to muster one Saturday on the town square as a way of forcing them to listen to a prosecessionist speech by Walter T. Colquitt, a Georgia planter and political leader.

This [sham muster sort of angered] me that I should be compelled to
have the same politics as my general, and I and some of my neighbors are
determined more than ever, that we will be for the [Unionists]. . . . I
should like to know whether this is a free country, or whether we are to
be dragged out from our business to gratify the military men and the political demagogues.

Other Southerners also questioned the wisdom of separating from
the Union. In the Upper South, both poor and prosperous whites were
less avid for secession than their brethren in the Deep South. The states of
Virginia, Arkansas, Missouri, North Carolina, Tennessee, Kentucky,
Delaware, and Maryland had a smaller percentage of slaves and slaveholders than their counterparts who first formed the Confederate States of
America. Most whites in the Upper South favored a compromise that
would maintain both slavery and the union. The presence of a large number of former Whigs and moderate, rather than secession-minded,
Democrats made the area more responsive to Unionist principles. The
recognition that geography placed them in the path of war and suspicions
about the ultimate power and goals of planters and politicians in the Deep
South also contributed to the concerns of whites in this region. In three
of these states, no formal discussion of secession occurred prior to the
outbreak of war; in three others, conventions met and rejected secession;
and in two, voters rejected the idea of even holding a convention.

Anticipating resistance in their home states and opposition in the upper South, secessionists did not propose a popular vote on the issue. Of
the seven states that seceded in early 1861, only Texas allowed voters to
speak directly on the question. A delegate to South Carolina's secession
convention observed that "the common people" did not understand the issues. "But who ever waited for the common people when a great
movement was to be made?," he asked. "We must make the move and
force them to follow."

Although some urban workers and small farmers remained loyal to
the Union, most southern yeomen—especially those in the Deep
South—did follow their leaders and support the Confederacy. They did
so voluntarily, mainly because of their ties to large planters. Many small
farmers had started farming cotton and tobacco in the 1850s, and in the
process grew dependent on large planters for help with marketing and labor. These close economic ties, reinforced by ties of kinship, the belief in
states' rights and white superiority, and hopes that they might one day
rise into the slaveholding class, led most yeoman farmers to support secession.

Moreover, the vast majority of southern whites, whatever their economic fortunes, supported slavery. And many, including small farmers

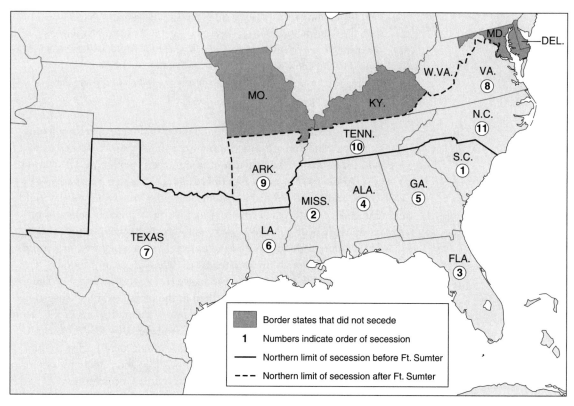

Border states that did not secede

1 Numbers indicate order of secession

—— Northern limit of secession before Ft. Sumter

- - - Northern limit of secession after Ft. Sumter

scratching out a living in the Upper South, defined their own liberty and independence in opposition to black bondage. The success of the secessionist appeal, then, can be attributed to fears that Republicans would free the slaves and introduce racial amalgamation in the South. One Georgia secessionist offered this typical warning to his nonslaveholding neighbors: "Do you love your mother, your wife, your sister, your daughter? If you remain in a nation ruled by Republicans, TEN years or less our CHILDREN will be the *slaves* of Negroes." With such images in mind, most nonslaveholding whites could agree with the slaveholder who said, "These are desperate means, but then we must recollect that we live in desperate times."

The North Assesses the Price of Peace

Times were desperate in the North as well. Southern secession threatened to throw the North into a financial panic. The cities of the Northeast and the towns along the Ohio River were hardest hit. Stock-market prices plummeted, banks shut their doors, factories laid off workers, and unsold

The Process of Secession. The first states to secede from the Union (as noted by the numbers on the map) were those with the highest concentration of slaves, all of which were located in the Deep South. The states of the Upper South, such as Virginia, Tennessee, and North Carolina, did not secede until after the firing on Fort Sumter. Several border states, that is, states in which slavery was legal but which were geographically closest to the North, remained in the Union throughout the war, although many whites in this area supported the Confederacy.

goods piled up on docks. Merchants and textile manufacturers worried about the permanent loss of the southern cotton crop, and bankers worried about whether Southerners would repay their loans. Adding these economic considerations to political concerns about national unity, many northern businessmen decided they could not afford the price of southern independence. They called for peace, at almost any price.

Northern working people also joined in the call for compromise, fearing that the economic strains of southern independence would lead to mass unemployment. Meeting in Philadelphia on February 22, a group of trade unionists from eight northern and border states denounced the secessionist "traitors" but also called for a peaceful resolution to the conflict. "Our Government never can be sustained by bloodshed," they proclaimed, opposing "any measures that will evoke civil war." Working-class support for compromise stemmed not only from economic considerations but also from a deep loyalty to the world's only political democracy. Sharing Lincoln's view, these Philadelphia laborers claimed that the United States had the "best form of government ever instituted by man."

But the price of peace would be high. In the most elaborate of various compromise schemes, Kentucky's Senator John J. Crittenden proposed that the North accept a return to the principles of the 1820 Missouri Compromise. In all western territory then held by the United States, slavery would be prohibited north of $36° 30'$ and permanently protected south of it, including land "hereafter acquired"—an open invitation to the acquisition of more southern territory for slavery. Crittenden also proposed constitutional amendments that would prohibit Congress from abolishing slavery in the District of Columbia, forbid federal interference with the internal slave trade, and provide compensation for any slaveholder prevented from recovering escaped slaves in the North.

Northern free blacks and abolitionists naturally opposed such measures. Frederick Douglass spoke for the opposition when he said, "If the Union can only be maintained by new concessions to the slaveholders, if it can only be stuck together and held together by a new drain on the negro's blood, then . . . let the Union perish."

The Republican leadership also opposed formulas that allowed for the expansion of slavery. "Free soil," after all, was a guiding principle of the party, and ordinary citizens flooded Congress with letters, demanding that their party leaders remain true to free-soil principles and reject compromise. "Artful politicians—rich merchants and speculators, whose god is money—will counsel peace, regardless of principle," wrote one citizen to his Republican congressman. "See that you yield not to their solicitations."

Chicago became a storm center of the fight against compromise. Led by the substantial population of German-American artisans and laborers, the city's Republican societies angrily denounced Chicago's wealthy businessmen, accusing them of "doing everything they possibly can . . . to support the compromisers." Trumpeting the city's commitment to anti-slavery principles, one newspaper proudly announced that, in Chicago at least, "Cotton has not usurped the function of Conscience."

Lincoln secretly advised Republican congressmen to "entertain no proposition for a compromise in regard to the extension of slavery." In the end, Congress defeated the Crittenden measures, and in doing so, expressed the political commitments of the Republican rank-and-file: the workers, farmers, and small businessmen who had elected Lincoln president. By March 1861, when Lincoln was sworn in as president, the voice of the Republican rank and file had been heard. Although Lincoln's new secretary of state, William Seward, continued to favor compromise, he had little room to maneuver in the face of such popular and congressional determination. As the Democratic *New York Herald* put it, there was "a power behind him, in the Republican camp, stronger than his own."

When Lincoln took control of the national government, he was not yet prepared to force the South back into the Union by military means. The new president nevertheless needed to demonstrate Union strength to satisfy his militant free-soil supporters. Attention now focused on Fort Sumter in South Carolina's Charleston Harbor, where a small Union garrison was running low on food and medical supplies. Lincoln dispatched reinforcements to Fort Sumter in April 1861, but he promised to use force only if the Confederates blocked a peaceful effort to send in supplies.

When a U.S. ship set sail for Charleston Harbor on April 8, the new Confederate government faced a major dilemma. It could either attack the Union vessel and bear the responsibility for firing the first shot of the war; or it could allow the supplies to be delivered, thus permitting what it had labeled a foreign power to maintain a fort in one of its key harbors. Jefferson Davis and his advisers chose the more aggressive course, demanding the unconditional surrender of the Fort Sumter garrison. The commanding offi-

Secessionist Spectators. Residents of Charleston watched the bombardment of Fort Sumter from the city's rooftops on April 12, 1861.

Source: *Harpers Weekly,* May 4, 1861—General Research Division, New York Public Library, Astor, Lenox and Tilden Foundations.

cer refused, and on April 12 Confederate guns opened fire on the fort. Two days later Fort Sumter surrendered. The Civil War had begun.

The North and the South would face very different tasks in this war. The South had to defend its own territory and force the North to halt military action. The North had to bring the South to its knees, which in military terms meant invading the South and isolating it from potential allies abroad. Most northern policymakers believed that these ends could be accomplished without challenging the institution of slavery. They certainly never intended to involve slaves in the war.

But from the first shot, enslaved Southerners knew that their future depended on the outcome of the Civil War, and they looked for chances to join the conflict. Their actions, both individually and collectively, had a profound impact not only on the course of the war but also on the aims for which it would be fought. The North went to war in April 1861 to preserve the Union and to stop the expansion of slavery, but, because of aggressive and largely unanticipated actions of African Americans and their abolitionist allies, by January 1863, the North would be fighting not merely to stop the expansion of slavery but to abolish the institution entirely.

The War for the Union

In the wake of Fort Sumter, Northerners across the social spectrum lined up behind Lincoln's war policy. The loudest advocates of compromise — manufacturers and merchants, intent upon maintaining economic links with the cotton South — now rushed to support Lincoln, hoping that force would succeed where compromise had failed.

The outbreak of fighting also galvanized northern workers, some of whom had also endorsed compromise. Many now expressed their concern for national unity through their firm support for the Union war effort. William Sylvis — who had advocated that Philadelphia workers endorse the Crittenden compromise — raised an army company among his fellow iron molders. Small unions across the country collapsed as their members rushed to recruiting stations. Foreign-born workers joined the patriotic muster. Germans organized ten regiments in New York State alone. New York City's Irish formed the soon-to-be-famous Sixty-Ninth Regiment and the Irish Brigade. Although over the long years of fighting, immigrants would be slightly underrepresented in military ranks, many foreign-born workers were initially eager to fight for the Union and prove to the world the soundness of a political democracy that recognized the rights of working people. Midwestern farmers and farm laborers, the backbone of the free-soil movement, also enlisted in large numbers, making up nearly half the Union Army.

The wives and daughters of these volunteers voiced concern for the safety of their loved ones. But they also waxed enthusiastic for the war, believing—as did their menfolk—that the fighting would be short-lived. Amanda Meshen, a young white woman raised in the abolitionist stronghold of Philadelphia, recorded her thoughts in July 1861. Mixing religious faith and political commentary, she wrote, "I believe that we shall prevail as I think we are on the Right side. I believe that as a Nation we have sinned and that we are making our just desert, but I believe finally victory shall be on the side of justice. . . ."

The March of the Seventh Regiment down Broadway. Newspaper artist Thomas Nast sketched the tumultuous send-off of New York's national guard regiment on April 19, 1861. Eight years later Nast completed this oil painting of the scene.

Source: Thomas Nast, 1869, oil on canvas, 5 feet 6 inches × 8 feet—The Seventh Regiment Fund, Inc.

Equally certain that justice was on their side were the 225,000 African Americans now living in the free states. One recalled that at the sound of the alarm bell, "Negro waiter, cook, barber, bootblack, groom, porter, and laborer stood ready at the enlisting office." An African-American recruitment meeting in Cleveland proclaimed, "Today, as in the times of '76, we are ready to go forth and do battle in the common cause of our country." Their country, however, was not yet ready for them. Secretary of War Simon Cameron quickly announced that he had no intention of calling up black soldiers. Local authorities drove his point home by prohibiting African-American recruitment meetings as "disorderly gatherings." "In Boston, Providence, New York, Philadelphia, Cleveland, and Columbus, black men have offered their services and been rejected," reported a leading African-American newspaper in May 1861.

Northern optimism contributed in part to this hasty rejection. Although four slave states that had previously rejected secession—Virginia, North Carolina, Arkansas, and Tennessee—joined the Confederacy after Fort Sumter, northern leaders remained confident that the South would be subdued easily. "Jeff Davis and Co. will be swingin' from the battlements at Washington at least by the 4th of July," predicted newspaperman Horace Greeley. "This much-ado-about nothing will end in a month," echoed a Philadelphia newspaper. The North did possess important advan-

---

". . . Will You Allow Us the Poor Priverlige of Fighting"

A letter to Secretary of War Simon Cameron from two Cleveland citizens seeking to raise a regiment for the Union Army suggests how eager many free black men in the North were to fight against the Confederacy.

Cleveland, O., 15 Nov. 1861

Sir:

The following particulars, hereafter mentioned, have been laid before the Hon. S. P. Chase, Sec of the Treas, and his reply to us is that "we apply to you direct."

Theirfore, we would humbly and respectfully State, that, we are Colard men (legal voters) all voted for the presant administration. The question now is will you allow us the poor priverlige of fighting—and if need be dieing—to suport those in office who are our own choise. We believe that a reigement of colard men can be raised in this State, who we are sure, would make as patriotic and good Soldiers as any other.

What we ask of you is that you give us the proper athroity to rais such a reigement, and it *can* and SHALL be done.

We could give you a Thousand names as ether signers or as referrance if required. . . .

W. T. Boyd,
J. T. Alston
P.S. we waite your reply.

Source: Herbert Aptheker, *A Documentary History of the Negro People in the United States*, Vol. 1 (1951).

---

tages—more than twice the population of the South, a growing industrial base, and a better transportation network, all of which had tremendous military value. Given these advantages, there seemed little need to call on the assistance offered by free black Northerners. Their rejection was also motivated in part by a fear that whites would not enlist if blacks were allowed to serve in the Union Army.

But there was a deeper reason. Lincoln and his advisers were wary lest the war for the Union become a war against slavery. Despite the quick secession of the upper South once war was declared, four crucial border slave states (Missouri, Kentucky, Maryland, and Delaware) had remained in the Union. Any threat to slavery might well drive these states into the Confederacy's waiting arms. Enlisting black soldiers would show that slavery's future in the Union was not entirely secure.

These concerns accounted for Lincoln's reaction to the exceedingly tense situation in Missouri. In August 1861, General John C. Frémont, the famous explorer and former Republican presidential candidate who now commanded Union military forces in the West, proclaimed martial law in Missouri and issued an order that freed the slaves of all Confederate sympathizers in the state. Abolitionists — black and white — hailed Frémont's action as a brilliant military move and a bold step for freedom. Furious Unionist slaveholders, however, called on Lincoln to reverse Frémont's order. Noting that Frémont's move would "alarm our Southern Union friends" and "perhaps ruin our rather fair prospects for Kentucky," the president quickly followed their advice. He insisted to Frémont and the Republican leadership that such a major policy issue must be determined in Washington rather than in the field.

African Americans and their white supporters nevertheless believed that the war had opened a door to freedom. As the fighting began, a black newspaper editor in the North spoke for most of his race when he concluded that "out of strife will come freedom, though the methods are not yet clearly apparent." Responding to the events at Fort Sumter, white anti-slavery agitator Amy Post proclaimed, "The abolitionists surely have a work to do now in influencing and directing the bloody struggle, that it may end in Emancipation, as the only basis of a true and permanent peace."

Although northern intentions remained unclear, most slaves realized that if Union troops came, they would undermine the authority of slaveholders and make freedom a distinct possibility. African Americans therefore carefully followed the course of the war, using the "grapevine telegraph" to learn about battles and follow Union troop movements. Even in the Deep South, far from the early battles, far from the Union Army, slaves were heartened by events. At the outset of the fighting, a white Alabama farmer wrote to Jefferson Davis that slaves in his region "very hiley hope that they will soon be free." Concealing their hopes from the slaveholders (as they had long concealed their real feelings), blacks in bondage awaited their chance.

The first of these chances appeared in tidewater Virginia, where the Confederate commander impressed (that is, seized) nearly all the male slaves in the area to build fortifications. Impressment, which became an official and widely used Confederate policy by 1863, allowed the army to take men, food, animals, and other property from farmers. Although farmers were paid for these goods, prices were fixed far below market value. Despite the payments, impressment angered area slaveholders, who objected to any infringement on what they regarded as their property rights. In response, the slaveholders began "refugeeing" male slaves, sending them out of the area. Knowing that either impressments or removal would mean separation from loved ones, some slaves chose another course: escape.

On the night of May 23, 1861, three escaped slaves paddled up the river to the Union outpost at Fortress Monroe, Virginia, requesting sanctuary from its commanding general, Benjamin Butler. Butler, a Democratic politician from Massachusetts, was no abolitionist, but he realized that the Confederacy would use slaves against the Union. He therefore offered the runaways military protection, refusing the owner's pleas for their return. The slaves, Butler proclaimed, were "contraband" of war, property that rebel slave owners had forfeited by the act of rebellion.

News of Butler's decision spread like wildfire. Two days later, eight runaway slaves arrived at what they called "Freedom Fort." The next day they were joined by another fifty-nine African-American men and women. Lincoln endorsed Butler's contraband policy in rebel Virginia as a legitimate tactic of war. The North now possessed a formula that allowed it to strike at the institution of slavery, the linchpin of the southern economy, without proclaiming general abolition and thus alienating the loyal border states.

Butler's policy was welcome news to the North. Union forces needed every weapon they could muster, even though from a statistical perspective, they controlled most of the material resources essential to war. The population of the Union states was considerably larger than that of the Confederate states, and the Confederacy included several million slaves who were not likely to be armed for combat. The Union also far outstripped the Confederacy in the production of commodities. Although the gap between the two sections was greatest in manufacturing, the North also led the South in the amount of land under cultivation and the quantity and value of agricultural products. The North had far more miles of railroad track, too, assuring greater facility in moving troops and supplies. And the Union could launch far more ships, a critical advantage in sustaining naval blockades of southern harbors.

Yet despite the North's material superiority, the South had many advantages that were critical in the early months and years of the war. Three were particularly significant. First, Southerners were fighting on their own ground. This gave them both a knowledge of the terrain and a distinct psychological edge, which was often expressed as arrogance about their military superiority. A wartime southern textbook proposed these problems for southern children to solve:

1. A Confederate soldier captured 8 Yankees each day on 9 successive days. How many did he capture in all?
2. If one Confederate soldier can kill 90 Yankees, how many Yankees can 10 Confederate soldiers kill?
3. If one Confederate soldier can whip 7 Yankees, how many soldiers can whip 49 Yankees?

Second, although the Confederate states held only thirty-nine percent of the total population of the United States, black and white, slave labor initially freed a much larger proportion of white working-age men

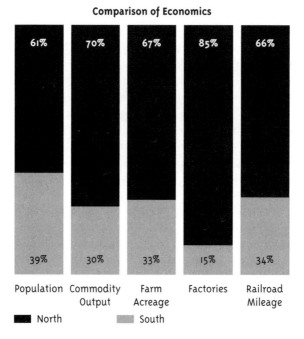

Comparison of Economics

Population	Commodity Output	Farm Acreage	Factories	Railroad Mileage
61%	70%	67%	85%	66%
39%	30%	33%	15%	34%

■ North ▒ South

Source: Stanley Engerman, "Economic Impact of the Civil War," in Robert W. Fogel and Stanley L. Engerman, *The Reinterpretation of American Economic History* (1971).

Economies of the North and South, 1860. The North entered the war with significant advantages in population, commodity output, farm acreage, factories, and railroad mileage. The advantages shown were even greater than this chart suggests since the southern population included slaves, who were not likely to be armed for combat, and since southern commodity production was dominated by farm products, which were less useful in military terms than manufactured goods. In addition, more southern farm acreage was unimproved, and southern factories were smaller than their northern counterparts.

for military service. And, third, the military tradition of the slaveholding class took on crucial significance. The Confederacy had the support not only of more than 280 officers trained at West Point but also nearly all of those trained at Virginia Military Institute, the Citadel, and other southern military academies. Among the officers who had gained their experience on the battlefields of the Mexican-American War, the best and the brightest (or at least most daring) joined the Confederate ranks: Pierre G. T. Beauregard, James Longstreet, George Pickett, Albert Sidney Johnston, Joseph E. Johnston, Thomas "Stonewall" Jackson, and Robert E. Lee.

All of the South's advantages were apparent in the first major battle of the Civil War. On July 21, 1861, at Bull Run in northern Virginia, twenty-two thousand Southerners pushed back an attack by thirty thousand Union troops. Although only six hundred men lost their lives, the battle of Bull Run gave Americans their first taste of the carnage that lay ahead. Northern civilians, who had traveled to the battle site to picnic and witness an afternoon of martial jousting, ended up fleeing for their lives to escape Confederate artillery.

"The Stampede from Bull Run—From a Sketch by Our Special Artist." Northern illustrated newspapers dispatched "special artists" to cover the war. These artists' sketches, engraved on wood blocks and published in *Harper's Weekly, Frank Leslie's Illustrated Newspaper,* and other periodicals, were the North's major source of war imagery. A few short-lived southern illustrated papers appeared, but it was the *Illustrated London News* that most actively portrayed the Confederate point of view. Its "special artist" Frank Vizetelly sketched this rout of Union forces on July 21, 1861.

Source: Frank Vizetelly, *Illustrated London News,* August 17, 1861—American Social History Project.

But the Battle of Bull Run was only one of many engagements in the early months of the war. In the others, which included confrontations in the western theater of war and the Union blockade of the South's deepwater ports, northern troops were considerably more successful. This mixture of failure and success on both sides suggested to those involved that the war might be a prolonged struggle after all.

The War against Slavery

The Union defeat at Bull Run shocked the North. In its wake, Congress began to move against slavery, expanding Butler's contraband policy. On August 6, 1861, Congress passed its first confiscation act, proclaiming that any slave owner whose bondsmen were used by the Confederate Army would thereafter lose all claim to those slaves. Although it was far from a clear-cut declaration of freedom, the act gave both slaves and abolitionists a foundation for further action.

In every region touched by the war, African-American men, women, and children moved quickly to reach the freedom offered by Union camps. In return for protection, they provided labor and knowledge of local terrain and Confederate troop movements. Slave owners also moved quickly, following runaways into the camps and demanding their return. Although no such demands were honored at Fortress Monroe, some Union commanders either returned slaves or simply denied them entrance.

The persistence of the slaves' attempts to gain freedom gradually led many Union officers and ordinary soldiers to help shield escapees from slave-catchers intent on returning them to servitude. In November 1861, Secretary of War Cameron, who had earlier opposed black enlistment, now publicly supported the radical idea of arming slaves to fight for the Union, labeling as "madness" the policy of leaving the enemy "in peaceful and secure possession of slave property." Lincoln, again acting to calm angry loyal slaveholders, forced Cameron to back down. Three months later, recognizing that the Secretary of War was inept and corrupt, the president removed him from office. Still, with the war dragging on and Union casualties rising, antislavery sentiment was growing in Congress, inside the Union army, and in the North as a whole.

Caught in the Middle. An illustration in a May 1862 issue of *Harper's Weekly* depicted one way that the institution of slavery contributed to the Confederacy's war effort. According to the caption, the northern newspaper artist observed this "struggle between two Negroes and a rebel captain" through a telescope. The captain "insisted upon their loading a cannon within range of [Union] Sharpshooters. . . . [He] succeeded in forcing the Negroes to expose themselves, and they were shot, one after the other."

Source: Mead, *Harper's Weekly,* May 10, 1862—American Social History Project.

The advocates of abolition, so long scorned by the majority of northern whites, now gained the hearing they had long sought. In January 1862, Philadelphia abolitionist Mary Grew reflected, "It is hard to believe the wondrous change that has befallen us." Grew had seen an antiabolitionist mob burn Pennsylvania Hall in 1838, and she had survived as well the castigations of northern whites who resented not only the antislavery movement but more specifically its encouragement of the participation of women and free blacks. Now, she responded with glee to the respect accorded her coworkers in the cause. One of them, Wendell Phillips, who had been among the abolitionists attacked in 1861 for supposedly provoking southern secession, was a year later accorded a formal introduction in the U.S. Senate.

At the forefront of those in Congress who applauded Phillips' presence was a handful of abolitionists—the so-called Radical Republicans—who sought to use the war to strike down the "peculiar institution." Although they never represented more than a minority in Congress, the Radical Republicans were able to help shape legislation. They did so by drawing on the North's growing support for abolition and by constantly emphasizing the military benefits to be gained by striking at the institution of slavery and by encouraging slaves to support the Union Army. The Radical Massachusetts senator Charles Sumner explained his strategy for success in November 1861: "You will observe that I propose no crusade for abolition. [Emancipation] is to be presented strictly as a measure of military necessity."

The military argument for emancipation intensified as the war dragged on through 1861 and 1862. The Union Navy began a blockade of southern ports that grew ever more effective, leading to the capture of the major port of New Orleans in April 1862. Even more significant, in the same month, Union troops commanded by Ulysses S. Grant won a battle at Shiloh in western Tennessee. Shiloh provided a critical victory in the Union's plan to control the Mississippi Valley, but it was a grisly bloodbath, a new kind of battle in which soldiers pushed forward yard by yard under heavy fire. When it was over, nearly four thousand men lay dead, and more than sixteen thousand were wounded. Grant's troops were too exhausted to follow up on their victory, but the Confederacy had lost a battle it could not afford to lose.

It was in these western campaigns that the diversity of the American populace became visible in army ranks. At the battles of Pea Ridge on the Arkansas-Missouri border, in the prolonged campaign for Vicksburg, Mississippi, and in the Union capture of Little Rock, Arkansas, the forces that faced each other were not composed simply of native-born whites whose only difference lay in whether they were raised on one side of the Mason-Dixon Line or the other. At Pea Ridge, for instance, General Earl van Dorn brought together a force of southern whites, three regiments of Choctaws and Chickasaws, two of Cherokees, and one of Seminoles and Creeks under the leadership of Cherokee General Stand Watie, who hoped that a Confederate victory would provide American Indians with greater autonomy. The Confederate forces were defeated, however, by Union troops that included both native-born white Midwesterners and Franz Sigel's German-American regiments. Similarly diverse forces would converge on Vicksburg in July 1863. And in the fighting around Little Rock, also in 1863, African Americans would join native-born whites, immigrant, and Indian soldiers on the Union side against regiments of white and Native American Confederates.

General Stand Watie. Leader of the southern Cherokee Nation, Degadoga gained fame as one of the most daring and successful Confederate commanders in the western theater of the war.
Source: Oklahoma Historical Society.

Union advances deep into the cotton belt during and after 1862 gave these diverse companies of Union soldiers a chance to observe slavery firsthand. Few white soldiers were abolitionists and some believed strongly in the necessity of enslaving African Americans, but many were nonetheless repulsed by what they saw. After visiting several captured plantations near New Orleans during which a number of instruments used to torture slaves were discovered, a Union soldier concluded that he had seen "enough

of the horror of slavery to make one an Abolitionist forever." A Union officer wrote from Louisiana, "Since I am here, I have learned what the
horrors of slavery was. . . . Never hereafter will I either speak or vote
in favor of slavery." Even though the majority of Union troops still questioned the wisdom of a complete emancipation, the changes in attitude
created by contact with slavery made some Union soldiers more sympathetic to the plight of runaways who sought protection behind Union
lines. There was also a growing sense that the Union could gain an advantage by employing African Americans as laborers and spies in return for a
promise of Union protection. "The Negroes are our only friends," wrote a
Union officer in northern Alabama. "I shall very soon have watchful
guards among the slaves on the plantations bordering the river from
Bridgeport to Florence, and all who communicate to me valuable information I have promised the protection of my Government."

As fighting continued in 1862, military reversals for the Union set
off a panic in the North, which further contributed to antislavery senti-
ment. In the summer of 1862, Confederate troops led by Stonewall
Jackson won a series of stunning victories in Virginia's Shenandoah Valley.
The panic in the North increased when Union General George B. Mc-
Clellan, known for his proslavery views and his vacillating approach to
military strategy, ordered a retreat following the crucial Seven Days' cam-
paign at Richmond, Virginia, in June and July. The Confederate Army in
Virginia, commanded by Robert E. Lee, now prepared to invade the
North itself.

As the war turned against the North, the North turned against slavery. In the spring of 1862, Congress had approved a measure to abolish
slavery in the District of Columbia, though they tried to mollify more
conservative colleagues by appropriating, at the same time, $600,000 to
assist in "colonizing" former slaves to Haiti, Liberia, and Central America.
The colonization efforts would collapse over the next year and a half, but
the eradication of slavery in the nation's capital stood as a symbol of a new
era. That July, Congress passed a second confiscation act, this one declaring that the slaves of anyone who supported the Confederacy should be
"forever free of their servitude, and not again held as slaves." This act encouraged more African Americans to head for freedom behind Union
lines. Acceding to pleas from free blacks, slaves, and some Union officers,
Congress also passed a militia act that allowed "persons of African descent" to be employed in "any military or naval service for which they may
be found competent." The first black Union regiment was organized before the end of 1862. And by 1863, African Americans would overcome
the objections of whites to their use as front-line soldiers, serving with
distinction in the Union Army and contributing directly to key northern
victories.

The Bittersweet Taste of Freedom

As the War moved south, slaves in greater and greater numbers deserted their owners to join the Union's advancing forces. Slave labor was crucial to the South's economy and military effort, and this massive transfer of labor from the Confederacy to the Union had a tremendous impact on the course of the war.

By the end of the summer of 1862, the numbers of African Americans employed by the Union Army increased dramatically. Black men built fortifications and roads, chopped wood, carried supplies, guarded ever-lengthening supply lines, and (on naval vessels) shoveled coal. They also worked in more skilled jobs, piloting boats and driving teams. Black women, employed in far smaller numbers, performed essential services as cooks, laundresses, seamstresses, and nurses. The work was often hard and heavy, and although pay was promised, black women and men often received their wages late—or not at all. They strongly protested this unfair treatment, since unpaid labor symbolized slavery. But they also believed that their labor played a central role in a military struggle for freedom.

For black men, who left families in bondage when they escaped to Union lines, joy in reaching freedom was mixed with the pain of separation. John Boston, a Maryland slave, ran to freedom early in the war and found employment as a servant to a Union officer. A letter to his still-enslaved wife in 1862 illustrates the mixed emotions of many runaways: "This day I can Address you thank god as a free man. . . . As the lord led the Children of Israel to the land of Canon So he led me to a land Whare freedom Will rain in spite of earth and hell." Then he added, "I trust the time Will Come When We Shall meet again. And if We don't meet on earth We Will meet in heven Whare Jesas ranes."

"Contrabands" in Cumberland Landing, Virginia. This photograph was taken in May 1862.

Source: James F. Gibson, May 14, 1862—United States Army Military History Institute.

613

Slaves Flee to Freedom

The following account of South Carolina slaves flocking to meet a regiment of black Union troops is drawn from the testimony of Harriet Tubman, famous for her success in helping hundreds of escaped slaves before the war. Tubman had joined forces with the First South Carolina Volunteers, made up largely of escaped slaves, in raiding plantations and leading slaves to freedom.

"I NEVER SAW such a sight," said Harriet; "we laughed, and laughed, and laughed. Here you'd see a women with a pail on her head, rice smoking in it just as if she'd taken it from the fire, young one hanging on behind, one hand hanging around her forehead to hold on, another hand digging into the rice pot, eating with all its might; holding on to her dress two or three more; down her back a bag with a pig in it. One woman brought two pigs, a white one and a black one; we took them all aboard; named the white pig Beauregard, and the black pig Jeff Davis [two prominent Confederate officials]. Sometimes the women would come with twins hanging around their necks; appears like I never seen so many twins in my life; bags on their shoulders, baskets on heir heads, and young ones tagging behind, all loaded; pigs squealing, chickens screaming, young ones squalling." And so they came pouring down to the gunboats. When they stood on the shore, and the small boats put out to take them off, they all wanted to get in at once. After the boats were crowded, they would hold onto them so that they could not leave the shore. The oarsmen would beat them on their hands, but they would not let go; they were afraid the gunboats would go off and leave them, and all wanted to make sure [that they were on] one of these arks of refuge. At length Col. Montgomery shouted from the upper deck, above the clamor of appealing tones, "Harriet you'll have to give them a song." Then Harriet lifted up her voice and sang:

> Of all the whole creation in the east or the west,
> The glorious Yankee nation is the greatest and the best.
> Come along! Come along! don't be alarmed,
> Uncle Sam is rich enough to give you all a farm.

Source: Joan Jensen, ed., *With These Hands: Women Working the Land* (1981).

There was cause for Boston's concern about his wife. Those slaves left behind often faced retaliation by owners furious over the escape of their most productive field hands. Women, the elderly, and children were subject to beatings and assaults, the brutality of which was intensified by the planters' outrage over the successful flight of the victim's husbands, sons, and fathers. When basic necessities grew scarce across the Confederacy in 1863 and 1864, slave owners claimed they had no responsibility for feeding and clothing workers whose relatives were earning wages from the Yankees. And when planters' families fled to avoid Yankee troops, slave families were once again torn apart, further reducing the chances of maintaining contact with their loved ones behind Union lines.

The Bright Side. Harper's Weekly "special artist" Winslow Homer's 1865 painting, based on his wartime sketches, depicted black teamsters relaxing in a Union campsite. While the teamsters were shown resting, the supply wagons and mules in the background reminded the viewer of the crucial role African Americans played in supplying ammunition and food to northern forces, and suggested that their relaxation was well earned.

Source: Winslow Homer, 1865, oil on canvas, 13 1/4 × 17 1/2 inches—The Fine Arts Museums of San Francisco, Gift of Mr. and Mrs. John D. Rockefeller 3rd (1979.7.56).

Escaping together was seldom a viable option for most slave families. While Union officers viewed the labor of black men as crucial, they often wanted little to do with black women and children, or elderly blacks. Many African-American men responded by making it clear that they would not work unless their families had food and shelter. To stem the general disorganization that would be created by large numbers of women and children congregating near military camps, Union commanders began to establish "contraband camps" in the fall of 1862. Life in these camps was often harsh. Provisions for food, clothing, shelter, and medicine were inadequate, given the number of slaves who sought refuge and the desperate condition in which many of them arrived.

In some places, such as Camp Nelson in Kentucky, conflicting orders created chaos. Fleeing women and children were first allowed entry, then driven outside the camp, and then readmitted a week later, by which time their original huts and cabins had been demolished. A northern missionary stationed at the camp described the bitterly cold weather and the inadequate provisions these fugitives confronted. He concluded, "As a clergyman I have no hesitation in pronouncing the treatment to which these poor people have been subjected as exceedingly demoralizing in its effects in addition to the physical suffering it entailed."

Some Northerners were moved by the plight of the fleeing women and children and began to organize on their behalf. Women abolitionists in Rochester, Philadelphia, and New York City sent packages of food, clothing, and medicine to a camp in Alexandria, Virginia. They also collected funds to pay the living expenses of two women who had volunteered to carry the goods south and distribute them—ex-slave Harriet Jacobs and white schoolteacher Julia Wilbur. Here as elsewhere, the women volunteers also offered medical care, established schools and sewing circles, and served as intermediaries with military and government officials. Jacobs had published her memoirs, *Incidents in the Life of a Slave Girl,* just as war had erupted. For Jacobs, the chance to assist southern blacks offered a way to make peace with her past and to provide other African Americans with the tools to create a new life in freedom.

Union Officials Consider Emancipation

By the fall of 1862, African Americans and abolitionists were no longer alone in advocating emancipation as a necessary outcome of the war. Congress, the larger public, and even President Lincoln were influenced by the unfavorable turn in the North's military fortunes. But Lincoln had to consider other factors. He wanted to prevent international recognition of southern independence, keep slaveholding border states in the Union, and unite northern whites behind the war effort.

The question of international recognition was paramount to the Confederacy. In the long run, support from European nations could undermine the Union cause and help persuade the North to accept southern independence. Of more immediate concern, the agricultural South was looking abroad for the manufactured products needed in a modern war. Southern attention focused mainly on Britain, the leading market for cotton and a potentially important supplier of goods. Many British political leaders sympathized with the Confederacy, particularly as the Union blockade of southern ports grew more effective, since the blockade had a disastrous effect on the British economy. In the Lancashire textile region, which depended entirely on the South for its raw cotton, thousands of workers lost their jobs, turning some of them into supporters of the Confederacy.

Nonetheless, working people throughout England had long maintained a hatred of both slavery and the southern slaveholding aristocracy. Lecture tours in England during the war by American abolitionists like Sarah Parker Remond, a free black activist from Philadelphia, intensified antislavery sentiments among Britons of all classes. But this powerful group of British abolitionists could not be fully mobilized until the North officially took a strong antislavery position. A firm Union commitment to the complete emancipation of the slaves might give the North an edge in the battle for British public opinion and prevent Britain's diplomatic recognition of the Confederacy.

Diplomacy. An 1862 cartoon from the northern satirical weekly, *Vanity Fair,* presented the Confederacy's president trying to gain diplomatic recognition from a skeptical Great Britain. "I hardly think it will wash, Mr. Davis," Britannia commented in the cartoon's caption, "We hear so much about your colors running."

Source: Howard, *Vanity Fair,* July 12, 1862—American Social History Project.

In response to these diplomatic considerations, the deteriorating military situation, and the unrelenting pressure from "contrabands," Lincoln decided in the summer of 1862 to issue a proclamation emancipating all slaves. He withheld its announcement, however, until a Union victory made the proclamation a sign of strength rather than one of weakness. Confederate troops in the eastern states had won numerous victories in the preceding months. In the Shenandoah Valley, Stonewall Jackson led Confederate troops to five victories against three Union armies. During June and July of 1862, General Robert E. Lee, commander of the Army of Northern Virginia, fought McClellan to a standstill in the Seven Days' battles. Lee and Jackson joined forces that August to defeat Union troops at the Second Battle of Bull Run. The chance to claim a victory finally came in the fall of 1862, when Lee led his army north into Maryland. On September 17, in the bloodiest battle yet, Union troops brought Lee's advance to a standstill at Antietam. Nearly five thousand men lost their lives on that day; another three thousand would die later of wounds. Although Antietam was the site of the bloodiest single day in American warfare, Lincoln viewed the battle as a victory. Five days later, he announced his preliminary Emancipation Proclamation to the assembled cabinet.

On January 1, 1863, Lincoln signed the final edict, proclaiming that slaves in areas still in rebellion were "forever free" and inviting them to enlist in the Union Army. Nonetheless, the proclamation was actually a conservative document, applying only to those slaves far beyond the present reach of federal power. Its provisions exempted 450,000 slaves in the loyal border states, 275,000 slaves in Union-occupied Tennessee, and tens of thousands more in areas controlled by the Union Army in Louisiana and Virginia. It also justified the abolition of southern slavery on military, not moral, grounds.

Despite its limitations, the Emancipation Proclamation prompted joyous "Watch Meetings" on December 31, 1862, as white and black aboli-

"Writing the Emancipation Proclamation." Surrounded by symbols of Satanism and paintings honoring John Brown and slave rebellions, an inebriated Lincoln trod on the Constitution as he drafted the document. This caricature was part of a collection of etchings, *Sketches from the Civil War in North America,* by Baltimore pro-South Democrat Adalbert Johann Volck.

Source: V. Blada (A. J. Volck), *Sketches from the Civil War in North America, 1861, '62, '63* (1863)—American Social History Project.

The Emancipation Proclamation

The Emancipation Proclamation is often presented as the act that ended slavery in the United States. In fact, the impact of the presidential pronouncement was considerably less dramatic, as a close reading of it will show. The Proclamation only freed slaves in Confederate states still in rebellion—states where the president's mandate carried little weight—and not in Union states. The president also urged newly freed African Americans to join the wage labor force and accept "reasonable wages" in doing so, without taking into account the ways that the history of racism and slavery would affect white notions of a reasonable wage for blacks.

By the President of the United States of America

A Proclamation

Whereas on the 22nd day of September, A.D. 1862, a proclamation was issued by the President of the United States, containing, among other things, the following, to wit:

"That on the first day of January, . . . 1863, all persons held as slaves within any State or designated part of a State the people whereof shall then be in rebellion against the United States, shall be then, thenceforward, and forever free; and the executive government of the United States, including the military and naval authority thereof, will recognize and maintain the freedom of such persons and will do no act . . . to repress such persons, . . . in any efforts they may make for their actual freedom.

"That the Executive will on the 1st day of January aforesaid, by proclamation, designate the States and parts of States, if any, in which the people shall then be in rebellion against the United States; and the fact that any State or the people thereof, shall on that day be in good faith represented in the Congress of the United States by members chosen thereto at elections wherein a majority of the qualified voters of such States shall have participated shall, in the absence of strong countervailing testimony, be deemed conclusive evidence that such State, and the people thereof are not then in rebellion against the United States."

And by virtue of the power and for the purpose aforesaid, I do order and declare that all persons held as slaves within said designated States and parts of States are and henceforward shall be free; and that the executive government of the United States, including the military and naval authorities thereof, will recognize and maintain the freedom of said persons.

And I hereby enjoin upon the people so declared to be free to abstain from all violence, unless in necessary self-defense; and I recommend to them that in all cases when allowed they labor faithfully for reasonable wages.

And I further declare and make known that such persons of suitable condition, will be received into the armed service of the United States to garrison forts, positions, stations, and other places and to man vessels of all sorts in said service.

And upon this act, sincerely believed to be an act of justice, warranted by the Constitution upon military necessity, I invoke the considerate judgment of mankind and the gracious favor of Almighty God.

tionists met to cheer and give thanks as the edict took effect. Fugitive slaves in Washington, D.C., gathered in celebration and prayer. There was even jubilation among the slaves in loyal border states who were exempted from the proclamation's provisions. African Americans, slave and free alike, understood, in ways that white Americans only partially did, that the aims of the war had now been dramatically changed. The Emancipation Proclamation augured a total transformation of southern society, rather than the mere reintegration of the slave states into the nation when the Union proved victorious. Although Lincoln had admonished Congress in 1861 that the war should not become "a violent and remorseless revolutionary struggle," that is precisely what it had become by 1863.

Soldiers' Lives

For soldiers caught in the midst of battle, political pronouncements did little to alleviate the dangers they daily faced. The fighting at Antietam in the summer of 1862 had given Lincoln the victory he needed to issue the Emancipation Proclamation and begin the active enlistment of black soldiers, but it did not mark an overall change in the North's fortunes on the battlefield. The war continued to go poorly for the Union on the eastern front. Against a superior force, Confederate troops won an important victory in December 1862 at Fredericksburg, Virginia, inflicting nearly thirteen thousand Union casualties while suffering only five thousand of their own. In the same month, Confederate cavalry cut Union supply lines in the West, preventing a much larger Union force from seizing the strategic river town of Vicksburg, Mississippi. By early 1863, the war had reached a stalemate. Then in May, Lee's army defeated a Union force twice its size at Chancellorsville, Virginia, setting the stage for a Confederate thrust north into Pennsylvania.

The South's victories reflected not only the Confederacy's advantages of fighting on its own terrain and its officers' greater talents, but also the generally disorganized nature of the Union war effort. Despite having more than twice as many soldiers under their command, northern officers seemed unable to press their advantages in the war's first two years. Early battles, while intense, were separated by long periods of inactivity. Tradition—shaped by impassable roads and the difficulty of providing food, clothing, and shelter—dictated that both armies refrain from fighting during the winter months. Instead, the armies built semipermanent camps to reside in while awaiting the spring thaw. One estimate suggests that in its first two years of operation, the Union's Army of the Potomac spent a total of only one month in actual battle.

"Cavalry Charge at Fairfax Court House, May 31, 1861"
Early in the war, artists often drew highly romantic and very inaccurate pictures. Such feats as firing from the saddle were viewed with great amusement by soldiers in the field, who enjoyed seeing illustrations of their exploits almost as much as they enjoyed criticizing the pictures' inaccuracies.

Source: *Harper's Weekly*, June 15, 1861—American Social History Project.

The war's casual pace fulfilled the expectations of both northern and southern soldiers. With the exception of those officers who had gained their experience in the Mexican-American war two decades earlier, most soldiers were too young to remember, much less to have experienced, any organized war. Their notions of battle were derived mainly from articles and pictures in popular magazines. Most young men expected war to be conducted in an orderly, even chivalrous fashion. They were in for a rude shock. A young private wrote home that his idea of combat had been that the soldiers "would all be in line, all standing in a nice level field fighting, a number of ladies taking care of the wounded, etc., etc., but it isn't so."

One reason that this soldier's idea of battle proved wrong had to do with the extraordinary range of the muzzle-loading rifles used by both sides, which quickly turned early battlefields into scenes of chaos and carnage. Although an individual soldier could fire only a few times a minute, their Enfield and Springfield rifles were murderously effective at great distances. The barrels of these guns were spirally grooved to spin the bullets, thereby extending their range and accuracy.

In early Civil War battles, soldiers marched in tight formation toward an enemy that began killing and wounding them from a quarter of a mile away. These battles thus put a premium on the courage of ordinary soldiers, valuing their willingness to move forward relentlessly under withering fire. In the face of such efficient killing, fixed infantry formations soon gave way to the realities of self-defense and self-protection. By

"Maryland and Pennsylvania Farmers Visiting the Battlefield of Antietam." As the war progressed and artist-reporters experienced battle firsthand, their illustrations often became more realistic. F. H. Schell sketched the carnage after the battle of Antietam and the morbid curiosity of local inhabitants.

Source: *Frank Leslie's Illustrated Newspaper,* October 18, 1862—American Social History Project.

1863 the nature of battle had changed considerably, relying on heavy fortifications, elaborate trenches, and distant heavy mortar and artillery fire—tactics that resembled World War I more than the American Revolution, or even the Mexican War.

In general, the Civil War proved to be an exhausting, trying experience for the ordinary infantrymen who bore the brunt of the fighting. After a major battle, one Vermont soldier described himself as "so completely worn out that I can't tell how many days . . . in the last two weeks . . . I went without sleeping or eating." The hardships and discomforts experienced on both sides extended far beyond the actual fighting. Many soldiers went into battle in ragged uniforms, some even without shoes. A Georgia major reported after the battle of Manassas that he "carried into the fight over one hundred men who were barefoot, many of whom left bloody foot-prints among the thorns and briars through which they rushed." Supplies of rations on both sides were sporadic at best; food was often adulterated, and even that was in short supply. Staples of the Union Army diet were bread—actually, an unleavened biscuit called hardtack—meat, beans, and coffee, the latter drunk in enormous quantities. Confederate troops got even less, subsisting on cornmeal and fatty meat. Vegetables and fruit were scarce on both sides, making scurvy common. Confederate rations were so short that after some battles, officers sent details of men to gather food from the haversacks of Union dead. As the war progressed, the Confederate government actually *reduced* rations to its soldiers. "I came nearer to starving than I ever did before," noted one soldier in Virginia. The Union soldiers' diet, in contrast, generally improved because of the greater scope and efficiency of the North's supply system.

Disease proved a greater adversary than enemy soldiers. "There is more dies by sickness than gets killed," a recruit from New York had complained in 1861. His assessment would prove chillingly accurate. For every soldier who died as a result of battle, three died of disease. Measles,

I Have Never Conceived of Such Trials . . .

Severe shortages of food, clothing, and medical care plagued soldiers in both the Union and Confederate armies throughout the war. Below are two letters from soldiers to their families, lamenting the travails of army life.

CONFEDERATE SOLDIER AFTER THE LONG MARCH FROM YORKTOWN TO RICHMOND, SEPTEMBER 1862

I have never conceived of such trials as we have passed through. We were for days together without a morsel of food, excepting occasionally a meal of parched corn. . . . The army was kept on the march day and night, and the roads were in some places waist deep in mud. . . . Many of the men became exhausted and some were actually stuck in the mud and had to be pulled out. . . . The men on the march ran through the gardens . . . devouring every particle of vegetables like the army worm, leaving nothing at all standing. Whenever a cow or hog were found it was shot down and soon despatched.

WOUNDED UNION SOLDIER, BATON ROUGE, JUNE 1863

I never wish to see another such time as the [day I was wounded]. The surgeons used a large Cotton Press for the butchering room and when I was carried into the building and looked about I could not help comparing the surgeons to fiends. It was dark and the building lighted partially with candles; all around on the ground lay the wounded men; some of them were shrieking, some cursing and swearing, and some praying; in the middle of the room was some ten or twelve tables just large enough to lay a man on; these were used as dissecting tables and they were covered with blood. Near and around the tables stood the surgeons with blood all over them and by the sides of the tables was a heap of feet, legs, and arms. On one of these tables I was laid, and being known as a colonel, the Chief Surgeon of the Department was called and he felt of my mouth and then wanted to give me chloroform: this I refused to take and he took a pair of scissors and cut out the pieces of bone in my mouth; then gave me a drink of whiskey and had me laid away.

Source: (a) Bell I. Wiley, *The Life of Johnny Reb: The Common Soldier of the Confederacy* (1943). (b) Bell, I. Wiley, *The Life of Billy Yank: The Common Solider of the Union* (1952).

---

dysentery, typhoid, and malaria became major killers, caused or made worse by contaminated water, bad food, and exposure. One soldier stationed in Louisiana described an outbreak of malaria:

> Two-thirds of the regiment are buried or in hospital. It is woeful to see how nearly destitute of comforts and of attendance the sick are. They cannot be kept in their wretched bunks, but stagger about, jabbering and muttering insanities, till they lie down and die in their ragged, dirty uniforms.

African-American troops fared worst of all. The death rate for black Union soldiers from disease was nearly three times greater than for white

Union soldiers, reflecting their generally poorer health upon enlistment, their meager food, the hard labor they performed, and the minimal medical care they received while in the field.

Even for white soldiers, medical assistance was primitive. One commentator described military hospitals in the war's early years as "dirty dens of butchery and horror." After the battle of Shiloh in 1862, General Ulysses S. Grant's medical director told of "thousands of human beings . . . wounded and lacerated in every conceivable manner, on the ground, under a pelting rain, without shelter, without bedding, without straw to lie upon, and with but little food. . . . The agonies of the wounded were beyond all description." Army doctors on both sides provided little relief. "I believe the Doctors kills more than they cure," wrote an Alabama private; "Doctors haint Got half Sence." Little wonder that ordinary soldiers often resisted being sent to hospitals, despite serious wounds or illness.

That the proportion of deaths from disease had been even higher during the Mexican-American War offered little solace to sick or wounded soldiers cared for by doctors who had not yet heard of antibiotics or antisepsis, who had no cure for peritonitis or gangrene, and who were perennially short of anesthetics. What solace was available came mostly to Union soldiers who had access to supplies and medical care provided by the U.S. Sanitary Commission. This commission, established by the federal government in 1861, had grown out of the efforts of the Women's Central Association for Relief, a volunteer organization that initially focused on training nurses. By 1862, tens of thousands of women had volunteered through hundreds of local chapters across the North and Midwest, hosting "Sanitary Fairs" to raise money; rolling bandages; shipping food, medicine, clothing, and bedding; and sending nurses to army camps along the battlefront. In the South, much of the medical care was also voluntary and also performed by women. The difference was that, without a government-sanctioned body to coordinate efforts and lobby for resources, a Confederate soldier's chances of dying from wounds or disease were even greater than those of his Union counterpart.

The morale of ordinary soldiers, Rebel and Yankee alike, reflected their performance on the battlefield and the relative comfort of camp life. As food, sanitation, and medical care deteriorated on both sides in the war's initial year and the horrors of battle sank in, a large number of soldiers deserted. At Antietam, in the fall of 1862, Confederate general Robert E. Lee estimated that one-third to one-half of his soldiers were "straggling"—that is, absent without leave. Early the next year, Union general Joseph Hooker reported that one in four soldiers under his command was similarly absent. Morale problems in the Union Army during this period were compounded by the fact that the North kept losing battles to seemingly inferior Confederate forces. By 1863, many Union soldiers were openly critical of their leaders. A Massachusetts private concluded that "there is very little zeal or patriotism in the army now; the men have seen so much more of defeat than of victory and so much bloody slaughter that all patriotism is played out."

Not until July 1863 would a string of Union victories, beginning at Gettysburg, Pennsylvania, and Vicksburg, Mississippi, improve Yankee morale and instill in the northern population a will to see the war through to victory. Confederate morale — both in the army and on the homefront — sank into despair at this same turn of events. What turned the tide for the Union was not simply improved army leadership and better military tactics, but a pronounced economic advantage over the South, which resulted in an improved supply of armaments, food, and clothing to Union troops, and of the necessities of life to their families and friends back home as well.

War Transforms the North

As the Civil War unfolded, it encouraged a quickening of economic change in the North. Despite military and economic setbacks in 1861 and 1862, the Union grew stronger as the war progressed. Northern factories turned out weapons, ammunition, blankets, clothing, shoes, and other products, and shipyards built the fleets that blockaded southern ports. Leading in the production of war materials, the North continued to serve as the center of American industrial development, a position it had held since the early 1800s. By 1860, manufacturing establishments in the North outnumbered those in the South six to one; and there were 1.3 million industrial workers in the North, compared with 110,000 in the South.

Initially, however, the effects of the war on northern industry had been little short of disastrous. New England textile production declined precipitously as the flow of raw southern cotton dried up. Shoe factories, which relied heavily on the orders of southern slaveholders, fell silent. The large seaboard cities of the Northeast, whose very lifeblood was trade, also suffered greatly. By 1863, however, the economic picture had changed dramatically. Coal mining and iron production boomed in Pennsylvania. In New England, woolen manufacturing took up the slack left by the decline of cotton. Merchants dealing in war orders made handsome profits, and industrialists ran their factories at a frenzied pace. The lower wages paid to desperate women and children, recently arrived immigrants, and free black Americans seeking entry into new occupations contributed to increases in both profits and the pace of work.

The economic boom of 1863 to 1864 was also linked to a vast expansion in the federal government's activities. Direct orders from the War Office for blankets, firearms, and other goods did much to spark the manufacturing upturn. The government also stimulated the economy by granting large contracts to northern railroads to carry troops and supplies, and by making loans and land grants that would finance the railroads' dramatic postwar expansion. Congress instituted a steep tariff on imported manufactured goods, giving American manufacturers protection from competition and encouraging industrial development, policies that northern industrialists had long demanded. With southern Democrats removed from the halls of Congress, Republicans now rushed to meet these demands.

Perhaps the federal government's most significant long-term contribution to the economy was the creation of a national currency and a national banking system. Before the Civil War, private banks (chartered by the states) issued their own banknotes, which were used in most economic transactions; the federal government paid all of its expenses in gold or silver. Various wartime acts of Congress revolutionized this system, giving the federal government the power to create currency, to issue federal charters to banks, and to create a national debt (which totaled $2 billion by the war's end). These developments had important long-term consequences: helping to shape the full flowering of industrial capitalism after the war.

They also had profound short-term effects. To finance the war, the government used its new power to flood the nation with $400 million in treasury bills, commonly called "greenbacks." The federal budget mushroomed—from $63 million in 1860 to nearly $1.3 billion in 1865. By the war's end, the federal bureaucracy had grown to be the nation's largest single employer. These federal actions provided a tremendous stimulus to industry, and northern manufacturers greeted them, on the whole, with enthusiasm.

But industrialists continued to face one daunting problem that government expansion only exacerbated: a shortage of labor. Over half a million workers left their jobs to serve in the Union Army, and others were drawn into jobs with the expanding federal bureaucracy, just as the need for increased production intensified the competition for workers. Employers dealt with the shortage in a variety of ways, primarily by joining the trend toward mechanizing industrial tasks and by increasing the participation of immigrants and women in the workforce. These developments had important consequences for northern society as a whole.

Then as now, mechanization could lessen the need for workers, although during the war agriculture benefitted more from this solution than industry. Reapers and mowers had been developed in the 1850s, but the shortage of labor greatly hastened their adoption by midwestern farmers. "The severe manual toil of mowing, raking, pitching, and cradling is now performed by machinery," noted *Scientific American* in 1863. "Man simply oversees the operations and conducts them with intelligence." The war similarly quickened the trend toward mechanization in the manufacture of clothing and shoes.

Industrial Work. Women filled cartridges at the U.S. Arsenal at Watertown, Massachusetts.

Source: Winslow Homer, *Harper's Weekly,* July 20, 1861—American Social History Project.

Northern industrialists also led the way in hiring immigrants to remedy the labor shortage. The industrialists formed organizations like the Boston Foreign Emigrant Aid Society and were extremely successful in encouraging migration from the European countryside to U.S. factories, mines, and mills. Immigration had fallen off sharply in the first two years of the war, with only about 90,000 immigrants arriving in 1861 and again in 1862—less than half the level of each of the preceding five years. By 1863, the number of immigrants—mostly Irish, German, and British—had again reached the pre-1860 level. The figure climbed to nearly 200,000 in 1864, and exceeded 300,000 in 1865.

The entry of women—immigrant and native-born—into both the agricultural and industrial workforce was a critical factor in easing the wartime labor shortage. On northern farms, women took over much of the work. A popular verse called "The Volunteer's Wife" described the situation:

> Take your gun and go, John,
> Take your gun and go,
> For Ruth can drive the oxen,
> And I can use the hoe.

A missionary traveling through Iowa in 1863 reported that he "met more women driving teams on the road and saw more at work in the fields than men." In the factories and armories, women were hired in ever-larger numbers to churn out northern war orders. Most important to the war effort were the thousands of "sewing women," who worked under government contract in their own homes (often in crowded tenements) to make the uniforms worn by Union soldiers. Opportunities for women also opened up in the fields of teaching and government clerical work. And northern women began their entry into retail sales and food processing, areas in which there would later be large concentrations of women workers.

Employment in some of the newer industrial jobs that women held was temporary; when the war ended, so did women's employment. But in other areas, such as the nursing profession, women made permanent inroads. Despite strong initial opposition, women struggled successfully to obtain work in northern hospitals and Union Army camps. This movement was led by such memorable figures as Clara Barton, Mary Ann "Mother" Bickerdyke, and Dr. Mary Walker, the first woman to be awarded the Medal of Honor. The work these women accomplished created popular support for their entrance into the medical profession. By

". . . And Then I Must Work for Myself"

The following letter, written by a sewing woman in November 1863 to the *New York Sun,* reveals the kinds of jobs and the low wages available to northern workingwomen during the war.

WHEN THIS REBELLION broke out, my brothers joined the Army, and then I must work for myself and help support my mother and my little sister. I would read the advertisements in the paper and go answer them. . . .

A well-known hat manufactory on Broadway wanted five hundred hands. I applied for work. The proprietor . . . promised me 62 cents per dozen. I knew I could not make a dozen per day; but what was I to do? I wanted work, and must get it, or starve. My mother and myself worked from early morning until late a night, but could not make more than $2.50 each per week. . . . Are we nothing but living machines, to be driven at will for the accommodation of a set of heartless, yes, I may say souless people . . . ? They ought to read the commandment, "Thou shall not kill." But they are murderers that die on feather beds. . . .

Men join the army and leave us with out employers to battle with. I trust that we will have kind friends to aid us; it is a good work. If we were paid better it would save many young girls from worse than poverty. Let us act as one, and I feel sure that with the blessings of God, and assistance of our fellow beings, we will succeed.

E.S.P., A Working Girl

Source: *New York Sun,* November 17, 1863.

the end of the war, women had almost entirely replaced men in nursing the sick and wounded.

Northern women played an astonishing array of roles over the course of the war. The Woman's National Loyal League gathered some four hundred thousand signatures on petitions calling for a constitutional amendment to end slavery. They served as spies, couriers, recruiting agents, and even soldiers. Some four hundred women, on both sides of the conflict, are known to have disguised themselves as men in order to join infantry companies; the identities of several were discovered only after they were wounded in battle. Although the financial rewards for such services were small, the efforts of women in wartime helped to transform popular notions of appropriate gender roles and set the stage for new debates in the postwar era over women's rights and responsibilities.

Dissent and Protest in the Union States

Despite an expanding economy, northern working people suffered tremendously during the war years. For those not facing enemy fire, the main problem was inflation. As greenbacks flooded the economy and as consumer goods fell into short supply, prices climbed rapidly—about twenty percent faster than wages. Skilled workers, whose labor was in high demand, might be able to keep up. But unskilled workers were hit hard by inflation, particularly the sewing women, who had almost no bargaining power and who were often exploited by unscrupulous contractors. "We are able to sustain life for the prices offered by contractors, who fatten on their contracts by grinding immense profits out of the labor of their operatives," wrote a group of Cincinnati seamstresses to President Lincoln in 1864.

Industrialists garnered huge profits as production boomed. Profits in the woolen industry nearly tripled. Railroad stocks climbed to unheard-of-prices. Government contractors made huge gains—sometimes by supplying inferior goods at vastly inflated prices. To working people suffering the ravages of inflation, such extraordinary profits seemed grossly unfair.

Northern workers tried to improve their plight in a variety of ways. From 1863 through 1865, there were dozens of strikes as

"The Irrepressible Conflict." In this cartoon from *Vanity Fair,* an Irish longshoreman told a black worker seeking employment on New York's waterfront: "Well, ye may be a man and a brother, sure enough; but it's little hospitality ye'll get out of yer relations on this dock, me ould buck!" The sharp competition for unskilled jobs contributed to the New York draft riot of 1863.

Source: *Vanity Fair,* August 2, 1862—American Social History Project.

628

workers began to form unions to demand higher wages. But wartime strikes could also exacerbate divisions among workers. In a number of cases, for example, the longshoremen's walkout in New York City in June 1863, the method of breaking strikes staged by largely immigrant workers, was to hire black workers for jobs from which they had traditionally been excluded.

Both black and white workers looked to Lincoln and the federal government for help. The Republicans, after all, had pledged themselves to protect the rights of free labor. But government proved to be a better friend of business. Employers successfully lobbied a number of state legislatures to pass laws prohibiting strikes. They also persuaded the increasingly powerful federal government to help block workers' efforts to organize. When workers at the Parrott arms factory in Cold Spring, New York, struck for higher wages in 1864, the government sent in two companies of troops, declared martial law, and arrested the strike leaders. The army similarly intervened in labor disputes in St. Louis and in the Pennsylvania coalfields. All three strikes were crushed. These and other experiences led many workers to criticize the federal government and its ruling Republican Party.

The widening unrest in the North raised the hopes of opposition Democrats in their continuing effort to bring the war to an end. The Civil War had deeply divided the Democratic Party in the North. Although some party leaders supported Lincoln and the war effort, many others — whom opponents called Copperheads, after the poisonous snake — rallied behind Ohio politician Clement L. Vallandigham in opposing the war. These antiwar Democrats sought desperately to build support for their position among midwestern farmers and eastern industrial workers. In areas of the Midwest where sympathy for the southern cause and antipathy to African Americans ran deep, both women and men enthusiastically joined the Copperhead campaign. Jane Evans, who worked the family farm in southern Ohio with her father and sisters, wrote to her brother in the Union Army, assuring him that she would do all in her power to see the peace party elected in 1864.

Democrats enjoyed considerable success in eastern cities, where inflation was running rampant and where immigrant workers had long supported Democratic political machines. Racism was the strongest weapon in the party's arsenal. As the Civil War increasingly became a war against slavery, many white workers found an outlet for their racism in supporting the peace wing of the Democratic Party.

The Republican draft law further fueled opposition to the war among many white Northerners. The Conscription Act of March 1863 provided that draftees would be selected by an impartial lottery. But the act contained a loophole that exempted men with $300 to spare. A man could pay that $300 to the government in place of serving, or to another man who served as the draftee's substitute. This option was unavailable to unskilled workers, who were lucky to earn $300 in an entire year. These workers deeply resented both the draft law's profound inequality and the recent expansion of the North's war aims to include emancipation of the slaves who, they assumed, would join already free blacks as competitors for scarce jobs after the war ended.

"Buying a Substitute in the North during the War." In his collection of etchings, *Sketches from the Civil War in North America*, A. J. Volck depicted the Union Army as composed of immigrant and native-born deviants and criminals. He was moved less by the inequities of the northern draft law than by his sympathy for the South.

Source: V. Blada (A. J. Volck), *Sketches from the Civil War in North America, 1861, '62, '63* (1863)—Print Collection, Miriam and Ira Wallach Division of Arts, Prints, and Photographs, New York Public Library, Astor, Lenox and Tilden Foundations.

The simmering resentment of the urban poor reached the boiling point in July 1863, when the new draft law went into effect. Riots broke out in cities across the North. In New York, where war-induced inflation had caused tremendous suffering and where a large immigrant population solidly supported a powerful Democratic machine, implementation of the draft triggered four days of the worst rioting Americans had ever seen. Violence quickly spread through the entire city, and even homes in wealthy neighborhoods were looted. Both women and men, many of them poor Irish immigrants, attacked and killed Protestant missionaries, Republican draft officials, and wealthy businessmen. New York City's small free-black population became the rioter's main target, however. Immigrants, determined not to be drafted to fight for the freedom of a people they despised, turned on black New Yorkers in rage. One observer reported that he saw "a black man hanged . . . for no offense but his Negritude." Rioters lynched at least a dozen African Americans and looted and burned the city's Colored Orphan Asylum. Leading trade unionists joined middle-class leaders in condemning the riots, but to no avail. The violence ended only when Union troops were rushed back from the front to put down the riot by force. The troops included New York's own Irish Brigade, whose members, in the process of securing the city's working-class wards, had to fire on their countrymen. At the end, over one hundred New Yorkers lay dead.

The New York Draft Riots. The lynching of a black man on Clarkson Street.

Source: *Illustrated London News,* August 8, 1863—American Social History Project.

The New York City draft riots, though bloody and brutal, lasted only a few days. A more prolonged battle—this one between prowar and antiwar forces—raged in Missouri for three years. This "inner civil war" dated not to the new Conscription Act but back to the earliest years of the North–South conflict. Confederate sympathizers, organized in militia bands under the Order of the American Knights, staged a guerrilla war against Unionists. From 1861 through 1864, when the Confederacy was finally on the verge of defeat, independent bands—with the tacit and sometimes strategic support of Confederate army commanders—terrorized the countryside, killing unarmed civilians and soldiers—white and black—and burning, robbing, and pillaging the homes and farms of those suspected of aiding the opposition. These attacks claimed thousands of lives, forced the Union Army to station troops in the area, and made clear that even in nominally Union states, especially those that bordered the Confederacy, many residents had southern sympathies. Many Confederate guerrillas were sons of southern farmers and planters, though the most infamous leader was William Clarke Quantrill, the son of an Ohio schoolteacher. The bands provided training for men like Frank James and his brothers, who would continue robbing and pillaging long after the war was over.

Building Consensus Through Victory

In July 1863, the Union won two decisive victories, marking the beginning of its military success. In the eastern theater, Union forces turned back a major Confederate drive, defeating Robert E. Lee's army at Gettysburg, Pennsylvania, on July 3. The battle was a disaster for the South: four thousand of its men were killed; another twenty-four thousand were wounded or missing. In the West, troops under General Ulysses S. Grant's command had been pounding Vicksburg, Mississippi. Then in June, Grant sent his men in a wide arc around the city and attacked from the east, setting the stage for a six-week siege and finally the capture of Vicksburg on July 4. Thirty thousand Confederate soldiers surrendered after Vicksburg's fall. In the long run, this victory was even more important than Gettysburg, for it gave the Union Army control of the richest plantation region in the South.

The circumstances in the weeks preceding these victories had not boded well for the Union. Following victories at Fredericksburg and Chancellorsville, Virginia, the Confederate army's premiere general, Robert E. Lee, had led his troops on the first direct invasion of northern territory. By late June 1863, the Confederate army had crossed into Pennsylvania. If Lee won a substantial victory there, European nations might be convinced to recognize the Confederacy and Peace Democrats might gain substantial support among war-weary Northerners. Union troops, forced to react to the movements of Confederate troops, pushed northwest from Washington, D.C., to remain between Lee's force and the nation's capitol. Union General Joseph Hooker, who had been in command of the Army of the Potomac since December 1862 and had faced defeat at Lee's hands before, was not eager to confront him again. As Confederate troops edged toward Gettysburg, Hooker resigned. Lincoln quickly appointed General George A. Meade as Hooker's replacement, but the new commander was only in place two days before the Battle of Gettysburg began.

Neither Lee nor Meade had set out to wage a major battle in this southern Pennsylvania town, but Lee was concerned about losing his supply lines if he moved further north, and Meade was anxious that the Confederates not gain control of the major roads that crossed at Gettysburg. So on July 1, the battle commenced, with Lee pushing Union forces to the south of town and Meade establishing his defense along a series of hills, known as Cemetery Ridge, on Gettysburg's outskirts. On July 2, Lee's attack against both Union flanks succeeded only in driving the Union forces into more secure locations. The next day, believing that Union troops were stretched thin across the ridge and were demoralized by Confederate victories, Lee ordered General George Pickett to take Cemetery Ridge by a frontal assault. Pickett's men undertook one of the most courageous attacks of the Civil War, and suffered one of its most crushing defeats. Moving across a mile of open terrain to reach Cemetery Ridge, they were mowed down by enemy fire. Some two-thirds of Pickett's division were killed or wounded in the assault, proving once again the effectiveness of the spirally grooved rifle against traditional massed infantry charges.

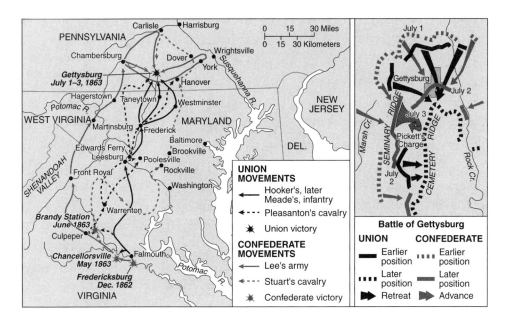

The Battle of Gettysburg. At the Battle of Gettysburg, Confederate forces threatened for the first time to gain a major victory in the North. Just before moving into Pennsylvania, the Confederate Army had won battles at Fredericksburg and Chancellorsville, Virginia. A victory at Gettysburg could have turned the tide of the war in the South's favor, and persuaded Europeans to support the Confederacy and allow the Peace Democrats to make a stronger case for ending the war without ending slavery.

The battle of Gettysburg was the bloodiest of the war. Twenty-three thousand Union soldiers were killed, wounded, or listed as missing, as well as twenty-eight thousand Confederate soldiers, more than a third of Lee's army. It was probably good that on July 4, as the weary and wounded Confederate troops retreated South, they had no idea of the events unfolding in Vicksburg, Mississippi. Exhausted and starving Confederate soldiers at Vicksburg had written a letter to their commander, General John C. Pemberton, stating: "If you can't feed us, you had better surrender, horrible as this idea is. . . ." Pemberton took their advice, and on July 4, a Union division raised the stars and stripes over the Vicksburg courthouse.

The capture of Vicksburg gave Union forces control of the Mississippi Valley. In November 1863, Grant's troops followed with a major victory at the battle of Chattanooga, Tennessee, opening up much of the South's remaining territory to Union invasion. As 1864 began, the Union had twice the forces in the field as did the Confederacy, and the southern armies were suffering from low morale, high mortality, and dwindling supplies, especially of food. While there were still difficult battles ahead for the North, the war of attrition (in which the larger, better-supplied Union forces slowly wore down their Confederate opponents) had begun to pay dividends.

The changing Union fortunes also helped turn the tide of northern public opinion, increasing support for Lincoln. At the same time, the

"A Harvest of Death, Gettysburg, July 1863."
Photographers also covered the war, following the Union Army in wagons that served as traveling darkrooms. Their equipment was bulky and the exposures had to be long, so they could not take action photographs during battle. But photography was graphic; this picture taken on the morning of July 4th showed the northern public that dying in battle lacked the gallantry often represented in paintings and prints.

Source: (Timothy H. O'Sullivan) Alexander Gardner, *Gardner's Photographic Sketch Book of the War*, Vol. 1 (1866)—Prints and Photographs Division, Library of Congress.

heroics of African-American soldiers, who in 1863 engaged in direct and often brutal combat against Confederate troops, encouraged wider support for emancipation. In addition, the Union victories at Vicksburg and Gettysburg convinced Great Britain not to recognize the Confederate States of America as an independent government.

The elections in the fall of 1864 offered the opportunity to test Northerners' support for the war and for Lincoln's policies. An aging generation of black and white abolitionists greeted the military and diplomatic developments of the previous year with enthusiasm. Many other white Northerners were now also convinced that the Republican Party could lead the Union to victory. This boded ill for the Democratic Party.

In 1864, the Democrats nominated George B. McClellan, the one-time Union commander, as their candidate for president. McClellan, running on a peace platform, managed to attract many working people who had traditionally supported the Democrats and who now bore the heaviest burden of the war. Meanwhile, Peace Democrats nominated the copperhead Clement Vallandigham for governor of Ohio, even though Lincoln had banished him from the North for his treasonous denunciations of the Union war effort.

Whatever hopes for victory these northern Democrats had were crushed when Union General William Tecumseh Sherman captured Atlanta just two months before the presidential election. Vallandigham was defeated, and Republicans won decisive elections in other key states. Lincoln's substantial victory over McClellan also won the president a clear mandate to continue the war to its conclusion. Combined with the victories at Gettysburg and Vicksburg, Lincoln's reelection raised the curtain on the most important act of the Civil War: the destruction, root and branch, of slavery.

African Americans in the War

African Americans intervened decisively in the Civil War in two interrelated ways. From January 1863 on, African-American soldiers were allowed to serve in the Union Army, and they helped ensure that nothing short of universal emancipation would be the outcome of the war. In addition, rapid Union advances after 1864 enhanced slaves' opportunities for seizing freedom, further disrupting Confederate war efforts.

When the Union finally began to recruit African Americans into the military, the response was overwhelming. By spring 1865, nearly two hundred thousand African Americans were serving in the Union Army or Navy, constituting about one-tenth of the total number of men in uniform. Nearly eighty percent of black soldiers had been recruited in the slave states. By fighting for the Union, these men struck a blow for their own and their people's freedom. George W. Hatton, a black sergeant with Company C, First Regiment, U.S. Colored Troops, captured the sense of momentous change when he observed in 1864 that "though the Government declared that it did not want Negroes in this conflict, I look around me and see hundreds of colored men armed and ready to defend the Government at any moment, and such are my feelings, that I can only say, the fetters have fallen — our bondage is over."

Of course, for many northern whites, recruitment of African Americans into the Union army was not so much a matter of giving blacks a chance to end slavery as it was a practical necessity. As Union manpower needs grew, even outright racists could support black recruitment. "When this war is over and we have summed up the entire loss of life it has imposed on the country," wrote Iowa's governor, Samuel Kirkwood, "I shall not have any regrets if it is found that a part of the dead are *niggers* and that *all* are not white men."

Recruitment policies sometimes reflected this racism. In Louisiana and Mississippi, for example, squads from the invading Union Army swept through plantation slave quarters, impressing all able-bodied men into the military. "The Soldiers have taken my husband away . . . and it is against

To Arms! A recruiting poster directed to free African Americans in Pennsylvania, 1863.

Source: Library Company of Philadelphia.

his will," protested one black women in a letter to the government. African Americans throughout the South condemned these policies, which undermined any real exercise of freedom and tore families apart. A handwritten manifesto distributed among New Orleans blacks in 1863 pointed to the similarities between "a rebel master and a Union master. . . . [The rebel master] wants us to make Cotton and Sugar . . . the Union master wants us to fight battles under white officers."

In the border states, however, slaves had less mixed feelings about recruitment into the Union Army. Because they had remained in the Union, four border slave states (Delaware, Kentucky, Maryland, and Missouri) had been exempted from the Emancipation Proclamation. But slaves in these states who enlisted in the Union Army were granted their freedom, nonetheless. Slaveholders in these loyal states did everything in their power to prevent their slaves from joining the army, including assault, harsh treatment of family members left behind, and even murder. Despite these actions, the proportion of military-age slave men in these four states joining the Union Army was staggering, ranging from twenty-five to sixty percent. By their enlistments, these men delivered to slavery in the border states a blow from which it could never recover.

African-American soldiers, wherever they were recruited, quickly distinguished themselves in battle. In May 1863, Louisiana black regiments fought with great gallantry and almost reckless disregard for their own lives in the assault on Port Hudson, downriver from Vicksburg. Two weeks later, ex-slaves helped fight off a Confederate attack at Milliken's Bend in the same region. The valor of African-American troops at Port Hudson and Milliken's Bend helped ensure Grant's victory at Vicksburg the following month.

African-American soldiers *had* to be courageous, for they faced not only death on the battlefield but torture and death if they were captured.

"Assault of the Second Louisiana (Colored) Regiment on the Confederate Works at Port Hudson, May 27, 1863." The bravery of black soldiers was extolled in the pages of *Frank Leslie's Illustrated Newspaper*.

Source: F. H. Schell, *Frank Leslie's Illustrated Newspaper*, June 27, 1863—American Social History Project.

The Confederate government threatened that any blacks taken prisoner would be treated as slaves in rebellion and be subject to execution. This policy was generally not enforced because Lincoln intervened and threatened northern retaliation. In some instances, however, as at Fort Pillow, Tennessee, in April 1864, Confederate troops cold-bloodedly murdered black Union soldiers who had surrendered. By the end of the war, thirty-seven thousand black soldiers had given their lives for freedom and the Union.

Northern whites began to acknowledge the courage of the African-American soldiers who served with them, helping to undermine the whites' ingrained racism. "The bravery of the blacks in the battle of Milliken's Bend completely revolutionized the sentiment of the army with regard to the employment of negro troops," wrote the assistant secretary of war. "I heard prominent officers who formerly in private had sneered at the idea of Negroes fighting express themselves after that as heartily in fa-

". . . I Hope to Fall with My Face to the Foe"

The heroism of black troops at Port Hudson and Milliken's Bend was only the first of a string of such examples of African-American bravery under fire. On July 18, 1863, the Massachusetts Fifty-Fourth, a regiment made up of free northern blacks and escaped slaves, unsuccessfully attacked Fort Wagner, the Confederate stronghold guarding the entrance to South Carolina's strategically vital Charleston Harbor. After the battle, Frederick Douglass's son Lewis, a sergeant in the Fifty-Fourth, wrote the following letter to his future wife.

My Dear Amelia:
I have been in two fights, and am unhurt. I am about to go in another, I believe to-night. Our men fought well on both occasions. The last was desperate—we charged that terrible battery on Morris Island known as Fort Wagoner, and were repulsed with a loss of [many] killed and wounded. I escaped unhurt from amidst that perfect hail of shot and shell. It was terrible. . . . Should I fall in the next fight killed or wounded I hope to fall with my face to the foe. . . .
My regiment has established its reputation as a fighting regiment—not a man flinched, though it was a trying time. Men fell all around me. A shell would explode and clear a space of twenty feet, our men would close up again, but it was no use we had to retreat, which was a very hazardous undertaking. How I got out of that fight alive I cannot tell, but I am here. My dear girl, I hope again to see you. I must bid you farewell should I be killed. Remember, if I die, I die in a good cause. I wish we had a hundred thousand colored troops—we would put an end to this war.

Source: Carter G. Woodson, ed., *The Mind of the Negro as Reflected in Letters Written During the Crisis, 1800–1860* (1926).

vor of it." Rank-and-file white soldiers, too, were often impressed with the valor of black troops. They gave three cheers to a Tennessee black regiment after one hard-fought battle. "One year ago the regiment was unknown, and it was considered . . . very doubtful whether Negroes would make good soldiers," a white commander noted. "Today the regiment is known throughout the army and is honored." John Evans, whose sister Jane was an ardent Copperhead back home in Ohio, was among the white officers leading black regiments. By war's end, he would be transformed into a defender of the Union, of emancipation, and even of economic and political rights for blacks.

Nevertheless, African Americans in the army felt the effects of continuing racism. They were segregated in camps, given all the most menial jobs, and treated as inferiors by white recruits and officers. "We are treated in a Different manner to what other Regiments is," a black recruit wrote to Abraham Lincoln. "Instead of the musket It is the spade and Whe[e]lbarrow and the Axe." Particularly galling was the early Union policy of paying black soldiers less than whites: $10 versus $13 per month. This inequality outraged African-American troops. Many now realized that their fight was not only against southern slavery, but against northern discrimination as well. Black soldiers who openly struggled against this discrimination, like Third South Carolina Volunteers' sergeant William Walker, paid dearly for their courage. Walker, who refused to take orders until given equal pay, was charged with mutiny and executed by firing squad in February 1864. But the protests continued. "The patient Trusting Descendants of Afric's Clime, have dyed the ground with blood, in defense of the Union, and Democracy," an African-American army corporal wrote to Lincoln. "We have done a Soldier's Duty. Why can't we have a Soldier's pay?"

In June 1864 the War Department finally equalized wages among black and white recruits. But the struggle itself had begun to transform African-American soldiers. They now understood that the battle for equality would go on after the war was over, and that it would be fought in the North as well as the South. Not surprisingly, black army veterans would lead many of the future struggles for African-American rights.

As Union soldiers, white and black, moved deeper into the South during 1863 and 1864, more and more blacks in bondage claimed their freedom. Thousands put down their tools, gathered up their belongings, and headed for the Union lines, joining those contraband who had escaped earlier in the war. Now, however, they sensed not only that they might flee to freedom, but that freedom was coming to them. A white woman noted how the Union Army's approach affected her mother's butler: "He won't look at me now. He looks over my head, he scents freedom in the air." Slaves became even less willing to work and refused to take punishment they had accepted in the past. And they began to talk openly of the advancing Union Army. "Now they gradually threw off the mask," a slave remembered of this moment, "and were not afraid to let it be known that the 'freedom' in their songs meant freedom of the body in this world."

By the end of the war, nearly a million ex-slaves, about one-quarter of the African Americans in the South, were under some kind of federal protection. This federal custody did not always mean improved conditions, however. By 1864, the military-run "contraband camps"—where ex-slaves were put to work for wages as government laborers—were badly overcrowded, disease-ridden, and poorly administered, and they created tremendous dissatisfaction among the ex-slaves. Despite those problems created by the massive influx of newly freed African Americans into Union camps and the continued exploitation of their labor, the advance of the Union Army offered the best hope for emancipation. And the heroic efforts of black soldiers alongside the critical labors of freed-women and men in the contraband camps provided the best argument for equality. The war had not only transformed the North, it had also transformed the lives and expectations of African Americans, North and South.

War Transforms the South

The destruction of slavery was the most dramatic, but by no means the only, effect the Civil War had on the South. In the South, as in the North, the war would intensify conflict between social classes, alter the role of women, increase the size of cities, and—at least temporarily—launch a small industrial revolution.

Although Southerners had gone to war to protect an essentially rural society, the war was beginning to transform that society. The growth of cities during the war years was evident throughout the South. Prior to the war, New Orleans had been the only really large southern city. Now Atlanta mushroomed, and Richmond's population more than doubled. Smaller cities also grew tremendously. The population of Mobile, Alabama, for example, climbed from twenty-nine thousand people in 1860 to forty-one thousand five years later.

Several factors encouraged the rapid growth of southern cities. One that was especially important in the capital city of Richmond was the creation of a large governmental and military bureaucracy. Hundreds of women were recruited to work in government offices there, such as the Treasury Department, a job considered sufficiently genteel to be respectable. Women, along with children and the elderly, also moved to cities during the war in hopes of finding protection from Union troops. These refugees trickled in during the early years of the war, but by 1863 and 1864, they were flooding cities like Richmond, Atlanta, and Savannah, sometimes moving two or three times in an effort to find safe haven from Union forces. Perhaps the most important contribution to urban growth was industrialization. Despite its traditional hostility to Yankee capitalists, the South was building factories. By 1863, for example, more than ten thousand people in Selma, Alabama, worked in war industries—industries that had not existed three years earlier.

Military necessity was the spur to industrialization. At the beginning of the war, the South contained only fifteen percent of the factories in the United States and produced only thirty percent of the nation's commodities. No longer able to buy industrial goods from the North and handicapped in its trade with Europe by the Union blockade, the South had either to industrialize or die. The thirty thousand troops that defended Vicksburg in 1863 depended almost exclusively on clothing and equipment manufactured in Mississippi, some of it by war widows and orphans. Factories in Natchez, Columbus, Jackson, and other southern towns turned out ten thousand garments and eight thousand pairs of shoes a week. According to a local newspaper, these factories, like those that made tents and blankets, had "sprung up almost like magic." At the base of the South's new industries was the huge Tredegar ironworks in Richmond, which, by January 1863, employed over twenty-five hundred men, black and white.

In the end, the South's industrial revolution would be aborted. The victorious Union Army destroyed factories and machinery all across the region as the war drew to a close. More important, even at its height, southern industrialization was a creation of government rather than of an independent class of industrial capitalists. The South remained only a pale reflection of industrial New England. Still, while it lasted, industrialization did trigger wider social change in the South.

One such change related to industrialization was an undermining of traditional gender roles when large numbers of southern women took jobs in the new factories. Women flocked to the mills

"Industry of Ladies in Clothing the Soldiers, and Zeal in Urging Their Beaux to Go to War." Southern white women's role in the Confederate cause as interpreted in *The South: A Tour of Battle-fields and Ruined Cities,* published a year after the end of the war.

Source: J. T. Trowbridge, *The South: A Tour of Battle-fields and Ruined Cities* . . . . (1866)—American Social History Project.

to make not only clothing but also powder, cartridges, and other armaments. When a roomful of explosives blew up in a Richmond factory in March 1863, most of the sixty-nine workers killed were women. Many women became the sole support of their families as fathers, husbands, and brothers joined the Confederate Army and received inadequate pay, died on the battlefield or of disease, or returned home as invalids.

Industrialization also led to a vast expansion of the region's small urban working class and to a new activism on its part. Led by skilled craftsmen in the war industries, workers formed unions, went on strike, and tried to put political pressure on the Confederate government. Although the labor movement was weaker and more isolated than in the North, its very existence showed how fast the South was changing in the midst of war.

With industrialization also came a breakup of the old social order—with its expected deference toward well-to-do whites—in southern cities. When Virginia legislators introduced a bill in the fall of 1863 to control food prices, a large crowd of Richmond workers expressed not only their support for price controls, but also their sense of resentment toward the rich. "From the fact that he consumes all and produces nothing," they proclaimed, "we know that without [our] labor and production the man with money could not exist." The lavish balls hosted by the wives of wealthy industrialists, planters, and politicians only reinforced the southern workers' disparaging views of their economic and political leaders. Although women like Mary Chesnut, a planter's wife and prolific diarist, insisted that such events were necessary to maintain morale and demonstrate to the Yankees that the South was far from defeated, the *Richmond Enquirer* argued that they were "shameful displays of indifference to national calamity . . . a mockery of the misery and desolation that covers the land." Yet, as the continuation of the social season in Richmond, New Orleans, Galveston, and elsewhere symbolized, the southern urban working class, despite its growing size, remained a relatively insignificant political force in the Civil War years.

Dissent and Protest in the Confederate States

Even more pronounced than the growing class antagonisms in the South was the growing popular dissatisfaction with the war itself. This dissatisfaction initially emerged when the Confederate Congress introduced a draft in April 1862, the first conscription act in the nation's history. It came a full year before the Union passed its own draft law. Concerned with the weariness of troops in the field and with Grant's successes in the West, Confederate president Jefferson Davis concluded that the war effort required conscription. Other Southerners disagreed, maintaining that the very idea of a national (that is, a Confederate) draft undermined the southern tradition of states' rights. Georgia's governor, Joseph E. Brown, for example, attempted to block implementation of the act, arguing that it conflicted with the very principles that had been used to justify secession in the first place. Many ordinary Southerners agreed. "I volunteered for six months and I am perfectly willing to serve my time out, and come home and stay awhile and go again," wrote a Georgia soldier to his family, "But I don't want to be forced to go."

As in the North, inequalities in the execution of the draft incited opposition. A draftee with money could hire a substitute to serve in his place. Morever, an October 1862 law exempted any white man owning twenty or more slaves from service in the army. This special exemption arose in part as a response to the growing unruliness of plantation slaves in the absence of overseers or owners. In practice, however, it meant that the large slave owners, the very ones who had led the South into war, had exempted themselves from dying in it.

The point was not lost on the non-slaveholding whites who fought and died for the Confederacy. Opposition to the draft grew rapidly, especially among small farmers in the mountains. "All they want is to get you pumpt up and go to fight for their infernal negroes," said one farmer from Alabama, "and after you do their fighting you may kiss their hine parts for all they care." Throughout the South, non-slaveholders used an increasingly popular phrase to describe the Civil War: "A rich man's war and a poor man's fight."

Impressment, which allowed the Confederate army to take whatever supplies it needed from farmers, planters, and other residents, also caused discontent. By 1863, the Confederate Congress had set prices for the goods taken at well below market value. A group of farmers from Floyd County, Georgia, told of "armed men traversing our 'neighborhoods' taking, in many instances, the last animal fit for beef, and insulting all who dare to claim their right to food." The farmers complained, "These seizures are not impressment, [they] are robbery." Along with a more stringent tax bill introduced the same year, impressment placed a heavy burden on the small, food-producing farm families that had the least to gain from a Confederate victory.

By taking farm products destined for the market and rerouting them to the army, impressment also brought to crisis proportions a food shortage that had been building for some time in southern cities. Although overwhelmingly agricultural, the South had built its economy primarily on cotton, tobacco, and other nonedible crops. Grain and livestock were produced in South Carolina, central Virginia, and middle Tennessee, but by 1863 the latter two areas had fallen under Union control. The absence

"Sowing and Reaping." The northern *Frank Leslie's Illustrated Newspaper* presented an unflattering portrait of southern white womanhood in a May 1863 illustration. The depiction contrasted sharply with the view promoted by plantation elites of virtuous southern white mothers and wives who obeyed and deferred to men. The panel on the left showed southern women "hounding their men on to Rebellion." The panel on the right depicted them "feeling the effects of Rebellion and creating Bread Riots."

Source: *Frank Leslie's Illustrated Newspaper,* May 23, 1863—General Research Division, New York Public Library, Astor, Lenox and Tilden Foundations.

of a good railroad or canal system in the South, coupled with the Union blockade of coastal shipping, hindered distribution of the remaining food. As the specter of starvation came to haunt the cities of the South, even people in Richmond, the capital of the Confederacy, went hungry. Richmond's urban poor had blamed their plight on the high prices charged by shippers, storekeepers, and others who profited from the food shortage. In March 1863, when government agents began using impressment to take scarce food from city markets to feed the Confederate Army, the poor found a new target for their anger.

Anger turned to protest on April 2, when a group of women, including the wives of Richmond ironworkers and mothers whose husbands were in the army, marched to the governor's mansion, demanding food. Asked by a curious passerby if the march was some sort of celebration, a young woman in the growing throng answered solemnly, "We celebrate our right to live. We are starving. As soon as enough of us get together we are going to the bakeries, and each of us will take a loaf of bread. This is little enough for the government to give us after it has taken all our men." Dozens of female clerical workers, hired by the government to serve in the Treasury Department in Richmond, gazed down through their office windows at the women demonstrators as the protest turned into a major riot. The conflict ended only when Jefferson Davis personally threatened to have troops open fire on the women. That spring, food riots broke out in Atlanta, Macon, and several other cities in Georgia and North Carolina. In Mobile, Alabama, crowds of rioters carried signs reading, "Bread or blood."

Food shortages were closely tied to another problem: inflation. Food shortages forced food prices up, while the blockade and the military focus of southern industry increased the prices of manufactured consumer goods. As the Confederate government issued more and more treasury notes to finance the war, inflation soared. By January 1864 it took twenty-seven Confederate dollars to buy what one dollar had bought in April

1861 — an inflation rate of 2,600 percent in less than three years! Southern urban workers were overwhelmed. In the aftermath of the Richmond
bread riots, a woman diarist declared, "I am for a tidal wave of peace —
and I am not alone. . . . if we can afford to give $11 for a pound of
bacon, $10 for a small dish of green corn, and $10 for a watermelon, we
can have a dinner of three courses for four persons. . . . Somebody,
somewhere, is mightily to blame for all this business, but it isn't you nor
I. . . ." The culprits, she saw, were the political leaders who had started
the war in the first place.

Small farmers and their families, too, bore a heavy burden because of
the war. On the whole, rural Southerners remained loyal to the Confederacy and its leaders, at least through the first three years of the war. Yet
eventually, taxation, impressment, inflation, and the inequities of the draft
began to take their toll. To these grievances was added the devastation of
war. Since most of the war was fought in the upper South rather than in
the cotton-growing regions of the lower South, small non-slaveholding
farmers saw their crops, their animals, and sometimes their very farms
destroyed. As the outcome of the war became clear by 1864, small farmers began to drift toward the cause of peace.

The phrase that had seemed so cynical in 1862 — "A rich man's war
and a poor man's fight" — had become the rallying cry of the southern
peace movement by 1864. The Washington Constitutional Union, a secret
peace society with a large following among farmers in Georgia, Alabama,
and Tennessee, elected several of its members to the Confederate Congress. The Heroes of America, another secret organization with strength
in North Carolina, provided Union forces with information on southern
troop movements and encouraged desertion from the Confederate Army.
By war's end, more Confederate soldiers had deserted than remained in
uniform. In some isolated mountainous regions of the South, draft
evaders and deserters formed guerrilla groups that not only killed draft
officials but actively impeded the war effort.

Many southern white women had also grown weary of the conflict.
They had provided essential services throughout the war years. Across the
Confederacy, women had organized aid societies, which provided bandages, blankets, clothing, ammunition, and food to the army. The women
also supplied hospitals, raised funds, and supported an increasing number
of widows and orphans. Individual women volunteered as nurses, served
as couriers and spies, picked up guns in defense of homes and farms, and
raised regiments. Among the slaveholding class, many mistresses became
"masters," taking over the management of fieldwork and field hands. As
one soldier wrote to his wife on a Georgia farm, "You must be a man and
woman both while the war lasts." Given the restrictions on women's activities before the war, the changes demanded by the protracted conflict

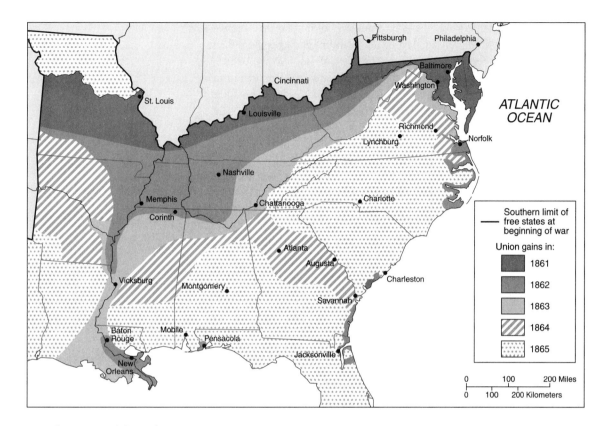

Map Legend:
— Southern limit of free states at beginning of war

Union gains in:
- 1861
- 1862
- 1863
- 1864
- 1865

0   100   200 Miles
0   100   200 Kilometers

The Conquest of the South, 1861–1865. Although Confederate forces maintained control over nearly half the area of the South until the end of the war, they did lose control over critical communication and supply lines. As Union forces penetrated the South from the North and the West, strategic railroad, communication, and shipping lines fell into Union hands. At the same time, bloody and prolonged military campaigns in many areas had devastated the Confederate Army, which was recruiting soldiers from a smaller, diminishing pool of men.

became too much to ask of more and more women. In addition to anxieties about the safety of their men on the front lines of battle, slaveholding southern white women feared the wrath of Yankee soldiers, the antipathy of slaves and free blacks, and the desperation of poor whites. They, like their countrywomen in general, found obtaining the necessities of life a heavier and heavier burden; and there was no relief, no victory, in sight.

With the military defeats of 1863 and 1864, many women who had once supported the Confederate cause began to pray for peace, whatever the price. Some even urged their sons and husbands to abandon the battlefield and return home. Though some women remained ardent supporters of secession, berating generals who ordered retreat or suffered defeat, a growing number agreed with Georgia plantation mistress Gertrude Thomas. In October 1864, she wrote in her diary, "It would be a brilliant thing to recapture Atlanta. And I wish it could be done." But she continued, "Am I willing to give my husband to gain Atlanta for the Confederacy? No, No, No, a thousand times No!"

Many white women who lived in non-slaveholding families, especially those in regions where neither slavery nor planters had ever gained a secure hold, had protested the war from the start. Women in western North Carolina, rather than aiding the Confederate cause, assisted male relatives and neighbors in avoiding recruitment and conscription agents or in hiding deserters. Like their counterparts in Missouri, families in western North Carolina fought a war within a war — in this case, one that expanded women's roles in both private and public arenas. White women in Bladen County complained about sending their sons, fathers, and husbands off to fight for the "big man's negroes," arguing that the war was begun without consulting "the voice of the people." Western North Carolina women raided grain depots, joined pro-Union organizations, and burned the property of Confederate officials. In retaliation, Confederate troops forced some women, including the Unionist farm wife Nancy Franklin, to watch as soldiers killed their sons and husbands in cold blood. Other women suspected of Unionist sympathies were reportedly beaten and whipped by soldiers or tortured to reveal the whereabouts of deserters.

In the eastern part of North Carolina, Indians fueled opposition to the Confederate cause. Native Americans from Robeson County were, like slaves, forced to labor for the Confederate Army. They used the knowledge they gained to mount guerrilla operations and pass information to Union officers. In the decades before the Civil War, whites in North Carolina had often lumped Indians with African Americans, a confusion fueled by extensive intermarriage between the two groups. The impressment of men from eastern North Carolina tribes and the deterioration of Indian communities as a result of the Confederate construction of ports and forts on their lands heightened tensions with whites. By 1864, Henry Berry Lowry, an Indian and, according to his supporters, the Robin Hood of Robeson County, had organized a band that consisted of his own people plus aggrieved whites and poor blacks to wage a guerrilla war against Confederate troops and the North Carolina Home Guard. Indians also helped guide Union General William Tecumseh Sherman and his troops — including a number of Oneidas serving with Company F — through the North Carolina swamps, helping to increase the devastation wreaked on the area but also to hasten the Union victory.

When they led the South out of the Union in 1861, slaveholders had ardently desired the loyalty of yeoman farmers. But the war seemed to have the opposite effect. Far from preserving social harmony between slaveholders and white farmers, or between slaveholders and white workers, the war undermined that harmony. Although dissent by white Southerners interfered with the war effort only to a limited extent, it did prepare the way for the much more massive disaffection of southern farmers and workers that would grow in the years to come.

The War's End

The war had now entered its final months. In March 1864, Lincoln placed General Ulysses S. Grant in charge of all Union forces. In early May, Grant embarked on a strategy that included attacks against military and civilian targets alike and that accepted huge casualties in order to achieve victory. Grant would lead his troops overland through the Wilderness, Spotsylvania, Cold Harbor, and Petersburg in attempts to take Richmond and defeat Lee's Confederate forces. General William Tecumseh Sherman, meanwhile, would push back the Confederate Army in Tennessee and invade Georgia. By August 1864, Sherman had forced Confederate General John Bell Hood's army to retreat to Atlanta, one of the most important cities in the South. Early the following month, Sherman's army swept into Atlanta, cutting the South in half. A sense of impending doom spread among those loyal to the Confederacy.

Sherman then began his now-famous three-hundred mile march across Georgia, from Atlanta to the sea, and then up through the Carolinas. His troops cut a path of destruction fifty to sixty miles wide, destroying crops, livestock, and houses before they reached Savannah in late December. Civilians—which often meant women and children—were now official targets of Union military strategists. Sherman's all-white army uprooted thousands of slaves, many of whom tried to attach themselves to the Union forces. In all, nearly eighteen thousand slaves—men, women, and children—left their plantations to join the victorious Union Army on its march to the sea. To the fleeing slaves' dismay, Sherman's troops turned many away. Marauding Confederate forces subsequently captured many of them, killing some and reenslaving others.

Sherman's callous actions caused a scandal in Washington. In January 1865, Lincoln dispatched Secretary of War Edwin Stanton to Georgia to investigate the charges. In an extraordinary meeting held in Savannah, Stanton and Sherman met with twenty black ministers to hear their complaints about mistreatment of contrabands and to inquire what, in their opinion, African Americans wanted, now that slavery was ending. The ministers spoke movingly of the war lifting "the yoke of bondage"; freed slaves now "could reap the fruit of their own labor" and, by being given land, could "take care of ourselves, and assist the Government in maintaining our freedom." Four days later, Sherman responded to the ministers' demands and issued his now-famous Field Order Number 15,

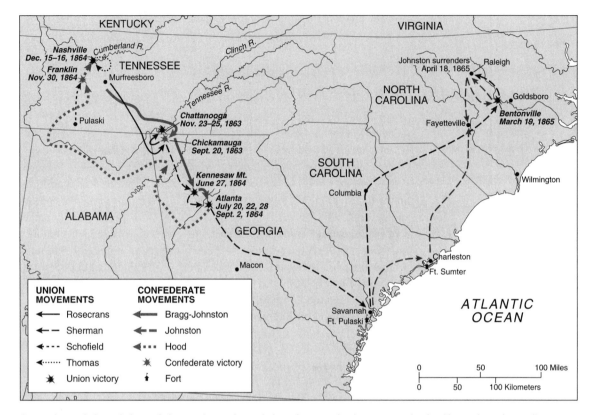

Sherman's March through the Confederacy. Sherman's March through Georgia has been memorialized in films and novels as well as in history books. The spectacular, if horrific, burning of Atlanta has gained particular attention. But for Sherman's troops, destroying Atlanta was only the beginning of a seven-month campaign of destruction that brought Union soldiers into the homes, kitchens, barns, and bedrooms of Confederate families from Atlanta, Georgia, through Columbia, South Carolina, and into Bentonville and Raleigh, North Carolina. The devastation Sherman's March wrought, moreover, was psychological as well as physical, and it drew women, black and white, into the center of the Civil War.

setting aside more than four hundred thousand acres of captured Confederate land to be divided into small plots for the freed slaves. Perhaps as significant as Sherman's order was the fact that a major official of the national government had traveled to Georgia to ask ordinary African Americans what they wanted. The Civil War had truly had revolutionary consequences.

Those consequences were far-reaching. At the end of 1864, as defeat loomed, Confederate leaders themselves began to talk of emancipating the slaves. At almost the same moment as Stanton and Sherman were meeting with African-American ministers in Savannah, Jefferson Davis was calling for the general recruitment of slaves into the Confederate

"Contrabands Accompanying the Line of Sherman's March through Georgia." This illustration from a March 1865 *Frank Leslie's Illustrated Newspaper* showed a stereotyped view of the men, women, and children who followed the Union Army's campaign through Georgia. But to northern readers, the engraving's significance may have lain in its unmistakable message about slaves' utter hatred of slavery. "The oft expressed fallacy that they preferred slavery to freedom," ran the picture caption, ". . . [has been] 'crushed to earth,' . . . never to rise again."

Source: *Frank Leslie's Illustrated Newspaper,* March 18, 1865 — General Research Division, New York Public Library, Astor, Lenox and Tilden Foundations.

Army, with their payment to include freedom for themselves and their families. The Confederate Congress ultimately passed such a law in early 1865, but it came too late to allow African Americans to actually enlist in the southern army. The event nonetheless demonstrated a startling fact: the southern planters who had seceded from the Union to protect the institution of slavery were now openly adopting policies that would inevitably destroy it. The Civil War had indeed turned southern society upside down.

In February, Sherman led his troops north from Georgia. They marched through South Carolina and North Carolina, wreaking havoc, destroying the remnants of the plantation system in the South. Meanwhile, in Virginia, Grant's troops were overwhelming Lee's besieged army in Richmond. In one of the war's most dramatic moments, seasoned African-American troops under Grant's command led the final assault on Richmond, and black soldiers were among the first Union troops to enter the capital of the Confederacy. They marched in carrying the Stars and Stripes and singing the anthem to John Brown, much to the amazement of Richmond's citizenry, black and white. Finally, in April 1865, with fewer than thirty thousand soldiers remaining under his command, Lee surrendered, signing the agreement along with Grant at the home of William McLean in Appomattox Court House, Virginia. Though two large Confederate armies continued to engage Union forces in North Carolina and west of the Mississippi, the Civil War, for all intents and purposes, had come to an end.

The legal abolition of slavery had been initiated in Washington a few months earlier. In 1864 the Republican Party had endorsed a constitutional amendment that would forever end slavery in the United States. On January 31, 1865, Congress finally passed the Thirteenth Amendment to the U.S. Constitution, prohibiting slavery and involuntary servitude anywhere within the jurisdiction of the United States.

Wartime experiences, moreover, had changed the attitudes of many Northerners, who had seen firsthand the "peculiar institution" and the suffering it inflicted on African Americans. By the end of the war, such

649

"A Jubilee of Freedom"

The meaning of freedom for enslaved African Americans can be glimpsed in the following report from Charleston, South Carolina, published in the *New York Daily Tribune* on April 4, 1865—just a few days before Lee's surrender. Charleston boasted one of the largest and most important African-American communities in the antebellum South. Two months after the Confederate Army fled, the city's black men and women organized a parade to celebrate their emancipation. The parade numbered thousands of marchers and included dramatic tableaux, banners, and songs. Like their white working-class counterparts who held similar events in the decades before the war, African Americans used such public celebrations to symbolize their deeply held beliefs and feelings.

It was a jubilee of freedom, a hosannah to their deliverers. First came the marshals and their aides, followed by a band of music; then the Twenty-First [U.S. Colored] Regiment; then the clergymen of the different churches, carrying open Bibles; then an open car drawn by four white horses. In this car there were fifteen colored ladies dressed in white—to represent the fifteen recent slave states. A long procession of women followed the car. Then the children—1,800 in line, at least. They sang:

> John Brown's body lies a mould'ring in the grave,
> *We* go marching on!

This verse, however, was not nearly so popular as one which rapidly supplanted all the others, until along the mile or more of children, marching two abreast, no other sound could be heard than

> We'll hang Jeff Davis on a sour apple tree!
> As we go marching on!

After the children came the various trades. The fisherman, with a banner bearing an emblematical device and the words, "The Fisherman welcome you, [U.S. Army] General [Rufus] Saxton." . . . The carpenters carried their planes, the masons their trowels, the teamsters their whips, the coopers their adzes. The bakers' crackers hung around their necks; the paper-carriers [had] a banner and each a copy of the Charleston *Courier;* the wheelwrights a large wheel; and the fire companies, ten in number, their foremen with their trumpets.

A large cart, drawn by two dilapidated horses, followed the trades. On this cart was an auctioneer's block and a black man with a bell represented a Negro trader. This man had himself been sold several times, and two women and a child who sat on the block had also been knocked down at auction in Charleston.

As the cart moved along, the mock-auctioneer rang his bell and cried out: "How much am I offered for this good cook? She is an excellent cook, gentlemen. . . . Who bids?"

"Two hundred's bid! Two-fifty. Three hundred."

"Who bids? Who bids?"

Women burst into tears as they saw this tableau and, forgetting that it was a mimic scene, shouted wildly:

"Give me back my children! Give me back my children!"

Source: *New York Daily Tribune*, April 4, 1865.

"Jefferson Davis as an Unprotected Female!" Union troops captured the former president of the Confederacy in May 1865. Whether Davis, who had eluded arrest for over a month, was actually wearing his wife's dress when he was caught is open to question. Nonetheless, the depiction of the captured Davis in woman's clothes was featured in many illustrations and cartoons in the northern press. These images—like earlier pictures of southern women sending their men to war and rioting— questioned the South's claims of courage and chivalry by showing its men and women reversing traditional sex roles.

Source: *Harper's Weekly,* May 27, 1865—American Social History Project.

experiences had been translated, at least in a limited way, into law. Ohio, California, and Illinois repealed statutes barring blacks from testifying in court and serving on juries. In May 1865, Massachusetts passed the first comprehensive public-accommodations law in U.S. history, ensuring equal treatment for blacks and whites in theaters, stores, schools, and other social spaces. Earlier, San Francisco, Cincinnati, Cleveland, and even New York City had desegregated their streetcars. The logic of a war against the enslavement of southern blacks was now extended to encompass at least limited rights for African Americans in the North.

Lincoln's assassination a week after Lee's surrender at Appomattox Court House seemed to mark the end of an era. Conflict between two social systems—one based on slavery, the other on free labor— had plagued the nation since the American Revolution. More than six hundred thousand Americans had died in this second revolution, in which once and for all the issue of slavery was resolved. In the process, nearly four million Americans who had once been slaves were freed. Now, in the spring of 1865, all Americans had to confront difficult new questions.

The Years in Review

1860
- Republican Abraham Lincoln elected President.
- South Carolina secedes from the Union.
- First dime novel, *Malaeska: The Indian Wife of the White Hunter* by Anna Sophia Stephens, sells more than three hundred thousand copies in its first year.

1861
- Confederacy established with Jefferson Davis as president.
- April 14: Fort Sumter surrenders to Confederate forces.
- Upper South states of Virginia, North Carolina, Arkansas, and Tennessee join the Confederacy.
- First Battle at Bull Run.
- U.S. Sanitary Commission established.
- Confederate sympathizers wage guerrilla war on Unionists.

1862

- Union Navy captures New Orleans.
- Congress approves abolition of slavery in the District of Columbia and appropriates $600,000 to assist in colonizing former slaves to Haiti, Liberia, and Central America.
- Congress passes a second confiscation bill, which declares the slaves of Confederate supporters free.
- Union commanders establish "contraband camps" for families of African-American soldiers.
- Lincoln announces preliminary Emancipation Proclamation five days after Union victory at Antietam on September 17.
- First black Union regiment organized.
- Confederate Congress passes first conscription act in American history.
- Robert E. Lee is appointed commander of Confederate Army.
- Nathaniel Allen opens first American kindergarten in West Newton, Massachusetts.

1863

- Emancipation Proclamation declares end of slavery in the rebellious states.
- North defeats South at Battle of Gettysburg (July 1 – 3); more than fifty thousand die.
- Draft riot in New York City (July 13 – 16); 105 die in bloodiest urban riot in U.S. history.
- Harriet Tubman becomes the first woman in U.S. history to lead troops into battle.
- Lincoln delivers Gettysburg Address.
- Lincoln, prompted by Union victory at Gettysburg and by lobbying of magazine editor Sarah Josepha Hale, proclaims Thanksgiving a national holiday to be celebrated on the last Thursday in October.
- The nation's first travelers' accident insurance company (Travelers Insurance) is organized; a Hartford banker pays first premium — two cents to insure him while walking home from the post office.
- "Tom Thumb" (the midget Charles Sherwood Stratton, who is 40 inches tall) marries Lavinia Warren (Mercy Bunn) who is 32 inches tall; showman P. T. Barnum, who has exploited the midget as a popular attraction since 1842, promotes the wedding, which draws huge crowds.
- James L. Plimpton wins patent for four-wheeled roller skates, which launches roller skating fad.
- Eddie Cuthbert of the Philadelphia Keystones becomes the first ballplayer to try to steal a base.
- U.S. government executes 38 Santee Sioux Indians; Lincoln approves the executions, although he angers local and military officials who want to execute 303 Sioux.
- North experiences economic boom, due to low wages and expansion of federal government power.
- Ulysses S. Grant captures Vicksburg, Mississippi.

- Battle of Chattanooga.
- Richmond women riot over severe food shortages.

1864

- Parrott arms factory strike crushed by federal government.
- Democratic Party nominates General George B. McClellan for president; he loses to Lincoln.
- African-American Union soldier William Walker is charged with mutiny and executed by firing squad after refusing to take orders until given equal pay.
- War Department equalizes pay between black and white recruits.
- Lumbee Indian Henry Berry Lowry organizes a band of Indians, aggrieved whites, and poor blacks and wages guerrilla war against Confederate troops and the North Carolina Home Guard.
- General William Tecumseh Sherman captures Atlanta and begins "March to the Sea."
- "In God We Trust" first appears on U.S. currency.
- Brooklyn Stars pitcher William A. "Candy" Cummings throws first curve ball.

1865

- Sherman issues Field Order Number 15, which sets aside over four hundred thousand acres of captured Confederate land to be divided into small plots for freed slaves.
- Thirteenth Amendment to the Constitution, which ends slavery, passes Congress, and is ratified by states.
- Lee surrenders to Grant at Appomattox Court House.
- John Wilkes Booth shoots President Abraham Lincoln while Lincoln is attending a play at Ford's Theater. Vice-President Andrew Johnson takes office when Lincoln dies the next day.

Suggested Readings

Berlin, Ira, et al., eds., *Free At Last: A Documentary History of Slavery, Freedom, and the Civil War* (1992).

Bernstein, Iver C., *The New York City Draft Riots* (1990).

Blair, William, *Virginia's Private War: Feeding Body and Soul in the Confederacy, 1861–1865* (1998).

Brumgardt, John R., ed., *Civil War Nurse: the Diary and Letters of Hannah Ropes* (1980).

Burr, Virginia Ingraham, ed., *The Secret Eye: The Journal of Ella Gertrude Clanton Thomas, 1848–1889* (1990).

Bynum, Victoria E., *Unruly Women: The Politics of Social and Sexual Control in the Old South* (1992).

Catton, Bruce, *A Stillness at Appomattox* (1954).

Degler, Carl, *The Other South: Southern Dissenters in the Nineteenth Century* (1974).

Donald, David, *Why the North Won the Civil War* (1960).

————, *Lincoln Reconsidered: Essays on the Civil War Era* (1966).

Faust, Drew, *Mothers of Invention: Women of the Slaveholding South in the American Civil War* (1996).

Fields, Barbara J., *Slavery and Freedom on the Middle Ground: Maryland During the Nineteenth Century* (1985).

Foner, Eric, *Politics and Ideology in the Age of the Civil War* (1980).

Foote, Shelby, *The Civil War: A Narrative,* 3 vols. (1958–1974).

Franklin, John Hope. *The Emancipation Proclamation* (1963).

Futch, Ovid L., *History of Andersonville Prison* (1968).

Ginzberg, Lori D., *Women and the Work of Benevolence: Morality, Politics and Class in the Nineteenth-Century United States* (1990).

Glatthaar, Joseph P., *Forged in Battle: The Civil War Alliance of Black Soldiers and White Officers* (1990).

Hahn, Steven, *The Roots of Southern Populism: Yeoman Farmers and the Transformation of the Georgia Upcountry, 1850–1890* (1983).

Hauptman, Laurence M., *Between Two Fires: American Indians in the Civil War* (1995).

Leonard, Elizabeth, *Yankee Women: Gender Battles in the Civil War* (1994).

McPherson, James M., *Battle Cry of Freedom: The Civil War Era* (1988).

Montgomery, David, *Beyond Equality: Labor and the Radical Republicans, 1862–1872* (1967).

Neely, Mark E., Jr., Harold Holzer, and Gabor S. Boritt, *The Confederate Image: Prints of the Lost Cause* (1987).

Paludan, Phillip Shaw, *"A People's Contest": The Union and the Civil War, 1861–1865* (1988).

Potter, David M., *Lincoln and His Party in the Secession Crisis* (1942).

Quarles, Benjamin, *The Negro in the Civil War* (1953).

Roark, James L., *Masters Without Slaves: Southern Planters in the Civil War and Reconstruction* (1978).

Rose, Willie Lee, *Rehearsal for Reconstruction: The Port Royal Experiment* (1964).

Silbey, Joel H., *A Respectable Minority: The Democratic Party in the Civil War Era, 1860–1868* (1977).

Stampp, Kenneth, *And the War Came: The North and the Secession Crisis, 1860–1861* (1950).

Tapert, Annette, ed., *The Brothers' Civil War: Civil War Letters to Loved Ones from the Blue and Gray* (1988).

Thorton, J. Mills, III, *Politics and Power in a Slave Society: Alabama, 1800–1860* (1978).

Trefousse, Hans L., *The Radical Republicans: Lincoln's Vanguard for Radical Justice* (1969).

Utley, Robert, *The Indian Frontier of the American West, 1846–1890* (1984).

Wiley, Bell Irvin, *The Life of Johnny Reb: The Common Soldier of the Confederacy* (1943).

———, *The Life of Billy Yank: The Common Soldier of the Union* (1952).

Woodward, C. Vann, ed., *Mary Chesnut's Civil War* (1982).

And on the World Wide Web

Edward L. Ayres, *Valley of the Shadow: Living the Civil War in Pennsylvania and Virginia*
(http://jefferson.village.virginia.edu/vshadow)

chapter *12*

Reconstructing an American Nation

1865–1877

With the Union victory in April 1865, the nation was preserved and slavery was dead. Now the United States faced a new task: healing the wounds of war and resuming life as one nation. For Benjamin Singleton, born into slavery in 1809 near Nashville, Tennessee, that task made possible opportunities that he could hardly have imagined before the war. Singleton had spent many years as a cabinetmaker in Tennessee, but in the 1850s he was sold to a planter in the Deep South. Soon after, he fled north and found refuge in Detroit, Michigan, where he operated a boardinghouse and assisted other fugitive slaves. When the Civil War ended, Singleton returned to Nashville and once again took up his occupation as a carpenter. But his hopes for a peaceful life as a free worker were dashed by the efforts of white Southerners to reassert their economic and political power in the region. As Singleton watched African Americans being forced by their old masters into wage labor or sharecropping, he came to believe that the best hope for southern blacks was land ownership, preferably in the North.

In 1871, Singleton founded the Tennessee Real Estate and Homestead Association to recruit African Americans for emigration to Kansas. Kansas held great promise for freedpeople. The state contained vast tracts of undeveloped farmland that, under provisions of the federal Homestead Act, could be obtained in 160-acre lots for $1.25 per acre. Kansas was well known as a home to ardent abolitionists, including John Brown, and as the site where the first black soldiers joined the Union Army. Postwar Kansas was dominated by the Republican Party, and the state legislature had been one of the first to ratify the Thirteenth Amendment, which ended slavery. After the Civil War, many white Quakers, Presbyterians, and Congregationalists from the Northeast, with a "sense of mission toward the Negro," had moved to Kansas, ensuring a warm welcome for freedpeople.

But by 1878, when Singleton arrived in Kansas with the first party of two hundred African-American emigrants, the railroad companies and speculators had already claimed the best land. The black homesteaders had to settle on less fertile lands, but even that proved difficult when, a year later, the Kansas Freedman's Relief Association sent four hundred new settlers to the same area to which Singleton and his followers had gone. Because plots were too small to sustain families, many of the African-American settlers ended up working for white ranchers and large

A Visit from the Old Mistress. In Winslow Homer's 1876 painting, an old plantation mistress visited the home of three of her former slaves. The coolness of the freedwomen's greeting, in sharp contrast to the reception the mistress would have received during slavery, suggests emancipation's impact on southern race relations.

Source: Winslow Homer, 1876, oil on canvas, 18 × 24 1/8 inches—National Museum of American Art, Washington, D.C.

farmers, or moving into local towns where most could find only menial employment.

The experiences of Benjamin Singleton and other African Americans who emigrated to Kansas reflect some of the difficulties generated by re-constituting a nation in the aftermath of a brutal civil war. No actions by individuals, groups, or the government could restore the nation to daily life as Americans remembered it. The country had changed, and it would continue to change, not only in the South but also in the Northeast, the Midwest, and the Far West. Over the course of little more than a decade—from 1865 to 1877—emancipation, migration, immigration, urbanization, industrialization, and economic depression would disrupt the patterns of life for millions of Americans in all regions of the country.

During this same period, the Republican Party would shift from be-ing the emancipator of the enslaved to being the guardian of economic expansion, and thus the representative and defender of northern, and at times, southern businessmen. The implications of such a shift for Ben-jamin Singleton and those who followed him were clear. Government subsidies would foster the growth of railroads and help to create the country's biggest corporations, leaving homesteaders and laborers with even less control over their lives than before. To many observers, it seemed that the Civil War had been fought to destroy the power of one ruling class, southern slaveholders, only to produce another—an indus-trial oligarchy.

All of these changes left their mark on the people who built America. In the Northeast and the South, innovations in transportation and manu-facturing fostered a shift from rural to urban life. As that shift occurred, poor whites, freedpeople, and new immigrants alike would see their dreams of land ownership wither in the shadow cast by rapidly growing cities, wage labor, and long workdays. Like the emigrants to Kansas, Americans of all colors would ride the newly laid railroad tracks west-ward, hoping for a fresh start in the vast expanses of land west of the Mississippi River. This land was not really vacant, however. Much of it was already occupied by American Indians, who would be forced to abandon their homes and livelihoods or fight a losing battle against removal. Mexi-can Americans also found themselves pushed to the margins, geographically, economically, and politically. Only the wealthiest families with Spanish surnames were accepted into western society once it be-came dominated by white Americans from back east. And as the United States extended its reach to the Pacific, Chinese immigrants found that despite the value of their labor to railroad and mining companies, they were despised as racially inferior foreigners.

As these developments unfolded, an American labor movement was being born. Workers in some areas and in some industries began to band together across differences of race and nationality to strengthen their position through collective action. It would not be an easy birth, however. Racial, ethnic, and gender conflicts continually surfaced within the labor movement as they did in society at large. Still, in 1877 the first national strike of industrial workers would spread like a forest fire across the continent.

Race and class relations in the dozen years after the Civil War were acted out against a backdrop of the longest period of uninterrupted economic contraction in U.S. history—fully sixty-five months, or over five years, beginning in 1873. The entire nation would suffer as businesses failed, banks collapsed, and massive unemployment became widespread. Many of the new-found freedoms enjoyed by African Americans in the late 1860s and early 1870s would slip away during the 1870s depression as political leaders focused their efforts on revitalizing the economy through reconciliation between North and South rather than protecting racial advancement in either region.

As the nation approached its one-hundredth anniversary, Americans would be engaged in open warfare with Indians in the West and on the brink of class warfare across the nation. And in the South, the old planter aristocracy—under the protection of the Democratic Party—would again return to power, controlling a nonslave but still exploitative system of agricultural labor. The freedpeople would be outgunned—both figuratively and literally. They were left with few alternatives. They could sustain autonomous institutions and their democratic hopes within an oppressive system. Or they could choose to migrate to other regions in search of better alternatives, but where they would also confront new problems.

Traveling. African Americans exercised their new freedom in many ways; one of them was traveling where and when they chose. This engraving was published in Edward King's *The Great South,* one of many postwar surveys of southern life. Northerners were curious to learn about the region that they had defeated in war.

Source: (J. Wells Champney [W. L. Sheppard, del.]), Edward King, *The Great South* . . . (1875)—American Social History Project.

Freedpeople Explore the Meaning of Freedom

Although the political and economic future of African Americans was undecided when the war ended in 1865, former slaves could still savor the taste of freedom on plantations and in towns and cities across the South. The meaning of freedom could be as specific and personal as the decision to take a new name, or the ability to dress as one pleased. Or it could take the form of refusing to be deferential to one's former owner. A Charleston, South Carolina, planter complained: "It is impossible to describe the condition of the city—It is so unlike anything we could imagine—Negroes shoving white persons off the walk—Negro women drest in the most outre style, all with veils and parasols, for which they have an especial fancy." In Richmond, Virginia, freedpeople held meetings without securing white permission. They also walked in Capitol Square, an

Wedding. An 1866 news engraving showed a chaplain marrying an African-American couple in the offices of the Vicksburg Freedmen's Bureau.

Source: Alfred R. Waud, *Harper's Weekly,* June 30, 1866—American Social History Project.

area previously restricted to whites, refusing to give up the sidewalks when whites approached. In countless ways, large and small, freedpeople demonstrated that the end of slavery meant the end of petty control by whites.

Freedom also meant the ability to reunite families. Thousands of freed slaves set out on searches for loved ones who had been sold away or displaced during the war's upheavals. A northern correspondent reported meeting a middle-aged ex-slave—"plodding along, staff in hand, and apparently very footsore and tired"—who had walked six hundred miles in search of his wife and children. As one government official noted, for many ex-slaves "the work of emancipation was incomplete until the families which had been dispersed by slavery were reunited." Emancipation also made it possible for thousands of couples to formalize long-standing relationships. People who had been unable to marry before the war because of separation or their master's objections, as well as those who had been allowed to "marry" only informally, sought out northern missionaries and Union officers to officially register and solemnize their unions. And many children who had lost their parents during the war were now legally adopted by relatives or friends.

The postwar years also saw a tremendous upsurge in African-American demands for education. Over ninety percent of black adults in the South were illiterate in 1860, and idealism and pragmatism now fueled their desire to secure an education. Some wanted to read "the word of God" on their own. Others wanted to read and do sums to protect themselves in a world of wage labor and signed contracts. In Savannah, a large number of black residents, led by a group of ministers, formed the Savannah Education Association in December 1864. Within three months, the association had raised nearly $1,000 and had hired fifteen black teachers, who began their work with six hundred pupils. Freedpeople built and maintained schools and hired black teachers all across the South in 1865 and 1866. Drawing on their own scarce resources, and with help from northern missionary groups and the federal government, African Americans converted some places that symbolized the oppression of slavery—such as the old slave markets in New Orleans and Savannah—into schoolhouses.

Freedpeople also quickly established churches independent of white control. Religion had been a fundamental institution before the war, but most slaves had been forced to worship in biracial churches headed by white preachers. Freedpeople now challenged white domination of biracial congregations and even replaced white preachers with black, as did the African-American members of the Front Street Methodist Church in Wilmington, North Carolina, early in 1865. When such efforts failed, as they frequently did, many black congregants pooled meager resources to construct new church buildings as permanent symbols of their desire to practice their religion as they chose. The African Methodist Episcopal (AME) Church was the most famous of these independent churches. But Baptist churches attracted the largest number of freedpeople after the war, mainly because this denomination's decentralized, democratic structure allowed for popular ministers, enthusiastic worship services, and local control of church affairs. "The Ebony preacher who promises perfect independence from White control and directions carries the colored heart at once," observed an officer of the American Missionary Association. The independent black church rapidly became the moral and cultural center of African-American life.

But maintaining black freedom demanded continual struggle, especially in rural areas still dominated by whites. On Henry Watson's plantation in Alabama, for example, workers had chosen to remain on the plantation after emancipation, but they quit work in June 1865. Watson responded in January 1866 by proposing a harsh labor contract that set up strict work rules and limited mobility. But

Reading, 'Riting, and Role Models. The textbooks prepared by northern reformers for freedmen and women contained more than practical lessons. Besides instructions on spelling, reading, and pronunciation, this page from *The Freedman's Second Reader* presented a "model" black household that exhibited the gentility of the northern middle-class ideal of the family.

Source: American Tract Society, *The Freedman's Second Reader* (1865)—American Social History Project.

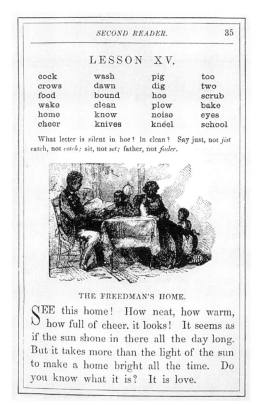

THE FREEDMAN'S HOME.

the freedpeople rejected this contract in a "most defiant manner." In disgust, Watson rented the plantation to his overseer, who leased individual plots to freed families.

That was not the only way Watson's workers demonstrated their interpretation of freedom. "The women," Watson complained in 1865, "say that they never mean to do any more outdoor work, that white men support their wives, and they mean that their husbands shall support them." All over the South, black women both embraced public efforts to gain a political voice and sought to move out of field labor and domestic service to concentrate on their own familial duties. Those employed in white households also tried to remove themselves from the dangers of sexual abuse that came with such employment. To black women these were crucial efforts to erase remnants of their slave past, but Watson saw them only as reflections of a desire to be "idle."

Other whites, long accustomed to African-American subservience, were enraged by the new assertiveness among blacks and resorted to violence to punish it. When in the course of a dispute an Arkansas ex-slave told her former white mistress, "I am as free as you, madam," the white

". . . It's Slavery Over Again"

In this speech, delivered in the summer of 1865 to the freedpeople of the South Carolina Sea Islands, Martin R. Delany, a longtime black abolitionist, a Union Army officer, and now a federal official, condemns those Northerners who purchased cotton plantations in the area, and exhorts resident African Americans to resist wage labor. Delany's words were recorded by Alexander Whyte, Jr., a white Union Army officer who thought Delany's views too radical.

I came to talk to you in plain words so as you can understand how to throw open the gates of oppression and let the captive free—In this state there are [hundreds of thousands] of able, intelligent, honorable negroes, *not an inferior race,* mind you, who are ready to protect their liberty. The matter is in your own hands. . . . I want to tell you one thing: Do you know that if it was not for the black man this war never would have been brought to a close with success to the Union, and the liberty of your race . . . ? I want you to understand that. Do you know it? Do you know it? Do you know it? (Cries of "Yes! Yes! Yes!") They can't get along without you. [Yet,] yankees from the North . . . come down here to drive you as much as ever. It's slavery over again: northern, universal U.S. slavery. But they must keep their clamps off. . . . They don't pay you enough. I see too many of you are dressed in rags and shoeless. These yankees talk smooth to you, oh, yes! Their tongue rolls just like a drum. (Laughter.) But it's slavery over again as much as ever it was.

Source: Herbert G. Gutman Archive, American Social History Project.

woman struck her. Later that day, learning that a "negro had sauced his wife," the planter horsewhipped the black woman. A North Carolina planter shot an employee, his former slave, after a quarrel over food. He later justified the murder by noting that the freedman's "language and manner became insolent." Such incidents were symptoms of the deep conflict generated between black and white Southerners by the lack of agreement on the meaning of emancipation, particularly in relation to political and economic freedoms.

Freedpeople Need Votes and Land

Most African Americans viewed political participation and land as the two most important foundations of freedom. To ensure that emancipation meant lasting change, southern blacks needed the power invested in the ballot and the independence that came with the ownership of property. Though in certain ways, this vision of political and economic independence echoed the republican ideals embraced by many white Americans, freedpeople imagined their advancement in collective as well as individual terms. Consequently, preachers, along with schoolteachers and ex-soldiers, emerged as community leaders, and churches often housed political meetings.

Religion and politics mixed easily in the first years after the war. In Richmond, Virginia, for example, African-American men, women, and children met at the four-thousand-seat African Baptist Church to discuss proposals to be presented to the 1867 state constitutional convention. With decisions made by standing votes or voice votes, women had their opinion counted alongside men. In Raleigh, North Carolina, a Freedmen's Convention was held at the AME church in 1865. Participants elected a black preacher from the North as their chairman and petitioned the white legislators to assist in the "education for our children," "protection for our family relations," and "the re-union of families which have long been broken up by war or by the operations of slavery."

Dozens of such conventions, meetings, and rallies were held across the South in 1865 and 1866. They raised demands for full civil equality and called for universal manhood suffrage, which, in the words of one delegate, was "an essential and inseparable element of self-government." In some communities, African Americans organized militia companies and "justice committees" as a way of both embracing their responsibilities and claiming their rights as American citizens. The statewide freedmen's conventions and the community-wide attempts to craft a collective agenda were the first steps that ex-slaves took toward the independent political activity that would characterize Reconstruction.

Freedpeople were equally committed to obtaining land. They realized that without property, they would remain in a fundamentally subservient position to their economically powerful former masters. "Every colored man will be a slave, and feel himself a slave," a black soldier argued, "until he can raise his own bale of cotton and put his own mark upon it and say this is mine." Freedpeople argued that they were entitled to land in return for their years of unpaid labor. "Our wives, our children, our husbands, have been sold over and over again to purchase the lands we now locates upon; for that reason we have a divine right to the land," argued freedman Baley Wyat in a speech in Yorktown, Virginia, protesting the eviction of blacks from land they had been assigned by the Union Army during the war. "And then didn't we clear the land, and raise the crops of corn, of cotton, of tobacco, of rice, of sugar, of everything? And then didn't them large cities in the North grow up on the cotton and the sugar and the rice that we made? . . . I say they has grown rich, and my people is poor."

Many southern blacks firmly believed that the federal government would help them achieve economic self-sufficiency. The Bureau of Freedmen, Refugees, and Abandoned Lands, known as the Freedmen's Bureau, was established by the Republican-dominated Congress just before the end of the war. It was created to assist freed slaves by issuing supplies, providing medical aid, establishing schools, dividing confiscated plantation lands, and supervising labor contracts. The bureau was headed by General Oliver O. Howard, and many of its nine hundred agents and officials were army officers. Committed to ideals of self-sufficiency, they did much to aid blacks with education and medical care. Blacks throughout the South turned to the bureau to protest brutality, harsh working conditions, and the hostility and inattention of local courts and police. Although such requests often went unanswered, most bureau agents were at least committed to guiding the South toward northern patterns of free labor

"Plowing in South Carolina."
An 1866 engraving portrayed a freedman as a farmer cultivating his homestead. For most mid nineteenth-century Americans, the image symbolized honesty, responsibility, and independence.

Source: James E. Taylor, *Frank Leslie's Illustrated Newspaper,* October 29, 1866—American Social History Project.

relations, what one Tennessee agent called "the noblest principle on earth."

But there were limits on how far the Bureau would go in supporting the economic interests of blacks against white planters. In fact, in many areas of the South, the Freedman's Bureau adopted extremely coercive labor policies. In the spring of 1865, for example, the Bureau issued stringent orders that restricted blacks' freedom of movement and required them to sign one-year labor contracts with large landowners. If freedmen refused to sign, the Bureau withheld relief rations. "Freedom

"The Presence of Some Authority"

Many agents of the Freedmen's Bureau viewed themselves as mediators between two deserving groups—former slaves and former masters. In the following report from October 1865, Colonel Eliphalet Whittlesey, an assistant commissioner for the Freedmen's Bureau in North Carolina, discusses the order imposed on black life and labor in the Raleigh area since his arrival the previous June when he had found "much confusion." Then freedpeople, "exhilarated by the air of liberty," had "committed some excesses" while planters, "suddenly stripped of their wealth," looked "upon the freedmen with a mixture of hate and fear."

. . . [M]any freedmen need the presence of some authority to enforce upon them their new duties. . . . The efforts of the bureau to protect the freedmen have done much to restrain violence and injustice. Such efforts must be continued until civil government is fully restored, just laws enacted, or great suffering and serious disturbance will be the result. Contrary to the fears and predictions of many, the great mass of colored people have remained quietly at work upon the plantations of their former masters during the entire summer. . . . In truth, a much larger amount of vagrancy exists among the whites than among the blacks. . . .

The report is confirmed by the fact that out of a colored population of nearly 350,000 in the State, only about 5,000 are now receiving support from the government. . . . Our officers . . . have visited plantations, explained the difference between slave and free labor, the nature and the solemn obligation of contracts. The chief difficulty met with has been a want of confidence between the two parties.

. . . Rev. F. A. Fiske, a Massachusetts teacher, has been appointed superintendent of education, and has devoted himself with energy to his duties. . . . the whole number of schools . . . is 63, the number of teachers 85, and the number of scholars 5,624. A few of the schools are self-supporting, and taught by colored teachers, but the majority are sustained by northern societies and northern teachers. The officers of the bureau have, as far as practicable, assigned buildings for their use, and assisted in making them suitable; but time is nearly past when such facilities can be given. The societies will be obliged hereafter to pay rent for school-rooms and for teachers homes. The teachers are engaged in a noble and self-denying work. They report a surprising thirst for knowledge among the colored people—children giving earnest attention and learning rapidly, and adults, after the day's work is done, devoting the evening to study. . . .

Source: *Report of the Joint Committee on Reconstruction,* 39th Cong., 1st sess. (1866).

means work," declared General Howard in 1865, and his policies ensured that African Americans would continue to work the lands of their former masters.

Despite the bureau's limitations, many southern blacks continued to believe that the federal government would confiscate the slaveowners' land and distribute it among the freedpeople. "This was no slight error, no trifling idea," reported an observer in Mississippi, "but a fixed and earnest conviction as strong as any belief a man can ever have." General William Tecumseh Sherman's distribution of confiscated plantation lands to African Americans during the final months of the war only reinforced this heartfelt conviction.

It was unclear whether President Lincoln would endorse Sherman's field order. Before he decided how to proceed, Lincoln was assassinated on April 14, 1865, by John Wilkes Booth. Vice-president Andrew Johnson, a southerner and a senator from Tennessee before the Civil War, was elevated to the presidency. By summer 1865, he had rescinded Sherman's field order.

Planters and freedpeople alike understood that black land ownership would destroy whites' basic control over labor and lead to the total collapse of the plantation economy. "The negroes will become possessed of a small freehold, will raise their corn, squashes, pigs, and chickens, and will work no more in the cotton, rice, and sugar fields," concluded one Alabama newspaper. If even a few independent black farmers succeeded, concluded one Mississippi planter, "all the others will be dissatisfied with their wages no matter how good they may be and thus our whole labor system is bound to be upset."

The labor system of the South had been based for a century and a half on the regimentation of slavery, and maintaining a similar system of regimentation became the most important objective of the planters. One northern observer concluded correctly that planters "have no sort of conception of free labor. They do not comprehend any law for controlling laborers, save the law of force." Planters looked to their state governments to secure this "law of force." Consequently, the struggle over the meaning and extent of freedom for African Americans shifted back to the arena of politics.

Reconstruction: President Johnson Versus Congress

Though Johnson was a Southerner, he had long viewed slaveholders as "an odious and dangerous aristocracy." A tailor by trade and entirely self-taught, Johnson resented the power that slaveholders held in his region, identifying personally and politically with the region's white yeoman farmers. When his state seceded from the Union, he remained in his Senate seat, the only senator from a seceding state to do so. This act led Lincoln to choose him as vice-president in 1864. But Johnson's hostility to the planters did not make him a supporter of African Americans, who he thought, as slaves, had participated with their masters in the oppression of yeoman farmers. One senator believed that he was "as decided a hater of the negro . . . as the rebels from whom he had separated."

In May 1865, with Congress in recess, Johnson calculated that he could win broad political support in the South by offering total amnesty to all white Southerners who would swear basic loyalty to the Union. Members of the social and political elite were excluded from this automatic amnesty but could petition the president for a pardon on a case-by-case basis.

For full readmission to the Union, southern states would have to hold constitutional conventions to ratify the Thirteenth Amendment, which abolished slavery; to repudiate Confederate debts; and to nullify the ordinances of secession. Once they had complied, the states were free to organize elections and reestablish governments. In the interim, Johnson appointed governors for the southern states, often conservatives hostile to the gains that African Americans had secured since 1863.

The readmission process proceeded rapidly, and elections were held in nearly all the southern states in the fall of 1865. Meanwhile, planters and Confederate officials flooded Johnson's desk with requests for pardons, most of which were granted. Although pleased to wield power over the South's former aristocrats, Johnson also believed that only planters possessed the experience, prestige, and power to "control" the volatile black population, and that they were therefore the best hope for the South's future.

Although in Johnson's view Reconstruction was now complete, many Northerners were shocked by the outcome of the 1865 elections. Ex-Confederates were elected to office in large numbers. Representatives chosen to fill vacated southern seats in Congress, for example, included the vice-president of the Confederacy, four Confederate generals, five Confederate colonels, six Confederate cabinet officers, and fifty-eight Confederate congressmen. The newly elected state governments in the South were dominated by more moderate elements, mainly former Whigs, Unionists, and "reluctant" secessionists, but these men—all white—shared with the ex-Confederates a determination to rebuild the South's plantation society.

Immediately after the elections in 1865, the new state governments began to pass legislation that became known as the Black Codes. The Codes attempted to ensure planters an immobile and dependent black labor supply through a series of rigid labor-control laws. Most states embraced the same basic provisions: a freedman found without "lawful employment" could be arrested, jailed, and fined. If he could not pay the fine, he could be hired out to an employer, who would pay the fine and deduct it from the worker's wages. In practice, this meant that any freedman who refused to work at a prevailing wage could be arrested as a vagrant. Other provisions prevented African Americans from entering any employment except domestic work or agricultural labor; allowed black children to be apprenticed to white employers for indefinite periods of time without parental consent; and set severe penalties even for petty theft. The overall effect of the Black Codes was to set the status of newly freed African Americans as landless agricultural laborers, with no bargaining power and restricted mobility.

The Black Codes were never effectively enforced, largely because of a labor shortage throughout the South and because of opposition from African-American workers and Freedmen's Bureau agents. Their passage did have one important result, however. Many members of Congress and their constituents became enraged that such laws could be passed in the first place.

In 1865, the Republicans held a three-to-one majority over Democrats in Congress. Representative Thaddeus Stevens of Pennsylvania and Senator Charles Sumner of Massachusetts led a group of Republican congressmen called Radicals, whose political roots lay in the prewar antislavery movement. They sought a vast increase in federal power to obtain new rights for the freedpeople and to revolutionize social conditions in the South.

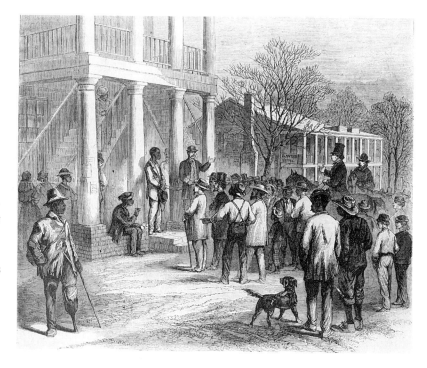

"Selling a Freedman to Pay His Fine." "Special artist" James E. Taylor toured the South for *Frank Leslie's Illustrated Newspaper* after the Civil War, when the notorious Black Codes were being enforced. He sketched this scene in front of the county courthouse in Monticello, Florida, during the winter of 1866–1867.

Source: James E. Taylor, *Frank Leslie's Illustrated Newspaper*, January 19, 1867—American Social History Project.

The Radical Republicans attracted only a minority of party members. The far greater number of "moderate" Republicans initially hoped for a rapid reunification of the nation and a return to good business relations between North and South. But, like the Radicals, they were profoundly disturbed by the return of many ex-Confederate leaders to positions of influence and the return of freedpeople to near-slave status by the terms of the Black Codes. Consequently, when Congress finally reconvened in December 1865, Radicals and moderates joined in refusing to seat the newly elected southern representatives, an act that initiated a confrontation with President Johnson and transformed the meaning of Reconstruction.

At the end of 1865, the Radicals established a joint committee of Congress to investigate the situation in the South. In the next few months, army officers, white southern Unionists, Freedmen's Bureau

---

"No Matter What His Race or Color. . . . an Equal Right to Justice"

In this speech made before the House of Representatives on January 3, 1867, Radical leader Thaddeus Stevens argued powerfully for Congress to take the initiative to impose suffrage for black men and to disfranchise all former Confederates.

We have broken the material shackles of four million slaves. We have unchained them from the stake so as to allow them locomotion, provided they do not walk in paths which are trod by white men. We have allowed the unwanted privilege of attending church, if they can do so without offending the sight of their former masters. We have even given them that highest and most agreeable evidence of liberty . . . , the "right of work." But in what have we enlarged their liberty of thought? In what have we taught them the science and granted them the privilege of self-government? We have imposed upon them the privilege of fighting our battles, of dying in defense of freedom, and of bearing their equal portion of taxes; but where have we given them the privilege of ever participating in the formation of the laws for the government of their native land? . . . Think not I would slander my native land; I would reform it. Twenty years ago I denounced it as a despotism. Then, twenty million white men enchained four million black men. I pronounce it no nearer a true Republic now when twenty-five million of a privileged class exclude five million from all participation in the rights of government. . . .

But it will be said, as it has been said, "This is negro equality!" What is negro equality . . . ? It means, as understood by honest Republicans, just this much, and no more: every man, no matter what his race or color . . . has an equal right to justice, honesty, and fair play with every other man; and the law should secure him those rights. . . .

Source: *Congressional Globe,* 39th Cong., 2nd Sess. (1867).

officials, newspaper reporters, and a handful of freedpeople testified to growing anti-Union sentiment, violence, and systematic oppression of the freedpeople. Joseph Stiles, a white Virginian loyal to the Union, complained, "It seems to me that the rapid promotion of rebels, the old politicians, to places of trust and honor, has had a great tendency to render treason popular instead of odious." Richard Hill, one of the few black witnesses, informed the joint committee that if the recently elected southern representatives were allowed to sit in Congress, "the condition of the freedmen would be very little better than that of slaves."

Such evidence convinced many congressmen that the rights of the freedpeople had to be guaranteed. The Republicans in Congress passed a bill that extended the life of the Freedmen's Bureau and expanded its powers. In addition, they passed a Civil Rights Bill that defined "all persons born in the United States (except Indians) as national citizens," granted freedpeople "full and equal benefit of all laws," and gave federal courts the power to defend their rights against interference from state governments. In this sweeping act, Congress nullified the Supreme Court's 1857 Dred Scott decision (which had denied citizenship to African Americans), undermined the Black Codes, and expanded the powers of the federal courts. Both bills marked a dramatic break from the deeply rooted American tradition of states' rights.

President Johnson was outraged and vetoed both bills as unconstitutional infringements of states' rights, arguing that the "distinction of race and color" had been "made to operate in favor of the colored and against the white race." For many Republicans, these vetoes were the last straw. "Those who formerly defended [the president] are now readiest in his condemnation," said one moderate Republican. On April 6, 1866, Congress overrode Johnson's veto of the Civil Rights Bill, the first time in U.S. history that a major piece of legislation was passed over the president's objection. Three months later, Congress also overrode Johnson's veto of the bill to extend the Freedmen's Bureau. And Congressional Republicans were prepared to go even further, preparing a constitutional amendment to guarantee civil rights to southern blacks.

The Radicals in Congress sought an even more sweeping approach. Stevens and Sumner envisioned not just civil rights for African Americans but a total transformation of southern society. Sumner wanted to make sure that blacks in the South, who were now citizens, would not be denied the right to vote for lack of property, for he believed that this was the only way to give the Republican Party political power in that region. Stevens argued that if the vote was to have any meaning, it needed to be backed up with economic power. Echoing the demands of freedpeople, he called for confiscating the land of planters and distributing it among the ex-slaves. "The whole fabric of southern society must be changed," he proclaimed, "and never can it be done if this opportunity is lost."

The best that the Radicals could achieve, however, was the Fourteenth Amendment, which passed both houses of Congress in June 1866. It granted full citizenship to African Americans and prohibited states from denying them "equal protection of the laws." This alone was a sweeping transformation of the constitutional balance of power. Until now, states had been seen as the guardians of the rights of their citizens against the power of the federal government. Now the roles were reversed.

Still, states were not required to grant black men suffrage. If they chose not to do so, however, their representation in Congress would be reduced in direct proportion. Most Republicans were not yet prepared to take the step of guaranteeing voting rights to black men, and the Radicals were forced to go along.

One group of political activists took a different position. As the members of Congress worked to pass the Fourteenth Amendment, women's rights activists called on them to place women and men—black and white—on an equal footing. Congress refused to pressure states to grant voting rights to women and instead, for the first time, inserted the word *male* into the Constitution. Although the movement for women's rights had long been intertwined with the abolitionist movement, women's rights' leaders Elizabeth Cady Stanton and Susan B. Anthony broke with the abolitionists and began searching for other allies in their drive for the vote. This would soon lead to a series of internal conflicts among suffragists and complicate their relationships with advocates of both racial equality and labor advancement.

The concerns of women suffrage advocates were overshadowed, however, by the president's appeal to southern legislatures to reject the Fourteenth Amendment. Encouraged by the president's position, all but one southern state (ironically, Johnson's home state of Tennessee) refused to ratify it. The congressional elections in the fall of 1866 thus became a referendum on the Fourteenth Amendment and Johnson's approach to Reconstruction. The Union had won the war, but it now appeared to be losing the peace.

On the eve of the campaign antiblack violence increased throughout the South. In Memphis in May and in New Orleans in July, local authorities stood by or actively participated as whites slaughtered blacks in orgies of racist violence. The Memphis riot took the lives of forty-six African Americans; the one in New Orleans left thirty-four blacks dead along with three of their white supporters. The riots revealed what one northern newspaper called "the demoniac spirit of the southern whites toward the freedmen." This naked brutality led to a stunning victory for the Republicans in the November elections. They held their three-to-one majority in Congress and retained power in every northern state as well

The Massacre at New Orleans. Thomas Nast's view of Andrew Johnson's role in the July 1866 riot.

Source: Thomas Nast, 1867, oil on canvas, 7 feet 10 3/4 inches × 11 feet 6 1/2 inches—Prints and Photographs Division, Library of Congress.

as in West Virginia, Missouri, and Tennessee. And among Republicans, the Radicals were the biggest winners.

The Republican mandate in 1866 encouraged the Radicals to present an even more sweeping agenda. They failed to achieve their most radical aim — the redistribution of land — but they did finally convince moderates to join them in embracing black voting rights. The Reconstruction Act of March 1867—the centerpiece of what became known as "Radical" Reconstruction—passed over President Johnson's veto. The Act divided the former Confederate states into five military districts. In each state there would be constitutional conventions in which blacks would participate, backed up by protection from federal troops. These conventions were mandated to draft new constitutions, which had to include provisions for African-American suffrage. Newly elected state legislatures were also required to ratify the Fourteenth Amendment as a condition for their readmission to the Union.

The guarantee of black voting rights seemed to many Americans to represent the final stage of a sweeping political revolution. In February 1867, a journalist writing in the *Nation* magazine summed up how the Civil War had revolutionized northern politics:

Six years ago, the North would have rejoiced to accept any mild restrictions upon the spread of slavery as a final settlement. Four years ago, it would have accepted peace upon the basis of gradual emancipation. Two years ago, it would have been content with emancipation and equal civil rights for the colored people without extension of the suffrage. One year ago, a slight extension of the suffrage would have satisfied it.

Now Congress had overridden a presidential veto to enshrine African-American suffrage in federal law.

African Americans Become a Political Force in Southern Politics

The onset of Radical Reconstruction inaugurated a massive and unprecedented movement of freedpeople into the political arena. They staged strikes, rallies, and protests in cities all over the South during 1867 — including Charleston, Savannah, Richmond, Mobile, and New Orleans, and small towns like Meridian, Mississippi, and Tuskegee, Alabama. The first organized expression of freedpeople's political activity was the dramatic growth of the Union (or Loyal) League. The League had started as a national organization that encouraged the Union cause during the war. With passage of the Reconstruction Act, the Union League dispatched white and black organizers all over the South to found local chapters. They functioned as political clubs, providing a civics education for new members and encouraging support for the Republican Party and its candidates.

These local chapters soon broadened the league's mission to include more aggressive economic and political activities. They helped build schools and churches, organized militia companies to defend communities from white violence, and called strikes and boycotts for better wages and fairer labor contracts. A number of local chapters were even organized on an interracial basis. One such racially mixed league in North Carolina debated questions such as disfranchisement, debtor relief, and public education, which members expected to be raised in the forthcoming state constitutional convention.

In the fall of 1867, Southerners began electing delegates to these constitutional conventions. The participation of freedpeople was truly astonishing: women joined in local meetings to select candidates, between seventy and ninety percent of eligible black males voted in every state in the South, and a total of 265 African Americans were elected as delegates. These conventions were of tremendous symbolic and practical importance. For the first time in U.S. history, blacks and whites met together to prepare constitutions under which they would be governed. The constitutions they produced were among the most progressive in the nation. They established public schools for both races, created social welfare agencies, reformed the criminal law, and drew up codes that more equitably distributed the burden of taxation. Most important of all, the constitutions guaranteed black civil and political rights, completing what one Texas newspaper called "the equal-rights revolution."

The intensity of black political participation demonstrated in these elections represented a dramatic turning point in southern politics. After 1867 the southern Republican Party won elections and dominated all of the new state governments. African Americans were prominent in many of these governments. Although they represented an actual majority only in South Carolina's legislature, blacks held a total of six hundred legislative seats in southern states. Between 1868 and 1876, southern states elected fourteen black representatives to the U.S. Congress, two black U.S. senators, and six black lieutenant governors. In addition, thousands of African Americans served local southern communities as supervisors, voter registrars, aldermen, mayors, magistrates, sheriffs and deputies, postal clerks, members of local school boards, and justices of the peace.

Unlike its northern counterpart, the southern Republican Party was, in the words of one black Republican leader, "emphatically the poor man's party." Ultimately, the party came to include poor white as well as poor black Southerners, but in 1867, nearly eighty percent of southern Republican voters were black. Because of the Republican Party's central role in emancipation and enfranchisement, freedpeople demonstrated a near fa-

White Supremacy Forever! An anti-Union League handbill, 1867.

Source: Prints and Photographs Division, Library of Congress.

"Electioneering in the South." A *Harper's Weekly* engraving captured freedmen and women actively engaged in the 1868 election campaign.

Source: W. L. Sheppard, *Harper's Weekly,* July 25, 1868—American Social History Project.

natical loyalty to it, placing the party with the church and the school as a central community institution. George Houston, an Alabama Union League organizer and Sumter County voter registrar, proudly asserted: "I am a Republican, and I will die one." The intensity of Houston's commitment echoed across the South.

Moreover, although only African-American men were granted the franchise, their wives and daughters considered voting to be a family affair. Some freedwomen continued to wield ballots in community meetings; and throughout the South, they influenced electoral politics by lobbying male voters, demanding that men use their new-found electoral rights, and accompanying voters to the polls on election day. Within African-American communities, then, the ballot was seen as a collective, rather than an individual possession, and the Republican Party as an organization to which women as well as men declared their loyalty.

Most blacks elected to state and federal offices were educated, and many were free-born. At the local level, however, black political leaders often emerged from the ranks of the freedmen. James Alston was a slave-born shoemaker and musician in Macon County, Alabama; he headed the Union League chapter in Tuskegee, became the county registrar of voters, and later represented Macon County in the state legislature. Such small-town artisans possessed the skill and independence to represent the growing African-American population in southern towns and villages as well as their rural constituents. Moreover, their work experience, which involved a good deal of contact with whites, helped them link the black community with potential white allies.

White allies were essential. Only in South Carolina and Mississippi were blacks in the majority. To survive in the South, the Republican Party would need to develop a coalition that included some white support. Most visible among the white Republicans were those labeled "carpetbaggers." Though the term was usually used by white Southerners to refer to white Northerners who came South to gain money and power, some so-called carpetbaggers were black and anything but greedy. This was true of Martin Delany, who had risen to the rank of major in the Union Army and then served in the Freedmen's Bureau before settling down in Charleston. Many white carpetbaggers were similarly sincere in their commitment to black rights and Republican government.

Even more important to Republican successes in the South were the "scalawags"—native white Southerners who supported the Republican Party. Some were wealthy planters who nevertheless believed that the South's future must be built on industrialization, urbanization, and the construction of a wage-labor system. They sought governmental support for railroads, industry, and the establishment of a stable banking and currency system. But far more of the scalawags were poor yeoman farmers from the southern mountains who had long resented the large planters' monopoly on land, labor, and political power. The southern mountain region became a stronghold of Unionist sentiment, providing a vital link to postwar Republicanism.

Economic changes added a new ingredient to yeoman support for the Republicans. Before the war, many small southern farmers had lived largely outside the market economy, producing most of their own food and necessities of life. But after the war, many of them were drawn into cotton planting, just in time to be hit hard by catastrophic crop failures in 1866 and 1867. The passage of new state constitutions containing provisions for homesteading and debtor relief led these struggling white farmers to become Union League and Republican supporters.

Most of the Republican Party's southern adherents, then, were poor people, black and white, with a strong hostility to the planter aristocracy. In Georgia, the Republicans called on "poor men" to vote for the party of "relief, homesteads, and schools"; their nominee for governor proclaimed himself the "workingman's candidate." The "bottom rail" among both races voted overwhelmingly in 1867 and 1868 to reconstruct state governments and design laws to benefit all citizens.

During their period in power—from two years in Tennessee to eight in South Carolina—these Republican governments constructed the beginnings of a welfare state for their citizens. They created a public school system where none had existed before. These schools remained segregated by race and were better in the cities than in the countryside, but there was real progress nonetheless. By 1876, about half of all southern children—white and black—were enrolled in school. And not only children went to school: a northern correspondent reported in 1873 that in

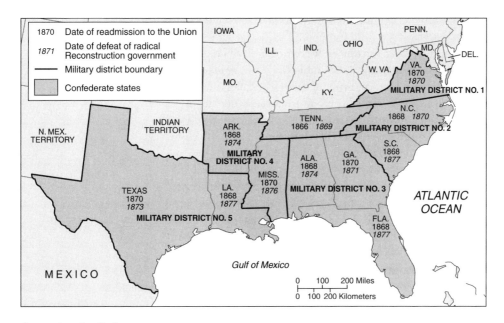

Map legend:

1870	Date of readmission to the Union
1871	Date of defeat of radical Reconstruction government
—	Military district boundary
(shaded)	Confederate states

IOWA

PENN.

ILL.   IND.   OHIO   MD.   DEL.

MO.   W. VA.   VA.
1870
1870

KY.   MILITARY DISTRICT NO. 1

N. MEX.
TERRITORY

INDIAN
TERRITORY

ARK.
1868
1874

TENN.
1866   1869

N.C.
1868   1870

MILITARY DISTRICT NO. 2

MILITARY
DISTRICT NO. 4

ALA.
1868
1874

GA.
1870
1871

S.C.
1868
1877

MISS.
1870
1876

TEXAS
1870
1873

LA.
1868
1877

MILITARY DISTRICT NO. 3

ATLANTIC
OCEAN

MILITARY DISTRICT NO. 5

FLA.
1868
1877

Gulf of Mexico

MEXICO

0   100   200 Miles
0   100 200 Kilometers

The Duration of Radical Reconstruction. The plan for Radical Reconstruction, including the establishment of military districts, was introduced in every state of the former Confederacy. But the duration of the Radical governments varied significantly. Radicals lasted only a few months in Virginia, but held on for several years in Louisiana, Florida, and South Carolina. Since African Americans had much more access to voting rights and political office under Radical governments, they had much greater opportunities to engage in formal politics in the states where those governments maintained control for the longest period.

Vicksburg, Mississippi, "female negro servants make it a condition before accepting a situation, that they should have permission to attend the night-schools."

Although school integration made little progress, several Radical governments did pass laws banning racial discrimination in other public accommodations, notably streetcars, restaurants, and hotels. Arkansas, Mississippi, Louisiana, and Florida made it illegal for railroads, hotels, and theaters to deny "full and equal rights" to any citizen. After 1869, South Carolina, with a black majority in the Republican-controlled legislature, required equal treatment in all public accommodations and in any business chartered or licensed by municipal, state, or federal authority. Much of this legislation proved unenforceable, but it showed that Republicans were committed to ending legal segregation.

Laws helping both black and white landless agricultural laborers were another achievement of Radical rule. Radical Republicans repealed the notorious Black Codes and passed lien laws that gave farmworkers (both black and white) a first claim on crops if their employers went bankrupt. South Carolina went further, creating a state Land Commission with the power to buy land and resell it to landless laborers on long-term credit. By 1876, despite this commission's initial mismanagement, fourteen thousand African-American families (about one-seventh of the state's black population) had acquired homesteads, as had a handful of white families. Other states chose to increase the property-tax rate paid by large

677

landowners, shifting some of the burden of new programs from poorer to wealthier residents.

Having local officials who sympathized with the plight of landless farmers proved especially beneficial to the rural poor. Locally elected magistrates and justices of the peace, many of them black, negotiated contract disputes between planters and laborers — and usually decided in favor of the laborers. The poor thus gained a significant bargaining edge in their economic relations with employers. This became particularly clear in the late 1860s, when the economy improved and black agricultural workers could command higher wages. With the repeal of the Black Codes by progressive legislatures, "the power to control [black labor] is gone," lamented one white southern newspaper.

Their new bargaining power enabled freedpeople to negotiate compromises with planters on how the land would be worked and who would reap its bounty. Rather than working in gangs for wages, individual black families now worked small plots independently, renting land from the planter for cash or, more commonly, for a fixed share of the year's crop. By 1870, "sharecropping" had become the dominant form of black agricultural labor, especially in the vast cotton lands. The system was a far cry from the freedpeople's objective of owning their own land, and, later in the century, it became connected to a credit system that drastically reduced the workers' economic freedom. But in the short run, sharecropping did free black workers from the highly regimented gang-labor system, allowing them a good deal of control and autonomy over their work, their time, and their family arrangements.

These very real economic and legal gains would be short-lived, however. Members and potential supporters of the southern Republican Party were constantly dissatisfied. Because the party was a fragile coalition of wealthy ex-Whigs, northern politicians, rural ex-slaves, free urban blacks, and poor white yeomen, it could not take any position without alienating at least part of its constituency. Its leaders, moreover, generally favored economic expansion. The promotion of transportation and industry, combined with large increases in state spending on schools and social programs, led to tremendous increases in taxes. This tax burden fell increasingly not only on the wealthy planters but also on poor whites who owned little property. Revelations of political corruption among southern Republicans seeking to gain from the state's involvement in capitalist enterprise also contributed to the growing disaffection of white voters. And perhaps most importantly at this critical moment, the corruption provided Northerners with a rationale for losing interest in southern affairs. In 1869, Tennessee and Virginia became the first states to return to Democratic control, in a process that conservative whites called "redemption."

Southern Democrats and the Klan "Redeem" the South

Two distinct forces converged to end Reconstruction. First, passage of the Reconstruction Act in 1867 had severely undercut the political power of the planter class, so they were now willing to turn to violence, economic intimidation, and fraud to regain political control of the South. Second, both northern public opinion and the northern Republican Party began to move sharply away from the original goals of Radical Reconstruction. Ordinary Northerners' commitment to the political and civil rights of African Americans had dwindled, as indicated by Republican defeats in a number of northern states in 1867. Delegates to New York's constitutional convention rejected a proposal to extend the franchise to African-American citizens. Editor Horace Greeley argued, "Thousands have turned against us because we propose to enfranchise the Blacks." Many Northerners, however, were simply worn out by the long military and political battles. They considered their obligation over when the most overt signs of southern intransigence were removed.

The first official sign of retreat from Reconstruction occurred on the economic front when Congress refused to confiscate planters' lands and distribute them among the freedpeople. Throughout 1867, Radicals Charles Sumner and Thaddeus Stevens had proposed a number of confiscation schemes. Echoing Thomas Jefferson, Stevens proclaimed, "Small independent landholders are the support and guardians of republican liberty." Northern businessmen and moderate Republicans effectively blocked land redistribution efforts for two reasons. First, many firmly believed that government had no business redistributing property. But second, and perhaps more important, they feared the economic consequences of ending plantation production of raw cotton, which remained the nation's single largest export and an important source of foreign revenue.

Other indications of waning enthusiasm for Reconstruction were apparent in the nation's capital. In 1868, Radical Republicans persuaded the House of Representatives to impeach the president for his efforts to subvert the Reconstruction program. In the subsequent trial before the U.S. Senate, however, moderate Republicans cast the deciding votes, narrowly acquitting Johnson. His successor, Ulysses S. Grant, elected in 1868, was a popular Union Army general. Grant's ascendancy to the presidency coincided with the emergence of a new group of moderate leaders in the Republican Party following the death of Thaddeus Stevens in 1868. These men, known as the "Stalwarts," had none of the idealism of the Radical Republicans. Their sole objective was to maintain the power of the Republican Party. By 1870, the Stalwarts had stripped Steven's Radical Republican ally, Charles Sumner, of power.

By 1872, the end of Grant's first term of office, it was starkly obvious that national Republican leaders were willing to abandon southern blacks in order to cultivate northern business support—support that depended on a revitalized southern economy. Northern politicians were prepared to retreat from social and political experimentation and leave the South's economic revitalization in the hands of the former slave owners. Now black Republican voters were the only remaining obstacle to the return of conservative white rule.

Initially, large planters tried to use their economic power to limit freedpeople's political activities. In Alabama, for example, one landlord required two black laborers to sign the following contract before he would hire them: "That said Laborers shall not attach themselves, belong to, or in any way perform any of the obligations required of what is known as the 'Loyal League Society,' or attend elections or political meetings without the consent of the employer." Without land, African Americans depended on planters for employment, but even so, this economic pressure was not very successful. Another planter complained bitterly that the Civil War and the Radical program had totally destroyed "the natural influence of capital on labor, of employer on employee." The result was that "negroes who will trust their white employers in all their personal affairs . . . are entirely beyond advice on all political issues."

When economic pressure proved inadequate, planters turned to more violent methods of intimidation. Their most important and effective weapon was the Ku Klux Klan. The Klan was, in essence, the paramilitary arm of the southern Democratic Party. Founded by Confederate veterans in Tennessee in 1866, the Klan grew rapidly after the advent of Radical Reconstruction. Although many of its rank-and-file members were poor men, its leaders were mainly prominent planters and their sons. As a white minister who traveled through Alabama reported in 1867:

Klansman. A captured member of the Ku Klux Klan posed for a Holly Springs, Mississippi, photographer after turning state's evidence in the 1871 prosecution of Klan members.

Source: Herb Peck, Jr. Collection.

They had lost their property, and worst of all, their slaves were made their equals and perhaps their superiors, to rule over them. They said there was an organization, already very extensive, that would rid them of this terrible calamity. . . . the organization of the Ku Klux Klan. . . . seemed to answer precisely the design expressed by these men.

By 1868 the Klan had a wide following across the South. The Klan terrorized individuals and freedpeople's organizations. Nightriders targeted black Civil War veterans and freedmen who had left their employers or complained about low wages. Freedpeople who had succeeded in breaking out of the plantation system and were renting or buying land on their own were in particular danger because they defied

"Dedicated to the Men of the South Who Suffered Exile, Imprisonment and Death for the Daring Service They Rendered Our Country as Citizens of the Invisible Empire." By the turn of the century, popular novels like Thomas Dixon, Jr.'s *The Traitor* transformed the bloody record of the Ku Klux Klan (now softened by the euphemism "Invisible Empire") into tales of gallantry, sacrifice, and latter-day knighthood.

Source: (L. D. Williams) Thomas Dixon, Jr., *The Traitor: A Story of the Fall of the Invisible Empire* (1907)— American Social History Project.

white supremacist assumptions of racial superiority and were often physically isolated. According to one Georgia freedman, "whenever a colored man acquires property and becomes in a measure independent, they take it from him."

Hooded Klansmen broke up meetings, shot and lynched Union League leaders, and drove black voters away from the polls all across the South. Abram Colby, a member of the Georgia legislature, testified that in October 1869 Klansmen took him to the woods and whipped him for hours when he insisted on his right to vote the Radical Republican ticket. His tormentors, he testified, included some of "the first-class men in our town. One is a lawyer, one a doctor, and some are farmers." Such targeted violence profoundly affected postwar politics. Even though African Americans fought back valiantly, the Klan succeeded in destroy-

"Kill Him, God Damn Him . . . "

The testimony offered by freedpeople at the 1871 congressional hearings on the Ku Klux Klan detailed a horrifying litany of brutal violence and intimidation. In her testimony before the committee in the courthouse in Demopolis, Alabama, Betsey Westbrook recounts the murder of her husband, Robin Westbrook.

They came up behind the house. One of them had his face smutted and another had a knit cap on his face. They first shot about seven [shotgun] barrels through the window. One of them said, "Get a rail and bust the door down." They broke down the outside door. . . . one of them said, "Raise a light." . . . Then they saw where we stood and one of them says, "You are that damned son of a bitch Westbrook." The man had a gun and struck him on the head. Then my husband took the dog-iron and struck three or four of them. They got him jammed up in the corner and one man went around behind him and put two loads of a double-barreled gun in his shoulders. Another man says, "Kill him, God damn him," and took a pistol and shot him down. He didn't live more than half an hour.

My boy was in there while they were killing my husband and he says, "Mammy, what must I do?" I says, "Jump outdoors and run." He went to the door and a white man took him by the arm and says, "God damn you, I will fix you too," but he snatched himself loose and got away.

Q—Did you know any of these men?
A—Yes, sir. I certainly knowed three.

Q—What were they mad at your husband about?
A—He just would hold up his head and say he was a strong Radical [Republican]. He would hang on to that.

_____

Source: *House of Representatives Report* 22, 42nd Cong., 2nd Sess.

"**Colored Rule in the Recon-structed (?) State.**" Although Thomas Nast was an ardent supporter of equal rights, he often resorted to racial and ethnic stereotypes in his *Harper's Weekly* cartoons. Questioning the actions of some southern black Republi-can legislators, Nast drew the figure of "Columbia," symbol of the nation, chiding: "You are aping the lowest whites. If you disgrace your race in this way you had better take back seats."

Source: Thomas Nast, *Harper's Weekly,* March 14, 1874—American Social History Project.

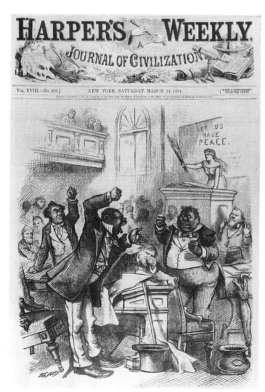

ing Republican organizations and demoralizing entire communities of freedpeople.

Despite the Republicans' general movement away from further inter-vention in the South, moderate Republicans were not yet ready to stand by and allow their party in the South to be terrorized and destroyed by vi-olence. Congress finally acted in 1869 when members approved the Fifteenth Amendment to the Constitution (ratified in 1870). This time, however, federal officials—already in retreat from Radical Reconstruction—enacted only a lukewarm compromise. The amend-ment declared that the right of U.S. citizens to vote could not "be denied or abridged" by any state "on account of race, color, or previous condition of servitude." This careful wording left open the possibility of using nu-merous "nonracial" means, such as poll taxes and literacy tests, to restrict black voting. Moreover, the amendment said nothing about the right to hold elective office.

In March 1871, a series of grisly events in Meridian, Mississippi, shocked the nation and galvanized Congress to act more forcefully. Three African-American leaders who were organizing freedpeople to resist Klan nightriders had been arrested by the Meridian authorities. Charged with delivering "incendiary speeches," they were put on trial. In the midst of the first day's proceed-ings, shots rang out in the courtroom—probably fired by a white spectator—killing two of the de-fendants and the Republican judge. In the rioting that followed, thirty African Americans were bru-tally murdered.

A joint congressional committee appointed to hear testimony in Washington and across the South (including in Meridian) listened while wit-nesses estimated that the Klan had killed or beaten thousands of freedpeople and their white allies in the previous four years. They heard the wives and daughters of black Republican leaders testify to being whipped and raped, often on more than one occasion and by more than one assailant.

Aghast at tales of such violence, and fearing the demise of the Republican Party in the South, Congress passed a series of enforcement acts im-posing harsh penalties on those who used organized terrorism for political purposes. In April the Ku Klux Klan Act became law. For the first time, certain individual crimes against citi-

zens' rights were punishable under federal law. Later in the year, President
Grant declared martial law in parts of
South Carolina, and, although having
earlier removed federal troops from
many parts of the South, he dispatched
U.S. Army units to the area. Hundreds
of Klansmen were indicted and tried by
the U.S. attorney general in South Carolina, North Carolina, and Mississippi.
The federal government had broken the
Klan's back, at least temporarily. The
election of 1872, which saw Grant re-
elected, was the most peaceful in the
Reconstruction period.

But other groups rapidly arose to
replace the KKK. The Democrats gambled that neither Congress nor the
president would act decisively to prevent further political violence and
fraud. The gamble paid off. After the
1872 election, Republicans in the
North continued their steady retreat
from the defense of African-American
rights.

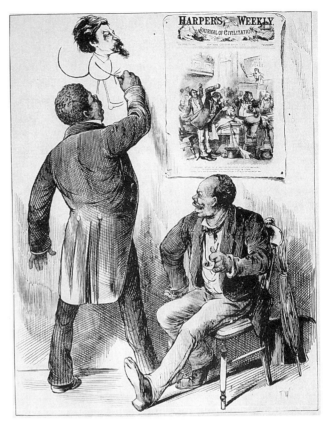

"I Wonder How *Harper's* Artist Likes To Be Offensively Caricatured Himself?" Nast got a taste of his own medicine in this answering cartoon on the cover of the *New York Daily Graphic*. Such consciousness in the press about offensive imagery would not last long. By the 1880s, with the end of a national commitment to black equality, racist stereotypes characterized most published cartoons and illustrations.

Source: Th. Wust, *New York Daily Graphic*, March 11, 1874—American Social History Project.

The national economy was expand-
ing rapidly, and the Republican Party now became closely attuned to the
interests of business. Concerned with investment possibilities in the
South, businessmen and their political allies became increasingly weary of
Reconstruction. A reunion between affluent whites North and South was
finally within reach. For African Americans and for poor whites, however,
this newfound national unity among economic and political leaders meant
that even the minimal protections afforded by federal troops and federal
laws in the late 1860s and early 1870s were gradually withdrawn. Though
small contingents of U.S. troops would remain in the South until 1877,
Northerners and the federal government were clearly in retreat from
their earlier support for Radical Reconstruction.

The large planters now engaged in their final battle to "redeem" the
South, struggling largely against freedpeople who had declining resources
and few allies. Planters initially justified their actions with overt appeals
to racism. As one planter put it, "God intended the niggers to be slaves."
But the racism of their rhetoric cloaked another motivation: planters
wanted a government-enforced system that would help them reassert

control over agricultural workers. As one leading southern Democrat declared, "We must get control of our own labor." In many areas of the South, the effort to regain control of blacks' lives and labors met substantial resistance from African Americans, sometimes in coalition with poor whites, throughout the late nineteenth century. Still, planters and their new industrial allies gradually achieved their main economic and political goals. As they did so, the South became a much more dangerous place for African Americans.

Railroads and Settlers Move West

By the late 1870s, thousands of African Americans across the South joined hundreds of thousands of new settlers — native-born and immigrant, black and white, women and men — and left their homes and headed west, hoping for a new start on the "open lands" of the frontier. Some hoped for wealth from newly discovered mineral resources. Others sought land for farming. Still others searched for a refuge from the confines and conflicts of their former homes.

The railroad turned these dreams of western expansion into a reality not only for eastern migrants but also for corporate investors. Between 1867 and 1873, railroad companies laid 35,000 miles of track in the United States — as much as was built in the three previous decades. In 1862, in the midst of the Civil War, Congress had chartered the Union Pacific and Central Pacific corporations to construct a line between Omaha, Nebraska, and Sacramento, California. In 1869, a golden spike — hammered into place with great ceremony at Promontory Point, Utah — marked the completion of the link between the Atlantic and Pacific coasts.

The largest government subsidies in U.S. history financed the railroad boom. Between 1862 and 1872, Congress gave the railroad companies more than 100 million acres of public land and over $64 million in loans and tax breaks. The Republican congressmen who had voted for these huge grants linked assistance to the railroads with what appeared to be a pathbreaking land bill, the Homestead Act of 1862. This act opened the West to settlement and allowed any adult citizen or permanent immigrant to claim 160 acres of public land for a $10 fee; final title to the land would be granted after five years of residence. Such a law had long been demanded by urban workers, and its supporters heralded it as the salvation of the laboring man. "Should it become a law," wrote the Radical Republican George Julian before it was passed, "the poor white laborers . . . would flock to the territories, where labor would be respectable, [and] our democratic theory of equality would be put in practice."

Railroad Mileage and the Expansion of Settlement, 1840–1860

State	1840 Railroads	1850 Railroads	1860 Railroads
New York	453	1,409	2,682
Pennsylvania	576	900	2,598
Massachusetts	270	1,042	1,264
New Jersey	192	332	560
Connecticut	94	436	601
Ohio	39	590	2,946
Indiana	20	226	2,163
Illinois	26	118	2,799
Missouri	. . .	4	817
Michigan	114	349	779
Iowa	. . .	. . .	655
Wisconsin	. . .	20	905
Virginia	341	341	1,731
North Carolina	247	249	937
Georgia	212	666	1,420
South Carolina	136	270	973
Maryland	273	315	386
Tennessee	. . .	48	1,253
Kentucky	32	80	534
Alabama	51	112	743
Mississippi	50	60	862
Louisiana	62	89	335
Texas	. . .	. . .	307

Railroad Mileage and the Expansion of Settlement, 1840–1860. The spread of railroads throughout the Northeast and to the West and South sometimes followed the path of settlement and at other times helped to set that path. In the years between 1840 and the Civil War rail lines were particularly important in establishing links between the Northeast and what we now think of as the Midwest. This chart illustrates the extension of railroad tracks to the West, particularly to Ohio, Indiana, Illinois, Missouri, Iowa, and Wisconsin in the mid nineteenth century. Although the railroad also reached several new southern states in this period, the number of miles of track laid was considerably smaller, especially given the size of the states involved.

Sources: *Hunt's Merchants' Magazine,* XXV (September, 1851), 381–382 for the years 1840, and 1850; and Henry V. Poor, *Manual of the Railroads of the United States for 1868–69* (1868).

A vast expansion of farming in the West did follow closely on the heels of the railroads. In the decade following the completion of the transcontinental line in 1869, Kansas attracted 347,000 new settlers. Similarly dramatic increases occurred in the other Plains states. Only about a tenth of the new farms in these years were acquired under the Homestead Act, however. The land was free, but a city laborer, making perhaps $250 a year, could not even pay the entry fees to file a claim, let alone raise the substantial funds necessary to buy farm equipment and move West. Indeed, many workingmen, including European and Asian immigrants, native-born whites, and African Americans, could only move west by signing on as laborers with the heavily subsidized railroad companies.

Instead of western lands going mainly to small farmers, some people who staked claims under the Homestead Act were in fact acquiring land for large mining and lumber companies. A provision of the act allowed homesteaders to obtain full and immediate title to their land by paying $1.25 or $2.50 an acre for it. The large companies paid individuals to stake claims, and quickly acquired huge tracts of land at prices well below their actual value. Later amendments to the act made the acquisition of western land by large companies even easier.

The dreams of small prospectors fared little better than those of small farmers. Major discoveries of silver and gold in Colorado and Nevada drew miners to the Rockies and eastern Sierras in the 1860s, as did subsequent such discoveries in Montana, Idaho, Wyoming, and the Black Hills of Dakota. Unlike the veins of precious metals found in California, however, those in Colorado and Nevada often ran three thousand feet deep or more and required extensive capital and technology to retrieve. As a result, the individual prospectors who discovered veins of gold or silver, for example, Nevada's spectacular Comstock Lode, were rapidly displaced by large mining companies. These enterprises employed large numbers of wage-earning miners in impersonal (and often unsafe) settings. The subsequent industrialization of hardrock mining, the emergence of powerful mining syndicates, and the movement of independent prospectors into the ranks of wage-earning employees stood in stark contrast to the dream of a free and open West.

Intergroup Conflict in the West

During the 1860s, the dreams of American Indians were also being destroyed. The rapid spread of railroads, mining companies, cattle ranchers, and settlers across the Plains and Far West led to violent conflict not only between tribal peoples and settlers from the East, but also among the various tribes themselves. Sioux, Pawnees, Apaches, Navajos, Comanches, and others were pushed off their ancestral lands and forced into greater contact with one another. Nomadic tribes that had survived by hunting now overran lands on which other groups had settled to farm. As more and more Native Americans were crowded into smaller and smaller areas, some tribes raided the stores and fields of others, touching off a series of mini-wars. Old animosities, like those between the Navajos and the Mescalero Apaches, flared when the U.S. government forced hostile groups to share the same reservation.

The clashes among the western tribes and between them and the growing numbers of white settlers ensured that, despite the Civil War, the federal government would bolster the U.S. Army's presence on the

Plains. Between 1860 and 1865, the number of U.S. troops stationed in the West increased from eleven thousand to nearly twenty thousand. The battle at Apache Pass in 1862 and the campaigns against the Mescalero Apaches, Navajos, and Sioux in 1863 made it clear that not even the war between whites in the East could deter the U.S. government's plans to conquer the West. In 1864, U.S. soldiers brutally attacked a sleeping village at Sand Creek, killing some two hundred Cheyennes—two-thirds of them women and children. As news of the massacre reached other Indian communities, confrontations with white settlers escalated.

In the spring of 1865, as the last battles of the Civil War were being fought, the Union Army mounted a new offensive on the Plains. Political leaders in Washington, D.C., now viewed the pacification or elimination of native societies as a necessary condition for the development of the West's economic potential. Army officers sent to quell uprisings included hardened veterans of the Civil War, men like William Tecumseh Sherman and Philip Sheridan, firm believers in the kind of total war against enemy populations that had proven so successful against the Confederacy. In 1867, Sherman assumed command of the Plains division of the U.S. Army.

Also in 1867, Congress declared a new policy, one that it claimed would assure peace. Although treaties signed in the 1830s pledged much of the Great Plains to tribal peoples, the federal government now withdrew that pledge. The remaining "free" Indians would now be concentrated on two reservations in the Dakota Territory and in the Oklahoma Territory. Officials persuaded a number of tribal leaders to accept the new terms, and many Native Americans felt that they had little choice. Iron Teeth, a Cheyenne woman, recalled that soldiers had built forts in "our Powder River country" and had resettled the Cheyennes, along with the Sioux, in "our favorite Black Hills country." But in 1874, "white people found gold on our lands. They crowded in, so we had to move out. My husband was angry about it, but he said the only thing we could do was go to other lands offered us. We did this."

Still, many Indians resisted the drastic reduction of their lands and (what was even worse) the destruction of their nomadic culture by the boundaries of the reservation system. For the next decade, these "non-treaty" Indians would conduct guerrilla warfare against white settlers and U.S. troops. Iron Teeth noted that "many Cheyennes and Sioux would not stay on the new reservations, but went back to their old hunting grounds in Montana." Attempts to circumvent the reservation system were quickly challenged, however, and in Montana, U.S. "soldiers were there to fight them."

In 1869, the same year that Sherman was appointed commander of the entire U.S. Army, the *Army Navy Journal* reported his suggestion for undermining Indian culture. Sherman remarked that "the quickest way to compel the Indians to settle down to civilized life was to send ten regiments of soldiers to the plains, with orders to shoot buffaloes until they became too scarce to support the redskins." The bison that roamed the West in giant herds provided the raw material for survival among nomadic tribes, and their destruction would be fully as devastating as open warfare. The army regularly staged buffalo "hunts" by soldiers and civilians and applauded soldiers who reported large kills. "Sportsmen," many outfitted at army posts, also killed many buffalo on the northern plains, as did railroad crews in search of meat. They were joined by professional hunters after a Pennsylvania tannery discovered in 1871 that buffalo hides could be used for commercial leather. By the mid-1880s, buffalo—once numbering over thirteen million—had all but disappeared from the Great Plains.

With the slaughter of the buffalo, the constant movement to either avoid or confront U.S. army troops, the periodic massacres of whole villages, the concentration of more diverse tribes in ever-smaller territories, and the disruption of normal patterns of hunting, agriculture, and trade, many Indian tribes found it impossible to sustain traditional ways of life. Others, whether from the confines of a reservation or amid the hazards of traveling the plains, worked hard to maintain some aspects of their religious ceremonies and kinship ties and their sense of themselves as a sovereign nation.

The pacification of the American Indians was not an easy process, and Indians fought back even when they were badly outnumbered and literally

Battle of the Little Big Horn. This is part of a series of pictures drawn by the Sioux warrior Red Horse recording his memories of the 1876 battle, drawn five years later at the Cheyenne River Agency.

Source: Tenth Annual Report, Bureau of Ethnology, #4700—National Anthropological Archive, Smithsonian Institution.

outgunned. One of the most notable stands made by Indians to fight off the U.S. Army's control of the West was that of the Sioux and Cheyennes at the Battle of Little Big Horn. In late June 1876, just a week before the nation celebrated its centennial, Sioux and Cheyenne warriors annihilated the U.S. 7th Cavalry led by General George Custer. The Sioux had

begun openly rebelling against the reservation system in the mid-1870s when white miners had rushed into the Black Hills, the site of the Sioux reservation, after gold was discovered there. Sioux chiefs Sitting Bull and Crazy Horse led the rebellious forces, and it was these that Custer was attempting to ferret out when he stumbled into a Sioux camp. Though taken by surprise, the Sioux, with the aid of Cheyennes camped nearby, won a major victory when they cut down Custer's troops and kept possible reinforcements pinned down on a nearby bluff.

The victory was short-lived, however. Facing a shortage of food and supplies and the certainty that the army would send fresh troops to avenge Custer's loss, the Sioux and Cheyennes headed north. Unable to imagine that the fault lay with Custer, many Americans who visited Philadelphia's Centennial Exposition in the summer of 1876 viewed the defeat at Little Big Horn as further evidence of Indian savagery. By the next fall, U.S. Army troops had captured the renegade leaders and defeated the Sioux and Cheyenne warriors, forcing these once powerful tribes back onto reservations that continued to shrink in the face of white interest in settling the Dakota Territory.

Another group long-settled in the West — Mexicans and Mexican Americans — also found their ways of life changed by the entrance of large numbers of eastern whites into the region. For instance, people who had once lived in settled villages along the Mexico–U.S. border were forced to migrate ever longer distances to find work. During the 1860s and 1870s, Mexican-American villagers established farming communities as far north as southern Colorado. The railroad, which had just begun to extend its reach into the Southwest in this period, offered seasonal wage labor for men in the region. This was new but also beneficial, providing a critical supplement to sheep raising and petty trade. Mexican and Mexican-American women, who had traditionally been considered economic partners with their husbands and sons and shared the use of communal pasturelands, continued to do so. Thus, although the expansion of the Anglo frontier in the 1870s transformed Mexican-American ways of life, the negative effects of wage labor and private property were not yet widespread.

More problematic in this period were the ongoing efforts by white politicians to establish racial supremacy. The majority of white settlers in the Southwest had migrated from the former Confederacy, and they sought to use the Black Codes developed in the South to restrict the political and economic rights of Mexican Americans. In addition, Mexicans and Mexican Americans had intermarried with various American Indian groups during the centuries that they occupied the same region. Those tribal peoples who had developed kinship ties with Mexican Americans may well have tried to bring members of their families into settled vil-

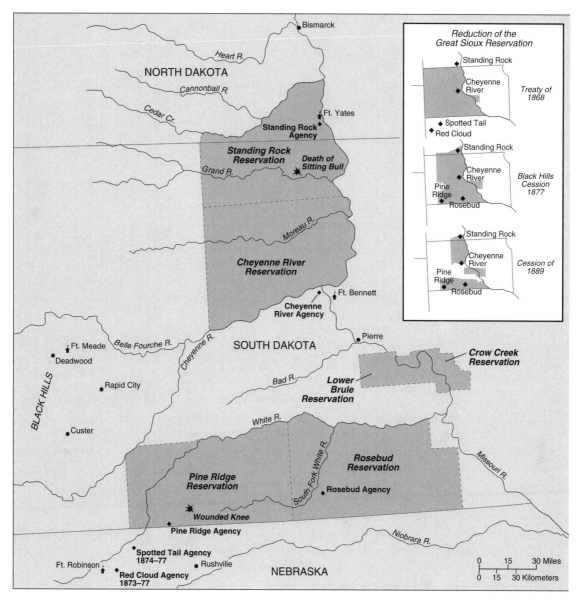

Reduction of the Great Sioux Reservation, 1868–1890. The Fort Laramie Treaty of 1868, signed between the Sioux Indians and the U.S. government, assured that the Sioux would henceforth confine themselves to a reservation, but it was a substantial reservation that covered roughly the western half of present-day South Dakota, with a portion also crossing the border into western North Dakota. With the discovery of gold in the Black Hills, however, the Sioux were forced to cede more territory, narrowing the lands on which they lived. A decade later, representatives of the federal government claimed that the Sioux, who had been forced to shift from holding land in common to individual homesteads and from hunting to farming, were not using much of the land granted them. In February 1890, President Benjamin Harrison stunned Sioux leaders by announcing a new agreement that broke up the existing reservation into six smaller reservations and opened the remaining land to white settlement. Reductions in food rations, epidemic disease, and a summer drought made 1890 one of the most devastating years in Sioux history.

Source: Robert Utley, *The Indian Frontier of the American West, 1846–1890* (1984).

lages as an alternative to reservation life. But Mexican Americans were wary of becoming embroiled in the bitter warfare between the U.S. Army and Indians. By the 1870s, forts were scattered across the New Mexico and Arizona territories, from which army units did battle with renegade members of the Comanche, Kiowa, and Apache tribes. These rebels, whose homes were in the Southwest, threatened to bring the fighting into Mexican-American villages, increasing the disruptions initiated by white settlement, mining companies, and the railroads.

Railroads Give Rise to Big Business

The railroads and mining companies that transformed life in the West also contributed to the acceleration of industrial growth after the Civil War. With this development, the ideal of economic independence and self-sufficiency became less and less possible for most Americans to attain, whatever the region in which they lived. In 1860 there had been about as many self-employed people as wage earners. Twenty years later, far more people relied on wages. The number of workers in manufacturing and construction, for instance, leapt from two million in 1860 to over four million in 1880.

The railroads were central to these changes in the very fabric of American economic life. Through large subsidies to the railroads, the federal government helped to create powerful corporations, which became America's first big businesses. The Pennsylvania Railroad, the nation's largest single business enterprise, employed over twenty thousand workers by the early 1870s. The railroads' tremendous need for capital led them to adopt and popularize a variety of modern managerial methods. One was the limited-liability corporation, which allowed wealthy men to buy shares in new ventures while limiting their financial responsibilities should the business fail. The number of railroad stockholders expanded exponentially, and large boards of directors—usually including several powerful bankers—replaced old-fashioned individual entrepreneurs. This new separation of ownership and control gave the railroad corporation a permanence and impersonality previously unknown, which made it more difficult for workers to negotiate problems and express their grievances.

The railroads were also the first businesses to face the problem of intense economic competition. This led periodically to disastrous rate wars. In some areas, groups of railroads formed "pools" that tried to end cutthroat competition by setting rates and dividing up traffic. From the standpoint of the railroad managers, pools seemed essential to survival. To others, such practices undermined the "free competition" that some lauded as the key to American prosperity. Critics contrasted the bankruptcy of some companies with the rise of a small group of wealthy entrepreneurs who had built immense personal fortunes through railroad promotion and consolidation. In the eyes of critics, these men — including Cornelius Vanderbilt, Jay Gould, Jim Fisk, and Collis P. Huntington, who together became known as the Robber Barons — symbolized all that was wrong with the capitalist system.

The industrial barons rapidly translated their economic might into political power. They hired armies of lobbyists whose activities gained the corporations even more subsidies and land grants, and protected them from regulation and taxation. "The galleries and lobbies of every legislature," observed a Republican leader, "are thronged with men seeking . . . an advantage" for one corporation or another. These developments made many Americans doubt the future of their nation. Having fought a war to destroy the power of one ruling class, Americans were now confronted with an even more powerful industrial oligarchy. This new power was emerging in part as a result of the rapid and uncontrolled development of the West, the very region where the dream of a free and open republic should have been fulfilled.

Railroads, which led in the development of big business, were vital in the opening up of the West. They developed the rapid, reliable shipping needed to create a truly national market. This in turn encouraged manufacturers to produce in larger quantities and to experiment with low-cost mass-production methods. Small producers that had once dominated local markets now faced competition from products made in distant factories and hauled to every area of the United States. By the late nineteenth century, carriages, wagons, furniture, and other wood products, as well as shoes, textiles, and cereals, were all mass-produced.

The most dynamic industries, such as oil refining, were those involved in processing the natural resources of the rapidly developing West. In 1859, Edwin Drake drilled America's first oil well in Pennsylvania. The lucrative business of refining crude oil grew up in the cities of Pittsburgh, Cleveland, and Philadelphia, leading to a period of intense competition similar to that which plagued the railroads. John D. Rockefeller, whose Standard Oil Company dominated the Cleveland petroleum business by 1871, saw this competition as the main problem facing the industry. Rather than support

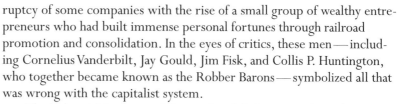

"The American Frankenstein." Inspired by Mary Shelley's novel about a man-made monster who turned upon its creator, this cartoon depicted the railroad trampling the rights of the American people. "Agriculture, commerce, and manufacture are all in my power," the monster roared in the cartoon's caption. "My interest is the higher law of American politics."

Source: Frank Bellew, *New York Daily Graphic,* April 14, 1874 — American Social History Project.

price-fixing pools like those used by railroad companies, Rockefeller brought pressure on smaller refiners to sell out to him. By the late 1870s, Standard Oil was a virtual monopoly, controlling about nine-tenths of the nation's oil-refining capacity.

Wage Earners: White Laborers, Immigrants, and Women

As industries grew, so did the need for workers. Many workers were still laboring under the old outwork system. Sewing women in particular still produced clothing the old-fashioned way in the tenements of New York, Boston, and Chicago. Feathers, paper flowers, cigars, and buttons were also made by women outworkers, and many male tailors also worked at home. Increased demand for their products did not improve the lives of these workers. For instance, between 1860 and 1880, textile manufacturers insisted that women homeworkers buy or rent newly invented sewing machines to speed up their work. Contractors then lowered the prices paid to the women for each piece of work completed, arguing that it was now easier to produce more. "I have worked from dawn to sundown, not stopping to get one mouthful of food, for twenty-five cents," reported one woman tailor in 1868.

Yet, it was the factory, not the outwork system, that represented the wave of the future. The history of shoemaking in Lynn, Massachusetts, is typical. As the national market expanded along with transportation and population, the outwork system seemed less efficient. The idea of concentrating workers in shoe-making factories was made possible with the invention of the McKay stitcher (an adaptation of the sewing machine) in 1862. The McKay stitcher allowed manufacturers to employ more machine operators, centralize production, and thus end outwork. Discipline became tighter and work was performed more steadily. "The men and boys are working as if for life," observed a visitor to one Lynn factory. So were the women and girls.

During this period, factory cities like Lynn were extremely dynamic. A similar city—Paterson, New Jersey—grew from a market town of eleven thousand people in 1850 into a sprawling city of over thirty-three thousand by 1873. Many of its residents labored in the new locomotive, iron, machinery, and textile industries. In the late 1860s, industry grew faster in smaller cities like Lynn and Paterson than in large cities like New York and Boston. Industrial centers began to emerge in the South as well. In Augusta, Georgia, for instance, textile factories provided work for growing numbers of families—especially widows and their daughters—

Changing Labor Patterns, 1810–1900. Although agriculture continued to employ the largest percentage of the workforce throughout the nineteenth century, both the number and the proportion of women and men working in manufacturing and service increased steadily. The Civil War was an important catalyst for this industrial leap, increasing the demand for guns, uniforms, shoes, and other war materiel. In the postwar period, textile factories multiplied exponentially in both the North and South. Laborers in the service category grew as a result of both the war and the expanding urban population. Government clerical workers, typists in city offices and factories, and sales clerks joined those workers long employed in service such as domestic servants and laundresses.

Changing Labor Patterns, 1810–1900

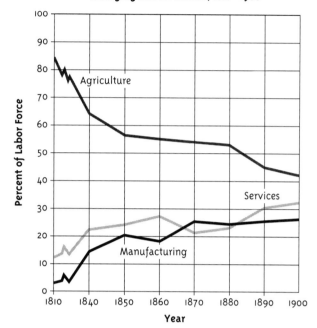

in the aftermath of the Civil War. By the 1870s, textile factories were opening across the South. Between the mid-1870s and the mid-1880s, six new mills opened in Augusta, and the work force jumped from seven hundred to three thousand workers.

Cities in the Midwest and Far West grew impressively as well. Chicago, which had thirty thousand people in 1850, became the sixth-largest city in the world a mere forty years later, with a population of over one million. Linked by the spreading railroad network, cities like St. Louis, Cleveland, and San Francisco also grew tremendously. The modern American city emerged in the first decade after the Civil War. During these years, urban services, including public transportation, professional fire and police protection, and rudimentary sanitation and health facilities were instituted.

Large cities, with their expanding services and job opportunities, also attracted the most immigrants. Immigration had slowed during the Civil War. Now it picked up again—and this time on an even more massive scale. About five million people entered the United States between 1815 and 1860, but more than double that figure came between 1860 and 1890. As before, most immigrants came from northern and western Europe, where agricultural crises prompted them to leave home. Tens of thousands of farm people, including many Irish families, emigrated to the

New World in the decade following the Civil War. Not all immigrants in this period were from the countryside, however; coal miners from Scotland and Wales and iron puddlers from England's Black Country brought crucial skills to the most dynamic sectors of the American economy. German immigrants worked as laborers and artisans in more traditional trades, such as baking, brewing, and upholstering. They made up the majority of skilled craftsmen in St. Louis, Chicago, and other large cities.

Most immigrants ended up working in the least-skilled sectors of the workforce: hauling goods on the docks and in warehouses, building roads and streetcar lines, and laboring at building sites. Most important, it was overwhelmingly immigrants who built America's railroad network — especially the Irish in the East and the Chinese in the West.

Chinese immigration to the Pacific Coast had surged in the 1850s, when famine in China had triggered an exodus to gold-rush California. By 1860, nearly one Californian in ten was Chinese. When the Central Pacific began to build the western end of the transcontinental railroad in the 1860s, it recruited laborers directly from China. Its agents paid a person's outfitting and passage in return for a $75 promissory note, the debt to be repaid within seven months of beginning work on the railroad. Eventually, over ten thousand Chinese laborers found their way to the grading camps and construction crews of the Central Pacific.

As the United States extended its reach into the Pacific — purchasing Alaska from the Russians and annexing the Midway Islands in 1867 — the Chinese continued to migrate eastward. By 1870, more than one in four people living in the Idaho Territory was Chinese. In mining towns, the Chinese had established their own communities and built businesses, particularly laundries. This allowed some to work for themselves rather than for American employers. Virginia City, Nevada, for instance, was home to about a thousand Chinese immigrants and twenty Chinese laundries in the mid-1870s. Whether working in

"On Stampede Pass, After the Blizzard." Chinese workers constructing a tunnel on the Northern Pacific Railway were photographed sometime in the 1880s as they cleared a switch-back (a zig-zag, uphill road) in the Cascade Mountains of Washington.

Source: Special Collections Division, University of Washington Libraries.

Chinese in the Western Mining Areas, 1870. The U.S. Census of 1870 demonstrated the massive impact Chinese men had on the mining industry. Their labor was critical to extracting the enormous mineral wealth of the western states and, in the process, providing raw materials for the entire nation's industrial development. Moreover, the number of miners represents only part of the contribution of Chinese immigrants to western and national economic growth. The Chinese also contributed by building railroads and serving as cooks, storekeepers, and laundry and domestic workers in the mining areas.

Source: Jack Chen, *The Chinese of America* (1980).

Chinese in Western Mining Areas (1870)

State or Territory	Total Mining Workforce	Chinese Miners	Percentage
Oregon	3,965	2,428	61.2%
Idaho	6,579	3,853	58.5
Washington	173	44	25.4
California	36,339	9,087	25.0
Montana	6,720	1,415	21.0
Nevada	8,241	240	2.9

mining towns or on the railroads, Chinese men, isolated from their families, struggled to survive the most brutal work conditions then known in the U.S. In the winter of 1866, heavy snows covered the Chinese encampments in the Sierra Nevada mountains. The laborers had to dig chimneys and air shafts through the snow and live by lantern light. Yet, under orders from Charles Crocker, who directed labor for the Central Pacific, construction continued. On Christmas Day, 1866, a local newspaper reported that "a gang of Chinamen employed by the railroad were covered up by a snow slide and four or five died before they could be exhumed." Even when not facing such dangers, the Chinese labored for ten grueling hours a day at roughly two-thirds the wages paid to whites. The experience of the Chinese in America at this time was harsher than that of other immigrant groups—partly because they were "contract laborers" and were recruited on a basis much like that of the indentured servants of the colonial period.

The dramatic increase in immigrants and wage laborers and the enormous expansion of industry and wealth raised fundamental questions about the survival of traditional American ideals and values. Business leaders and their intellectual supporters tried to create a rationale for these vast changes in American economic and social life by combining two concepts: "laissez-faire" and "Social Darwinism." The theory of laissez-faire (roughly, "leave it alone" in French) rested on a belief that economic growth could result only from the free and unregulated development of a market that was governed entirely by laws of supply and demand and kept free from any interference by government or unions. Social Darwinism applied British scientist Charles Darwin's ideas about animal evolution to social relations. Its proponents used Darwin's concept of "the survival of the fittest" to explain the economic success of a few capitalists ("the strong") and the increasing impoverishment of many workers ("the weak"). They argued that this "natural" process resulted in society's continuing improvement.

Not all Americans agreed, however. Even the generally conservative *New York Times* expressed concern in 1869 that the increasingly rapid descent of the independent mechanic to the level of a dependent wage-earner was producing "a system of slavery as absolute if not as degrading as that which lately prevailed [in] the South." In the North, the *Times* noted, "capitalists threaten to become the masters, and it is the white laborers who are to be slaves." More than any other single fact, the development of industrial capitalism and the attendant deterioration of working conditions lay behind the rapid growth of the American labor movement in the years after the Civil War.

An American Labor Movement Emerges

The period from 1866 to 1873 marked a new stage in the development of the American labor movement. A greater proportion of industrial workers joined trade unions during these years than in any other period in the nineteenth century, and more of them than ever belonged to unions that were national rather than local in scope. By 1872, there were thirty national trade unions in the United States and hundreds of local ones, with a total membership of over three hundred thousand workers.

Trade unions emerged out of a series of intense struggles with employers over wages, hours, and working conditions. The struggle to limit the length of the workday to eight hours was especially important, and it triggered union organization in a number of trades. Workers' ideological traditions also helped to spark the labor upsurge. Native-born workers, white and black, drew on the egalitarian ideals and republican traditions of the American Revolution in building both individual unions and the labor movement as a whole. German, Irish, and British immigrants carried with them from their home countries new, often radical, ideas about collective action and forms of struggle and organization, including socialism and anarchism. The melding of these traditions shaped the politics and ideology of the post–Civil War American labor movement.

The National Molders' Union, founded in 1859, became one of the most important of the new unions. The power of the iron molders lay in their possession of valuable skills in a rapidly expanding industry. Led by president William H. Sylvis, they were also deeply committed to an egalitarian legacy. "We assume to belong to the order of men who know their rights, and knowing, dare maintain them," proclaimed a Troy, New York, molder. They had organized locals during the inflation-ridden Civil War, most notably among Chicago's giant McCormick reaper workers.

Through a series of successful strikes, the union managed to maintain its members' real wages and even obtain wage increases for the unskilled workers in the plant. By 1867, the molders' union stood at the head of efforts to shorten the workday to eight hours.

Manufacturers were unified in their opposition to labor's demand. "As long as the present order of things exists, there will be poor men and women who will be obliged to work," noted one employer who wanted to maintain a ten-hour workday, "and the majority of them will not do any more than necessity compels them to do." Concerned with the effect of a shortened workday on their profits, factory owners vowed to fight the eight-hour day.

The Illinois legislature presented a major test of employers' resolve. The Republican-controlled state legislature passed a law declaring eight hours to be "the legal workday in the State," and the governor signed it into law in March 1867. Employers were required to conform to the new legislation beginning May 1. Chicago workers, elated with the seeming victory, took to the streets on May first in a spectacular parade that featured six thousand marchers, elaborate floats, and exuberant brass bands.

Chicago employers, however, encouraged by the legislature's failure to institute a penalty for noncompliance, simply refused to comply. Workers once again took to the streets, this time in a massive citywide work stoppage, to demand that the new law be enforced. The iron molders led the way, followed by German and native-born machinists, and Irish workers from the packinghouses and rolling mills. On May 6, a crowd of strikers estimated at five thousand, many of them armed, marched through the city's industrial areas, closing factories and battling police.

But the strike was badly weakened by hostility from the same politicians who had passed the law. Calling for the liberation of Chicago from "the riot element," Illinois Republicans united behind the mayor when he called out the Dearborn Light Artillery on May 7 to suppress the strik-

"Serenading a 'Blackleg' on His Return from Work."
Jonathon Lowe of *Frank Leslie's Illustrated Newspaper* sketched coalminers and their families harassing a scab during a strike in the Cherry Valley region of Ohio in 1874.

Source: *Frank Leslie's Illustrated Newspaper,* September 5, 1874—American Social History Project.

ers. Chicago workers bitterly denounced Republican politicians, but by the middle of June most workers, including the molders, had gone back to work on a ten-hour-day basis.

Coal miners also built powerful unions in this period. In 1868, miners organized an effective trade union, the Workingmen's Benevolent Association (WBA) under the leadership of Irish-born John Siney. A year later, the organization had a membership of over thirty thousand, including skilled and unskilled workers throughout the entire industry. By 1873, the Miners' National Association was formed, with Siney as its president, to organize all American mine workers into one great industrial union.

A third group, shoemakers, similarly built upon traditions of struggle going back to the early 1800s. Forced into factories, they found themselves working under a new order, subjected to the control of manufacturers and machines. In 1867, the shoe-factory workers organized the Knights of St. Crispin, named after the patron saint of shoemakers. Through a series of successful strikes, the organization grew rapidly, and by 1870 it had a membership of nearly fifty thousand—making it the largest labor union in the nation. Women shoe workers organized the Daughters of St. Crispin to fight what they called "the unjust encroachments upon our rights." Defying the wave of anti-Asian feeling sweeping the nation, the Crispins also organized a local of Chinese workers who had been brought to Massachusetts to break a shoemakers' strike in 1870.

Despite the Chinese local, however, many racial and ethnic groups organized into separate unions. Ethnic concentrations in particular industries or workplaces, as well as language and cultural differences, proved difficult obstacles for unions to overcome, assuming they were even willing to make the effort. Many foreign-born workers chose to join associations organized by their countrymen. German immigrants, for instance, created separate craft unions, trades councils, and political organizations. In 1868, Adolph Douai and Friedrich Sorge established a section of the International Workingmen's Association (IWA) in New York, and by 1872, there were twenty sections in the city.

Founded by the German revolutionary Karl Marx in London in 1864, the IWA held that "the final object" of the labor movement was "the abolition of all class rule." Members sought the abolition of private ownership of production and its replacement by a socialist system in which workers would hold political power and run the nation's industries in a democratic fashion. German-American socialists also played a leading role in the great eight-hour-day strikes. Despite the strong opposition of employers and politicians, the eight-hour strikes were partially successful, and organized socialism continued to grow.

Many native-born workers shared the German immigrants' distrust of industrial capitalism and the wage system, if not their more militant ideology. Some turned to cooperation as an alternative to capitalist competition. To circumvent the monopolistic power of the railroads, small farmers had organized in the late 1860s local chapters of the Grange, or Patrons of Husbandry, for the cooperative distribution and purchase of agricultural products. Worker-run cooperative stores and factories that mimicked the Granger co-ops appeared all over the nation in the early 1870s, particularly in textile, shoemaking, and mining towns.

Though members of the middle class hailed cooperation as an alternative to strikes, working-class cooperatives reflected a deep dissatisfaction with the unfettered individualism celebrated by industrial capitalism. Co-operation, argued one advocate, would make workers "independent of the capitalist employer," end "ceaseless degradation," and establish a new civilization in which "reason directed by moral principle" would prevail and universal brotherhood would flourish. Yet it was not clear whether such a brotherhood could bring together workers of different ethnic and racial backgrounds, different skill levels, and different sexes.

Racism and Sexism Stall the Labor Movement

The resurgence of working-class militancy was capped by the formation of a new federation of labor organizations, the National Labor Union (NLU), which covered workers in diverse craft and industrial occupations. It was founded in Baltimore in 1866 and led initially by iron molder William Sylvis. The NLU marked a new stage in labor organization: the emergence of a nationwide institution that linked wage workers together in a broad community of interest. Its vision of this community was limited in crucial respects, however. Reflecting the racism and sexism of most white workingmen, it condemned the Chinese and gave only lip service to the rights of African-American and women workers. These very exclusions gave rise to alternative movements that both expanded organization among workers and tested the power of labor unions and the law to create a more democratic society.

Many of the trade unions affiliated with the NLU had policies that excluded blacks from membership, and in 1867 the NLU ground to a halt on the question of pushing these trade unions to organize African-American workers. NLU head Sylvis took a pragmatic line, arguing that "if the workingmen of the white race do not conciliate the blacks, the black vote will be cast against them." But a committee assigned to study the question took no action, leaving black workers to fend for themselves.

African-American workers had already set about creating their own labor institutions, calling the exclusion of blacks from trade unions "an insult to God and injury to us, and disgrace to humanity." In 1869, a national convention of African Americans created the Colored National Labor Union (CNLU). Led by the onetime Baltimore caulker Isaac Myers, the new organization attracted the backing of Frederick Douglass and other prominent African Americans. The CNLU, like Douglass, also actively supported the Republican Party.

The NLU, hoping to create a working-class party, could not understand the political stance of African-American workers. White labor leaders refused to recognize that the discrimination practiced by their unions had a far greater effect than did partisan differences in hindering class solidarity. At the same time, the NLU had good reasons for doubting the efficacy of labor's alliance with the Republican Party. Focusing attention on the central demand of white workers, the NLU attempted to obtain a national eight-hour-day law for industrial workers. It ran up against intense opposition not only from employers, but also from Republicans.

Ira Steward, a self-educated Boston machinist and a leader in the eight-hour movement, met this opposition head-on. He maintained that the system of wage labor undermined freedom and civilization. Steward, a veteran of the antislavery movement, likened northern industrial capitalism to southern slavery. Just as the motive for "making a man a slave was to get his labor, or its results, for nothing," Steward argued, so "the motive for employing wage-labor is to secure some of its results for nothing. . . ." The eight-hour day, he said, would totally transform this system. As hours were shortened and wages rose, profits would decline, leading to the gradual elimination of the capitalist "as we understand him." Cooperation would replace the wage system, and "a republicanization of labor, as well as a republicanization of government" would occur.

Steward had taken a long step toward adapting the antislavery and republican traditions of thought to the new industrial age. White working people quickly took up his argument, stressing the comparison between southern racial slavery and northern "wage slavery." Only an eight-hour day would allow the worker to feel "full of life and enjoyment," asserted a Massachusetts bootmaker, because "the man is no longer a slave, but a man."

Drawing this parallel to slavery, however, did not necessarily put white workers on the side of black workers. Although some farsighted leaders, like William Sylvis, recognized the potential power of interracial coalitions, any calls for unity were drowned out by those who viewed unionization as a right for whites only. Discrimination against Chinese workers was especially intense. Almost every important native-born labor leader opposed Chinese immigration, and advocated, instead, their absolute exclusion. The primary argument was that employers would use "docile" Chinese labor to lower the standard of living of U.S. workers and take the Americans' jobs away.

The "docility" of the Chinese, like the penchant for strikebreaking among blacks, was largely mythical. In the spring of 1867, for example, thousands of Chinese railroad workers in the Sierras went on strike, demanding higher wages and an eight-hour day. Management condemned the strike as a "conspiracy," and it considered the possibility of transporting ten thousand southern blacks to replace the Chinese. But Charles Crocker, who managed labor for the Central Pacific Railroad, developed a more powerful strategy, similar to Sherman's policy of slaughtering the buffalo to defeat American Indians. Crocker decided to starve the workers into submission. "I stopped the provisions on them, stopped the butchers from butchering, and used [other] such coercive measures," Crocker bragged. The strike was broken within a week.

Most white workers argued for the exclusion of the Chinese from jobs on the same grounds that they argued against African Americans — economic competition. In most cases, the issue of competition was largely illusory, since Chinese immigrants gravitated to the lowest-paying jobs at the bottom of the employment ladder — the occupations largely abandoned by whites. This fact mattered little, however, since the underlying hostility toward the Chinese had as its basis the same deep belief in white racial supremacy that shaped attitudes toward African Americans. Labor editor John Swinton, a humane working-class leader in other ways, spoke for many workers when he argued that the "Mongolian type of humanity is an inferior type — inferior in organic structure, in vital force or physical energy, and in the constitutional conditions of development." Such racial classification schemes were pervasive in the postwar period, when educated middle-class Americans used Social Darwinism and other pseudoscientific theories to justify their belief in the inevitability of their social and political dominance. Anti-Chinese sentiment was equally pervasive among white working-class labor leaders.

Opposition to the organization of working women — even white, native-born, working women — was also strong. Nonetheless, wage-earning women, who formed nearly one-quarter of the total nonfarm labor force in 1870, used a variety of tactics to defend and improve their conditions and wages during this period. In 1869, for example, sewing women in Boston petitioned the Massachusetts legislature to provide them with public housing. Although the legislature ignored the request, the petition broke new ground in demanding state intervention to remedy oppressive working conditions.

Many working women, however, turned to trade unions rather than the state to gain protection. Female cigarmakers, umbrella-sewers, and textile and laundry workers all formed short-lived local unions in these years, but they received little support from white male workers. Of the thirty national unions that existed in the early 1870s, only two — the cigarmakers and the printers — admitted women into their ranks. Most organized workingmen believed that the presence of women in the paid labor force was either a temporary phenomenon or, like the employment of African Americans and Chinese immigrants, part of a strategy of employers to lower wages. Clinging to the myth that "all men support all women," they kept women out of their unions in an effort to keep them out of their trades.

This opposition came to a head in 1869, when the NLU, which initially welcomed women to its ranks, expelled women's rights advocate Susan B. Anthony. The conflict behind the expulsion was complex, and stemmed in part from Anthony's efforts to train female workers to take the jobs of striking New York printers, who at the time excluded women from apprenticeships in their trade. But many workingmen opposed Anthony because her vision of total female equality — including women's right to vote — threatened male domination. In arguing for Anthony's expulsion, one NLU member noted, "The lady goes in for taking women away from the washtub, and in the name of heaven who is going there if they don't? I believe in woman doing her work and men marrying them, and supporting them."

Women's rights advocates shared the interest of Boston's sewing workers in using state power to improve the lives of women. They argued that the Reconstruction-era amendments to the U.S. Constitution could be interpreted in broad and inclusive ways that would gain rights for women without limiting the rights of African Americans or of workers. Known as the New Departure, this legal strategy was developed by a husband and wife team of Missouri suffragists, Francis and Virginia Minor, in 1869. The Minors emphasized the new idea of federal power as positive and as supportive of individual rights broadly defined.

The argument for universal suffrage backed up by the power of the national government was tested by hundreds of women. Between 1870 and 1872, freedwomen, female antislavery veterans, women taxpayers, and women wage-earners attempted to register and vote in South Carolina coastal communities; in Vineland, New Jersey; Detroit, Michigan; St. Louis, Missouri; Washington, D.C.; Santa Cruz, California; and dozens of other cities and towns. These attempts to vote led to a number of arrests, the most famous being that of Susan B. Anthony in Rochester, New York, in 1872. Anthony's case came to trial in a federal district court at Canandaigua, New York, in the spring of 1873. The judgment — rendered by a judge rather than a jury — repudiated an inclusive interpretation of the Reconstruction amendments.

"**A lady delegate reading her argument in favor of woman's voting, on the basis of the Fourteenth and Fifteenth Constitutional Amendments.**" A delegation of women, including Victoria Woodhull (standing) and Elizabeth Cady Stanton (seated behind her), argued for voting rights before the Judiciary Committee of the House of Representatives in January 1871.

Source: *Frank Leslie's Illustrated Newspaper,* February 4, 1871—American Social History Project.

This narrowing of the U.S. Constitution had important implications for African Americans and workers as well as for women. In 1873, for example, the U.S. Supreme Court upheld both the right of Illinois to bar women from practicing law in the state (*Bradwell* v. *Illinois*) and the right of Louisiana to regulate the work of butchers (the *Slaughterhouse* cases). The two opinions, handed down on the same day, assured that the federal powers granted under the Fourteenth Amendment would not be employed to advance the interests of either women or workers. By 1875, the rights accorded under the Fifteenth Amendment would be similarly narrowed, with the U.S. Supreme Court arguing, in a case brought by Virginia Minor (*Minor* v. *Happersett*), that the Constitution "does not confer the right of suffrage upon any one." Shortly afterward, the Court used this logic in *United States* v. *Reese* and *United States* v. *Cruikshank* to reject the claims of two freedmen who sought protection of their political rights under the Fifteenth Amendment.

The judicial redress that women, workers, and African Americans sought in the early 1870s demonstrated that members of these groups viewed both the federal government and union organization as avenues for improving the lives of their families and communities. The rulings that the courts handed down, reinforced by Congress's retreat from the egalitarian implications of Reconstruction-era laws, belied these hopes to forge broad alliances in the fight for equal rights. The failure of postwar coalitions across racial, gender, or class lines haunted efforts at collective action for decades to come.

The Panic of 1873 and Its Effects

But working people in America faced an even more immediate challenge in the mid-1870s: five years of serious deflation and the longest and most severe depression of the century. An economic crisis of such magnitude not only dealt a heavy blow to labor activism but also delivered a fatal blow to Reconstruction. In the South, the depression drove many black landowners and renters back into the ranks of laborers, sharply reduced wage levels for African Americans, and helped transform sharecropping into a system of peonage. In the North, the depression encouraged northern businessmen and workers to focus their attention on problems at home and away from divisive racial politics in the South.

The crisis, which began on September 18, 1873, was triggered by the collapse of Jay Cooke and Company, one of the country's great investment houses. In a matter of days, panic led to runs on a number of banks across the country, and, for the first time, the New York Stock Exchange closed. By 1874, construction of railroads and buildings ground to a halt, and tens of thousands of businesses, large and small, went bankrupt. Two years later, in 1876, half the nation's railroads had defaulted on their bonds, and half the iron furnaces were idle. Those businesses that survived did so by engaging in cutthroat competition to keep customers, causing the prices of capital and consumer goods to spiral downward.

The nation had experienced economic downturns before, but this one differed in both kind and degree. Not only was it the longest period of uninterrupted economic contraction in U.S. history — a full sixty-five months — but it also exacted an extraordinary human toll. This was because so many more Americans were now dependent on industry for their survival. By 1874 fully a million workers were without jobs. City dwellers were hit hardest. In some cities, unemployment approached twenty-five percent of the workforce. New York alone counted some 100,000 unemployed workers in the winter of 1873 – 1874. "The sufferings of the working classes are daily increasing," wrote one Philadelphia worker the following summer. "Famine has broken into the home of many of us, and is at the door of all." Workers in small towns could — and did — tend little garden plots or engaged in hunting as a way to survive the hard times. The countryside was flooded, however, with urban men, and a few women, wandering from town to town in search of jobs. The wanderers often used the network of railroads that earlier had linked the nation in a single prosperous

"Panic, as a Health Officer, Sweeping the Garbage out of Wall Street." Despite the ghastly appearance of the figure representing financial panic, this *New York Daily Graphic* cover cartoon of September 29, 1873, subscribed to the belief that such financial "busts" cleansed the economy.

Source: Frank Bellew, *New York Daily Graphic,* September 29, 1873 — American Social History Project.

". . . A 'Tramp and Vagabond' "

In a September 7, 1875, letter to the *National Labor Tribune,* an unemployed mechanic described his year-long search for work and the rejection he faced.

Twelve months ago, left penniless by misfortune, I started from New York in search of employment. . . . During this year I have traversed seventeen states and obtained in that time six weeks' work. I have faced starvation; been months at a time without a bed, when the thermometer was 30 degrees below zero. Last winter I slept in the woods, and while honestly seeking employment I have been two and three days without food. When, in God's name, I asked for something to keep body and soul together, I have been repulsed as a "tramp and vagabond."

Source: *National Labor Tribune,* September 7, 1875.

---

market, which led to the birth of the popular image of the rail-riding "tramp."

The struggle for public relief now became far more pressing than that for the eight-hour day. In mass meetings, workers in cities across the nation demanded jobs. New York labor leaders in the winter of 1873 demanded to know what would be done "to relieve the necessities of the 10,000 homeless and hungry men and women of our city." They called on officials to create jobs financed by the sale of government bonds. Their request was denied, and subsequent meetings of the unemployed in New York were brutally suppressed by the police. In Chicago, St. Louis, and other large cities, many in the West, socialists took a leading role in the protests of the unemployed. It was during this period that socialism moved out of its relative isolation in German neighborhoods and began to build a larger following among native-born workers. In these cities, too, demonstrators demanding relief and jobs were often met with violence from public officials and open hostility from the press.

Employers and their supporters, drawing on Social Darwinist theories, viewed the depression as a necessary, if painful, process that would weed out inefficient businesses and allow only the strongest and most creative capitalists (and, by extension, workers) to survive. Business and government leaders were inclined to blame the suffering of working people on "the ignorance, indolence, and immorality" of the poor, and they attacked public-works schemes as a form of imported "communism."

Business leaders and editors spoke scornfully of the "debased bread of charity." The *Nation* magazine summed up this attitude when its editor, E. L. Godkin, wrote in its Christmas 1875 issue that "free soup must be prohibited, and all classes must learn that soup of any kind, beef or turtle, can be had only by being paid for."

The depression nearly destroyed the

young labor movement. At the depression's beginning in 1873, there were almost thirty national trade unions, with three hundred thousand members. By the end of the decade, the numbers had dropped to eight or nine unions, with only about fifty thousand members. Any wage gains won since the Civil War were lost: New York building tradesmen, for example, had earned $2.50 to $3.00 for an eight-hour day in 1872; three years later, they were working a ten-hour day for $1.50 to $2.00.

Northern white working-class voters, preoccupied by the depression and still unconvinced by arguments for racial equality, turned away from the radicalism of the mid-1860s. Capitalizing on this weariness, Democrats scored important victories in the North in the elections of 1874 and subsequently took control of the House of Representatives.

For African Americans in the South, the depression coincided with the end of Reconstruction. The leverage of black workers collapsed, and they had no alternative but to accept white rule and white control of the economy. One of the most significant effects of the depression in the South was, ironically, the consolidation of a capitalist economy in that region. After 1873, merchants unwilling to accept the financial risks of extending credit to poor farmers and farm laborers — black or white — instead charged goods to the accounts of large planters. The planters then resold the goods to workers, usually at inflated prices. Lien laws ensured that any debts to planters and merchants would be paid before workers could take profits for themselves. This meant that in a season of bad harvests or low prices, both of which were frequent in the 1870s, black farm

"The Red Flag in New York— Riotous Communist Workingmen Driven from Tompkins Square by the Mounted Police, Tuesday, January 13th, 1874." Demonstrations by workers and their allies demanding relief and job programs often were met with official violence—and were treated with hostility by the nation's press.

Source: Matthew Somerville Morgan, *Frank Leslie's Illustrated Newspaper,* January 31, 1874—American Social History Project.

families who had slowly and painfully accumulated a little capital, or even a piece of land, were likely to lose everything.

At the same time, southern manufacturers increased their holdings as falling cotton prices and a growing supply of unskilled wage labor created the possibilities for industrial profits. The Bibb Manufacturing Company in Macon, Georgia, for instance, opened a massive cotton mill in the midst of the depression. Between 1870 and 1880, the number of Macon's African-American household heads who worked as artisans or professionals fell precipitously. Among their white neighbors, many men left the skilled trades as well. Some moved into clerical, professional, or proprietary positions. Others joined white women and children in the cotton mills, which flourished despite the economic crisis.

The dual transformation of black landowners, renters, and sharecroppers into day laborers and of poor whites into industrial wage-earners created a southern workforce that mirrored, more closely than ever before, that of the North and West. This same transformation ensured that, even in the midst of hard times, activism among some workers—white and black—would continue. Most activism was local and short-lived, but its very persistence suggested the potential for a new labor insurgency that could respond to the needs of working people throughout the country. Particularly as industrial development moved south and growing numbers of southern workers moved north and west, the preconditions were developed for the creation of a national working class and a national labor movement.

Though insurgencies that crossed lines of region or race were still rare, railroad workers launched a wave of strikes across the nation between November 1873 and July 1874. Engineers, brakemen, and machinists on eighteen railroads walked off their jobs—mainly in response to wage cuts. The workers effectively disrupted railroad traffic through a variety of actions: removing coupling pins from freight cars, tearing up sections of track, and cutting telegraph lines. Railroad companies in turn convinced a number of state governors to send in the militia, and nearly all of the strikes were eventually defeated. Despite those defeats, the strikes indicated the determination of rank-and-file workers to resist attacks on their livelihood.

More characteristic in the mid-1870s were regional labor protests, like the dramatic Long Strike in the eastern Pennsylvania coalfields. Franklin Gowen, president of the Reading Railroad, had bought up small mines in the area and by 1874 had become the largest coal operator in eastern Pennsylvania. In a plan to break labor's power, he stockpiled coal and then, in the winter of 1874–1875, he shut down his mines. The bitter struggle that followed lasted five months, caused tremendous hardships for the miners and their families, and was marked by violence on both sides. "Coal and Iron Police" hired by Gowen shot indiscriminately into crowds of workers, while members of the Workingmen's Benevolent Association (WBA), the union that represented the miners, attacked strikebreakers with clubs and stones. Gowen also hired the Pinkerton National Detective Agency to infiltrate the miners' organization, providing further ammunition against the workers. Despite their courage and determination, the miners finally had to concede defeat, and reluctantly accept a twenty percent wage cut.

In the winter of 1876, Pennsylvania coal miners were again confronted by the anger of mine owners, now cloaked in the robes of law. James McParlan, a Pinkerton Agency operative who had lived among the Irish miners of eastern Pennsylvania for several years, stepped forward and became a leading witness in a series of sensational murder trials. Mc-Parlan testified that the murders were the result of a conspiracy by the Molly Maguires, a shadowy organization of Irish immigrant workers reputed to be willing to redress their grievances through violence. He also claimed that the "Mollies" dominated the WBA. Despite questions about the validity of McParlan's testimony, twenty miners were found guilty and sentenced to death in the spring of 1876. A year later, ten were hanged. Because of widespread press coverage, these trials helped link in the public mind trade unionism and terrorism. As a result, unionism in Pennsylvania mining was totally destroyed for twenty years.

The lack of responsiveness to workers' needs on the part of the two existing political parties also increased working-class dissatisfaction with traditional politics during the depression years. With the disfranchisement of African Americans in the South and the disaffection of northern working men, the Republican Party increasingly emphasized business development and looked to businessmen as its most important social base. Politicians of both parties were accepting bribes from big business to guarantee the politicians' support on critical issues. Consequently, the two major

The Molly Maguires. An illustration from *The Mollie Maguires and the Detectives,* Allan Pinkerton's self-serving account of his detective agency's infiltration of the secret society of Irish miners. Pinkerton's work in the service of the Reading Railroad typified the widespread use of private police by railroads and other businesses to suppress unions.

Source: Allan Pinkerton, *The Mollie Maguires and the Detectives* (1877)—American Social History Project.

parties, which had been diametrically opposed a mere decade earlier, now seemed indistinguishable.

As working-class activists grew increasingly dissatisfied with both parties, they looked for other, more independent roads to political influence. What they found was the Greenback Party, organized on a national level by farmers in 1875. The new party stood for governmental action to expand the currency with paper "greenbacks" that were not tied to the nation's gold reserves—a reform that was intended to inflate prices, thus benefiting debtors and providing capital needed for economic growth. Despite the protests of eight-hour advocates like Ira Steward, many labor leaders—including Richard Trevellick, A. C. Cameron, and John Siney—rallied to the Greenback cause, marking their final rejection of the Republican Party.

Other workers, mainly from the cities and including a large core of immigrants, based their hopes on the Workingmen's Party of the United States. The Socialists who founded this party in 1876 put aside their differences and took a major step toward bringing immigrant and native-born workers together in the same political organization. The Prohibition Party, inspired by grassroots campaigns against saloons in Ohio in 1874 and 1875, also began nominating candidates for state and national elections. Neither the Greenback nor the Workingmen's Party offered any real threat to Republican dominance, however. The Prohibitionists were limited by women's lack of voting rights, since it was women who had led the attacks on "rum sellers" across the Midwest. Nonetheless, the willingness of workers to experiment with party affiliations suggested a new awareness of their place in national politics.

The Final Assault on Reconstruction

Meanwhile, in the South, the final assault on Radical Reconstruction was taking place. Southern landowners and employers, under the protection of the newly elected Democratic Party, curtailed the potential for mass mobilization of poor whites and blacks in rural areas or their unionization in urban ones. New criminal codes in Georgia and elsewhere declared insurrection and incitement to insurrection to be capital offenses. Most southern legislatures increased penalties for theft, broadened the definition of arson, made it illegal to ride a horse or mule without the owner's permission, and restricted traditional access to land for the purpose of gathering wood, hunting, and fishing.

These codes were part of a larger pattern of discrimination that Democrats also directed against black Republicans and their white allies. In 1875, the Democrats' "Mississippi Plan" became a model for "redemption" in what was left of the reconstructed South: South Carolina, Louisiana, and Florida. The first step in this plan was to use economic pressure, social ostracism, and threats of physical violence to force the remaining white Republicans back into the Democratic Party. Democrats simply made it "too damned hot for [us] to stay out," explained one white Republican who gave in to the pressure. The second step was to use a combination of economic and physical coercion to prevent African Americans from voting. One Democratic newspaper pledged to "carry the election peacefully if we can, forcibly if we must." Landlords informed African-American sharecroppers that they could expect no further work if they voted Republican. Democrats also organized rifle clubs and physically attacked Republican picnics and rallies. Such violence proved to be the Democrats' most effective tool.

Vicksburg, Mississippi, was the scene of the worst political violence since the Klan murders in Meridian, Mississippi, in 1871. In December 1874, responding to the continuing harassment of Republicans, Vicksburg's African-American sheriff called on local blacks to help maintain the peace. But they were outnumbered and outgunned. White terrorists attacked a group of armed black deputies, killing thirty-five of them. With black voters intimidated, the Democrats won the county elections that same month, and the violence continued. It was directed primarily at local Republican leaders such as Richard Gray in Noxubee County. According to a fellow black Republican, Gray was "shot down walking on the pavements . . . because he was nominated for treasurer, and furthermore, because he made a speech and said he never did expect to vote a Democrat ticket, and also advised the colored citizens to do the same."

In response to this terrorism and to the appeals of African Americans, Mississippi governor Adelbert Ames organized a state militia. Black men all around the state volunteered to serve in it, but Ames hesitated to arm them, perhaps fearing that this step would only result in greater violence. Although Ames requested President Grant's administration to send in federal troops, his request was denied. On election day, Republican supporters were thoroughly intimidated. Many stayed away from the polls, and the Democratic Party carried the state by thirty thousand votes. Mississippi had been "redeemed."

As one southern state after another was "redeemed," many African Americans could no longer tolerate staying in the South. Beginning in the mid-1870s, colonization schemes, which proposed migration to Africa or to midwestern states such as Kansas, became popular among freedpeople. Henry Adams, a Union Army veteran from Louisiana and a colonization organizer, claimed to have signed up sixty thousand blacks from all parts of the South. "This is a horrible part of the country," he wrote. "It is impossible for us to live with these slaveholders of the South and enjoy the

All Colored People

THAT WANT TO

GO TO KANSAS,

On September 5th, 1877,

Can do so for $5.00

IMMIGRATION.

WHEREAS, We, the colored people of Lexington, Ky,. knowing that there is an abundance of choice lands now belonging to the Government, have assembled ourselves together for the purpose of locating on said lands. Therefore,

BE IT RESOLVED, That we do now organize ourselves into a Colony, as follows:— Any person wishing to become a member of this Colony can do so by paying the sum of one dollar ($1.00), and this money is to be paid by the first of September, 1877, in installments of twenty-five cents at a time, or otherwise as may be desired.

RESOLVED, That this Colony has agreed to consolidate itself with the Nicodemus Towns, Solomon Valley, Graham County, Kansas, and can only do so by entering the vacant lands now in their midst, which costs $5.00.

RESOLVED, That this Colony shall consist of seven officers—President, Vice-President, Secretary, Treasurer, and three Trustees. President—M. M. Bell; Vice-President —Isaac Talbott; Secretary—W. J. Niles; Treasurer—Daniel Clarke; Trustees—Jerry Lee, William Jones, and Abner Webster.

RESOLVED, That this Colony shall have from one to two hundred militia, more or less, as the case may require, to keep peace and order, and any member failing to pay in his dues, as aforesaid, or failing to comply with the above rules in any particular, will not be recognized or protected by the Colony.

Exodusters. An 1877 handbill urged African Americans to leave Kentucky and join a new settlement in Kansas.

Source: Kansas State Historical Society.

right as they enjoy it." Although not many made the journey to Africa, tens of thousands of southern blacks, taking the biblically inspired name Exodusters, did migrate to Kansas. Few succeeded in establishing themselves on Kansas farmland, however, and most Exodusters had to settle for menial jobs in the state's towns. But few returned to the "redeemed" South, and growing numbers entered the industrial labor force, though most often in the least skilled positions. Unfortunately, they joined the industrial age at the moment of its worst crisis of the century, which drastically limited African Americans' opportunities to secure employment, much less to join labor unions.

The presidential election of 1876 brought down the final curtain on the long drama of Reconstruction. The Republicans nominated Rutherford B. Hayes, governor of Ohio, as their candidate. He was a moderate Republican with a respectable Civil War record and a reputation for honesty. The Democrats, focusing on the corruption scandals that had rocked the Grant administration, chose New York's reform governor Samuel J. Tilden. Tilden had helped to break the grip of the notorious Tweed Ring in New York City. Although initial returns gave Tilden the election—including victories in New York, New Jersey, Connecticut, Indiana, and most of the former Confederacy—disputes about the votes from three southern states still in Republican hands (Louisiana, South Carolina, and Florida) threw his victory into question. A specially appointed electoral commission composed of ten congressmen and five Supreme Court justices—eight Republicans and seven Democrats—ruled 8 to 7 in February 1877, that the disputed votes in the three states belonged to Hayes. But there was no guarantee that the Democratic majority in the House of Representatives would accept this decision, and many felt the nation faced another civil war. Leading Republicans now moved to the

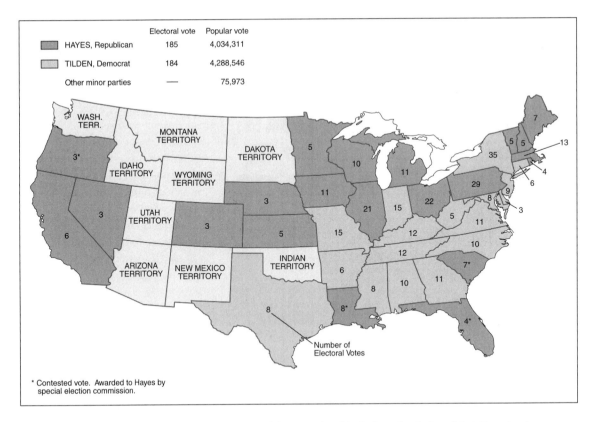

The Election of 1876. Initially it appeared that Democratic candidate Samuel J. Tilden had won the election of 1876. He captured a majority of the popular vote and was leading in electoral votes. Only a series of political maneuvers and a compromise by Republicans that involved the final withdrawal of federal troops from the former Confederacy allowed Rutherford B. Hayes to gain all of the contested electoral votes in Florida, Louisiana, and South Carolina. With those votes in the Hayes column, he won the presidency by a single electoral vote.

fore, however, working out an understanding with southern Democrats in Congress to assure Hayes's inauguration. In exchange for Democratic support, the Republicans promised to give southern Democrats a fair share of federal appointments and to remove the remaining federal troops from the South. They also agreed to provide federal assistance for southern railroad development, as a boon to industrialization and the creation of truly national markets.

Hayes was inaugurated in March 1877, and in April he pulled out the few remaining federal troops from the capitals of Louisiana and South Carolina, allowing Democrats to return to power. Neither the southern Republican Party nor the freedpeople who were its most ardent supporters could rely any longer on federal protection against violence and intimidation. And those who sought to escape the ravages of "redemption" by moving to the North or West found themselves increasingly hemmed in by the legal, political, and economic constraints that had characterized the South.

The Great Uprising of 1877

The very events that crushed the aspirations of many black and working-class Americans — the "redemption" of southern state governments, the opening of new investment opportunities in the former Confederacy, the tainted victory of the Republican Party in the 1876 presidential election, and the defeat of labor radicalism by the trials of the Mollie Maguires — buoyed the hopes of businessmen. Although the country had not yet emerged from the depression, the major problem of cutthroat competition was gradually being eliminated by the emergence of large monopolies in a number of basic industries. And unionism was clearly in retreat. The public hanging of ten Molly Maguires in June 1877 seemed to close the book on a defeated post–Civil War labor movement.

Within a month of the hangings, however, it would be clear that business confidence was profoundly misplaced. In July 1877 a massive railroad strike, the first truly national strike in the country's history, shook the very foundations of the political and economic order. On July 16, 1877, in Martinsburg, West Virginia, workers on the Baltimore and Ohio (B&O) railroad staged a spontaneous strike in response to yet another wage cut imposed by the railroad company. Three days later, as the strike intensified, President Hayes ordered federal troops into West Virginia to protect the B&O and the nation from "insurrection."

The use of federal troops in a domestic labor dispute incited popular anger across the country. In Baltimore, the Maryland state militia fired on huge crowds of angry workers, leaving eleven

715

dead and forty wounded. Work stoppages rapidly spread north and west along the railroad lines to Pennsylvania, where in Pittsburgh the strike reached its most dramatic climax. Because many Pittsburgh citizens sympathized with the railroad workers, the Pennsylvania Railroad sought help from outside the city. But when the state militia reached Pittsburgh on July 21, a large and angry crowd of strikers and sympathizers met them. Unnerved by their reception, the soldiers suddenly thrust their bayonets at members of the crowd. When rocks were thrown at the troops, they answered with a volley of rifle fire. When the gunfire finally ended, twenty Pittsburgh citizens, including a woman and three small children, lay dead.

News of the killings quickly spread. Pittsburgh residents, including thousands of workers from nearby mills, mines, and factories, converged on the Pennsylvania Railroad yards. By dawn they had set fire to the railroad roundhouse to which the militiamen had retreated. Twenty more Pittsburgh residents and five soldiers were killed in the ensuing gun battle.

In the next few days the strike spread across the Midwest. Workers took over entire towns, shutting down work until employers met their demands. The same railroad and telegraph lines that had unified the nation and laid the groundwork for the full emergence of industrial capitalism also linked and unified workers' protests. Without any central organization (most national unions were defunct as a result of the 1870s depression), the conflict spawned local committees, many led by anarchists and socialists, that provided unity and direction to the strike. In Chicago, for example, the strike quickly became a citywide general strike that touched off open class warfare. In St. Louis, by contrast, thousands of workers participated in a largely peaceful general strike that shut down virtually all of the city's industries, while government officials fled. Black workers in St. Louis took an active role in the strike, closing down canneries and docks. When an African-American steamboat worker, addressing a crowd of white workers, asked, "Will you stand to us regardless of color?" the crowd responded, "We will! We will! We will!" In other strikes, however, racism prevailed, particularly in the Far West. In San Francisco, a crowd gathered to discuss strike action but ended up rampaging through the city's Chinese neighborhoods, killing several residents and burning buildings.

But the massive national strike was directed mainly against the railroads and the unchecked cor-

"Waiting for the Reduction of the Army." As this 1878 cartoon from the *New York Daily Graphic* indicated, in the aftermath of the "Great Uprising" of 1877, Indians, trade unionists, immigrants, and tramps were increasingly grouped together in the press as symbols of disorder and opposition to the nation's progress.

Source: Ph. G. Cusachs, *New York Daily Graphic*, June 14, 1878—American Social History Project.

porate power they typified. Most working people in 1877 were seeking not to overthrow capitalism as a whole, but to set limits on the system's unbridled economic power and to assert workers' right to an equitable share of the extraordinary economic bounty they helped produce. Despite the nationwide mobilization of workers in the first truly national strike in American history, in the end the strike failed when faced with the massive power of the railroads and their allies in state and national government.

To fully engage in successful collective action, workers would have to create a labor movement in the future that would welcome a national and increasingly diverse labor force. Native-born and immigrant workers, men and women, African Americans, Asians, Indians, Mexican Americans, and whites, skilled and unskilled, industrial, agricultural, and domestic workers would have to find common cause in the same way that planters and industrialists, railroad magnates and coal operators, moderate Republicans and New South Democrats had. And they would have to do so in a nation that now embraced lands from the Atlantic to the Pacific Coast and beyond; that was increasingly defined by industrial and urban developments; and that was venturing ever further into international arenas of commerce, labor, and war.

The Years in Review

1859

- National Molders' Union founded as part of nationwide growth of trade unions.

1862

- Homestead Act.
- McKay stitcher allows manufacturers to end outwork, employ more male workers, and centralize production.

1863

- Newly freed black Sea Island residents purchase two thousand acres of deserted land from the federal government in an effort to distance themselves from the plantation system.
- Lincoln's Proclamation of Amnesty and Reconstruction allows any Confederate state to seek readmission to the Union if ten percent of its voters take an oath of loyalty to the Union.

1864

- U.S. soldiers massacre Cheyennes at Sand Creek, leaving two hundred men, women, and children dead.

1865

- Lincoln endorses limited black suffrage.
- Bureau of Freedmen, Refugees, and Abandoned Lands created to assist freed slaves.
- President Johnson offers total amnesty to white Southerners who would swear basic loyalty to the Union.
- Ex-Confederate officials elected in large numbers to federal and state positions. Enraged Radical Republicans establish a joint committee of Congress to investigate.

1866

- Fourteenth Amendment, granting full citizenship to African Americans, passes both houses of Congress. Encouraged by President Johnson, all but one southern state refuses to ratify it.
- Confederate veterans in Tennessee found Ku Klux Klan.
- National Labor Union (NLU) founded.

1867

- Reconstruction Act of March 1867 passes over President Johnson's veto.
- Congress declares new Indian policy that aims at concentrating Indians on two reservations in Dakota Territory and Oklahoma Territory.
- Shoemakers organize the Knights of St. Crispin. By 1870 the Knights of St. Crispin is the largest labor union in the nation.
- Edward P. Weston sets a new long-distance walking record by walking from Portland, Maine, to Chicago in twenty-six days.

1868

- Republican Ulysses S. Grant elected president.
- German immigrants Adolph Douai and Friedrich Sorge organize the socialist International Workingmen's Association in New York.
- President Johnson impeached by U.S. House of Representatives and acquitted by Senate.
- Patent is issued for the "QWERTY" keyboard that is still used today. The arrangement was developed to avoid jamming by separating the most widely used keys. Remington & Sons Fire Arms Co. will acquire the rights and begin producing typewriters in 1874.
- First celebration of Memorial Day—a holiday to commemorate the Union dead in the Civil War.

1869

- Transcontinental railroad completed.

1870

- Fifteenth Amendment, granting all citizens the right to vote regardless of color, is ratified.
- William W. Lyman patents the can opener.

1872

- Ulysses S. Grant reelected. Republican Party continues its retreat from the defense of African-American rights.
- German-American brewer Adolph Coors launches Golden Brewery in Colorado, which will produce Coors Beer.

1873

- Economic depression, triggered by the collapse of Jay Cooke and Company, begins.
- Miners' National Association forms under the leadership of John Siney.

1875

- President Grant denies Mississippi Governor Adelbert Ames's request for federal troops to end the violence directed at Republican voters.
- Farmers looking to artificially inflate prices and create capital needed for economic growth organize Greenback Party.
- Charles G. Waite wears the first baseball glove at a game in Boston.
- Charles Elmer Hires develops "Hires Rootbeer" from a recipe for herb tea. A friend advises him that "rootbeer" would more likely attract sales from coal miners than "herb tea."

1876

- Initial returns in election give victory to Democrat Samuel J. Tilden, but in February 1877 a special commission makes Republican Rutherford B. Hayes president.
- Centennial Exposition in Philadelphia.
- Sioux warriors defeat General George Custer's 7th Calvary at the Battle of Little Big Horn in Dakota Territory.
- Twenty miners—alleged members of the Molly Maguires—are found guilty of murder and sentenced to death in spring 1876; ten are later hanged.
- Socialists form the Workingmen's Party of the United States.
- First fraternity house, Kappa Alpha, opened at Williams College in Massachusetts.

1877

- Railroad strike, the first national strike, spreads coast-to-coast in two weeks. One hundred people die and millions of dollars' worth of property is destroyed. President Hayes sends federal troops in to protect the interests of the railroad owners.

Suggested Readings

Berlin, Ira, et al., eds., *Free at Last: A Documentary History of Slavery, Freedom, and the Civil War* (1992).

Bruce, Robert V., *1877: Year of Violence* (1959).

Carter, Dan T., *When the War Was Over: The Failure of Self-Reconstruction in the South, 1865–1867* (1985).

Chandler, Alfred D., *The Visible Hand: The Managerial Revolution in American Business* (1977).

Chen, Jack, *The Chinese of America* (1980).

Commons, John R., ed., *A Documentary History of American Industrial Society* (1958).

DuBois, W. E. B., *Black Reconstruction in America, 1860–1880* (1935).

Dubofsky, Melvin, *Industrialism and the American Worker, 1865–1920* (1985).

DuBois, Ellen Carol, *Woman's Suffrage and Women's Rights* (1998).

Edwards, Laura, *Gendered Strife and Confusion: The Political Culture of Reconstruction* (1997).

Foner, Eric, *A Short History of Reconstruction, 1863–1877* (1990).

Foner, Philip S., *Organized Labor and the Black Worker, 1619–1973* (1974).

Frankel, Noralee, *Freedom's Women: Black Women and Families in Civil War Era Mississippi* (1999).

Franklin, John Hope, *Reconstruction: After the Civil War* (1961).

Gordon, Ann, et al, eds., *African American Women and the Vote, 1837–1965* (1997).

Gutman, Herbert G., *Work, Culture and Society in Industrializing America* (1976).

Harris, William, *The Harder We Run: Black Workers Since the Civil War* (1982).

Holt, Thomas, *Black Over White: Negro Political Leadership in South Carolina During Reconstruction* (1977).

Jacobson, Matthew Frye, *Whiteness of a Different Color: European Immigrants and the Alchemy of Race* (1998).

Jones, Jacqueline, *Labor of Love, Labor of Sorrow: Black Women, Work and the Family from Slavery to the Present* (1985).

Kessler-Harris, Alice, *Out to Work: A History of Wage-Earning Women in the United States* (1982).

Kousser, Morgan J., *The Shaping of Southern Politics: Suffrage Restriction and the Establishment of the One-Party South, 1880–1910* (1974).

Lens, Sidney, *The Labor Wars: From the Molly Maguires to the Sitdowns* (1973).

Licht, Walter, *Working for the Railroad: The Organization of Work in the Nineteenth Century* (1983).

Litwack, Leon, *Been in the Storm So Long: The Aftermath of Slavery* (1979).

McCrary, Peyton, *Abraham Lincoln and Reconstruction: The Louisiana Experiment* (1978).

McFeeley, William S., *Yankee Stepfather: General O. O. Howard and the Freedmen* (1968).

McKittrick, Eric L., *Andrew Johnson and Reconstruction* (1960).

McPherson, James M., and J. Morgan Kousser, eds., *Region, Race, and Reconstruction: Essays in Honor of C. Vann Woodward* (1982).

Miller, Stuart C., *The Unwelcome Immigrant: American Images of the Chinese, 1785–1882* (1969).

Montgomery, David, *Beyond Equality: Labor and the Radical Republicans, 1862–1872* (1967).

Nee, Victor, and Brett de Barry Nee, *Longtime Californ': A Documentary Study of an American Chinatown* (1972).

Painter, Nell Irvin, *Exodusters: Black Migration to Kansas after Reconstruction* (1971).

Perman, Michael, *The Road to Redemption: Southern Politics, 1869–1879* (1984).

Ransom, Roger L., and Richard Sutch, *One Kind of Freedom: The Economic Consequences of Emancipation* (1977).

Reidy, Joseph P., *From Slavery to Agrarian Capitalism in the Cotton Plantation South: Central Georgia, 1800–1880* (1992).

Roark, James, *Masters Without Slaves: Southern Planters in the Civil War and Reconstruction* (1977).

Rose, Willie Lee, *Rehearsal for Reconstruction: The Port Royal Experiment* (1964).

Saville, Julie, *The Work of Reconstruction: From Slave to Wage Laborer in South Carolina, 1869–1870* (1994).

Saxton, Alexander, *The Indispensable Enemy: Labor and the Anti-Chinese Movement in California* (1971).

Silber, Nina, *The Romance of Reunion: Northerners and the South, 1865–1900* (1993).

Sterling, Dorothy, ed., *We Are Your Sisters: Black Women in the Nineteenth Century* (1984).

Takaki, Ronald, *Iron Cages: Race and Culture in Nineteenth-Century America* (1979).

Taylor, Quintard, *In Search of the Racial Frontier: African Americans in the American West, 1528–1990* (1998).

Trachtenberg, Alan, *The Incorporation of America: Culture and Society in the Gilded Age* (1982).

Trelease, Allen W., *White Terror: The Ku Klux Klan Conspiracy and Southern Reconstruction* (1971).

Utley, Robert M., *The Indian Frontier of the American West, 1846–1890* (1984).

Williamson, Joel, *After Slavery: The Negro in South Carolina During Reconstruction, 1861–1877* (1965).

Woodward, C. Vann, *Reunion and Reaction: The Compromise of 1877 and the End of Reconstruction* (1951).

And on the World Wide Web

Freedmen and Southern Society Project
(http://www.inform.umd.edu/ARHU/Depts/History/Freedman/home.html)

Appendix

The Declaration of Independence

IN CONGRESS, July 4, 1776.

The unanimous Declaration of the thirteen united States of America,

When in the Course of human events, it becomes necessary for one people to dissolve the political bands which have connected them with another, and to assume among the powers of the earth, the separate and equal station to which the Laws of Nature and of Nature's God entitle them, a decent respect to the opinions of mankind requires that they should declare the causes which impel them to the separation.

We hold these truths to be self-evident, that all men are created equal, that they are endowed by their Creator with certain unalienable Rights, that among these are Life, Liberty and the pursuit of Happiness. — That to secure these rights, Governments are instituted among Men, deriving their just powers from the consent of the governed, — That whenever any Form of Government becomes destructive of these ends, it is the Right of the People to alter or to abolish it, and to institute new Government, laying its foundation on such principles and organizing its powers in such form, as to them shall seem most likely to effect their Safety and Happiness. Prudence, indeed, will dictate that Governments long established should not be changed for light and transient causes; and accordingly all experience hath shewn, that mankind are more disposed to suffer, while evils are sufferable, than to right themselves by abolishing the forms to which they are accustomed. But when a long train of abuses and usurpations, pursuing invariably the same Object evinces a design to reduce them under absolute

Despotism, it is their right, it is their duty, to throw off such Government, and to provide new Guards for their future security. — Such has been the patient sufferance of these Colonies; and such is now the necessity which constrains them to alter their former Systems of Government. The history of the present King of Great Britain is a history of repeated injuries and usurpations, all having in direct object the establishment of an absolute Tyranny over these States. To prove this, let Facts be submitted to a candid world.

He has refused his Assent to Laws, the most wholesome and necessary for the public good.

He has forbidden his Governors to pass Laws of immediate and pressing importance, unless suspended in their operation till his Assent should be obtained; and when so suspended, he has utterly neglected to attend to them.

He has refused to pass other Laws for the accommodation of large districts of people, unless those people would relinquish the right of Representation in the Legislature, a right inestimable to them and formidable to tyrants only.

He has called together legislative bodies at places unusual, uncomfortable, and distant from the depository of their public Records, for the sole purpose of fatiguing them into compliance with his measures.

He has dissolved Representative Houses repeatedly, for opposing with manly firmness his invasions on the rights of the people.

A

He has refused for a long time, after such dissolutions, to cause others to be elected; whereby the Legislative powers, incapable of Annihilation, have returned to the People at large for their exercise; the State remaining in the mean time exposed to all the dangers of invasion from without, and convulsions within.

He has endeavoured to prevent the population of these States; for that purpose obstructing the Laws for Naturalization of Foreigners; refusing to pass others to encourage their migrations hither, and raising the conditions of new Appropriations of Lands.

He has obstructed the Administration of Justice, by refusing his Assent to Laws for establishing Judiciary powers.

He has made Judges dependent on his Will alone, for the tenure of their offices, and the amount and payment of their salaries.

He has erected a multitude of New Offices, and sent hither swarms of Officers to harrass our people, and eat out their substance.

He has kept among us, in times of peace, Standing Armies without the Consent of our legislatures.

He has affected to render the Military independent of and superior to the Civil power.

He has combined with others to subject us to a jurisdiction foreign to our constitution, and unacknowledged by our laws; giving his Assent to their Acts of pretended Legislation:

For Quartering large bodies of armed troops among us:

For protecting them, by a mock Trial, from punishment for any Murders which they should commit on the Inhabitants of these States:

For cutting off our Trade with all parts of the world:

For imposing Taxes on us without our Consent:

For depriving us in many cases, of the benefits of Trial by Jury:

For transporting us beyond Seas to be tried for pretended offences

For abolishing the free System of English Laws in a neighbouring Province, establishing therein an Arbitrary government, and enlarging its Boundaries so as to render it at once an example and fit instrument for introducing the same absolute rule into these Colonies:

For taking away our Charters, abolishing our most valuable Laws, and altering fundamentally the Forms of our Governments:

For suspending our own Legislatures, and declaring themselves invested with power to legislate for us in all cases whatsoever.

He has abdicated Government here, by declaring us out of his Protection and waging War against us.

He has plundered our seas, ravaged our Coasts, burnt our towns, and destroyed the lives of our people.

He is at this time transporting large Armies of foreign Mercenaries to compleat the works of death, desolation and tyranny, already begun with circumstances of Cruelty & perfidy scarcely paralleled in the most barbarous ages, and totally unworthy the Head of a civilized nation.

He has constrained our fellow Citizens taken Captive on the high Seas to bear Arms against their Country, to become the executioners of their friends and Brethren, or to fall themselves by their Hands.

He has excited domestic insurrections amongst us, and has endeavoured to bring on the inhabitants of our frontiers, the merciless Indian Savages, whose known rule of warfare, is an undistinguished destruction of all ages, sexes and conditions.

In every stage of these Oppressions We have Petitioned for Redress in the most humble terms: Our repeated Petitions have been answered only by repeated injury. A Prince whose character is thus marked by every act which may define a Tyrant, is unfit to be the ruler of a free people.

Nor have We been wanting in attentions to our Brittish brethren. We have warned them from time to time of attempts by their legislature to extend an unwarrantable jurisdiction over us. We have reminded them of the circumstances of our emigration and settlement here. We have appealed to their native justice and magnanimity, and we have conjured them by the ties of our common kindred to disavow these usurpations, which, would inevitably interrupt our connections and correspondence. They too have been deaf to the voice of justice and of consanguinity. We must, therefore, acquiesce in the necessity, which denounces our Separation, and hold them, as we hold the rest of mankind, Enemies in War, in Peace Friends.

We, therefore, the Representatives of the united States of America, in General Congress, Assembled, appealing to the Supreme Judge of the world for the rectitude of our intentions, do, in the Name, and by Authority of the good People of these Colonies, solemnly publish and declare, That these United Colonies are, and of Right ought to be Free and Independent States; that they are Absolved from all Allegiance to the British Crown, and that all political connection between them and the State of Great Britain, is and ought to be totally dissolved; and that as Free and Independent States, they have full Power to levy War, conclude Peace, contract Alliances, establish Commerce, and to do all other Acts and Things which Independent States may of right do. And for the support of this Declaration, with a firm reliance on the protection of divine Providence, we mutually pledge to each other our Lives, our Fortunes and our sacred Honor.

John Hancock

Georgia
Button Gwinnett
Lyman Hall
George Walton

North Carolina
William Hooper
Joseph Hewes
John Penn
South Carolina
Edward Rutledge
Thomas Heyward, Jr.
Thomas Lynch, Jr.
Arthur Middleton

Maryland
Samuel Chase
William Paca
Thomas Stone
Charles Carroll of Carrollton
Virginia
George Wythe
Richard Henry Lee
Thomas Jefferson
Benjamin Harrison
Thomas Nelson, Jr.
Francis Lightfoot Lee
Carter Braxton

Pennsylvania
Robert Morris
Benjamin Rush
Benjamin Franklin
John Morton
George Clymer
James Smith
George Taylor
James Wilson
George Ross

Delaware
Caesar Rodney
George Read
Thomas McKean

New York
William Floyd
Philip Livingston
Francis Lewis
Lewis Morris

New Jersey
Richard Stockton
John Witherspoon
Francis Hopkinson
John Hart
Abraham Clark

New Hampshire
Josiah Bartlett
William Whipple

Massachusetts
Samuel Adams
John Adams
Robert Treat Paine
Elbridge Gerry

Rhode Island
Stephen Hopkins
William Ellery

Connecticut
Roger Sherman
Samuel Huntington
William Williams
Oliver Wolcott

New Hampshire
Matthew Thornton

Constitution of the United States of America

Note: The following text is a transcription of the Constitution in its original form.

We the People of the United States, in Order to form a more perfect Union, establish Justice, insure domestic Tranquility, provide for the common defense, promote the general Welfare, and secure the Blessings of Liberty to ourselves and our Posterity, do ordain and establish this Constitution for the United States of America.

Article I

Section 1

All legislative Powers herein granted shall be vested in a Congress of the United States, which shall consist of a Senate and House of Representatives.

Section 2

The House of Representatives shall be composed of Members chosen every second Year by the People of the several States, and the Electors in each State shall have the Qualifications requisite for Electors of the most numerous Branch of the State Legislature.

No Person shall be a Representative who shall not have attained to the Age of twenty five Years, and been seven Years a Citizen of the United States, and who shall not, when elected, be an Inhabitant of that State in which he shall be chosen.

Representatives and direct Taxes shall be apportioned among the several States which may be included within this Union, according to their respective Numbers, which shall be determined by adding to the whole Number of free Persons, including those bound to Service for a Term of Years, and excluding Indians not taxed, three fifths of all other Persons. The actual Enumeration shall be made within three Years after the first Meeting of the Congress of the United States, and within every subsequent Term of ten Years, in such Manner as they shall by Law direct. The Number of Representatives shall not exceed one for every thirty Thousand, but each State shall have at Least one Representative; and until such enumeration shall be made, the State of New Hampshire shall be entitled to chuse three, Massachusetts eight, Rhode-Island and Providence Plantations one, Connecticut five, New-York six, New Jersey four, Pennsylvania eight, Delaware one, Maryland six, Virginia ten, North Carolina five, South Carolina five, and Georgia three.

When vacancies happen in the Representation from any State, the Executive Authority thereof shall issue Writs of Election to fill such Vacancies.

The House of Representatives shall chuse their Speaker and other Officers; and shall have the sole Power of Impeachment.

Section 3

The Senate of the United States shall be composed of two Senators from each State, chosen by the Legislature thereof for six Years; and each Senator shall have one Vote.

Immediately after they shall be assembled in Consequence of the first Election, they shall be divided as equally as may be into three Classes. The Seats of the Senators of the first Class shall be vacated at the Expiration of the second Year, of the second Class at the

Expiration of the fourth Year, and of the third Class at the Expiration of the sixth Year, so that one third may be chosen every second Year; and if Vacancies happen by Resignation, or otherwise, during the Recess of the Legislature of any State, the Executive thereof may make temporary Appointments until the next Meeting of the Legislature, which shall then fill such Vacancies.

No Person shall be a Senator who shall not have attained to the Age of thirty Years, and been nine Years a Citizen of the United States, and who shall not, when elected, be an Inhabitant of that State for which he shall be chosen.

The Vice President of the United States shall be President of the Senate, but shall have no Vote, unless they be equally divided.

The Senate shall chuse their other Officers, and also a President pro tempore, in the Absence of the Vice President, or when he shall exercise the Office of President of the United States.

The Senate shall have the sole Power to try all Impeachments. When sitting for that Purpose, they shall be on Oath or Affirmation. When the President of the United States is tried, the Chief Justice shall preside: And no Person shall be convicted without the Concurrence of two thirds of the Members present.

Judgment in Cases of Impeachment shall not extend further than to removal from Office, and disqualification to hold and enjoy any Office of honor, Trust or Profit under the United States: but the Party convicted shall nevertheless be liable and subject to Indictment, Trial, Judgment and Punishment, according to Law.

Section 4

The Times, Places and Manner of holding Elections for Senators and Representatives, shall be prescribed in each State by the Legislature thereof; but the Congress may at any time by Law make or alter such Regulations, except as to the Places of chusing Senators.

The Congress shall assemble at least once in every Year, and such Meeting shall be on the first Monday in December, unless they shall by Law appoint a different Day.

Section 5

Each House shall be the Judge of the Elections, Returns and Qualifications of its own Members, and a Majority of each shall constitute a Quorum to do Business; but a smaller Number may adjourn from day to day, and may be authorized to compel the Attendance of absent Members, in such Manner, and under such Penalties as each House may provide.

Each House may determine the Rules of its Proceedings, punish its Members for disorderly Behaviour, and, with the Concurrence of two thirds, expel a Member.

Each House shall keep a Journal of its Proceedings, and from time to time publish the same, excepting such Parts as may in their Judgment require Secrecy; and the Yeas and Nays of the Members of either House on any question shall, at the Desire of one fifth of those Present, be entered on the Journal.

Neither House, during the Session of Congress, shall, without the Consent of the other, adjourn for more than three days, nor to any other Place than that in which the two Houses shall be sitting.

Section 6

The Senators and Representatives shall receive a Compensation for their Services, to be ascertained by Law, and paid out of the Treasury of the United States. They shall in all Cases, except Treason, Felony and Breach of the Peace, be privileged from Arrest during their Attendance at the Session of their respective Houses, and in going to and returning from the same; and for any Speech or Debate in either House, they shall not be questioned in any other Place.

No Senator or Representative shall, during the Time for which he was elected, be appointed to any civil Office under the Authority of the United States, which shall have been created, or the Emoluments whereof shall have been encreased during such time; and no Person holding any Office under the United States, shall be a Member of either House during his Continuance in Office.

Appendix

Section 7

All Bills for raising Revenue shall originate in the House of Representatives; but the Senate may propose or concur with Amendments as on other Bills.

Every Bill which shall have passed the House of Representatives and the Senate, shall, before it become a Law, be presented to the President of the United States: If he approve he shall sign it, but if not he shall return it, with his Objections to that House in which it shall have originated, who shall enter the Objections at large on their Journal, and proceed to reconsider it. If after such Reconsideration two thirds of that House shall agree to pass the Bill, it shall be sent, together with the Objections, to the other House, by which it shall likewise be reconsidered, and if approved by two thirds of that House, it shall become a Law. But in all such Cases the Votes of both Houses shall be determined by yeas and Nays, and the Names of the Persons voting for and against the Bill shall be entered on the Journal of each House respectively. If any Bill shall not be returned by the President within ten Days (Sundays excepted) after it shall have been presented to him, the Same shall be a Law, in like Manner as if he had signed it, unless the Congress by their Adjournment prevent its Return, in which Case it shall not be a Law.

Every Order, Resolution, or Vote to which the Concurrence of the Senate and House of Representatives may be necessary (except on a question of Adjournment) shall be presented to the President of the United States; and before the Same shall take Effect, shall be approved by him, or being disapproved by him, shall be repassed by two thirds of the Senate and House of Representatives, according to the Rules and Limitations prescribed in the Case of a Bill.

Section 8

The Congress shall have Power To lay and collect Taxes, Duties, Imposts and Excises, to pay the Debts and provide for the common Defence and general Welfare of the United States; but all Duties, Imposts and Excises shall be uniform throughout the United States;

To borrow Money on the credit of the United States;

To regulate Commerce with foreign Nations, and among the several States, and with the Indian Tribes;

To establish an uniform Rule of Naturalization, and uniform Laws on the subject of Bankruptcies throughout the United States;

To coin Money, regulate the Value thereof, and of foreign Coin, and fix the Standard of Weights and Measures;

To provide for the Punishment of counterfeiting the Securities and current Coin of the United States;

To establish Post Offices and post Roads;

To promote the Progress of Science and useful Arts, by securing for limited Times to Authors and Inventors the exclusive Right to their respective Writings and Discoveries;

To constitute Tribunals inferior to the supreme Court;

To define and punish Piracies and Felonies committed on the high Seas, and Offences against the Law of Nations;

To declare War, grant Letters of Marque and Reprisal, and make Rules concerning Captures on Land and Water;

To raise and support Armies, but no Appropriation of Money to that Use shall be for a longer Term than two Years;

To provide and maintain a Navy;

To make Rules for the Government and Regulation of the land and naval Forces;

To provide for calling forth the Militia to execute the Laws of the Union, suppress Insurrections and repel Invasions;

To provide for organizing, arming, and disciplining, the Militia, and for governing such Part of them as may be employed in the Service of the United States, reserving to the States respectively, the Appointment of the Officers, and the Authority of training the Militia according to the discipline prescribed by Congress;

To exercise exclusive Legislation in all Cases whatsoever, over such District (not exceeding ten Miles square) as may, by Cession of particular States, and the Acceptance of Congress, become the Seat of the Government of the United States, and to exercise like Authority over all Places purchased by the Consent of the Legislature of the State in which the Same shall be, for the Erection of Forts, Magazines, Arsenals, dock-Yards, and other needful Buildings; — And

To make all Laws which shall be necessary and proper for carrying into Execution the foregoing Powers, and all other Powers vested by this Constitution in the Government of the United States, or in any Department or Officer thereof.

Section 9

The Migration or Importation of such Persons as any of the States now existing shall think proper to admit, shall not be prohibited by the Congress prior to the Year one thousand eight hundred and eight, but a Tax or duty may be imposed on such Importation, not exceeding ten dollars for each Person.

The Privilege of the Writ of Habeas Corpus shall not be suspended, unless when in Cases of Rebellion or Invasion the public Safety may require it.

No Bill of Attainder or ex post facto Law shall be passed.

No Capitation, or other direct, Tax shall be laid, unless in Proportion to the Census or enumeration herein before directed to be taken.

No Tax or Duty shall be laid on Articles exported from any State.

No Preference shall be given by any Regulation of Commerce or Revenue to the Ports of one State over those of another; nor shall Vessels bound to, or from, one State, be obliged to enter, clear, or pay Duties in another.

No Money shall be drawn from the Treasury, but in Consequence of Appropriations made by Law; and a regular Statement and Account of the Receipts and Expenditures of all public Money shall be published from time to time.

No Title of Nobility shall be granted by the United States: And no Person holding any Office of Profit or Trust under them, shall, without the Consent of the Congress, accept of any present, Emolument, Office, or Title, of any kind whatever, from any King, Prince, or foreign State.

Section 10

No State shall enter into any Treaty, Alliance, or Confederation; grant Letters of Marque and Reprisal; coin Money; emit Bills of Credit; make any Thing but gold and silver Coin a Tender in Payment of Debts; pass any Bill of Attainder, ex post facto Law, or Law impairing the Obligation of Contracts, or grant any Title of Nobility.

No State shall, without the Consent of the Congress, lay any Imposts or Duties on Imports or Exports, except what may be absolutely necessary for executing it's inspection Laws: and the net Produce of all Duties and Imposts, laid by any State on Imports or Exports, shall be for the Use of the Treasury of the United States; and all such Laws shall be subject to the Revision and Controul of the Congress.

No State shall, without the Consent of Congress, lay any Duty of Tonnage, keep Troops, or Ships of War in time of Peace, enter into any Agreement or Compact with another State, or with a foreign Power, or engage in War, unless actually invaded, or in such imminent Danger as will not admit of delay.

Article II
Section 1

The executive Power shall be vested in a President of the United States of America. He shall hold his Office during the Term of four Years, and, together with the Vice President, chosen for the same Term, be elected, as follows:

Each State shall appoint, in such Manner as the Legislature thereof may direct, a Number of Electors, equal to the whole Number of Senators and Representatives to which the State may be entitled in the Congress: but no Senator or Representative, or Person holding an Office of Trust or Profit under the United States, shall be appointed an Elector.

The Electors shall meet in their respective States, and vote by Ballot for two Persons, of whom one at least shall not be an Inhabitant of the same State with themselves. And they shall make a List of all the Persons voted for, and of the Number of Votes for each; which List they shall sign and certify, and transmit sealed to the Seat of the Government of the United States, directed to the President of the Senate. The President of the Senate shall, in the Presence of the Senate and House of Representatives, open all the Certificates, and the Votes shall then be counted. The Person having the greatest Number of Votes shall be the President, if such Number be a Majority of the whole Number of Electors appointed; and if there be more than one who have such Majority, and have an equal Number of Votes, then the House of Representatives shall immediately chuse by Ballot one of them for President; and if no Person have a Majority, then from the five highest on the List the said House shall in like Manner chuse the President. But in chusing the President, the Votes shall be taken by States, the Representation from each State having one Vote; A quorum for this purpose shall consist of a Member or Members from two thirds of the States, and a Majority of all the States shall be necessary to a Choice. In every Case, after the Choice of the President, the Person having the greatest Number of Votes of the Electors shall be the Vice President. But if there should remain two or more who have equal Votes, the Senate shall chuse from them by Ballot the Vice President.

The Congress may determine the Time of chusing the Electors, and the Day on which they shall give their Votes; which Day shall be the same throughout the United States.

No Person except a natural born Citizen, or a Citizen of the United States, at the time of the Adoption of this Constitution, shall be eligible to the Office of President; neither shall any Person be eligible to that Office who shall not have attained to the Age of thirty five Years, and been fourteen Years a Resident within the United States.

In Case of the Removal of the President from Office, or of his Death, Resignation, or Inability to discharge the Powers and Duties of the said Office, the Same shall devolve on the Vice President, and the Congress may by Law provide for the Case of Removal, Death, Resignation or Inability, both of the President and Vice President, declaring what Officer shall then act as President, and such Officer shall act accordingly, until the Disability be removed, or a President shall be elected.

The President shall, at stated Times, receive for his Services, a Compensation, which shall neither be increased nor diminished during the Period for which he shall have been elected, and he shall not receive within that Period any other Emolument from the United States, or any of them.

Before he enter on the Execution of his Office, he shall take the following Oath or Affirmation: — "I do solemnly swear (or affirm) that I will faithfully execute the Office of President of the United States, and will to the best of my Ability, preserve, protect and defend the Constitution of the United States."

Section 2

The President shall be Commander in Chief of the Army and Navy of the United States, and of the Militia of the several States, when called into the actual Service of the United States; he may require the Opinion, in writing, of the principal Officer in each of the executive Departments, upon any Subject relating to the Duties of their respective Offices, and he shall have Power to grant Reprieves and Pardons for Offences against the United States, except in Cases of Impeachment.

He shall have Power, by and with the Advice and Consent of the Senate, to make Treaties, provided two thirds of the Senators present concur; and he shall nominate, and by and with the Advice and Consent of the Senate, shall appoint Ambassadors, other public Ministers and Consuls, Judges of the supreme Court, and all other Officers of the United States, whose Appointments are not herein otherwise provided for, and which shall be established by Law: but the Congress may by Law vest the Appointment of such inferior Officers, as they think proper, in the President alone, in the Courts of Law, or in the Heads of Departments.

The President shall have Power to fill up all Vacancies that may happen during the Recess of the Senate, by granting Commissions which shall expire at the End of their next Session.

Section 3

He shall from time to time give to the Congress Information of the State of the Union, and recommend to their Consideration such Measures as he shall judge necessary and expedient; he may, on extraordinary Occasions, convene both Houses, or either of them, and in Case of Disagreement between them, with Respect to the Time of Adjournment, he may adjourn them to such Time as he shall think proper; he shall receive Ambassadors and other public Ministers; he shall take Care that the Laws be faithfully executed, and shall Commission all the Officers of the United States.

Section 4

The President, Vice President and all civil Officers of the United States, shall be removed from Office on Impeachment for, and Conviction of, Treason, Bribery, or other high Crimes and Misdemeanors.

Article III

Section 1

The judicial Power of the United States shall be vested in one supreme Court, and in such inferior Courts as the Congress may from time to time ordain and establish. The Judges, both of the supreme and inferior Courts, shall hold their Offices during good Behaviour, and shall, at stated Times, receive for their Services a Compensation, which shall not be diminished during their Continuance in Office.

Section 2

The judicial Power shall extend to all Cases, in Law and Equity, arising under this Constitution, the Laws of the United States, and Treaties made, or which shall be made, under their Authority; — to all Cases affecting Ambassadors, other public Ministers and Consuls; — to all Cases of admiralty and maritime Jurisdiction; — to Controversies to which the United States shall be a Party; — to Controversies between two or more States; — between a State and Citizens of another State; — between Citizens of different States; — between Citizens of the same State claiming Lands under Grants of different States, and between a State, or the Citizens thereof, and foreign States, Citizens or Subjects.

In all Cases affecting Ambassadors, other public Ministers and Consuls, and those in which a State shall be Party, the supreme Court shall have original Jurisdiction. In all the other Cases before mentioned, the supreme Court shall have appellate Jurisdiction, both as to Law and Fact, with such Exceptions, and under such Regulations as the Congress shall make.

The Trial of all Crimes, except in Cases of Impeachment, shall be by Jury; and such Trial shall be held in the State where the said Crimes shall have been committed; but when not committed within any State, the Trial shall be at such Place or Places as the Congress may by Law have directed.

Section 3

Treason against the United States, shall consist only in levying War against them, or in adhering to their Enemies, giving them Aid and Comfort. No Person shall be convicted of Treason unless on the Testimony of two Witnesses to the same overt Act, or on Confession in open Court.

The Congress shall have Power to declare the Punishment of Treason, but no Attainder of Treason shall work Corruption of Blood, or Forfeiture except during the Life of the Person attainted.

Article IV

Section 1

Full Faith and Credit shall be given in each State to the public Acts, Records, and judicial Proceedings of every other State. And the Congress may by general Laws prescribe the Manner in which such Acts, Records and Proceedings shall be proved, and the Effect thereof.

Section 2

The Citizens of each State shall be entitled to all Privileges and Immunities of Citizens in the several States.

A Person charged in any State with Treason, Felony, or other Crime, who shall flee from Justice, and be found in another State, shall on Demand of the executive Authority of the State from which he fled, be delivered up, to be removed to the State having Jurisdiction of the Crime.

No Person held to Service or Labour in one State, under the Laws thereof, escaping into another, shall, in Consequence of any Law or Regulation therein, be discharged from such Service or Labour, but shall be delivered up on Claim of the Party to whom such Service or Labour may be due.

Section 3

New States may be admitted by the Congress into this Union; but no new State shall be formed or erected within the Jurisdiction of any other State; nor any State be formed by the Junction of two or more States, or Parts of States, without the Consent of the Legislatures of the States concerned as well as of the Congress.

The Congress shall have Power to dispose of and make all needful Rules and Regulations respecting the Territory or other Property belonging to the United States; and nothing in this Constitution shall be so construed as to Prejudice any Claims of the United States, or of any particular State.

Section 4

The United States shall guarantee to every State in this Union a Republican Form of Government, and shall protect each of them against Invasion; and on Application of the Legislature, or of the Executive (when the Legislature cannot be convened), against domestic Violence.

Article V

The Congress, whenever two thirds of both Houses shall deem it necessary, shall propose Amendments to this Constitution, or, on the Application of the Legislatures of two thirds of the several States, shall call a Convention for proposing Amendments, which, in either Case, shall be valid to all Intents and Purposes, as Part of this Constitution, when ratified by the Legisla-

tures of three fourths of the several States, or by Conventions in three fourths thereof, as the one or the other Mode of Ratification may be proposed by the Congress; Provided that no Amendment which may be made prior to the Year One thousand eight hundred and eight shall in any Manner affect the first and fourth Clauses in the Ninth Section of the first Article; and that no State, without its Consent, shall be deprived of its equal Suffrage in the Senate.

Article VI

All Debts contracted and Engagements entered into, before the Adoption of this Constitution, shall be as valid against the United States under this Constitution, as under the Confederation.

This Constitution, and the Laws of the United States which shall be made in Pursuance thereof; and all Treaties made, or which shall be made, under the Authority of the United States, shall be the supreme Law of the Land; and the Judges in every State shall be bound thereby, any Thing in the Constitution or Laws of any State to the Contrary notwithstanding.

The Senators and Representatives before mentioned, and the Members of the several State Legislatures, and all executive and judicial Officers, both of the United States and of the several States, shall be bound by Oath or Affirmation, to support this Constitution; but no religious Test shall ever be required as a Qualification to any Office or public Trust under the United States.

Article VII

The Ratification of the Conventions of nine States, shall be sufficient for the Establishment of this Constitution between the States so ratifying the Same.

The Word, "the," being interlined between the seventh and eighth Lines of the first Page, the Word "Thirty" being partly written on an Erazure in the fifteenth Line of the first Page, The Words "is tried" being interlined between the thirty second and thirty third Lines of the first Page and the Word "the" being interlined between the forty third and forty fourth Lines of the second Page.

    Attest William Jackson Secretary

    Done in Convention by the Unanimous Consent of the States present the Seventeenth Day of September in the Year of our Lord one thousand seven hundred and Eighty seven and of the Independence of the United States of America the Twelfth In witness whereof We have hereunto subscribed our Names,

G°. Washington
Presidt and deputy from Virginia

Delaware
    Geo: Read
    Gunning Bedford jun
    John Dickinson
    Richard Bassett
    Jaco: Broom

Maryland
    James McHenry
    Dan of St Thos. Jenifer
    Danl. Carroll

Virginia
    John Blair——
    James Madison Jr.

North Carolina
    Wm. Blount
    Richd. Dobbs Spaight
    Hu Williamson

South Carolina
    J. Rutledge
    Charles Cotesworth Pinckney
    Charles Pinckney
    Pierce Butler

Georgia
    William Few
    Abr Baldwin

New Hampshire
    John Langdon
    Nicholas Gilman

Massachusetts
    Nathaniel Gorham
    Rufus King

Connecticut
    Wm. Saml. Johnson
    Roger Sherman

New York
    Alexander Hamilton

New Jersey
    Wil: Livingston
    David Brearley
    Wm. Paterson
    Jona: Dayton

Pennsylvania
    B Franklin
    Thomas Mifflin
    Robt. Morris
    Geo. Clymer
    Thos. FitzSimons
    Jared Ingersoll
    James Wilson
    Gouv Morris

The Preamble to the Bill of Rights

Congress of the United States
begun and held at the City of New-York, on Wednesday the fourth of March, one thousand seven hundred and eighty nine.

The Conventions of a number of the States, having at the time of their adopting the Constitution, expressed a desire, in order to prevent misconstruction or abuse of its powers, that further declaratory and restrictive clauses should be added: And as extending the ground

Note: The capitalization and punctuation in this version is from the enrolled original of the Joint Resolution of Congress proposing the *Bill of Rights,* which is on permanent display in the Rotunda of the National Archives Building, Washington, D.C.

of public confidence in the Government, will best ensure the beneficent ends of its institution.

Resolved by the Senate and House of Representatives of the United States of America, in Congress assembled, two thirds of both Houses concurring, that the following Articles be proposed to the Legislatures of the several States as amendments to the Constitution of the United States, all, or any of which articles, when ratified by three fourths of the said Legislatures, to be valid to all intents and purposes, as part of the said Constitution; viz.

Articles in addition to, and Amendment of the Constitution of the United States of America, proposed by Congress and ratified by the Legislatures of the several States, pursuant to the fifth Article of the original Constitution.

The First 10 Amendments to the Constitution as Ratified by the States

Amendment I

Congress shall make no law respecting an establishment of religion, or prohibiting the free exercise thereof; or abridging the freedom of speech, or of the press; or the right of the people peaceably to assemble, and to petition the Government for a redress of grievances.

Amendment II

A well regulated Militia, being necessary to the security of a free State, the right of the people to keep and bear Arms, shall not be infringed.

Amendment III

No Soldier shall, in time of peace be quartered in any house, without the consent of the Owner, nor in time of war, but in a manner to be prescribed by law.

Amendment IV

The right of the people to be secure in their persons, houses, papers, and effects, against unreasonable searches and seizures, shall not be violated, and no Warrants shall issue, but upon probable cause, supported by Oath or affirmation, and particularly describing the place to be searched, and the persons or things to be seized.

Amendment V

No person shall be held to answer for a capital, or otherwise infamous crime, unless on a presentment or indictment of a Grand Jury, except in cases arising in the land or naval forces, or in the Militia, when in actual service in time of War or public danger; nor shall any person be subject for the same offence to be twice put in jeopardy of life or limb; nor shall be compelled in any criminal case to be a witness against himself, nor be deprived of life, liberty, or property, without due process of law; nor shall private property be taken for public use, without just compensation.

Amendment VI

In all criminal prosecutions, the accused shall enjoy the right to a speedy and public trial, by an impartial jury of the State and district wherein the crime shall have been committed, which district shall have been previously ascertained by law, and to be informed of the nature and cause of the accusation; to be confronted with the witnesses against him; to have compulsory process for obtaining witnesses in his favor, and to have the Assistance of Counsel for his defence.

Amendment VII

In suits at common law, where the value in controversy shall exceed twenty dollars, the right of trial by jury shall be preserved, and no fact tried by a jury, shall be otherwise reexamined in any Court of the United States, than according to the rules of the common law.

Amendment VIII

Excessive bail shall not be required, nor excessive fines imposed, nor cruel and unusual punishments inflicted.

Amendment IX

The enumeration in the Constitution, of certain rights, shall not be construed to deny or disparage others retained by the people.

Amendment X

The powers not delegated to the United States by the Constitution, nor prohibited by it to the States, are reserved to the States respectively, or to the people.

Amendments 11 – 27 to the Constitution of the United States

Amendment XI

Passed by Congress March 4, 1794. Ratified February 7, 1795.

The Judicial power of the United States shall not be construed to extend to any suit in law or equity, commenced or prosecuted against one of the United States by Citizens of another State, or by Citizens or Subjects of any Foreign State.

Amendment XII

Passed by Congress December 9, 1803. Ratified June 15, 1804.

The Electors shall meet in their respective states and vote by ballot for President and Vice-President, one of whom, at least, shall not be an inhabitant of the same state with themselves; they shall name in their ballots the person voted for as President, and in distinct ballots the person voted for as Vice-President, and they shall make distinct lists of all persons voted for as President, and of all persons voted for as Vice-President, and of the number of votes for each, which lists they shall sign and certify, and transmit sealed to the seat of the government of the United States, directed to the President of the Senate; — the President of the Senate shall, in the presence of the Senate and House of Representatives, open all the certificates and the votes shall then be counted; — The person having the greatest number of votes for President, shall be the President, if such number be a majority of the whole number of Electors appointed; and if no person have such majority, then from the persons having the highest numbers not exceeding three on the list of those voted for as President, the House of Representatives shall choose immediately, by ballot, the President. But in choosing the President, the votes shall be taken by states, the representation from each state having one vote; a quorum for this purpose shall consist of a member or members from two-thirds of the states, and a majority of all the states shall be necessary to a choice. [And if the House of Representatives shall not choose a President whenever the right of choice shall devolve upon them, before the fourth day of March next following, then the Vice-President shall act as President, as in case of the death or other constitutional disability of the President. —]* The person having the greatest number of votes as Vice-President, shall be the Vice-President, if such number be a majority of the whole number of Electors appointed, and if no person have a majority, then from the two highest numbers on the list, the Senate shall choose the Vice-President; a quorum for the purpose shall consist of two-thirds of the whole number of Senators, and a majority of the whole number shall be necessary to a choice. But no person constitutionally ineligible to the office of President shall be eligible to that of Vice-President of the United States.

Amendment XIII

Passed by Congress January 31, 1865. Ratified December 6, 1865.

Section 1

Neither slavery nor involuntary servitude, except as a punishment for crime whereof the party shall have been duly convicted, shall exist within the United States, or any place subject to their jurisdiction.

---

*Superseded by section 3 of the 20th amendment.

Section 2

Congress shall have power to enforce this article by appropriate legislation.

Amendment XIV

Passed by Congress June 13, 1866. Ratified July 9, 1868.

Section 1

All persons born or naturalized in the United States, and subject to the jurisdiction thereof, are citizens of the United States and of the State wherein they reside. No State shall make or enforce any law which shall abridge the privileges or immunities of citizens of the United States; nor shall any State deprive any person of life, liberty, or property, without due process of law; nor deny to any person within its jurisdiction the equal protection of the laws.

Section 2

Representatives shall be apportioned among the several States according to their respective numbers, counting the whole number of persons in each State, excluding Indians not taxed. But when the right to vote at any election for the choice of electors for President and Vice-President of the United States, Representatives in Congress, the Executive and Judicial officers of a State, or the members of the Legislature thereof, is denied to any of the male inhabitants of such State, being twenty-one years of age,* and citizens of the United States, or in any way abridged, except for participation in rebellion, or other crime, the basis of representation therein shall be reduced in the proportion which the number of such male citizens shall bear to the whole number of male citizens twenty-one years of age in such State.

Section 3

No person shall be a Senator or Representative in Congress, or elector of President and Vice-President,

*Changed by section 1 of the 26th amendment.

or hold any office, civil or military, under the United States, or under any State, who, having previously taken an oath, as a member of Congress, or as an officer of the United States, or as a member of any State legislature, or as an executive or judicial officer of any State, to support the Constitution of the United States, shall have engaged in insurrection or rebellion against the same, or given aid or comfort to the enemies thereof. But Congress may by a vote of two-thirds of each House, remove such disability.

Section 4

The validity of the public debt of the United States, authorized by law, including debts incurred for payment of pensions and bounties for services in suppressing insurrection or rebellion, shall not be questioned. But neither the United States nor any State shall assume or pay any debt or obligation incurred in aid of insurrection or rebellion against the United States, or any claim for the loss or emancipation of any slave; but all such debts, obligations and claims shall be held illegal and void.

Section 5

The Congress shall have the power to enforce, by appropriate legislation, the provisions of this article.

Amendment XV

Passed by Congress February 26, 1869. Ratified February 3, 1870.

Section 1

The right of citizens of the United States to vote shall not be denied or abridged by the United States or by any State on account of race, color, or previous condition of servitude —

Section 2

The Congress shall have the power to enforce this article by appropriate legislation.

Amendment XVI

Passed by Congress July 2, 1909. Ratified February 3, 1913.

The Congress shall have power to lay and collect taxes on incomes, from whatever source derived, without apportionment among the several States, and without regard to any census or enumeration.

Amendment XVII

Passed by Congress May 13, 1912. Ratified April 8, 1913.

The Senate of the United States shall be composed of two Senators from each State, elected by the people thereof, for six years; and each Senator shall have one vote. The electors in each State shall have the qualifications requisite for electors of the most numerous branch of the State legislatures.

When vacancies happen in the representation of any State in the Senate, the executive authority of such State shall issue writs of election to fill such vacancies: Provided, That the legislature of any State may empower the executive thereof to make temporary appointments until the people fill the vacancies by election as the legislature may direct.

This amendment shall not be so construed as to affect the election or term of any Senator chosen before it becomes valid as part of the Constitution.

Amendment XVIII

Passed by Congress December 18, 1917. Ratified January 16, 1919. Repealed by amendment 21.

Section 1

After one year from the ratification of this article the manufacture, sale, or transportation of intoxicating liquors within, the importation thereof into, or the exportation thereof from the United States and all territory subject to the jurisdiction thereof for beverage purposes is hereby prohibited.

Section 2

The Congress and the several States shall have concurrent power to enforce this article by appropriate legislation.

Section 3

This article shall be inoperative unless it shall have been ratified as an amendment to the Constitution by the legislatures of the several States, as provided in the Constitution, within seven years from the date of the submission hereof to the States by the Congress.

Amendment XIX

Passed by Congress June 4, 1919. Ratified August 18, 1920.

The right of citizens of the United States to vote shall not be denied or abridged by the United States or by any State on account of sex.

Congress shall have power to enforce this article by appropriate legislation.

Amendment XX

Passed by Congress March 2, 1932. Ratified January 23, 1933.

Section 1

The terms of the President and the Vice President shall end at noon on the 20th day of January, and the terms of Senators and Representatives at noon on the 3d day of January, of the years in which such terms would have ended if this article had not been ratified; and the terms of their successors shall then begin.

Section 2

The Congress shall assemble at least once in every year, and such meeting shall begin at noon on the 3d day of January, unless they shall by law appoint a different day.

Section 3

If, at the time fixed for the beginning of the term of the President, the President elect shall have died, the Vice President elect shall become President. If a President shall not have been chosen before the time fixed for the beginning of his term, or if the President elect shall have failed to qualify, then the Vice President elect shall act as President until a President shall have qualified; and the Congress may by law provide for the case wherein neither a President elect nor a Vice President shall have qualified, declaring who shall then act as President, or the manner in which one who is to act shall be selected, and such person shall act accordingly until a President or Vice President shall have qualified.

Section 4

The Congress may by law provide for the case of the death of any of the persons from whom the House of Representatives may choose a President whenever the right of choice shall have devolved upon them, and for the case of the death of any of the persons from whom the Senate may choose a Vice President whenever the right of choice shall have devolved upon them.

Section 5

Sections 1 and 2 shall take effect on the 15th day of October following the ratification of this article.

Section 6

This article shall be inoperative unless it shall have been ratified as an amendment to the Constitution by the legislatures of three-fourths of the several States within seven years from the date of its submission.

Amendment XXI

Passed by Congress February 20, 1933. Ratified December 5, 1933.

Section 1

The eighteenth article of amendment to the Constitution of the United States is hereby repealed.

Section 2

The transportation or importation into any State, Territory, or Possession of the United States for delivery or use therein of intoxicating liquors, in violation of the laws thereof, is hereby prohibited.

Section 3

This article shall be inoperative unless it shall have been ratified as an amendment to the Constitution by conventions in the several States, as provided in the Constitution, within seven years from the date of the submission hereof to the States by the Congress.

Amendment XXII

Passed by Congress March 21, 1947. Ratified February 27, 1951.

Section 1

No person shall be elected to the office of the President more than twice, and no person who has held the office of President, or acted as President, for more than two years of a term to which some other person was elected President shall be elected to the office of President more than once. But this Article shall not apply to any person holding the office of President when this Article was proposed by Congress, and shall not prevent any person who may be holding the office of President, or acting as President, during the term within which this Article becomes operative from holding the office of President or acting as President during the remainder of such term.

Section 2

This article shall be inoperative unless it shall have been ratified as an amendment to the Constitution by the legislatures of three-fourths of the several States within seven years from the date of its submission to the States by the Congress.

Amendment XXIII

Passed by Congress June 16, 1960. Ratified March 29, 1961.

Section 1

The District constituting the seat of Government of the United States shall appoint in such manner as Congress may direct:

A number of electors of President and Vice President equal to the whole number of Senators and Representatives in Congress to which the District would be entitled if it were a State, but in no event more than the least populous State; they shall be in addition to those appointed by the States, but they shall be considered, for the purposes of the election of President and Vice President, to be electors appointed by a State; and they shall meet in the District and perform such duties as provided by the twelfth article of amendment.

Section 2

The Congress shall have power to enforce this article by appropriate legislation.

Amendment XXIV

Passed by Congress August 27, 1962. Ratified January 23, 1964.

Section 1

The right of citizens of the United States to vote in any primary or other election for President or Vice President, for electors for President or Vice President, or for Senator or Representative in Congress, shall not be denied or abridged by the United States or any State by reason of failure to pay poll tax or other tax.

Section 2

The Congress shall have power to enforce this article by appropriate legislation.

Amendment XXV

Passed by Congress July 6, 1965. Ratified February 10, 1967.

Section 1

In case of the removal of the President from office or of his death or resignation, the Vice President shall become President.

Section 2

Whenever there is a vacancy in the office of the Vice President, the President shall nominate a Vice President who shall take office upon confirmation by a majority vote of both Houses of Congress.

Section 3

Whenever the President transmits to the President pro tempore of the Senate and the Speaker of the House of Representatives his written declaration that he is unable to discharge the powers and duties of his office, and until he transmits to them a written declaration to the contrary, such powers and duties shall be discharged by the Vice President as Acting President.

Section 4

Whenever the Vice President and a majority of either the principal officers of the executive departments or of such other body as Congress may by law provide, transmit to the President pro tempore of the Senate and the Speaker of the House of Representatives their written declaration that the President is unable to discharge the powers and duties of his office, the Vice President shall immediately assume the powers and duties of the office as Acting President.

Thereafter, when the President transmits to the President pro tempore of the Senate and the Speaker of the House of Representatives his written declaration that no inability exists, he shall resume the powers and duties of his office unless the Vice President and a majority of either the principal officers of the executive department or of such other body as Congress may by law provide, transmit within four days to the President pro tempore of the Senate and the Speaker of the House of Representatives their written declaration that the President is unable to discharge the powers and duties of his office. Thereupon Congress shall decide the issue, assembling within forty-eight hours for that purpose if not in session. If the Congress, within twenty-one days after receipt of the latter written declaration, or, if Congress is not in session, within twenty-one days after Congress is required to assemble, determines by two-thirds vote of both Houses that the President is unable to discharge the powers and duties of his office, the Vice President shall continue to discharge the same as Acting President; otherwise, the President shall resume the powers and duties of his office.

Amendment XXVI

Passed by Congress March 23, 1971. Ratified July 1, 1971.

Section 1

The right of citizens of the United States, who are eighteen years of age or older, to vote shall not be denied or abridged by the United States or by any State on account of age.

Section 2

The Congress shall have power to enforce this article by appropriate legislation.

Amendment XXVII

Originally proposed Sept. 25, 1789. Ratified May 7, 1992.

No law, varying the compensation for the services of the Senators and Representatives, shall take effect, until an election of representatives shall have intervened.

Emancipation Proclamation

January 1, 1863

By the President of the United States of America:

A Proclamation.

Whereas, on the twenty-second day of September, in the year of our Lord one thousand eight hundred and sixty-two, a proclamation was issued by the President of the United States, containing, among other things, the following, to wit:

"That on the first day of January, in the year of our Lord one thousand eight hundred and sixty-three, all persons held as slaves within any State or designated part of a State, the people whereof shall then be in rebellion against the United States, shall be then, thenceforward, and forever free; and the Executive Government of the United States, including the military and naval authority thereof, will recognize and maintain the freedom of such persons, and will do no act or acts to repress such persons, or any of them, in any efforts they may make for their actual freedom.

"That the Executive will, on the first day of January aforesaid, by proclamation, designate the States and parts of States, if any, in which the people thereof, respectively, shall then be in rebellion against the United States; and the fact

that any State, or the people thereof, shall on that day be, in good faith, represented in the Congress of the United States by members chosen thereto at elections wherein a majority of the qualified voters of such State shall have participated, shall, in the absence of strong countervailing testimony, be deemed conclusive evidence that such State, and the people thereof, are not then in rebellion against the United States."

Now, therefore I, Abraham Lincoln, President of the United States, by virtue of the power in me vested as Commander-in-Chief, of the Army and Navy of the United States in time of actual armed rebellion against the authority and government of the United States, and as a fit and necessary war measure for suppressing said rebellion, do, on this first day of January, in the year of our Lord one thousand eight hundred and sixty-three, and in accordance with my purpose so to do publicly proclaimed for the full period of one hundred days, from the day first above mentioned, order and designate as the States and parts of States wherein the people thereof respectively, are this day in rebellion against the United States, the following, to wit:

Arkansas, Texas, Louisiana, (except the Parishes of St. Bernard, Plaquemines, Jefferson, St. John, St. Charles, St. James Ascension, Assumption, Terrebonne, Lafourche, St. Mary, St.

Martin, and Orleans, including the City of New Orleans) Mississippi, Alabama, Florida, Georgia, South Carolina, North Carolina, and Virginia, (except the forty-eight counties designated as West Virginia, and also the counties of Berkley, Accomac, Northampton, Elizabeth City, York, Princess Ann, and Norfolk, including the cities of Norfolk and Portsmouth[)], and which excepted parts, are for the present, left precisely as if this proclamation were not issued.

And by virtue of the power, and for the purpose aforesaid, I do order and declare that all persons held as slaves within said designated States, and parts of States, are, and henceforward shall be free; and that the Executive government of the United States, including the military and naval authorities thereof, will recognize and maintain the freedom of said persons.

And I hereby enjoin upon the people so declared to be free to abstain from all violence, unless in necessary self-defence; and I recommend to them that, in all cases when allowed, they labor faithfully for reasonable wages.

And I further declare and make known, that such persons of suitable condition, will be received into the armed service of the United States to garrison forts, positions, stations, and other places, and to man vessels of all sorts in said service.

And upon this act, sincerely believed to be an act of justice, warranted by the Constitution, upon military necessity, I invoke the considerate judgment of mankind, and the gracious favor of Almighty God.

In witness thereof, I have hereunto set my hand and caused the seal of the United States to be affixed.

Done at the City of Washington, this first day of January, in the year of our Lord one thousand eight hundred and sixty three, and of the Independence of the United States of America the eighty-seventh.

By the President: ABRAHAM LINCOLN
WILLIAM H. SEWARD, Secretary of State.

Population, Labor Force, and Wealth

Population of the United States, 1790–2000

Year	Population	Percentage Increase	Year	Population	Percentage Increase
1790	3,929,214	41.3	1900	75,994,575	20.7
1800	5,308,483	35.1	1910	91,972,266	21.0
1810	7,239,881	36.4	1920	105,710,620	14.9
1820	9,638,453	33.1	1930	122,775,046	16.1
1830	12,866,020	33.5	1940	131,669,275	7.2
1840	17,069,453	32.7	1950	150,697,361	14.5
1850	23,191,876	35.9	1960	179,323,175	19.0
1860	31,443,321	35.6	1970	203,235,298	13.3
1870	39,818,449	26.6	1980	226,545,805	11.5
1880	50,155,783	26.0	1990	248,709,873	9.8
1890	62,947,714	25.5	2000	273,482,000	10.0

Note: These figures largely ignore the Native American population. Census takers never made any effort to count the Native American poplation that lived outside their political jurisdictions and compiled only casual and incomplete enumerations of those living within their jurisdictions until 1890. In that year the federal government attempted a full count of the Indian population: the Census found 125,719 Indians in 1890, compared with only 12,543 in 1870 and 33,985 in 1880.

Source: *Historical Statistics of the United States, Colonial Times to 1970* (1975); *Statistical Abstract of the United States, 1998.*

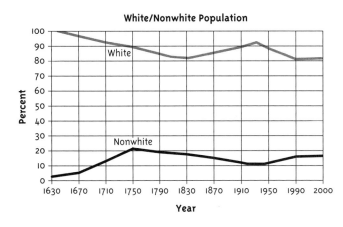

White/Nonwhite Population

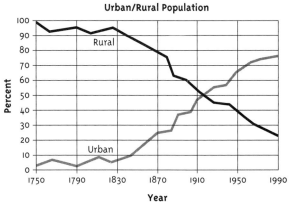

Urban/Rural Population

Immigrant Origins of the American Population, 1825–1985

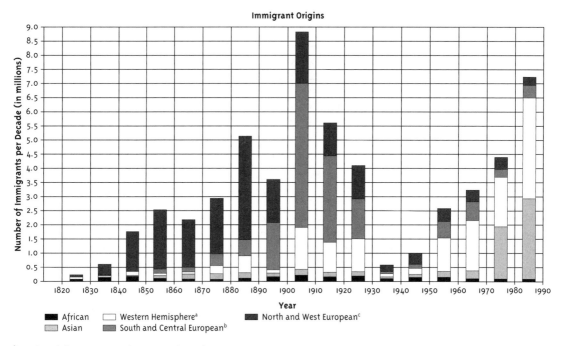

Immigrant Origins

Legend:
- African
- Asian
- Western Hemisphere[a]
- South and Central European[b]
- North and West European[c]

Y-axis: Number of Immigrants per Decade (in millions)

X-axis: Year (1820–1990)

[a]Canada and all countries in South America and Central America.

[b]Italy, Spain, Portugal, Greece, Germany (Austria included, 1938–1945), Poland, Czechoslovakia (since 1920), Yugoslavia (since 1920), Hungary (since 1861), Austria (since 1861, except 1938–1945), former USSR (excludes Asian USSR between 1931 and 1963), Latvia, Estonia, Lithuania, Finland, Romania, Bulgaria, Turkey (in Europe), and other European countries not classified elsewhere.

[c]Great Britain, Ireland, Norway, Sweden, Denmark, Iceland, Netherlands, Belgium, Luxembourg, Switzerland, France.

Source: Stephan Thernstrom, ed., *Harvard Encyclopedia of American Ethnic Groups* (1980), 480; U.S. Bureau of the Census, *Statistical Abstract of the United States, 1991.*

The Labor Force (Thousands of Workers)

Year	Agriculture	Mining	Manufacturing	Construction	Trade	Other	Total
1810	1,950	11	75	—	—	294	2,330
1840	3,570	32	500	290	350	918	5,660
1850	4,520	102	1,200	410	530	1,488	8,250
1860	5,880	176	1,530	520	890	2,114	11,110
1870	6,790	180	2,470	780	1,310	1,400	12,930
1880	8,920	280	3,290	900	1,930	2,070	17,390
1890	9,960	440	4,390	1,510	2,960	4,060	23,320
1900	11,680	637	5,895	1,665	3,970	5,223	29,070
1910	11,770	1,068	8,332	1,949	5,320	9,041	37,480
1920	10,790	1,180	11,190	1.233	5,845	11,372	41,610
1930	10,560	1,009	9,884	1,988	8,122	17,267	48,830
1940	9,575	925	11,309	1,876	9,328	23,277	56,290
1950	7,870	901	15,648	3,029	12,152	25,870	65,470
1960	5,970	709	17,145	3,640	14,051	32,545	74,060
1970	3,463	516	20,746	4,818	15,008	34,127	78,678
1980	3,364	979	21,942	6,215	20,191	46,612	99,303
1990	3,223	724	21,346	7,764	24,622	60,849	117,914
1997	3,399	634	20,835	8,302	26,777	69,611	129,558
1998	3,378	620	20,733	8,518	27,203	71,011	131,463

Source: *Historical Statistics of the United States, Colonial Times to 1970* (1975), 139; *Statistical Abstract of the United States, 1998,* table 675.

Wealth Held by Richest Americans, 1774–1995

Year	Percentage of Total Net Worth Held by Richest 1%
1774	12.6
1860	29.0
1870	27.0
1912	56.4
1923	45.7
1929	44.2
1949	27.1
1962	26.0
1969	31.1
1979	20.5
1980	35.7
1995	40.0

Sources: James L. Huston, *Securing the Fruits of Labor: The American Concept of Wealth Distribution, 1765–1900* (1998); Edward Wolff, *Top Heavy* (1996), cited in Steve Brouwer, *Sharing the Pie* (1998).

Index

Page numbers in *italics* refer to illustrations or sidebar documents

Index

Index

Index

Index

Index

Morse, Samuel, 531
Mortgages, 370
Mott, Lucretia, 464
Mott family, 555
Mulattos, 477
Mummers, 451
Murphy, Bridget (Bridget Murphy Kennedy), 419
Murray, Judith Sargent, 263
Myers, Isaac, 702

Nantucket Island, 53
Narango, Pedro, *55*
Narragansett Indians, *12*, 54, 131, *132*
Nashoba community, 459
Nast, Thomas, *452*, *604*, *672*, *683*, *684*
Natchez, Miss., 480, 494, 495, 640
"nabobs" in, 480–483, 500
Natchez Indians, 114
Nation magazine, 672–673, 708
National Era, 557, 575
National Industrial Congress, 556–557
National Labor Union (NLU), 701, 704
National Molders' Union, 576–579, 698–699
National Republican Party, 379
National Trades Union (NTU), 402, 403, 405, 462
Native Americans. *See* Indians, American
Nativism, 300, 420–421, 443–447, 573. *See also* American Party
Navajo Indians, 542, 543, 687, 688
Navigation Acts, 78, 115, 165
"Negro Election Day," 162–163
Neolin, 199
Netherlands. *See* Holland
Nevada, 550
Newark, N.J., 188
New Brunswick, 226
New Departure, 704
New England
    antislavery sentiment in, 524
    industrialization in, 298, 299, 306, 372–73, 384, 393–395 (*see also* Lowell, Mass.; Lynn, Mass.)
    migration from, 426–427
    and War of 1812, 313
    see also New England colonies; *specific states and cities*
New England colonies, 45–47, 124–135, 139–140, 144–149, 170–171
    government and politics in, 151–152, 163, 171–172
    immigration to, 46, 136, 181
    and Indians, 53–54, 130–135, 140–141

landholding in, 125–127, 129–130, 149, 170–171
    religion in, 127, 128, 164, 172–173, 187 (*see also* Puritans)
    towns in, 125–127, 144
    women in, 127–129
    see also specific cities and towns
New England Farmer, 369–370
Newfoundland, 34, 186
New Hampshire, 171, 210, 251, 260, 426. *See also* New England; New England colonies
New Harmony, Ind., 459
New Jersey, 239, 251, 263–264, 280, 432
    in colonial era, 121, 136, 188–189
New Mexico, 531
    as Spanish colony, 25, 26, 54, 58, 60, 69, 185, 284
New Netherland, 136
New Orleans, La., 304, 309, 311, 514, 576
    battle of, 313
    in Civil War, 611, 639
    diverse population of, 515–516, 517
    free blacks in, 348, 494
    as French settlement, 69, 185–186
    in Reconstruction era, 661, 671, 673
Newport, R.I., 151, 153, 281
Newsom, Robert, 584
Newspapers, 377–378, 423
    foreign-language, 436
New York City, 278, 377, 409–410, 454–455, 630–631
    in American Revolution, 205, 208–209, 212, 215, *225*, 227, 228, 239, 240
    in colonial era, 152, 154–155, 169, 202
    and Constitution, 270, *273*
    in economic depressions, 409, 706, 708
    free blacks in, 558, 651
    growth of, 374, 427, 431
    labor movement in, 403, 405–406, *408*, 461
    leisure activities in, 448–451
    manufacturing in, 374, 375, 391, 427, 694
    slaves in, 123, 162, 177
New York City Children's Aid Society, 452, 456
New York colony, 36, 166
    government and politics in, 136, 163–164, 169, 186
    landholding in, 136, 138, 142–143, 154–155, 164, 190, 194
    see also New York City: in colonial era

New York Evening Post, 454
New York Herald, *378*, 602
New York Laborers' Union Benevolent Association, 561
New York Manumission Society, 260
New York state, 251, 252, 343, 367–369, 370, 376, 380, 382, 432
    see also specific cities
New York State Mechanic, 387–388
New York Tailoresses' Society, 402
New York Times, 698
New York Tribune, 441–442, 582, *650*
Nez Perce Indians, 543–544
Nicaragua, 517, *581*
Nieuw Amsterdam, 35, 60
Nipmuck Indians, 134
Nisenan Indians, 544, 546
NLU (National Labor Union), 701, 704
Nonimportation agreements, 210–212
Norfolk, Va., 494
North Carolina, 191–193, 304, 308, 334, 335, 336, 499–500, 502
    during and after Civil War, 604, 684
    slavery in, 108–109, 346
    see also Carolina colony
Northern colonies
    class conflict in, 166–168, 187–190, 194–195
    class differences in, 151, 154–164
    families in, 121, 124–125, 144
    government and politics in, 151–152, 163–166, 169, 171–172, 186
    immigration to, 46, 121–122, 125, 136, 143–144, 160, 181
    indentured servants in, 160–161
    and Indians, 53–54, 123, 130–135, 140–141, 191
    landholding in, 122, 125–127, 129–130, 136–139, 142–143, 154–155, 164, 190, 194
    population growth of, 123, 170
    port towns in, 122–123, 129, 151–154 (*see also specific towns and cities*)
    rural societies in, 144–151
    slavery in, 122–123, 150–151, 162, 167
    women in, 124, 144–147, 164
    see also New England colonies
Northup, Solomon, 327
Northwest Ordinance, 269, 287, 293
Norwegians, 436–437
Nova Scotia, 186, 197, 226
Nugent, Polly, 282
Nursing profession, 627–628
Nzinga Mbemba (Affonso I), king of Congo, *30*

Index

Poverty, 282–283
  in colonial era, 157–159, 202
  of many wage earners, 374–375, 390, 391, 433–434, 441–442, 628, 694
  worsening of, in periodic depressions, 202, 409, 706–709
Powhatan, *40*, 43, 52
Powhatan Indians, *42*, 43–44, 70
Pownall, Thomas, 197
"Praying Indian" towns, 131, 134
Pregnancy, premarital, 171
Prendergast, William, 190, 194
Presbyterians, 336
"Press gangs," 187. *See also* Impressment
Price setting
  by colonial governments, 165–166
  by crowds, 166, 253–254, 263, 409–410
Primogeniture, 77–78
Printers, 385, 436, 704
Proclamation Line of 1763, 200, *201*, 245
Productivity, 422
Profits, 391, 395, 628
  from slavery, 328–329, 332, 502, 521
Prohibition Party, 711
Prostitution, 158, 454–455
  reformers and, 455–456
Protestant Reformation, 15–16, 37, 45, 59
Providence, R.I., 215, 278, 372, 407
Public education, 73, 76–77, 443, 457–458
Pueblo Indians, 9–10, 26, 54, 542, 543. *See also* Pueblo Revolt
Pueblo Revolt (1680), 9–10, 52, 54, *55*, 61, 69
Punch, John, 73
Puritans
  in England, 45, 47–49, 125, 136
  in New England colonies, 45–47, 122, 123–135, 139–140, 154, 164
"Putting out" system, 390. *See also* Outwork
Pynchon, John, 129

Quakers, 48–49, 50, 128, 171, 336, 496
  in England, 48–49
  in Pennsylvania colony, 122, 138, 143, 194
  and slavery, 340, 342, 257, 555
  and women's rights, 164, 463–464
Quantrill, William Clarke, 631
Quartering Act, 205
Quebec, 34, 185, 197
Quebec Act (1774), *201*
Quinnipiac Indians, 131

Racism, 281, 629, 635–636, 703
  against Chinese, 549–550, 648
  against Mexican Americans, 658, 690
  see also Free blacks: discrimination against; Slavery
Radical Republicans, 610, 668–672
  eclipse of, 536, 679–680
Railroads, 369, 565, *686*, 706–707
  after Civil War, 537, 625, 685, 692–693, 695
  importance of, in westward expansion, 422–423, 693, 695
  strikes on, 537, 703, 709–710, 715–717
  workforce composition of, 686, 696
Raleigh, N.C., 663
Raleigh, Sir Walter, 34
Ramsay, David, 240
Randolph, John, 109, 339
Reading, Pierson B., 519
Reconstruction, 536
  and depression of 1870s, 706, 708
  and Republican Party politics, 536, 668–672, 674–680, 683–684, 713–715
  state governments formed in, 673–678
  undermining of, by terror, 536, 680–684
  see also Freedpeople
Reconstruction Act of March 1867, 672–673, 679
"Redemption," 678–685, 711–712
"Red Sticks," 319
Reed, John C., 328
Reform, moral, 383–384, 443, 473
Reform movements, 421
  class differences in, 375, 383–385, 456–458
  and evangelical Protestantism, 382–384, 421, *444*, 456–458
  see also Abolitionists
Regulators, 226
  in North Carolina colony, 191–193
  in South Carolina colony, 191
Religion
  African Americans and, 66–67, 85, 112, 336–340, 342, 347, 439–440, 484–487, 661, 663
  American Indians and, 289, 316–317
    (*see also* Missionaries)
  class differences in, 112–113, 173, 187, 383–384, 456–458
  differences in, among workers, 561–562
  and party politics, 469, 573
  in West Africa, 17–18
  women and, 112, 128, 164, 338, 383

  see also Catholic Church; Evangelical Protestantism; Great Awakening; Moravians; Quakers
Remond, Charles, 467
Remond, Sarah Parker, 616
Republicanism, 266–267, 358
  Constitution and, 266–267
  invoking of, by labor movement, 405–407, 698
  and wage labor, 395–398
  see also Independence: republican ideal of
"Republican mothers," 358
Republican Party, 535, 572–575
  planters' fear of, 574–575, 576
  Radical wing of, 610, 668–672, 679–680
  and Reconstruction, 536, 668–672, 674–680, 683–684, 713–715
  rise to power of, 574, 588–589
  shifting emphasis of, 658, 684, 710
  social base of, 573–574, 675–676
Revolution. *See* American Revolution
Revenue Act of 1767 (Townshend Duties), 205, 210
Revere, Paul, 157, *181*, *213*, 214, 221, 272
Rhode Island, 15, 46, 61, 150, 210, 258, 376. *See also* New England; New England colonies; Providence, R.I.
Rice, 90–91, 92–94, 304
  as export, 90, 105–106, 183
  slave labor and, 90–91, 93, 95–96, 304, 324–325, 326
Rice, Sally, 395
Richardson, Ebenezer, 212
Richmond, Va., 337, 494, 515–516
  African Americans in, 281, 339–340, 513, 516
  in Civil War, 639, 640, 641, 643
  factories in, 513, 514, 640–641
  in Reconstruction era, 660, 663, 673
Rifles, 620, 632
Rights of Englishmen. *See* "English liberties"
Ripley, George, 458
Roanoke Island, 34
"Robber Barons," 693
Robeson County, N.C., 646
Robinson, Colonel Beverly, 143
Rochester, N.Y., 427, 455
Rockefeller, John D., 693–694
Rogers, Thomas, 374
Rolfe, John, 43, 52
Roman Catholic Church. *See* Catholic Church
Rood, Hannah, 148
Ropes, Hannah Anderson, 570
Ross, John, 321

Index

Index